MW01006865

OXFORD EARLY CHRISTIAN TEXTS

Praise for *Leontius of Byzantium*

'Scholars have awaited this long-heralded edition for decades . . . The significance of these Completed Works is not to be understated: there really is no equal to be found among the monographs on Leontius cited in the bibliography, especially since this is the first complete edition of the Greek in modern times. This critical edition opens many new avenues for future scholarship, provides a far more reliable text than one finds in the Patrologia Graeca, and attempts a correction of a number of longstanding assumptions about Leontius . . . Daley's volume would qualify as anyone's magnum opus, even his own, and posterity will ever be in his debt for this work.'

Kevin Clarke, *Reading Religion*

OXFORD EARLY CHRISTIAN TEXTS

The series provides reliable working texts of important early Christian writers in both Greek and Latin. Each volume contains an introduction, text, and select critical apparatus, with English translations *en face*, and brief explanatory references.

Titles in the series include:

Justin, Philosopher and Martyr
Apologies
Edited by Denis Minns and Paul Parvis

Priscillian of Avila
The Complete Works
Edited by Marco Conti

The Case Against Diodore and Theodore
Texts and their Contexts
Edited by John Behr

Jerome's Epitaph on Paula
A Commentary on the *Epitaphium Sanctae Paulae*
Edited by Andrew Cain

The Life of Saint Helia
Critical Edition, Translation, Introduction, and Commentary
Edited by Virginia Burrus and Marco Conti

Nonnus of Panopolis
Paraphrasis of the Gospel of John XI
Edited by Konstantinos Spanoudakis

Damasus of Rome
The Epigraphic Poetry
Edited by Dennis Trout

Greek and Latin Narratives about the Ancient Martyrs
Edited by Éric Rebillard

Adrian's *Introduction to the Divine Scriptures*
An Antiochene Handbook for Scriptural Interpretation
Edited by Peter W. Martens

Faith in Formulae
A Collection of Early Christian Creeds and Creed-related Texts
Edited by Wolfram Kinzig

Gregory of Nyssa

On the Human Image of God

JOHN BEHR

Great Clarendon Street, Oxford, OX2 6DP,
United Kingdom

Oxford University Press is a department of the University of Oxford.
It furthers the University's objective of excellence in research, scholarship,
and education by publishing worldwide. Oxford is a registered trade mark of
Oxford University Press in the UK and in certain other countries

First Edition published in 2023

Published in the United States of America by Oxford University Press
198 Madison Avenue, New York, NY 10016, United States of America

British Library Cataloguing in Publication Data
Data available

Library of Congress Control Number: 2022937791

ISBN 978–0–19–284397–5

Printed and bound in the UK by
Clays Ltd, Elcograf S.p.A.

For Metropolitan Savas of Pittsburgh

Our Best Man!

Preface

'Every *logos*'—word, argument, treatise—'is like a living being, with a body of its own', so that each member is 'composed in fitting relation to each other and to the whole' (*Phaedr.* 264c2–5). These words of Plato are certainly true of the treatise presented here, *On the Human Image of God* by Gregory of Nyssa (otherwise known as *On the Making of Man*). It is one of the most remarkable treatises from the golden era of Patristic literature, presenting a sophisticated analysis of the human being that draws upon both Scripture and the prior Christian tradition, above all Origen, and also the tradition of philosophical and medical reflection going back to Anaxagoras, and above all Plato's *Timaeus*. Although attention is rarely given to the treatise as a whole, it is, like its subject, a skilfully composed and arranged complex work, with its own economy, that is, the working together of the different parts of the text (paralleling, I argue, those of Timaeus' speech); an economy, moreover, which reflects, and so contributes to, the economy of God that is the growth of human being, in the workshop of nature, towards the final realization of God's project from the beginning, that of making the human being, individually and collectively, in his image and likeness.

This treatise has long been a source of fascination for me; indeed, it was the subject of one of my first published pieces. What is presented in the introduction to this volume is a substantial revision of my first attempt to try to make sense of how the whole fits together. It has benefitted from other work done along the way—on the Gospel of John, Irenaeus, and Origen—and especially by the opportunities I have had to work through this text numerous times with others, in semester-long seminars or short summer intensives—at St Vladimir's Seminary, Nashotah House, Regent's College, Trinity School for Ministry, St Andrew's Greek Orthodox Theological College, and St Irenaeus Institute for Orthodox Theology. I am truly grateful to all those with whom I have had the pleasure of reading through the text, learning from them at each stage. My especial thanks go to Fr Andrew Louth for his guidance, Sophia Theodoratos for checking through the critical apparatus, Brad Jersak for reading through the introduction, and Tom Perridge for his encouragement, and all those at Oxford University Press for their work on this volume.

Contents

Abbreviations

Abbreviations for classical and Patristic texts are given in the Bibliography following the title; they are based on those found in the following:

The SBL Handbook of Style for Ancient Near Eastern, Biblical and Early Christian Studies, ed. P. H. Alexander et al. (Peabody, MA: Hendrickson, 1999).

And:

H. G. Liddell and R. Scott, *A Greek-English Lexicon*, rev. H. S. Jones with R. McKenzie. 9th edn. with revised supplement (Oxford: Clarendon Press, 1996).
G. W. Lampe, *A Patristic Greek Lexicon* (Oxford: Clarendon Press, 1961).

When a text is not conveniently divided according to chapter and paragraph, reference has been given to the editor's name, page and line number of the edition given in the Bibliography. Scriptural references have been given according to the LXX; this principally affects the numeration of the Psalms and the naming of 1 & 2 Samuel and 1 & 2 Kings as 1–4 Reigns.

ACA	Ancient Commentators on Aristotle
ACO	*Acta Conciliorum Oecumenicorum*
ACW	Ancient Christian Writers
ANF	Ante-Nicene Fathers
CAG	Commentaria in Aristotelem Graeca
CBQ MS	*Catholic Biblical Quarterly* Monograph Series
CCCM	Corpus Christianorum: Continuatio Mediaevalis
CCSG	Corpus Christianorum: Series Graeca
CCSM	Corpus Christianorum: Series Mediaevalis
CÉA, SA	Collection des Études Augustiniennes, Série Antiquité
CLA	Christianity in Late Antiquity
CMG	Corpus Medicorum Graecorum
CPG	Clavis Patrum Graecorum, vol. 2, ed. Maurits Geerard (Turnhout: Brepols, 1974)
CTC	Christian Theology in Context
CWS	Classics of Western Spirituality
D–K	Herman Diels, *Die Fragmente der Vorsokratiker*, ed. Walther Kranz, 6th edn., 3 vols (Berlin, 1951–2)
DL	Diogenes Laertius
DOMP	Dumbarton Oaks Medieval Library
DOP	Dumbarton Oaks Papers

EcRev	*Ecclesiastical Review*
ET	English translation
FC	Fathers of the Church
FChr	Fontes Christiani
GCS	Die griechische christliche Schriftsteller der ersten [drei] Jarhunderte
GNO	Gregorii Nysseni Opera
HTR	*Harvard Theological Review*
IJST	*International Journal of Systematic Theology*
JECS	*Journal of Early Christian Studies*
JTI Suppl.	*Journal of Theological Interpretation* Supplements
JTS	*Journal of Theological Studies*
LCL	Loeb Classical Library
M–R	Emmanuel Amand de Mendieta and Stig Y. Rudberg, *Basile de Césarée: La tradition manuscrite directe des neuf homélies sur l'Hexaéméron*, TU 123 (Berlin: Akademie, 1980).
MTh	*Modern Theology*
NHC	Nag Hammadi Codices
NPNF	Nicene and Post Nicene Fathers
OCA	Orientalia Christiana Analecta
OCT	Oxford Classical Texts
OECS	Oxford Early Christian Studies
OECT	Oxford Early Christian Texts
OLP	*Orientalia Lovaniensia Periodica*
PPS	Popular Patristic Series
PTS	Patristiche Texte und Studien
RevScRel	*Revue des Sciences Religieuses*
RSR	*Recherches de Science Religieuse*
SA	Studia Anselmiana
SBL	Society of Biblical Literature
SC	Sources chrétiennes
SCE	*Studies in Christian Ethics*
SLA	*Studies in Late Antiquity*
SPM	Studia Patristica Mediolanensia
SROC	*Studi e Richerche sull'Oriente Cristiano*
STAC	Studien und Texte zu Antike und Christentum
StP	*Studia Patristica*
Suppl. *VC*	Supplements to *Vigiliae Christianae*
SVF	*Stoicorum Veterum Fragmenta*
TS	*Theological Studies*
TTH	Translated Texts for Historians
TU	Texte und Untersuchungen
UCPCP	University of California Publications in Classical Philology
VC	*Vigiliae Christianae*
WGRW	Writings from the Greco-Roman World
ZAC	*Zeitschrift für Antikes Christentum/Journal of Ancient Christianity*

'We are, clearly, transitory beings and our existence on earth is, clearly, a process, the uninterrupted existence of a chrysalis transitioning into a butterfly.'

Stavrogin to Shatov in appendix to Dostoevsky's *The Demons*

INTRODUCTION

Chapter 1
The Text, Manuscripts, and Editions

If, as Werner Jaeger suggested, a side effect of the French Revolution was that the Maurist Fathers, having produced monumental editions of Basil, Gregory of Nazianzus, and John Chrysostom, were not able to do the same for Gregory of Nyssa,[1] it is apt that amongst all the critical editions of Patristic texts in the various series produced during the past century, Gregory's works are distinguished by the fact that he alone has an equally magnificent edition dedicated solely to his works, overseen by Jaeger himself—the Leiden Brill Corpus, Gregorii Nysseni Opera (GNO). The project was launched by Ulrich von Wilamowitz-Moellendorff at the beginning of the 20th century, initially resulting in editions of Gregory's *Contra Eunomium* (ed. Jaeger, 1921) and his letters (ed. Pasqualis, 1925).[2] The project was continued by Jaeger after his move to the United States and founding the Institute for Classical Studies at Harvard University in 1939. After decades of gathering and examining copies of more than 1,000 manuscripts containing Gregory's texts, volumes of GNO began to appear from the 1950s, numbering 18 individual volumes by 2014 (the date of the most recent volume). In a paper delivered in 1969, Hadwig Hörner recalled how Jaeger had given her the task of editing the *Apologia in Hexaemeron* and then, after Hermann Langerbeck's death (1964), the work now customarily known as *De hominis opificio* in addition, noting that 'until then only the collations have been made'.[3] The edition of the *Apologia* appeared five decades later; the *De hominis opificio* is the last announced work yet to appear.[4] Fortunately, however, we do have an edition of this work published in the mid-19th century, well in advance of any other edition from the period of this

[1] Werner Jaeger, *Two Rediscovered Works of Ancient Christian Literature: Gregory of Nyssa and Macarius* (Leiden: Brill, 1954), 5–6.

[2] The earliest announcement of a new critical edition of Gregory's corpus seems to be the notice, in *Byzantinische Zeitschrift* 18 (1909), 711–12, of a gathering in honour of Ulrich von Wilamowitz-Moellendorff on the occasion of his 60th birthday. For more details of the history of the GNO edition, see Hadwig Hörner, 'Über Genese und Derzeitigen Stand der Grossen Edition der Werke Gregors von Nyssa', in Marguerite Harl, *Écriture et culture philosophique dans la pensée de Grégoire de Nysse: Actes du Colloque de Chevetogne (22–25 Septembre 1969)* (Leiden: Brill, 1971), 18–50.

[3] Hörner, 'Über Genese', 48.

[4] Hubert R. Drobner, *Gregorii Nysseni in Hexaemeron*, GNO 4.1 (Leiden: Brill, 2009). In Margarete Altenburger annd Friedhelm Mann, *Bibliographie zu Gregor von Nyssa: Editionen—Übersetzungen—Literatur* (Leiden: Brill, 1988), x, Martin Henniges is listed as the editor for the *Apologia* and Hadwig Hörner for *De hom. op.*

or any other work of Gregory, produced by the remarkable Scottish scholar, George Hays Forbes.[5]

Gregory's *De hominis opificio* was written between the death of Basil in September 378 and Easter 379.[6] It was very popular in antiquity as is clear from the numerous manuscripts and translations of the treatise. The work was first translated into Latin by Dionysius Exiguus (*c*.470–540) and then several centuries later by Eriugena (completed *c*.862–4), who also used the work extensively in his *Periphyseon*, referring to it as Gregory's *Sermo de imagine*. The work was also translated into Syriac, Arabic, Georgian, Armenian, and Slavonic.[7] The first printed edition of the work, entitled simply *Βίβλος περὶ ἀνθρώπου*, was by the Aldus Press in 1536.[8] In the following year, Dionysius' Latin translation was

[5] George Hay Forbes, *Τοῦ ἐν ἁγίοις πατρὸς ἡμῶν Γρηγορίου ἐπισκόπου Νύσσης* (*ἀδελφοῦ τοῦ μεγάλου Βασιλείου*) *τὰ εὑρισκόμενα πάντα. Sancti patris nostri Gregorii Nysseni Basilii Magni fratris quae supersunt omnia. In unum corpus collegit, ad fidem codd. mss. recensuit, Latinis versionibus quam accuratissimis instruxit et genuina a supposititiis discrevit,* Tomus primus, Fasc. 1 and 2 (Burntisland: Pitsligo Press, 1855, 1861). The *Περὶ κατασκευῆς ἀνθρώπου—De hominis conditione id est de imagine* is found in Fasc. 1, 102–Fasc. 2, 319; it is preceded by Forbes' 'Monitum', Fasc. 1, 96–101.

[6] For the dating of Gregory's works, I have used the ranges given in *The Brill Dictionary of Gregory of Nyssa*, ed. Lucas Francisco Mateo-Seco and Giulio Maspero, Suppl. *VC* 99 (Leiden: Brill, 2010), 153–69, 'Chronology of Works', by Pierre Maraval.

[7] For the Syriac version, see M. Parmentier, 'Syriac Translations of Gregory of Nyssa', *Orientalia Lovaniensia Periodica* 20 (1989), 143–93, at 164. Translations of, and comments on, *Vat. sir. 106*, dated *c*.700 CE (noted, but not studied by Forbes, cf. 'Monitum', 99), appeared in a series of articles, entitled 'La versione siriaca del "De opificio hominis" di Gregorio di Nissa' in *SROC*: T. Clementoni, on chapters 13–14, *SROC* 5 (1982), 81–101, 157–71; M. R. De Deo, further on chapter 14, *SROC* 3 (1983), 39–56, 181–95; F. Grassi, on chapters 9–11, *SROC* 7 (1984), 25–50, 191–206; and A. Bonanni, on chapter 22, *SROC* 10 (1987), 149–70.

For the Arabic version, see Joseph Nasrallah, 'Dossier arabe des oeuvres de saint Basile dans la littérature melchite', *Proche-Orient Chrétien* 29 (1979), 17–43, at 27–9, on the existence of an 8th-century Arabic translation of Basil's *Hexaemeron* and Gregory's *De hom. op.*, which was then used for the Georgian translation (see below).

For the Georgian version, see Tina Dolidze and Ekvtime (Tamaz) Kochlamazanashvili, 'Old Georgian Translations of Gregory of Nyssa's Works', in *Gregory of Nyssa: The Minor Treatises on Trinitarian Theology and Apollinarism*, ed. Volker Henning Drecoll and Margitta Berghaus, Suppl. *VC* 106 (Leiden: Brill, 2011), 577–92, at 577–8 and 581, which dates the first, anonymous, translation of *De hom. op.* to the 8th–9th centuries, though preserved in the 10th-century Shatberdi collection and the 12th–13th-century manuscript Codex Jerusalem, Greek Patriarchal Library Collection 44 (now edited by and published Ilia Abuladze: Tbilisi, 1979; in Georgian); the second translation is that by George the Athonite (1009–65), a critical edition, edited by Ekvtime Kochlamazanashvili, is forthcoming in *Christian Archaeology* 2. See Ekvtime Kochlamazanashvili and Tina Dolidze, *Description of Georgian Manuscripts Including St. Gregory of Nyssa's Works* (Tbilisi, 2009; in Georgian).

For the Armenian version, Forbes, 'Monitum', 99, notes an Armenian version held by the Mekhitarists monks in Venice; see also R. P. Casey, 'Armenia Inedita', in *Le Muséon, Revue d'études orientales* 68 (1955), 55–9, at 59, on an ms in the Tübingen collection, and M. van Esbroeck and U. Zanetti, 'Le manuscrit Érevan 993. Inventaire des pièces', *Revue des études Arméniennes* 12 (1977), 123–67, at 139 (no. 118, regarding *De hom. op.* 25).

The Slavonic translation has now been critically edited by Lara Sels, *Gregory of Nyssa,* De hominis opificio О Образѣ Чловѣка*: The Fourteenth-Century Slavonic Translation: A Critical Edition with Greek Parallel and Commentary*, Bausteine zur Slavischen Philologie und Kulturgeschichte NF 21 (Köln: Böhlau, 2009).

[8] *Gregorii Nazanzeni Theologi orationes novem elegantissimae, Gregorii Nysseni liber de homine, quae omnia nunc primum, emendatissima, in lucem prodeunt* (Aldus, 1536); and in the final colophon: *Venetiis, in aedibus haeredum Aldi, et Andreae Asulani soceri. MDXXXVI.*

published (Cologne, 1537, reprinted in 1551; subsequently re-edited by Laurentius Sifanus, Basel, 1562), with the title *De creatione hominis*, although in the explicit (fol. 23^{v}) it is referred to as *De imagine*.[9] Two further Latin translations were produced in the mid-16th century, that of the Cassinese monk Ambrosius Ferrarius in 1553, and then, apparently without knowledge of Ferrarius's work, by Johannes Löwenklau (Levvenklaius).[10] Löwenklau's edition was published in Basel in 1567, along with the Greek text from Aldus' edition, under the title *De hominis opificio—Περὶ κατασκευῆς ἀνθρώπου*; this Latin translation and these titles thereafter became standard.[11] It was this text that was included by Claudius Morellus in the first publication of the collected known works of Gregory in 1615.[12] An appendix to this work, containing newly discovered works, was published in 1618, and an enlarged edition, the expanded *editio Morelliana*, in 1638, which was then used as the basis for Gregory's works in the series Patrologia Graeca.[13] Eriugena's translation was only rediscovered in the years before the Second World War, when Dom Maïeul Cappuyns noticed it in the manuscript *Bamberg B.IV.13* and published an edition of the text, comparing it also to the translation found in Eriugena's *Periphyseon* (in the three principal recensions: Reims, Bibliothèque Municipale, *875*; Bamberg, Staatsbibliothek, *Patr. 78* [*olim B.IV.13*]; and Paris, Bibliothèque nationale de France, *Lat. 12964–5*); the work has recently been re-edited by Giovanni Mandolino, with recourse to both the critical edition of the *Periphyseon* by Édouard Jeauneau and the Greek text of Forbes.[14]

Although not having yet appeared in the GNO, we are fortunate, as already noted, to have the exceptional edition of this work of Gregory, along with the *Apologia in Hexaemeron* and the *Vita Moysis*, edited by George Forbes and published in 1855/61 at his own private press (Pitsligo Press, named after his ancestor Lord Pitsligo) in Burntisland, a small town on the northern shore of the

[9] For details of these and other editions, see Altenburger and Mann, *Bibliographie*, 11–12, 15, 23–4. The *editio princeps* was included in PL (67.347–408), with two titles: *Ad fratrem suum Petrum Presbyterum: De imagine, id est de hominis conditione quae a fratre eorum Sancto Basilio episcopo in Hexaemeron sunt omissa*, and then *De creatione hominis*.

[10] For more details see P. Levine, 'Two Early Versions of St. Gregory of Nyssa's *Περὶ κατασκευῆς ἀνθρώπου*', *Harvard Studies in Classical Philology* 63 (1958), 473–92, at 475 and 484 n. 24, relating also the scathing comments of Ferrarius and Löwenklau on Dionysius' translation and betraying their ignorance of the identity of Dionysius.

[11] *Γρηγορίου τοῦ Νύσσης ἐπισκόπου θαυμαστὴ βίβλος, περὶ κατασκευῆς ἀνθρώπου. Opus admirandum Gregorii Nysseni antistitis de hominis opificio.* Interprete Iohanne Levvenklaio, annotationibus estiam necessariis additis. Liber medicinae, philosophiae sacrarumque litterarum studiosis perutilis (Basel: Ioannis Oporini, 1567). Ferrarius's translation (*Cod. Vat. Otto lat. 776*) remains unpublished.

[12] For details, see Altenburger and Mann, *Bibliographie*, 50–1.

[13] Ibid. 55, 58–60. Gregory's treatise is found in PG 44, 123–256 (Paris, 1858).

[14] M. Cappuyns, 'Le 'De imagine' de Grégoire de Nysse traduit par Jean Scot Érigène', *Recherches de théologie ancienne et médiévale* 32 (Louvain, 1965), 205–62. Iohannis Scotti Eriugenae, *Carmina; De Imagine*, ed. Michael W. Herren, Andrew Dunning, Giovanni Mandolino, and Chiara O. Tommasi, CCCM 167 (Turnhout: Brepols, 2020). Iohannes Scottus Eriugena, *Periphyseon*, ed. É. Jeauneau, CCCM 161–5 (Turnhout: Brepols, 1996–2003).

Firth of Forth.[15] Despite his physical handicap (paralysed from the knees downward), Forbes travelled extensively, not only to Oxford and London but also to Paris, Turin, Nancy, and Venice, to collate numerous manuscripts for his edition. He settled on 20 manuscripts, from the 10th to 16th centuries, collating most of them himself, but also benefitting from the kind services of others: J. G. Krabinger collated the Munich manuscripts; J. B. Pitra also inspected manuscripts on his behalf; and E. B. Pusey helped finance this work.[16] Although it was the expanded *editio Morelliana* that ultimately served as the basis for the Patrologia Graeca, it seemed possible for a while that Abbé Migne, at the urging of Cardinal J. B. Pitra, was willing to engage Forbes (despite being 'a Protestant and a heretic') to edit the works of Gregory for his monumental series.[17] Forbes consulted the 1536 Aldus Press edition and that of Löwenklau, and also prepared his own edition, published on the facing page, of Dionysius' Latin translation using Sifanus' edition and himself collating two further manuscripts found in Oxford and the readings of three Parisian manuscripts supplied by Pitra.

In the 19th century, the work was translated once into English (entitled *On the Making of Man*; it has not been retranslated since),[18] twice into Russian,[19] and no less than three times into German (under the titles: *Ueber die Schöpfung des Menschen, Abhandlung von der Erschaffung des Menschen, Über die Austattung des Menschen*).[20] In the mid-20th century, the first French translation appeared in the Sources chrétiennes series, by Jean LaPlace (*La création de l'homme*, without a facing Greek text as later became customary for SC), a second translation four decades later in the series Les Pères dans la foi,[21] then an Italian translation (simply called *L'uomo*),[22] and most recently a new Russian translation (*Об устроении человека*).[23]

[15] For Forbes himself, see W. Perry, *George Hay Forbes: A Romance in Scholarship* (London: SPCK, 1927).

[16] Cf. Forbes, 'Monitum', 97; Perry, *George Hay Forbes*, 77–8.

[17] See the account, together with letters exchanged between Pitra and Migne, in Perry, *George Hay Forbes*, 76–85.

[18] Translation by Henry Austin Wilson in William Moore and Henry Austin Wilson, *Select Writings and Letters of Gregory, Bishop of Nyssa*, NPNF, second series, vol. 5 (1893; reprinted Grand Rapids, MI: Eerdmans, 1994); Wilson utilized some of the alternate readings noted by Forbes.

[19] Cf. Cyprien Kern, *Les traductions russe des textes patristiques: Guide bibliographique* (Chevetogne: Éditions de Chevetogne, 1957), 32: the complete works of Gregory first appeared in Християнское Чтение (Moscow, 1826–47), and then in the series Творения Святых Отцов издаваемых в русском переводе при Московской Духовной Академии vols. 37–45 (Moscow, 1861–72), vol. 37, pp. 76–222.

[20] The first title is from the series Sämmtliche Werke der Kirchen (Väter aus dem Urtexte in das Teutsche übersetzt), Bd. I (Kempten 1851); second title, trans. F. Oehler, Bibliothek der Kirchenväter, Bd. III (Leipzig, 1859), 202–315; third title, trans. H. Hayd, Bibliothek der Kirchenväter, Bd. I (Kempten, 1874), 207–317. Cf. Altenburger and Mann, *Bibliographie*, 85, 88–9, 93–4, respectively.

[21] J. LaPlace and J. Daniélou, *Grégoire de Nysse: La création de l'homme*, SC 6 (Paris: Cerf, 1943, reprinted 2002). J. Y. Guillaumin and A. G. Hamman, *Grégoire de Nysse: La création de l'homme* (Paris: Deslcée de Brouwer, 1982).

[22] B. Salmona, *Gregorio di Nissa. L'uomo*, Collana di testi patristici 32 (Rome: Città Nuova, 1982, reprinted 2000).

[23] В. Лурье, *Об устроении человека* (St Petersburg, 2000).

While we eagerly await a full *editio maior* in GNO, Forbes' edition remains the unparalleled basis from which to work. Regarding the 20 manuscripts used by Forbes and his editorial judgement, Hörner was very positive: 'All—nearly all—the important strands of transmission were available to Forbes, whose judgment in evaluating them was extraordinarily good.'[24] The manuscripts used by Forbes, together with his sigla, are:[25]

a 'Nesselii ccxvii' (i.e. Vienna, Österreichische Nationalbibliothek, *theol. gr. 222*)
α 'Burneianus 52' (i.e. London, British Library, *Burney MS 52*)
b 'Lambecii tomi iv. cod. 110' (i.e. Vienna, Österreichische Nationalbibliothek, *theol. gr. 278*)
β 'Regius 1277' (i.e. Paris, Bibliothèque nationale de France, *grec 1277*)
c 'Lamb. t. iii. cod. 63' (i.e. Vienna, Österreichische Nationalbibliothek, *theol. gr. 113*)
d 'Lamb. t. iii. cod. 62' (i.e. Vienna, Österreichische Nationalbibliothek, *theol. gr. 160*)
e 'Lamb. t. iii. cod. 64' (i.e. Vienna, Österreichische Nationalbibliothek, *theol. gr. 168*)
f 'Lamb. t. iii. cod. 65' (i.e. Vienna, Österreichische Nationalbibliothek, *theol. gr. 134*)
g 'Ædis Christi Oxonii' (i.e. Oxford Christ Church Library, *grec 45*)
h 'Codex in Museo Hunteriano Glasguae asservatus' (i.e. Glasgow, University Library, *MS Hunter 447*, contains only extracts)
i 'Mon. 192' (i.e. Munich, Bayerische Staatsbibliothek, *Cod. graec. 192*)
k 'Monac. 206' (i.e. Munich, Bayerische Staatsbibliothek, *Cod. graec. 206*, incomplete)
l 'Monac. 240' (i.e. Munich, Bayerische Staatsbibliothek, *Cod. graec. 240*)
m 'Monac. 570' (i.e. Munich, Bayerische Staatsbibliothek, *Cod. graec. 570*)
n 'Marcianus 58' (i.e. Venice, Biblioteca Nazionale di San Marco, *grec 58*)
p 'Regius 476' (i.e. Paris, Bibliothèque nationale de France, *grec 476*)
q 'Coislinianus 235' (i.e. Paris, Bibliothèque nationale de France, *Coislin grec 235*)

[24] Letter to Lara Sels, dated 20 May 2003 (Sels, *Gregory of Nyssa*, 95, ftn. 352); Sels reused Forbes' text for her parallel Greek–Slavonic edition of this treatise, but only noted those variants pertinent to the Slavonic translation.

[25] For a, b, c, d, e, and f, Forbes refers to Daniel de Nessel, *Catalogus sive Recensio specialis omnium codicum manuscriptorum graecorum, nec non linguarum orientalium, Augustissimae Bibliothecae Caesareae Vindobonensis* (Vienna: L. Voigt & J. B. Endteri, 1690), 321 (Forbes has misidentified 'a' as 'ccxvii'; Sels, *Gregory of Nyssa*, 95, gives 'ccxxvii'; it should be ccxxii), and Peter Lambeck, *Commentariorum de augustissima bibliotheca caesarea Vindobonensis, Liber Tertius, editio altera* (Vienna: J. Thomae, 1776), 286 (cod. 62), 289 (cod. 63), 294 (cod. 64), and *Liber Quartus, editio altera* (Vienna: J. Thomae, 1778), 126–7 (cod. 110).

r 'Musæ Britannici xvi. D 1' (i.e. London, British Library, *Royal MS 16 D I*)
s 'Baroccianus 144' (i.e. Oxford, Bodleian, *Barocci grec 144*)
t 'Vaticanus 408' (i.e. Vatican City, Biblioteca Apostolica Vaticana, *grec 408*)

In his brief introductory comments, Forbes suggested that these manuscripts formed two basic families: first, abcikmnqrt and, second, def, with which ghpl and s are closely connected. Further, in his assessment a/α and b/β are so close that he only recorded α or β when the reading of a or b had not been noted (and he occasionally notes when they disagree with each other).[26] Forbes also notes that '*Regius 956*' (i.e. Paris, Bibliothèque nationale de France, *grec 956*, 14th century) concurs very closely with n,[27] and he occasionally includes variant readings in his apparatus from three other manuscripts he had read: '*Regius 940*' (i.e. Paris, Bibliothèque nationale de France, *grec 940*, 14th century); '*coislin 228*' (i.e. Paris, Bibliothèque nationale de France, *coislin grec 228*, 11th century); and '*Mon. 562*' (i.e. Munich, Bayerische Staatsbibliothek, *Cod. graec. 562*, 11th century).[28] Forbes' apparatus is very complete and full of details, though his method of reference is sometimes unclear and occasionally incorrect.[29] Moreover, when his choice of text differs from those of previous editors, he notes the mss supporting his reading but not those supporting the earlier editions; but, as he does note all other variants, one can probably assume that the remaining unnamed mss align with the previous editions. Notably, Forbes also printed the list of headings following the Letter to Peter, prefacing the work, which had not been done in the *editio Morelliana* or PG (nor in the translation of Moore and Wilson), but had been included by Löwenklau in his edition.

We have further information about the manuscript tradition of Gregory's treatise, indirectly, from the study of the manuscript tradition of Basil's *Hexaemeron*, undertaken by Emmanuel Amand de Mendieta and Stig Y. Rudberg in preparation for their own edition of Basil's work.[30] They identified three different forms of collections in which Basil's work has been handed down in the manuscript tradition: first, a small collection, including Basil's *Hexaemeron* and the two homilies *In Verba: Faciamus Hominem* (also called *Sermones de creatione hominis*)[31] to which

[26] Forbes, 'Monitum', 98. [27] Forbes, 'Monitum', 97.

[28] Paris BNF *coislin grec 228*, 62–74^{v} contains chaps. 1–12.11. Munich, BSB *Cod. graec. 562*, contains only chap. 12, at 113^{r}–117^{v}, between Nemesius of Emesa's *De natura hominis* and Gregory's *De Anima*, followed by a short work of John of Damascus on those who have fallen asleep in faith.

[29] Forbes placed a superscript letter above the Greek word in the text, with the variants noted below, frequently followed by variants of subsequent words in the text in the lines that follow, before the next superscript letter.

[30] Emmanuel Amand de Mendieta and Stig Y. Rudberg, *Basile de Césarée: La tradition manuscrite directe des neuf homélies sur l'Hexaéméron*, TU 123 (Berlin: Akademie, 1980); referred to below as M–R. Emmanuel Amand de Mendieta and Stig Y. Rudberg eds, *Basilius von Caesarea: Homilien zum Hexaemeron*, GCS NF 2 (Berlin: Akademie Verlag, 1997).

[31] CPG 3215 and 3216. Ed. Alexis Smits and Michel van Esbroeck, *Basile de Césarée: Sur l'origine de l'homme*, SC 160 (Paris: Cerf, 1970); Hadwig Hörner, GNO Supplement (Brill, 1972), 2–40, 41–72; ET Nonna Verna Harrison, *St Basil the Great: On the Human Condition*, PPS (Crestwood, NY: SVS Press, 2005), 31–48, 49–64.

the apocryphal homily *De Paradiso* is sometimes added;[32] second, what they described as being the normal collection, in which the *Hexaemeron* is supplemented by *De hominis opificio* and sometimes Gregory's *Apologia in Hexaemeron*; and, third, a larger collection, which brings together all the texts that are in the small and normal collection: *Hexaemeron, De hominis opificio*, the two homilies *In Verba: Faciamus Hominem*, and occasionally the *Apologia in Hexaemeron* and the *De Paradiso*. Of the manuscripts they list, 68 contain Gregory's treatise (18 in the large collection; 50 in the normal collection), 14 of which had been used by Forbes; a full list of these 68 manuscripts and details they supplied is given in the Appendix.[33]

1. Manuscripts Used in this Edition

In the list provided on the website database 'Pinakes|*Πίνακες* Textes et manuscrits grecs', there are 166 manuscripts of Gregory's treatise.[34] For this present edition, I have re-examined several of the manuscripts used by Forbes, especially when his reading seemed questionable or he was in doubt or when his apparatus was unclear. I have also collated four of the earliest manuscripts, not used by Forbes, now digitized and available online: Vatican City, Biblioteca Apostolica Vaticana, *Vat. grec 2053* and *Vat. grec 2066*, to the latter of which also belongs Washington, Library of Congress, *Ms 60*; Oxford, Bodleian, *Barocci grec 228*; and Florence, Biblioteca Laurenziana, *grec Plut. 4.27*. I have also taken note of Paris, Bibliothèque nationale de France, *grec 1356*, two fly-leaves of which, dating from the 9th to 10th centuries, contain two passages from Gregory's treatise. For printed editions, I have compared the text as given in the Patrologia Graeca, the text which, due to the scarcity of Forbes' edition, has become the standard one in modern times, and also the *editio princeps* (Aldus, 1536). Passages from the text as they appear in Justinian's *Ep. ad Mennam*, the *Doctrina Patrum de Incarnatione Verbi*, John of Damascus' *De Sacris Imaginibus*, and the *Sacra Parallela* attributed to John of Damascus, have also been noted.

I have retained Forbes' sigla for the manuscripts, modifying *α* to Æ and *β* to ß, to avoid confusion. The information provided below is drawn from the manuscripts themselves, when available online (on the websites of the various libraries in which they are held, together with supplementary information contained therein), 'Pinakes', the study of A. de Mendieta and S. Rudberg (= M–R), Forbes, and the

[32] CPG 3217, ed. Hörner, GNO Supplement (Brill, 1972), 75–84.

[33] The mss used by Forbes are given the following designations by M–R: *β*/D 5, c/F 5, d/C 3, e/H 7, f/D 4, g/A*16, i/H 4, l/E 17, m/E 22, n/E 3, p/A 1, q/I 1, s/A*15, t/C 1. For their own edition of Basil's *Hexaemeron*, M–R used: A 1, A 2, A 3, B 1, B 2, C 1, E 1, E 2, E 3, G 1, G 2.

[34] https://pinakes.irht.cnrs.fr (accessed 23 October 2020); the information it supplies, however, should be treated with caution: it lists the 8th–9th-century Athens, *EBE 223* as containing exclusively works by Basil but also as including Gregory's treatise; and it dates Moscow, Musée historique, *grec 81 Vladimir* to the 10th century, which as M–R observe is correct for folios 2–120, but folios 121–235, in which we have Gregory's work, date to the 12th century.

catalogues of Nessel and Lambeck. Listed in date order, the manuscripts used for this edition are as follows:

9th–10th centuries

Z—Paris, Bibliothèque nationale de France, *grec 1356* (images online)

The manuscript dates from the 14th century, but two fly-leaves of this volume, containing passages from Gregory's work, date to the late 9th to early 10th centuries:[35]

fol. A[r-v] *πρῶ]τον μὲν εἰπῶν—χαρακτῆρα*: chapter 16.8–13 (16, lines 62–109).

fol. 340[r-v] *Καίσαρος εἰκόνα—ἄν(θρωπ)οι*: chapters 16.13–*titulus* 17 (16, lines 110–17, line 2).

fol. 341[r-v] *τοῖς διορατικωτέροις—σπουδαζό[μενα*: chapters 19.3–20.2 (19, line 25–20, line 26).

fol. B[r-v] *σπουδαζό]μενα Ἐπειδὴ—ἀλλ'ἀνα[γκαίοις*: chapters 20.3–21.1 (20, line 26–21, line 16).

W—Vatican City, Biblioteca Apostolica Vaticana, *grec 2053* (M–R G 1; images online)

No initial title. 248[r] (M–R and Pinakes have 247[r]) *Τῷ ἀδελφῷ δούλῳ Θεοῦ Πέτρῳ ἐπισκόπῳ Γρηγόριος ἐπίσκοπος Νύσης*. 248[rv] Ep. to Peter. 248[v] *Τοῦ ὁσίου πατρὸς ἡμῶν Γρηγορίου Νύσης. σύνταξις κεφαλαίων λ*, but no list of headings. 248[v]–283[v] treatise in 30 chapters, with headings and numbers ornately marked out. Text breaks off a few lines before the end of the treatise, at last line of 283[v], with *ὑποτίθεται, λέγων ἀπεκδύσασθαι* (chapter 30, line 301).

V—Vatican City, Biblioteca Apostolica Vaticana, *grec 2066* (M–R E 1; images online)

No initial title. 299[r] *Τῷ ἀδελφῷ δούλῳ Θεοῦ Πέτρῳ ἐπισκόπῳ Γρηγόριος ἐπίσκπος Νύσης*. 299[r]–300[r] Ep. to Peter. 300[r]–301[r] list of 30 headings with numbers in margin. 301[r] heading *Τοῦ ἁγίου Γρηγορίου ἐπίσκοπου Νύσης*, then title of first chapter. 301[r]–316[v] incomplete text, containing first 11 chapters and part of chapter 12; text of treatise breaks off at last line of 316[v], with *κάτοπτρον γινομένην κρατεῖ* (chapter 12, lines 119). Chapter divisions are clearly indicated by line of ornamentation and the chapter numbers are written in the margin.

[35] Identified by Charles Astruc, 'Deux fragments anciens (en minuscule de type "Anastase") du *De hominis opificio* de Grégoire de Nysse', *Scriptorium: revue internationale des études relatives aux manuscrits*, 39.1 (1985), 265–9, who also provides a list of variants.

To this manuscript belong the two folios that constitute Washington, Library of Congress, *Ms 60* (images online with *grec 2066*):[36]

fol. 1^{rv} *ἀσώμα]τον; πῶς—τῶν γεγραμμένων αἰνίττεται* chapter 16.3–8 (16, lines 21–62).

fol. 2^{rv} *ἐν οἷς τόινυν—δοχεῖ τὸν μέγαν* chapters 18.8–19.4 (18, line 71–19, line 29).

N—Venice, Biblioteca Nazionale di San Marco, *grec 58* (M–R E 3)

65^{v} title in red uncials: *Τοῦ μακαρίου καὶ ἐν ἁγίοις Γρηγορίου ἐπισκόπου Νύσσης· εἰς τὴν ἀναπλήρωσιν τῶν προκειμένων τῆς ἑξαημέρου.* 65^{v}–66^{v}: *πρόλογος τῷ ἀδελφῷ δούλῳ Θεοῦ Πέτρῳ ἐπισκόπῳ Γρηγόριος ἐπίσκοπος Νύσης.* 66^{v}–67^{v} list of 31 headings, under the title: *κεφάλαια ἐμπιλόσοφα περὶ τῆς τοῦ ἀνθρώπου κτίσεως· καὶ περὶ τῆς τοῦ κόσμου δὲ μερικῶς· ἅπερ ἦν λείποντα τῇ ἑξαημέρῳ· ἥν προείρηκεν ὁ μακάριος καὶ ἐν ἁγίοις Βασίλειος.* 67^{v}–116^{r} text in 31 chapters, with scholia.

10th century

X—Florence, Biblioteca Medicea Laurenziana, *grec 4.27* (M–R A 3; images online)

(Dated to the first part of the 10th century) No initial title. 186^{v} *Τῷ ἀδελφῷ δούλῳ Θεοῦ Πέτρῳ ἐπισκόπῳ Γρηγόριος ἐπίσκπος Νύσης.* 186^{v}–187^{v} Ep. to Peter. 187^{v}–188^{v} list of 30 headings with numbers. 188^{v}–240^{v} treatise in 30 chapters with numbers in the margins, and scholia.

P—Paris, Bibliothèque nationale de France, *grec 476* (M–R A 1; images online)

(Dated to the first part of the 10th century) No initial title. 64^{v} *Τῷ ἀδελφῷ δούλῳ Θεοῦ Πέτρῳ ἐπισκόπῳ Γρηγόριος ἐπίσκπος Νύσης.* 64^{v}–65^{v} Ep. to Peter. 65^{v}–66^{v} list of 30 headings. 66^{v}–116^{v} treatise in 30 chapters, with numbers in the margins, and scholia. 116^{v} *explicit*: *Τοῦ ἁγίου Γρεγορίου ἐπισκόπου Νύσης θεώρια εἰς τὴν κατασκευὴν τοῦ ἀνθρώπου*, written around an image of the cross.

S—Oxford, Bodleian, *Barocci grec 144* (M–R A*15; images online)

(Dated to the second part of the 10th century) No initial title. 98^{v} *Τῷ ἀδελφῷ δούλῳ Θεοῦ Πέτρῳ ἐπισκόπῳ Γρηγόριος ἐπίσκπος Νύσης.* 98^{v}–100^{r} Ep. to Peter. 100^{r}–101^{r} list of 30 headings. 101^{v}–174^{v} treatise in 30 chapters, with numbers in

[36] See Werner Jaeger, 'Greek Uncial Fragments in the Library of Congress in Washington', *Traditio*, 5 (1947), 79–102, with plates, and a full and fascinating study of the manuscript's history. Jaeger identifies the ms as having come from Constantinople and calculates that these folios would have been fols. 325 and 332 of *Vat. grec* 2066.

the margins. 174^{v} *explicit* in black uncials: *τοῦ ἐν ἁγίου Γρηγορίου ἐπισκόπου νύσης θεωρία εἰς τὴν κατασκευὴν τοῦ ἀνθρώπου.*

T—Vatican City, Biblioteca Apostolica Vaticana, *grec 408* (M–R C 1; images online)

(Dated to the second part of the 10th century) No initial title. 89^{v} *Τῷ ἀδελφῷ δούλῳ Θεοῦ Πέτρῳ ἐπισκόπῳ Γρηγόριος ἐπίσκπος Νύσσης.* 89^{v}–91^{r} Ep. to Peter. 91^{r}–92^{v} list of 31 headings. 92^{v}–161^{v} treatise in 31 chapters, with numbers written in the margins and scholia.

10th–11th centuries

O—Oxford, Bodleian, *Barocci grec 228* (M–R E 6; images online)

65^{r} two dodecasyllables in the hand of the copyist: *ὡς αὐτάδελφος καὶ ὁμότροπος πέλων, πληροῖ τὸ λεῖπον τοῦ σοφοῦ Βασιλείου.* 65^{r} title: *περὶ εἰκόνος ἀνθρώπου τοῦ μακαρίου Γρηγορίου ἀδελφοῦ τοῦ ἁγίου Βασιλείου.* 65^{r}: *Τῷ τιμιωτάτῳ ἀδελφῷ δούλῳ Θεοῦ Πέτρῳ ἐπισκόπῳ Γρηγόριος ἐν κυρίῳ χαίρειν.* 65^{r}–66^{r} Ep. to Peter. 66^{r}–67^{r} list of 31 headings. 67^{r}–118^{v} treatise in 31 chapters, with numbers in margin, and scholia. 118^{v}, *explicit* in black uncials: *Γρηγορίου ἐπισκόπου Νύσσης ἀδελφοῦ τοῦ ἁγίου Βασιλείου θεωρία εἰς τὴν τοῦ ἀνθρώπου κατασκευήν.*

Q—Paris, Bibliothèque nationale de France, *Coislin 235* (M–R I 1; images online)

No initial title. 121^{r} *Τῷ ἀδελφῷ δούλῳ Θεοῦ Πέτρῳ ἐπισκόπῳ Γρηγόριος ἐπίσκπος νύσης εἰς τὸν ἄνθρωπον.* 121^{r}–123^{r} Ep. to Peter. 123^{r}–124^{v} list of 31 headings. 124^{v}–208^{v} treatise in 31 chapters, with numbers in the margins. Text breaks off a few lines before the conclusion of chapter 31, with *ἐν τῷ ἀτελεῖ καὶ ἐν* (chapter 30, line 278).

D—Vienna, Österreichische Nationalbibliothek, *theol. gr. 160* (M–R C 3)

Beginning damaged; Ep. to Peter missing. 60^{r} *Τοῦ ἐν ἁγίοις πατρὸς ἡμῶν Γρηγορίου ἐπισκόπου Νύσσης κεφάλαια τριάκοντα εἰς τὴν τοῦ ἀνθρώπου κατασκευήν*, followed by list of 30 headings. 61^{r}–113^{v}, text of treatise missing first seven chapters and first part of chapter 8.

11th century

J—Munich, Bayerische Staatsbibliothek, *Cod. graec. 562* (113^{v}–117^{r}; images online)

Chapter 12 only.

12th–13th centuries

Æ—London, British Library, *Burney MS 52* (Forbes α; images online)

No initial title. 88^{v} *Πρὸς Πέτρον τὸν ἴδιον ἀδελφὸν θεωρία εἰς τὴν τοῦ ἀνθρώπου κατασκευήν*. 88^{v}–89^{r} Ep. to Peter; 89^{r}–90^{r} list of 31 headings (missing no. 19). 90^{v}–130^{r} treatise in 31 chapters. Chapter titles, and the numbers in margins, written in red ink.

13th century

R—London, British Library, *Royal MS 16 D I* (images online)

117^{v}, two headings: *'Επιστολὴ Γργορίου ἐπισκόπου Νύσης πρὸς Πέτρον τὸν ἴδιον ἀδελφὸν εἰς τὰ λοιπὰ τοῦ ἐξαημέρου τοῦ ἀδελφοῦ αὐτῷ Βασιλείου* then *Τῷ ἀδελφῷ αὐτοῦ Πέτρῳ ἐπισκόπῳ Γρηγόριος ἐπίσκοπος Νύσης προοίμιον τῶν λα κεφαλαίων τῶν ἐν τῇ ἐξαημέρῳ λεχθέντων τὰ παραλειπόμενα τοῦ μεγάλου Βασιλείου*. 117^{v}–118^{r} Ep. to Peter. No list of headings, but instead another heading: *τοῦ ἐν ἁγίοις πατρὸς ἡμῶν Γρηγορίου ἐπισκόπου Νύσης* followed by heading for chapter 1. 118^{v}–143^{r} treatise in 31 chapters; headings marked by large capitals, only 11 marked by numbers in the margins.

G—Oxford Christ Church Library, *grec 45* (M–R A*16)

No initial title. 115^{r}–116^{v} Ep. to Peter. 116^{v}–118^{r} list of 30 headings; 118^{r}–194^{r} text in 30 chapters, with scholia. 194^{r} *explicit*: *Τοῦ ἐν ἁγίου Γρηγορίου ἐπισκόπου Νύσης θεωρία εἰς τὴν κατασκευὴν τοῦ ἀνθρώπου* and this dodecasyllable verse: + *ὁ σταυρὸς ἀρχὴ καὶ τέλος καλῶν πέλει.*

F—Vienna, Österreichische Nationalbibliothek, *theol. gr. 134* (M–R D 4; images online)

(Dated by ÖNB to 1200 Constantinople; by Pinakes to *c*.1300) No initial title. 95^{r} *τῷ ἀδελφῷ δούλῳ Θεοῦ Πέτρῳ ἐπισκόπῳ Γρηγόριος ἐπίσκπος νίσης*. 95^{r}–96^{v} Ep. to Peter. 96^{v}–98^{r} list of 30 headings. 98^{r}–150^{v} text; headings and numbers, in margins, in red ink.

14th century

H—Glasgow, University Library, *MS Hunter 447 (V.5.17)*

Extracts: chapters 1, 3, 6, 7 (with lacunae), 10, 11, 12; then three excerpts from chapter 8, under the title: *Διά τι τελευταῖος κατεσκευάσθη ὁ ἄνθρωπος*; then chapters 13, 14, 15, and fragments from chapters 16, 20, 21, then chapters 24 and 30.

I—Munich, Bayerische Staatsbibliothek, *Cod. graec. 192* (M–R H 4; images online)

(Dated *c.*1370) 111^{v} title: *Τοῦ ἁγίου Γρηγορίου ἐπισκόπου Νύσης, εἰς τὴν ἑξαήμερον· τοῦ μακαρίου Γρηγορίου ἐπισκόπου Νύσης ἀδελφοῦ τοῦ ἁγίου βασιλείου περὶ εἰκόνος ἀνθρώπου τῷ τιμιωτάτῳ ἀδελφῳ δούλῳ τοῦ Θεοῦ Πέτρῳ γρηγόριος ἐν Κυρίω χαίρειν.* 111^{v}–112^{v} Ep. to Peter. 112^{v}–113^{v} list of 31 headings. 114^{r}–166^{v} treatise in 31 chapters, with headings and numbers (placed before the heading) in red ink.

M—Munich, Bayerische Staatsbibliothek, *Cod. graec. 570* (M–R E 22)

108^{r}–170^{v} title *Τοῦ ἐν ἁγίοις πατρὸς Γρηγορίου ἐπισκόπου Νύσσης πρὸς Πέτρον ἴδιον ἀδελφὸν εἰς τὰ λοιπὰ τῆς ἑξαημέρου τοῦ ἀδελφοῦ αὐτῷ Βασιλείου· τουτέστιν εἰς τὴν κατακσκευὴν τοῦ ἀνθρώπου.* Ep. to Peter. List of 30 headings. Treatise in 30 chapters.

ß—Paris, Bibliothèque nationale de France, *grec 1277* (Forbes *β*; M–R D 5; images online)

54^{v}–55^{r} list of 30 headings. 55^{r}–56^{r} Ep. to Peter: *Τοῦ ἐν ἁγίοις πατρὸς ἡμῶν Γρηγορίου ἐπισκόπου Νύσσης θεωρία εἰς τὴν τοῦ ἀνθρώπου κατασκευὴν· πρὸς τὸν ἐπίσκοπον ἀδελφὸν αὐτοῦ Πέτρον.* 56^{r}–82^{v} treatise in 30 chapters, with chapter numbers in the margins.

E—Vienna, Österreichische Nationalbibliothek, *theol. gr. 168* (M–R: H 7)

(Pinakes 14th century; M–R 15th century) Lacking Ep. to Peter and list of headings. 73^{v} title: *εἰς τὴν τοῦ ἀνθρώπου κατασκευήν.* 73^{v}–120^{r} treatise in 30 chapters.

A—Vienna, Österreichische Nationalbibliothek, *theol. gr. 222*

134^{r} *Τοῦ Γρηγορίου ἐπισκόπου Νύσσης πρὸς πέτρον τὸν ἴδιον ἀδελφὸν εἰς τὰ λοιπὰ τῆς ἑξαημέρου τοῦ ἀδελφοῦ αὐτῷ Βασιλείου περὶ τῶν προγεγονότων τῶν τοῦ ἀνθρώπου γενέσεως.* 134^{r}–187^{r} treatise in 30 chapters.

B—Vienna, Österreichische Nationalbibliothek, *theol. gr. 278*

2^{r} *Τοῦ ἐν ἁγίοις πατρὸς ἡμῶν Γρηγορίου ἐπισκόπου Νύσσης θεωρία εἰς τὴν τοῦ ἀνθρώπου κατασκευὴν· πρὸς τὸν ἐπίσκοπον καὶ ἀδελφὸν αὐτοῦ Πέτρον.* 2^{r}–49^{v} treatise in 30 chapters.

15th century

C—Vienna, Österreichische Nationalbibliothek, *theol. gr. 113* (M–R F 5)

(Dated 27 August 1412) 79^{r} title: *περὶ εἰκόνος ἀνθρώπου· τοῦ μακαρίου Γρηγορίου ἀδελφοῦ τοῦ ἁγίου Βασιλείου τῷ τιμιωτάτῳ ἀδελφῷ δούλῳ Θεοῦ πέτρῳ ἐπισκόπῳ Γρηγόριος ἐν Κυρίῳ χαίρειν.* 79^{r}–80^{r} Ep. to Peter. 80^{r}–81^{r} list of 31 headings. 81^{v}–138^{r} treatise in 31 chapters.

L—Munich, Bayerische Staatsbibliothek, *Cod. graec. 240* (M–R E 17; images online)

(Dated by BSB and Pinakes to the 15th century; by M–R to the 14th century) 65^{r} title: *Τοῦ ἐν ἁγίοις πατρὸς ἡμῶν Γρηγορίου ἐπισκόπου Νύσης κεφάλαια τριάκοντα εἰς τὴν τοῦ ἀνθρώπου κατασκευήν.* 65^{r}–66^{r} Ep. to Peter. 66^{r}–109^{v} text divided into 30 chapters; headings marked by large capital in the margin together with number, in red ink.

16th century

K—Munich, Bayerische Staatsbibliothek, *Cod. graec. 206*

(Dated to the second half of the 16th century) 1^{r}–34^{r} incomplete. Forbes gives the title as: *περὶ εἰκόνος ἀνθρώπου τοῦ μακαρίου Γρηγορίου ἀδελφοῦ τοῦ ἁγίου Βασιλείου.* On 17^{v} there is the title of chapter 18 (19), with number *ιθ̅* given in the margin, and on 31^{r} title of chapter 30 (31) without an accompanying number; the manuscript would thus have originally been in 31 chapters.

Indirect Witnesses

Justinian, *Ep. ad Mennam*

28.4–14 (*τάχα—ἐνφυσήματος*) = *Ep. ad Mennam* (ACO 3, 199.22–31)

28.28–74 (*οἱ τῷ προτέρῳ—σώμασι*) = *Ep. ad Mennam* (ACO 3, 199.32–200.37)

Doctrina Patrum de Incarnatione Verbi

4.6–9 (*ἡ μὲν γὰρ—διοικουμένην*) = 19, VII (Diekamp, 122.14–15)

15.7–10 (*πᾶν τὸ—προσηγορίαν ἔχει*) = 22, XI (Diekamp, 140.13–18)

15.16–17 (*ἃ μὴ—τὴν κλῆσιν*) = 22, XII (Diekamp, 140.1–2)

John of Damascus, *De Sacris Imaginibus*

4.11–17 (*ὥσπερ—ὀνόματος*) = *Imag.* 1.49/2.45 (Kotter, 3.153.4–11)

5.2–6 (*Τὸ δὲ—τὸ ὁμοίωμα*) = *Imag.* 1.50/2.46 (Kotter, 3.154.3–9)

John of Damascus (?), *Sacra Parallela*

4.6–11 (*ἡ μὲν γὰρ ψυχὴ—φύσιν*) = II^{1}98/K cap. A 2, 20 (Thum, 117.3–9)

4.11–5.3 (*ὥσπερ—θεωρεῖται*) = $\Pi^1$38/K cap. A 1, 38 (Thum, 67.11–68.5)

13.12–25 (*ὕπνος—ἄνεσις*) = $\Pi^1$2122/K cap. *Υ* 3, 8 (Thum, 1122.3–19)

16.89–98 (*ἐπεὶ δὲ—τὴν γνώμην*) = $\Pi^1$99/K cap. A 2, 21 (Thum, 117.12–118.5)

23.6–7 (*ὁ γὰρ—τέλους*) = $\Pi^1$52/K cap. A 1, 52 (Thum, 86, 10)

28.4–17, 28.20–29.98 (*τάχα—γίνεται, ἐπεὶ—βλαστημάτων ἐγένετο*) = $\Pi^1$39/K cap. A 1, 39 (Thum, 68.8–74.21)

30.90–6 (*ἐπειδὴ—πνεῦμα*) = $\Pi^1$1218/K cap. K 1, 19 (Thum, 687.2–11)

30.250–1 (*ἀλλὰ—φύσεως*) = $\Pi^1$40/K cap. 1, 40 (Thum, 74.24–5)

30.253–78 (*τὸ γὰρ—τέλειον*) = $\Pi^1$40/K cap. 1, 40 (Thum, 74.25–75.27)

As mentioned earlier, Forbes had already noted that his manuscripts fell into two main groups. On the basis of the analysis of variant readings noted in this edition, it appears that his second group, D E F, occurs 12 times, always in combination with other manuscripts, never as the only three witnesses. However, D G L P S X occur together as the sole witnesses to a variant reading 29 times, and together with other manuscripts 79 times (with E 10 times; F 10 times; H 25 times). These manuscripts, moreover, all divide the text into 30 chapters. Listed in date order, they are:

X 10th century, first half
P 10th century, first half
S 10th century, second half
D 10th–11th centuries (missing last part of chapter 7 and first part of chapter 8)
G 13th century
F 13th century
E 14th century
H 14th century
L 15th century (missing list of chapters after the Letter to Peter).

The remaining manuscripts, A Æ B ß C I K M N O Q R T V W Z, also form a distinct group. This group contains manuscripts having both 30 chapters (A B ß M V W) and 31 chapters (Æ C I K N O Q R T). However, their variant readings are so close that it seems impossible to differentiate them into two distinct subgroups. Indeed, as mentioned earlier, Forbes had noticed that two pairs are particularly close, A (with 30 chapters) and Æ (with 31), and B-ß, so that he only recorded Æ or ß when A or B had not been noted, and the few times when they disagree with each other. On the seven occasions noted in this edition where A differs from Æ, it shares readings with the other group (always with D with one exception, when it agrees with G P X).[37] A full examination of the various groupings of manuscripts, their transmission, and the reason behind some having 30 chapters while others have 31, must await a full examination of all 166 known manuscripts.

For our purposes here, it is sufficient to note that whereas Forbes' group of A/Æ B/ß C I K M N Q R T occurs together, either by themselves or with other manuscripts, only ten times, the group Æ A B ß I K N O Q T occurs 67 times, and with C a further 25 times, with M 32 times, with R 41 times, with V 14 times, with W 12 times; the fragmentary Z, on the two occasions when it shares variant readings with other manuscripts, does so with W once, and N T V W once. In date order they appear as follows:

W	9th–10th centuries	30 chaps	N	9th–10th centuries	31 chaps + list
V	9th–10th centuries	30 chaps + list	O	10th–11th centuries	31 chaps + list
A	14th century	30 chaps	Q	10th–11th centuries	31 chaps + list
ß	14th century	30 chaps + list	T	10th century, second half	31 chaps + list
B	14th century	30 chaps	Æ	12th–13th centuries	31 chaps + list
M	14th century	30 chaps + list	R	13th century	31 chaps
I	14th century	31 chaps + list			
C	15th century	31 chaps + list			
K	16th century	31 chaps			

Latin Translations

The Latin translations of Dionysius and Eriugena have also been collated for this edition. For that of Dionysius, I have used the edition of Forbes, who used the following manuscripts:

Oxford, *Laud Misc. 123* (12th century, English, Gloucester), incip. f. 94^{v}; in 31 chapters, missing list of headings.

Oxford, *Ms Bodl. 238* (14th century, English), f. 185^{r}–197^{r}; in 31 chapters, with list, but different set of headings.

[37] Chapter 23, line 40 *εὑρήσοι* A (*sed non* Æ) D G^{2} P S; 25, line 5 *νῦν om.* A (*sed non* Æ) D L; 25, line 7 *ἀνάστασιν*] *διάστασιν* A (*sed non* Æ) G P X; 29, line 72 *τοῦ φυτοῦ*] *τούτου* A (*sed non* Æ) D E F L N^{mg} P S X; 29, line 77 *ψυχικὰς*] *τῆς ψυχῆς* A (*non* Æ) D E F L P S X; 30, line 16 *τὴν ἀνθρωπίνην συστῆναι ζωὴν* A (*non* Æ) D E F H L P S X: *τὴν ἀνθρωπίνην ζωὴν συστῆναι* I. There are ten occasions when B differs from ß, only one of which is shared with other mss (N and P) at 13, line 156. For A/Æ, the similar case is 30, line 112 *τῆς om.* A (*non* Æ) B D E G H P X.

Paris, Bibliothèque nationale de France, *Lat. 2633* (12th–13th centuries), incip. f. 98^{v}; in 31 chapters with list of headings.

Paris, Bibliothèque nationale de France, *Lat. 1710* (14th century), incip. f. 1^{r}; in 31 chapters with list of headings.

Paris, Bibliothèque nationale de France, *Lat. 1701* (13th century), incip. f. 42^{v}; in 31 chapters with list of headings.

For the translation of Eriugena, we now have the critical edition of Giovanni Mandolino with the extensive introduction by Chiara Tommasi.[38] For their edition of *De Imagine*, the following manuscripts were used:

Bamberg, Staatsbibliothek, *Patr. 78* (*olim* B.IV.13), f. 88^{r}–114^{r}

Paris, Bibliothèque nationale de France, *n.a. Lat. 2664*, f. 122^{r}–139^{v}

Paris, Bibliothèque nationale de France, *Lat.* 18095, f. 40^{v}–41^{r}

Berlin, *Lat. Qu. 690* (Görres 87), f. 186^{r}–186^{v} (fragment)

Reims, Bibliothèque Municipale, *875*

Vatican City, *Vat. Reg. lat.* 195, f. 61^{v}–62^{r}

Mandolino also collated the previous edition of Cappuyns, together with Forbes' edition of the Greek text and his edition of Dionysius' translation, the translation of Löwenklau (Levvenklaius) in PG, and the text as it appears in Eriugena's *Periphyseon*, as edited by Édouard Jeauneau. Comparing Eriugena's translation to the variant readings of the Greek manuscripts provided by Forbes, Tommasi concludes that the manuscript to which Eriugena's translation has greatest affinity is Q (Paris, Bibliothèque nationale de France, *Coislin* 235). For this edition, notice has only been made of substantive differences (which are indeed significant, especially regarding how Gregory's text has been translated in chapter 16). Notice has not been made, for instance, of differences of word order or matters more properly pertaining to the transmission of the Latin manuscripts themselves; for example, in chapter 16.14 (line 112) *πρὸς ὅ τι* is rendered *aliquid*, which Mandolino corrected to *ad quid*, based on the translation of this passage given in Eriugena's *Periphyseon* and the Greek text.

This edition thus represents an intermediary stage while we await the full *editio maior* from GNO. I have transcribed Forbes' text and critical apparatus, putting the latter into a more familiar and accessible format, and checked his readings when his apparatus was unclear, when he was himself in doubt, or when his

[38] Iohannis Scotti seu Eriugenae, *Carmina; De Imagine*, ed. Michael W. Herren, Andrew Dunning, Giovanni Mandolino, and Chiara O. Tommasi, CCCM 167 (Turnhout: Brepols, 2020).

reading seemed questionable. I have further collated five of the earliest manuscripts, which were not available to Forbes but are now online (O V W X Z), and also collated the Latin translations of Dionysius and Eriugena, both of which had been done by their previous editors (Forbes and Mandolino, respectively), but now brought together with further observations.

2. Title

Aspects of the four elements of the work—title, Letter to Peter, list of headings, and the divisions within the treatise—have many variations from the earliest testimonies to the work and within the manuscript traditions. The division of works into chapters, the use of chapter titles, the development of a table of contents, and other similar matters were unfortunately not of much interest to previous generations of editors. These 'paratexts' have, however, garnered more interest in recent decades and are important, for they have much to offer us in our understanding of the work itself and the history of its reception.[39]

The earliest witness to Gregory's treatise, writing only a century and a half after Gregory himself, is Dionysius Exiguus (*c*.470–540) in his letter to Eugippus which accompanied his translation of this treatise of Gregory. In the letter he refers to the work as *De conditione hominis* and mentions that it is divided into 31 chapters (PL 67, 345c). However, the manuscripts of his translation used by Forbes (for the work has yet to be fully edited) have the title *De imagine id est de hominis conditione* as well as *De conditione hominis*; the manuscripts consistently divide the work into 31 chapters, but differ as to whether

[39] Most of the recent work has concentrated on the Latin tradition. See J.-C. Fredouille, Marie-Odile Goulet-Cazé, Philippe Hoffmann, and Pierre Petitmengin, *Titres et articulation du texte dans les ouvrages antiques: Actes du Colloque International de Chantilly, 13–15 décembre 1994*, CÉA, SA 152 (Paris: Institut d'Études Augustiniennes, 1997); Bianca-Jeanette Schröder, *Titel und Text: Zur Entwicklung lateinischer Gedichtüberschriften. Mit Untersuchungen zu lateinischen Buchtiteln, Inhaltsverzeichnissen und anderen Gliederungsmitteln* (Berlin: De Gruyter, 1999); Andrew M. Riggsby, 'Guides to the Wor(l)d', in Jason König and Tim Whitmarsh, eds., *Ordering Knowledge in the Roman Empire* (Cambridge: Cambridge University Press, 2007), 88–107; Laura Jansen, *The Roman Paratext: Frame, Texts, Readers* (Cambridge: Cambridge University Press, 2014); Joseph A. Howley, 'Tables of Contents', in Dennis Duncan and Adam Smith, *Book Parts* (Oxford: Oxford University Press, 2019), 67–79; Nicholas Dames, 'Chapter Heads', in Duncan and Smith, *Book Parts*, 153–64; and for the Greek tradition, Patrick Andrist, 'Towards a Definition of Paratexts and Paratextuality: The Case of Ancient Greek Manuscripts', in Liv Ingeborg Lied and Marilena Maniaci, eds., *Bible as Notepad: Tracing Annotations and Annotation Practices in Late Antique and Medieval Biblical Manuscripts*, Manuscripta Biblica 3 (Berlin: de Gruyter, 2018), 130–50; Jeremiah Coogan, 'Transforming Textuality: Porphyry, Eusebius, and Late Ancient Tables of Contents', *SLA* 5.1 (2021), 6–27. See also the fascinating series of postings on this topic by Roger Pearse over the last decade at www.roger-pearse.com (accessed 7 March 2020), tagged 'chapter headings'. For a critical study of the importance of such phenomena, see Gérard Genette, *Paratexts: Thresholds of Interpretation*, trans. Jane E. Lewin, Literature, Culture, Theory 20 (Cambridge: Cambridge University Press, 1997 [French edn. 1987]).

or not they have a list of headings following the Letter to Peter.[40] Three centuries later, Eriugena, who also translated the work, refers to it in his *Periphyseon* as Gregory's *Sermo de imagine*; his translation seems to have contained 31 chapters and lacks a list of headings.[41] In the case of both Dionysius and Eriugena, however, their rendering of Gregory's Letter to Peter concludes with the sentence introducing a list of headings. Regarding translations, it should be noted that *Vat. sir. 106*, dated to approximately 700 CE, has the title *On the Formation [twqn'] of the Human Being* and is divided into 31 chapters, with a list of headings following the Letter to Peter. We will return to this important manuscript later.

Our earliest reference to the work in Greek is provided by Justinian in his *Epistle to Mennas* (543 CE), where he refers to it as ἡ εἰς τὸν ἄνθρωπον πραγματεία, and quotes two passages from chapter 28, without providing a chapter number.[42] The 7th–8th-century text known as *Doctrina Patrum de Incarnatione Verbi* gives three passages from this work of Gregory, together with chapter numbers. The first, from chapter 4, refers to the work as ἡ εἰς τὸν ἄνθρωπον θεωρία. For the second and third quotations, Diekamp gives the title as ἡ εἰς τὸν ἄνθρωπον κατασκευή, although the 15th-century manuscript *Vaticanus gr. 1102* gives it as ἡ εἰς τὸν ἄνθρωπον ὅτι κατ' εἰκόνα; these two passages are said to have come from chapter ις (16, which is chapter 15 in this edition), indicating that the manuscripts used were divided into 31 chapters.[43] In the 8th century, John of Damascus, despite quoting from it in his *Apology for the Holy Icons*, refers to it as περὶ κατασκευῆς ἀνθρώπου.[44] John also provides references to the chapter number from which he quotes, although as these are from chapters 4 to 5, it is not possible to determine whether his text had 30 or 31 chapters. The *Sacra Parallela*, attributed to John of Damascus, also has a number of passages from Gregory's work, referring to it as ἡ εἰς τὸν ἄνθρωπον θεωρίας. Suidas also refers to this work of Gregory as τεῦχος θαυμάσιον εἰς τὴν τοῦ ἀνθρώπου κατασκευὴν. As noted earlier, the first printed edition of the work, that of the Aldus Press (1536), entitled the

[40] Oxford, *Laud Misc. 123* (12th century), on 94[r] has the title *De imagine id est de hominis conditione* and is divided into 31 chapters, with no list of chapters; Oxford *Ms Bodl. 238* (14th century), on 285[v] has the title *De conditione hominis*, and is also divided into 31 chapters, but has a list of headings different to any other mss.

[41] John Scottus Eriugena, *Periphyseon (De divisione naturae)*, ed. I. P. Sheldon-Williams, Scriptores Latini Hiberniae, 7, 9, 11, 13 (Dublin: Dublin Institute for Advanced Study, 1999 [1968], 2017 [1972], 2005 [1981], 2009 [1995]): vol. 3: 735d5 (p. 292), 737a17 (p. 294); vol. 4: 758c1 (p. 40), 788a2 (p. 110), 788b2 (p. 112), 793c1 (p. 124). The only complete manuscript of Eriugena's translation (Bamberg, Staatsbibliothek *Patr. 78*) has for the title: *Sermo Gregorii Episcopi Nysae de <Imagine> in ea quae relicta sunt in Examero a beato Basilio suo fratre*; the ms has a space where Mandolino has supplied *imagine*. A number of the later chapters numbers are missing (e.g. 24–6, 30); however, as chapter 12 (in the division into 30 chapters) is divided into two, it seems certain that Eriugena's translation originally contained 31 chapters, as does Q, which Tommasi identifies as having the greatest affinity with his translation, though Q also has a list of headings.

[42] Ed. Eduard Schwartz, *ACO* 3, 199.21–200.37.

[43] Ed. Franz Diekamp, rev. B. Phanourgakis and E. Chrysos (Münster: Aschendorff, 1981), 122, 140–1.

[44] Ed. Kotter, 3, 153.3–11, 154.3–9.

treatise *Βίβλος περὶ ἄνθρωπον*. This edition is divided into 30 chapters (though they are not numbered), and it places the list of headings at the end of the work, after the colophon, rather than after the Letter to Peter. It was only with Löwenklau's edition (1567) that it became customary to refer to the work as *περὶ κατασκευῆς ἀνθρώπου*—*De hominis opificio*—and to present it in 30 chapters with a list of headings following the Letter to Peter, although the list was then omitted in both the *editio Morelliana* and the PG, but included by Forbes.

While we await a full study of the Greek manuscript tradition, from those inspected for this volume and the information regarding those manuscripts belonging to the *Hexaemeron* tradition given by de Mendieta and Rudberg, it is clear that the manuscripts are themselves divided regarding the title and the number of chapters (and that this difference cuts across the two main manuscript groups). The earliest manuscripts which have a title for this work give it as *περὶ εἰκόνος ἀνθρώπου*: that is, from the 9th to 10th centuries, *Vat. grec 413*, which lacks the Letter to Peter but does have a list of 31 headings between the initial title and chapter 1;[45] and, from the 10th to 11th centuries, *Bodl. Barocci grec 228*, again with 31 chapters but also supplying a list of headings. From the 11th to 16th centuries, there are four other manuscripts (one of which is incomplete) which use *περὶ εἰκόνος ἀνθρώπου* as the title, each with 31 chapters and two with a list of headings.[46]

The title *θεωρία εἰς τὴν κατασκευὴν τοῦ ἀνθρώπου* is first found in the *explicit* of two 10th-century manuscripts, neither of which have an initial title to the treatise, but each of which have 30 chapters and a list of headings: *Bodl. Barocci grec 144*, and Paris, BNF, *grec 476*.[47] The earliest manuscript with 31 chapters which uses the designation *θεωρία εἰς τὴν κατασκευὴν τοῦ ἀνθρώπου*, although again only in the *explicit* (for it has as the title *περὶ εἰκόνος ἀνθρώπου*), is Bodleian *Barocci grec 228* from the 10th to 11th centuries. Also from the same period, Paris, BNF, *Coislin 228* uses an abbreviated form of this designation, though as a concluding phrase in the heading to the Letter to Peter it has: *Τῷ ἀδελφῷ δούλῳ Θεοῦ Πέτρῳ ἐπισκόπῳ Γρηγόριος ἐπίσκπος νύσης εἰς τὸν ἄνθρωπον*. The first clear example of a

[45] According to de Mendieta and Rudberg, *Basile de Césarée*, 119, *Vat. grec 413* (which is not online) is missing the Letter to Peter, but has the list of 31 headings (374^v–375^v), and has the treatise under the title *περὶ εἰκόνος ἀνθρώπου* (375^v–413^r); folios 1–2 and 412–13 of this ms were replaced in the 16th century.

[46] Athos, Lavra, *grec B.77* (11th century), with no list of headings; Munich, BSB, *Cod. graec. 192* (14th century) and Vienna, ÖNB, *theol. gr. 113* (15th century), both with a list of headings; and the incomplete 16th-century Munich, BSB, *Cod. graec. 206*, which, as chapter 18/19 is designated as 19, would also have been in 31 chapters. It is interesting to note that this is also the title given in the Slavonic translation (О Образъ Чловѣка); see Sels, *Gregory of Nyssa*.

[47] *Vat. grec 2053* (9th–10th centuries) is also divided into 30 chapters but has no initial title; after the Letter to Peter it has the heading *Τοῦ ὁσίου πατρὸς ἡμῶν Γρηγορίου Νύσης. σύνταξις κεφαλαίων λ*, but then goes straight to chapter 1, without providing a list of headings. Likewise *Vat. grec 2066* (9th–10th centuries), without an initial title, is also divided into 30 chapters and provides a list of headings following the Letter to Peter. The remaining ms from this period, Venice, Biblioteca Nazionale di San Marco, *grec 58*, has 31 chapters and has a different title, mentioned below.

manuscript with 31 chapters, a list of headings, and the title *θεωρία εἰς τὴν τοῦ ἀνθρώπου κατασκευήν*, given after the Letter to Peter and before the list of headings, is the 12th-century Moscow, Musée historique, *grec 81 Vladimir*.[48] Besides the five manuscripts mentioned here, 20 other manuscripts use this title, variously having either 30 or 31 chapters (see Appendix).

It should also be noted that other manuscripts refer to Gregory's work in yet other ways. Some present the work simply as a completion of the *Hexaemeron* of Basil.[49] The 12th-century manuscript Paris, BN, *grec 479* has the title *εἰς τὸν ἄνθρωπον θεωρία*, which is closest to that used in the Aldus edition (*Βίβλος περὶ ἀνθρώπου*): it, however, is divided into 31 chapters and includes a list of headings. Several manuscripts use other words than *κατασκευή*: *διάπλασις*,[50] *κτίσις*,[51] or even just *ἡ γένεσις*.[52] Finally, to conclude this survey, two outliers should be noted. First, the 15th-century manuscript Milan, Biblioteca Ambrosiana, *grec 668 (Q. 14 sup.)* which contains 32 chapters. Second, the 14th-century ms of English provenance, Oxford, *Ms Bodl. 238*, which has a list of headings not found in any other manuscript, the origin of which is totally obscure.[53]

Regarding the title of the treatise, then, although John of Damascus refers to it as *περὶ κατασκευῆς ἀνθρώπου*, no manuscript examined, or noted by Mendieta and Rudberg, has these words; rather the title given in the majority of manuscripts is *θεωρία εἰς τὴν κατασκευὴν τοῦ ἀνθρώπου*. It is possible that the preposition *εἰς* together with the word *θεωρία* is derived from the Letter to Peter, where Gregory describes his task as completing what is lacking in Basil's *Hexaemeron* (Ep. Pet. 2: *Εἰ γὰρ λειπούσης τῇ Ἑξαημέρῳ τῆς εἰς τὸν ἄνθρωπον θεωρίας*...), and then continues by saying that 'our effort would be convicted of failing its promise, if,

[48] Pinakes gives this manuscript a date in the first half of the 10th century, but M–R note that while this is so for folios 2–120, folios 121–235 (Gregory's treatise is 189ʳ–234ʳ) date to the 12th century.

[49] Venice, Biblioteca Nazionale di San Marco, *grec 58* (10th century), *εἰς τὴν ἀναπλήρωσιν τῶν προκειμένων τῆς ἑξαημέρου*. London, British Library, *Royal MS 16 D I* (13th century) has two headings on 117ᵛ: *Ἐπιστολὴ Γργορίου ἐπισκόπου Νύσης πρὸς Πέτρον τὸν ἴδιον ἀδελφὸν εἰς τὰ λοιπὰ τοῦ ἑξαημέρου τοῦ ἀδελφοῦ αὐτῷ Βασιλείου*. Then, immediately following the first: *Τῷ ἀδελφῷ αὐτοῦ Πέτρῳ ἐπισκόπῳ Γρηγόριος ἐπίσκοπος Νύσης προοίμιον τῶν λα κεφαλαίων τῶν ἐν τῇ ἑξαημέρῳ λεχθέντων τὰ παραλειπόμενα τοῦ μεγάλου Βασιλείου*.

[50] All from the 14th century: Moscow, Musée historique, *grec 132 Vladimir*, *Κεφάλαια τριάκοντα εἰς τὴν τοῦ ἀνθρώπου διάπλασιν*. Paris, BN, *grec 503*, *πρόγραμμα εἰς τὴν περὶ διαπλάσεως τοῦ ἀνθρώπου φιλοσοφίαν ἢ φυσιολογίαν*. Paris, BN, *grec 940*, and *grec 777 A*, 14th *πρόγραμμα εἰς τὴν περὶ διαπλάσεως τοῦ ἀνθρώπου φυσιολογίαν*. The use of the word *φυσιολογία* in these two Paris manuscripts suggests a connection or derivation from the first chapter title.

[51] Venice, Biblioteca Nazionale di San Marco, *grec 58* (10th century), which gives a list of 31 headings under the title: *κεφάλαια ἐμπιλόσοφα περὶ τῆς τοῦ ἀνθρώπου κτίσεως· καὶ περὶ τῆς τοῦ κόσμου δὲ μερικῶς· ἅπερ ἦν λείποντα τῇ ἑξαημέρῳ· ἥν προείρηκεν ὁ μακάριος καὶ ἐν ἁγίοις Βασίλειος.*

[52] Brussels, Bibliothèque Royale, *11.354* (12th century): *Τοῦ ἐν ἁγίοις πατρὸς ἡμῶν Γρηγορίου ἀρχιεπισκόπου Νύσης ἡ γένεσις*. See also Vienna, ÖNB, *theol. gr. 222* (14th century): *Τοῦ Γρηγορίου ἐπισκόπου Νύσσης πρὸς πέτρον τὸν ἴδιον ἀδελφὸν εἰς τὰ λοιπὰ τῆς ἑξαημέρου τοῦ ἀδελφοῦ αὐτῷ Βασιλείου περὶ τῶν προγεγονότων τῶν τοῦ ἀνθρώπου γενέσεως*. This title is clearly derivative from the first chapter title.

[53] It should also be noted that ß (Paris, Bibliothèque nationale de France, *grec 1277*) is also anomalous in that it alone has the list of headings preceding the Letter to Peter.

when the human being is proposed for contemplation, anything contributing to the topic were to be omitted' (Ep. Pet. 3: *εἰ τοῦ ἀνθρώπου προκειμένου τῇ θεωρίᾳ, παρεθείη τι τῶν συντεινόντων πρὸς τὴν ὑπόθεσιν·*). It is also possible that the title *περὶ κατασκευῆς ἀνθρώπου*, or variations thereon, may in turn derive from Gregory's *Hexaemeron*, written soon after *On the Human Image*: towards the end of the *Hexaemeron*, Gregory refers back to the present treatise, noting that Basil 'left aside nothing of the things requiring a contemplation, except the formation of the human being [*πλὴν τῆς τοῦ ἀνθρώπου κατασκευῆς*] which we laboring over in a particular book before these, sent to your perfection'.[54] On the other hand, the title found in the earliest manuscripts, *Περὶ εἰκόνος ἀνθρώπου*, and in the translations of Dionysius and Eriugena, does not appear to be derived from either the Letter to Peter or Gregory's *Hex.*, or even from any part of the text of the treatise itself, but is in fact, as we shall see in Chapter 3, very much the central theme of the work itself. Moreover as the title *θεωρία εἰς τὴν κατασκευὴν τοῦ ἀνθρώπου* is first found in the *explicit* of a manuscript, in which the title heading the treatise is *Περὶ εἰκόνος ἀνθρώπου*, and following Dionysius (*De imagine id est de hominis conditione*), I have adopted as the title of the work: *Περὶ εἰκόνος ἀνθρώπου ἤτοι θεωρία εἰς τὴν κατασκευὴν τοῦ ἀνθρώπου* (or in Latin *De hominis imagine, id est contemplatio de hominis conditione*, abbreviated to *De hom.*).

One final problem remains: how best to translate the word *κατασκευή*? Dionysius rendered it as *conditio*, while Löwenklau chose *opificium*, which, while not evidenced in any manuscript, has become the standard designation. As noted above, the term has been rendered variously in modern languages, more often than not focusing on the idea of making or creating.[55] The term *κατασκευή*, however, has a far wider range of meanings: preparation, construction, fitting-out, state, condition, constitution, and, in the field of rhetoric, artistic treatment, elaboration.[56] Although often read as a treatment on how the human being came to be made and what happened after the fall, the work is, as we will see, more concerned with the form and constitution of the human being and how and why it is that the human being is said to be made in the image and likeness of God when this is not really self-evident in the present. In this, Gregory's treatise is indeed continuous with Basil's *Hexaemeron* as understood by Gregory, who describes Basil as having 'by his own contemplation made the sublime adornment

[54] *Hex.* 77: *τοῖς δὲ λοιποῖς ἐπεξιέναι τῶν κατὰ τὴν ἑξαήμερον κοσμογένειαν πεποιημένων μάταιον ἐνομίσαμεν, τῆς ὑψηλῆς τοῦ διδασκάλου φωνῆς μηδὲν τῶν ζητουμένων εἰς θεωρίαν παραλειπούσης πλὴν τῆς τοῦ ἀνθρώπου κατασκευῆς, ἣν ἡμεῖς ἐν ἰδιάζοντι βιβλίῳ πρὸ τούτων πονήσαντες ἀπεστείλαμέν σου τῇ τελειότητι.* Maraval, 'Chronology of Works', would place it in the early months of 379, but after the present treatise which was composed between September 378 and Easter 379.

[55] The Russian translation by B. Lurie is a case apart: *Об устроении человека*, which has the sense of order/ordering or arranging/arrangement or structure. My thanks to John Mikitish for his insights on this. B. Salmona entitled his Italian translation simply: *L'uomo*.

[56] Cf. H. G. Liddell and R. Scott, *A Greek-English Lexicon*, rev. H. S. Jones with R. McKenzie. 9th edn. with revised supplement (Oxford: Clarendon Press, 1996), s.v. (hereafter, LSJ).

of the universe accessible to many, making the world established by God in true wisdom known to those who are led, by means of his understanding, to contemplation' (Ep. Pet. 1). To capture both the sense of form/constitution as well as forming or fashioning, I have chosen the word 'formation'. As such, the title I propose for this work is: *On the Human Image of God, that is, A Contemplation on the Formation of the Human Being.*

3. Headings and Divisions

Variations regarding an introductory letter and a list of headings also occur in the manuscript tradition of other works of Gregory.[57] In his edition of the *De Virginitate* (written between 371 and 378), J. P. Cavarnos, principally on the basis of the 12th-century manuscript *Ω* (*Escorialensis Ω III 14*), in which the text is not divided into chapters and which lacks the introductory letter and list of headings, hypothesized two different editions of the work from the hand of Gregory himself: the first being simply the treatise itself and the second that of the treatise together with the cover letter and list of headings.[58] Given the fact that both *Ω* and another 12th- or 13th-century manuscript, S (*Vat. grec 1907*), have an alternative opening to chapter 1, and that S, which has the epistolary preface and list of headings, also has an apparently redundant heading after the list and before the title of chapter 1, Cavarnos sees in this heading the original title of the work and characterizes its opening section as being rather 'youthfully enthusiastic' and even polemical, having in view Basil of Ancyra, while the second edition, with its more general prefatory letter, tones down this aspect.

However, as Michel Aubineau points out, the process could equally well have been the reverse: that the Letter to Peter and its list of headings was dropped at some point, perhaps as an adaptation for reading in a monastic context.[59] Given the importance of such letters in antiquity, as a seal of authenticity, it is much more likely, Aubineau argues, that it belonged to the first edition of the work. Moreover, as the epistolary preface to Cavarnos' 'second edition' refers to Basil as living and a bishop, it cannot have come from a much later date than a postulated earlier edition.[60] As such, Aubineau argues that it is more plausible to hold that the

[57] In his edition of *De anima et resurrectione* (cf. GNO 3.3, CXLI–CXLIV and 125–36), Spira provides an appendix giving the 96 *argumenta* (125–36), which he attributes to the 'bibliothekarische Tradition', noting also that only three mss (dating from the 11th to 14th centuries) have placed the *argumenta* numbers in the margins of the text (CXLI).

[58] See J. P. Cavarnos' introduction to his edition of *De Virg.* in GNO 8.1, *Opera Ascetica* (Leiden: Brill, 1986), 238–40.

[59] M. Aubineau, ed. *De Virg.*, SC 119 (Paris: Cerf, 1966), 229–35.

[60] Following Jaeger (*Two Rediscovered Works*), Aubineau also points to the idea that the 'Great Letter' of Macarius was a reworking of Gregory's *De instituto Christiano*, a position that has been abandoned since Reinhart Staats, *Gregor von Nyssa und die Messalianer: Die Frage der Priorität zweier altkirchlicher Schriften*, PTS 8 (Berlin: De Gruyter, 1968).

introductory letter is original to the work, written in 371 at the urging of his brother, newly made a bishop and responsible for the ascetics living in Pontus and Cappadocia; then, as the work was recopied in this monastic milieu, various modifications were introduced, resulting in a 'second edition', independent of Gregory himself, and then at a later point (but before the Syriac translation was made in the 6th century) summaries were formulated, often based upon elements within the text, and written in the margins as a guide for the reader, and only later were these utilized to divide the treatise itself up into 'chapters'.[61]

Another interesting point of comparison is Gregory's *Contra Eunomium*, the first two books of which were written in 17 days in 380 and the third between 381 and 383. As Matthieu Cassin has pointed out, while each book opens with an exordium, the editions of the work, including the ground-breaking edition of Jaeger, do not include any general prefatory letter: the work is presented as opening with a list of the headings of the three books, despite the fact that '[a]lmost all the manuscripts put the two letters just before the list of headings or before the first book *Contra Eunomium*'.[62] However, in this case it seems that, although these two letters survive independently of the *Contra Eunomium* in a single manuscript, they were only included in the manuscripts of the *Contra Eunomium*, as a preface, as late as the 11th century.[63] Moreover, these letters, from Gregory to Peter (*Ep.* 29) and Peter's reply (*Ep.* 30), are highly specific: Gregory wrote to his brother asking his advice about the wisdom of releasing his work against Eunomius to a general readership (*Ep.* 29.2–6). This letter is clearly not meant as a general preface to the work itself, although as Cassin notes, it has many fascinating things to say about how Gregory understood his own work. Moreover, building upon the work of J. A. Röder, Cassin argues that the headings of the first book go back to Gregory himself and their positioning within the treatise as chapter divisions goes back to at least the 6th century.[64] So, in this case, we have an example of a work by Gregory that does not include a general prefatory address or letter, but does have a list of headings, going back to Gregory himself, prefacing the work, which are then positioned within the treatise itself as headings

[61] Aubineau, ed. *De Virg.*, 235–8.

[62] Matthieu Cassin, 'Text and Context: The Importance of Scholarly Reading: Gregory of Nyssa, "Contra Eunomium"', in Scot Douglass and Morwenna Ludlow, *Reading the Church Fathers* (London: T&T Clark, 2011), 109–31, 161–5, at 113.

[63] Cf. G. Pasquali, *Gregorii Nysseni Epistulae*, GNO 8.2, 2nd edn. (Leiden: Brill, 1998), IX, and Anna M. Silvas, *Gregory of Nyssa: The Letters. Introduction, Translation, and Commentary*, Suppl. *VC* 83 (Leiden: Brill, 2007), 206–10.

[64] For the headings going back to Gregory himself see J. A. Röder, *Gregor von Nyssa, Contre Eunomium I, 1–146, eingeleitet, übersetzt und kommentiert*, Patrologia 2 (Frankfurt am Main: Peter Lang, 1993), 73–4; for further analysis of the chapter divisions of *Contra Eunomium* see Matthieu Cassin, *L'écriture de la polémique à la fin du IVe siècle: Gregoire de Nysse,* Contra Eunome III (PhD thesis; Paris: Sorbonne, 2009), vol. 1, 135–7 and 'Contra Eunome III: une introduction', in Johan Leemans and Matthieu Cassin, eds., *Gregory of Nyssa: Contra Eunomium III. An English Translation with Commentary and Supporting Studies*, Suppl. VC 124 (Leiden: Brill, 2014), 3–33, esp. 12–18.

a few centuries later. It should also be noted that there are other works of Gregory that include an introduction addressed to a person, but they do not include lists of headings.[65]

Returning to our treatise, we have seen that two manuscripts do not contain the Letter to Peter: the 9th–10th-century *Vat. grec 413* and the 14th-century Vienna, ÖNB *theol. graec. 168*, the former having a list of headings, the latter lacking also the list. However, as the treatise presented in both is divided into chapters (the former with 31, the latter with 30), if we (safely) assume that an initial list of headings predates their inclusion within the text of the treatise itself as chapter headings, we can infer that the prototype for Vienna, ÖNB *theol. graec. 168* would originally also have had a list of headings. In the case of the two other manuscripts that do not have the list of headings, both do, nevertheless, indicate a list: *Vat. grec 2053* has the words, set in an ornate box, *σύνταξις κεφαλαίων λ* immediately after the Letter to Peter and before chapter 1, and BL *Royal 16 D I* includes the Letter to Peter which concludes with the words announcing such a list of headings. We can thus conclude that a list of headings following the Letter to Peter belonged to their prototypes but was omitted by their scribes for whatever reason.

If we accept Aubineau's point about the importance in antiquity of a cover letter as a 'seal of authenticity', and that the absence of the Letter to Peter or a list of headings in the manuscripts noted above is the result of their falling out or failing to be copied, then we can also conclude that the Letter to Peter was intended as the original preface to the treatise, as it indeed states. Moreover, the fact that we have no examples of the treatise not divided into chapters, would suggest that not only was the letter original and integral to the treatise, but so too was the list of headings. Aubineau, on the basis of earlier studies of chapter divisions and headings, assumed that the development of this phenomenon was later than Gregory himself. However, that earlier authors did indeed preface their work with an introduction (usually in the form of a letter) followed by a list of headings is evidenced by several texts from the 1st to 2nd centuries CE, as we will see later. Lists of headings are also found in manuscripts of earlier Patristic works, though not in connection with an introductory address by the author himself; the nearest comparable example we have might be Origen's Preface to his *On First Principles*, where he outlines the topics he will treat and which he does thereafter follow.[66]

[65] Cf. To Peter, a 'man of God', *Hex.* (early 379 CE) and *Inscr.* (*c.*376–8 CE), and to Olympias, *Cant.* (*post* 391 CE).

[66] For Irenaeus, see the introductions to the SC vols (for *Haer.* 1, SC 263, 30–41; for *Haer.* 2, SC 293, 51–80; for *Haer.* 3, SC 210, 47–8; for *Haer.* 4, SC 100, 42–3, 186–91). Many of Eusebius's works also include such lists: *Praep. ev.*, *Dem. ev.*, *Marc.*, *Eccl. theol.*, *Mens.*, and *Eccl. hist.*; for the latter see Eduard Schwartz, GCS 9.3 (1909), chap. 4, 'Überschriften und Kephalaia', pp. CXLVII–CLII. For Eusebius's canon tables for the Gospels, see Matthew R. Crawford, *The Eusebian Canon Tables: Ordering Textual Knowledge in Late Antiquity*, OECS (Oxford: Oxford University Press, 2019) and Jeremiah Coogan, *Eusebius the Evangelist* OECS (Oxford: Oxford University Press, 2022). For chapters in Origen, see John Behr, *Origen: On First Principles*, OECT (Oxford: Oxford University Press, 2017), xxxvi–xxxviii.

It is thus not impossible, and indeed quite likely, that Gregory himself appended to his introductory letter a list of topics that he discussed in the treatise.

In all our Greek and Latin manuscripts of the treatise, including *Ms Bodl.* 238 which differs from every other manuscript in the headings it gives, the headings given in the list correspond to the headings given in the treatise itself, where almost invariably they have a number. However, in the earliest manuscript we have, *Vat. sir. 106*, 41^{r}–74^{v}, dating to around 700 CE, we have a very different pattern.[67] Here, following the Letter to Peter, we have a list of 31 headings preceded by the word *ršʾ* (certainly translating κεφάλαιος) and the number (41^{v}–42^{r}); these correspond somewhat to those of the Greek text.[68] Following this list, the title of the treatise is restated and chapter 1 then begins (on 42^{r}, right column), without any numeration or heading. What we have as chapter 2 in the Greek and Latin manuscript traditions begins (on 43^{r}, left column) with no break, heading, enlarged capital or other manner of signifying a transition, but as a direct continuation of chapter 1. Chapter 3, however, is marked by the words 'chapter three' (on 44^{r} right column), but with no repetition of the heading given in the list or any other heading. Over the course of the rest of the treatise, only 18 other 'chapters' are out marked in the same way (missing are: 4, 6, 7, 8, 9, 17, 24, 25, 27–31). That the manuscript has the word 'chapter' and 'number' within the body of the treatise would seem to indicate that, while accepting that the list of headings was composed by Gregory himself, concluding his letter to his brother, they were not used by Gregory as dividing marks within the treatise itself. It is also likely that numbers were added to the list at the point when scribes began to identify points in the treatise correlating to the topics listed earlier. Either the scribe of *Vat. sir. 106* was careless in transcribing each of these numbered headings or perhaps this manuscript might even mark a stage at which the points of correlation had not yet been fully established. Once these numbers were in the text, it is but a small step to repeat the words given in the list at the beginning, but now as 'headings' within the treatise itself.

Whatever the actual history behind this development is, one point should be clearly borne in mind: these κεφαλαία are not 'chapters' in the modern sense and the headings are not chapter titles. The earliest examples we have of such lists are those of Scribonius Largus, Columella, Pliny the Elder, and Aulus Gellius, and each of them introduces the list with an explanatory note, thereby indicating the

[67] The manuscript is available online at the Digital Vatican Library (https://digi.vatlib.it/view/MSS_Vat.sir.106, accessed 3 June 2021): 41^{r} Title and Ep. to Peter; 41^{v}–42^{r} list of headings; 42^{v} restated title; 42^{v}–74^{r} text; 74^{r} *explicit.* Cf. S. E. Assemanus and J. S. Assemanus, *Bibliothecae Apostolicae Vaticanae: Codicum manuscriptorum catalogus, in tres partes distributus* (Rome: 1759; reprinted Paris: Libraire Orientale et Américaine, 1926), Partis primae, tomus tertius, 42–3.

[68] The first three headings of the list are: 1, 'Concerning the making of the world and the correct account of those things prior to the creation of the human being'; 2, 'Concerning what creatures were created following the human being', clearly thinking of Gen. 2 rather than 1; 3, 'Concerning the fact that the substance and formation [*twqnʾ*] of the human being was better than all creatures'.

relative novelty of the undertaking and also its purpose. Pliny concludes the letter to Titus prefacing his *Natural History* by stating that 'I have appended to this letter what is contained in each of the books' (*quid singulis contineretur libris huic epistulae subiunxi*), so that the recipient and others 'will not need to read right through them either, but only look for the particular point that each of them wants and will know where to find it. This Valerius Soranus did before me, in our literature, in the books he entitled ἐποπτίδων.'[69] The primary purpose of these lists, then, is indexical, enabling the locating of specific material and the sequence of topics treated rather than being indicative of the structure of the treatment.[70] In reverse, however, the list enables the segmentation of the text, so that it can be viewed as a series of separate, discrete even, topics, a process which continues with the headings being transcribed into the text itself as chapter titles: as Dames notes, commenting on Pliny's work, 'a trajectory seems dimly evident, in which a table becomes *chapterized*, finding its way into the text itself and thus becoming a kind of segmentation rather than an index'.[71]

Gregory, however, introduces his list by stating a different purpose:

> For the sake of clarity, I think it well to set out the treatise [τὸν λόγον] for you by headings [ἐπὶ κεφαλαίων], that you may be able to know in brief the force of each of the arguments [τῶν καθέκαστον ἐπιχειρημάτων … τὴν δύναμιν] of the whole work [πάσης τῆς πραγματείας]. (Ep. Pet. 3)

The language here echoes that of Porphyry's account of his editorial work on Plotinus' *Enneads*, when he states that for all the books except *On Beauty* he has composed not only τὰ κεφάλαια, translated in Gerson's edition as 'key-point summaries' but also the ἐπιχειρήματα, 'lines of argument'.[72] The 'headings' given by Gregory are clearly not meant as a table of contents which would enable the reader to jump to a discrete topic within a segmented or 'chapterized' text. Neither do they function to indicate of the structure of the treatise as a whole; with a few exceptions, when integrated into the body of the text they do not neatly correspond to a division within the text, as might be indicated by a summary of what has been discussed or the announcement of a new topic, with a reflection on how it fits into the structure of the treatise as a whole. Rather, Gregory says, the

[69] Pliny, *Nat. His.* Pref. 33; ed. and trans. H. Rackham, LCL (Cambridge: Harvard University Press, 1967). Cf. Riggsby, 'Guides to the Wor(l)d', 90–1, for the other statements. See also Aude Doody, *Pliny's Encyclopedia: The Reception of the Natural History* (Cambridge: Cambridge University Press, 2010), 92–131.

[70] Cf. Howley, 'Tables of Contents', 68; Dames, 'Chapter Heads', 154–7.

[71] Dames, 'Chapter Heads', 157, italics original.

[72] Porphyry, *Vita Plot.* 26; ed. Paul Henry and Hans-Rudolf Schwyzer, Oxford Classical Texts (Oxford: Clarendon Press, 1964); Lloyd P. Gerson, ed., *Plotinus: The Enneads* (Cambridge: Cambridge University Press, 2018). On Porphyry's editorial work in arranging the text, see Jeremiah Coogan, 'Transforming Textuality'.

purpose of these 'headings' is that the reader might know 'the force of each argument'.

As such, the items in the list provided by Gregory take on a variety of forms, beyond the usual 'about' (περὶ) or 'that' (ὅτι) statements. Some are introduced with 'why' (διὰ τί), others are designated as 'an examination' (ἐξέτασις), and others again are addressed to particular interlocutors and their own claims (πρὸς τοὺς λέγοντας). Nicholas Dames draws attention to a similar phenomenon in the *Discourses* of Epictetus, as edited by his disciple Arrian, and in particular the way in which Arrian has applied Epictetus' understanding of 'preconceptions' to the headings he introduces. As Dames puts it, Arrian's headings 'seem in fact to be a series of experiments on the relation between title and unity, or initial perception and later understanding.... Arrian's seemingly inapposite heads could be thought of as provoking a constant testing or evaluation.'[73] Gregory, who at a key moment in his treatise tells us that he is writing in the form of an exercise for the reader (*De hom.* 15), seems to be doing the same with some of his headings. For instance, the heading for *De hom.* 18 asserts 'That our irrational passions have their starting-point from kinship with the irrational nature'. However, as he makes clear in the ensuing discussion, while irrational passions are indeed occasioned from such kinship, the real problem is not the shared animality but 'the evil husbandry of the intellect' (*De hom.* 18.4).

Two particular headings, however, deserve closer attention. Chapter 16 has the only heading beginning with the word θεωρία—'A contemplation of the divine word which says, "Let us make the human being in accordance with our image and likeness"; in which is examined what the definition of the image is, and how the passible and mortal is liken to the blessed and impassible, and how the male and female are in the image, these not being in the Prototype.' The words 'in which it is examined...' are clearly a summary of what follows, suggesting that the previous words have more status as an actual 'title', marking a θεωρία.[74] And then again, the heading for chapter 30 is also designated as a θεωρία: 'A brief, more medical contemplation regarding the formation of our body'.

Chapter 16 clearly constitutes a new beginning in Gregory's treatise: he explicitly announces a new beginning: 'Let us now take up again [ἐπαναλάβωμεν πάλιν] the divine saying, "Let us make the human being in accordance with our image and likeness".' It is possible that this heading might indicate a structure of the treatise similar to that of *De Vita Moysis* (written mid-380s to *c.*392) which (at least in one manuscript) has a twofold title (περὶ ἀρετῆς ἤτοι εἰς τὸν βίον Μωϋσέως) and consists of two λόγοι, the second of which is described as a

[73] Dames, 'Chapter Heads', 159–60.

[74] A similar consideration might explain how chapter 12 came to be divided into two in those manuscripts that have 31 chapters, for those manuscripts which do so, also divide the heading of chapter 12 as well, with what now becomes chapter 13 beginning with the word θεώρημα.

θεωρία.[75] Towards the end of that Preface, Gregory describes his task as being twofold: 'Let Moses then be proposed as our example in life, first going through his life as we have learned it from the divine Scripture, then we shall seek out the meaning corresponding to the history, useful as providing suggestions for virtue, through which we will come to know the perfect life for human beings.'[76] The pattern of narrative followed by contemplation, however, does not really adequately describe the distinction between *De hom.* 1–15 and 16 onwards.

An alternative model is Plato's *Timaeus*. The proposed subject of Timaeus' great speech is 'to speak beginning from the coming-to-be of the world and end with the nature of human beings'.[77] This is, of course, directly the theme of Gregory's own work. Moreover, the two chapters, 16 and 30, of Gregory's treatise designated as *θεωρίαι* correspond, as we will see more fully in the following chapters, to the major divisions within Timaeus' speech. The first part of Timaeus' speech gives an account of 'the things crafted by Intellect' (*Tim.* 47e7), though with several detours and anticipations of points made later; the first 15 chapters of Gregory's treatise gives a beautiful description of the cosmos and the human being as the image of God, again with various detours. Halfway through his speech, Timaeus proposes to 'go back once again to the beginning and start my inquiry from there', to consider further dimensions, 'necessity' and 'the straying cause', which were not directly treated, though intimated, in the first part of his speech (*Tim.* 47e3–48b2); in a similar way Gregory, in *De hom.* 16, explicitly returns to his own starting point, Genesis 1:27, to consider thereafter further dimensions implicit in that scriptural verse not directly treated, though also intimated, in *De hom.* 1–15, ones moreover which play upon the errant ways of human beings. The third part of Timaeus' speech, in which he says he will bring together the first two parts and so put a 'head' on his account (*Tim.* 69a8–b2), is an extensive psychophysical account of the human being; likewise Gregory's final lengthy chapter (*De hom.* 30), offers a medical account of the formation and actual coming into being of the human being. The structural parallels with the *Timaeus* seem certain. Within a year or two of writing *On the Human Image*, Gregory wrote *On the Soul and Resurrection*, which is clearly modelled on Plato's *Phaedo*; it

[75] Edited by H. Musurillo, GNO 7.1 (Leiden: Brill, 1991). Two of the manuscripts used indicate in their titles that it was addressed to either Peter or Olympias. For the heading of the second part of the treatise, two of the five manuscripts noted in the edition use the word *θεωρία*: *θεωρία τῆς ἐκτεθείσης ἱστορίας* and *θεωρία εἰς τὸν τοῦ Μωϋσέως βίον*. Musurillo settles for simply: *θεωρία*. The other three manuscripts at this point have headings describing what follows as the second *λόγος* on virtue.

[76] *Vit. Mos.* pp. 6.25–7.3. It should be noted that Musurillo's edition does not mark out the opening paragraphs as a 'preface'; the critical apparatus indicates that it is preserved in various manuscripts as addressed to Olympias or Peter; most titles noted there have a similar twofold pattern to the one given above.

[77] Plato, *Timaeus*, 27a5–6; ed. J. Burnet, Oxford Classical Texts, Platonis Opera 4 (Oxford: Clarendon Press, 1902); trans. Donald J. Zeyl (Indianapolis, IN: Hackett, 2000), occasionally modified.

is likely, then, that in *On the Human Image of God*, Gregory had his eye towards the *Timaeus*.

We will turn to Gregory's treatise itself in Chapter 3. For now, I would simply note that although I have retained the headings for the different parts of the work, it should be borne in mind that these are not 'chapter titles' for discrete topics. But before we turn to Gregory's *On the Human Image of God*, we should explore the philosophical and theological background he inherited and built upon, for although he presents this work to Peter as the completion of Basil's *Hexaemeron*, it is, as we will see, far more complex.

Chapter 2
Philosophical and Theological Background

1. Anaxagoras

Although Socrates ultimately found his account lacking, and Aristotle treated him rather dismissively, it was Anaxagoras (sixth century BCE), as Socrates reports, who was the first to argue 'that it is intellect [νοῦς] that arranges and causes all things', and, according to Simplicius, he also taught that creation was 'two-fold'.[1] There are many obscurities and contentious points of interpretation regarding Anaxagoras' teaching, but there are also several points of importance for understanding the background of Gregory's work. Although the fragments of Anaxagoras' writings are primarily preserved in the writings of Simplicius in the sixth century CE, extracting these fragments from that context and attempting to make sense of them in terms of Aristotle's presentation of Anaxagoras leads to numerous problems and inconsistencies; indeed, Simplicius occasionally points out that Aristotle had misunderstood or misrepresented Anaxagoras. Simplicius, of course, was writing in a very different context than either Anaxagoras or Aristotle, with the whole history of Neoplatonism behind him. But this doesn't necessarily mean that he has turned a Presocratic into a Neoplatonist; his commentary on Aristotle is a fair account of the Stagirite, and we have no reason to doubt that Simplicius is equally faithful in his representation of Anaxagoras whose writings he knew. It is just as likely, as Tzamalikos argues, that 'some Neoplatonists saw in Anaxagoras the real source of a consistent solution to the ancient problem of how exactly did the material universe come to be from immaterial principles'.[2]

[1] Plato, *Phaedo* 96c; text and ET Harold North Fowler, Loeb Classical Library, Plato 1 (Cambridge, MA: Harvard University Press, 1914). For a brief but lucid account of Anaxagoras, see David Sedley, *Creationism and its Critics in Antiquity* (Berkeley, CA: University of California Press, 2007), 8–30, and for a recent massive (almost 1800-page) account arguing that Anaxagoras was the genius behind later developments in philosophy, culminating in Origen and through him the Neoplatonists, see Panayiotis Tzamalikos, *Anaxagoras, Origen, and Neoplatonism: The Legacy of Anaxagoras to Classical and Late Antiquity*, Arbeiten zur Kirchenggeschichte 128, 2 vols (Berlin: De Gruyter, 2016), especially, for the topic treated here, Chapter 4, 'A Two-Fold Creation'. The best treatment of Anaxagoras is Anna Marmodoro, *Everything in Everything: Anaxagoras' Metaphysics* (Oxford: Oxford University Press, 2017).

[2] Tzamalikos, *Anaxagoras*, 58.

Anaxagoras opened his book *On Nature* with the words: 'All things were together' (ἦν ὁμοῦ πάντα χρήματα).[3] The fullest passage preserved from Anaxagoras' own writings (though in fact compiled from different parts of Simplicius' work) describes the cosmogenic activity of intellect [νοῦς] in terms echoed by Gregory in the opening chapter of his *On the Human Image*, and deserves to be quoted in full.

> The other things possess a portion of every thing, but intellect is unlimited and master of itself, it has not been mixed with any thing, but is the only one to be itself by itself. For if it were not by itself, but had been mixed with some other thing, it would participate in all things, if it had been mixed with any; for in every thing is present a part of every thing, as I said earlier. And the things that would be mixed with it would prevent it from having control over any thing in the same way as it does being alone by itself. For it is at the same time both the thinnest of all things, and the purest, and in particular it retains the full decision [γνώμην or 'understanding'] concerning every thing and possesses the greatest power; and of the things that have life [ψυχὴν], whether they are larger or smaller, of these intellect is master; and intellect has been master of the whole rotation, so that there would be rotation at the beginning [καὶ τῆς περιχωρήσιος τῆς συμπάσης νοῦς ἐκράτησεν, ὥστε περιχωρῆσαι τὴν ἀρχὴν]. And the rotation began at first from the small, then it rotates more broadly, and it will continue to become even broader. And the things that mix as well as those that are detached and separate out—all these intellect decided [ἔγνω or 'knew']. And as things were going to be, and as all things were that now are not, and as all things are now, and as they will be, intellect separated and ordered them all, as well as this rotation, which is being performed now by the heavenly bodies, the sun, the moon, the air, and the aether, which are separating out. And the rotation itself caused the detachment [ἡ δὲ περιχώρησις αὕτη ἐποίησεν ἀποκρίνεσθαι]. And from the rarefied the dense separates out, from the cold the warm, from the dark the bright, and from the moist the dry. Numerous are the parts of numerous things; yet nothing is completely detached or separates out from one another, except intellect. But all intellect is similar, the larger and the smaller, and nothing else is similar to anything else, but that of which each thing contains the most, this is what each thing is and was most manifestly.[4]

[3] Simplicius, *In Phys.* 3.4 (Diels, 460.26); ET J. O. Urmson, *On Aristotle Physics 3*, ACA (London: Bloomsbury, 2013), 79, occasionally modified.

[4] Herman Diels, *Die Fragmente der Vorsokratiker*, ed. Walther Kranz, 6th edn., 3 vols (Berlin: Weidmann, 1951–2), B12 (= Simplicius, *In Phys.*, ed. Diels, 164.24–5; 156.13–157.4); text and ET, André Laks and Glenn W. Most, *Early Greek Philosophy*, vol. 6, LCL 529 (Cambridge, MA: Harvard University Press, 2016), modified. I should note that while translators of Anaxagoras almost uniformly translate νοῦς as 'mind', I have chosen 'intellect', not to project back to him later developments, but for consistency across this volume. References to the fragments of the Presocratics will be given by the Diels-Kranz numeration.

Intellect is thus a distinct cosmogenic force, separate from everything else, and so able to work upon all things. Unlimited, autonomous, and unmixed with anything else, it is the active agent in the process of separating, segregating, ordering, and thus bringing into being, that is, creating.[5] But what are the things (χρήματα) that were originally all together? Aristotle, perhaps led by comments that Anaxagoras makes about nourishment which we will consider momentarily, called these 'things' 'homoeomeries', referring to 'elements, such as bone, flesh, and marrow, and anything else of which the part bears the same name as the whole'.[6] However, in the above passage Anaxagoras is clearly speaking about various sets of incorporeal powers (cold and hot, moist and dry, etc.).[7] By rotating or spinning the unified whole, intellect separates out these powers, so that, as Simplicius reports Anaxagoras concluding, 'the dense, <the> wet, the cold, and the dark came together here, where earth now is, while the rare, the hot, <the bright>, and the dry retreated to the farther parts of the aether'.[8] Anaxagoras, as Simplicius rightly understood, 'posited as elements the simple qualities, which have the nature of principles [τὰς ἁπλᾶς καὶ ἀρχοειδεῖς ποιότητας], but not the compounds . . . these most simple things which have the character of principles are separated off and other things of a more compound nature are in some cases compacted as compounds [συμπήγνυσθαι ὡς σύνθετα], in others separated off, as earth'.[9] Earth, and the other elements, are thus the resultant products of this segregating-by-spinning activity of intellect; they are compounds compacted from particular incorporeal powers. However, even when separated in this manner, the various powers are not completely sundered or severed from each other: never being able to be absolute heat or wetness (for heat could always, in principle, be hotter), their opposite always remains present, so that as Anaxagoras put it above, 'other things [apart from intellect] possess a portion of every thing'.[10]

The revolving effected by intellect is one that, according to the above passage (B12), operates even now and will continue to do so; it began small and increases

[5] As Tzamalikos (*Anaxagoras*, 287–8) notes, Simplicius (*In Phys.*, 300.27–30) quotes from Alexander of Aphrodisias' lost commentary on Aristotle's *Physics*, to the effect that Aristotle did not mention Anaxagoras, because even though he posited intellect, he 'does not make use of this in genesis' (ἐν τῇ γενέσει), although, Simplicius argues, it is plain that Anaxagoras does, for he says that 'genesis is nothing other than separation itself' (τὴν γένεσιν οὐδὲν ἄλλο ἢ ἔκκρισιν εἶναι φησί).

[6] Aristotle, *Gen. corr.* 314a18–21. For Aristotle's misreading of Anaxagoras, see Sedley, *Creationism*, 26–30, and Tzamalikos, *Anaxagoras*, 264–5, 272–3.

[7] That these pairs of opposites (cold/warm, dark/bright, moist/dry) should be designated as 'powers' rather than 'properties' (the latter being 'properties' that inhere in something else) is strongly argued by Marmodoro, *Everything in Everything*, 17–24, and *passim*.

[8] B15 (Simplicius, *In Phys.* 1.4; Diels, 179.3–6; ET 79; where it follows the relevant passage from B12). D–K marked 'earth' as an editorial addition; but David Sider, *The Fragments of Anaxagoras*, 2nd edn. (Sankt Augustin: Academia Verlag, 2005), 149, demonstrates that it is unanimously present in the manuscript tradition, of which only one ms includes a definite article: it is 'earth', not 'the earth'.

[9] Simplicius, *In Phys.* 3.4 (Diels, 178.33–4, 179.6–7; ET 86).

[10] Cf. B8 (Simplicius, *In Phys.* 1.4; Diels, 176.29 and 175.12–14): 'The things that are in one world order have not been separated from one another and they have not been chopped apart by an ax, neither the hot from the cold, nor the cold from the hot.'

in breadth. The separation of the unified whole into incorporeal powers is not a primordial creation of a different world or realm, nor in fact is it Anaxagoras' own starting point. On Simplicius' telling, Anaxagoras began from the observation that bread, when taken as nourishment, becomes separated out into flesh, bones, sinews, veins, hair, and so on.[11] From this, he concluded that 'everything was mixed in everything and genesis happens by separation [*τὴν γένεσιν κατὰ ἔκκρισιν γίνεσθαι*]'.[12] This genesis, moreover, has an order and a proper time: Anaxagoras 'saw that everything comes from everything, if not immediately, but in order [*κατὰ τάξιν*]'.[13] And from such observation, according to Simplicius, Anaxagoras reasoned by analogy to the universe: 'So just as in each thing there is at some time a principle to distinguish it, so also in the universe. And just as from each, something appears to come to be at some time, so, since everything comes to be, the genesis of all things was separated out from the universal mixture, even if not all together.'[14] It was this that led Anaxagoras, finally, to postulate a 'principle and cause' superior to bodies, which are moved externally, and he called this intellect.[15] Finally, intellect, 'that which was distinguishing the complex and bringing out in order the distinction from the complexity, had first to contain itself the existent as a complex and reveal the distinction in itself'.[16] Thus, intellect establishes the incorporeal principles that both cause and are embodied in the material universe we inhabit.

Tracing the order of his thought in this way—from empirical observation to postulating intellect as the primary cause—as Simplicius suggests, Anaxagoras' hypothesis about principles becomes clear. Whereas Aristotle had presented the superficial aspect of his thought (*τὸ προφαινόμενον ἱστορεῖν τῆς Ἀναξαγόρου δόξης*), Anaxagoras was, according to Simplicius, in fact pointing to something more:

> Anaxagoras, being wise, hinted at a twofold orderly arrangement: the one united and intelligible, pre-existing, not in time (for that one is not temporal), but in superiority of being and potentiality; the other distinct from this; and in accordance with this it comes to be through the demiurgic intellect.[17]

[11] Simplicius, *In Phys.* 3.4 (Diels, 460.22–5; ET 79).

[12] Simplicius, *In Phys.* 3.4 (Diels, 460.19–20; ET 79).

[13] Simplicius, *In Phys.* 3.4 (Diels, 460.12–13; ET 79).

[14] Simplicius, *In Phys.* 3.4 (Diels, 460.32–5; ET 80): *ὥσπερ οὖν ἐν ἑκάστῳ ἀρχὴ γίνεταί ποτε τῆς διακρίσεως, οὕτως καὶ ἐν τῷ παντί. καὶ ὥσπερ ἀπὸ ἑκάστου φαίνεταί τις γένεσίς ποτε γινομένη, οὕτως ἐπειδὴ καὶ πάντων ἐστὶ γένεσις, ἀπὸ τοῦ πάντων μίγματος ἡ πάντων γένεσις ἐξεκρίθη, εἰ καὶ μὴ ἅμα.*

[15] Simplicius, *In Phys.* 3.4 (Diels, 460.35–461.1; ET 80).

[16] Simplicius, *In Phys.* 3.4 (Diels, 461.1–3; ET 80): *ἔδει γὰρ τὸ τὰ συνῃρμένα διακρῖνον καὶ προάγον ἐν τάξει τὴν διάκρισιν ἀπὸ τῆς συναιρέσεως αὐτὸ συνῃρημένην ἔχον τὴν οὐσίαν πρώτως ἀναφαίνειν ἐν ἑαυτῷ τὴν διάρκσιν.*

[17] Simplicius, *In Phys.* 3.4 (Diels, 461.11–14; ET 80): *ὁ δὲ Ἀναξαγόρας σοφὸς ὢν διττὴν ᾐνίττετο τὴν διακόσμησιν, τὴν μὲν ἡνωμένην καὶ νοητὴν προϋπάρχουσαν οὐ χρόνῳ (οὐ γὰρ ἔγχρονος ἐκείνη), ἀλλ' ὑπεροχῇ οὐσίας καὶ δυνάμεως, τὴν δὲ διακεκριμένην ἀπὸ ταύτῃ· καὶ κατὰ ταύτην ὑφίστασθαι ὑπὸ τοῦ δημιουργικοῦ νοῦ…*

Simplicius continues by referring back to his first book, where he had given the evidence from words of Anaxagoras himself, and in which, after quoting the passage with which we began (B12), he makes a similar observation:

> He posits a twofold world-order, one intellectual, the other perceptible, derived from the former [*διττήν τινα διακόσμησιν τὴν μὲν νοεράν, τὴν δὲ αἰσθητὴν ἀπ' ἐκείνης*]: that is clear both from what he has previously said and from the following: 'Intellect is now too where all the other things are as well [*ὁ δὲ νοῦς καὶ νῦν ἔστιν ἵνα καὶ τὰ ἀλλὰ πάντα*], in the surrounding mass, in the things that have separated more, and in those that are separating' [=B14].[18] Further, after [saying] 'in all the things that are combined there are many things of all kinds and seeds of all things with all kinds of shapes and colours and flavours, and human beings have been compacted [*ἀνθρώπους γε συμπαγῆναι*] and the other animals which have life [*ψυχὴν*]' [=B4, 2–5], he goes on 'and human beings have built cities and devised works [*ἔργα κατεσκευασμένα*], as we do, and they have a sun and a moon and the rest, as we do, and the earth brings forth for them many things of all kinds, the most useful of which they collect in their dwellings and use' [=B4, 5–10]. That he is hinting at a different world order from ours [*ἑτέραν τινὰ διακόσμησιν παρὰ τὴν παρ' ἡμῖν αἰνίττεται*] is made clear from the phrase 'as we do', which he uses more than once. That he thinks that it is not a perceptible world, preceding this world in time, is made clear by [the words] 'the most useful of which they collect in their dwellings and use'. For he does not say 'used' but 'use'. But he is not talking about a civilisation similar to ours located elsewhere.[19]

The word 'twofold' (*διττὴν*) does not occur in any preserved text of Anaxagoras; it does, however, describe accurately the distinction between the spinning out of the incorporeal powers and the compacted resulting products (such as earth). And, if Simplicius is right in describing the order of Anaxagoras' train of reflection (from how, for instance, bread separates out into flesh and bones, to the originary separation of incorporeal powers, such as hot and cold), this movement is not two separate stages but two aspects of the same revolving effect of intellect. The distinction of world orders between the intellectual and the perceptible is not a matter of chronological priority (he emphasizes the present tense), nor are they located in different realms. The perceptible is derived from the intellectual, and the latter is embodied in the former; it is this world order, other than our empirical one but embodied in it, at which Anaxagoras is 'hinting'. More will be said presently about Anaxagoras' words in the above passage from Simplicius

[18] Following the emendation of B14 proposed by Sider and adopted by Laks and Most.

[19] Simplicius, *In Phys.* 1.4 (Diels, 157.5–20), adopting D–K's emendation; Simplicius' has *ὁ δὲ νοῦς ὅσα ἐστί*... Trans. Pamela Huby and C. C. W. Taylor, *On Aristotle Physics 1.3–4*, ACA (London: Bloomsbury, 2011), 65–6, modified.

(constituting fragment B4). Regarding the first quotation given there (B14), Tzamalikos argues that the ἵνα clause should be taken purposively rather than locatively, so that it would read: 'intellect exists *so that* others exist too'.[20] It is through the activity of intellect that everything is ordered—that is, brought into being; everything brought into being is ontologically different from intellect, yet totally dependent upon intellect, and while intellect is 'alone all by itself' (B12, above), intellect co-exists with that which it has brought into being, and, indeed, is embodied in it.

Although, as we have seen, Anaxagoras emphasizes the distinction of intellect from everything else, he also affirms that intellect masters (*κρατεῖ*) 'things that have life, whether they are larger or smaller' (B12, above), so that 'in every thing there is a portion of every thing except of intellect; but there are things in which intellect too is present [*ἔστιν οἷσι δὲ καὶ νοῦς ἔνι*]'.[21] As Sedley comments, with Anaxagoras 'the reference of the word *nous* ranges, without clear demarcation, over both intelligence as a power resident in each of us, whose properties we therefore know at first hand, and the great cosmic intelligence which created the world. The ambiguity is permissible because Anaxagoras almost certainly holds that the great cosmic intelligence, having created the world, apportioned at least some of itself into individual living beings, ourselves included.'[22] As Gregory would put it later, 'intellect' is not simply 'given' (*ἔδωκεν*) by God to human beings, but rather 'he gives a share' (*μετέδωκε*, *De hom.* 9.1).

Anaxagoras seemed to Socrates and Plato to have failed in giving an account of why the result of the activity of intellect is the best structure for the cosmos—that is, a fully adequate teleology. Sedley, however, argues that there is in fact a teleological orientation in the subtext of Anaxagoras' thought: 'when intelligence creates worlds, it designedly constructs them so as to be hospitable to agricultural civilizations like Anaxagoras's own'.[23] The 'seeds of all things', which Anaxagoras sees implanted in all things should, according to Sedley, be taken simply as ordinary biological seeds, in accord with his agricultural model. Moreover, translating B4 (quoted above) as 'and that human beings, for their part, have cities that they have populated and farms that they have constructed [*ἔργα κατεσκευασμένα*], just as where we are', Sedley infers that this 'mirrors accurately enough the purposive construction of the great cosmic farm by *nous*'.[24] Moreover, as Aristotle reports that 'Anaxagoras asserts that it is his possession of hands that makes the human being the most intelligent of animals', whereas Aristotle would

[20] Cf. Tzamalikos, *Anaxagoras*, 284–5; his full translation of the passage is: 'Mind, which always is, certainly is also now, so that all the other things also should exist, namely, in the encompassing multitude [of the principles] and in the things that have been joined together, and in the things that have been separated off.'

[21] B11; Simplicius, *In Phys.* 1.4 (Diels, 164.23–4; ET 72).

[22] Sedley, *Creationism*, 11. [23] Sedley, *Creationism*, 22.

[24] Sedley, *Creationism*, 23; the translation is given on p. 14. Laks and Most translate *ἔργα κατεσκευασμένα* similarly: 'cultivated fields'.

have it that it is 'because the human is the most intelligent animal that he has hands', it would seem that Anaxagoras shared in the commonplace assumption that the human being is the culmination or high point of the works of intellect within nature.[25] And so, Sedley concludes, 'it therefore seems implicit in Anaxagoras' text that *nous* constructs and, as it were, farms worlds primarily in order to generate human beings. The teleology proves to have an anthropocentric bias.'[26]

There are many themes in what we have seen that recur in Gregory's treatise *On the Human Image* (and elsewhere in his corpus): that incorporeal properties are combined to make matter; that a process of revolving results in the genesis of things in an ordered and temporal sequence; that creation is twofold; that intellect is not simply given to humans, but that they have a share of it; and that humans, the culmination of this process, have hands as befits an intellectual being.

It is possible that there is a further allusion, through the word used in the opening sentence of Anaxagoras' book, a leitmotif of his thought (though obscured by Aristotle's 'homoeomeries'): 'All things [*χρήματα*] were together.' This word also occurs in the LXX text of Prov. 17:6 'The faithful one has the whole world of money [*ὅλος ὁ κόσμος τῶν χρημάτων*], but the faithless not even a farthing', which Origen paraphrases: 'the faithful, he says, will see the principles of this world, which he figuratively called the things of the intellect [*ὄψεται τοὺς λόγους τοῦ κόσμου τούτου, οὕστινας χρήματα τροπικῶς τοῦ νοῦ προσηγόρευσεν*]'.[27] This characteristically Anaxagorean word (along with other points) indicates, for Tzamalikos, Origen's 'discipleship' to Anaxagoras.[28] This verse from Proverbs, through this 'Anaxagorean' interpretation, is thus taken as a metaphor, speaking of the vision that the faithful one will have: the *λόγοι* of the world are the *χρήματα* of the intellect (that is, for Origen, God), and they are held together in his Logos. Similarly, for Origen the *λόγοι* are the words of Scripture, woven together as the 'garment' of the Word and as his body (for, according to Origen, 'the Word always becomes incarnate in Scripture'); they are a garment, moreover, which appears one way to those at the foot of the mountain, but brighter than the sun to those who climb Tabor to see the transfigured Christ in every passage.[29] Intriguingly, Gregory opens his letter to Peter, introducing the work *On the Human Image*, using the same word, *χρήματα*: 'If it is necessary to honour with rewards of *χρήματα* those who excel in virtue, "the whole world of *χρήματα*"' would not match his brother's virtue; but as the feast of Pascha requires a gift, Gregory offers him a treatise (*λόγος*), 'woven not without toil from our poor mind'. Moreover, the very subject of this treatise points to the same indebtedness, for according to

[25] Aristotle, *Parts of animals*, 4.10, 687a8–10; text and ET A. L. Peck and E. S. Forster, Loeb Classical Library, Aristotle 12 (Cambridge, MA: Harvard University Press, 1937). Gregory too employs this topos in *De hom.* 8.8.

[26] Sedley, *Creationism*, 24.

[27] Origen, *Exp. Prov.* PG 17, 197c9–11.

[28] Tzamalikos, *Anaxagoras*, 827.

[29] Origen, *Philoc.* 15.19; cf. *Com. Matt.* 12.38.

Gregory, 'in accordance with the image, then, the human being came to be, that is, the universal nature, the godlike thing [*ὁ ἄνθρωπος, ἡ καθόλου φύσις, τὸ θεοείκελον χρῆμα*]' (*De hom.* 22.4). It is not impossible that he is playing with these words, and thus intimating his own indebtedness to, and standing within, the same tradition as had, according to Tzamalikos, Origen.

2. Plato

According to Plato, Socrates was dissatisfied with Anaxagoras' book because it did not seem to him to provide what is most needed in an account of cosmology—that is, how and why Intellect 'arranges everything and establishes each thing as it is best [*βέλτιστα*] for it to be' (*Phaed.* 97c4). Apart from a single passage of Diogenes of Apollonia (late fifth century BCE), consideration of the goodness of the intellect and its cosmogenic activity seems not to have been treated by the Presocratics.[30] While the good was, of course, central to Socrates' concerns, and although he gave a story (*μῦθος*) at the end of the *Phaedo* which gestures towards such an account (*Phaed.* 107c1–115a8), his wish, even in his last hours, to 'be a pupil of one who would teach me of such a cause' (*Phaed.* 99c7–8) is only fulfilled, as Sedley points out, when Plato has him listen to Timaeus, presumably a Pythagorean, so that Plato thereby 'legitimates his own lifetime project, portraying his later move into physics not as a betrayal of Socrates but as the very development that Socrates himself would above all else have welcomed'.[31] Without a doubt, Plato's *Timaeus* was the most important text in the ancient world, and beyond, regarding the universe, the structure of the cosmos, and the human being within it, the nature of the soul, and providence. There are, of course, many difficult points of interpretation regarding this work, some of which have been debated from the earliest times onwards, such as the status of the 'Craftsman' or 'Demiurge' (a 'creator god' or a mythical figure personifying divine reason within creation working towards good ends?) and the account of time (did the world come to be in time or time with the creation of the world?), or, in more recent times, the setting of *Timaeus* in relation to the *Republic*, the relation between the speeches in the *Timaeus*, the parts of Timaeus' own speech, and the way in which meaning evolves as it unfolds in dialogue.[32] I suggested in the previous chapter, and will argue more in what is to come, that the three parts of Timaeus' speech are paralleled by the divisions within

[30] Cf. Diogenes of Apollonia B3 (= Simplicius, *In Phys.* 1.4; Diels, 152.11–16): 'for without intelligence [*ἄνευ νοήσιος*], he says, it would not be possible for it to be distributed in such a way as to possess the measures of all things, of winter and summer, of night and day, of rains and winds and fine weather; if one wishes to think intelligently [*ἐννοεῖσθαι*] about them, one would find that they are arranged in the finest way [*κάλλιστα*] that could be achieved'. For Diogenes, see Sedley, *Creationism*, 75–8.

[31] Sedley, *Creationism*, 92.

[32] For many of the former points, Francis MacDonald Cornford, *Plato's Cosmology: The* Timaeus *of Plato* (Indianapolis, IN: Hackett, 1997 [1937]) remains essential. For the latter questions, see

Gregory's work *On the Human Image*. As such, it is necessary to give a sketch of the train of thought in each part of Timaeus' speech, or at least key aspects of them, in order to see how they relate and the overall picture that is given thereby.

The subject proposed for Timaeus is 'to speak beginning from the genesis of the world and end with the nature of human beings' (27a5–6). Following his introductory prelude (27d5–29d3), there are three main parts to Timaeus' speech. The first (29d7–47e2) sets out 'the things that have been crafted by Intellect' (47e4: *τὰ διὰ νοῦ δεδημιουργημένα*). Although intimations are already given in this first part that he is anticipating what will come later (cf. 34b10, 44c4–5), midway through his speech Timaeus announces he will make a new beginning, so as to give an account of 'Necessity' (*ἀνάγκη*) and the 'Straying Cause' (*πλανωμένη αἰτία*), that over which Intellect 'prevailed', 'persuading it to direct most of the things that come to be towards what is best' (48a2–3); this is the subject of the second part of his speech (47e3–69a5). The third part (69a6–92c9) is again signalled likewise: he announces that as all the materials are now ready for construction, 'from them we are to weave together the remainder of our account; so let us briefly return to our starting point and quickly proceed to the same place from which we arrived at our present position and let us try to put a final head on our story, one that fits with our previous discussion' (69a7–b2). The bulk of what follows is a detailed psychophysical account of the parts of the body, their functions and purposes, the diseases of body and soul, and the need for proper care of each, ending with an account of the differentiation into male and female (90e–92d6) and the appearance of the lower animals. Timaeus concludes his speech in *Critias* with a prayer 'to the god [i.e. the world] who previously of old came to be in reality and just now comes to be in words'.[33] Timaeus' speech is not, then, simply an account of the formation of the cosmos and the human being within it, but a verbal representation or enactment of its order and harmony. Moreover, by showing 'the reasons and forethought [*αἰτίας καὶ προνοίας*] of the gods in causing them to be' (44c7), it enables others, through the right nurture of instruction, to calm the irrational movements of their souls and so become 'perfectly whole and healthy' (44b8–c1).

In the prelude, Timaeus sets out the general metaphysical structure for his account and indicates the status of the account itself. He begins by making a firm distinction between 'that which is grasped by intellection through a rational

Hans-Georg Gadamer, 'Idea and Reality in Plato's *Timaeus*', in idem, *Dialogue and Dialectic: Eight Hermeneutical Studies on Plato*, trans. P. Christopher Smith (New Haven, CT: Yale University Press, 1980), 156–93, and Dominic J. O'Meara, *Cosmology and Politics in Plato's Later Works* (Cambridge: Cambridge University Press, 2017), 1–84. In addition, I have found the following particularly helpful: Donald J. Zeyl's introduction to his translation of the *Timaeus* (Indianapolis, IN: Hackett, 2000), xiii–lxxxix (I have largely followed Zeyl's translation, consulting others, and modifying as necessary); T. K. Johansen, *Plato's Natural Philosophy: A Study of the* Timaeus-Critias (Cambridge: Cambridge University Press, 2004); and David Sedley, *Creationism and Its Critics in Antiquity* (Berkeley, CA: University of California Press, 2007), 93–132.

[33] Plato, *Crit.* 106a3–4: *τῷ δὲ πρὶν μὲν πάλαι ποτ' ἔργῳ, νῦν δὲ λόγοις ἄρτι θεῷ γεγονότι.*

account [νοήσει μετὰ λόγου], always unchangeably being', and 'that which is conceived of by opinion through unreasoning sense-perception, coming to be and passing away but which never really is' (28a1–3). As the heaven or the cosmos can be seen and touched, it has a body, and thus has come to be, and necessarily has done so because of some cause (28a7–c2). In bringing this about, Timaeus argues, 'the maker and father of this universe' must have looked to the eternal for his model, for indeed this world 'is the most beautiful of the things that have come to be and he is the best of causes'.[34] As such, what came to be must have been crafted 'with reference to that which is graspable by reason (λόγῳ) and wisdom', and it is thus 'a likeness [εἰκόνα] of something' (29a6–b2). These metaphysical principles, finally, have a direct impact on how Timaeus understands his own speech: with regard to this likeness and its model (παράδειγμα), he argues that as 'the accounts [τοὺς λόγους] we give of things have the same character as the subjects they set forth', so accounts of that which is 'stable and fixed and transparent to understanding are themselves stable and unshifting', whereas an account of that which is but a 'likeness' (εἰκών) will itself only be a 'likely story' (εἰκὸς μῦθος, 29b2–c1) and also have a tendency to be 'casual and random', for we too 'greatly partake of the casual and random' (34c2–4).

Turning to the first part of his speech, there are a number of points to note. Most important is the affirmation that the framer of the universe, being good and therefore without jealousy, 'wanted everything to become as much like himself as possible', and that this is 'the most preeminent reason [ἀρχὴν κυριωτάτην] for the origin of the world's genesis' (29e1–30a2). This being his desire, 'the god took over all that was visible—not at rest but in discordant and unordered motion—and brought it from a state of disorder to one of order, because he believed that order was in every way better than disorder' (30a2–6). Reasoning that among visible things, those that have intellect are better than those that do not and that intellect can only be present in those things that have souls, when the god framed the universe he thus placed intellect within the soul and soul within the body—at least, 'according to the likely story, this is how we must say that this world came to be by the god's providence [πρόνοιαν], as a truly living thing, endowed with soul and intellect' (30a6–c1). The result is that this world 'resembles more closely than anything else that Living Thing of which all other living things are parts, both individually and by kinds. For that Living Thing comprehends within itself all intelligible living things, just as our world is made up of us and all the other visible creatures' (30c5–d1).

After having established that the world must be singular and unique, as is its model (31a1–b2), Timaeus turns to the four elements (fire, earth, water, and air) of the cosmic body, made spherical in shape and rotating upon its axis. Within

[34] Plato, *Tim.* 28c3–29a6: ὁ μὲν γὰρ κάλλιστος τῶν γεγονότων, ὁ δ' ἄριστος τῶν αἰτίων.

that body, the god 'set a soul in its center, which he extended throughout the whole body and with which he then covered the body outside' so that 'this world which he begat for himself is a blessed god' (34b3–9). Catching himself, however, Timaeus emphasizes that although he has treated the body of the world before its soul, because of the 'random and casual' character of his speech, 'priority and seniority' is in fact given by the god to the soul, for it is preeminent and to rule the body (34b10–35a1). In Plato's telling, the soul of the world is made by combining 'the Same'—that is, that which is indivisible and always changeless—with 'the Different'—that is, that which comes to be in the corporeal realm and is divisible—by means of a third, an 'intermediary form of being derived from the other two', 'conforming by force [βίᾳ] the different, which was hard to mix, into conformity with the Same' (35a1–9). After describing the creation of time, as 'a moving image of eternity' (37c6–38b5), Plato notes that although the world, up to the birth of time, had been made in all other respects like its model, it was still 'unlike' in that 'it did not yet contain all the living things that it were to have come to be within it', that is, the four kinds of living things: the heavenly race of gods, those that have wings and fly, those that live in the water, and those that have feet and live on land (39e3–40a2). He himself made the heavenly gods—sun, moon, stars, and planets—who regulate time, and also earth as our 'nurturer' and the guardian of day and night (40a2–d5); the coming to be of other gods, he notes briefly, has been described by their descendants (40d6–41a3).

With this accomplished, 'the begetter of the universe' directed all these gods regarding their work in forming mortal beings, 'without whom the heaven will be incomplete [ἀτελὴς]' (41a5–b8). He announces that he will 'begin by sowing that seed' and then specifies that 'the rest of the task is yours: weave what is mortal to what is immortal, fashion and beget living things. Give them food, cause them to grow, and when they perish, receive them back again' (41c8–d3). When he finished his speech to his children, the father of the universe, according to Timaeus, returned to the mixing bowl, mixing together the same ingredients, although no longer ones that are 'invariably and constantly pure, but of a second and third grade of purity'; after dividing the mixture into the same number of souls as there are stars in the heavens and assigning each one to a star, he 'mounted each soul in a carriage, as it were, and showed it the nature of the universe' (41d4–e1). He then 'described to them the laws that had been ordained', that is, 'that they would all be assigned one and the same initial birth [γένεσις]', so that all would be treated by him equally, and said that 'he would then sow each of the souls into that instrument of time suitable to it, where they were to acquire the nature of being the most god-fearing of living things', adding that 'since human beings have a two-fold nature' (διπλῆς δὲ οὔσης τῆς ἀνθρωπίνης φύσεως), it should be the superior kind that would from then on be called 'man' (ἀνήρ, 41e1–42a3).

But, importantly, before describing the work of the gods in constructing the mortal frames for these souls, Timaeus immediately continues by spelling out how these 'laws' are, as it were, existentially experienced. 'Once the souls were of necessity implanted in bodies', as these bodies have things coming in and going out, 'the first innate capacity they would of necessity come to have would be sense-perception, which arises out of forceful disturbances', and secondly 'love [ἔρως], mingled with pleasure and pain', with fear [φόβος] and spiritedness [θυμός], together with whatever goes with having these emotions and their natural opposites (42a3–b1). 'If they could master them, their lives would be just, whereas if they were mastered, they would be unjust. And if a person lived a good life throughout the due course of time, he would at the end return to his dwelling place in his companion star.' Failing this, 'he would be born a second time, now as a woman', and if even then he could not refrain from wickedness, he would be changed again, into some wild animal (42b1–c4). There would be, moreover, 'no rest from these toilsome transformations until, by dragging into conformity with the revolution of the same and uniform within him that massive accretion of fire and water and air and earth, controlling that turbulent irrational mass by means of reason, he would return to the form of his first and best condition' (42c4–d2).

Only after having given these ordained laws setting out the growth that is required of mortal embodied beings does Timaeus turn to describing how the gods wove what is mortal to the immortal, fastening together the elements drawn from the world with rivets rather than indissoluble bonds. And the result of their work is what we now see: human beings who begin their existence by moving 'in a disorderly, random, and irrational manner' (43b1–2), because 'at this stage souls do not have a ruling orbit taking the lead' (44a4–5): 'all these disturbances are no doubt the reason why even today and not only at the beginning, whenever a soul is bound with a mortal body, it at first lacks intelligence' (ἄνους ψυχὴ γίγνεται τὸ πρῶτον 44a7–b1). 'But', Timaeus continues, 'as the stream that brings growth and nourishment diminishes and the soul's orbits regain their composure, resume their proper courses, and establish themselves more and more with the passage of time, their revolutions are set straight, to conform to the configuration each of the circles takes in its natural course; they then correctly identify what is the same and what is different, and render intelligent the person who possesses them' (44b1–7). In this way, finally, 'if such a person also gets proper nurture to supplement his education, he'll turn out perfectly whole and healthy' (44b8–c1).

Yet, once again, Timaeus then catches himself: 'But this doesn't happen till later. Our present subject, on the other hand, needs a more detailed treatment. We must move on to treat the prior questions' (44c4–5)—that is the construction, form, and functioning of the various bodily parts, especially eyes and sight, and also music, which by its rhythm assists us, for most of us 'have lost all sense of measure and are lacking in grace'; several pages are devoted to this (43d3–47e2), full of extensive details that need not detain us here.

In the prelude and the first part of his speech, then, Timaeus has given us a 'likely story' expounding a cosmology that accounts for the world and human beings in terms of what is 'best' or 'most beautiful', tracing this back to the father of the universe and the intelligible and eternal model upon which this world is fashioned: this, or rather he, is 'the best of causes' and the world is indeed 'the most beautiful of the things that have come to be' (29a5–6), and 'the preeminent reason' for the becoming of the world is that it should be as like the god as possible (29e2–30a2). However, as a 'likely story' the speech is itself rather 'casual and random', with Timaeus apparently running ahead of himself and catching himself: the formation of the body is described before that of the soul, although the priority is in fact the other way round; the growth expected of embodied souls is detailed before their embodiment is treated; and, most importantly, while the world is indeed most beautiful, human beings, he points out, do not come into existence in that way. Although as souls they are shown the nature of the universe and have 'one and the same initial birth', as embodied beings the first impression that strikes them is not 'the movement of the same within them' but the forceful disturbances that arise from outside by means of the senses, and so they come into being in a rather disordered manner, with limbs flailing about rather than moving in an orderly manner—they are at first souls lacking intelligence (44a8). But this means that the world, while being indeed the most beautiful of things that have come to be, is also a proving ground, as it were, where souls implanted in bodies have the task of mastering the irrational movements stimulated by external impressions, and for whom pleasure is mixed with pain so as to provide a stimulus for growth in self-mastery; indeed, it is this 'instrument of time' into which the souls are sown that provides the guidance for their growth, so that, conforming their irrational movements to 'the revolution of the Same and uniform within him', they will thereby return (though in what sense, as the account of creation is not yet complete?) to the 'first and best condition' and 'acquire the nature of being the most god-fearing of living things'.[35] By arranging things this way, moreover, directing the gods to give mortal beings 'the finest, the best possible guidance they could give', the father and maker of the universe provides the means for their growth, yet 'without being responsible for any evil that these creatures might bring upon themselves' (42e1–4).

Having concluded this part of his speech by referring to our present condition, in which we have 'lost all sense of measure and are lacking in grace' (47d7–e2), Timaeus then announces:

[35] As Cornford (*Plato's Cosmology*, 6) notes: 'The *Republic* had dwelt on the structural analogy between the state and the individual soul. Now Plato intends to base his conception of human life, both for the individual and society, on the inexpugnable foundation of the order of the universe. The parallel of macrocosm and microcosm runs through the whole discourse. True morality is not a product of human evolution, still less the arbitrary enactment of human wills. It is an order and harmony of the soul; and the soul itself is a counterpart, in miniature, of the soul of the world, which has an everlasting order and harmony of its own, instituted by reason. This order was revealed to every soul before its birth (41e); and it is revealed now in the visible architecture of the heavens.'

> Now in all but a brief part of the discourse I have just completed I have presented what has been crafted by Intellect. But I need to match this account by providing a comparable one concerning the things that have come about by Necessity [ἀνάγκη]. For this ordered world is of mixed birth: it is the offspring of a union of Necessity and Intellect. Intellect prevailed over Necessity by persuading it to direct most of the things that come to be towards what is best, and the result of this subjugation of Necessity to wise persuasion was the initial formation of this universe. So, if one is to speak of how it really came to be in this way [εἴ τις οὖν ᾗ γέγονεν κατὰ ταῦτα ὄντως ἐρεῖ], one would also have to introduce the character of the Straying Cause [τὸ τῆς πλανωμένης εἶδος αἰτίας]—how it is its nature to set things adrift. I shall have to retrace my steps, then, and, armed with a second starting point that also applies to these same things, I must go back once again to the beginning and start my present inquiry from there, just as I did with my earlier one. (47e3–48b3)

Although narrated first in his 'likely story', the way in which Timaeus has already included elements of the countervailing forces operative in the world and the genesis of human beings, and also the passing mentions of 'auxiliary' or 'contributory' causes (*συναίτιαι* 46c7, d1; *συμμεταίτια* 46e6), disrupting, though surely not purposelessly, the flow of his speech, indicates that 'what was crafted by Intellect' is not separate, temporally or spatially, from the world that actually is, as he says here, 'of mixed birth'. It is, however, only in this second part of his speech that Timaeus sets about to examine systematically, from the same starting point, what these are—that is, 'Necessity' or 'Constraint' and 'the Straying Cause'. What is meant by this 'Necessity' and 'Straying Cause' has been a matter of considerable debate.[36] On one level it seems most likely, as Sedley argues, that they consist in matter and its properties: 'when intelligence operates in the world it has to rely on the intrinsic properties of matter, but matter, having no inherent tendency towards good ends, acts in a purposeless way unless it is directed, or in Timaeus' preferred idiom "persuaded", by intelligence'.[37] But this does not simply indicate, he further argues, the 'intransigence of matter, its resistance to intelligent persuasion, the cause of evil in the world', for after all, according to the 'likely story', the creator had 'carte blanche' in organizing the stuff from which he would build the cosmos.[38] The key point is that, as Johansen puts it, this cause is 'wandering' in that in itself 'it is not teleological'; yet, while its operation is not of itself directed towards the best outcome, nevertheless when 'persuaded' by Intellect it becomes a 'contributory cause'.[39]

[36] Cf. Cornford, *Plato's Cosmology*, 162–77; Johansen, *Plato's Natural Philosophy*, 92–116; Sedley, *Creationism*, 113–27.

[37] Sedley, *Creationism*, 114–15.

[38] Sedley, *Creationism*, 115.

[39] Johansen, *Plato's Natural Philosophy*, 93.

Besides the question of matter and its own properties, there is also a further dimension of necessity at play in the growth of the human being, already alluded to by Timaeus in 41d4–42d2. Whether the 'necessity' by which souls are implanted into bodies (42a4) or the 'necessity' by which they come first to experience violent impressions from without (42a5) is related to the 'Necessity' in 47e3–48b3 or not,[40] the point that embodied souls are to undergo a process of growth under 'the finest, the best possible guidance' (42e2–3) is a given, a 'foreordained law' laid down by the maker of the universe, even before their embodiment, or at least before the narration of the construction of their bodies (41e2–3). While the maker of the universe can use force (*βίᾳ*, 35a9) in constructing souls, their growth cannot be forced but requires guidance and especially time: 'sown into the instrument of time' (41e5), souls are able to conform their movements with the revolution of the Same within each, and so return 'to their original condition of excellence' (42d2).

It is in this part of the speech that Timaeus introduces the third factor in his account: in the first part he had distinguished two kinds (*δύο εἴδη*), the intelligible changeless model and the visible imitation of that model that comes to be, but now he needs to distinguish 'a third, one of a different sort' (*τρίτον ἄλλο γένος*), and this is 'a receptacle of all genesis, its wetnurse, as it were' (*πάσης εἶναι γενέσεως ὑποδοχὴν αὐτὴν οἷον τιθήνην*, 48e2–49a6). Plato's account of this receptacle is perhaps the most obscure part of the *Timaeus*, it being debated whether he is speaking of 'space' or 'stuff'. Zeyl suggests that the way to resolve these two interpretations is to think rather of 'room', in the sense of 'room to move about in': while it is necessarily the case that movement requires room in which to move, this is, for Plato, both the stuff and the room in which the stuff moves, as when a liquid in a container is agitated, forming currents, 'parts' of the liquid will travel through other 'parts' of it, travelling through the room, so that 'the parts through which the currents travel is the room. But any part of the room may become a traveller as well.'[41] If the connection between movement and time has been explored in the first part of Timaeus' speech, it is the connection between movement and space that is explored here further, opening out into a detailed examination of the mathematical and geometrical properties constituting the elements in the realm of becoming. However, while time is of great importance to Gregory in *On the Human Image*, space does not seem to be an important factor for him, at least in that work, and so this aspect of the *Timaeus* can be left aside here.

The third part of Timaeus' speech (69a6–92c9), as already noted, brings the speech together by returning to the starting point, but now 'weaving together' the materials developed in the first two parts, so as to put a 'head' upon his story (69b1). The bulk of what follows is a detailed psychophysical account of the

[40] Cf. Sedley's comment about the very common word *ἀνάγκη* in *Creationism*, 114 ftn. 48.
[41] Zeyl, *Timaeus*, lxiii.

human being, analysing the functions and purposes of the various bodily parts and how they contribute to human well-being, together with an examination of the diseases of body and soul, and the need for the care of each. Accepting that 'the *Timaeus* is not easy reading', Cornford adds that 'the physiological and medical chapters towards the end would be repellent to many'.[42] However, the purpose of this extensive psychophysical investigation is indicated towards the end of the speech, when Timaeus reflects that it should suffice for 'the subject of the living thing as a whole and its bodily parts, and how a man should both lead and be led by himself in order to have the best prospects for living a rational life' (89d2–4). Moreover, we are to make sure that the motions of the 'three distinct types of soul that reside within us' are kept in due proportion (89e3–90a2). It is 'the most sovereign part of our soul [that is] god's gift to us, given to be our guiding spirit', which resides in our heads, raising us up from the earth, 'as plants grown not from the earth but from heaven. For it is from heaven, the place from which our souls were originally born, that the divine part suspends our head, that is, our root, and so keeps our whole body erect' (90a2–b1). Rather than becoming absorbed in the appetites or ambitions, and so become thoroughly mortal, we should devote ourselves to the love of learning and true wisdom, thereby nourishing that part of our soul, and 'redirect the revolutions in our heads that were thrown off course around the time of our birth' by learning the harmonies and revolutions of the universe, bringing our understanding into conformity with what it contemplates (90b1–d5). And so, Timaeus, concludes, 'when this conformity is complete, we shall have achieved our goal: that most excellent life offered to humankind by the gods, both now and forevermore' (90d5–7).

Although it seems that Timaeus has completed his assignment of tracing the formation of the universe and culminating in the coming to be of humankind, he recalls that there are other things whose coming to be is necessary for this world to be fully like its model (cf. 39e3–40a2)—that is, the appearance of women and the other animals. 'According to the likely account', as Timaeus tells it and as we have already seen, 'males who lived lives of cowardice or injustice were reborn in the second generation as women' (90e6–91a1). This explains why, according to Timaeus, it is only at this time that 'the gods fashioned the desire for sexual union' by constructing the reproductive organs, which in turn 'produced the love of procreation', and which are 'unruly and self-willed', refusing to be subject to reason, but seeking to overpower everything else, until 'finally the woman's desire and the man's love bring them together, and, like plucking the fruit from the tree, they sow the seed into the ploughed field of her womb, living things too small to be visible and still without form' (91a1–d5).[43] Birds in turn, are reincarnations of

[42] Cornford, *Plato's Cosmology*, 20.

[43] As Zeyl, *Timaeus*, lxxxviii, observes: 'Sexual desire, then, is not a desire of the male or female proper—not even of the appetitive part of his or her soul—but of the reproductive organs.'

simpler souls who have studied the heavens through visible observation rather than mathematical calculation; land animals are those who followed the lower parts of the soul rather than reason; and aquatic animals are derived from those who were 'the most stupid and ignorant of all' (91d6–92c3). Although in this 'likely story' women are derived from the moral failings of males, and the groups of animals from human intellectual failure, it nevertheless remains the case that for the world to be a perfect likeness of its intellectual model, it must contain all these beings. Only now has Timaeus' speech come to an end: 'This world of ours has received and teems with living things, mortal and immortal. A visible living thing containing visible ones, a perceptible god, image of the intelligible Living Thing, its grandness, goodness, beauty and perfection are unexcelled. Our one heaven, indeed the only one of its kind, has come to be' (92c4–9). Although it had 'previously of old come to be in reality', it is indeed in Timaeus' speech that it 'just now comes to be in words' (*Crit.* 106a3–4), and so his task, 'to speak beginning from the genesis of the cosmos and end with the nature of human beings' (27a5–6), is discharged.

While there are many particular points of similarity between the *Timaeus* and Gregory's treatise, which are noted in the following translation, most striking is the parallel threefold division of each work, together with the numerous foreshadowings, backtracking, and apparent detours, and switching between different modes of speech. Gregory's treatise begins with an ideal description of creation and the human being as the image of God (*De hom.* 1–15), with a lengthy excursion into the apparent relapse from rational control exhibited in tears, laughter, yawning and dreaming, which provides an occasion for a brief (and deeply embedded in a lengthy discussion about the slackening of rational control in such bodily phenomena) treatment of the genesis of evil (*De hom.* 12–13). But then, noting that the image he has just described is not in fact what we see when looking at actual human beings, he returns again to his starting point, the scriptural verses of Gen. 1:26–7, discerning this time a distinction between the image and the prototype inscribed in these verses (*De hom.* 16.1–9). Thus begins a lengthy and complex analysis of the waywardness of human beings, God's providence, the division into male and female, the arising of the passions, and the time needed to reach the fullness (both intensively and extensively) of the human being that will happen together with the end of time at the universal reconstitution and the transformation of humanity from the corruptible and earthy to the impassible and eternal. The economy of creation is thus for Gregory, as it is for Plato, a pedagogy, God 'persuading' human beings by providing them with the occasion, the time, and the means for growth in understanding and virtue. The third part of Gregory's treatise, the final lengthy chapter (*De hom.* 30), as with the third part of Timaeus' speech, draws extensively upon medical knowledge, describing the various organs and their functions, showing how they contribute to the growth of the human being. This chapter is as hard a read as Cornford found the final chapters of the *Timaeus*, replete with extensive and detailed discussions of medical and physiological matters, and it only overtly returns in the last paragraphs (if one gets that far!) to important threads pulling the whole treatise together. His purpose, Gregory says as he nears the end, acknowledging that he has 'wandered far from the matters of hand', was to show that 'the seminal cause of our constitution is neither soul without a body nor a body without a soul, but that, from animated and living bodies a being, living and animated from the first, is generated, human nature receiving it to be cherished, like a nursling, with her own powers', so that each part grows appropriately and together, and the soul, which initially appears somewhat obscurely, 'by this artistic and scientific process of formation', gradually 'increases in radiance concurrently with the perfecting of the organism' (*De hom.* 30.28–9). In a similar manner to the way in which a statue is fashioned, he argues, so too 'the all-contriving nature, taking from the kindred matter within herself the part that comes from the human being, crafts the statue', and, as with the carver and his stone, 'in the carving of the organism the form of the soul, by the analogy, is displayed in the substratum, incompletely in that which is incomplete, and perfectly in that which is perfect; but it would have been perfect from the beginning had nature not been maimed by evil' (*De hom.* 30.30). What Gregory understands by evil maiming nature must wait for the examination of his treatise itself, but the analogy with the statue emerging from the stone—in this case, a living embodied soul requiring growth in both body and soul to reach completeness—indicates that we are within the realm of necessity and pedagogy, and, above all, time and the possibilities for transformation that time opens up.

3. Philo

With Philo of Alexandria (*c.*20 BCE–50 CE) we see for the first time the cosmological reflections of the Greek philosophers applied to the opening chapters of Genesis. His work, *On the Creation of the Cosmos according to Moses*, is of particular interest for understanding the background of Gregory's treatise, as, unlike the later hexaemeral tradition it inspired, Philo deals with both creation accounts (and, indeed, Gen. 3), holding them in tension, yet also providing a unitary account.[44] As Moses is primarily the lawgiver, the work is not simply a treatise on cosmology and the place of the human being within the cosmos, but is

[44] Greek text ed. F. H. Colson and G. H. Whitaker, *Philo* vol. 1, Loeb Classical Library, Philo 1 (Cambridge, MA: Harvard University Press, 1929); ET David T. Runia, *Philo, On the Creation of the Cosmos according to Moses: Introduction, Translation, and Commentary*, Philo of Alexandria Commentary Series 1 (Atlanta: Society of Biblical Literature, 2001); I have used Runia's translation, modifying it occasionally. On the title, see Runia, *Creation*, 96–8. For the relation between Philo and the *Timaeus*, see David T. Runia, *Philo of Alexandria and the Timaeus of Plato*, Philosophia Antiqua 44 (Leiden: Brill, 1986); and for a survey of his influence in later Christian writers, see idem, *Philo in Early*

framed rather in terms of the law. So it begins with Philo pointing out that, unlike all the others who either 'simply drew up unadorned regulations' or 'enclosed their thoughts with a mass of verbiage and so deceived the masses by concealing the truth with mythical fictions' (*Opif.* 1), Moses did not simply state what was to be done, 'nor did he, since it was necessary to form in advance the minds [*προτυπῶσαι τὰς διανοίας*] of those who were to make use of the laws, invent myths or express the approval of those composed by others' (*Opif.* 2). Moses' account of creation (*κοσμοποιίαν*) is thus a pedagogy, showing how 'the cosmos is in harmony with the law and the law with the cosmos', so that 'the man [*ἀνδρὸς*] who observes the law is at once [*εὐθὺς*] a citizen of the cosmos [*κοσμοπολίτου*], directing his actions towards the purpose of nature [*πρὸς τὸ βούλημα τῆς φύσεως*], in accordance with which the entire cosmos also is administered' (*Opif.* 3). And the work concludes, in turn, by drawing out five lessons that Moses teaches by means of his account of the creation of the cosmos (*Opif.* 170–2).

Before turning to the opening verses of Genesis, Philo begins, much like Timaeus, by laying out a fundamental distinction. Moses, according to Philo, taught that it is 'absolutely necessary that among existing things there is an activating cause on the one hand, and a passive object on the other [*ἐν τοῖς οὖσι τὸ μὲν εἶναι δραστήριον αἴτιον, τὸ δὲ παθητόν*]': 'the activating cause is the absolutely pure and unadulterated Intellect [*νοῦς*] of the universe superior to excellence and superior to knowledge and even superior to the good and the beautiful itself' (*Opif.* 8), while the passive element 'when set in motion and shaped and ensouled by the Intellect [*ψυχωθὲν ὑπὸ τοῦ νοῦ*] changes into the most perfect piece of work, this cosmos' (*Opif.* 9). To deny this and say that the world is ungenerated, according to Philo, would eliminate the most important aid towards piety, which is the idea of providence, for 'reason demands that the Father and Maker of all exercise care for that which has come into being', just as a father does for his children or a craftsman for his work (*Opif.* 10). Moreover, as the ungenerated 'was of a totally different order' than the visible and 'the entire sense-perceptible realm is in a process of genesis and change [*ἐν γενέσει καὶ μεταβολαῖς*] and never remains in the same state, [Moses] assigned eternity to the invisible and intelligible, as being akin and related to it', but to the sense-perceptible 'he ascribed the appropriate name "genesis" [*γένεσιν οἰκεῖον ὄνομα ἐπφήμισεν*]' (*Opif.* 12)—the name, of course, of the book under discussion.

Turning to the opening verses of Genesis, Philo emphasizes that although the fashioning of the cosmos is described as taking place over six days, this was not because the maker needed a length of time, 'for God surely did everything simultaneously [*ἅμα*], not only in giving commands but also in his thinking',

Christian Literature: A Survey, Compendia rerum judaicarum ad Novum Testamentum, Section III, Jewish Traditions in Early Christian Literature 3 (Assen, Netherlands: Van Gorcum; Minneapolis: Fortress Press, 1993).

whereas things that come into existence require 'order' (*Opif.* 13). Noting a distinction in the text between the beginning, designated by the cardinal number 'one' (μία), and the ordinal numbers used for the following days (*Opif.* 15; Gen. 1:5), Philo emphasizes that 'day one' stands alone, distinct from the following sequence of days. Day one contains innumerable things, preeminent among which is 'the intelligible cosmos [νοητὸν κόσμον]' (*Opif.* 15). Using similar reasoning to Timaeus, he continues:

> For God, because he is God, understood in advance [προλαβὼν] that a beautiful copy [μίμημα καλὸν] would not come into existence apart from a beautiful paradigm, and that none of the objects of sense-perception would be without fault, unless it was modelled on the archetypal and intelligible idea. Therefore when he had decided to construct this visible cosmos, he first marked out the intelligible [προεξετύπου τὸν νοητόν], so that he could use it as an incorporeal and most god-like paradigm and so produce the corporeal, a younger likeness of the older [πρεσβυτέρου νεώτερον ἀπεικόνισμα], which would contain as many sense-perceptible kinds as there were intelligible ones in that other. (*Opif.* 16)

It is noteworthy that the intention of God is to create the visible, and thus bodily, cosmos, and it is in order to do this that he first marks out the intelligible pattern. This intelligible paradigm, Philo continues, should not be thought to exist 'in some place' (*Opif.* 17). It exists, rather, in the way that a plan of a city, ordered to be founded by a king, first exists in the head of the architect, who then constructs the city out of stones and timber, all the while 'looking at the model and ensuring that the corporeal objects correspond to each of the incorporeal ideas' (*Opif.* 17–18). In the same way, when God 'decided to found the great cosmic city, he first conceived of its outlines', from which 'he composed the intelligible cosmos, which served him as a model when he completed the sense-perceptible cosmos as well' (*Opif.* 19). And as the archetype for the city was engraved in the soul of the architect, so also 'the cosmos composed of the ideas would have no other place than the divine Logos who gives these [ideas] their ordered disposition' (*Opif.* 20); the location of the intelligible cosmos is not in space, nor, as we will see, in time, but rather 'in' or even 'as' the Logos. The analogy with an architect is modified a few lines later when Philo states that if one wanted to speak more simply, 'one would say that the intelligible cosmos is nothing other than the Logos of God as he is actually making the cosmos'.[45] While the analogy implies a distinction between the king and the architect, Philo drops that implication thereafter: God alone is the creator—apart from when the plural of Gen. 1:26 and other considerations, as we will see, demand others (although the Logos is not in fact introduced as a

[45] *Opif.* 24: οὐδὲν ἂν ἕτερον εἴποι τὸν νοητὸν κόσμον εἶναι ἢ θεοῦ λόγου ἤδη κοσμοποιοῦντος. For the translation of ἤδη as 'actually', see Runia, *Creation*, 148.

collaborator in the creation of the human being). The Logos is the 'place' of all the powers of God, especially that 'cosmos-producing power which has as its source that which is truly good' (*Opif.* 20–1), containing in or as itself the intelligible cosmos as the blueprint for the work being effected. Philo concludes this reflection by drawing an analogy from the part to the whole: as the human being is made in the image of God, so too must be the whole, so that 'this entire sense-perceptible cosmos... is a representation of the divine image', and as such, 'it is plain that the archetypal seal, which we affirm to be the intelligible cosmos, would itself be the model and archetypal idea of the ideas, the Logos of God' (*Opif.* 25). As Runia observes, Philo seems to be deliberately rejecting any attempt to introduce subordinate deities: 'the intelligible world and the Logos—as object and subject of thought, respectively—may be identified because they are both intrinsically tied to God's creative activity'.[46]

Turning to the reason why the universe was constructed, Philo again follows Plato, 'one of the ancients', to affirm that as 'the Father and Maker was good', 'he did not begrudge a share of his own excellent nature to an existence [οὐσίᾳ] which did not possess any beauty of its own but was able to become all things' (*Opif.* 21). However, although the distinction between the active cause and passive object is bridged through God's creative activity, that which has come into being is nevertheless too weak to be able to receive 'the unstinting riches of his beneficence' in their own infinite measure. God thus conferred his blessings 'in proportion to the capacities of those who receive them,... dispensing with fine tuning to each thing its allotted portion' (*Opif.* 23), a proportional measuring out presumably effected through the Logos.

Only now does Philo turn to the full phrase of Gen. 1:1: 'In the beginning God made heaven and earth.' Regarding the term 'beginning', Philo is emphatic that this should not be taken in a temporal sense: 'for there was no time before the cosmos, but rather it either came into existence together with the cosmos or after it', and thus time is 'the extension [διάστημα] of the movement of the cosmos' (*Opif.* 26). While all things were made 'simultaneously' (ἅμα), what comes into 'beautiful existence', however, possesses 'order' (τάξιν), 'for there is no beauty in disorder' (*Opif.* 28). At this stage of the Genesis account and Philo's exposition, we are still in the realm of the intelligible cosmos, for the earth is 'invisible and unformed' (Gen. 1:2: ἀόρατος καὶ ἀκατασκεύαστος), and the heaven is likewise, according to Philo, 'bodiless' (*Opif.* 29). In this 'one day', God also made 'a form [ἰδέαν] of air and of void', which is the 'darkness' and the 'abyss', respectively, and also 'the incorporeal being of water and of spirit, and as seventh and last of all light', the latter being the 'intelligible model' of the sun and the stars which would be placed in the heavens (*Opif.* 29). The 'invisible and intelligible light', moreover,

[46] Cf. Runia, *Creation*, 154.

'has come into being as an image of the divine Logos which communicated its genesis' (*Opif.* 31), so that when the light appeared, 'its rival darkness proceeded to withdraw', and God built a wall between them to keep them separate, thus establishing morning and evening, which are thus also intelligible realities (*Opif.* 33–4). All this is contained in 'day one', which 'was named in this way because of the aloneness of the intelligible cosmos which has the nature of the unit' (*Opif.* 35).

With the intelligible cosmos thus 'completed and established in the divine Logos', 'the sense-perceptible cosmos was ripe for birth, with respect to the model of the incorporeal'.[47] That what follows is 'sense-perceptible' is implied by the first thing made after 'day one', that is, the 'firmament', called 'heaven' by the Creator (*Opif.* 36; Gen. 1:6–8): the word *στερέωμα* is related to *στερέος*, meaning 'firm', 'solid', with three dimensions. With the earth created on the third day (*Opif.* 38–44), Philo then catches himself, in a similar manner to the way in which Timaeus does when noting that he has spoken about the body before the soul, to affirm that their priority is in fact the other way round. Philo argues that although it is only once the earth is finished that God sets about adorning the heavens, this is 'not because he placed it after the earth in rank... but rather in order to give a very clear demonstration of the might of his sovereignty' (*Opif.* 45). However, Philo's explanation of this demonstration involves him anticipating further the course of his exposition. The creator, he continues, 'understood in advance what the humans who had not yet come into existence would be like in their thinking', that is, that 'they would focus their aim on what is likely and convincing and contains much that is reasonable, but not on the unadulterated truth, and they would put their trust in appearances rather than on God, thereby showing admiration for sophistry rather than wisdom' (*Opif.* 45). Anticipating that by looking at the revolutions of the sun and the moon, and deducing that they cause the seasons, humans would conclude that they were also the 'first causes' for created beings, God said (to whom is not specified): 'Let them turn back in their minds to the first genesis of the universe', for such reflection, he continues, should lead them to God and his providence (*Opif.* 46–7). In other words, the rationality, as it were, of the cosmos and the order of its production is already that of providing a suitable pedagogy and correction to human beings.

Philo blurs somewhat the distinction between the fifth and the sixth day, so as to set apart the creation of the human being.[48] After describing the creation of the animals that inhabit the waters, the air, and the land, God, then, 'to crown all proceeded to "make the human being"' (*Opif.* 65). However, before turning directly to this, Philo makes an observation about Moses' account of these days that would be picked up by Gregory: Moses 'employed a truly excellent sequence

[47] *Opif.* 36: *Ὁ μὲν οὖν ἀσώματος κόσμος ἤδη πέρας εἶχεν ἱδρυθεὶς ἐν τῷ θείῳ λόγῳ, ὁ δ' αἰσθητὸς πρὸς παράδιεγμα τούτου ἐτελειογονεῖτο.*

[48] Cf. Runia, *Creation*, 211, 222.

of succession in describing the birth of the animal realm', beginning with 'the most sluggish and least delineated type of soul', that which is found in fishes, and ending with 'the most developed and in every respect best type [which] has been assigned to the kind of the human beings' (*Opif.* 65). For all living beings, he points out, 'seed is the starting-point of genesis', but it is only when deposited in the womb that it obtains movement and natural growth, the latter being superior to seed 'since movement is superior to quiescence in created things [ἐν γενητοῖς]' (*Opif.* 67). Philo compares 'nature' to a craftsman, or, better, 'an irreproachable art' (ἀνεπίληπτος τέχνη) which 'moulds living beings' (ζῳοπλαστεῖ), distributing the moist substance to the limbs and organs of the body and 'the life-giving substance' or 'air' to the faculties of the soul (τὴν δὲ πνευματικὴν εἰς τὰς τῆς ψυχῆς δυνάμεις), that is, 'nourishment and sense-perception' (*Opif.* 67): beginning with seed, nature thus 'ended with what is most precious, the structure of an animal and a human being' (*Opif.* 68: τὴν ζῴου καὶ ἀνθρώπου κατασκευήν). This ordering is also exemplified in the coming into existence of the universe: when the creator decided to form living beings, he did so in an ordered sequence, beginning with 'insignificant' animals and ending with 'the best, human beings' (*Opif.* 68).

Returning to the question of how God made the human being, Philo focuses on three aspects of the description given in Gen. 1:26–7: the dimension of image and likeness; the plurality of the verb; and the specification that the result of this work, the human being, is also male and female. Regarding the first point, Philo comments:

> After all these other creatures, as has been stated, he says that the 'human being' has come into existence 'in accordance with God's image and in accordance with his likeness'. This is most excellently said, for nothing earthborn bears a closer resemblance to God than the human being [ἐμφερέστερον γὰρ οὐδὲν γηγενὲς ἀνθρώπου θεῷ]. But no one should infer this likeness from the characteristics of the body, for God does not have a human shape and the human body is not God-like. The term 'image' has been used here with regard to the director of the soul, the intellect. (*Opif.* 69)

It is noteworthy that although Philo has not yet turned to Genesis 2 and the moulding of the human being from the earth described there, and although his point here is that it is possession of intellect that marks the human being as 'in accordance with the image and likeness', the human being that he speaks about is 'earthborn'—that is, embodied in a material body. This is particularly striking given that later on (*Opif.* 134), as we will see, Philo distinguishes Gen. 1:26–7 and 2:7 in terms of the 'vast difference' between the human being made 'after the image' and the human being 'moulded from the earth'.

What exactly this 'intellect' is, by virtue of which the human being is said to be 'after the image and likeness', is described by Philo in the paragraphs that follow:

'On that single intellect of the universe, as on an archetype, the intellect in each individual human being was modelled. In a sense it is a god of the person who carries it and bears it around as a divine image.' As such, the human intellect has the same position in the human being that God has in the cosmos: it is invisible, yet it sees all; its own nature is unclear, yet it comprehends the nature of other things (*Opif.* 69). In line with the ordering of creation in terms of human pedagogy, seen above, Philo continues here by setting before the intellect the path of growing in knowledge: by the arts and sciences, the intellect comes to know all aspects of the earthly creation, and then it is led to the revolutions of the heavens and their 'perfect music', and then, attaining to the intelligible realm, where it becomes 'possessed by sober drunkenness', and stimulated by 'a higher form of desire,... it thinks it is heading to the Great King himself', yet finds itself overwhelmed by brightness and suffering from vertigo (*Opif.* 70–1).

Regarding the question why the human was not created by God alone, Philo offers an answer 'through a likely conjecture' (δ' εἰκότι στοχασμῷ, *Opif.* 72). Noting that plants and animals without reason do not share in goodness or evil, he concludes that 'intellect and reason [νοῦς καὶ λόγος] may be regarded as the home where goodness and evil naturally reside' (*Opif.* 73). As such, he surmises, creatures with a 'mixed nature', capable of both these opposite characteristics, must have been created with the assistance 'of other collaborators' in order that their good decisions can be attributed to God, while the opposite cases can be attributed to 'the others who are subordinate to him' (*Opif.* 75). Although Philo introduced the Logos when he touched upon Gen. 1:26–7 in *Opif.* 25 (discussed above), it is striking that Philo does not do the same, as one might have expected to him to do, when discussing here the plurality of Gen. 1:26.

Finally, regarding the creation of the human being as male and female, Philo simply observes that 'even though individual members had not yet taken shape' (μήπω τῶν ἐν μέρει μορφὴν λαβόντων), 'after he had called the genus "human being", he separated its species and stated that it was created "male and female"' (*Opif.* 76). This is, he says, 'because the most proximate of the species are present in the genus and become apparent as if in a mirror to observers with sharp vision'. As with the first point regarding this scriptural verse, where the term 'image' refers to the intellect, distinguishing human beings from other 'earthborn' creatures as the one most resembling God (even though Gen. 2:7 has not yet been discussed), so here, in reverse, while the focus is on the genus 'human being' prior to particular individuals, nevertheless the species, male and female, found in the particular individuals, are already accounted for in the intelligible realm. Given the scriptural verse before him, he could not reasonably have concluded, as Timaeus did, that women are reincarnated males with moral failings; nor could he, as we will see Gregory do, take the analysis a step further, on the ground that in Christ, the archetype, there is 'neither male and female' (Gal. 3:28).

Following his analysis of Gen. 1:26–7, Philo gives four reasons why the human being was created last, several of which are picked up by Gregory. The first of these is that 'the Director of the universe, like an organizer of games and a holder of a banquet, when he was about to invite the human being to a lavish feast and a spectacle', made all the necessary preparations first, 'so that, when the human being entered the cosmos, he would immediately encounter both a festive meal and a most sacred theatre' (*Opif.* 77–8). The second is that the human being would find all the means needed for living, without toil or trouble, as shown in 'the example of the original ancestor of their race', but which will become a present reality 'when unreasoning pleasures fail to gain the upper hand by constructing gluttony and lust as battle stations in the soul'. The 'present time', however, is one in which 'all these vices flourish and human beings have unconditionally surrendered themselves to the passions', the punishment for which is that 'the necessities of life are difficult to obtain'; what lies before us is thus the acquisition of self-control, in the hope that God 'will cause the good things of life to be supplied to the race spontaneously and ready for consumption' (*Opif.* 79–81).

The third reason given by Philo is that 'God, having reasoned that the beginning and end of creation should be harmonized together in a necessary and loving relationship, proceeded to make heaven as its beginning [ἀρχὴν] and the human being as its end [τέλος], the former as the most perfect of immortal beings in the sense-perceptible realm, the latter as the best of earthborn and mortal creatures' (*Opif.* 82); it is again already the earthborn mortal being that he has in mind as the end of creation. In this way, the human being is 'a miniature heaven who carries around in himself numerous star-like beings as divine images'. The fourth and final reason, the only one said to be 'necessary', is that the human being had to appear last so as to instil astonishment in all other creatures, rendering them tame and demonstrating his kingly rule, despite his lack of armour or weapons (*Opif.* 83–8).

Following the text of the LXX, which has God completing his works on the sixth day, rather than the seventh (Gen. 2:2), Philo concludes his exposition of the first creation account by describing the seventh day, which alone is called 'holy' (Gen. 2:3), as a universal festival, 'the birthday of the cosmos' (*Opif.* 89). Although Philo concedes that 'I do not know whether anyone can give sufficient praise to the nature of the seven; it is superior to every form of speech' (*Opif.* 90), he continues to sing the praises of the hebdomad for many pages, drawing in all sorts of numerological reflections.

Reaching Gen. 2:4–5 (LXX), Philo notes a particularity in the text: 'this is the book of the genesis of heaven and earth when it came to be on the day that God made heaven and earth and all the green of the field before it came to be upon the earth and all the grass of the field before it sprang up'. As this verse speaks of God having 'made heaven and earth' as an action already accomplished, Philo takes it as a 'summarizing statement' uttered by Moses reflecting upon his account of the creation of the cosmos.[49] The 'book of the genesis of heaven and earth' mentioned in Gen. 2:4 thus refers to the preceding verses.[50] But, although Philo had previously described the creation that begins on the second day as 'sense-perceptible' (*Opif.* 36), if Scripture at this point says that God has 'made' (past tense) all the 'green' and 'grass' of field '*before* it came to be upon the earth', the vegetation mentioned earlier (Gen. 1:11–12) must, Philo now concludes, refer to 'the incorporeal and intelligible ideas, which are in fact the seals of the completed products perceived by the senses'. Moreover, although Moses in his brevity did not say more, this is a principle which holds for all things: 'It should be understood that for each of the other things which the senses judge, anterior forms and measures also pre-existed [*τὰ πρεσβύτερα εἴδη καὶ μέτρα . . . προϋπῆρχε*], by means of which the things that come into being are given form and measured', so that 'the nature of the whole of reality' is such that nothing among sense-perceptible things is brought to completion without an incorporeal paradigm (*Opif.* 130).

This observation enables Philo, as he continues his exposition, to contrast the creation account thus far, as intelligible and incorporeal, with what follows. The account in Genesis 2 clearly centres upon the creation of human beings from the earth. The only item to be mentioned before the human being is the spring of water rising up to water the earth (Gen. 2:6), which Philo explains, using the procreative imagery we have already seen him use, by the idea that 'moist substance has to be part of the earth which gives birth to all things', so that 'the earth too is a mother' (*Opif.* 132–3). Only now do we get to the formation of actual, material human beings:

> After this, he says that God 'moulded the human being taking clay from the earth and he inbreathed onto his face the breath of life.' By means of this text too he shows in the clearest fashion that there is a vast difference between the human being 'who has been moulded' and the one who previously came into being 'in accordance with the image of God'. For the one 'moulded' is sense-perceptible, already participating in quality, consisting of body and soul, either man or woman, by nature mortal; the one 'in accordance with the image' is a kind of idea or genus or seal, intelligible, incorporeal, neither male nor female, by nature immortal.[51]

[49] *Opif.* 129: *Ἐπιλογιζόμενος δὲ τὴν κοσμοποιίαν κεφαλαιώδει τύπῳ φησιν . . .*

[50] *Opif.* 129. On the difference between the LXX and the Hebrew text, and the way in which Philo treats this verse in comparison to modern scholarship, see Runia, *Creation*, 309.

[51] *Opif.* 134: *Μετὰ δὲ ταῦτα φυσιν ὅτι "ἔπλασεν ὁ θεός τὸν ἄνθρωπον χοῦν λαβὼν ἀπὸ τῆς γῆς, καὶ ἐνεφύσησεν εἰς τὸ πρόσωπον αὐτοῦ πνοὴν ζωῆς". ἐναργέστατα καὶ διὰ τούτου παρίστησιν ὅτι διαφορὰ παμμεγέθης ἐστὶ τοῦ τε νῦν πλασθέντος ἀνθρώπου καὶ τοῦ κατὰ τὴν εἰκόνα θεοῦ γεγονότος πρότερον· ὁ μὲν γὰρ διαπλασθεὶς αἰσθητὸς ἤδη μετέχων ποιότηος, ἐκ σώματος καὶ ψυχῆς συνεστώς, ἀνὴρ ἢ γυνή, φύσει θνητός· ὁ δὲ κατὰ τὴν εἰκόνα ἰδέα τις ἢ γένος ἢ σφαγίς, νοητός, ἀσώματος, οὔτ' ἄρρεν οὔτε θῆλυ, ἄφθαρτος φύσει.*

The contrast between the human being of Gen. 1:26–7 and 2:7 is clear, but what is the meaning of the designation of the difference between them as 'previously'? As we have already noted, when describing the human being who has come into being 'after the image', Philo was already speaking about the 'earthborn': it was the possession of intellect that distinguished the human being from all other earth-born creatures, giving the human a 'closer resemblance to God' than any other (*Opif.* 69), making them 'the best of earthborn and mortal creatures' (*Opif.* 82). The 'species' male and female are also present in the intellectual realm, although at that point there were no concrete individual humans. The two accounts, though distinct, are thus also interwoven with each other.[52] That they cannot be separated too sharply is further underscored by Philo's emphasis that God does everything 'simultaneously' (ἅμα), even though things come to be in sequence and order, and that God's primary intention is in fact to make the visible, bodily cosmos, with the intelligible cosmos being the 'prior' design for this, or, better, the intelligible cosmos 'is nothing other than the Logos of God actually making the cosmos' (*Opif.* 24). The 'previously' is thus not temporal: time measures the sequence of days measuring the emergence of things within creation, not the relationship between the intellectual world (in itself in day one) and the material world. It also takes time to narrate the unfolding of God's simultaneous action; that Genesis 1 necessarily comes before Genesis 2 does not mitigate the fact that, as Runia puts it, Philo takes 'the creation account as a unified whole'.[53] There nevertheless does remain a fundamental priority of elements within this unified account, in that it is the possession of intellect—incorporeal, neither male nor female, immortal—that renders the earthborn, moulded human 'in accordance with the image and likeness' of God. Finally, it must also be recalled that Philo reads Moses' account as a pedagogy, 'preparing minds' so that human beings can be 'citizens of the cosmos'.[54]

Rather than a 'double creation' as such, Philo's interest is thus, as becomes clear in what immediately follows, on 'the composite structure [τὴν κατασκευὴν σύνθετον] of the sense-perceptible and individual human being, composed of earthly substance and divine spirit' (*Opif.* 135). In this composite, the body came to be 'when the Craftsman took clay and moulded a human shape out of

[52] For full discussion of the scholarly positions regarding the relation between 'the one in accordance with the image' in Gen. 1 and 'the one moulded from the earth' in Gen. 2, see Runia, *Creation*, 321–3. I would concur with Runia that 'the human being after the image' of Gen. 1:27 should not be taken as the 'idea of the human being', in a technical sense, and that the intellect spoken of in *Opif.* 69–71 should not be too readily equated with the divine part inbreathed into the composite human being of Gen. 2:7, but rather, in Runia's words (*Creation*, 323), that 'the former is an idealization, i.e. the "true human being" such as he should and can be when the cares of the body and earthly life have entirely fallen away ... an idealization of human nature in terms of the intellect'.

[53] Runia, *Creation*, 309.

[54] Runia, *Creation*, 224: 'Philo is answering a specific question raised by the biblical text. For this reason, perhaps, he is not concerned to give a full anthropology. His doctrine is that humankind is above all characterized by its intellectual powers is significant enough.'

it', while, on the other hand, 'the soul obtained its origin from nothing which has come into existence at all', but comes from the Father and Director of all things, when he breathed into its face the divine spirit, 'which has emigrated here from that blessed and flourishing nature for the assistance of our kind'. As such, while the composite human being is mortal in its visible part, 'it would be immortalized [ἀθανατίζεται] with regard to its invisible part' (*Opif.* 135). The human being thus 'is the borderline [εἶναι μεθόριον] between mortal and immortal nature, sharing in both to the extent necessary, he has come into existence as a creature which is mortal and at the same time immortal, mortal in respect of the body, immortal in respect of the mind' (*Opif.* 135).

The first human born of earth, Philo further asserts, excelled those who followed in both body and soul. Philo gives three reasons why this was the case for the body: first, that the earth was new and so 'unmixed and undefiled and pure as well as receptive and easy to work with' (*Opif.* 136); second, because God took 'from pure matter the purest and utmost refined part' (*Opif.* 137); and third, as the creator excelled in knowledge, the proportions were carefully fashioned to be harmonious (*Opif.* 137). Regarding the excellence of the soul, Philo introduces again the Logos of God:

> For it is fitting that for his construction God used no other model belonging to the realm of becoming, but only, as I said, his own Logos. For this reason, he says that the human being has come into existence as its likeness and representation [ἀπεικόνισμα καὶ μίμημα] by being inbreathed into the face, which is the location of the senses.... The representation of a splendid model must be splendid itself. The Logos of God is even superior to the beauty which is beauty as it occurs in nature. It is not adorned with beauty, but, if the truth be told, it is itself beauty's preeminent adornment. (*Opif.* 139)

It is again striking that Philo did not introduce the Logos in his examination of Gen. 1:26–7 in *Opif.* 69, when his claim that the image relates to the human possession of intellect and the plurality of the verb might have invited him to do so, but does so here, in consideration of how the moulded human of Gen. 2:7, by being 'inbreathed', is the likeness and imitation of the Logos. Concluding his discussion of Gen. 2:7, Philo puts the matter thus: 'every human being, as far as his mind is concerned, is akin to the divine Logos and has come into being as a casting or fragment or effulgence of the blessed nature, but in the structure of his body he is related to the entire cosmos' (*Opif.* 146).

Regarding the formation of the woman, this turns out to be, for Philo, a mixed blessing. Although, as we have seen, the 'species' male and female are present in the intelligible realm, Philo begins his treatment of the appearance of the woman in Genesis 2 with the statement: 'But, since nothing is stable in the world of genesis and mortal beings necessarily [ἀναγκαίως] undergo reversals and changes, the first human being had to enjoy some ill fortune [ἐχρῆν... ἀπολαῦσαί τινος κακοπραγίας]', and this is woman, who is 'for him the starting-point of a blameworthy life' (*Opif.* 151). He continues: 'As long as he was single, he resembled God and the cosmos in his solitariness, receiving the delineations of both natures in his soul, not all of them, but as many as a mortal constitution could contain.' When the woman was moulded, seeing in her 'a sisterly form and a kindred figure', he rejoiced at the sight and greeted her; she, in turn, seeing that he resembled herself more than any other living creature, was also glad and responded modestly (*Opif.* 151–2). Echoing Aristophanes' speech in Plato's *Symposium*, Philo continues: 'Love [ἔρως] ensues bringing together the two separate halves of a single living being as it were, and joins them together into unity, thereby establishing in both a desire [πόθον] for union with the other in order to produce a being similar to themselves.' But as this is also the desire which begets bodily pleasure, which is the starting point of wickedness, they thereby 'exchange the life of immortality and well-being for the life of mortality and misfortune' (*Opif.* 152).

Finally, Philo notes that as 'the garden of delights' was planted by God while the man was still solitary, these delights bear no resemblance to pleasures we experience; the garden instead 'hints at the ruling part of the soul', while the tree of life hints at the most important of virtues, reverence for God (*Opif.* 153–4). But when the first couple had their attention caught by that which was 'highly attractive to behold', offered by the serpent, they passed by the tree of immortal life, 'through which they could have enjoyed the fruits of an age-long life of well-being', and chose instead 'that ephemeral and mortal existence, not a life but a time span full of misfortune', suffering the punishments that the outraged Father determined fit (*Opif.* 156).

Philo has, thus, given us a multi-layered account of creation and the human being, which also seems to shift as he works his way through the scriptural text: 'day one' is distinct from the sequence of days that follow, for it contains 'the intelligible cosmos', while the others describe the successive appearances of sense-perceptible creation; but then, from Gen. 2:4–5 onwards, the first account becomes the creation of the intelligible paradigm, while the second account is of that which is moulded from the earth. In both cases, however, the accounts are thoroughly interwoven: it is as the best of earthborn creatures that the human being mentioned in Gen. 1:26–7 is, by virtue of the intellect, 'in accordance with the image', and the species of that human being, male and female, is already accounted for in the intelligible realm, even though, when particular earthborn individuals, men and women, are created (or, at least, when their creation is narrated), it is made clear that being male and female is on a different level than their common possession of intellect, and the appearance of the woman, for Philo, disrupts the solitary (godlike) existence of the man. Holding these interweavings together is the fact that, for Philo, God's act is 'simultaneous', encompassing his thinking and doing, while those things which come into being have their own proper sequence and order, just as they must also be narrated sequentially. That all things are held together in God's 'simultaneous' act, yet unfold in time, is perhaps best captured in the statement which Philo himself designates as stating his position in the simplest, 'most naked', words: 'the intelligible cosmos is nothing other than the Logos of God as he is actually making the cosmos' (*Opif.* 24).

There are numerous particular themes in this work which are picked up by Gregory (and noted in the footnotes to the translation): the sequential appearance of increasing levels of life narrated by Moses, with 'nature' being 'an irreproachable art moulding living beings' (*Opif.* 65–8); that though our intellect sees all and comprehends the nature of other things, it remains unseen and not understood by itself (*Opif.* 69); that the intellect and reason are the seat of goodness and evil (*Opif.* 73); that although the human being is created in Gen. 1:27, the individual does not come into existence until Gen. 2:7 (*Opif.* 176); and that the cosmos has been prepared as a feast for the human being, and that the human being is to be an unarmed king before whom animals become tame (*Opif.* 77–83). More generally, the importance of this text of Philo for understanding Gregory's treatise lies in the way in which we see, for the first time, an attempt to combine the two creation accounts in Genesis into a unified account, but one that accounts for 'the composite structure' (*τὴν κατασκευὴν σύνθετον*) of the human being, the 'borderline' between the mortal and the immortal (*Opif.* 135), and, of course, how they respectively deal with the question of male and female. Finally, if Moses' own account, in and as Philo's telling of this, is meant to aid in the forming of the human being, by observing the law, to be a citizen of the cosmos, Gregory's account pushes further towards something more, an economy that provides a pedagogy leading from Adam to Christ.

4. Origen

While Origen's influence on Gregory is indisputable, Origen's understanding of creation is anything but, being instead a subject of controversy almost from the time he first put pen to paper. Following his detractors, Origen has been presented as teaching that there was an eternal realm of intellects existing alongside God, which then fell away from God and into bodies, from which they will eventually be liberated to return to their original state of unity together and with God. This depiction, which dominated twentieth-century scholarship, has more recently been challenged and a new picture is gradually gaining acceptance.[55] We cannot

[55] Cf. Ronald E. Heine, *Origen: An Introduction to His Life and Thought* (Eugene, OR: Wipf and Stock, 2019), 106–7: 'Most later scholars, including myself, have presented this as Origen's view. I now believe we were mistaken and that a continued careful reading of Origen's texts will provide further confirmation of this.' He refers to Marguerite Harl, 'La préexistence des âmes dans l'oeuvre d'Origène',

here enter into a detailed engagement with the scholarly debate, but will rather try to present as clear and coherent a picture as possible, with an eye both backwards to what we have seen so far and forward to Gregory's *On the Human Image*. Origen was not the first Christian writer to focus attention on the opening verses or chapters of Genesis: according to Eusebius, Rhodo wrote a 'treatise on the hexaemeron'—that is, on the six days of creation—as also did Apion and Candidus, and, according to Anastasius of Sinai, Papias, Clement, Pantaenus, and Ammonius 'thought that the entire hexaemeron referred to Christ and the Church'.[56] Although there is no record of Origen having written a 'hexaemeron', his seminal and controversial work on this topic, the *Commentary on Genesis*, seems to have focused on the first four chapters of Genesis. It is now lost, however, with only a few fragments surviving in the Catenae and elsewhere.[57] It seems to have consisted of thirteen books, the first eight of which had been composed in Alexandria, in the same period as his *On First Principles* and the first five books of his *Commentary on John*, and the final five books in Caesarea between 232 and 235 CE.

In his *Contra Celsum*, begun some time after 246 CE, Origen refers back to his earlier work, saying that 'if anyone wants to see the arguments, with clear demonstration, that persuade us regarding the creation of the cosmos according to Moses [περὶ κατὰ Μωϋσέα κοσμοποιΐας], let him take our studies on Genesis from the beginning of the book down to the words "This is the book of genesis of humans" [Gen. 5:1]', further specifying that he had there identified what was 'the heaven and earth' made 'in the beginning', 'the invisible and unformed of the

in Lothar Lies, ed., *Origeniana Quarta* (Innsbruck-Vienna: Tyrolia, 1987), 238–58, at 238–48; Mark Edwards, *Origen against Plato* (Aldershot: Ashgate, 2002), 82–92; Ilaria L. E. Ramelli, '"Preexistence of Souls"?: The ἀρχή and τέλος of Rational Creatures in Origen and Some Origenians', *Studia Patristica*, 56.4, *Rediscovering Origen*, ed. Markus Vinzent (Leuven: Peeters, 2013), 167–226, at 167–81; Panayiotis Tzamalikos, *Origen: Cosmology and Ontology of Time*, Suppl. *VC* 77 (Leiden: Brill, 2005), 92–4, and my edition of Origen's *On First Principles*, OECT (Oxford: Oxford University Press, 2017), vol. 1, lvi–lxii. See also the other works of Panayiotis Tzamalikos: *The Concept of Time in Origen* (Bern: Peter Lang, 1991); *Origen: Philosophy of History and Eschatology*, Suppl. *VC* 85 (Leiden: Brill, 2007); and *Anaxagoras*.

[56] Eusebius, *Hist. eccl.* 5.13.8; 5.27; Anastasius of Sinai, *Hexaemeron*, 6.1, ed. and ET Clement A. Kuehn and John D. Baggarly, OCA 278 (Rome: Pontificio Istituto Orientale, 2007), 18, 322–5. It should also be noted that Theophilus of Antioch has a lengthy section dealing with creation and the hexaemeron (*Ad. Auto.* 2.10–30), and that Gen. 1–3 provides the scriptural matrix for much of Irenaeus' work explicating Christ and the economy, for which see Thomas Holsinger-Friesen, *Irenaeus and Genesis: A Study of Competition in Early Christian Hermeneutics*, *JTI* Supp. 1 (Winona Lake, IN: Eisenbrauns, 2009).

[57] For a complete collection of fragments and testimonia, see Karin Metzler ed. and German trans., *Origenes: Die Kommentiering des Buches Genesis*, Origenes Werke Mit Deutscher Übersetzung 1/1 (Berlin: De Gruyter, 2010). See also the survey given by Ronald E. Heine, 'The Testimonia and Fragments Related to Origen's Commentary on Genesis', *ZAC* 9 (2005), 122–42. For the contextual setting of the *Commentary on Genesis*, see Ronald E. Heine, *Origen: Scholarship in Service of the Church*, CTC (Oxford: Oxford University Press, 2010), 104–15.

earth', 'the abyss', 'the darkness upon it', and so on.[58] A few paragraphs later, Origen takes up Gen. 5:1 again, combining it now with 2:4—'this is the book of the genesis of humans, in the day in which God made the heaven and the earth'—pointing out that 'the day' mentioned here cannot refer back to Gen. 1:1, for that verse occurs before the appearance of light and God calling the light 'day' (Gen. 1:3–5)—and then continues: 'it is not our present task to explain the doctrine about intelligible and sense-perceptible things [νοητῶν καὶ αἰσθητῶν], and the way in which the natures of the days have been divided between both forms, or to study the text of the passage. We would need whole treatises to explain Moses' account of creation of the cosmos; we did this as well as we could a long time before writing the present treatise against Celsus' (*Cels.* 6.50–1). A little earlier in the same book, Origen had equated the distinction between 'intelligible' and 'sense-perceptible' with Paul's distinction between those 'things which are seen' and those 'which are not seen', the former being 'temporal' and the latter 'eternal' (2 Cor. 4:18), further specifying that the latter are 'intelligible, comprehensible by the intellect alone'.[59] Origen thus, as with those we have examined so far, distinguishes two realms, the intelligible and the sense-perceptible; however, like Philo, he did not align these realms straightforwardly with the two creation accounts, for he took the 'firmament' and the 'dry land', made on the second and third day, respectively, to be the sense-perceptible 'heaven' and 'earth' distinct from, but named after, the 'heaven and earth' made on 'day one'.[60] The distinction between the 'intelligible' and 'sense-perceptible' realms falls rather between 'day one', outside of time, and that which follows, marked as it is by the succession of time.[61] This, moreover, enables Origen, as it did Philo, to read the two creation accounts together, especially as it pertains to the human being, differentiating between the accounts to distinguish different aspects of the human being.

One further preliminary point needs to be made regarding Origen's awareness of the limitations of our knowledge in speaking about creation. Ronald Heine points to a passage from Origen's *Homilies on Isaiah*, where Origen specifies what

[58] Origen, *Contra Celsum* (*Cels.*), 6.49; ed. Paul Koetschau, GCS 2 and 3, Origenes Werke 1 and 2 (Leipzig: Hinrichs, 1899); ET H. Chadwick (Cambridge: Cambridge University Press, 1953), modified. Heine, *Origen: Scholarship*, 107–8, points to *The Testimony of Truth* (*NH* IX.3, 41.28–42.3; *The Nag Hammadi Library in English*, ed. James M. Robinson [Leiden: Brill, 1988], 453), the *Apocryphon of John* (*NH* II.1, 13.14–14.34; Robinson, 112), and Irenaeus' account of Ptolemy (*Haer.* 1.4.1–5, and 1.8.2) for a similar concern to identify what each word refers to.

[59] *Cels.* 6.20. Cf. *Commentary on John* (*Com. John*) Frag. 13; ed. E. Preuschen, GCS 10, Origenes Werke 4 (Leipzig: Hinrichs, 1903), 494: our perception is, correspondingly, 'twofold, sense-perceptible and intelligible' (διττοῦ τοῦ θεωρεῖν ὄντος αἰσθητικοῦ τε καὶ νοητικοῦ); by the former we apprehend bodily objects, with the second incorporeal realities, which are not simply 'not seen', but rather those that 'by nature are not to be seen'.

[60] Gen. 1:1, 8–10. Cf. *On First Principles* (*Princ.*) 2.9.1. Ed. and trans. J. Behr, OECT (Oxford: Oxford University Press, 2017), translation occasionally modified.

[61] Cf. *Homilies on Genesis* (*Hom. Gen.*), 1.2; ed. W. A. Baehrens, GCS 29, Origenes Werke 6 (Leipzig: Hinrichs, 1920), 2.17–19; ET Ronald E. Heine, FC 71 (Washington, DC: Catholic University of America, 1981).

can be known.[62] There, Origen identifies the two seraphim veiling God with their wings (Isa. 6:2) as 'my Lord Jesus and the Holy Spirit', covering both the face of God, 'for God's beginning is unknown', and also his feet, 'for what could be understood as the end in our God?', and concludes:

> Only the middle is visible. What was before this, I do not know. I understand God from those things that are. What will come about after this, in accordance with what is coming, I know not. 'Who has declared to him?' said Ecclesiastes [6:12]. 'Declare to me the former things and the last things that shall be, and I will say that you are gods' [Isa. 41:22–3]. Therefore if someone shall tell past things and shall be able to speak of the last things, he is a 'god'. Who then besides the seraphim can say this? Who can say 'Holy, Holy, Holy!' besides the seraphim? But what part of God have they left exposed, so to speak? His middle.[63]

The beginning and end are veiled; only the middle, the present state of things, is directly available to us. The end, however, has been revealed, even if it is yet to be realized. So Origen continues: 'The coming of my Lord Jesus Christ is being announced; and so, now "all the earth is full of his glory".' Or rather, he adds, 'it is not yet full, but will be so', for 'in those who sin he does not yet reign, but when authority even over these has been given to him, when all things have been subjected to him [cf. Phil. 3:21; 1 Cor. 15:28], then the authority will be fulfilled when he goes about subjecting all things to himself'. It is in the light of the end that has already been announced, that is, the subjection of all to Christ, and then to God, so that he will be 'all in all' (1 Cor. 15:28), that we can make sense of what we know of 'the middle', that which is presently visible, and contemplate the beginning. As Origen puts it succinctly elsewhere: 'the phenomenal world is an image of the intellectual and invisible: the truth is in the future'.[64]

This orientation is repeatedly underscored by Origen, most forcefully in *On First Principles* 1.6.2:

> Seeing, then, that such is the end, when all enemies will be subjected to Christ, and when the last enemy, death, will be destroyed and when the kingdom shall be delivered to the God and Father by Christ, to whom all things have been subjected [cf. 1 Cor. 15:24–7], let us, I say, from such an end as this contemplate the beginning of things. For the end is always like the beginning, and, therefore,

[62] Heine, *Origen: An Introduction*, 96–7.

[63] Origen, *Homilies on Isaiah*, 1.2; ed. W. A. Baehrens, GCS 33, Origenes Werke 8 (Leipzig: Hinrichs, 1925); ET Thomas P. Scheck, ACW 69 (New York/Mahwah, NJ: Newman Press, 2015).

[64] *καὶ φαινόμενος κόσμος εἰκῶν ἐστι τοῦ νοητοῦ καὶ ἀορατοῦ· ἐν τῷ μέλλοντι γὰρ ἡ ἀλήθεια.* In J. B. Cardinal Pitra, *Analecta Sacra Spicilegio Solesmensi Parata* tome 3, *Patres Antenicaeni* (Venice: Mechitaristarum Sancti Lazari, 1883), 30, commenting on Ps. 37:3, 'Indeed everyone passes through like an image; surely for nothing they are in turmoil...'

> as there is one end of all things, so ought there to be understood one beginning of all things, and as there is one end of many things, so also from one beginning there are many differences and varieties, which, in turn, through the goodness of God and by subjection to Christ and through the unity of the Holy Spirit, are recalled to one end which is like the beginning: that is, all those who 'bending the knee at the name of Jesus' have displayed by this the proof of their subjection to him, those who are 'of the heavens and of the earth and of the regions under the earth' [Phil. 2:10].

It is important to note that although Origen says that 'the end is always like the beginning', he does not start from the beginning to envision an end that is straightforwardly a return to the same beginning; it is, rather, 'from such an end' that he proposes to 'contemplate the beginning of things'. This eschatological starting point for theological reflection is one he says he has 'frequently' affirmed (*Princ.* 3.5.4, cited below).[65] It must also be recognized that the end is said to be 'like', not identical to, the beginning, for there has been a path traversed from one to the other, which in turn implies time and growth. Finally, the combination of 1 Cor. 15:24–8 and Phil. 2:10 to explain this end, with every knee bowing in subjection to Christ so that God can be 'all in all', is one that, as we will see, is fundamental for Origen's understanding of the end and, on its basis, the beginning.

4.1 Christ, The Archē, and Intelligible World

As similar as Origen is to Philo on many points, the fundamental difference, of course, is that he reads Genesis in the light of the end, that is, Christ. As Christ is 'the wisdom of God' (1 Cor. 1:24), and it is 'in wisdom' that 'God made all things' (Ps. 103:24), 'the beginning' in which God made heaven and earth is, for Origen, none other than Christ himself. It is likely that Origen drew this conclusion already in his *Commentary on Genesis*;[66] it is emphatically stated in his first homily on Genesis.

> 'In the beginning, God made heaven and earth'. What is the beginning of all things, except our Lord and Saviour of all, Jesus Christ the firstborn of every

[65] This point is forcefully argued by Alexander H. Pierce, 'Apokatastasis, Genesis 1.26–27, and the Theology of History in Origen's *De Principiis*', *JECS* 29 (2021), 169–91.

[66] Heine ('The Testimonia', 124) draws attention to a passage from John Philoponus, who likely knew Origen's *Commentary on Genesis*, which reports: 'Some say that "in the beginning" means "in wisdom". For God "made all things in wisdom" [Ps. 103:24], that is, in the Son. "For Christ is the power of God and the wisdom of God" [1 Cor. 1:24]. And "all things came to be through him and without him not one thing came to be" [John 1:3]. And again, "In him all things visible and invisible were created" [Col. 1:16].' John Philoponus, *De Opificio Mundi*, 1.3. Ed. and German translation by C. Scholten, FChr 23, 3 vols (Freiburg i. Br. 1997), 1.90–2. That cf. John knew Origen's work, ibid. 63, 439.

> creature [1 Tim. 4:10; Col. 1:15]? In this beginning, therefore, that is in his Word, God made heaven and earth, as the evangelist John also says at the beginning of his Gospel: In the beginning was the Word and the Word was with God and the Word was God. This same was in the beginning with God. All things were made by him and without him nothing was made [John 1:1–3]. Scripture is not speaking here of any temporal beginning [*Non ergo hic temporale aliquod principium dicit*], but it says that the heaven and the earth and all things which were made were made in the beginning, that is, in the Saviour. (*Hom. Gen.* 1.1)

Origen clearly understands the term 'beginning' (ἀρχή) not as a temporal 'beginning', but rather as 'origin', 'first principle', or 'source' (to make this clear, I will hereafter transliterate the term: *archē*). In his *Homily on the Passover*, Origen points out that there is a difference in the way in which Scripture uses the term '*archē*' and 'first' (πρῶτος). Commenting on Exod. 12:2 ('This month is for you the *archē* of months; it is the first month of the year for you'), Origen argues that 'properly speaking, "first" applies only when nothing comes before, while "*archē*" applies to those which are beginning, even if they come last. What is "first" is always "*archē*", but "*archē*" is not always "first".'[67] He then points out the similar pairing of words in Christ's self-identification, 'I am the Alpha and Omega, the first and the last, the *archē* and the end' (Apoc. 22:13), and concludes that Christ is the 'first' as 'the first-born of all creation' (Col. 1:15), but the '*archē*' as Wisdom, for Wisdom says of herself, 'The Lord created me the *archē* of his ways' (Prov. 8:22).[68] As it is 'in Wisdom' that God creates, it is as Wisdom that Christ is 'the *archē* of the ways of God', 'the *archē* of the creation of God' (Apoc. 3:14), or, more simply and absolutely, 'the *archē*' (Col. 1:18), while he is 'first' as 'the firstborn of all creation' (Col. 1:15) and 'the firstborn of the dead' (Col. 1:18), a title he points out which clearly does not apply to him as *archē*.[69]

Origen gives a further insight into how it is that God made all things 'in Wisdom' when he examines the divine titles or aspects of Christ in *On First Principles* 1.2. Here he again takes 'Wisdom' as being the first of these titles, making clear that he is not speaking of Christ as 'Wisdom' by a participation in wisdom but rather as being 'God's Wisdom subsisting substantially'. He then continues:

[67] Origen, *On Pascha* [*Pasch.*] 8.24–32: *τ[ὸ μὲν] [γ]ὰρ πρῶ[τον μό]νον μη[δένος] προάγο[ντος κυρίω]ς λέγ[εται], ἡ δὲ ἀρχὴ ἐπὶ τ[ῶν ἀρ]χεμέ[νων] κἂν τελευταῖ[α γέ]νηται, συμαίνεται. Κ[αὶ ὅ τι] μὲν πρῶτόν ἐστιν, τοῦ[τ]ο κ[αὶ] ἀρχή ἐστιν, οὐχ ὅ τι δὲ ἀρχή, ἤδη καὶ πρῶτον*. Ed. and French trans. O. Guéraud and P. Nautin, *Origène: Sur la Pâque: Traité inédit publié d'après un papyrus de Toura*, Christianisme Antique 2 (Paris: Beauchesne, 1979); ET Robert J. Daly, ACW 54 (New York: Paulist Press, 1992).

[68] Origen, *Pasch.* 10.4–11.4.

[69] Cf. Origen, *Com. John*, 1.117; ET Ronald E. Heine, 80, 89 (Washington, DC: Catholic University of America Press, 1989, 1993).

> And since within this very subsistence of Wisdom was every capacity and form of the creation that would come to be—both of those things which exist primarily and of those which occur in consequence, having been formed beforehand and arranged by the power of foreknowledge regarding these very created things, which had been as it were outlined and prefigured in Wisdom herself—Wisdom herself says through Solomon that she was 'created the beginning of the ways' [Prov. 8:22] of God, that is, containing within herself the beginning and the reasons and the species of the entire creation. Now, in the same way in which we have understood that Wisdom is 'the beginning of the ways' of God, and is said to be 'created', that is, forming beforehand and containing within herself the species and reasons of the whole creation, in the same manner must she be understood to be the Word of God, as she discloses to all other beings, that is, to the entire creation, the reason of the mysteries and secrets which are contained within the Wisdom of God, and so she is called the Word, because she is, as it were, the interpreter of the secrets of the Intellect. (*Princ.* 1.2.2–3)

As Wisdom, Christ contains all 'the beginnings and the reasons and the species' of the cosmos that was to be, prefigured or outlined in him, and as such has been 'created the beginning of the ways of God'; then, as Word, he discloses these secrets of the Intellect.[70] Christ is the 'location', as it were, of the 'beginnings, reasons, and species' of the things that would come to be, already existing in himself, the *archē*, as the Wisdom of God. Christ is, as we will see, the 'intelligible world'. In his *Commentary on John*, Origen employs similar imagery to Philo to describe this: 'just as a house or ship are built according to the plans of the architect, the house and the ship having as their beginning the plans and thoughts in the craftsman, so all things have come to be according to the principles of what will be, which were prefigured by God in Wisdom' and so, he concludes: 'we must say that after God had created living Wisdom, if I may put it this way, from the models in her he entrusted to her [to present] to the things which exist and to matter [both] their confirmation and forms, but I stop short of saying their essences'[71]—the hesitation presumably being because it is God who is the 'Maker of heaven and earth'.

The analogy with an architect or a ship-builder is limited, however, for as Origen insists, in an extract from the *Commentary on Genesis* regarding the 'invisible and unformed earth' made in the *archē* on day one, God was not in

[70] Cf. *Com. John* 1.118: 'And if we should carefully consider all the concepts applied to him, he is the *archē* only insofar as he is Wisdom. He is not even the *archē* insofar as he is Word, since "the Word" was "in the beginning," so that someone might say boldly that Wisdom is older than all the concepts in the names of "the firstborn of all creation".'

[71] *Com. John* 1.113–15: . . . *οὕτω τὰ σύμπαντα γεγονέναι κατὰ τοὺς ἐν σοφίᾳ προτρανωθέντας ὑπὸ θεοῦ τῶν ἐσομένων λόγους· "Πάντα γὰρ ἐν σοφίᾳ ἐποίησε." καὶ λεκτέον ὅτι κτίσας, ἵν' οὕτως εἴπω, ἔμψυχον σοφίαν ὁ θεὸς, αὐτῇ ἐπέτεψεν ἀπὸ τῶν ἐν αὐτῇ τύπων τοῖς οὖσι καὶ τῇ ὕλῃ <παρασχεῖν καὶ> τὴν πλάσιν καὶ τὰ εἴδη, ἐγὼ δὲ ἐφίστημι εἰ καὶ τὰς οὐσίας.*

need of some pre-existing matter. Inquiring about the power of God, specifically 'whether God, by willing, gives subsistence to that which he wills, his will not lacking or being weak, not able to cause to subsist that which he wills', he asserts, 'on the ground that he, by his inexpressible power and wisdom, establishes the qualities (according to all who, on their own ground, introduce providence), when they did not exist, so as to adorn the universe as he wills, on the same ground also his will to create is sufficient for as much substance to come into existence as he needs'.[72] In the concluding paragraphs of *On First Principles*, Origen explores further what is meant by 'matter' (ὕλη), noting that it is not used in Scripture 'for that substance which is said to underlie bodies' (*Princ.* 4.4.6). An exception is Wisdom of Solomon, where it says, 'For your all-powerful hand that created the world out of formless matter [ἀμόρφου ὕλης]' (Wisd. 11:17), which naturally leads Origen back to the 'invisible and unformed [ἀκατασκεύαστος]' earth of Gen. 1:1. Origen continues by asserting that 'bodily nature is nothing other than qualities', and it is these qualities that are created by God and which are brought together in various ways to form bodies (*Princ.* 4.4.7). Bodies, for Origen, are essentially malleable or transformable, capable of existing in different states—a point of importance, as we will see, for understanding the consummation of all things and, on its basis, the beginning and 'the middle' state. He continues by saying that God has created 'two universal natures, a visible, that is, bodily nature, and an invisible nature, which is bodiless', both of which undergo different changes, the latter changing 'in mind and purpose, as it is endowed with free will', the former undergoing substantial changes, 'so that, in whatever he wishes to undertake or fashion or to rework, the Artificer of all things, God, has the service of matter in every way, so that he can transform and apply it in whatever forms and species he desires, as the merits of things require. The prophet evidently points to this when he says "God who makes and transforms all things"' (*Princ.* 3.6.7; Amos 5:8).

A final point with regard to the term *archē* is that while in the LXX, Wisdom says of herself that 'The Lord created me *archē*' (Prov. 8:22: ἔκτισέν με ἀρχὴν), the Hebrew text has the verb 'acquire' or 'possess', and Origen knew of other Greek translations that rendered the verse as such: 'the Lord acquired me *archē*....'[73] It is, intriguingly, in this form that he cites the verse in his newly rediscovered homilies on the Psalms, when discussing Ps. 73:2a: 'Remember your congregation, which you acquired from the *archē* [ἧς ἐκτήσω ἀπ' ἀρχῆς]'. Referring to Paul's

[72] D3, from Eusebius, *Prep. Evang.* 7.19 (ed. Metzler, 62–4): εἰ θελήσας ὑποστῆσαι ὅ τι βούλεται ὁ θεός, τῆς θελήσεως αὐτοῦ οὐκ ἀπορουμένης οὐδὲ ἀτονούσης, οὐ δύναται ὑποστῆσαι ὃ βούλεται. ᾧ γὰρ λόγῳ τὰς ποιότητας (κατὰ πάντας τούς πρόνοιαν εἰσάγοντας τῷ ἰδίῳ λόγῳ) οὐκ οὔσας ὡς βούλεται εἰς διακόσμησιν τοῦ παντὸς ὑφίστησι τῇ ἀφάτῳ αὐτοῦ δυνάμει καὶ σοφίᾳ, τούτῳ τῷ λόγῳ καὶ τὴν οὐσίαν ὅσης χρῄζει ἱκανή ἐστιν αὐτοῦ ἡ βούλησις ποιῆσαι γενέσθαι.

[73] Cf. Origen, *Hexapla* (ed. Frederick Field, *Origenis Hexaplorum*, 2 vols, Oxford: Clarendon Press, 1875), 2.326: κύριος ἐκτήσατό με (using κτάομαι rather than κτίζω).

words about 'those whom he foreknew', 'called', 'justified', and 'glorified' (Rom. 8:29–30), Origen comments:

> When God foreknew, he foreknew in the *archē* and by his foreknowledge acquired everything that was going to come to be present by him, and this is what is said in 'Remember your congregation, which you acquired from the *archē*'. And I said this, being economical with the word, for I know the *archē* from which God acquired each of us; I know that this *archē* is animate, is alive, and says 'God acquired [*ἐκτήσατο*] me, the *archē* of his ways, for his works'. The *archē* is Christ; [God] acquired from the *archē*, from Christ, the real *archē* and the real end, the real alpha and the real omega [cf. Apoc. 22:13].[74]

God 'acquired' Christ as the *archē* of his works, thereby in his foreknowledge also 'acquiring everything that was going to come to be present with him', that is, everything that, as he had put it in *Princ.* 1.2.2–3 (cited above), was 'outlined and prefigured in Wisdom herself', 'every capacity and form of the creation that would come to be', formed and arranged beforehand by the power of God's foreknowledge.

This eschatological dimension of the work of Wisdom in creation is brought out a little further on in the same chapter on Christ in *On First Principles*, this time with reference to the description of Wisdom as 'a breath of the power of God and the emanation of the purest glory of the Almighty' (Wisd. 7:25, in *Princ.* 1.2.10). Origen brings up again Ps. 103:24 and John 1:3 to conclude that 'the title of "Almighty" cannot be older in God than that of Father, for it is through the Son that the Father is Almighty'—One God, Father, Almighty, as the Creed of Nicaea puts it. He continues by noting that the Son is also called 'Almighty' (Apoc. 1:8), and then reflects on what 'the glory of omnipotence' is:

> The God and Father is 'Almighty' because he has power over all things, that is, over heaven and earth, sun and moon, and all things in them. And he exercises power over them through his Word, for 'at the name of Jesus every knee bows, of things in heaven, and things on earth, and things under the earth' [Phil. 2:10]. And, if 'every knee bows' to Jesus, then, without doubt, it is Jesus to whom 'all things have been subjected', and he it is who exercised power over all things, and through whom 'all things have been subjected' to the Father [1 Cor. 15:27–8.]; for

[74] Origen, *Homilies on the Psalms*, homily 1.4 on Ps. 73; GCS *Origenes* 13, 230 (ET 182–3): *Ὁ θεὸς ὅτε προέγνω, ἐν ἀρχῇ δὲ προέγνω καὶ ἐκτήσατο τῇ προγνώσει αὐτοῦ πάντα τὰ μέλλοντα ἥκειν ὑπ' αὐτὸν, καὶ τοῦτό ἐστιν τὸ λεγόμενον· μνήσθητι τῆς συναγωγῆς σου ἧς ἐκτήσω ἀπ' ἀρχῆς. Καὶ τοῦτο λέγω οἰκονομῶν τὸν λόγον· οἶδα γὰρ ἐγὼ ἀρχὴν ἀφ' ἧς ἐκτήστατο ἕκαστον ἡμῶν ὁ θεός, οἶδα ταύτην τὴν ἀρχὴν ἔμψυχον οὖσαν καὶ ζῶσαν καὶ λέγουσαν· ὁ θεὸς ἐκτήσατό με ἀρχὴν ὁδῶν αὐτοῦ εἰς ἔργα αὐτοῦ. Ἡ ἀρχὴ Χριστός ἐστιν· ἐκτήσατο οὖν ἀπ' ἀρχῆς, ἀπὸ Χριστοῦ τοῦ ὄντος ἀρχῆς καὶ τοῦ ὄντος τέλους, τοῦ ὄντος ἄλφα καὶ τοῦ ὄντος ὦ.* Ed. Lorenzo Perrone, GCS NF 19; Origenes Werke 13 (Berlin: De Gruyter, 2015); ET Joseph W. Trigg, FC 141 (Washington, DC: Catholic University of America Press, 2020), modified.

> it is through Wisdom, that is by Word and Reason, not by force and necessity, that they have been subjected. And therefore his glory is in the very fact that he possesses all things, and this is the 'purest and most clear glory' of omnipotence, that by Reason and Wisdom, not by force and necessity, all things have been subjected.

Although, as we saw earlier, Origen employs the image of an architect building a house, the 'omnipotence' by which the Father is 'Almighty' is not simply that of 'force and necessity', and, in turn, his creation is not simply inert matter brought into existence and shaped into forms. God, rather, exercises his 'omnipotence' through the persuasion of Word or Reason and Wisdom, and his 'creation' (those whom he has 'acquired' from the *archē*) is those who have been persuaded to subject themselves willingly to their Creator. Moreover, this is, again, explained by reference to the combination of Phil. 2:10 and 1 Cor. 15:27–8: when all knees bow at the name of the one who was exalted above all because of his obedient acceptance of death upon a cross, then God will, in turn, be 'all in all'. If the *archē* of Gen. 1:1 is 'our Lord and Saviour Jesus Christ', the creation that is brought into being, reflecting the will of God perfectly, is eschatological.

4.2 The Human Being, Made in the Image and Fashioned from the Earth

We do not have any significant passages from Origen's *Commentary on Genesis* to elucidate how he treated the various days of creation.[75] They are covered in his first homily on Genesis, where they are presented in terms of the spiritual growth of the human being. Origen, as already mentioned, does not align the two creation accounts with the distinction between the intelligible and the sense-perceptible worlds. His words on these matters are very careful and precise, and need to be read carefully; as we will see, he occasionally prefaces his thoughts by an extended caution and exhortation.

Although he was repeatedly accused of teaching that pre-existing incorporeal souls fell into embodied existence, Origen emphatically denies that he taught any such thing, ridiculing it as 'folly', 'myth', 'false teaching', 'introduced by the Greeks', borrowed by Pythagoras and Plato from the Egyptians.[76] He insists that

[75] Metzler includes from the second book of the *Commentary*, short passages from John Philoponus on Gen. 1:9 (D5), from the Collectio Coisliniana on Gen. 1:11 (D6), and an extensive passage from the *Philoc.* 23, on Gen. 1:14 (D7), discussed above; from the third book of the *Commentary*, a passage from Eusebius *Hist. eccl.* 3.1.1–3 on Gen. 1:14–18 (D8) discussed below, and from the *Philoc.* 14 on Gen. 1:16–18 (D9); and from somewhere in the fourth to eighth book of the *Commentary*, a sentence from the Catenae on Gen. 1:22 (D10).

[76] Cf. *Cels.* 1.13 [*Philoc.* 18.7]; *Cels.* 1.20 [*Philoc.* 18.5], *Cels.* 5.49; *Com. John* 6.66.

if Celsus had understood 'what is appropriate for a soul which will be in everlasting life, and what it is necessary to think regarding its essence and about its principles, he would not have ridiculed in this way the immortal entering a mortal body [τὸν ἀθάνατον εἰς θνητὸν ἐρχόμενον σῶμα]', adding that his view on this is 'not according to the Platonic transmigration [μετενσωμάτωσιν] but according to a more sublime contemplation', and, further, that Celsus would also have understood how 'in his great love for humanity [God] made one special descent [κατάβασιν] to convert those whom the divine scripture mystically calls "the lost sheep of the house of Israel", which had strayed down from the mountain'.[77]

What particularly catches Origen's interest in the two accounts of the origin of human beings, as it did Philo, is the different verbs used, 'make' (ποιέω) and 'mould' (πλάσσω), respectively, and the materiality implied by the latter. In his *Homilies on Jeremiah* (preserved in Greek), commenting on the words 'Before I moulded you in the womb, I knew you' (Jer. 1:5), Origen points out that the text of Genesis speaks 'in a way exceedingly dialectic' (πάνυ διαλεκτικώτατα) by differentiating between the verbs 'to mould' and 'to make'. It is, Origen observes, only 'when he is created "in accordance with the image" that God says, "Let us make..."', whereas, when he takes clay from the earth, God did not 'make' but 'moulded the human being'. Accordingly, God did not say to Jeremiah, 'Before I made you in the womb', because, he explains, 'what is made [τὸ ποιούμενον] does not arise in a womb, but what is moulded [τὸ πλασσόμενον] from the clay of the earth is created [κτίζεται] in the womb'.[78] That is, the human 'made' by God is not strictly identical with the human 'moulded' from clay and 'created' in the womb.

This distinction is the subject of an extensive passage from the *Dialogue with Heraclides*, also preserved in Greek. Origen has been asked whether the soul is blood, on the grounds of the verse 'the soul of all flesh is its blood' (Lev. 17:11), but he hesitates to speak directly about this, as the problem is 'rather delicate'.[79] He urges his audience: 'I beseech you, therefore, be transformed; resolve to learn that you can be transformed and put aside the form of swine... let us learn from the Apostle that the transformation depends on us. This is how he puts it: "We all, with unveiled face, beholding the glory of the Lord, are being changed into his likeness" [2 Cor. 3:18]. If you were a barker, and the Word moulded you and changed you, you were transformed from a dog into a human. If you were impure, and the Word touched your soul, and if you offered yourself to be shaped by the

[77] *Cels.* 4.17, Matt. 15:24. In *Com. John* 6.68, Origen proposes to examine how 'transmigration' (μετενσωμάτωσις) is different from 'incarnation' or 'embodiment' (ἐνσωμάτωσις).

[78] *Homilies on Jeremiah*, 1.10; ed. Erich Klostermann, rev. P. Nautin, GCS 6, Origenes Werke 3, 2nd edn. (Berlin: Akademie Verlag, 1983); ET John Clark Smith, FC 97 (Washington, DC: Catholic University Press, 1998).

[79] *Dialogue with Heraclides* (*Dial.*), 10.20–12.20; ed. Jean Scherer, *Entretien D'Origène avec Héraclide et les évêques ses colleges sur le Père, le Fils, et l'âme*, Publications de la Société Fouad I de Papyrologie, Textes et Documents 9 (Cairo: Institute Français d'Archéologie Orientale, 1949); ET Robert J. Daly, ACW 54 (New York/Mahwah, NJ: Paulist Press, 1992).

Word, you were changed from a swine into a human' (*Dial.* 13.26–14.16). After such exhortation, Origen continues with his subject, the human being, whether the soul is its blood, and, by consequence, 'the doctrine of the two humans', again urging his hearers that 'since we have come to a mystical subject, I appeal to you not to make me guilty on your account of casting pearls before swine' (*Dial.* 14.26–15.1). After further exhortation, and admitting that 'I am worried about speaking; I am worried about not speaking... You see how long my preamble is to prepare my hearers. I hesitate to put off speaking, and when I do speak I change my mind again. What is it that I really want? To treat the matter in a way that heals the souls of my hearers' (*Dial.* 15.9–27).

Only after such lengthy exhortation to be transformed into a human, and specifying his purpose, does Origen give his account:

> The human, therefore, created first [*κτιζόμενος πρότερον*] was created 'according to the image' in whom is found no matter [*οὗ ὕλη οὐκ εὑρίσκεται*], for that which is 'according to the image' is not made from matter. 'And God said, "Let us make the human being in accordance with our image and according to our likeness and let them have dominion"' and so forth. 'And God made the human' not by 'taking dust from the ground' as he did the second [*ὡς ἐπὶ τοῦ δευτέρου*], but made him 'in accordance with the image of God'. That Moses was not the only one to know that his being 'in accordance with the image of God' is nonmaterial [*ἄϋλον*], superior to every bodily existence [*κρεῖττον πάσης σωματικῆς ὑποστάσεως*], but that the Apostle also knew this, is shown in his text which says, 'Seeing that you have put off the old human with its practices and have put on the new which is being renewed in knowledge after the image of its Creator' [Col. 3:9–10]. There are, therefore, two humans regarding each of us [*Δύο οὖν καθ' ἕκαστον ἡμῶν εἰσιν ἄνθρωποι*].[80]

This distinction then leads into a lengthy discussion on the spiritual senses, based on the homonymity of the word 'human', applying both to 'the outer human' and 'the inner' (*Dial.* 16.15–16; cf. 2 Cor. 4:16), so that each member or faculty of the outer human has a corresponding member or faculty in the inner human (*Dial.* 16.16–24.23). Important in all this, for our purposes, is that Origen is not speaking of two separate or separable entities (a pre-existing soul and a material body), but, as Paul, a distinction between 'the old human' and the new, 'the outer human' and 'the inner': the 'two humans', with their members and faculties, are 'regarding each of us'.

[80] *Dial.* 15.30–16.17. Cf. Origen, *Commentary on Song of Songs*, Prologue. Ed. W. A. Baehrens, GCS 33, Origenes Werke 8 (Leipzig: Hinrichs, 1925), 63.31–68.3; ET R. P. Lawson, ACW 26 (New York/Mahwah, NJ: Newman Press, 1956), 25–30.

Origen's primary concern in all this is that we should not identify the 'making' of the human being 'in the image' of God with the shape or figure in which the clay is 'moulded'. We have a lengthy fragment from Origen's *Commentary on Genesis* emphasizing this very point, arguing against those, like Melito, who, he says, took the scriptural descriptions of the bodily parts of God only 'according to the letter'.[81] For Origen, being 'in accordance with the image' resides instead 'in the rational soul' (*ἐν δὲ τῇ λογικῇ ψυχῇ*), in its various faculties: 'for there is in the human a faculty of knowing, of judging and of doing good, of doing righteousness and of flourishing, and, comprehensively, of completing every good: these bring about, by God, the "according to the image" in him; for actions characterize the "according to the image" and not the form of the body'.[82] It is, Origen further specifies, by living according to the flesh and doing its works that the human bears the image of the earthly (cf. Rom. 8:13; Gal. 5:19; 1 Cor. 15:49), while the one who 'by the Spirit puts to death the deeds of the body bears the image of the heavenly'. Only in this way, he concludes, by being merciful, compassionate, righteous, and holy, as the Father in heaven, will we 'become in all things an image of God' (*εἰκὼν γίνεται κατὰ πάντα τοῦ θεοῦ*).[83] That is, although it is in their intellectual capacities, not the form of the body, that humans are 'in accordance with the image', this is not set in opposition to the body, for it is in their actions that human beings demonstrate this likeness. As Origen put it elsewhere, 'the saint alone is rational' (*Com. John* 2.114), where the content of the term 'rational' (*λογικός*) is clearly derived from the 'Logos', Jesus Christ, the image of the invisible God.

There is one intriguing passage in the *Commentary on John* where Origen not only differentiates but seems to coordinate the three verbs we have seen used so far—'to create' (*κτίζω*), 'to make' (*ποιέω*), and 'to mould' (*πλάσσω*)—and introduces a new element:

> Because, therefore, the first human fell away from the superior things and desired a life different from the better life, he deserved to be an *archē* neither of something created nor made [*οὔτε κτίσματος οὔτε ποιήματος*], but 'of something moulded [*πλάσματος*] by the Lord, made [*πεποιημένον*] to be mocked by the angels' [Job 40:19]. Now, our superior existence [*ἡ προηγουμένη ὑπόστασις*] is in our being made [*κτίσαντος*] 'in accordance with the image' of the Creator, but that resulting from a cause [*ἡ ἐξ αἰτίας*] is in the thing moulded [*ἐν τῷ... πλάσματι*], which was received from the dust of the earth. And if, forgetful, as it were, of the superior essence [*οὐσίας*] in us, we subordinate ourselves to that which is moulded from dust, even the superior part will take on the image of the

[81] D11, from the Collectio Coisliniana (Metzler, 158–62).

[82] Metzler, 160.24–6: *ἡ γὰρ γνωστικὴ δύναμις ἡ ἐν τῷ ἀνθρώπῳ, κριτική τε καὶ εὐποιητική, δικαιοπρακτική τε καὶ ἐρρωμένη, καὶ ἀπαξαπλῶς παντὸς καλλοῦ ἐπιτελεστική, "κατ' εἰκόνα" ὑπὸ τοῦ θεοῦ γεγόνασιν αὐτῷ. ὅτι δὲ τὸ κατ' εἰκόνα αἱ πράξεις χαρακτηρίζουσι καὶ οὐχὶ ἡ τοῦ σώματος μορφή,...*

[83] Metzler, 162.5–6.

> earthly. But if, once we have understood what has been made 'in accordance with the image' and what has been received 'from the dust of the earth', we should completely incline to him in whose image we have come into existence, we will also be in accordance with the likeness of God, having abandoned every passionate desire for matter and bodies, and even for some of those beings who are according to the likeness. (*Com. John* 20.182–3)

As Marguerite Harl points out, Origen seems to indicate a hierarchy of terms describing the different aspects of 'creation', a descending gradation of 'create' (*κτίζειν*), 'make' (*ποιεῖν*), and 'mould' (*πλάσσειν*).[84] This should not be thought of so much as distinct or discrete acts, but rather as different aspects of God's act of creating, much the same way as Origen analyses the different titles of Christ as various aspects of the one Christ. Our 'superior existence' is being created according to the image of God—a distinction, as we have seen, that resides in our intellectual faculties, but which is manifest in our actions as embodied beings; it is 'superior' not only in an ontological sense but also in a literary sense (for Gen. 1 comes before Gen. 2). That which is moulded from the earth, on the other hand, is not simply 'created or made', but 'results from a cause'. To understand what this 'cause' is, and the further dimension that it adds to Origen's understanding of human embodiment, we must introduce one further word that Origen employs to speak about the origin of the world and human beings within it. But before that, to conclude what we have seen so far, it is clear that for Origen, human beings find themselves caught between the two aspects of their existence, able to incline in either direction, either downwards, subordinating the superior aspect of their existence so that even this takes on the image of the earthly, or, abandoning their desire for things of sense-perception, inclining rather towards the one in whose image we have come into existence, to be made also in his likeness.

One final and perhaps surprising point, regarding the difference between that made in the image and that formed from the earth, is the way in which Origen handles the remaining aspect of how the human being is described in the text of Scripture. In his *Commentary on Matthew*, he notes that while Christ had combined Gen. 1:27 and 2:24 together (Matt. 19:4–5), 'male and female' (*ἄρρεν καὶ θῆλη*) are in fact said regarding 'those who came into being according to the image of God', while those moulded from the dust of the earth and from the rib are called 'man and woman' (*ἀνὴρ καὶ γυνὴ*). He further points out that 'it is never said that woman was made in the image, nor man, for that matter, but those who are superior, namely male, and second, female'.[85] Origen doesn't follow Philo in

[84] Harl, 'Préexistence des âmes', at 244.

[85] *Com. Matt.*, 14.16: *οὐδέποτε γὰρ γυνὴ κατ' εἰκόνα οὐδὲ ἀνήρ, ἀλλ' οἱ μὲν διαφέροντες ἄρρεν οἱ δὲ δεύτεροι θῆλυ*. Ed. Erich Klostermann and Ernst Benz, GCS 40, Origenes Werke 10, two parts (Leipzig: Hinrichs Verlag, 1935, 1937), 321–3; ET Ronald E. Heine, OECT, 2 vols (Oxford: Oxford University Press, 2018), 177–8:

describing 'human' as the genus, and 'male and female' as the species, but 'male' and 'female' are indeed proper designations of those made in the image. He also seems to have a higher appreciation for the distinction of the sexes than Philo. That 'the two become one flesh', when there is 'oneness of mind, agreement, and harmony between husband and wife', he continues, is a 'gift of God' equivalent to the gift of celibacy spoken about by Paul. In his first homily on Genesis, Origen further explains the distinction of the human as 'male and female' by reference to the blessing that follows: 'since, indeed, man could not otherwise increase and multiply except with the female. Therefore, that there might be no doubt about his blessing that is to come, the text says "Male and female he made them"' (*Hom. Gen.* 1.14).

Having noted the 'literal sense', Origen then goes on in his homily to consider how, allegorically, 'the human, made in the image of God, is male and female'. As the inner human consists of spirit and soul, the former is said to be 'male', while the latter is 'female', so that 'if these have concord and agreement among themselves, they increase and multiply, by the very accord among themselves and they produce sons, good inclinations and understandings or useful thoughts, by which they fill the earth and have dominion over it' (*Hom. Gen.* 1.15). In his *Commentary on Matthew*, following many Christian writers before him (noted above) going back to Paul, Origen also takes the 'male' and 'female' to refer to Christ and the Church: 'he, who in the beginning created the one who is in the image (as "he is in the form of God"), made him male and the church female, and gave the "being in the image" to both as to one'.[86] It is, then, for the sake of the Church that Christ left the father and his mother ('for he is a son of the "Jerusalem above"') to join himself to his wife, ('who had fallen hence') so that, down here, the two became one flesh, when 'the Word became flesh and dwelt in us', forming 'the body of Christ and individually members of it'.[87]

4.3 The Throwing Down of the World and the Descent of the Human

Origen was particularly struck by the way in which the writers of the New Testament employed the word *καταβολή*. It is used eleven times in the New Testament (once implied), where in all but one it is in the phrase usually translated 'the foundation of the world'; the word, however, really means a 'throwing down'.[88] Although the most

[86] *Com. Matt.* 14.17 (325.27–32; ET 179): *ὁ κτίσας γε ἀπ' ἀρχῆς τὸν κατ' εἰκόνα (ὡς "ἐν μορφῇ" θεου ὑπάρχων) ἄρρεν αὐτὸν ἐποίησε καὶ θῆλυ τὴν ἐκκλησίαν, ἓν τὸ κατ' εἰκόνα ἀμφοτέροις χαρισάμενος.*

[87] Ibid; Gal. 4:26, John 1:14; Eph. 5:31; Gen. 2:24, 1 Cor. 12:27. Cf. Origen, *Com. Songs*, 2.8 (Baehrens, 157–8; ET 149–50).

[88] Matt. 25:34; Lk. 11:50; John 17:24; Eph. 1:4; Heb. 4:3; 9:26; 11:11; 1 Pet. 1:20; Apoc. 13:8; 17:8; in Matt. 13:35 'of the world' is implied; it is used one other time, in Heb. 11:11, where it refers to human reproduction.

controversial passages of Origen regarding this 'throwing down' are in *On First Principles*, it is better to start, as Heine suggests, with a lengthy passage from the nineteenth book of Origen's *Commentary on John*, which, although written in his Caesarean period, and thus after *On First Principles*, is preserved in the original Greek.[89] As we will see, the 'throwing down of the world' has as much to do with human orientation as it does with the relationship between the intelligible realm and the sense-perceptible world. In this passage, Origen is treating Christ's words: 'You are from below, I am from above; you are of this world, I am not of this world' (John 8:23). He begins by quoting Christ's other words, 'He who is of the earth is of the earth and speaks of the earth. He who comes from heaven is above all; what he has seen and heard, to this he bears testimony' (John 3:31–2), and asks whether being 'of the earth' in the latter text is equivalent to being 'from below' in the former (*Com. John* 19.127). Origen points out that in John 3, Christ did not put his statements about being 'of the earth' and coming 'from heaven' in direct parallel (by saying 'of heaven' instead of 'comes from heaven'), and suggests as a possible reason for this that 'the Saviour was not "of heaven", especially insofar as he was "firstborn of all creation"', while the phrase 'of heaven' is used by Paul to speak of the second human in contrast to the first.[90] To be 'from above', he concludes, is not the same thing as to be 'not of this world'.

Likewise, being 'from below' and being 'of the earth' are also different, in that while 'from below' can refer to a place, it can also refer to 'a way of thinking' (*Com. John* 19.131). 'Of the world' can certainly be used as a spatial designation, for the visible, material world has places 'of the world' that are above and others that are below. On the other hand, as referring to 'a way of thinking', he points out, 'the one from below is necessarily of the world, but the one who is of this world is not necessarily from below' (*Com. John* 19.132–3); that is, one who is 'of this world' can still be a 'citizen of the heavens', and one who is 'from below' can change to become 'one who is from above and is no longer of this world' (*Com. John* 19.134–5). The difference turns, for Origen, upon where one's heart is: 'if someone stores up treasure on earth, he is from below; but if someone stores up treasure in heaven, that person is born from above and assumes "the image of the heavenly" ... He is not of this world, however, who does not love the world nor the things in the world, but who says, "God forbid that I should boast except in the cross of my Lord Jesus Christ"' (*Com. John* 19.138–9). The descent and ascent of souls must

[89] Heine, *Origen: An Introduction*, 111–12.

[90] *Com. John* 19.128: *τάχα γὰρ ὁ σωτὴρ οὐκ ἐκ τοῦ οὐρανοῦ ἦν, μάλιστα καθ' ὃ "προτότοκος πάσης κτίσεως" ἦν. τὸ γὰρ "ἐκ τοῦ οὐρανοῦ" ὁ δεύτερος ἄνθρωπος ἦν ἐξ οὐρανοῦ, ὡς καὶ ὁ Παῦλός πού φυσιν·* referring to Col. 1:15, and then 1 Cor. 15:47. The Gospel of John might also indicate such a distinction in the way it speaks of the ascending and descending Son of Man; cf. John Behr, *John the Theologian and His Paschal Gospel: A Prologue to Theology* (Oxford: Oxford University Press, 2019), 148–60, 218–44.

therefore, according to Origen, be understood 'in a more mystical manner not spatially' (*Com. John* 19.144–5).[91]

He continues by affirming that there must therefore be 'another world' besides this sense-perceptible one, one which 'in its entirety is an invisible world, a world which is not seen, an intelligible world [*νοητὸς κόσμος*]', yet which is beheld by the pure in heart, that is, those being prepared to seek God (*Com. John* 19.146). This then raises the question, for Origen, of whether Christ, 'the first-born of all creation' (Col. 1:15) 'can be a world, and especially in so far as he is "the manifold wisdom"' (*Com. John* 19.147; Eph. 3:10). He then comments:

> For by being the principles [*τοὺς λόγους*] of absolutely everything according to which all things made by God in Wisdom have come to be (as the prophet says 'you made all things in wisdom') in himself he would also be a 'world' that surpasses the world of sense-perception in its diversity and excels it as much as the principle stripped of all the material of the whole world differs from the material world, [a world constituted] not on the basis of matter, but on the basis of the participation of the things that have been set in order in the Word and Wisdom, which set matter in order.[92]

It is here that Origen now introduces the term 'throwing down' (*καταβολή*):

> That world has nothing below even as this world has nothing above, to the one who examines it as to its exact nature. For how can this world, whose creation is a throwing-down, have anything above? For one must not hear the phrase, 'Before the throwing-down of the world' [John 17:24; Eph. 1:4] in just any way, [but] advisedly because the saints coined the expression 'throwing-down' to express such a concept, although they could have said, 'Before the creation of the world', and not used the expression 'throwing down'. The whole world, therefore, and the things in it are included in the 'throwing down'. But the genuine disciples of Jesus, whom he chose out of the world that, by bearing their own cross and following him, they might no longer be of the world, but come to be outside the throwing down of the world in its entirety. (*Com. John* 19.149–50)

[91] Cf. Heine, *Origen: Introduction*, 113: 'We should note here that this is not a statement about an original fall of souls from the heavenly realm that occurred before the earth was created. This is a statement about the condition that people experience in life because of choosing to live with their thoughts focused on material realities rather than on immaterial realities.'

[92] *Com. John* 19.147: *τῷ γὰρ εἶναι παντὸς οὑτινοσοῦν τοὺς λόγους, καθ' οὓς γεγένηται πάντα τὰ ὑπὸ τοῦ θεοῦ ἐν σοφίᾳ πεποιημένα (ὥς φησιν ὁ προφήτης· "Πάντα ἐν σοφίᾳ ἐποίησας"), ἐν αὐτῷ, εἴη ἂν καὶ αὐτὸς κόσμος, τοσούτῳ ποικιλώτερος τοῦ αἰσθητοῦ κόσμου καὶ διαφέρων, ὅσῳ διαφέρει γυμνὸς πάσης ὕλης τοῦ ὅλου κόσμου λόγος τοῦ ἐνύλου κόσμου, οὐκ ἀπὸ τῆς ὕλης ἀλλὰ ἀπὸ τῆς μετοχῆς τοῦ λόγου καὶ σοφίας τῶν κοσμούντων τὴν ὕλην κεκοσμημένων.*

The distinction between the world 'thrown down' and the world above is thus not spatial or even temporal, but rather the distinction between the world of sense-perception, what we can see physically as it currently is, and the principles (*τοὺς λόγους*) of absolutely everything according to which God made all things in Wisdom, the intellectual world that is Christ. The descent has not been of incorporeal intellects into material bodies, but rather, in a 'more mystical manner', the turning of attention and desire from the world made by God in Wisdom to the world that sense-perception sees and desires. And, in turn, the ascent from below to above is made by bearing the cross and following Christ. As we have already seen Origen assert: 'the phenomenal world is an image of the intellectual and invisible: the truth is in the future'.[93]

The 'throwing down of the world' is also treated extensively in a passage in *On First Principles*, although only available as translated by Rufinus. It begins by noting that the Scriptures speak of the creation of the world 'by a new and particular name, terming it the *καταβολή* of the world', a word which Rufinus then explains (to his Roman readers) has been mistranslated into Latin (as *constitutio* rather than *deicere*). Then, after the quotation of a passage from John (in fact, Matt. 24:21; 25:34, but cf. John 17:24) and Paul (Eph. 1:4), Origen continues:

> It seems worthwhile, therefore, to inquire what is indicated by this new term. And I am of the opinion that as the end and the consummation of the saints will be in those [worlds] that are 'not seen and eternal' [2 Cor. 4:18.], it must be supposed, from a contemplation of that very end, as we have frequently pointed out above, that rational creatures have also had a similar beginning. And if they had a beginning such as the end for which they hope, they were undoubtedly from the beginning in those [worlds] that are 'not seen' and 'eternal'. And if this is so, then there has been a descent from the higher conditions to the lower, not only on the part of those souls who have by the variety of their own movements deserved it, but also on that [part] of those who, to serve the whole world, were brought down from the higher and invisible conditions to these lower and visible ones, even against their will. 'Because the creation was subjected to futility, not willingly, but by the one who subjected it in hope' [Rom. 8:20], so that both the sun and the moon and the stars and the angels of God might fulfil an obedient service for the world; and for those souls which, because of their excessive spiritual defects needed these denser and more solid bodies, and because of those for whom this was necessary, this visible world was founded. From this, therefore, a descent of everyone alike would seem to be indicated by the meaning of the word, that is, of *καταβολή*. The whole creation indeed entertains the hope

[93] Pitra, *Analecta Sacra*, 30.

> of freedom, of being 'set free from the bondage of corruption when the children of God' [Rom. 8:21], who either fell away or were scattered abroad, shall be gathered together into one, or when they shall have fulfilled their other duties in this world, which are known to God alone, the Artificer of all things. It must be supposed that the world was created of such a kind and of such a size as to be able to contain all those souls which were appointed to be trained in this world, and also those powers which were prepared to attend, to serve, and to assist them. For it is proved by many assertions that all rational creatures are of one nature; on which ground alone can the justice of God in all his arrangements concerning them be defended, when everyone has within himself the reasons he has been placed in this or that rank of life. (*Princ.* 3.5.4)

There are a number of important points in this passage. First, Origen again emphasizes (and notes that he has repeatedly made the point) that it is by looking to the end that human beings contemplate the beginning, and if the end is similar to the beginning, then their beginning is in that 'world' which was 'not seen and eternal', that is, they are chosen in Christ 'before the throwing down of the world' (Eph. 1:4). Second, although the whole creation has been 'thrown down', this is not uniformly the result of sin. As Origen put it in the opening line to his homilies on Ezekiel, 'Not everyone who is a captive endures captivity on account of his sins.'[94] Some have certainly deserved it, on account of 'their own movements' as the above passage puts it, but others were brought down, sometimes against their will, to serve others. Third, this descent is described not in terms of incorporeal intellects or souls taking a body or being embodied, but rather as entering a 'denser and more solid' form of embodiment. While some have certainly 'needed' this condition, because of their 'excessive spiritual defects', the whole of creation has been subjected to this 'futility'—not willingly, however, but in hope, as Origen quotes Paul. As such, in reference to the same verse in his *Commentary on John*, Origen suggests that as Paul himself 'wishes "to remain in the flesh", not willingly but in hope', it is possible that 'some can exist in a body not in this way'.[95] What is meant by bodies become 'denser and more solid' is a question that we will return to later.

The questions we must first address are: why is the world 'thrown down' in this manner, and what relationship might this have to the 'cause', mentioned above, resulting in the body being formed from the dust of the earth? Origen is particularly vexed by any imputation to God of partiality, whether in the form of making different 'kinds' of soul, some destined for salvation and others for damnation, or in the form of suggesting that he is directly (and arbitrarily) responsible for the

[94] *Homilies on Ezekiel*, 1.1; ed. W. A. Baehrens, GCS 33, Origenes Werke 8 (Leipzig: Hinrichs, 1925); ET Thomas P. Scheck, ACW 62 (New York: Newman Press, 2010).

[95] *Com. John* 1.98–100, Phil. 1:24: δυναμένων τινῶν ὑπάρχειν ἐν σώματι οὐχ οὕτως.

different conditions in which people find themselves through their birth. Origen's answer to this is to emphasize the role of human free will and to clarify the nature of God's foreknowledge. Both of these points are treated in a passage from the third book of his *Commentary on Genesis*, preserved for us in Greek in the *Philocalia*, where Origen is concerned to refute the idea that our fortunes are determined by the stars (made as 'signs', Gen. 1:14). According to Origen: 'When God in the *archē* projected the creation of the world [ἐπιβάλλων ὁ θεὸς τῇ ἀρχῇ τῆς κοσμοποιΐας], inasmuch as there is nothing without a cause, his thoughts traversed the whole course of the future', so that he foresaw all the various trains of events that would occur and which would cause others to occur—without this, however, implying that he caused them, no more than when we see someone stepping out onto a slippery path, we can foresee that they will fall without causing that fall.[96] As Origen concludes, 'the future event is the cause of God's particular knowledge concerning it; for it does not happen because it is known, but it is known because it will happen'.[97] On this basis, Origen can argue in a passage from his *Commentary on Romans*, also preserved in the *Philocalia*, with respect to Paul's 'election' by God before his birth (Rom. 1:1; Gal. 1:15), that 'anyone who is predestined through the foreknowledge of God is the cause of the events known', rather than as a result of 'the absurd doctrine' of being saved 'by nature', as his opponents taught (*Philoc.* 25.1–2). The 'antecedent causes' invoked by Origen to reconcile the diversity in which human beings find themselves with the justice of God thus do not refer to the actions of souls prior to falling into bodies, as he was often charged with teaching, but rather to the anteriority of the foreknowledge of God.[98]

Origen can thus distinguish between what is created by God 'in the *archē*' and what results from ourselves. In another important passage from *On First Principles*, Origen further explains:

> When, 'in the *archē*', he created those beings that he desired to create, that is, rational beings, he had no other reason for creating them other than himself, that is, his own goodness. As, then, he himself, in whom was neither variation nor change nor inability, was the cause of all those things which were to be created, he created all whom he created equal and alike, since there was in himself no ground

[96] *Philoc.* 23.8; ed. J. Armitage Robinson (Cambridge: Cambridge University Press, 1893); ET George Lewis (Edinburgh: T & T Clark, 1911), modified.

[97] *Philoc.* 23.8. Cf. *Cels.* 2.20: 'We say that the one who made the prediction was not the cause of the future event, because he foretold that it would happen; but we hold that the future event, which would have taken place even if it had not been prophesied, constitutes the cause of its prediction by the one with foreknowledge.' See also, *On Prayer* 3. As Panayiotis Tzamalikos, *Origen: Philosophy of History and Eschatology*, Suppl. *VC* 85 (Leiden: Brill, 2007), 119, argues, regarding the phenomenon of prophecy, in the intersection of eternity and temporality, causality works backwards: 'though odd as it may appear, the prospective fulfilment of certain prophecy is the *cause*, whereas the utterance of prophecy is the *result*, although it temporally precedes the event itself.... it is the future that determines the past'.

[98] Cf. Harl, 'Préexistence des âmes', 252.

> for variety and diversity. But since these rational creatures, as we have frequently shown and will nevertheless show yet again in the proper place, were endowed with the faculty of free will, this freedom of will either incited each one to progress by the imitation of God or drew him to defection through negligence. And this, as we have already said before, is the cause of the diversity among rational creatures, drawing its origin not from the will or judgment of the Creator, but from the freedom of the individual will. (*Princ.* 2.9.6)

Our existence is owed to God, or more specifically God's goodness, while the condition of our existence results from ourselves and our free will. Yet, Origen continues from the above passage, God does not simply leave the resulting diversity to unravel further, but rather 'drew these diversities of intellects into the harmony of one world', as vessels not only of gold and silver but also of wood and clay, some unto honour and others unto dishonour, all adorning one house (cf. 2 Tim. 2:20), with 'divine providence arranging each individual according to the variety of their movements or of their intellects and purposes'. In this way, he argues, the Creator will not appear unjust when, 'according to the antecedent causes', each is arranged according to their merit, nor will the particular circumstances of each one's birth or condition be held to be merely accidental, nor again will one be led into believing in different creators or diverse natures of souls. He has thus given an account of 'how the great variety and diversity of the world may appear to be consistent with the whole rationale of righteousness', though in general terms only, 'for it is', he cautions, 'the mark of an ignorant person to seek, and of a foolish person to give, the particular rationale for each being' (*Princ.* 2.9.4, cf. 2.9.8).

One final point regarding the world as it is in this throwing down must be noted, and that is that the world is arranged suitably for 'all those souls which were appointed to be trained in this world' (*Princ.* 3.5.4, cited above)—that is, although resulting from a (future) cause, the throwing down of the world, and those in it, is pedagogically oriented, leading towards the final return to the end which is 'like' the beginning, but not identical with it because of the path that has now been trodden. The position in which each finds themselves within this orderly arrangement is thus not permanently fixed: there is no distinction of nature between vessels of honour and those of dishonour; it lies, rather, in the scope of each to 'purify himself from what is dishonourable', so as to be 'a vessel of honour, consecrated and useful to the master of the house, ready for any good work' (2 Tim. 2:21; cf. *Princ.* 3.1.21–4). In this situation, while urging each to 'be transformed' by attending to their higher calling, Origen also, provocatively, suggests that it would be better for the soul to descend fully into the flesh than to remain in a middle state, 'neither hot nor cold' (Apoc. 3:15): 'if it adheres to the flesh, then, at some time it will be satiated and filled with those very evils which it suffers from the vices of the flesh, and wearied, as it were, by the heavy burden of luxury and lust, it may more easily and rapidly be converted from the squalor of material things to a desire for heavenly things and to spiritual grace' (*Princ.* 3.4.3; cf. 1.3.8). As 'the spirit wars against the flesh, and the flesh against the spirit, that we may not do that which we would' (Gal. 5:17), 'it is better', Origen concludes, 'for a human being to be either in a condition of virtue or wickedness than in neither of these', if possible, of course, 'to be rendered spiritual by adhering to the spirit; but, if this is not possible, it is more expedient to follow even the wickedness of the flesh than, fixed in the sphere of its own will, to hold the position of an irrational animal' (*Princ.* 3.4.3). Evil will run its course, being finite, resulting, in the end, in the return to God.

There is one further passage, in the fourth book of *On First Principles*, that, while not using the term 'thrown down', explores the contrast between the intelligible world and the sense-perceptible world not only vertically but also horizontally, as it were, in terms of two lineages. It has been argued, rightly I think, that the exposition of 'first principles' given in the first three books, the framework that we have been exploring in the above pages, serves to provide the framework for the kind of scriptural exegesis that Origen propounds in the fourth book.[99] Reading from the light of the end conditions Origen's reading of the text of Genesis, and this is played out in the coordination of the beginning and the end, the below and above, just as it had done for Paul: the first human being, Adam, was from below, animated earth, while the last Adam, from above, is a life-giving spirit (1 Cor. 15:45–7), so that while all die in Adam, death having come by a human being, in Christ all are made alive, through the resurrection of the dead effected by a human being (1 Cor. 15:22), with the consequence that the perishable, animated body, which is sown in weakness and dishonour, is raised as an imperishable spiritual body in glory and power for 'what you sow does not come to life unless it dies' (1 Cor. 15:35–44). Reading in the light of the end opens up a double narrative in Scripture, similar to the way, for example, that Joseph's being sold into slavery as a sinful action of his jealous brothers is revealed, only at the end, to have really been the action of God, sending him into Egypt to preserve life (Gen. 37; 45:4–9). So, when Paul says, 'Behold Israel according to the flesh' (1 Cor. 10:18), Origen concludes that 'there is an Israel according to the Spirit' (*Princ.* 4.3.6), a distinction also indicated by Paul's statement that 'it is not the children of the flesh that are the children of God, for not all who are descended from Israel belong to Israel' (Rom. 9:8, 6) and the contrast between one who is 'a Jew openly' and the one who is 'a Jew in secret' (Rom. 2:28–9). Origen then continues:

[99] Cf. Brian E. Daley, 'Origen's *De Principiis*: A Guide to the Principles of Scriptural Interpretation', in John Petruccione, ed., *Nova et Vetera: Patristic Studies in Honor of Patrick Halton* (Washington, DC: Catholic University of America Press, 1998), 3–21, at 6, and Behr, *Origen*, *On First Principles*, xlv–liii.

> Jacob was the father of the twelve patriarchs, and they of the rulers of the people, and these again of the rest of the Israelites. So, then, the bodily Israelites have reference to [τὴν ἀναγωγὴν ἔχουσιν] the rulers of the people, and the rulers of the people to the patriarchs, and the patriarchs to Jacob and those still higher up; the intelligible Israelites, on the other hand, of whom the bodily were a type [οἱ δὲ νοητοὶ Ἰσραηλῖται, ὧν τύπος ἦσαν οἱ σωματικοί], are they not from the clans, the clans having come from the tribes, and the tribes from some one individual [i.e. Jacob] having a birth not of a bodily kind but of the better kind, he too being born from Isaac, and he being descended from Abraham, all referring back up to Adam, whom the Apostle says is Christ [πάντων ἀναγομένων ἐπὶ τὸν Ἀδαμ, ὃν ὁ ἀπόστολος εἶναι φησι τὸν Χηριστόν]? For every beginning of lineages as [referring] to the God of all began lower down from Christ [πᾶσα γὰρ ἀρχὴ πατριῶν τῶν ὡς πρὸς τὸν τῶν ὅλων θεὸν κατωτέρω ἀπὸ Χριστοῦ ἤρξατο], who is next to the God and Father of all, being thus the father of every soul, as Adam is the father of all human beings. And if Eve is touched on by Paul as referring to the Church, it is not surprising—Cain being born of Eve and all after him having reference to Eve—to have here types of the Church, they all being born from the Church in a preeminent sense.[100]

These two lineages, that of the human bodily descent from Adam and that of the soul descending from Christ, perhaps allude to the difference between the genealogy given in Matthew, where 'the genesis of Jesus' (Matt. 1:1, 18) is described as a descending line from Abraham, and that of Luke (3:28–38), which traces the lineage backwards or upwards to Adam the son of God, the former being the descent of Israel according to the flesh, the latter being the descent (or rather ascent) of the spiritual Israel, arriving at the end, when all are subject to Christ, so that 'Adam is Christ'. In the meantime, before the end, to quote Origen's comment one more time: 'the phenomenal world is an image of the intellectual and invisible: the truth is in the future'.[101]

4.4 Embodiment and Transformation

We can now turn to the question of what might be meant by the 'denser and more solid bodies' inhabited by those who need this form of education in their fall away

[100] *Princ.* 4.3.7; it is notable that this striking passage is preserved in Greek in the *Philocalia*, but omitted by Rufinus in his Latin translation. Origen continues by extending this correspondence to include a corresponding topography; while 'the mother city' in Judah is Jerusalem (*Princ.* 4.3.6), for Paul 'our mother' is 'the Jerusalem above' (*Princ.* 4.3.8; Gal. 4:26; and Heb. 12:22–3); and likewise 'If there are spiritual Israelites, it follows that there are also spiritual Egyptians and Babylonians', as what Ezekiel says about Pharaoh or the Prince of Tyre clearly does not refer to a human being ruling over Egypt or Tyre (*Princ.* 4.3.9; cf. Ezek. 29:1–9; 28).

[101] Pitra, *Analecta Sacra*, 30.

from the cause of their existence. The question of human embodiment is probably the most debated aspect of Origen's teaching.[102] One might have thought that he had in mind the 'garments of skin' with which God clothed Adam and Eve upon their expulsion from paradise (cf. Gen. 3:21). But in fact, Origen's references to the 'garments of skin' are extremely sparse.[103] And although Origen was repeatedly accused of teaching that when incorporeal souls fell, they were embodied by being clothed in 'garments of skin', in a passage from his *Commentary on Genesis* preserved in the Catenae, he ridicules this as 'silly' and 'unworthy of God', for it would turn God into a tanner, and contradict the scriptural account in which Adam had previously described Eve as being 'bone of my bone and flesh of my flesh' (Gen. 2:23).[104] Neither can it be the process of dying (νέκρωσις), he adds, for it would be difficult to explain how God, not sin, caused this, and such an answer would also require an account of how flesh and bones, which previously existed in paradise, could have been immortal in themselves. There is no other passage in Origen's surviving works that really explains how he might have understood the 'garments of skin'. However, there is a passage in Procopius of Gaza's *Commentary on Genesis* that might well refer to Origen. Procopius mentions those who ridicule the idea that God slaughtered cattle or sheep and undertook the craft of a tanner, and then gives an account of their view:

> But the allegorists, after the previously mentioned ridicule, say the one 'in accordance with the image' refers to the soul, and the one 'formed from the dust' refers to the body, composed of fine particles and worthy of the way of life in paradise, and which some call luminous [τὸ λεπτομερὲς σῶμα...ὅ τινες αὐγοειδὲς ἐκάλεσαν]. The garments of skin, on the other hand, refer to 'you clothed me with skin and flesh and enveloped me with bones and sinews' [Job 10:11]. They say, furthermore, that the soul is borne upon the first luminous body, which later is clothed with the garments of skin [τῷ δὲ αὐγοειδεῖ τὴν ψυχὴν ἐποχεῖσθαι πρώτῳ λέγουσιν, ὅπερ ὕστερον ἐνεδύσατο τοὺς δερματίνους χιτῶνας].[105]

Origen uses similar words in his *Commentary on Matthew* in explaining Christ's words about those raised from the dead being 'like the angels': their bodies 'of

[102] See, for examples, the following exchange: Peter W. Martens, 'Origen's Doctrine of Pre-Existence and the Opening Chapters of Genesis', *ZAC* 16 (2012), 516–49; Mark Edwards, 'Origen in Paradise: A Response to Peter Martens', *ZAC* 23 (2019), 163–85; Martens, 'Response to Edwards', *ZAC* 23 (2019), 186–200. Pierce, 'Apokatastasis, Genesis 1:26–27, and the Theology of History in Origen's *De Principiis*', 174–5, ftn. 13, astutely suggests that Martens and others have taken Origen 'to be reasoning about eschatology on the basis of protology' rather than the other way round.

[103] Cf. Anders Lund Jacobsen, 'Genesis 1–3 as Source for the Anthropology of Origen', *VC* 62 (2008), 213–32, at 223.

[104] D 22, from the Collectio Coisliniana (Metzler, 190–2).

[105] Procopius of Gaza, *Com. Gen.* 3.21; ed. Karin Metzler, GCS NF 22, Prokop von Gaza 1 (Berlin: De Gruyter, 2015), 151.

humiliation' are transformed to be like the bodies of angels, 'ethereal and luminous' (*αἰθέρια καὶ αὐγοειδὲς φῶς*).[106] Given that for Origen, the end is 'like' the beginning, it would not be surprising at all if he had speculated about Adam in paradise possessing a 'luminous body' that is modified in the garments of skin.[107]

In explaining the transformation of Christ's human body and soul in the resurrection, Origen has recourse to the understanding of matter that we considered earlier. 'Matter', he points out, 'by its own principle is without quality, but is clothed with qualities such as the Creator wishes to give it, and that it often puts aside its former qualities and receives better and different ones', so that 'it is nothing remarkable if in the resurrection the quality of mortality in the body of Jesus, by the providence of God, should have been changed into an ethereal and divine quality'.[108] It is, moreover, this capacity of matter to be changed, altered, and transformed, that explains, for Origen, the different forms of Jesus, appearing 'without form or comeliness' to the multitude, in the 'folly' of his preaching, but glorious, luminous, and exceedingly beautiful to those who ascend the mountain with him.[109] God is, as we have seen Origen quote Amos, the one 'who makes and transforms all things' (Amos 5:8; *Princ.* 3.6.7).

How the 'ethereal and luminous body' in the resurrection, and one like it in the beginning, relate to the 'denser and more solid body' in the 'throwing down' of the sense-perceptible world and the 'garments of skin' is simply not explained in any surviving text of Origen. However, it is likely that his account of the soul in *On First Principles* 2.8.3 gives an indication. There he suggests, on the basis of the supposed etymology of the word 'soul' (taking *ψυχή* as derived from *ψυχόω*, which, as a passive verb, can mean 'to become cool'), that the intellect becomes a soul through cooling down. Origen further points out that as God is a 'consuming fire', whenever Scripture speaks of God in relation to creation, it does so in

[106] *Com. Matt.*, 17.30; Matt. 22:30; Phil. 3:21. See also *Cels.* 2.60, where Origen explains apparitions of the dead on the grounds of the existence of the souls 'in what is called the luminous body' (*τοῦ κατὰ τὴν ὑφεστηκεῖαν ἐν τῷ καλουμένῳ αὐγοειδεῖ σώματι ψυχήν*).

[107] For the idea of Adam's luminous body in Jewish thought, see David H. Aaron, 'Shedding Light on God's Body in Rabbinic Midrashim: Reflections on the Theory of a Luminous Adam', *HTR* 90 (1997), 299–314; and for an older, but succinct, survey of the 'ethereal' body in Neoplatonism and its background, see E. R. Dodds, *Proclus: The Elements of Theology*, 2nd edn. (Oxford: Clarendon Press, 1963), 313–21. For the 'garments of skin' more generally, see Gary A. Anderson, *The Genesis of Perfection: Adam and Eve in Jewish and Christian Imagination* (Louisville, KY: Westminster John Knox Press, 2001), 117–34.

[108] *Cels.* 3.41: Celsus should listen to what is said by the Greeks: *ἐπιστησάτω τοῖς ὑπὸ Ἑλλήνων λεγομένοις περὶ τῆς τῷ ἰδίῳ λόγῳ ἀποίου ὕλης, ποιότητας ἀμφισκομένης, ὁποίας ὁ δημιουργὸς βούλεται αὐτῇ περιτιθέναι, καὶ πολλάκις τὰς μὲν προτέρας ἀποτιθεμένης κρείττονας δὲ καὶ διαφόρους ἀναλαμβανούσης. εἰ γὰρ ὑγιῆ τὰ τοιαῦτα, τί θαυμαστὸν τὴν ποιότητα τοῦ θνητοῦ κατὰ τὸ τοῦ Ἰησοῦ σῶμα προνοίᾳ θεοῦ βουληθέντος μεταβαλεῖν εἰς αἰθέριον καὶ θείαν ποιότητα*; cf. *Cels.* 4.57: 'All of us who have accepted the existence of providence maintain that the underlying matter is capable of receiving qualities which the Creator wills to give it. And by God's will a quality of one kind is imposed upon this particular matter, but afterwards it will have a quality of another kind, one, let us say, which is better and superior.'

[109] *Cels.* 6.77, referring to Isa. 53:2, 1 Cor. 1:21; Matt. 17:2. Cf. *Com. Matt.* 12.36–8.

fiery terms (the burning bush, for example, or 'making' his ministers 'burning fire' in Ps. 103:4), whereas when it speaks of the effects of the adverse powers, and these powers themselves, it is as 'cold'. Moreover, when it speaks of that which is lost and in need of salvation, Scripture speaks of 'soul', but when it speaks in terms of praise or as approaching God, it speaks instead of 'intellect', as for instance Paul, saying, 'I will pray with the Spirit and I will pray with the intellect' (*Princ.* 2.8.2; 1 Cor. 14:15). It is to 'throw fire upon the earth' that Christ has come, and so he sets Simon and Cleopas' hearts aflame on the road to Emmaus.[110] In Origen's analogy, borrowed from the Stoics, of iron placed in a fire, where the iron, while remaining iron, 'has become wholly fire, since nothing else is discerned in it except fire', so too Christ's own human soul, 'like iron in the fire, was placed in the Word forever, in Wisdom forever, in God forever, is God in all that it does, feels, and understands', and from him something of the warmth of the Word of God passes to others.[111] So too, when all have become subject to Christ, and then to God, such that God will be 'all in all', the rational mind 'will no longer sense anything else apart from God: it will think God, see God, hold God; God will be the mode and measure of its every movement; and thus God will be all to it' (*Princ.* 3.6.3). The 'mystery' proclaimed by Paul, at the end of his treatment of the resurrection and the transition from bearing the image of the earthy to that of the heavenly, is this change: 'we shall all be changed in a moment, in the twinkling of an eye, at the last trumpet.... we shall all be changed' (1 Cor. 15:49–52). It is this transformation that is the heart of Origen's vision of the human being and the culmination of God's act of creating, as is clear from his long preamble in the *Dialogue with Heraclides* discussed above: 'I beseech you, be transformed!'

There are many points from this survey of Origen's understanding of creation and the human being that are of importance for understanding Gregory. For Origen, the human being is emphatically twofold, so much so that he can speak, following Paul, of each being 'two humans', the inner and the outer, or the old putting on the new. 'What is moulded from the clay of the earth is created in the womb' (*Hom. Jer.* 1.10), while that which is accordance with the image is 'made' by God, residing in the intellectual capacities of the soul but only as embodied in virtue. The former belongs to the world as 'thrown down', its diversity resulting from the free actions of those made equally in the image, but a 'throwing down' which, in the foresight and providence of God, is a 'harmonious world', configured to be suitable as a realm of instruction where, by the persuasion of the Word or Reason and Wisdom, all come to learn to subject themselves to Christ, so that he

[110] Luke 12:49; 24:32; brought together by Origen in *Hom. Jer.* 20.8 and *Hom. Ex.* 13.4, ed. W. A. Baehrens, GCS 29, Origenes Werke 6 (Leipzig: Hinrichs, 1920), ET Ronald E. Heine, FC 71 (Washington, DC: Catholic University Press, 1981).

[111] *Princ.* 2.6.6. Chrysippus had previously used the image of iron and fire; cf. Alexander of Aphrodisias, *Mixt.* 3–4, for his theory of blending (image of iron and fire at 218.1–2); ed. and ET Robert B. Todd (Leiden: Brill, 1976), 216.14–218.10 (= *SVF* 2.473).

can subject all to God, so that God, in turn, can be 'all in all'. It is, above all, this eschatological orientation, the end which enables us to discern properly what we know of the present and contemplate the beginning, that is adopted by Gregory, with the difference that he sees the point of tension between the two clauses of Gen. 1:27 ('God made the human, in accordance with the image of God he made it' and 'male and female he made them'), for as Gregory points out, the latter has no point of reference in its archetype, for in Christ there is not 'male and female' (Gal. 3:28). But both are equally concerned with transformation; indeed, Gregory concludes his treatise with the same verse repeatedly used by Origen, urging us 'to put off the old human with its practices and put on the new, which is being renewed in knowledge according to the image of the one who created it' (Col. 3:9–10).

Chapter 3
Gregory's Treatise, *On the Human Image of God*

Written between the death of his brother Basil (September 378) and Easter in the following year, Gregory's treatise *On the Human Image* was composed, so he tells us in his covering letter to Peter, to complete Basil's *Hexaemeron*. While Basil had made known 'the world established by God in true wisdom' to those who are led by his words to a true contemplation of its 'sublime adornment', he had not continued to 'the contemplation of the human being' (Ep. Pet. 1). However, Gregory does much more than supplement Basil's own treatment. In this work and in his own *Hexaemeron*, a companion piece written about same time,[1] Gregory provides a comprehensive cosmology and anthropology, drawing upon the traditions of classical philosophy and earlier theology that we have traced from Anaxagoras to Origen and also inspiring later writers such as Maximos the Confessor and John Scotus Eriugena.

But in *On the Human Image*, Gregory also addresses a specific problem. At the heart of the treatise, structurally and thematically, lies the question of how the human being is in the image of God: having given, in the first 15 chapters, a beautiful description of the human being, decked in virtue, as the high point of creation, Gregory then asks: where, in fact, do we see this? Scripture does not lie when it says that the human being came to be in accordance with the image of God, yet neither can the 'pitiable wretchedness of human nature be likened to the blessedness of the impassible life' (*De hom.* 16.4). Intriguingly, the same problematic surfaces again a couple of decades later in the 'anthropomorphite' controversy. Although the ecclesiastical historian Socrates describes the controversy as being caused by Theophilus of Alexandria's assertion, in his Paschal Address for 399, that the incorporeal God cannot be described in human form, there are indications that the real issue was the reverse.[2] According to the dialogue between Apa Aphou and Theophilus of Alexandria, it was the bishop's assertion that 'it is not the image of God which we humans bear' which prompted Apa Aphou to go

[1] According to Maraval, 'Chronology of Works', it should be placed in the early months of 379, after the *On the Human Image*.

[2] Cf. Socrates, *Historia ecclesiastica* 6.7. Ed. G. C. Hansen, with M. Širingan, GCS NF 1 (Berlin: Akademie Verlag, 1995); ET in NPNF 2.

to Alexandria to correct Theophilus.[3] When Aphou told him that 'this sentence is not correct; for my part, I confess that all humans have been created in the image of God', Theophilus replied incredulously: 'How could you say of an Ethiopian that he is the image of God, or of a leper or of a cripple or of a blind man?' And when Aphou countered to say otherwise would be to contradict the statement in Genesis, Theophilus argued: 'Not so! I believe that Adam alone was created in his likeness and his image, but that the children whom he begot after him do not resemble him', adding, 'I hesitate to say of a human being, subject to sickness and to tiredness, that he bears the image of the impassible and simple God.' Pointing to the eucharistic gifts, which are affirmed to be the body and blood of Christ, Aphou argued that 'just as it is necessary to believe this, so also it is necessary to believe the authority [that says] "the human being was created in the likeness and image of God"', and gave the further example of a king and his image, for although the portrait is nothing but wood and paint, everyone nevertheless pays it due respect. That Gregory's treatise deals with the same issues suggests that although the 390s was, as Elizabeth Clark memorably described it, 'the decade of the image', the roots of the problem began earlier.[4]

However, Gregory doesn't resolve this problematic by simply affirming that 'it is necessary to believe' that the human being is in the image of God, despite the evidence of our eyes. While acknowledging that 'only the very Truth knows the true answer to this question' Gregory seeks an account (*logos*) which enables both realities to be affirmed, describing how the human being is indeed the image of God but also the economy of God that leads, finally, to this reality.

As suggested in Chapter 1, on the basis of the headings in the manuscripts (of which only two, 16 and 30, are designated as a 'contemplation') Gregory's treatise is divided into three parts and as we intimated when examining Plato's *Timaeus* these divisions mirror the corresponding threefold account in that work.[5] Gregory begins, in Chapters 1–15, by presenting a beautiful picture of the human being as the apex of creation and more than that, the very image of God (as Timaeus had first given an account of 'what is crafted by intellect', *Tim.* 47e3).

[3] The Coptic text is edited with a French translation, by Étienne Drioton, 'La Discussion d'un moine anthropomorphite Audien avec le patriarche Théophile d'Alexandrie en l'année 399', *Revue de l'Orient Chrétien*, 2nd series 10 (=20) (1915–17), 92–100, 113–28. The ensuing discussion is on pp. 95–9. A partial English translation is given by Georges Florovsky, 'The Anthropomorphites in the Egyptian Desert', in idem, *Aspects of Church History*, Collected Works 4 (Belmont MA: Büchervertiebsanstalt, 1987), 89–96. For further discussion, see Paul A. Patterson, *Visions of Christ: The Anthropomorphite Controversy of 399 CE*, STAC 68 (Berlin: Mohr Siebeck, 2012).

[4] Elizabeth A. Clark, *The Origenist Controversy: The Cultural Construction of an Early Christian Debate* (Princeton, NJ: Princeton University Press, 1992), 55.

[5] That Chapter 16 begins a new section of the work has previously been noted; scant attention has been paid to Chapter 30. Cf. Gerhardt B. Ladner, 'The Philosophical Anthropology of St Gregory of Nyssa', DOP 12 (1958), 61–94, at 78, who holds that Chapter 27 begins a 'final section, which deals with the body-mind relationship in view of the resurrection of the bodies'. The structural comparison with the *Timaeus* has not, to my knowledge, previously been noted.

In Chapter 16, Gregory explicitly returns to the key scriptural text, Gen. 1:26–7, with the question: where do we in fact see this? His response is long and complex, involving changes of voice and detours, explaining the provision of God with respect to the waywardness of human beings (like Timaeus' account of 'the straying cause', *Tim.* 48a7), ensuring that the *pleroma*, the plenitude of the human being and human beings, the image of God, is attained at the end. Finally, in Chapter 30, Gregory gives a medical account of the formation of the human being in concrete terms, just as Timaeus had 'put a final head on our story' (*Tim.* 69b1) by bringing the two preceding accounts together. Because our concern is with the economy of the text—how the treatise as a whole works, how the different parts fit and work together, and to what end—it will be necessary to review the development of Gregory's argument in detail, only occasionally bringing in other texts of Gregory (his first homily on Ecclesiastes to expound further the relationship between the beginning and end touched upon in the Letter to Peter, and his *Hexaemeron* to illustrate his understanding of creation), reserving further comment and comparison to other texts, of both Gregory and others, to the concluding section of this chapter. And although we will see plenty of similarities with what we have found in the earlier writers we have examined, they will generally not be noted, nor will parallels with a further range of literature (which are given in the footnotes to the translation).

1. The Letter to Peter

In his cover letter to Peter, offering him this treatise as a paschal gift, Gregory promises to complete the work of Basil, 'who by his own contemplation made the sublime adornment of the universe accessible to many, making the world established by God in true wisdom known to those who are led, by means of his understanding, to contemplation' (Ep. Pet. 1), that is, he will now provide 'the contemplation of the human being' (Ep. Pet. 2). The scope of the proposed contemplation, he points out, is greater than anything else in creation, for the human being alone is made in the image of God (Ep. Pet. 3). Gregory then makes a couple of important points regarding how he understands his particular task. First, that he must examine everything pertaining to the human being, specifically: 'of what we believe to have taken place previously, of what we now contemplate, and of what we expect to transpire afterwards' (Ep. Pet. 3). This threefold categorization, with three different verbs, echoes what we saw in Origen: while we can contemplate that which presently is, what comes afterwards is expected, while that which took place previously is believed. The beginning, middle, and end, therefore, are not equally in view, subject to similar scrutiny, or placed on the same plane or horizon of investigation.

Gregory provides a further analysis on the relationship between the end, the beginning, and the middle, in the concluding paragraphs of his first homily on Ecclesiastes, written about the same time.[6] Here he is commenting on verses 1:9–11, beginning with: 'What is it that has come to be? The same as what shall be. And what is it that has been made? The same as shall be made'. To the rhetorical question 'Do you wish to know what it is that came to be?', Gregory replies: 'Think what it is that will be, and you will know what has been.'[7] He then continues more fully and clearly:

> 'Think, you human being', he says, 'what you will become by exalting yourself [σεαυτὸν ὑψώσας] through virtue. If you shape your soul in every respect with good characteristics ... what will you become as you beautify yourself in such ways? What loveliness will you put on? If you carefully consider this with your mind, you will have been taught what came to be in the first [things], which indeed will truly come to be [τὸ ἐν τοῖς πρώτοις γενόμενον, ὅ γε ἀληθῶς ἐστι γενησόμενον], that which is "in the image and likeness of God"'. (295.8–16)

It is by looking to the end, and becoming beautified by exaltation through virtue (ὑψώσας, with its unmistakable allusions back to Isa. 52:13 and John 3:14; 8:28; 12:34), that we come to know what came to be 'in the first [things]' and 'will truly come to be' in the future. Gregory continues by arguing that in using two different verbs—'what has come to be' and 'what is made'—the Ecclesiast indicates a distinction between them: 'the soul has come to be and the body has been made' (296.4–8). And this is done, moreover, so that we might understand 'what is advantageous in each case'. Specifically:

> The soul came to be in accordance with the *archē* [κατ' ἀρχὰς] the same as it will again appear hereafter, when it has been purified. The body moulded by the hands of God was made what the resurrection of the dead in due time will reveal it to be. For such as it is after the resurrection from the dead, just such it was made at the first [παρὰ τὴν πρώτην]. The resurrection of the dead is nothing but the complete restoration to the original [state] [εἰς τὸ ἀρχαῖον ἀποκατάστασις]. (296.12–18)

Gregory's theological outlook is thoroughly eschatological. By considering what we are called to be, exalting ourselves through virtue, we finally, 'truly', come to be in the image, that which was made in the *archē*.

[6] Maraval, 'Chronology of Works', places it *c*.379–80 CE.

[7] Ed. J. McDonough and P. Alexander GNO 5 (Leiden: Brill, 1986), 295.6–8: τί ἐστι τὸ γενόμενον; νόησον, τί ἐστι τὸ ἐσόμενον, καὶ ἐπιγνώσῃ ὃ γέγονε. ET Stuart G. Hall, in idem, ed., *Gregory of Nyssa, Homilies on Ecclesiastes* (Berlin: De Gruyter, 1993), 45–6, modified occasionally.

Returning to the Letter to Peter, Gregory concludes by giving a further note regarding how he sees his task:

> ...it is also proper to fit together, from scriptural guidance and from that discovered by reasoning, the things concerning the human being that seem to be opposed (as what is now seen pertaining to nature by a kind of necessary sequence is not the same as those that occurred from the beginning) so that our whole subject may be consistent with itself in train of thought and order, with things seemingly contrary being brought together to one and the same end, and with the divine power finding a hope for things beyond hope and a means of accomplishing things unworkable. (Ep. Pet. 3)

That which needs fitting together are not Scripture and reason, but rather, using both of these resources, to try to explain those things about the human being that seem to be opposed, that is, the scriptural affirmation that God created the human in his image and likeness, and what we presently and empirically see. Guided by both Scripture and reason, Gregory hopes to provide an account that brings both of these truths to one and the same end, so that what seems impossible is brought into reality.

2. The Human Image of God (1–15)

Gregory opens his treatise by quoting Gen. 2:4, 'This is the book of the genesis of heaven and earth', and devotes a few paragraphs to describing a very dynamic picture of the world. Everything that appears, he says, was completed and each separate being had withdrawn to its own place, the heaven above, encompassing all things, and the heavy bodies drawn downwards, with the earth and water taking middle place and holding each other back, 'while the divine art and power was implanted in the nature of things as a sort of bond and stability for the things that came to be, guiding the universe by a twofold activity, for by rest and motion it devised the genesis of the things that were not and the continuance of things that are', driving the celestial sphere in a circle, like a wheel around an axle, so that 'the circling substance by its rapid motion compresses the solid body of the earth in a circle' (*De hom.* 1.1). Moses' words that the heaven and earth were made 'in the beginning' thus indicate that they are 'a kind of beginning of the whole machine', 'so that all things appearing in the creation are the offspring of rest and motion, brought to genesis in accordance with the divine will' (*De hom.* 1.2). Moreover, things that come into being, lying between the opposites of heaven and earth, mediate between the two and so have a 'twofold quality'. Air imitates the perpetual motion and subtlety of the fiery substance, yet it is not alien to solid substance; it is 'a kind of borderland in the opposition between activities, in itself at once mixing and dividing things distinct by nature' (*De hom.* 1.2). The same also goes for liquid which, as heavy, is borne downwards, yet has a fluid and mobile activity, so that 'things most extremely opposite in nature combine with one another, being united by those mediating between them' (*De hom.* 1.3). Indeed, as Gregory puts it, he says more accurately, 'the very nature of contrary things is not entirely unmixed with the properties of the other, so that, I think, everything that appears in the world mutually converges and the creation, though found in properties of contrary things, coheres with itself' (*De hom.* 1.4). What we will shortly see in Gregory's understanding of the human being, as a combination of opposites, is thus writ large in the structure of the cosmos as a whole.

Gregory develops his cosmology at greater length in the *Hexaemeron* composed shortly after this treatise.[8] There, after arguing that matter is nothing other than properties combined together (*Hex.* 7; a point also elaborated in *De hom.* 24), Gregory notes that Aquila had translated the opening two words of Genesis as 'in summary' (ἐν κεφαλαίῳ), which, he says, has the same meaning as 'in the *archē*' but with a different nuance,

> since both equally indicate 'everything all at once' [τὸ ἀθρόον]; for in the word 'summary' there is the connotation of everything coming into being collectively, while instantaneity and absence of spacing [ἀδιάστατον] are evoked by the '*archē*'. For *archē* is alien from any idea of spacing; as a point is the *archē* of a line, and the atom [the *archē*] of mass, so is what is instantaneous [the *archē*] of temporal spacing. So the simultaneous foundation of beings [ἡ οὖν ἀθρόα τῶν ὄντων... καταβολή], through the indescribable power of God is called by Moses either '*archē*' or 'summary'; it is from that origin that everything is said to have been composed. (*Hex.* 8–9)

This being 'the *archē* of the cosmogony' [ἡ ἀρχὴ τῆς κοσμογονίας] implies, for Gregory, that God 'laid down [κατεβάλετο] the starting points and the causes and the potentialities of all things, collectively and instantaneously, and that in the initial impulse of his will the essence of each of the beings came together concurrently', that is, heaven, ether, stars, fire, air, sea, earth, animals, and plants (*Hex.* 9; he notably doesn't here mention the human being). Everything being seen by his power of foreknowledge, for 'he knows everything before it comes into being' (Sus. (*Θ*) 42), and with his power and wisdom as the foundation, 'a certain necessary order follows on, according to a certain sequence, with a view to bringing to completion each part of the world' (*Hex.* 9). Gregory returns to the idea of an instantaneous creation combined with the ordered sequence of their

[8] Ed. Hubertus R. Drobner, GNO 4.1 (Leiden: Brill, 2009); ET Robin Orton, FC Shorter Works 1 (Washington, DC: Catholic University of America Press, 2021), modified occasionally.

appearance later in the work, when discussing the lights created after the third day. He phrases the same point slightly differently this time:

> everything was constituted simultaneously, in the plenitude of creation, by God's initial will [παντὸς ἀθρόως τοῦ κατὰ τὴν κτίσιν πληρώματος ἐν τῷ πρώτῳ τοῦ θεοῦ θελήματι συστάντος], [and] the ordered series that necessarily arose, in consequence of the wisdom that is found within everything that exists, brought each of the elements into its manifestation [ἀνάδειξιν] as a consequence of the divine commands. Moses indicated the totality [τὸ πᾶν] when he summarized it in an inclusive expression referring to the first subsistence of the sense-perceptible creation [τῇ πρώτῃ τῆς αἰσθητικῆς κτίσεως ὑποστάσει], saying 'In the *archē* God created the heaven and the earth'. Saying, therefore, that God created the plenitude of beings [τὸ οὖν πλήρωμα τῶν ὄντων], he indicates in his account that the manifestation [ἀνάδειξιν] of each existing thing happened in a naturally ordered series. (*Hex.* 64)

This interplay between a simultaneous creation and its gradual manifestation, and also the idea of the former constituting a 'plenitude', are themes of great importance in *On the Human Image of God.*

Returning to the first chapter of *On the Human Image of God*, with the heaven and earth being 'finished' (Gen. 2:1), and all things having 'arrived at their end', Gregory rhapsodizes about the beauty of the world, but concludes by noting that 'there was no one to share it' (*De hom.* 1.5), for 'the human being had not yet occupied its place in the world of beings' (*De hom.* 2.1). The Maker having prepared the world as a royal lodging for a king, with all the preparations, 'presents [ἀναδείκνυσιν] the human being to the world', to behold the wonders in it and by his enjoyment know the Benefactor (*De hom.* 2.1). Alternatively, Gregory continues, the world is like a banquet prepared by a munificent host, into which God 'introduces [εἰσάγει] the human being' (*De hom.* 2.2). The verbs that Gregory uses here are striking, and important for what comes later: he does not speak here of the 'creation' or 'making' of the human being, but of the human as being 'presented', 'introduced', and 'occupying' its place, just as he had spoken in the *Hexaemeron* of the 'manifestation' of particular things in their proper order and sequence.

As 'the work' of the human being is 'not the acquisition of things absent but the enjoyment of things present', Gregory continues, God 'establishes for him a twofold point origin for his formation [διπλᾶς αὐτῷ τῆς κατασκευῆς τὰς ἀφορμὰς καταβάλλεται], blending the divine with the earthy, so that by means of both he may, congenitally and appropriately, have enjoyment of each, enjoying God by means of the more divine nature and the good things of the earth by the sense akin to them' (*De hom.* 2.2). In Chapter 3, Gregory further praises the dignity of the human being as the only act of creation preceded by divine counsel, and in that 'what he will be is foreshadowed by the Artist through the writing of the account [διὰ τῆς τοῦ λόγου γραφῆς], and what kind of being it is fitting he should be, and to what archetype he should bear a likeness, and for what purpose he shall come into being, and, having come to be, what activity, and what he shall rule'—all this is sketched out in Gen. 1:26, before the human comes into being (*De hom.* 3.1). Only in the case of the human being 'does the Maker drawn near with circumspection', preparing the material beforehand, likening his form to an archetypal beauty, and 'setting before him the goal for which he will come to be' (*De hom.* 3.2: προθέντα τὸν σκοπὸν οὗ χάριν γενήσεται). The human being is not simply made, but has a task set before him.

This goal, Gregory continues in the following two chapters, is the exercise of royalty, imaging the King of all. It is striking that for Gregory, while the human being is a 'vessel fit for the exercise of royalty', with the 'superior advantages' of having a self-governing soul, 'swayed autocratically by its own will', and a body whose 'very form' is 'adapted for royalty' (*De hom.* 4), the human is in the image not because of these, but through the exercise of virtue that they enable. The human being is to be 'a living image, sharing with the Archetype in both rank and name', clothed in virtue, instead of a purple raiment, leaning upon immortality instead of a sceptre, and adorned with the crown of righteousness instead of a royal diadem (*De hom.* 4). While the divine beauty does not reside in a particular shape or form, the Maker of all, as one painting a portrait, 'by the addition of virtues, as it were with colours, shows in us his own sovereignty... purity, freedom from passion, blessedness, estrangement from all evil... with such lustres did the Craftsman of his own image mark our nature' (*De hom.* 5.1). There are, indeed, certain other characteristics of divine beauty in which the image shares a likeness: for as 'the divinity is intellect and word' (νοῦς καὶ λόγος), so also we can see in ourselves 'word and mind' (τὸν λόγον καὶ τὴν διάνοιαν), an imitation (μίμημα) of the very Intellect and Word. Moreover, as 'God is love' (1 John 4:7, 8), if this is absent 'the whole stamp of the image is transformed' (*De hom.* 5.2). For Gregory it is emphatically in the free exercise of virtue that the human being manifests their existence as the image of God. Gregory concludes his discussion about the image by arguing that the fact that the human being is made as the image of God should not be taken, in reverse, to imply that the divine acts in a similar way to human beings, that is, through different faculties. Even in the case of humans, Gregory points out, this is misleading, for in fact 'there is one faculty, the implanted intellect itself, which passes through each of the organs of sense and grasps the beings beyond' (*De hom.* 6.1). Finally, he argues, that the human being is made in the image also disproves the 'Anomoean' teaching about the unlikeness of the different natures of Father and Son, for it is impossible for a single image to resemble two different archetypes.

In the following chapters, Gregory turns his attention to the form of the body, arguing that its very weakness renders the human being suitable for royal rule, but one which is exercised through the cooperation, rather than domination, of his subjects (*De hom.* 7), that its upright form, looking upwards to the heavens rather than down towards the ground, is a mark of royal dignity (*De hom.* 8.1), and that 'the ministry of the hands is a particular property of the rational nature' (*De hom.* 8.2). However, pulling himself up short, in terms which echo Timaeus (*Tim.* 34b10–35a1, where after discussing the body, Timaeus reminds himself that he should really treat the soul first), Gregory comments 'before discussing this point, however, let us consider the subject passed over, for the subject of the order of the things that came to be almost escaped us' (*De hom.* 8.3; the discussion about hands is deferred until *De hom.* 8.8). What catches his attention now is the sequence narrated by Moses: first the plants sprouting up from the earth, then the irrational animals, and only after that the human being. By this order, Gregory suggests, 'Moses reveals a certain doctrine about hidden things and secretly delivers the philosophy concerning the soul' which is 'that the vital and animating power is contemplated in three divisions': the first, simply the faculty of growth and nutrition, which is called 'the vegetative', for it is seen in plants; the second includes also, in addition to the faculty of growth and nutrition, the ability to regulate sense-perception, such as we find in irrational animals; while 'the perfect embodied life is seen in the rational, I mean the human, nature, which is both nourished and endowed with sense-perception and partakes of reason and is ordered by intellect' (*De hom.* 8.4). Thus Moses, having introduced inanimate matter, proceeds to speak of animate beings, beginning with plants, and then animals with sense-perception, and finally the human being, with 'nature advancing in a certain way sequentially to perfection'. In Gregory's estimation Paul does the same in his threefold distinction between body, soul, and spirit (*De hom.* 8.5; Thess. 5:23), or carnal, animated, and spiritual (*De hom.* 8.6; 1 Cor. 3:3, 2:14–15). Gregory's conclusion from all this is that 'reasonably, nature makes an ascent, as it were by steps, I mean the various properties of life, from the lower to the perfect' (*De hom.* 8.7). Having spoken about the development or evolution of the soul, Gregory then returns to the discussion about hands, pointing out that it is because humans have hands that their mouths can be fashioned for speaking words, as befits a 'rational animal', rather than for grazing grass or tearing meat (*De hom.* 8.8).

Gregory's emphasis on the body continues in the following chapters. Since God, he says,

> has bestowed upon our moulded figure [*τῷ πλάσματι ἡμῶν*] a certain godlike grace, by implanting in the image [*ἐνθεὶς τῇ εἰκόνι*] the likeness of his own good gifts, for this reason he gave, of his munificence, the other good gifts to human nature; yet it is not strictly right to say that he 'gave' [*δέδωκεν*] of intellect and practical wisdom [*νοῦ δὲ καὶ φρονήσεως*], but that he 'gave a share' [*μετέδωκε*] of them, adding to the image the proper adornment of his own nature [*τὸν ἴδιον αὐτοῦ τῆς φύσεως κόσμον ἐπιβαλὼν τῇ εἰκόνι*]. (*De hom.* 9.1)

It is striking that here, for Gregory, intellect and practical wisdom are not the locus of the image of God in the human being: it is 'that which is moulded' (the πλάσμα, an allusion to Gen. 2:7) that is the image. It is into this image that God implants the likeness of his own good gifts, which in turn merit the further gifts, or rather not a gift of but a share in intellect and reason, adding to the image the distinctive adornment of the divine nature itself. But even this inestimable share would remain ineffectual without the body, for as Gregory immediately continues: 'since the intellect is a thing intelligible and incorporeal, its grace would have been incommunicable and isolated, without its movement being made manifest by some contrivance', that is, this 'instrumental formation' that, like the vocal organs struck by a plectrum, indicates by the sound it produces 'the movement within' (*De hom.* 9.1). And so, 'since the intellect produces the music of reason by means of this instrumental construction within us, we have become rational [λογικοὶ γεγόναμεν]', which would not have happened had our mouths been shaped in such a way as to supply the needs of the body rather than being 'well-adapted for the service of reason' (*De hom.* 10.1). It is, then, the body in its very structure, and its weakness, that enables human beings to 'become rational', manifesting the divine gifts in which they share, a point which is picked up dramatically at the end of the treatise.

The activity of this bodily instrument is also 'twofold', allowing the intellect to express itself and communicate its movements, but also allowing for all the impressions which flow in to the 'inner receptacle' through the senses, as entrances into a city, while the intellect 'distinguishing and examining each of the things that enters, stores them in their proper departments of knowledge' (*De hom.* 10.3–4). In its own nature, the intellect must, therefore be something other than the senses (*De hom.* 11.1), but is itself incomprehensible: '"Who has known the intellect of the Lord?" asks the apostle; and I ask further, who has understood his own intellect?' (*De hom.* 11.2). But this should not be surprising, he adds, for made in the image of God, it lacks nothing that is perceived in the archetype, so that if one of the aspects perceived in the divine nature is incomprehensibility, this too will be found in the image (*De hom.* 11.3–4).

Gregory returns to the subject of the soul, especially the rational soul, in chapters 14–15. But before that he sets out on a long discussion about the location of the intellect, whether it should be thought of as residing in a particular part of the body, such as the heart or the brain. His examination of the matter leads him to consider those occasions where 'the calculating faculty is blunted in its natural activity by some bodily accident' (*De hom.* 12.3), or when the membranes around the side are diseased, so producing 'frenzy' (*De hom.* 12.4), or, less dramatically, in moments of 'gladness and laughter', where parts of the body are relaxed, producing involuntary movements (*De hom.* 12.5), or, later on, what happens in sleep, yawning, and the phenomenon of dreams (*De hom.* 13). Placed discretely within this extensive excursus (note *De hom.* 14.1: 'we have wandered far from our subject'), Gregory introduces a discordant element into this first part of his treatise, which has otherwise been devoted to a wholly positive description of the human being. His conclusion regarding the placement of the intellect is that it is not spatially located in one part of the body, but rather that the intellect 'passing throughout the instrument and touching each of the parts in a manner appropriate to its intellectual activities, according to its nature', effects its proper movement on such parts. In those parts, on the other hand, 'too weak to accept the movement of its art it remains ineffective and inactive', for as he concludes, 'the intellect is naturally somehow familiar with that which is disposed according to nature, but to be alien from that which is removed from it' (*De hom.* 12.8). This train of reflection leads Gregory to speak a little about 'the more refined teachings' to be learnt from this (*De hom.* 12.9). They are:

> Since the most beautiful and supreme good of all is the divinity itself, to which incline all things that have the desire [ἔφεσιν] for the beautiful, we therefore say that the intellect, as being in accordance with the image of the most beautiful, as long as it partakes so far as possible in its likeness to the archetype also remains in the beautiful; but if it were in some way to be outside this, it will be stripped bare of the beauty in which it was. And just as we said that the intellect was adorned by the likeness of the archetypal beauty, being formed, as though it were a mirror, by the figure of that which appears in it, so we consider that the nature administered by the intellect possesses something of the intellect in the same proportion and that it is adorned by the beauty issuing from the intellect, such that it becomes, as it were, a mirror of a mirror; by it, the material element of existence, in which nature is contemplated [τὸ ὑλικὸν τῆς ὑποστάσεως, περὶ ἣν θεωρεῖται ἡ φύσις], is ruled and sustained. (*De hom.* 12.9)

If this order is preserved, he continues, 'the communication [κοινωνία] of the true beauty extends proportionally [ἀναλόγως] through the whole series, beautifying by the superior that which comes next', but if there is 'an interruption [διασπασμός] of this beneficial connection', or when the superior element follows the inferior, 'then the unseemliness [τὸ ἄσχημον] of matter itself is exposed, when it is isolated from nature (for in itself matter is something formless and unwrought [ἄμορφον...ἀκατάσκευον]), and by its formlessness is also destroyed the beauty of the nature which was beautified by the intellect; and in this way the transmission of the ugliness of matter reaches back through the nature to the intellect itself, so that the image of God is no longer beheld in the figure of that which was moulded' (*De hom.* 12.10: ἐν τῷ χαρακτῆρι καθορᾶσθαι τοῦ πλάσματος). Instead, turning its back on 'the lustrous rays of the good', the intellect receives into itself 'the shapelessness of matter' (*De hom.* 12.10). This is, for Gregory, 'the genesis of evil', occurring through 'the withdrawal of the good': the intellect, as 'having come to be in accordance with the image of the good', is able itself to be good, and, as long as it does so, 'the nature sustained by the intellect is like an image of the image', with the material part holding together and regulated by nature; but this will be dissolved and fall apart if it were no longer to be sustained by the intellect, and so be 'severed from its connection to the good' (*De hom.* 12.11). This does not happen, Gregory adds, 'except when an overturning [ἐπιστροφή] of nature to the opposite state occurs, in which desire [ἐπιθυμία] does not incline towards the good but towards that which is in need of being beautified; for it is absolutely necessary that that being made like to matter, which is destitute of its own form, it should be conformed to it in respect of its unseemliness and absence of beauty' (*De hom.* 12.12). This account of 'the genesis of evil', however, was only given, Gregory immediately adds, because he was 'following a certain line of argument, since they were introduced by our contemplation of the point before us; for the subject of enquiry was whether the intellectual faculty has its seat in any of the parts within us or extends equally over them all' (*De hom.* 12.13).

After exploring further, as already noted, the subject of sleep, yawning and dreams (*De hom.* 13), observing that 'we have wandered far from our subject', he returns to the point that the intellect should not be thought of as residing in a particular part of the body, 'but is equally in touch with the whole, producing its movement according to the nature of the part under its influence' (*De hom.* 14.1). Recalling that his exposition had discerned 'three different forms regarding the vital faculty'—that is 'the vegetative', the 'sense-perceptive', and 'third, the rational and perfect, pervading the whole faculty'—he emphasizes that these should not be thought of as 'three souls welded together': 'the true and perfect soul is one by nature, the intellectual and immaterial, which mingles with the material nature through the senses' (*De hom.* 14.2). It is only, he adds, by 'a misuse of language' that, while 'the soul has its perfection in that which is intellectual and rational, everything that is not so may indeed have the homonym of "soul", yet is not really soul but a certain vital energy associated with the appellation of "soul"' (*De hom.* 15.1–2). But again, he notes, 'the course of our argument has diverged to another point', his concern being to emphasize that 'the intellect is not confined to any one part of us, but is equally in all and through all' (*De hom.* 15.3). Of the connection between the material and immaterial, Gregory comments:

> The communion of the intelligible with the bodily is a conjunction unspeakable and inconceivable, neither being within it (for the incorporeal is not enclosed in a body) nor yet surrounding it from outside (for things incorporeal do not surround [something else]), but the intellect, approaching our nature in some inexplicable and incomprehensible way and coming to touch it, is to be thought of as both in it and around it, neither seated in it nor enfolded within it, but in a way which we cannot speak or think. (*De hom.* 15.3)

All we can say, he concludes, is that while nature is in proper order, the intellect is active; if any misfortune (πλημμέλημα) comes upon it, then the movement of thought falters accordingly.

In these first 15 chapters, Gregory has presented us with a wholly positive picture of the human being as the image of God, the culmination of, and reason for, creation, whose body is adapted in its very structure for the exercise (through weakness) of kingly sovereignty, fashioned in such a way as to enable this animal to become rational, sharing in the intellect and reason that adorns the divine nature itself, and so to be the living image, decked out in virtue. But of whom is Gregory speaking? It is notable that Gregory does not speak in the way that Philo and Origen do, in their own ways, of the 'intelligible' or 'inner' human, contrasted with the bodily or outward one (though, as we have seen, in their case they are also speaking of the single human being in two aspects). Nor has he been speaking about the 'prelapsarian' Adam (for despite allusions to Gen. 2:7, Adam has not been mentioned), and his analysis of 'the genesis of evil'—in the midst of a detour and thoroughly and discretely padded within an extensive discussion about bodily phenomena, all of which was aimed to show that the intellect pervades the human being throughout—is not straightforwardly the narration of an event called 'the Fall'. Given that he has spoken about 'the goal' for which the human being was to come into existence (*De hom.* 4), and that it is in the exercise of virtue that the human being becomes a 'living image', is he in this first part speaking of the eschatological reality that will come to be at the end (and as such, as he put it in his first homily on Ecclesiastes, is that which was made in the *archē*)? Or perhaps he is talking about Christ? His language at the end of *De hom.* 15 about how the incorporeal interacts with the body—pervading the body but not being contained by it, united to it through an 'unspeakable and inconceivable conjunction', not confined to any one part but 'equally in all and through all'—might be taken to intimate this. To go further, we must turn to the next section.

3. The Prevision and Provision of God (16–29)

Gregory begins the second part of his treatise, designated as 'a contemplation', by saying: 'Let us now take up again [ἐπαναλάβωμεν πάλιν] the divine saying, "Let us make the human being in accordance with our image and likeness"' (*De hom.* 16.1). What follows is not a mere resumption of a continuous analysis. Rather Gregory now turns to the central problematic of his treatise. The dignity of the human being is not, as some say, in being 'a little cosmos' made of the same elements as the universe, for so too are gnats and mice; rather, 'according to the ecclesiastical teaching', the dignity is shown in the human being coming to be 'in accordance with the image' of God (*De hom.* 16.2). However, what is 'the definition of the image', and how can the incorporeal be likened to the body, the temporal to the eternal, that which grows up with evil with that which is unmixed with evil (*De hom.* 16.3)? 'How, then, is the human being, this mortal being, subject to passions and short-lived, an image of that undefiled and pure and everlasting nature?' (*De hom.* 16.4). While only 'the very Truth clearly knows the true account regarding this', Gregory nevertheless ventures to explain what 'we, so far as we are able, tracking down the truth by guesses and suspicions, apprehend' regarding these things (*De hom.* 16.4). To do so, he must navigate his way between an apparent contradiction, both elements of which must be maintained: that the divine word doesn't lie in saying that the human being came to be in accordance with the image of God, and yet that one cannot liken 'the pitiable wretchedness of human nature' to 'the blessedness of the impassible life'. Nevertheless, an account must be given to hold these two truths together, and so, as he put it in the Epistle to Peter, bring things that seem contradictory 'to one and the same end'.

So, Scripture must be 'taken up again'. In so doing, Gregory focuses not on the difference between the two creation accounts, that made in the image (Gen. 1:26–7) and that moulded from earth (Gen. 2:7), as did Philo and Origen in their own ways, but on a tension between the clauses of Gen. 1:27: '[a] And God made the human, [b] according to the image of God he made it, [c] male and female made he them'. These clauses, he says, 'must be examined with precision', and so his analysis must also be given in full and examined precisely:

> [16.7] For we find that what came to be [*γενόμενον*] 'in accordance with the image' is one [*ἕτερον μέν*], and what is now manifest in wretchedness is another [*ἕτερον δὲ*]. 'God made [*ἐποίησεν*]', it says, 'the human being, in accordance with the image of God he made it'. The creation of that which came to be 'in accordance with the image' has an end [*τέλος ἔχει ἡ τοῦ κατ' εἰκόνα γεγενημένου κτίσις*]; then it makes a repetition [*ἐπανάληψιν*] of the account regarding the formation [*τοῦ κατὰ τὴν κατασκευὴν λόγου*], and says, 'male and female he made them'. I think it is known to everyone that this is understood to be outside the Prototype, 'for in Christ Jesus', as the apostle says, 'there is neither male nor female' [Gal. 3:28], but the account [*ὁ λόγος*] says that the human being is indeed divided [*διῃρῆσθαι*] into these. Therefore, the formation of our nature is in a sense twofold [*Οὐκοῦν διπλῆ τίς ἐστιν ἡ τῆς φύσεως ἡμῶν κατασκευὴ*], that being likened to the divine [*ἥτε πρὸς τὸ θεῖον ὡμοιωμένη*], [and] that being divided according to this difference [*ἥτε πρὸς τὴν διαφορὰν ταύτην διῃρημένη*]; for something like this the account hints at by the syntax of what is written, first saying, 'God made the human being, in accordance with the image of God he made it', and then, adding to what has been said, 'male and female made he them', something that is foreign to what is conceived about God. (*De hom.* 16.7–8)

In each clause of Gen. 1:27, the word used for God's action is the same: he 'made' (*ἐποίησεν*). What it is that is 'made' in these causes, however, is expounded by

Gregory with different words.[9] With Gen. 1:27ab, Gregory uses the word 'creation' (*κτίσις*) for 'that which has come to be [*τοῦ... γεγενημένου*] in accordance with the image'. He does not say that this 'creation' has 'come to an end', but rather 'has an end', that is, it has an end in view, a goal or final cause, which is, as he puts it in the next sentence, its Prototype, that is, Christ Jesus. It is very important to register this point: it is Christ who is the Prototype, not Adam, who in fact has not yet been mentioned, either by Scripture or by Gregory (until *De hom.* 16.16 and 22.3, in both cases specifying that he is not talking about Adam). Gregory then takes v. 27c as being an '*ἐπανάληψις* of the account of the *κατασκευή*': both words used here need to be carefully considered. The word *ἐπανάληψις* can mean either a 'resumption' or a 'repetition', while the word *κατασκευή*, as noted in Chapter 1, can mean 'construction' in the sense of 'fitting-out' or 'preparing', but also in the sense of 'state, condition, constitution' (cf. LSJ s.v.). The result of God's 'making' in v. 27c is, in Gregory's words, the 'division' of the human being into male and female. Finally, the conclusion he draws from all this is that 'the *κατασκευή* of our nature is in a sense twofold', that 'being likened to the divine' and that divided into male and female. Gregory continues in the next sentence (*De hom.* 16.9, cited below) by reiterating this twofold aspect of the human being, as the 'span', sharing in both the divine, by its intellect, and in the irrational, by its bodily construction, which in turn is divided into male and female. As such, it would seem that we should take the word *κατασκευή*, 'formation', in the sense of 'constitution', so that it is the structure of human nature that is 'twofold' (the rational and intellectual, and the irrational and corporeal), rather than God's act of 'making', played out in two distinct stages.[10] As we saw in Gregory's *Hexaemeron*, and as we will see again with regard to the human plenitude discussed shortly, God's act of making is instantaneous, encompassing all that is to be, while what comes into being is 'manifested' (*Hex.* 64), and the human being 'presented' and 'introduced' (*De hom.* 2), in proper order, a sequence moreover, in which, according to Moses'

[9] Wilson translated all these words simply as 'create' or 'creation': '"God created man..." There is an end of the creation of that which was made in the image; then it makes a resumption of the account of creation...'

[10] Cf. Eugenio Corsini, 'Plérôme humain et plérôme cosmique chez Grégoire de Nysse', in Marguerite Harl, ed., *Écriture et culture philosophique dans la pensée de Grégoire de Nysse: Actes du Colloque de Chevetogne (22–26 Septembre 1969)* (Leiden: Brill, 1971), 111–26, at 115: 'Il ne dit nullement qu'il y a eu deux créations pour les deux aspects: il dit tout simplement qu'il y a deux expressions de l'Écriture pour indiquer que l'acte créateur de Dieu s'est porté sur deux aspects différents de l'homme. Grégoire ne dit pas, non plus, que l'homme «à l'image» n'avait pas de sexe: il veut dire que dans l'archétype (Dieu) il n'y a pas de sexe et que le sexe est, en conséquence, exclu du *κατ' εἰκόνα*.' For a valiant attempt to argue that the *διπλῆ κατασκευή* denotes a 'two stage creation' in *De hom.* 16, see Johannes Zachhuber, *Human Nature in Gregory: Philosophical Background and Theological Significance* (Leiden: Brill, 2014), 166–74, yet this leads him to conclude that 'there ultimately remains a grave tension between this theory and the role of man as a mediator between the sensible and the intelligible envisaged in the earlier parts of his writing... the rudimentary nature of Gregory's Origenism itself is responsible for a number of severe inconsistencies' (166), and that therefore 'Gregory here effectively undermines his own previous argument' (171).

'philosophy of the soul', 'nature makes an ascent' from the lower to the perfect (*De hom.* 8.4–7).

This, in turn, would suggest that ἐπανάληψις has the force of 'repetition' not 'resumption': rather than continuing to a second stage of a two-step account of creation, Gen. 1:27c repeats the account of God's single act of making, but now under a different aspect, one that includes human existence as male and female. There would then be a parallel between these two clauses of Genesis (1:27ab and 1:27c), on the one hand, and, on the other, the first 15 chapters and what follows: this part of the treatise presents a 'repetition' of the 'construction' of the human being but under a different aspect or from a different perspective; indeed, it really only now becomes apparent that he had said nothing about male and female when describing the human being in the first part of the treatise. Finally, as such, this second part of Gregory's treatise corresponds to the second part of Timaeus' speech, when, realizing that he has so far given an account of 'what was crafted by Intellect', he notes that he must start again, for 'if one is to speak of how it really came to be [γέγονεν . . . ὄντως] one would have to introduce the character of the Straying Cause' (cf. *Tim.* 47e3–48b3)—which is precisely what Gregory does in what follows.

Concluding this examination of the verse of Scripture, Gregory sets out unambiguously what its teaching is:

> I think that by these words, Holy Scripture conveys to us a certain great and lofty doctrine [δόγμα]; and the doctrine is this. While two [elements]—the divine and incorporeal nature [φύσεως], and the irrational and animal life [ζωῆς]—are separated from each other as extremes, humankind is the span [μέσον]. For there is to be beheld in the human compound a share of each of those mentioned—of the divine, the rational and intelligent, which does not admit the distinction of male and female; of the irrational, the bodily formation and construction, divided into male and female—for each of them is certainly in all that partakes of human life [ζωῆς]. But the intellectual takes precedence [προτερεύειν], as we have learnt from one who gives in detail an ordered account of the origin of the human being [ἀνθρωπογονίαν]; participation and kinship with the irrational is concomitant to being human [ἐπιγεννηματικὴν δὲ εἶναι τῷ ἀνθρώπῳ], for he first says that 'God made the human being in accordance with the image' of God, showing by what was said, just as the Apostle says, that in such a being 'there is no male and female', then he adds the particularities of human nature [τῆς ἀνθρωπίνης φύσεως τὰ ἰδιώματα], that 'male and female he made them'. (*De hom.* 16.9)

The explicit teaching of Scripture, for Gregory, is that the human being is the 'span' between the divine nature and animal life, participating in both. The 'precedence' or 'priority' of the intellectual over the irrational, bodily, and sexed, in the twofold human formation or construction is not, however, chronological (as would be implied by a two-step creation); indeed, as we have already seen, he regards Moses' 'philosophy of the soul' in terms of an advance in the other direction, from the nutritive to the sense-perceptive to, lastly, the intellectual (*De hom.* 8.4–7), a pattern we will see again in medical terms at the end of his treatise. The 'precedence' is certainly an ontological priority: it is this that distinguishes the human being from the irrational animals and so it should take the lead; the overturning of this order, indeed, results in the 'genesis of evil' (*De hom.* 12.11). But in this passage, the priority primarily pertains to the literary order, for, as Gregory explains, it is spoken of first in Moses' 'anthropogony': it is written first, but it only comes into actual existence at the end.

This being stated first, what then follows, human existence as male and female, is ἐπιγεννηματικήν. Wilson, following Dionysius Exiguus' Latin translation, rendered this word as 'a provision for reproduction'.[11] The word in fact means 'of the nature of an ἐπιγέννημα, resulting, consequential', it is that which comes upon something else, something that is concomitant to something else; it does not define what it is to be, in this case, a human being, but is, nevertheless, as Gregory puts it at the end of the sentence, the 'particularities of human nature'.[12] The verbal form of the word is used by Gregory in *De hom.* 17.4 and 30.33, and in the latter, as we will see, the subject is again Moses' 'anthropogony'. There is no explicit purpose assigned here, where Gregory presents the teaching of Scripture, to human existence as male and female; in distinction to God, they are simply 'the particularities of human nature', part of the bodily construction and formation, and are found in everything that partakes of human life.

Turning next to what we can learn from this, Gregory emphasizes that God, being good or beyond any good we can understand, created the human being for no other reason than his own goodness, and bestowed upon human beings all possible goods, which is summed up in the assertion that the human being is made 'according to the image' of God, so that there is in the human being 'a form of every beauty, all virtue and wisdom', and especially the 'self-determining deliberation' without which there would be no virtue (*De hom.* 16.10–11). But there must also be a difference between the archetype and the image, Gregory notes, for otherwise they would be the same. Strikingly, however, given what he has just said

[11] Dionysius rendered the sentence thus: 'But from one who speaks about the very order of creation we have learnt that what is intellectual in us takes precedence before that which we see serves for the propagation of the human race [taking ἀνθρωπογονία as a reference to sexual reproduction], for in fact there is some kind of innate conjunction of the human with irrational things for the accomplishing of generation'. Eriugena, on the other hand, translated the word ἐπιγεννηματικὴν as 'supergenituam'.

[12] Cf. LSJ s.v. In philosophy, the terms seems to have been a Stoic term, for whom joy, cheerfulness, and the like are 'by-products' of virtue (*SVF* 3.19.29); according to Cicero, 'In the other arts, when we speak of an "artistic" performance, this quality must be considered as in a sense subsequent to and a result of the action, it is what the Stoics call ἐπιγεννηματικόν'. *On Ends* (*Fin.*) 3.9.32; ed. and ET H. Rackham, LCL 40, Cicero 17 (Cambridge, MA: Harvard University Press, 1914).

about the distinctive property of human nature, Gregory does not point to human existence as male and female as the locus of this difference, but rather to the fact that, as created, the human being cannot exist without change, 'for its very passage from non-being into being is a kind of movement and alteration of the non-existent being changed by the divine purpose into being' (*De hom.* 16.12). As such, while the attributes bestowed by God upon the human being are indeed his own, the difference between the two is found in the substratum seen in the uncreated and created (*De hom.* 16.13).

It is on this basis that Gregory can now respond to the predicament he posed at the beginning of the chapter, and he does so by appealing to the wavering, mutable will of human beings (the equivalent of Timaeus' 'straying cause'), foreseen by God in his prevision of and provision for the waywardness of the human will. According to Gregory:

> Since, then, as the one always remains as it is, while the other, having come into being though creation, began to exist from alteration and has kinship with such change, on this account 'he who knows all things before their genesis', as the prophecy says [Sus. (*Θ*) 42], following, or rather knowing beforehand, by his faculty of foreknowledge towards what the movement of human choice inclines, in accordance with its independence and self-determination—since he knows what is to be, he devised for the image the difference of male and female, which no longer looks to the divine archetype but, as was said, assimilates [προσῳκείωται] to the less rational nature. (*De hom.* 16.14)

What is striking about this paragraph is that it is not only a response to the problem of why we don't (immediately) see the image of God in human beings, but that it is phrased as an aetiological account for what he has just established as the scriptural teaching regarding the human as a twofold being, intellectual and corporeal, with the particularities of being male and female. That is, if the purpose of God is to make a human being in accordance with his image (Gen. 1:26), and in the Prototype there 'is not male and female' (Gal. 3:28), why and for what purpose did God *also* make the human being 'male and female'? That God has done so, and that the human being is such, is not in question: the issue is why? And his answer here is that this assimilation to the less rational is a provision made in anticipation of the divinely foreseen waywardness of the human will.

However, this is immediately followed by Gregory registering a change in his mode of his discourse:

> The reason [τὴν αἰτίαν] for such a device only those who were 'eyewitnesses' of the truth 'and ministers of the Word' [Luke 1:2] can know; but we, as far as is possible, by means of some guesses and images picturing the truth [εἰκόνων φαντασθέντες τὴν ἀλήθειαν], do not set forth categorically what comes to mind,

> but add it in a form of an exercise [ἐν γυμνασίας εἴδει] for our well-disposed hearers. (*De hom.* 16.15)

This is strong language indeed, contrasting greatly with the categorical 'great and lofty doctrine' given by Scripture a few paragraphs earlier. The 'exercise' that he offers, moreover, is not simply his best conjecture at that which cannot ultimately be known except by those who were eyewitnesses, for it is combined with the assertion that he is *not* going to say directly what comes to mind, but instead offer images that 'picture the truth'.[13] Gregory offers two further aetiological accounts of the relationship between God's prevision and human existence as male and female (*De hom.* 17.4–5 and 22); it is only in the latter where he finally states 'what comes to our mind' (*De hom.* 22.3). The sequence of Gregory's argument over these chapters is, moreover, convoluted, with apparent detours tackling a range of topics (in the same way that when Timaeus' treats what is only a 'likely story' his account tends to be 'casual and random'; cf. *Tim.* 34c2–4), before he is prepared to state his position.

Gregory begins by observing that the statement 'God made the human being' does not in fact refer to Adam; he is introduced later in the narrative (*De hom.* 16.16). Rather 'the indefinite character of the term' indicates, for Gregory, that the text is not speaking of the particular but the universal, and so 'we are led by the universal name of the nature to suppose something such as this, that by divine foreknowledge and power all humanity is included in the first formation' (*De hom.* 16.16: πᾶσα ἡ ἀνθρωπότης ἐν τῇ πρώτῃ κατασκευῇ περιείληται). But, as God does not make anything indeterminate, each being made by him must have 'some limit and measure' prescribed by the wisdom of God. And so, 'the entire plenitude of humanity [ὅλον τὸ τῆς ἀνθρωπότητος πλήρωμα] was included by the God of all, by his power of foreknowledge, as in one body', and this, in turn, means that 'the image is not in part of our nature', but rather 'extends equally to the whole genus', as is shown by the fact that 'the intellect is seated alike in all' (*De hom.* 16.16–17), that is, in both males and females alike, and in each and all. He then concludes this

[13] Cf. Gregory of Nyssa, *De Anima et resurrectione* (*An. et res.*), 3.36, where the subject is similarly the question of the status of the 'concomitants' (translated by Silvas as 'accretions'): 'All these we reckon as accretions from without, because no such characteristics are to be found in the beauty of the archetype. In the meantime, let the following argument of these matters be offered as a kind of training exercise (ὁ δὲ δὴ περὶ τούτων λόγος ἡμῖν τέως ὡς ἐν γυμνασίῳ προκείσθω), to avoid the sneers of contentious hearers. The Word tells us that the divine proceeded by a certain gradual and orderly sequence to the creation of man.' Ed. Andreas Spira, GNO 3.3 (Leiden: Brill, 2014), 40; ET in Anna M. Silvas, *Macrina the Younger: Philosopher of God*, Medieval Women: Texts and Contexts, 22 (Turnhout: Brepols, 2008). The Greek text is not divided into chapters and paragraphs; these are supplied by Silvas. See also *Hex.* 9 and *De Tridui Spatio*, ed. E. Gebhardt, GNO 9 (Leiden: Brill, 1967), 286.15–16; ET Stuart Hall, in Andreas Spira and Christoph Klock, *The Easter Sermons of Gregory of Nyssa: Translation and Commentary: Proceedings of the Fourth International Colloquium on Gregory of Nyssa, Cambridge, England: 11–15 September, 1978*, Patristic Monograph Series, 9 (Cambridge, MA: Philadelphia Patristic Foundation, 1981), 31–50, at 38.

reflection on the pleromatic character of the human being created in the image this way:

> The human being manifested together with the first formation of the world [ὅ τε τῇ πρώτῃ τοῦ κόσμου κατασκευῇ συναναδειχθεὶς ἄνθρωπος], and he who shall come to be after consummation of all [ὁ μετὰ τὴν τοῦ παντὸς συντέλειαν γενησόμενος], both likewise have this: they equally bear in themselves the divine image. For this reason the whole was called one human being, because to the power of God nothing has either passed or is to come, but even that which is looked for is held fast equally with the present by his all-embracing activity. The whole nature [πᾶσα ἡ φύσις], then, extending from the first [πρώτων] to the last [ἐσχάτων], is a kind of single image of He Who Is. But the difference between male and female was additionally fashioned for the creature last, I suppose, for this reason. (*De hom.* 16.17–18)

This very strong understanding of the unity of all human beings—past, present, and future—as one human being is, again, an expression of God's instantaneous and comprehensive act of making which unfolds through its own sequence and order. Embracing all that would come to be, the human being 'manifested' at the beginning, and the one who 'comes to be after the consummation of all', bear the divine image. Here now we see the significance of the fact that to this point Gregory has *not* been speaking of Adam, the first particular human being in the Genesis narrative, but only appearing in its second chapter: to apply a point we noted when discussing Origen, Adam might be the first, but he is not the *archē*.[14] The image of God in accordance with whom God makes the human being in Gen. 1:27 is, as we saw in *De hom.* 16.7, Christ Jesus, the 'Prototype'. Yet so too is the one who 'comes to be' at the end, but then, 'after the consummation of all', in 'the entire plenitude of humanity' foreseen by God from or in the beginning, the *archē*. Or, as von Balthasar more elegantly put it: 'The total Christ is none other than the total humanity'.[15]

Although Gregory says that he will next turn to the reason for creatures also being fashioned as male and female, he in fact defers that discussion, turning first to another matter, that is the argument of his 'opponents' who teach that as there

[14] Zachhuber (*Human Nature*, 35–40, 128–44) makes a strong case that Gregory's understanding of the 'plenitude' of humanity derives ultimately from the idea of a 'derivative genus' ('a class of things that share their derivation from the same being, which is thus both the first element of the class and of the genus itself', p. 37), developed by Apollinarius, with the important difference that (p. 161) 'Their chief divergence appears to consist in the fact that with Apollinarius the principle (ἀρχή) of humanity is identical with the first human individual, whereas with Gregory it is not. Thus, Apollinarius would see Adam as both the *archē* and the first individual person, while for Gregory the *archē* is as distinct from Adam as from all other men.'

[15] Hans Urs von Balthasar, *Presence and Thought: An Essay on the Religious Philosophy of Gregory of Nyssa*, trans. Mark Sebanc (San Francisco, CA: Ignatius Press, 1995 [1944]), 87.

is no account of procreation before the sin, marriage did not exist in paradise, and so humanity would not have come to plurality if the grace of immortality had not fallen away and the fear of death impelled the first-formed to provide succession of the race (*De hom.* 17.1). Gregory, again accepting that 'the true account' is only known to those like Paul who had been initiated into the mysteries of Paradise, responds by citing the word of Christ to the Sadducees, that in the resurrection there will be no more 'marrying and giving in marriage... for they are like the angels' (Luke 20:35–6), arguing that 'if the life [ζωή] of those restored is akin to that of the angels, it is clear that the mode of life [βίος] before the transgression was something angelic, and hence our ascent to the primordial condition of life [ἡ πρὸς τὸ ἀρχαῖον τῆς ζωῆς ἡμῶν ἐπάνοδος] is likened to the angels' (*De hom.* 17.2). Gregory seems to be playing here, as we will see more clearly later, between two different words for 'life': ζωή, that which characterizes the nature of something (as for instance it seems to do in *De hom.* 16.9, cited above) and βίος, which has more the sense of 'mode of life'. This would suggest that, at least in this rhetorical argument, before the transgression humans lived a human life in an angelic manner, and ascending to this ancient condition it will be such again. And so, Gregory argues, as the angels clearly exist in multitudes, 'if there had not come upon us as a result of sin a turning away and a displacement from equality of honour with the angels, neither should we have needed marriage for multiplying, but whatever the mode of increase [τοῦ πλεονασμοῦ τρόπος] is in the nature of the angels (unspeakable and inconceivable by human guesses, except that it assuredly exists), it would have operated also in the case of human beings, "made a little lower than the angels", increasing humankind to the measure determined by the will of the Maker' (*De hom.* 17.2; Ps. 8:6).

'Having cleared up these matters', at least as far as it serves his purpose, Gregory then offers his second aetiological account of God's prevision and provision as it pertains to human existence as male and female:

> He who brought all things into being, and modelled the human being as a whole by his own will into the divine image, did not wait to see the number of souls made complete in its proper plenitude by the gradual addition of those subsequently coming to be, but considering the human nature as a whole, in its plenitude, by the activity of foreknowledge, and honouring it with an allocation exalted and equal to the angels, since he foresaw by his visionary power the [human] will not keeping a straight course towards the good and, because of this, falling away from the angelic life [ζωή], in order that the multitude of human souls should not be cut short, by falling from that mode [τοῦ τρόπου] by which the angels increased to a multitude, for this reason he formed in our nature that device for increase [τῆς αὐξήσεως ἐπίνοιαν ἐγκατασκευάζει τῇ φύσει] appropriate to those who had slipped into sin, implanting in humanity, instead of the angelic nobility, the animal and irrational mode of succession from one another. Hence

> also, it seems to me, the great David, lamenting the misery of the human being, mourns over his nature with such words as these, that, 'the human being in honour knew it not' (meaning by 'honour' the equality of honour with the angels), [and] therefore, he says, 'he was compared to senseless beasts, and made like them' [Ps. 48:13]. For the one who received in his nature this genesis subject to flux on account of his inclination to things material truly became like a beast [ὄντως γὰρ κτηνώδης ἐγένετο ὁ τὴν ῥοώδη ταύτην γένεσιν τῇ φύσει παραδεξάμενος διὰ τὴν πρὸς τὸ ὑλῶδες ῥοπήν]. (*De hom.* 17.4–5)

The brief aetiology given in *De hom.* 16.14, which made no connection between existence as male and female and procreation (human or angelic), is now further developed, but has also become somewhat circular: God, foreseeing the waywardness of the human will, that it would fall away from the angelic life and their mode of increase, formed for humans 'that device for increase' befitting those who had fallen into sin, although it is only because God thus creates the human twofold that they are able to fall away in this way. There is, moreover, an ambiguity in the last line: Does the human become like a beast when (and because) God implants this device for increase, or when the (twofold) human no longer directs his will towards the good, but assimilates himself to the animals, and in that way becomes like a beast? And if God did indeed form in our nature this device for procreation before the human turned away from the good, were humans in fact ever able to multiply 'as the angels'? And, finally, whom has Gregory been speaking about so far, or even, for that matter, is he saying what he actually thinks (recall *De hom.* 16.15)?

Gregory goes on in the following chapter to give a very nuanced account of how the passions arise in human beings. It is 'from this beginning' (referring back to the last line of *De hom.* 17.5, cited above), that 'the passions of each one issue as from a spring, to flow over in human life' (*De hom.* 18.1). It cannot be, he argues, that 'the first beginnings of the impassioned disposition' derive from that modelled in the divine form; rather, as the irrational animals entered the world first, 'the human being, for the reason already mentioned, has something of their nature (I mean regarding genesis)', and therefore also partakes of the other attributes of that nature, such as the incensive faculty, cowardice, rashness, and so on (*De hom.* 18.1). But, while animals possess these attributes for the sake of 'self-preservation', 'when transferred to human life [they] become passions' (*De hom.* 18.2). The human being is, again, twofold, modelled on divine beauty but 'also bearing, in the passionate impulses that arise in him, a relationship to the animal-like [form]' (*De hom.* 18.3). Because of this, 'the love of pleasure had its beginning from the likeness to the irrational animals, but was increased by human transgressions [πλημμελήμασι], begetting such varieties of sinning for pleasure' that are not found amongst the animals; more specifically it is 'the evil husbandry of the intellect' that perverts 'the impulses of the irrational animals', turning them into the vices (*De hom.* 18.4)—it is the intellect that is the problem, not the body (made male and female) and its impulses that humans share with the animals. But, on the other hand, Gregory continues, 'if the passion were stripped of the alliance with calculating thoughts, the anger that is left behind is short-lived and weak, like a bubble, bursting as soon as it comes into being' (*De hom.* 18.4). Even more, the impulses of the irrational nature, rather than becoming vices through misuse by the intellect, can instead be transformed into virtue: anger produces courage, cowardice caution, and so on: in fact, 'every such movement, when elevated by the loftiness of mind, is conformed to the beauty of the divine image' (*De hom.* 18.5). Within the twofold compound that is the human being, however, the soul is more frequently drawn downwards by the weight of the irrational nature than is the earthy element raised by loftiness of mind. What we thus more frequently see is the passions covering over the beauty of the image, though it is nevertheless possible to see the divine form in those who have ordered their lives aright, such as Moses (*De hom.* 18.6–8).

Gregory then turns his reflection to the question of eating, another feature we share in common with the irrational animals, and those who feel ashamed that our life is sustained by food (*De hom.* 18.9). We might, Gregory suggests, hope that this function (along with procreation) will pass away in the age to come, as is perhaps suggested by various scriptural verses (Rom. 14:17 and Matt. 4:4), and by the idea that 'as the resurrection indicates to us a life equal to the angels, and with the angels there is no food' (*De hom.* 18.9). Gregory, however, points out that there are many other ways in which 'eating' is spoken of in Scripture, and that the 'tree' in Paradise, called 'all' (*τὸ πᾶν ξύλον*; cf. Gen. 2:16) from which we are invited to eat, is none other than Wisdom herself, who is 'a tree of life' (Prov. 3:18; *De hom.* 19.1–4). Opposed to this tree is the tree of 'the knowledge of good and evil' (which also stands at the centre of the garden), offering a mixed fruit, that is, one that appears to be good but contains evil (*De hom.* 19.5; Gen. 2:9, 17). Noting that Scripture makes a distinction between 'knowledge' and 'discernment', Gregory argues that in fact the latter is the higher condition: 'for to "discern" skilfully "the good from the evil", the Apostle says is of a more perfect condition and "of exercised senses", on which account he also gives the injunction "test all things" and says that "discernment" belongs to the "spiritual"' (*De hom.* 20.1; Heb. 5:14; 1 Thess. 5:21; 1 Cor. 2:15). However, as 'the majority judge the good to be in that which gratifies the senses', they are attracted by the appearance of the mixed fruit, and so receive also the evil within, 'the knowledge of which, that is, its reception by experience, is the beginning and ground of death and destruction' (*De hom.* 20.3). It is this 'evil poison' working its effect upon the human being, likening the human being to 'vanity' and the result is all that which is 'painful and wretched' in our mode of life (*βίος*) in its estrangement from likeness to the divine (*De hom.* 20.4–5; Ps. 143:3). However, as evil is finite and God infinite, it must needs be, Gregory points out, that, as the very character of our nature and life is mutability and movement, we will all ultimately return to God: 'as evil does not extend to infinity, but is bounded by necessary limits, the accession of the good consequently succeeds the limit of evil, and thus, as we have said, the ever-moving character of our nature runs its journey once more at last towards the good, chastened by the memory of its former misfortunes so that it will never again be in the same circumstances' (*De hom.* 21.2). Paradise will be restored, and so too the tree of life, and the grace and dignity of the image (*De hom.* 21.4).

It is only now, having explored in a rather rambling manner these different issues, that Gregory returns, for the third and final time, to the question of God's prevision and provision, the relationship between the plenitude of the human race, as one human being, and particular human beings, and the relationship between human existence as male and female and procreation, angelic or human—doing all this now, moreover, in accord with 'what comes to our mind' rather than as an 'exercise'. He begins by posing a problem, in the form of a question from someone complaining, like a vexed child, about the delay of the good things promised: 'What is this reason, in accordance with which the transformation of our painful mode of life [*βίος*] to that which is desired does not take place immediately, but that this heavy and corporeal life [*ζωὴ*] itself waits, extended to some determined time, for the limit of the consummation of all things, in order that then the human life [*ζωὴ*] may be set free, as it were from the bridle, ascending again, released and free, to the blessed and impassible mode of life [*βίος*]? (*De hom.* 22.2). Saying now 'what comes to our mind' in returning again to Gen. 1:26–7, Gregory begins with the observation that 'the image of God, then, that which is contemplated in the universal nature, had its end [*τὸ τέλος ἔσχεν*], but as yet, Adam was not', for it is 'the earthy moulded figure' (*τὸ γὰρ γήϊνον πλάσμα*) that is called, etymologically, 'Adam', as Paul, who knew Hebrew, designates 'the human being from the earth "earthy" as though translating the name Adam into the Greek language' (*De hom.* 22.3; 1 Cor. 15:47). Gregory then continues:

> In accordance with the image, then, the human being came to be, that is, the universal nature [*ἡ καθόλου φύσις*], the godlike thing; by the omnipotent wisdom not a part of the whole, but the plenitude of nature as a whole came to be [*γέγονε... ἅπαν ἀθρόως τὸ τῆς φύσεως πλήρωμα*]. He who holds all limits in his grasp saw, as the Scripture says, 'all the ends of the earth in his hands' [Ps. 94:4], he 'who knows all things even before their genesis' [Sus. (*Θ*) 42] saw, embracing in his knowledge, how many in number humanity will be in its individuals. Since he perceived in our moulded figure [*ἐν τῷ πλάσματι ἡμῶν*] the inclination towards the worse, and that, voluntarily falling from equality of honour with the angels, it would appropriate fellowship with the lowly nature, he mingled [*κατέμιξε*], for this reason, an element of the irrational with his own image, for the distinction

> between male and female is not in the divine and blessed nature; but, when transferring [μετενεγκὼν] the property of the irrational formation to the human being, he bestowed upon our race the power of multiplying [τὸν πλεονασμὸν], not according to the lofty character of our creation, for it was not when he made that which was in accordance with the image that he added the power to increase and multiply, but when he divided it [διέκρινε] by the distinction of male and female that he then said, 'Increase and multiply and fill the earth' [Gen. 1:28]. For such is not a property of the divine nature, but of the irrational element, as the narrative indicates, when it narrates that this was first said by God in the case of the irrational animal [cf. Gen. 1:22]; since if, before putting on our nature the distinction between male and female, he had added the power for 'increase' expressed by this utterance, we should not have needed this form of birth, by which the irrational animals are born. (*De hom.* 22.4)

It is the plenitude of human beings, not simply as an abstract category ('the universal nature'), but also the 'number humanity will be in its individuals', that is created in accordance with the image. Gregory again appeals to the prevision of God, foreseeing the voluntary fall from equality with the angels, and his provision by dividing the human into male and female, a property not belonging to the high character of human existence as made according to the image but that which is shared with the animals. But this time Gregory notes a further dimension in the scriptural text, bringing in the following verse: it is only when God 'divided' the human being into male and female that he bestowed the power of increasing and multiplying, just as he had earlier done with the animals, so that any suggestion that humans might have multiplied otherwise is finally, scripturally, and definitively excluded. Only now—after 'exercising' our reasoning powers, so that we might no longer think, like his 'opponents', that procreation is for the sake of preserving the human race (cf. *De hom.* 17), or that the problem lies with the body and its impulses shared with the irrational animals rather than with the 'evil husbandry of the intellect' (cf. *De hom.* 18.4), taking 'what gratifies our senses' as the criterion of the good, but have instead learnt 'discernment' (cf. *De hom.* 20)—can we perhaps sense how 'every movement, when elevated by loftiness of mind, is conformed to the beauty of the divine image' (*De hom.* 18.5), for sexual procreation (and it was never otherwise) thus contributes to the completion of the plenitude of humanity in its individuals that is the divine image of God.[16]

[16] Cf. Balthasar, *Presence and Thought*, 174: 'The introduction of the realm of possibilities remains licit, henceforth, only if it is understood as a "mythical" way of expressing the real. We had reason to believe that the myth of an asexual generation of humanity was understood by Gregory as being just such.' Though at an earlier stage in the development of his analysis, Balthasar had commented (73–4): 'Not that procreation is bad in itself, but it is, as it were, the sacrament of sin.'

Gregory continues by returning to the question of his interlocutor: why the delay?

> With the plenitude of human beings, then, preconceived by the activity of foreknowledge, coming into life by means of this more animal form of birth, God, who guides all things in a certain order and sequence—since the inclination of our nature to what is lowly (which he who beholds, equally with the present, what is to be before it happens) made this form of birth absolutely necessary [ὅλως . . . ἀναγκαῖον] for humanity—therefore also foreknew the time coextensive with the formation of human beings: so that the extent of time should be adapted for the entrance of the predetermined souls, and that the flowing movement of time should then halt, when humanity is no longer produced by it; and when the genesis of human beings is completed, time should stop together with the end of it, and then should take place the reconstitution of all things, and with the changing of the whole, humanity should also be changed, from the corruptible and earthy to the impassible and eternal. (*De hom.* 22.5)

What was seen earlier (*De hom.* 21) as the wayward movement of human beings running its course in finite evil, to return, necessarily, to the good but now with experienced discernment, a higher state than mere knowledge, is now also seen as the completion of God's own work of making the human being in his image, the completion of the plenitude of human beings, the end of time, and 'the reconstitution of all things'. It is this promise, Gregory says, that the divine Apostle holds out before us: 'Behold I tell you a mystery: we shall not all sleep, but we shall all be changed, in a moment, in the twinkling of an eye, at the last trumpet' (1 Cor. 15:51–2), the 'moment' and the 'twinkling of an eye' designating 'an instant of time', that limit 'which has no parts or extension', and the transformation through the resurrection effecting a change so that 'the weight of the flesh no longer weighs downwards nor does its burden hold them to the earth' and they can arise through the air, 'caught up in the clouds to meet the Lord in the air, and so we shall ever be with the Lord' (*De hom.* 22.6; 1 Thess. 4:17). So, he concludes, we must 'wait the time necessarily co-extensive with human increase' (*De hom.* 22.7), as did the Patriarchs, who desired to see the good things and sought the heavenly homeland, but waited with patience and hope, for as the Apostle said 'God having foreseen something better for us, that without us they would not be made perfect' (*De hom.* 22.7; Heb. 11:40).

In the remaining chapters of this second part of the treatise, Gregory deals with various sundry points that arise out of further reflection on the end and the transformation to be effected through the resurrection. In Chapter 23, he addresses the point that if one holds that the world had a beginning, one must also hold that it has an end. Although the heading for Chapter 24 suggests that its concern is with those who say that matter is co-eternal with God, its main theme (though it is 'a digression', cf. *De hom.* 24.3) is one that we considered earlier when looking at Gregory's *Hexaemeron* (and Anaxagoras and Origen), that is, that matter is nothing other than a combination of intellectual qualities, brought together by God, and so can be changed into another state. Chapter 25 discusses the way in which others can be persuaded regarding the resurrection, appealing to the course of nature, with seeds dying and rising to bear fruit (*De hom.* 25.5), and suggesting that the Gospel narratives can be read as a gradually increasing instruction into the mystery of the resurrection, with Christ first healing illnesses, then curing one about to die, then raising the dead, and finally, as the Physician, healing himself (*De hom.* 25.7–12). In the following two chapters, Gregory argues that the resurrection is not beyond probability, even with dead bodies dissolving into the elements of the earth, for he who brought all things into being to begin with must certainly have the power to bring them back into existence (*De hom.* 26–7). And then finally, the issue currently being discussed in the churches, he says, that is whether soul or body has priority (*De hom.* 28), with Gregory taking the position that 'as the human being is one, consisting of soul and body, it is to be supposed that the principle of his constitution is one and common to both', so that 'the whole human plenitude' can be affirmed 'to have pre-existed in the power of God's foreknowledge (according to the account given a little earlier)' (*De hom.* 29.1), just as 'in the grain, or in any other seed, the whole form of the ear of corn is potentially included' (*De hom.* 29.3).

This image of the seed, in which the fullness of the whole is already contained and which only comes to its fullness by being sown in the earth, used by Paul to provide an account of the resurrection and final transformation (1 Cor. 15:35–54), is something that Gregory uses repeatedly. Here he points out that the coming to be of both soul and body together, and their growth together, is what we see in the case of each particular human being: the seed is 'warm and active' so that we must conclude that it is not inanimate. And even if we don't see in it flesh, bones, hair, and all the other things we see in human beings, 'it is potentially each of these things, although it does not yet visibly appear to be so', and so also with respect to the animated part, the faculties of the soul are not yet visible, but rather 'analogously to the formation and perfection of the body, so also the activities of the soul grow with the subject' (*De hom.* 29.6). In this process, we can see, once again, the threefold power of the soul that Moses, according to Gregory, narrates:

> For just as the body proceeds from a very small original to the perfect state, so also the activity of the soul, growing in step with the subject, gains and increases with it. For in its first formation, first of all comes the power of growth and nourishment alone, as though some root buried in the ground, for the smallness of the one receiving does not admit of more; then, as the plant comes to light and shows it shoot to the sun, the gift of the sense-perception blossoms; and when at last it is ripened and has grown up to its proper height, the rational faculty begins

> to shine, just like some fruit, not all appearing at once, but by diligence growing with the perfection of the instrument, always bearing as much fruit as the power of the subject grants. (*De hom.* 29.8)

There is, once again, a proper order and sequence for the growth of both body and soul: nourished in the womb, when it is sufficiently grown it emerges, through parturition, into the world of sense-perception, and then in this world (as another womb, as Maximos, as we will see, puts it) the newborn human takes time to grow in stature of body and reasoning power of soul, and, further, to learn the discernment that is needed with regard to sense-perception (for that which appears is 'mixed'). As such it is only with time that the power of the soul reaches perfection with the body. 'Take heed to yourself' says Moses, and Gregory adds that in doing so 'you will read, as in a book, the account of the works of the soul' (*De hom.* 29.9; Deut. 4:23). Finally, as the end of human beings in this world is to be placed in the earth, we can learn from what we see in agriculture: what is sown in the earth—'kernels of fruit and portions torn from roots, not deadened [by being deprived] of the vital power naturally residing in them, but preserving in themselves, hidden, indeed, but certainly living, the property of their prototype'—is surrounded by the earth, not in such a way as to give it life (for then even dead wood would grow), but rather such that it 'makes manifest that which resides within them, nourishing by its own moisture, perfecting the plant' in all its dimensions (*De hom.* 29.11).

4. The Life of the Human Being (30)

In the third and final part of the work (a lengthy chapter, designated along with Chapter 16 as 'a contemplation'), Gregory turns, just as did Timaeus in the third part of his speech, to a detailed medical account of the human being. Gregory notes that there are many books on the topic, but as those inside the church prefer not to hear those outside, he has taken it upon himself to give an account also of these matters (*De hom.* 30.1). As mentioned earlier, Cornford, while accepting that the *Timaeus* as a whole is not an easy read, thought that 'the physiological and medical chapters towards the end would be repellent to many.'[17] It is likely that this last chapter of Gregory had the same effect; indeed, it is one of the least commented on parts of this treatise. But, as with the *Timaeus*, where the third part puts a 'head' on the two preceding parts, both of which only give a partial account and need to be combined, so too this part of Gregory's treatise now gives the

[17] Cornford, *Plato's Cosmology*, 20.

account of the actual constitution of the human being, in anatomical terms, and how the human being comes into life and grows.

He begins by noting that there are three things pertaining to the nature of the human body for the sake of which the particular parts are formed: 'some are for the sake of living, others for living well, others are adapted towards the succession of descendants'; those without which we cannot live, such as the brain, the heart, and the liver, fall in the first category; the organs of sense bestow the gift of living well and so fall in the second group; while the third group 'looks to what comes after and the succession of life' (*De hom.* 30.2). Gregory then spends many pages exploring the anatomical arrangement and purposes of the parts of the body, until he pulls himself short, commenting that 'our argument, however, has wandered far from the matters at hand, going deep into the works of nature' to describe the constitution of the organs, 'those intended for life, and those for the good life, and any other category after these that we considered in the first division' (*De hom.* 30.28).

His purpose, he notes, alluding back to the concluding chapters of the second part of the work, was to show that 'the seminal cause of our constitution is neither a soul without body, nor a body without soul, but that, from animated and living bodies a being, living and animated from the first, is generated, human nature receiving it to be cherished, like a nursling, with her own powers' so that it grows appropriately in each part, 'for it immediately displays, by this artistic and scientific process of formation, the power of the soul interwoven with it, appearing at first somewhat obscurely, but afterwards increasing in radiance concurrently with the perfecting of the organism' (*De hom.* 30.29).

Gregory then goes on to compare this process to that of a sculptor: intending to produce the figure of an animal in stone, the sculptor first separates the stone from its quarry, then chips away the superfluous parts, proceeding through the various steps of the first outline, when even an inexperienced observer can conjecture what the final figure will be; and then working again at the material, till at last 'producing in the material the perfect and exact form, he brings his art to its conclusion', and what had been shapeless stone is now a perfect figure of a lion or a human, 'not by the material being changed into the figure, but by the figure being wrought upon the matter' (*De hom.* 30.30). In the same way, Gregory proposes,

> we say that the all-contriving nature taking from the kindred matter within herself the part that comes from the human being crafts the statue [*τὴν γὰρ πάντα τεχνιτεύουσαν φύσιν ἐκ τῆς ὁμογενοῦς ὕλης λαβοῦσαν, ἐν ἑαυτῇ τὸ ἐκ τοῦ ἀνθρώπου μέρος δημιουργεῖν ἀνδριάντα φαμέν*]. And just as the form follows upon the gradual working of the stone, at first somewhat indistinct, but more perfect after the completion of the work, so also in the carving of the organism the form of the soul, by the analogy, is displayed in the substratum, incompletely in that

which is incomplete, and perfectly in that which is perfect; but it would have been perfect from the beginning had nature not been maimed by evil [ἀλλ᾽ ἐξ ἀρχῆς ἂν τέλειον ἦν εἰ μὴ διὰ τῆς κακίας ἡ φύσις ἐκολοβώθη]. For this reason our sharing in that impassioned and animal-like genesis brings it about that the divine image does not shine forth immediately in the moulded figure, but, by a certain method and sequence, through those material and more animal-like properties of the soul, brings to perfection the human being [διὰ τοῦτο ἡ πρὸς τὴν ἐμπαθῆ καὶ ζωώδη γένεσιν κοινωνία οὐκ εὐθὺς ἐκλάμπειν ἐν τῷ πλάσματι τὴν θείαν εἰκόνα ἐποίησεν ἀλλ᾽ ὁδῷ τινι καὶ ἀκολουθίᾳ διὰ τῶν ὑλικῶν τε καὶ ζωωδεστέρων τῆς ψυχῆς ἰδιωμάτων ἐπὶ τὸ τέλειον ἄγει τὸν ἄνθρωπον]. (*De hom.* 30.30)

There are two things that need to be carefully considered in this climactic paragraph. First, the 'maiming by evil' that has prevented the end result from being perfect from the beginning. What this refers to is not stated by Gregory. However, it is important to note that it is not 'our nature' (as Wilson translated it) that has been 'maimed', which might be taken to refer to a 'fall'. Rather it is 'nature' as the 'all-contriving', the active agent of the process of that which comes into being, as it has been frequently throughout the treatise (e.g. *De hom.* 8.4–7). Moreover, as we have seen, 'the genesis of evil' for Gregory lies in the turning of intellect from the good to matter, receiving its shapelessness into itself rather than beautifying matter as 'an image of an image' (*De hom.* 12.9–13); and, as we have further seen, this has been played out across the second part of the treatise in terms of the waywardness of the inclination of the human will, learning discernment through experience so that it returns, in the end, to what it was made in the beginning, the *archē*. As such, if the analogy with sculpting is to be followed, then the 'evil' which 'maims' nature, such that the human being is not brought to perfection at the beginning but at the end, is more like the recalcitrance of that upon which nature is working, which in this case is the waywardness of the human will. Like Timaeus' 'straying cause', it needs to be persuaded by intellect, or, in Origen's terms, by the omnipotence of the Almighty Creator working through the 'persuasion of Word and Wisdom'.

The second point is Gregory's striking concluding words: it is not simply by 'sharing in the impassioned and animal-like genesis' that the human race reaches the plenitude foreseen by God (cf. *De hom.* 22.4), but that this entails that the human being is brought to perfection in a proper order and sequence, and, Gregory now adds, this happens 'through those more material and animal-like properties of the soul'.[18] If it is 'the evil husbandry of the intellect' that has

[18] Cf. Eric Daryl Meyer, 'On Making Fleshly Difference: Humanity and Animality in Gregory of Nyssa', *Relegere: Studies in Religion and Reception*, 7.1–2 (2017), 39–58, at 56: 'Animal flesh, then, is the foil that generates the fragile space of human virtue, freedom, and discursiveness, while simultaneously serving as a threatening example of what may become of those who fail to exercise these gifts.'

perverted all the motions and impulses shared with the animals into forms of passion not known amongst the animals, it is the intellect which needs training, to raise all these motions so that they too are 'conformed to the beauty of the divine image' (*De hom.* 18. 4–5), so that the beauty of the divine image in the moulded figure can truly shine forth. It is, as we noted earlier, through the body, both its excellent structure and its weakness, that 'we have become rational' (*De hom.* 10.1).

And so, in the concluding paragraphs of the work, Gregory exhorts his reader to be like Paul, putting away childish things (1 Cor. 13:11): not that the soul of the adult is other than that in the child, 'but that the same soul displays its imperfect condition in that one and the perfect state in this' (*De hom.* 30.31). After reiterating the account of the ascent of nature through the different levels of life, Gregory again points out that 'the true and perfect soul is the human', whereas anything else is only called 'soul' by 'customary misuse of language', for in those cases the soul is not perfect 'but only certain parts of the animated activity which, we have learnt, have also arisen [ἐπιγεγενῆσθαι] in the human being, according to Moses' mystical account of the human origin [ἀνθρωπογονίαν], through kinship [οἰκειότητα] with the impassioned' (*De hom.* 30.32–3). And so, Gregory concludes his work with the same words of Paul that Origen cited in his exhortation to 'Be transformed!' (*Dial.* 13.26–16.17): if we wish to reach perfection 'it is necessary "to put off the old human being" and "put on the one being renewed in accordance with the image of God"' (*De hom.* 30.33; Col. 3:9–10), and so, 'let us all ascend [ἐπανέλθωμεν or 'return'] to the divine grace in which God created the human being in accordance with the *archē* [κατ' ἀρχὰς], saying, 'Let us make the human being in accordance with our image and likeness' (*De hom.* 30.34).

Gregory has presented us with a very sophisticated analysis of the human being. It is, however, emphatically not presented as a description of a 'prelapsarian' Adam, followed by 'the Fall' and 'postlapsarian' existence, awaiting for the redeeming work of salvation, as commentators, myself included, have assumed.[19] At its heart, thematically and structurally, it is an account of the condition in which we find ourselves, in which it is hard to see the truth of the scriptural affirmation that the human being is made in the image of God. Structuring his treatise in parallel with the *Timaeus*, Gregory offers, in the first part, a vision of the human being (Chapters 1–15); in the second part, an analysis of the prevision and provision of God with respect to the wavering inclination of our will and the evil husbandry of the intellect, sketching out the economy, or the 'anthropogony', on the one hand, traced in the ascent of nature to the more perfect form of life, and, on the other hand, leading to the completion of the plenitude of the human race as the image of God, the total Christ, a process which requires, and is co-extensive

[19] See my earlier piece, 'The Rational Animal: A Rereading of Gregory of Nyssa's *De hominis opificio*', *JECS* 7 (1999), 219–47.

with, time itself, resulting in the final transformation heralded by Paul (chapters 16–29); and, in the third part, a description of how this economy is recapitulated in the life of each human being, from the seed being implanted in the womb and growing there through the power of nutrition, then coming into the world of sense-perception, where it continues to grow in both body and soul, learning discernment by experience and growing in virtue, yet needing to be exhorted to put away childish things, the old human being, and put on instead the one being renewed in accordance with the image of God. Gregory does indeed seem to have accomplished the task he set himself, of bringing together, through scriptural guidance and human reason, things that appear contrary, 'to one and the same end, with the divine power finding a hope for things beyond hope and a means of accomplishing things unworkable' (Ep. Pet. 3).

5. 'The Fall' and 'Male and Female'

5.1 The Fall

Having paid close attention to the economy of Gregory's text, how he develops his argument, we can now turn to a couple of points that have perplexed interpreters and see how Gregory's position fits with those before and after. Firstly, the question of 'the Fall'.[20] Concluding his analysis of human nature in Gregory, in particular his strong understanding of 'universal human nature', Zachhuber comes to the conclusion that here 'there is no room for a Fall of the "nature":...Human individuals...would not have been able to change that nature on account of its ontological priority (it was complete before Adam was there!)'.[21] The particular question that interests Zachhuber is: 'Does Gregory, then, or does he not, know of original sin and a single act of disobedience which has caused human nature to be damaged in such a way that it has affected every human being since?'[22] Noting that there are 'possible theories of universal sin different from Augustine's', for which one can find some evidence in other texts of Gregory (*De Virginitate* for the 'Neoplatonic pattern'; a number with the 'Origenist pattern; and even some that follow an 'Apollinarian pattern'), Zachhuber concludes: 'A further view might be identified in *De Hominis Opificio* 16 where

[20] For an exhaustive survey of every possible expression pertaining to 'the Fall' in Gregory's writings, see Manfred Hauke, *Heilsverlust in Adam: Stationen griechischer Erbsündenlehre: Irenäus-Origenes-Kappadozier* (Paderborn: Bonifatius, 1992), 572–692. His conclusion is that while Gregory has all the 'building blocks', he lacks the connection of them into a systematic whole and the resolution of the inner contradictions by a proper theology of grace, so that while some aspects of his thought point towards a distinct conception of original sin, others are in tension with it (686–7); at most, Gregory 'is on the way to original sin' (692).

[21] Zachhuber, *Human Nature*, 174.

[22] Ibid., 175.

Gregory all but says that God himself created the "fallen" state in anticipation of the fall.'[23]

But perhaps this is the wrong way of phrasing the question, for, after all, Gregory has not spoken of 'a' or 'the Fall' as an event describing 'a single act of disobedience' corrupting human nature and beings thereafter; indeed, as Zachhuber notes, 'there was no sign that he attempted an application of his own genuine theory to this doctrinal question'.[24] Rather than succumbing to what Skinner describes as 'the mythology of doctrine', that is, assuming that certain topics are constitutive for a particular discipline, in this case theology, and looking to each historical author to see what they said about it, we should perhaps take Gregory on his own terms.[25] To start by looking for the prelapsarian state and the fall and its effect is to begin with protology, as many interpreters of Gregory (and also Origen, as we noted in the last chapter) do, rather than eschatology. Looking to the end to see what it is that the human being is to become—the one who is first in the foreknowledge of God, the *archē* that is Christ, but the end in our own temporal horizon of growth, our *telos*—Gregory contemplates the current state of existence, but also provides a vision of the singular economy of God that leads, in the end, to the outcome envisioned from the beginning. This perspective was not unique to Gregory, and before him, as we have seen, Origen, but was also, of course, clearly held by Irenaeus.

In fact, in *Against the Heresies* 4.37–39, Irenaeus addresses this very point, responding to his opponents' complaint: God, they say, should not have created 'human beings such that they immediately became ungrateful towards him, because they were created rational and capable of examining and judging and not like irrational or inanimate creatures which are not able to do anything of their own will but are drawn by necessity and force towards the good, with one inclination and tendency, unable to deviate and without the power of judging, and unable to be anything other than what they were created'.[26] The last clause is the most important, for, as he argues, only a free, independent, and temporal creature is able to grow, and so change its mode of existence while remaining what it is by nature: in other words, while an uncreated creature is a logical impossibility, God can create those who come to share in his uncreated life, but this requires change, growth, and time. And so, Irenaeus argues, if we had been created

[23] Ibid., 176–86; the first quotation is from 176, the second from 186. [24] Ibid., 185.

[25] Cf. Quentin Skinner, 'Meaning and Understanding in the History of Ideas', *History and Theory* 8 (1969), 3–53; reprinted in a much abbreviated and extensively revised version in Quentin Skinner, *Visions of Politics*, vol. 1, *Regarding Method* (Cambridge: Cambridge University Press, 2002), 57–89, esp. 59–67.

[26] *Haer.* 4.37.6. Ed. and French trans. A. Rousseau et al., *Haer.* 1–3, SC 263–4, 293–4, 210–11 (Paris: Cerf, 1979, 1982, 1974); *Haer.* 4 SC 100 (Paris: Cerf, 1965); *Haer.* 5 SC 152–3 (Paris: Cerf, 1969). ET in A. Roberts and J. Donaldson eds., ANF 1 (Grand Rapids, Mich.: Eerdmans, 1987 [1887]). For full exposition, see Behr, *Irenaeus of Lyons: Identifying Christianity*, CTC (Oxford: Oxford University Press, 2013), 144–203.

as his opponents desired, we would have thought that communion with God is 'by nature', rather than a result of their own proper endeavour, care, or study; it would be misunderstood and no pleasure would be found in it, and so it would have benefitted neither God nor the human being. Instead, Irenaeus points out, 'the violent take it by force' (Matt. 11:12), and we must run the race (1 Cor. 9:24–7). Moreover, he notes, something is only truly valued once one has experienced its loss, such as the faculty of sight by temporary blindness, health by sickness, and, finally, life by death (*Haer.* 4.37.7). In all of this, God has been patient, knowing that, as the prophet put it, 'your own apostasy shall instruct you' (*Haer.* 4.37.7; Jer. 2:19). He concludes this section thus:

> God, thus, determined all things beforehand for the perfection of the human being, and towards the realization and manifestation of his economies, that goodness may be displayed and righteousness accomplished, and that the Church may be 'conformed to the image of his Son' [Rom. 8:29], and that, finally, the human being may be brought to such maturity as to see and comprehend God. (*Haer.* 4.37.7)

Worked out in and through the life of each individual human being, the conclusion is, as it is with Gregory, corporate: it is the Church that is conformed to Christ as each human being is brought to see God.[27]

Irenaeus argues similarly in *Haer.* 3.20.1–2, using the sign of Jonah to describe the whole economy, from beginning to end. As 'strength is made perfect in weakness' (2 Cor. 12:9), 'foreseeing the victory which would be granted to [the human being] through the Word', God 'was patient' with the human being, 'allowing' him 'from the beginning to be swallowed up by the great whale, who was the author of the transgression', not in ignorance of what would happen and so having to find a remedy later on, but 'arranging and preparing the economy of salvation which was accomplished by the Word through the sign of Jonah', so that the whole economy is arranged in such a way to acquaint human beings with their own weakness in order that they might simultaneously know the strength of God, and having known the experience of death they might thereafter hold ever more firmly to the source of life. There is, thus, for Irenaeus 'an author of the transgression' (though if the analogy with the whale is to hold, God in fact appointed the whale, just as he also sent Satan to tempt Job), and the human race is indeed in apostasy, although seen from the point of view of the end, Christ, the apostasy and death now function pedagogically, the whole being embraced by 'the sign of

[27] For Gregory on the Church as the 'manifold wisdom of God', weaving together opposites, life mingled with death, established by Christ as his body through 'the addition of those being saved... until we all attain to mature humanity', see his eighth homily on the Song of Songs (Langerbeck, 255–7; ET 269).

Jonah', who represents both the suffering human race and the Saviour. In other words, the whole economy, including apostasy and death, begins (with God) and ends (for us) with Jesus Christ, who by his death brings eternal life; or, as Irenaeus says a little later, 'Since the Saviour pre-exists, it was necessary that he who would be saved should come into existence so that the Saviour doesn't exist in vain'.[28]

In *Haer.* 4.39, Irenaeus develops his analysis further by contrasting two different types of knowledge: that gained, on the one hand, through experience, and that, on the other hand, learned through hearsay (*Haer.* 4.39.1). It is, he points out, only through experience that the tongue comes to learn of both bitterness and sweetness, and likewise, it is only through experience of both good and evil, the latter being disobedience and death, that the mind receives the knowledge (*disciplina*) of the good, that is, obedience to God, which is life for human beings. By experiencing both, and casting off disobedience through repentance, the human being (as in the case of Jonah) becomes ever more tenacious in obedience to God, growing into the fullness of life. The alternative, Irenaeus says dramatically, is that 'if anyone shuns the knowledge of both of these, and the twofold perception of knowledge, forgetting himself he destroys the human being' (*Haer.* 4.39.1: *latentur semetipsum occidit hominem*).

Between *Haer.* 4.37 and 39 lies chapter 38, which tackles the question from a different angle. Here he suggests that it would have been possible for God to have created the human being perfect, or as a 'god', from the beginning, for all things are possible to him. Yet, as created, human beings are initially 'infantile', and so 'unaccustomed to and unexercised in perfect conduct' (*Haer.* 4.38.1). Just as a mother could give solid food to a newborn infant, though it would not benefit the infant, 'so also,' Irenaeus continues, 'it was possible for God himself to have made the human being perfect from the first, but the human being could not receive this, being as yet an infant' (*Haer.* 4.38.1). What is needed is, again, growth, a process of accustoming the human being to bear the life and glory of God. This pattern of growth is spelled out a few paragraphs later. By definition, of course, the created cannot be uncreated, but this is not a restriction upon the omnipotence of God, for this omnipotence is demonstrated, for Irenaeus, in the way that the created *is* in fact brought *in time* to share in the uncreated life of God, a change in the 'fashion' of its existence or the mode of its life, which requires preparation and training, and it is to this end that the whole economy has aimed and been tending from the beginning. He begins:

> With God power, wisdom, and goodness are demonstrated simultaneously: power and goodness in that he willingly created and made things previously not existing; wisdom in having made those things that have come into being rhythmical and harmonious and elaborate [εὔρυθμα καὶ ἐμμελῆ καὶ

[28] *Haer.* 3.22.3; cf. Behr, '"Since the Saviour Pre-exists": A Reconsideration of Irenaeus 3.22.3', *StP* 109, vol. 6 (Leuven: Peeters, 2021), 43–54.

> ἐγκατάσκευα], which, through the superabundance of his goodness, receiving growth [αὔξησιν] and continuing for a long period [ἐπὶ πλεῖον], obtain the glory of the Uncreated [ἀγενήτου δόξαν ἀποίσεται], of the God who ungrudgingly bestows good. By virtue of being created, they are not uncreated; but by virtue of continuing in being throughout a long course of ages, they shall receive the power of the Uncreated [δύναμιν ἀγένητου προσλήψεται], of the God who freely bestows upon them eternal existence. (*Haer.* 4.38.3)

It is, he continues, by 'this order and such rhythms and such a movement [that] the created and moulded human becomes in the image and likeness of God', with God 'planning everything well', the Son 'executing', the Spirit 'nourishing and increasing', and 'the human making progress day by day, and ascending towards perfection, that is approaching the Uncreated one'. Then, spelling out these stages:

> Now, [1] it was first necessary for the human being to be created;
> [2] and having been created, to increase;
> [3] and having increased, to become an adult;
> [4] and having become an adult, to multiply;
> [5] and having multiplied, to become strong;
> [6] and having been strengthened, to be glorified;
> [7] and being glorified, to see his Master;
> for God is He who is yet to be seen, and the vision of God produces incorruptibility, and "incorruptibility renders one close to God." (*Haer.* 4.38.3; Wisd. 6:19)

It is striking that the arc of the economy, as sketched here, is patterned upon the life of each human being, the 'seven stages' of life. Such reflection seems to have gone back to John the Evangelist, and the discussions he had with 'the Elders', such as Papias, at the end of the first century. Irenaeus alludes to this elsewhere (cf. *Haer.* 2.22.4), and Victorinus of Pettau records the same tradition independently of Irenaeus, saying that Christ 'consummates his humanity [*humanitatem... consummat*] in the number seven: birth, infancy, boyhood, youth, young-manhood, maturity, death'.[29] As with Gregory, the lifespan of each human being recapitulates the whole arc of the economy that culminates in the human plenitude, in the image and likeness of God.[30]

[29] *De Fabrica mundi*, 9; for full discussion, see Behr, *John the Theologian*, 211–13.

[30] This recapitulation calls to mind Ernst Haeckel's formulation that 'ontogeny recapitulates phylogeny'; although this has been debunked as an account of a possible similarity of the embryonic development to evolutionary history, it has, however, been picked up by evolutionary anthropologists: as Mary LeCron Foster put it: 'both biological evolution and the stages in the child's cognitive development follow much the same progression of evolutionary stages as that suggested in the archaeological record'. Mary LeCron Foster, 'Symbolism: the Foundation of Culture' in *Companion Encyclopedia of Anthropology: Humanity, Culture, Social Life*, ed. Tim Ingold (London: Routledge, 1993), 366–95, at 386.

It is, thus, at the end that the human being becomes 'according to the image and likeness of God': 'never at any time did Adam escape the Hands of God', that is the Word and the Wisdom of God, to who he speaks saying 'Let us make the human being in our image after our likeness. And for this reason, at the end [*fine*], "not by the will of the flesh nor by the will of men" [John 1:13], but by the good pleasure of the Father, his Hands perfected a living human being, in order that Adam might become in the image and likeness of God' (*Haer.* 5.1.3). It is intriguing that for Irenaeus it is Adam who at the end becomes the perfected living human being, in the image and likeness of God, whereas for Gregory (at least in *De hom.* 22.3, though he does not provide a full, positive exposition of Adam even there), Adam is the first particular human being, for the head or *archē* is always Christ, while at the end Christ encompasses the totality of humanity. The difference can perhaps be reconciled in terms of how Origen understood Paul to assert that 'Adam is Christ' (*Princ.* 4.3.7); seen from the point of view of the end Adam is indeed (the total) Christ, whereas from our own beginning we first know Adam in humanity's infancy and subjection to sense-perception and the resulting passions.

A further possible similarity to Irenaeus can perhaps be seen in the way in which both speak of the relationship between the *text* of Gen. 1:26–7 and the human being that is to come about at the end. What the human being 'will be', we saw Gregory say, 'is foreshadowed by the Artist through the writing of the account [διὰ τῆς τοῦ λόγου γραφῆς]', along with what kind of being he should be, his archetype, and for what purpose he shall come into being (*De hom.* 3.1). In a similar manner, Irenaeus describes how Christ recapitulates Adam 'so that he might also demonstrate the likeness of enfleshment to Adam [i.e. Virgin birth// virgin earth], and might become the human being, written in the beginning [γένηται ὁ γεγραμμένος ἐν ἀρχῇ ἄνθρωπος] "according to the image and likeness of God"'.[31] Or, as he puts it elsewhere, previously it was only 'said, that the human being was created according to the image of God, but it was not shown', and for this reason, not seeing what the image looks like, the human being 'easily lost the similitude'; but when the Word became flesh, he confirms both, truly showing the image of God, 'since he became himself what was his image', and so also 'he reestablished the similitude in a sure manner, assimilating the human being to the invisible Father through the visible Word' (*Haer.* 5.16.2). In the same way, for Gregory, although it was certainly foreshadowed in the writing of Genesis 1:26–7 what the human being was called to be, this was not shown until Christ, enabling human beings now to put off the old human being and put on the one being renewed in accordance with the image of God. If this is so, then, while Gregory's treatise structurally parallels the *Timaeus*, he has nevertheless reversed the task of their respective texts. If Timaeus concludes his speech with a prayer 'to the god

[31] Irenaeus, *Demonstration of the Apostolic Preaching*, 32; trans. John Behr, PPS 17 (New York: Saint Vladimir's Seminary Press, 1997); the Greek is Rousseau's retroversion from the Armenian.

[i.e. the world] who previously of old came to be in reality and just now comes to be in words' (*Crit.* 106a3–4), for Gregory it is that which was in words that comes to be in reality at the end, doing so through the economy sketched out in Gregory's words and the exhortation he gives at the end.

That human beings have been in apostasy 'from the beginning', as Irenaeus put it, yet that this is in fact a pedagogy, is maintained in the later tradition. Indeed, Maximos puts this idea in a more emphatic form, which does not permit taking the expression 'from the beginning' as meaning no more than 'from of old', 'a long time ago', but before which there nevertheless was a primordial age of perfection. Maximos opens his response to Thalasius's question about the meaning of a passage in First Peter, with this striking paragraph:

> When God crafted [*δημιουργήσας*] the nature of human beings, he did not co-create with it sense-perceptive pleasure and pain [*οὐ συνέκτισεν αὐτῇ κατὰ τὴν αἴσθησιν οὔτε ἡδονὴν οὔτε ὀδύνην*], but a certain capacity for pleasure according to the intellect [*δύναμίν τινα κατὰ νοῦν αὐτῇ πρὸς ἡδονήν*], by which [the human] would be able to enjoy him ineffably. Together with coming into being [*ἅμα τῷ γενέσθαι*], the first human, by sense-perception [*τῇ αἰσθήσει*], gave this capacity—the natural desire [*ἔφεσιν*] of the intellect towards God—to things of sense-perception [*τὰ αἰσθητὰ*], activating, in the very first movement [*κατ' αὐτὴν τὴν πρώτην κίνησιν*], an unnatural pleasure [*ἡδονήν*] through the medium of sense-perception. Being, in his providence, concerned for our salvation, God therefore affixed pain alongside this sensible pleasure as a kind of punitive faculty [*ὥσπερ τινὰ τιμωρὸν δύναμιν*], whereby the law of death was wisely implanted in our corporeal nature to curb the folly of the intellect [*τῆς τοῦ νοῦ μανίας*] moving desire [*ἔφεσιν*], against nature, toward sense-perceptible things.[32]

Given the simultaneity between the movement towards sense-perceptible things, squandering the desire for God and the intellectual pleasure he provides, and 'coming into being', it would seem that what Maximos is speaking about here correlates to what Gregory describes as the parturition of the infant: after human seed has been deposited in the womb, and the body has grown by the soul's power of nutrition and growth, it then emerges into the world of sense-perception, where both body and soul are to grow further, not only in stature but also learning discernment through experience, and especially coming to learn that what appears to be good is not the true criterion for what is good, so as to attain proper intellectual understanding.[33] The world of sense-perception is like a womb,

[32] Maximos, *Ad Thalassium* (*Ad Thal.*) 61. Ed. C. Laga and C. Steel, CCSG 22 (Turnhout: Brepols, 1990), 86.8–21; ET Maximos Constas, *On Difficulties in Sacred Scripture: The Responses to Thalassios*, FC 136 (Washington, DC: Catholic University of America Press, 2018), 434, modified.

[33] See also Gregory of Nyssa, *De Mortuis*: 'For since the perfect power of the soul is still not contained in the infantile body, while the operation of the senses is born immediately perfect together

a space for this further growth, resulting in the emergence of a fully mature human being. As Maximos puts it:

> For it is true—though it may be a jarring and unusual thing to say—that both we and the Word of God, the Creator and Master of the universe, exist in a kind of womb, owing to the present conditions of our life. In this sense-perceptible world, just as if he were enclosed in a womb, the Word of God appears only obscurely, and only to those who have the spirit of John the Baptist, while, on the other hand, human beings, gazing through the womb of the material world, catch but a glimpse of the Word who is concealed within beings (and this, again, only if they are endowed with John's spiritual gifts). For when compared to the ineffable glory and splendor of the age to come, and to the kind of life that awaits us there, this present life differs in no way from a womb swathed in darkness, in which, for the sake of us who were infantile in mind, the infinitely perfect Word of God, who loves mankind, became an infant.[34]

Returning to *Ad Thal.* 61, the act of expending the capacity meant for the enjoyment of God upon things of sense-perception in themselves results in the pedagogic cycle of pleasure and pain, established by the provision of God, culminating in death, but a death which Christ has now turned inside out, changing its 'use': when Christ 'naturally willed to undergo death itself in the passibility of his human nature, clearly suffering, he converted the use of death, so that henceforth in him death would no longer be a condemnation of nature but clearly of sin', and in this way, 'the baptised', that is, those who conform themselves to Christ's death (cf. Rom. 6:3), also 'acquires the use of death to condemn sin, which in turn mystically leads that person to divine and unending life'.[35] Whereas in our 'genesis' (*γένεσις*) we are passive, our 'birth' (*γέννησις*) into life through death is active.

Rather than seeing Gregory as having the building blocks of an Augustinian understanding of 'the Fall' and 'original sin', but not yet having put them together

with the baby, because of this reasoning in judging of the good is prejudged by sense-perception and what already appears to the senses is also supposed to be good' (*τούτου χάριν προλαμβάνεται ὑπὸ τῆς αἰσθήσεως ἡ διάνοια ἐν τῇ τοῦ καλοῦ κρίσει καὶ τὸ τοῖς αἰσθητηρίοις φανὲν ἤδη καὶ νομισθὲν εἶναι καλὸν*). Ed. Gunter Heil, in GNO 9.1 (Leiden: Brill, 1967), 28–68; ET by Rowan A. Greer in *One Path for All: Gregory of Nyssa on the Christian Life and Human Destiny* (Eugene, OR: Cascade, 2014), 94–117. The text is not divided into sections. Here, Heil 48 (ET 105).

[34] Maximos, *Ambiguum* (*Ambig.*) 6; ed. and ET Nicholas Constas, *On Difficulties in the Church Fathers: The Ambiguum*, DOML 2 vols (Cambridge, MA: Harvard University Press, 2014), vol. 1, 72–3, modified.

[35] Maximos, *Ad Thal.* 61 (95.187–91): *αὐτὸν δὲ κατὰ φύσιν θέλων ἐν τῷ παθητῷ τῆς φύσεως καταδεξάμενος τὸν θάνατον, δηλονότι πάσχων, τὴν τοῦ θανάτου χρῆσιν ἀντέστρεψεν, οὐκ ὄντα λοιπὸν ἐν αὐτῷ τῆς φύσεως, ἀλλὰ τῆς ἁμαρτίας προδήλως, κατάκρισιν·* (99.247–9): *εἰς κατάκρισιν τῆς ἁμαρτίας τὴν αὐτοῦ* [i.e. *τοῦ θανάτου*] *καταδέχεται χρῆσιν, πρὸς τὴν θείαν καὶ ἀτελεύτητον ζωὴν μυστικῶς αὐτὸν παραπέμπουσαν.*

coherently, Gregory's understanding of the economy of creation, from its beginning (in Christ) to its end (in and as Christ), clearly falls within the pattern developed before him by Irenaeus and after him by Maximos, and also, as we saw in the previous chapter, with Origen. It is, as we have seen, thoroughly teleological, based on the pattern of growth that we see in the case of each human being. It does not attempt to look back to a lost golden age of primordial perfection in any kind of actualized state, any more than one might, by the customary misuse of language as Gregory would say, describe a newborn infant as 'perfect'. This growth towards perfection of the human being is bound up, for Gregory, with the dynamics of the cosmos: cosmology and anthropology form an integral way of thinking for him, just as it did for Anaxagoras, Timaeus and Philo. But whereas for them the goal of the pedagogy was to produce rational citizens of the polis or the cosmos, for Gregory (as for Irenaeus, Origen, and Maximos), the teleology is eschatological, that is, the coming to be of the entire plenitude of human beings that is the total Christ, the human being, the very image of God, something achieved, as we have seen Maximos say, but not yet Gregory, through the conversion of death.

5.2 Male and Female

The question of death, and resurrectional transformation, raises the second problem perplexing commentators of Gregory, and that is, what becomes of the distinction between male and female in the resurrection. It has been argued above, that the division of the human being into male and female is not a second act in a two-stage creation, belonging only to the second stage so that the resurrectional transformation is a restoration to what was actually and temporally from the beginning, and thus a resumption of a sexless existence. If, instead, existence as male and female is the condition in which God 'made' the human being from the beginning, and is indeed both the means for growth to the plenitude of human beings and, together with the more material and animal-like attributes of the soul, the horizon for the growth of each to the perfection of being human, what then happens to the division into male and female in the resurrectional transformation? Gregory does not address this issue directly in *On the Human Image*; the nearest he gets is when he suggests that the human need to eat would be fulfilled in the other forms of eating spoken about by Scripture (*De hom.* 20). In two other works from around the same period, *On the Soul and Resurrection* and especially *On Those Who Have Fallen Asleep*, however, Gregory addresses the issue directly.

In *On the Soul*, Gregory, taking the part of those who object to the teaching of the resurrection, phrases the problem in a distinctively bodily manner: if there is to be no procreation in the resurrection (cf. Matt. 22:30), and the resurrectional life will not be maintained by eating and drinking (cf. Rom. 14:17), then 'what use shall there be for these parts of our body, if the activities for which our members now exist are no longer to be expected in that life?' Specifically: 'If the organs for marriage exist for the sake of marriage, then when this is no more, we shall have no need of those organs for this purpose', and similarly for the hands, feet, mouth, and teeth.[36] Gregory is, however, rebuffed by Macrina, as arguing 'not without gallantry using the rhetorical art as it is called, running around the truth with attractively subversive arguments' (*An. et res.* 10.64). She resorts to saying that 'the true rationale [*λόγος*] of these things is still laid up in the hidden treasuries of Wisdom, and will not come to light until we are taught the mystery of the resurrection by the deed' (*An. et res.* 10.66). Pointing out, she continues, that as the body of one travelling in icy conditions becomes cold, while the bodily complexion of those under the hot sun becomes darkened, in the same way, if 'all that was mingled with our human nature from the irrational life was not in us before our humanity fell through vice into passion, then of necessity when we abandon passion, we shall also abandon all that is observed in company with it' (*An. et res.* 10.74). As such, 'when we have put off that dead and repulsive tunic made for use from the skins of irrational animals—for when I hear "skins" [cf. Gen. 3:21], I take it to mean the aspect of the irrational nature with which we clothed when we became habituated to passion.... And what we received from the skin of the irrational animals was sexual intercourse, conception, childbearing, sordidness, breastfeeding, nourishing, excreting, gradual growth into maturity, the prime of life, old age, disease, and death' (*An. et res.* 10.75). The resurrection is not about the resumption of such activities, however much they have enabled attaining the plenitude of human beings and 'the gradual growth into maturity'. Rather, 'the rationale of the resurrection requires only one thing, that a human being is brought forth through birth [*ἓν ζητεῖ μόνον ὁ τῆς ἀναστάσεως λόγος τὸ φυῆναι διὰ γεννήσεως ἄνθρωπον*], or rather as the Gospel says, that "a human being is born into this world"'.[37] It is this birth through death that Macrina then further expounds upon, reflecting upon Paul's words about that which is sown and raised in 1 Cor. 15:38–44, especially the play between the continuity and discontinuity from the seed of corn to the full ear that is raised, a full ear which is implicitly already there in the seed, but is transformed into its fullness through death and resurrection. In all this, however, Macrina does not directly return to the question of male and female.

In his work *On Those Who Have Fallen Asleep*, Gregory deals extensively with the question of the role of death in life and the transformation that comes about

[36] *An. et res.* 10.58–9 (Spira, 110.16–111.3). The material discussed in this paragraph extends to the end of the treatise; hereafter, reference will be given to Silvas' chapter and section numbers.

[37] *An. et res.* 10.78 (Spira, 114.14–15); John 16:21. For this passage in John, see Behr, *John the Theologian*, 211–17.

through resurrection. Those displeased by this forthcoming transformation are, he says, like those who would prefer to remain as embryos in the womb, 'for since the birth-pangs of death serve as the midwife assisting the birth of humans to another life, when they go forth to that light and draw in the pure Spirit they know by experience what a great difference there is between that life and the present one, while those left behind in this moist and flabby life, since they are simply embryos and not humans [ἔμβρυα ὄντες ἀτεχνῶς καὶ οὐκ ἄνθρωποι]', call the departed 'unhappy' (*Mort.*, 47; ET 104–5). Just as with the newborn infant, so too 'an eye is opened for him when he leaves what now afflicts him', and also the other spiritual senses—hearing (quoting 2 Cor. 12:4), taste (Ps. 33:9), smell (2 Cor. 2:14), and touch (1 John 1:1)—'if these and such things are stored up for humans after the birth through death [τὸν διὰ τοῦ θανάτου τόκον], what is the purpose of grief, sorrow, and dejection' (*Mort.*, 47; ET 105)? According to Gregory:

> nature always trains us by death [ἐμμελετᾷ τῷ θανάτῳ] and death has been made to grow together with life as it passes through time. For since life is always moved from the past to the future, and never does away with what follows afterwards, death is what always accompanies the life-giving activity by being united with it. For in past times every life-giving movement and activity certainly ceases. Since, then, impotence and inactivity are the special property of death, and certainly this always follows after the life-giving activity, it is not outside the truth to say that death has been woven together with life.... That is why, according to the words of the great Paul, 'we die daily' (1 Cor. 15:31), not remaining constantly the same in the same house of the body, but from time to time we become different from something else, by addition and subtraction, being constantly changed as though to a new body [οὐχ οἱ αὐτοὶ διὰ παντὸς ἐν τῷ αὐτῷ διαμένοντες οἴκῳ τοῦ σώματος ἀλλ' ἑκάστοτε ἄλλοι ἐξ ἄλλου γινόμενοι, διὰ προσθήκης τε καὶ ἀλλοιούμενοι]. Why, then, are we astonished at death when the life existing through the flesh has been demonstrated to be its constant care and its training ground? (*Mort.* 52–3; ET 107–8)

If we were what we became from the *archē*, Gregory continues, we would not have needed the garments of skin, for the divine image would have shone upon us (*Mort.* 52; ET 108). But, in order to maintain human autonomy and to ensure that evil would in due course pass away, 'God's wisdom found this device to permit humanity to become what it wished, so that by tasting the evils it desired and learning by experience what sort of things it had exchanged for the kinds it chose, it might return willingly by desire to its first blessedness' (*Mort.* 54; ET 109).

With regard to the final transformation that will be effected when our desire returns again to God, Gregory begins urging that 'since the craftsman of the universe will at the appropriate time forge the lump of the body into a "weapon of good pleasure" [Ps. 5:13], "the breastplate of righteousness" as the apostle says, and the "sword of the Spirit" and the "helmet" of hope, and the whole armor of God" [Eph. 6:14–17], love your own body [ἀγάπα τὸ ἴδιον σῶμα] according to the law of the apostle who says "no one has hated his own body"' (*Mort.* 61–2; ET 113; cf. Eph. 5:29). But if, as Paul says, we will have a 'house not made by hands, eternal in the heavens' (2 Cor. 5:1), a worthy 'dwelling place of God in the Spirit' (Eph. 2:22), how can that be described physically as our present state of embodiment can be?

> Let no one describe to me the mark, shape, and form of that house not made with hands according to the likeness of the characteristic marks that now appear to us and that distinguish us from one another by special properties. For since it is not only the resurrection that has been preached to us by the divine oracles, but also that those who are being renewed by the resurrection pledged by divine scripture must be changed [cf. 1 Cor. 15:51], it is entirely necessary that what we shall be changed to has been hidden from absolutely everyone and is unknown, because no example of what is hoped is to be seen in the life we now live.
>
> (*Mort.* 62; ET 113)

The heaviness now characteristic of the body will be transformed for those 'whose elements of their bodies have been changed to a more divine condition' so that they may rise in the air to meet the Lord (*Mort.* 62, ET 113–14; 1 Thess. 4:17). In this condition, 'there will be one kind for all when all of us become one body of Christ, having been shaped by one characteristic mark' so that 'since the divine image shines equally on all, as to what will become ours in the change of nature instead of such properties we shall appear to be something better than any thought can guess' (*Mort* 63; ET 114).

Then, finally:

> But lest our account of this should be left entirely unexercised, we say that since the difference between male and female functions with our nature for nothing other than the procreation of children, perhaps it is possible to adopt some guess worthy of God's promised blessing of good things by saying about this that the procreative power of nature will be changed to that service of birth [εἰς τὴν ἐκείνου τοῦ τόκου ὑπηρεσίαν μεταβήσεται ἡ γεννητικὴν τῆς φύσεως δύναμις] in which the great Isaiah participated when he said, 'From fear of you, Lord, we have received in the womb, have undergone labor-pangs, and have given birth; we have conceived the spirit of salvation on earth" [Isa. 26:18]. If such a birth is good, and the procreation of children becomes the cause of salvation, as the apostle says [cf. 1 Tim. 2:15], someone who has once by such a birth produced as children for himself a multitude of good things never ceases begetting the spirit of salvation. (*Mort.* 63; ET 114)

In a similar way to Origen, then, who took the male and female in the 'inner human being' to refer to the spirit and the soul, respectively, which, if 'they have concord and agreement among themselves, they increase and multiply by the very accord among themselves and they produce sons, good inclinations and understandings and good thoughts, by which they fill the earth and have dominion over it' (*Hom. Gen.* 1.15), for Gregory, while the bodily forms of male and female are transformed into the one body of Christ, in whom there is neither male nor female, 'the procreative power of nature' continues, now elevated by the intellect rather than brought down by its 'evil husbandry', so that even this movement is conformed to the beauty of the divine image (*De hom.* 18.4–5), and the spirit of salvation is constantly begotten.[38] To say otherwise, and to try to hold on to our current experience of what it is to be human, is ultimately futile, for, again, 'a human does not always remain the same as himself with respect to the form of his characteristic mark', as he is 'refashioned by the stages of life', from infancy to maturity, to old age (*Mort.* 64; ET 114).

With respect to the question of male and female, we might profitably conclude by turning once again to Maximos, who develops these reflections of Gregory in his *Ambiguum* 41. Maximos opens this text by asserting that 'the existence (*ὑπόστασιν*) of all things that have come into being is distinguished by five divisions: created/uncreated, intelligible/perceptible, heaven/earth, paradise/inhabited world', and finally, 'the fifth is that according to which the human being who is above all—like a most capacious workshop containing all things and naturally mediating through itself all the divided extremities, having been placed amidst beings according to genesis [*κατὰ γένεσιν*]—is divided into male and female'.[39] Maximos seems to be playing upon the word genesis, referring both to how the human being comes to be, and also to the book which relates this. Mediating between all these extremities the human being has the potential, and vocation to bring them all into unity, and so 'establish clearly through itself the great mystery of the divine goal [*τοῦ θείου σκοποῦ*]'.[40] These divisions, it shouldn't need stating, are not the result of a 'fall', but rather the God-given structure and framework for the vocation of the human being.

[38] For spiritual generation more generally in the Cappadocians, see Verna E. Harrison, 'Gender, Generation, and Virginity in Cappadocian Theology', *JTS* NS 47 (1997), 38–68.

[39] Maximos, *Ambig.* 41; Constas, vol. 2, 102–21 (and notes on 345–6); and PG 91.1304d–1316a. Here, vol. 2, 102.20–104.4 (PG 91.1305ab): the clause between the dashes in Greek occurs between the article and the noun: *ὁ ἐπὶ πᾶσιν, ὥσπερ τι τῶν ὅλων συνεκτικώτατον ἐργαστήριον καὶ πᾶσι τοῖς κατὰ πᾶσαν διαίρεσιν ἄκροις δι' ἑαυτοῦ φυσικῶς μεσιτεύων ἀγαθοπρεπῶς κατὰ γένεσιν τοῖς οὖσιν ἐπεισαχθεὶς* **ἄνθρωπος** *διαιρεῖται εἰς ἄρρεν καὶ θῦλη*. As will become clear, I have heavily modified parts of Constas' translation. A further ET by Andrew Louth, *Maximus the Confessor*, Early Christian Fathers (London: Routledge, 1996), 156–62; French translation by Emmanuel Ponsoye, with an introduction by Jean-Claude Larchet and commentary by Dumitru Staniloae, *Saint Maxime le Confesseur: Ambigua*, Collection l'Arbre de Jessé (Paris–Suresnes: Éditions de l'Ancre, 1994), 292–99.

[40] Constas, 104.7–10 (PG 91.1305b).

In what follows, there are three passages where Maximos addresses how the distinction between male and female is to be overcome, each of which requires close attention to matters of translation. The first occurs when describing the task set before the human being, that is, to unite all things in God, beginning from their own division by:

> τὴν μηδαμῶς ἠρτημένην δηλαδὴ κατὰ τὸν προηγούμενον λόγον τῆς περὶ τὴν γένεσιν τοῦ ἀνθρώπου θείας προθέσεως κατὰ τὸ θῆλυ καὶ τὸ ἄρσεν ἰδιότητα τῇ περὶ τὴν θείαν ἀρετὴν ἀπαθεστάτῃ σχέσει πάντῃ τῆς φύσεως ἐκτιναξάμενος, ὥστε δειχθῆναί τε καὶ γενέσθαι κατὰ τὴν θείαν πρόθεσιν ἄνθρωπον μόνον, τῇ κατὰ τὸ ἄρρεν καὶ τὸ θῆλυ προσηγορίᾳ μὴ διαιρούμενον, καθ' ὃν καὶ προηγουμένως γεγένηται λόγον, τοῖς νῦν περὶ αὐτὸν οὖσι τμήμασι μὴ μεριζόμενον διὰ τὴν τελείαν πρὸς τὸν ἴδιον, ὡς ἔφην, λόγον, καθ' ὅν ἐστιν, ἕνωσιν,[41]
>
> completely shaking off from nature, by means of a supremely dispassionate condition of divine virtue, the property according to the female and the male, which clearly in no way depends, according to the foregoing account [or: the guiding principle], upon the divine purpose concerning the genesis of the human being, so that it might be shown to be, and becomes, simply a human being according to the divine purpose, not divided by the designation according to the male and the female, in accordance with the principle by which it primarily came to be, nor divided into the parts that now appear around it, thanks to the perfect union, as I said, with its own principle, according to which it exists.

Translators and commentators have invariably read this passage, and the two following, against the background of Gregory's supposed teaching of a two-stage creation and the possibility of multiplying sexlessly, 'as the angels', and so rendered the expression τῆς περὶ τὴν γένεσιν τοῦ ἀνθρώπου θείας προθέσεως in terms that suggest this: the divine purpose concerning human generation or procreation. The Greek, however, is simpler and more direct: the divine purpose concerns 'the genesis of the human being'. It is not a divine intention about how humans should multiply (angelically or otherwise), but rather that the human being should come to be, which alone is given as the divine purpose in Gen. 1:26, or, as Maximos had put it earlier, the accomplishment of the task set before the human being to reconcile all things, bringing them into union, and so establish 'the great mystery of the divine goal'. The preceding words, then, κατὰ τὸν προηγούμενον λόγον, could refer to the 'preceding account', that is, most immediately, Maximos' own account of the divisions found in creation needing to be reconciled, and behind that Gen. 1:26 (the text of Genesis already perhaps being alluded to earlier); but it can also refer to the 'governing principle' of that divine

[41] Constas, 104.23–106.4 (PG 91.1305cd, which has γνῶσιν as the last word rather than ἕνωσιν).

purpose, which, as it concerns the genesis of the human being, is a governing principle that is common to both male and female. This division into male and female, Maximos says, is clearly in no way at all dependent [*μηδαμῶς ἠρτημένην δηλαδή*] upon the divine purpose concerning the genesis of the human being: that is, this divine purpose is not the reason for the division of the human being into male and female, for, as Gregory already pointed out, the purpose of Gen. 1:27c ('male and female made he them') is given in Gen. 1:28 ('increase and multiply'; cf. *De hom.* 22.4), and such multiplication, in turn, does not for Maximos (at least here) seem to contribute to the completion of the plenitude of human beings as it did for Gregory. In other words, in the opening clauses of this sentence, Maximos is not speaking about the means or modes of procreation, but rather about the divine purpose that the human being should come to be: it is this that God proposes or 'purposes' to make (Gen. 1:26), not 'male and female' (Gen. 1:27c), though of course this too is of his making, but for a different purpose (given in Gen. 1:28). In *Ambig.* 41, existence as male and female is, nevertheless, established by God, and forms part of the framework, the fivefold divisions, that the human is to reconcile. Finally, in the passage under consideration, Maximos says that we are to 'shake off from nature the property according to the female and the male'. Why Maximos puts it in this order is unclear, other than that it forms a chiasm: female-male—simply human—male-female. But, importantly, this 'shaking off' is accomplished not through a transition into a sexless existence, but through the acquisition of virtue and the removal of the 'designation' of male and female that currently divides the human being. In this way, 'it is shown to be and becomes simply human [*ἄνθρωπον μόνον*] in accordance with the divine purpose'.[42]

After describing how the human being did not accomplish the task set before it, but rather overturned 'the natural power to unite what was separated...for the division rather of what was united', Maximos then turns to Christ's work of unification. Christ initiates the universal union of all things with himself: 'beginning with our own division, he became the perfect human [*γίνεται τέλειος ἄνθρωπος*]', like us in every way except sin (Heb. 4:15), and 'needing for this [i.e. becoming the perfect human] nothing of the natural process of marital intercourse' (*τῆς κατὰ τὴν φύσιν γαμικῆς ἀκολουθίας οὐδόλως εἰς τοῦτο προσδεηθείς*). Maximos continues:

> *καὶ κατὰ τὸ αὐτὸ δεικνύς, ὡς οἶμαι, τυχόν, ὡς ἦν ἄλλος τρόπος τῆς εἰς πλῆθος τῶν ἀνθρώπων αὐξήσεως προεγνωσμένος Θεῷ, εἰ τὴν ἐντολὴν ὁ πρῶτος ἐφύλαξεν ἄνθρωπος καὶ πρὸς κτηνωδίαν ἑαυτὸν τῷ κατὰ παράχρησιν τρόπῳ τῶν οἰκείων δυνάμεων μὴ κατέβαλε*

[42] Is it possible that in the phrase *ἄνθρωπον μόνον* Maximos enigmatically hints towards Gen. 2:18, where this is the first and only thing said to be 'not good'? For this human life of virtue, see Doru Costache, 'Living Above Gender: Insights from Maximus the Confessor', *JECS* 21.2 (2013), 261–90.

> In this way, he showed, I think, that there was perhaps another mode, foreknown by God, for the growth to the multitude of human beings, had the first human kept the commandment and not cast himself down to the level of irrational animals by misusing the mode of his proper power[43]

Again, Maximos is not simply speaking about 'the multiplication of human beings', which might be taken as suggesting that there was another means for procreation had things been otherwise, but rather about the *αὔξησις* towards the multitude of human beings, a word which simply means 'growth' or 'increase'. Most importantly, Maximos' point here is that God could 'perhaps' have arranged things in such a way that the desired number of human beings was attained otherwise, for all things are possible for God, but that he has in fact chosen the route we do indeed have. And, moreover, as we have seen, as the way in which we 'are shown to be and become simply human' is through the acquisition of virtue, so attaining the perfection of being human, as exemplified in Christ, it is not the result of, nor does it even need, 'the natural process of marital intercourse'. Maximos then continues the sentence:

> *καὶ τὴν κατὰ τὸ ἄρρεν καὶ θῆλυ διαφοράν τε καὶ διαίρεσιν τῆς φύσεως ἐξωθούμενος, ἧς πρὸς τὸ γενέσθαι, καθάπερ ἔφην, ἄνθρωπος, οὐδόλως προσεδεήθη, ὧν δὲ ἄνευ εἶναι τυχόν ἐστι δυνατόν.*
>
> and so he drove out from nature the difference and division into male and female, which he in no way needed to become human, as I have said, and without which existence would perhaps have been possible.

Clearly, for Maximos the distinction between male and female is not needed to become human—virtue is—and existence without this distinction is 'perhaps' possible. He then concludes this sentence by citing, as Gregory does, Gal. 3:28: 'there is no need for this division to last perpetually, for in Christ Jesus, says the divine apostle, there is neither male nor female.'

The third mention of this discussion is in the section devoted to describing Christ's work of recapitulation, how 'as human' Christ appears before the God and Father, he who, 'as Word' can never be separated from the Father, 'fulfilling as human, in deed and truth, and with perfect obedience, all that he himself as God had preordained should take place, having completed the whole plan of God the Father for us'. Maximos now describes how Christ's work of unification is effected in us, beginning again from the division into male and female:

> Thus he united, first of all, ourselves in himself, through the removal of the difference according to the male and the female [*τῆς κατὰ τὸ ἄρρεν καὶ τὸ θῆλυ*

[43] Constas, 110.5–21 (PG 91.1308d–1309b).

> διαφορᾶς], and instead of men and women [ἀντὶ ἀνδρῶν καὶ γυναικῶν], in whom this mode of division is especially evident [ἐνθεωρεῖται μάλιστα], he showed us as properly and truly to be simply human beings, thoroughly formed according to him, bearing his image intact and completely unadulterated, touched in no way by any marks of corruption.[44]

For the first time in this treatise, Maximos now speaks of 'men' and 'women', and it is in these that the division between 'male and female' is most particularly seen. Quite what Maximos means by this is not clear, apart from the fact that he is evidently not equating 'male and female' with 'men and women', raising the question of whether he has even been talking about the latter in the previous passages. One final point of interest in *Ambig.* 41, for us in this volume, is that in concluding his description of how Christ has divinely 'recapitulated all things in himself' (Eph. 1:10), Maximos comments that Christ 'shows that the whole creation exists as one, like another human being [μίαν ὑπάρχουσαν τὴν ἅπασαν κτίσιν δείξας, καθάπερ ἄνθρωπον ἄλλον]' brought to perfection through the convergence of all its parts, united 'according to the one and simple and undefined and undifferentiated concept of its derivation from non-being, in accordance with which the whole of creation admits of one and the same absolutely undiscriminated *logos*, that non-being is prior to being'.[45]

Elsewhere in his writings, Maximos almost invariably takes 'male and female' in a 'spiritual' sense. For instance, in his *Commentary on the Our Father*, he simply and directly takes the 'male and female' of Gal. 3:28 to indicate 'anger and desire' (τουτέστι θυμός καὶ ἐπιθυμία).[46] When these contrary dispositions are put aside, so that the *logos* is not enslaved by them, he continues, the divine image shines forth, remoulding the soul to the divine likeness, according to its will. In this way, 'it comes to be [γενέσθαι] in the great kingdom, subsisting essentially [συνυφισταμένης οὐσιωδῶς] with the God and Father of all, as a radiant dwelling place of the Spirit, wholly receiving, if one may so speak, the power of the knowledge of the divine nature as far as possible', and it is in this way, finally, that 'Christ always wills to be born mystically, becoming incarnate in those being saved, and rendering the soul begetting him to be a virgin mother, not having, to speak concisely, according to the comparison, as male and female, the properties of nature subject to corruption and genesis'.[47]

[44] Constas, 114.1–8 (PG 91.1309d–1312a).

[45] Maximos, *Ambig.* 41; Constas, 114.16–23 (PG 91.1312ab).

[46] Ed. Peter van Deun, CCSG 23 (Turnhout: Brepols, 1991), 47.342–3; ET George Berthold, CWS (London: SPCK, 1985), 108, modified.

[47] Ibid., 50; ET 109. For Maximos' cosmological understanding of 'incarnation', see Jordan Wood, *The Whole Mystery of Christ: Creation as Incarnation in Maximus Confessor* (Notre Dame, IN: Notre Dame Press, 2022).

What then, finally, of existence as men and women (if not male and female) in the resurrection as understood by the authors we have been considering? Much of what we have seen in Gregory and Maximos is primarily concerned with modes of identification: it is by the mark of Christ, that the human being is known, not by the properties of male and female, and this, they would argue, is based upon a careful consideration of the different clauses in Gen. 1:27 (and, of course, Gal. 3:28). It might be helpful to borrow the image of Origen: when iron is in the fire, although it remains iron, it is no longer known by its own properties but is now known by the properties of the fire (*Princ.* 2.6.6). Origen, so far as we can tell, did not use this image with regard to Gal. 3:28, though he did speak of how, when God is 'all in all', the human being 'will no longer sense anything else apart from God: it will think God, see God, hold God; God will be the mode and measure of its every movement; and thus "God" will be "all" to it' (*Princ.* 3.6.3). Gregory, in the passages especially from *De Mortuis* considered above, similarly holds that there will be no 'mark, shape, and form of that house not made with hands'; it is only by the characteristic mark of Christ that we are known in the resurrection. Whether Gregory intends that the resurrectional transformation is such that the reweaving of the elements of the body (i.e. intellectual properties) actually eradicates bodily differences or whether such differences no longer, as it were, register, in the way that, to adapt Origen's image, iron and bronze in the fire would be indistinguishable, is not clear. But Gregory does allow, as we have seen, that the procreative power remains, now giving birth to virtue and the spirit of salvation.

Maximos, however, adapts the image of fire in a most interesting way. When a sword is heated in a fire, he points out:

> the quality of sharpness assumes the quality of heat, and the quality of heat that of sharpness (for just as the fire is united to the iron, so too is the heat of the fire diffused throughout the cutting edge of the sword), and the iron becomes burning hot through its union with the fire, and the fire acquires a cutting edge through its union with the iron. Yet neither of the elements undergoes any change in the exchange that results from the union, but each remains secure in its own natural properties, even though it has acquired the property of the other to which it has been joined.[48]

Maximos' purpose here is to argue that in the mystery of the divine incarnation divinity and humanity, united in the one hypostasis, maintain both their natural properties and energies, or rather, that it is here, in the union, that we see what their natural properties are, for after all, if the sharpness of the sword has assumed the quality of heat, the coldness that would have identified the iron, with which the

[48] Maximos, *Ambig.* 5; Constas, vol. 1, 54.25–55.8.

sword is made, outside the fire would no longer be present when united with it. That there 'is not male and female' in Christ, as the word of the Apostle, is a given for our figures; what becomes of men and women, for Maximos, when they finally become and are shown to be simply human, and how he would adapt the iron sword and fire analogy, remains another question. Undoubtedly, each of the figures we have considered take seriously Paul's mysteriological proclamation that 'we all shall be changed' (1 Cor. 15:51), and would have regarded any attempt to hold on to our current experience of existence as, in Gregory's striking image, embryos wanting to remain in the womb rather than becoming human.

The further legacy of Gregory's work in Maximos and beyond him in Eriugena is, however, for another work. Given Gregory's conclusion prior to his final exhortation at the end of *On the Human Image*, that it is 'through those material and more animal-like attributes of the soul' that the human being is brought to perfection, it seems apt to end this introduction with the words of Stavrogin, the last line of which was used as an epigraph for this volume:

> 'I don't understand why you consider the possession of a mind, that is, consciousness, the greatest of all possible existences?...Why do you reject the possibility of a secret? Note also that, perhaps, unbelief is natural for man, and this precisely because he puts mind above all; since mind is a property only of the human organism, he thereby neither understands nor wishes to understand life in another form, that is, life beyond the grave—he does not believe that that life is higher. On the other hand, by nature the sense of despair and wretchedness is proper to man, for the human mind is so constituted that at every moment it doubts itself, is not satisfied with himself, and man is therefore prone to consider his existence inadequate. We are, clearly, transitory beings and our existence on earth is, clearly, a process, the uninterrupted existence of a chrysalis transitioning into a butterfly.'[49]

[49] Dostoevsky, in appendix to eighth volume of sixth printing of *The Demons*, Stavrogin to Shatov; quoted in Bulgakov, *The Sophiology of Death*, essay 1, pp. 1–2, ftn. 1.

Manuscripts, Abbreviations, Sigla, and Translation

Manuscripts

A Vienna, Österreichische Nationalbibliothek, *theol. gr. 222* (134^{r}–187^{r})

Æ London, British Library, *Burney MS 52* (88^{v}–130^{r})

B Vienna, Österreichische Nationalbibliothek, *theol. gr. 278* (2^{r}–49^{v})

ß Paris, Bibliothèque nationale de France, *grec 1277* (54^{v}–82^{v})

C Vienna, Österreichische Nationalbibliothek, *theol. gr. 113* (79^{r}–138^{r})

D Vienna, Österreichische Nationalbibliothek, *theol. gr. 160* (60^{r}–113^{v})

E Vienna, Österreichische Nationalbibliothek, *theol. gr. 168* (73^{v}–120^{r})

F Vienna, Österreichische Nationalbibliothek, *theol. gr. 134* (95^{r}–150^{r})

G Oxford Christ Church Library, *grec 45* (115^{r}–194^{r})

H Glasgow, University Library, *MS Hunter 447* (1–52), extracts

I Munich, Bayerische Staatsbibliothek, *Cod. graec. 192* (111^{v}–166^{v})

J Munich, Bayerische Staatsbibliothek, *Cod. graec. 562* (113^{v}–117^{r}), chapter 12

K Munich, Bayerische Staatsbibliothek, *Cod. graec. 206* (1^{r}–34^{r}), incomplete

L Munich, Bayerische Staatsbibliothek, *Cod. graec. 240* (65^{r}–109^{v})

M Munich, Bayerische Staatsbibliothek, *Cod. graec. 570* (108^{r}–170^{v})

N Venice, Biblioteca Nazionale di San Marco, *grec 58* (65^{v}–116^{r})

O Oxford, Bodleian, *Barocci grec 228* (65^{r}–118^{v})

P Paris, Bibliothèque nationale de France, *grec 476* (64^{v}–116^{v})

Q Paris, Bibliothèque nationale de France, *Coislin grec 235* (121^{r}–208^{v})

R London, British Library, *Royal MS 16 D I* (117^{v}–143^{r})

S Oxford, Bodleian, *Barocci grec 144* (98^{r}–174^{v})

T Rome, Biblioteca Vaticana, *grec 408* (89^{v}–161^{v})

V Vatican, Biblioteca Apostolica Vaticana, *Vat. grec 2066* (299–316^{v}), incomplete + Washington, Library of Congress, *Ms 60*

W Vatican, Biblioteca Apostolica Vaticana, *Vat. grec 2053* (247–283^{v})

X Florence, Biblioteca Laurenziana, *grec Plut. 4.27* (186^{v}–240^{v})

Z Paris, Bibliothèque nationale de France, *grec 1356*—9th-century fragments (Astruc)

Λ Oxford, Bodleian, *Ms Bodl. 238* (185^{r}–197^{r})

Σ Vatican, Biblioteca Apostolica Vaticana, *Vat. sir. 106* (42^{r}–75^{r})

Editions and Translations

Ald Aldus (1536)

Dion *Dionysius*, ed. Forbes (1855–61)

Eri Eriugena, ed. Mandolino (2020)

Forb Forbes (1855–61)

Mign	Migne PG (1858)
Wils	Wilson NPNF (1893)

Indirect Witnesses

Dam	John of Damascus, ed. Kotter (1973)
Inc	*De Incarnatione*, ed. Diekamp, rev. Phanourgakis and Chrysos (1981)
Ius	Justinian, ed. Schwartz, ACO 3 (1940)
SP	*Sacra Parallela*, ed. Thum (2018)

Abbreviations Used in Critical Apparatus

ac	ante correctionem
add.	addidit, addiderunt
al.	alia
cap.	capitula
codd.	codices
corr.	correxit, correxerunt
def.	deficit, deficiens
des.	desinit, desinunt
edd.	editores
eras.	erasit
exp.	expunxit
inc.	incipit
inscr.	inscriptio
l.	linea
lit.	littera
man.	manus
mg	in margine
om.	omisit, omiserunt
pc	post correctionem
pon.	ponit, ponunt
rel.	reliqui
supr.	supra

Sigla

[ ] Words supplied by the translator.

Translation

The translation provided owes a lot to that of Wilson (NPNF 2.5; 1893), especially with regard to the passages containing medical and astronomical descriptions. As noted in the Introduction and in the annotations that follow, it corrects several significant errors of translation. In general, as with my previous translations, I have attempted to provide as literal a translation as possible, while still respecting the rules of English grammar. As such, there are longer sentences, more numerous sub-clauses, and a greater use of the passive voice than will please some. This is done, however, in the conviction that the mode of expression, how an author holds together various clauses in a single sentence, conveying as it does patterns of thought, is essential to understanding what is being said.

ΤΟΥ ΕΝ ΑΓΙΟΙΣ ΓΡΗΓΟΡΙΟΥ ΝΥΣΣΗΣ

ΠΕΡΙ ΕΙΚΟΝΟΣ ΑΝΘΡΩΠΟΥ
ΗΤΟΙ
ΘΕΩΡΙΑ ΕΙΣ ΤΗΝ ΚΑΤΑΣΚΕΥΗΝ ΤΟΥ ΑΝΘΡΩΠΟΥ

Saint Gregory of Nyssa

On the Human Image of God
That is
A Contemplation of the Formation of the Human Being

Τῷ ἀδελφῷ δούλῳ Θεοῦ Πέτρῳ Γρηγόριος ἐπίσκοπος Νύσσης.

[1] [125] *Εἰ ταῖς διὰ τῶν χρημάτων τιμαῖς ἔδει γεραίρειν τοὺς κατ' ἀρετὴν διαφέροντας, μικρὸς ἄν, καθώς φησιν ὁ Σολομών,* ***ὅλος ὁ κόσμος τῶν χρημάτων*** *ἐφάνη πρὸς τὸ γενέσθαι τῆς σῆς ἀρετῆς ἰσοστάσιος. Ἐπει δὲ κρείττων ἢ κατὰ πλούτου τιμὴν ἡ χρεωστουμένη τῇ σεμνότητί σου χάρις ἐστίν· ἀπαιτεῖ δὲ τὸ ἅγιον πάσχα τὴν συνήθη τῆς ἀγάπης δωροφορίαν·* [B] *προσάγομέν σου τῇ μεγαλοφροσύνῃ δῶρον, ὦ ἄνθρωπε τοῦ Θεοῦ, μικρότερον μὲν ἢ ὡς ἄξιον εἶναί σοι προσκομίζεσθαι· τῆς γε μὴν δυνάμεως ἡμῶν οὐκ ἐνδεέστερον. Τὸ δὲ δῶρον λόγος ἐστὶν, οἷον ἱμάτιόν τι πενιχρὸν ἐκ τῆς πτωχῆς ἡμῶν διανοίας οὐκ ἀπόνως ἐξυφασμένον· ἡ δὲ τοῦ λόγου ὑπόθεσις τολμηρὰ μὲν ἴσως τοῖς πολλοῖς εἶναι δόξει, πλὴν οὐκ ἔξω τοῦ πρέποντος ἐνομίσθη· μόνος μὲν γὰρ ἀξίως τὴν κτίσιν τοῦ Θεοῦ κατενόησεν ὁ κατὰ Θεὸν κτισθεὶς ὄντως καὶ ἐν εἰκόνι τοῦ κτίσαντος τὴν ψυχὴν μεμορφωμένος, Βασίλειος, ὁ κοινὸς ἡμῶν πατὴρ καὶ διδάσκαλος, ὃς τὴν ὑψηλὴν τοῦ παντὸς διακόσμησιν εὔληπτον τοῖς πολλοῖς διὰ τῆς ἰδίας θεωρίας ἐποίησε, τὸν ἐν τῇ ἀληθινῇ σοφίᾳ παρὰ τοῦ Θεοῦ συστάντα κόσμον γνώριμον τοῖς διὰ τῆς συνέσεως αὐτοῦ τῇ θεωρίᾳ προσαγομένοις ποιήσας·* [C] *ἡμεῖς δὲ οἱ καὶ τοῦ θαυμάζειν αὐτὸν κατ' ἀξίαν ἐνδεῶς ἔχοντες, ὁμῶς τὸ λεῖπον τοῖς τεθεωρημένοις τῷ μεγάλῳ προσθεῖναι διενοήθημεν· οὐχ ὡς νοθεύοντες δι' ὑπερβολῆς τὸν ἐκείνου πόνον (οὐδὲ γὰρ θέμις τὸ ὑψηλὸν ἐκεῖνο καθυβρισθῆναι στόμα τοῖς ἡμετέροις ἐπιφημιζόμενον λόγοις), ἀλλ' ὡς μὴ δοκεῖν ἐλλειπῆ τοῦ διδασκάλου τὴν δόξαν ἐν τοῖς μαθηταῖς αὐτοῦ εἶναι.*

[2] *Εἰ γὰρ, λειπούσης τῇ Ἑξαημέρῳ τῆς εἰς τὸν ἄνθρωπον θεωρίας, μηδεὶς τῶν μαθητευσάντων αὐτῷ σπουδήν τινα πρὸς τὴν τοῦ λείποντος ἀναπλήρωσιν εἰσηνέγκατο, ἔσχεν ἂν εἰκότως κατὰ τῆς μεγάλης αὐτοῦ δόξης ὁ μῶμος λαβὴν, ὡς μὴ βουληθέντος ἕξιν τινὰ κατανοητικὴν τοῖς ἀκροαταῖς ἐνεργάσασθαι· νυνὶ δὲ κατὰ δύναμιν ἡμῶν ἐπιτολμησάντων τῇ ἐξηγήσει τοῦ λείποντος, εἰ μέν* [D] *τι τοιοῦτον ἐν τοῖς ἡμετέροις εὑρεθείη οἷον τῆς ἐκείνου διδασκαλίας μὴ ἀνάξιον εἶναι, εἰς τὸν*

2 *τῶν om.* R *κατ'*] *κατὰ* L 3 *καθώς*] *ὡς* B G L M P R² S T V X *σολομὼν*] *ita* Æ I K L M O R V W X *Ald Mign* : *σολομῶν Forb* *ὅλος ὁ κόσμος τῶν χρημάτων* : sermo sicut ex rebus *Eri* 4 *ἰσοστάσιον* L *ἐπει δὲ*] *ita* Æ B C I K L M N O P² Q R S T V W *Forb* : *ἐπειδὴ* X *Ald Mign* *κρείττων*] *ita* Æ ß I K M P O Q R T^{ac} *Forb* : *κρείττον* S^{ac} (*ω sup. l.*) : *κρεῖττον* V W X *Ald Mign* 5 *πλοῦτον* B 6 *προσάγομέν*] *ita* Æ B C I K M N O Q R T W *Forb* : *ἣν προσάγομέν* V W^{ac} *Eri Ald Mign* 7 *ὦ ἄνθρωπε τοῦ θεοῦ* : uidelicit homo dei *Eri* *τοῦ*] *ita* Æ B C G I K L M N O P Q R S T V W X *Ald Forb* : *om. Mign* *ὡς*] *ὥστε* N *προσκομίζεσθαι*] *προσάγεσθαι* R² 9 *τι om.* Æ C G K S *οὐκ ἀπόνως om.* I *ἐξυφασμένον οὐκ ἀπόνως* B 10 *εἶναι ἴσως τοῖς πολλοῖς δόξει* Æ C K O : *τοῖς πολλοῖς ἴσως δόξει εἶναι* B 11 *μὲν*] *ita* Æ B C G I K L M N O P Q R S T V W X *Forb* : *om. Ald Mign* *γὰρ om.* B *ἀξίως om.* N 12 *βασίλειος*] *om.* G I P^{ac} T X *Eri* 13 *πατὴρ ἡμῶν* G K 14 *τὸν*] *ita* Æ B C G I K L M N O P Q R S X *Forb* : *καὶ τὸν* V W *Ald Mign* 15–16 *τοῖς διὰ τῆς συνέσεως αὐτοῦ τῇ θεωρίᾳ προσαγομένοις ποιήσας*] *διὰ τῆς συνέσεως αὐτοῦ ποιήσας τοῖς τὴν τούτου θεωρίαν* B 15 *τοῖς post αὐτοῦ pon.* N 16 *οἱ*] *ita* B G L N O P R S T V W X *Forb* : *εἰ* M : *om. Ald Mign* 17 *ἔχοντες*] *ἔχομεν* M *ὁμῶς*] *ita* Æ B C G I K L M N O P Q R S T V W X *Forb* : *ὁμοῦ Ald Mign* 18 *ὑπερβολῆς*] *ita* Æ C G I K L N^{mg} O P R S X *Forb* : *ὑποβολῆς* V W *Ald Mign* 19 *καθυβρίσαι* C K O : *καθυβρίζεσθαι* I 20 *ἐλλειπῆ*] *ita* G I K L P Q T V W X *Forb* : *ἐλλιπῆ Ald Mign* 21 *τῇ ἑξαημέρῳ*] *ita* Æ^{ac} B C G K L M N O P Q R S T V W X *Forb* : *τῆς ἑξαημέρου Ald Mign* *εἰς τὸν ἄνθρωπον θεωρίας*] de conditione hominis expositio *Dion* : theoria hominis *Eri* 23 *εἰσηνέγκατο*] *ita* Æ I K L M N O Q R S V W *Ald Forb* : *εἰσενέγκατο* ß G P R (*in mg a 2ª man. ἀποπλήρωσιν ἀπηνέγκατο*) : *εἰσενέγκαιτο Mign* *μεγάλης αὐτοῦ*] *ἐκείνου μεγάλης* N 24 *κατανοητικὴν*] *διανοητικὴν* B G L N^{mg} P R S T V X 25 *μέν τι*] *μέντοι* B P² : *μέν* Æ (*τ sup. l.*) *ἐν om.* B 26 *μὴ ἀνάξιον*] *ἄξιον* Æ C O Q : *μὴ om.* K *εἶναι ἀνάξιον* B *Dion*

Gregory, Bishop of Nyssa, to his brother Peter, the servant of God.

[1] If it is necessary to honour with rewards of money those who excel in virtue, *the whole world of money*, as Solomon says,[1] would seem to be small in equivalence to your virtue. Since, however, the favour owed to your Reverence is greater than can be valued in money, yet the holy Pascha demands the accustomed gift of love, we offer to your magnanimity, O man of God,[2] a gift too small indeed to be worthy of being presented to you, but one not falling short of our ability. The gift is a treatise, like a mean garment, woven not without toil from our poor mind; the subject of the treatise, while it will perhaps seem to many to be audacious, yet was not deemed beyond what is fitting. For he alone has worthily considered the creation of God who truly was created according to God and whose soul was formed in the image of the Creator—Basil, our common father and teacher—who by his own contemplation made the sublime adornment of the universe accessible to many, making the world established by God in true wisdom known to those who are led, by means of his understanding, to contemplation; but we, while falling short even of worthily admiring him, nevertheless intend to add what is lacking in the reflections of the great one, not interpolating his work by insertion (it not being right for that lofty mouth to be insulted by being attributed with our words), but so that the glory of the teacher may not seem lacking among his disciples.[3]

[2] As the contemplation of the human being is lacking in his *Hexaemeron*, if none of those who had been his disciples contributed any effort towards the completion of what was lacking, the scoffer would perhaps have had a pretext against his great fame, for not having wished to produce in his hearers a certain disposition of understanding. But now that we venture according to our ability

[1] Prov. 17:6. [2] That is, Peter; cf. Gregory of Nyssa, *Hex.* 1, 77 (Drobner, 5.3; 83.10).
[3] Cf. Gregory of Nyssa, *Hex.* 77 (Drobner, 83–4).

διδάσκαλον πάντως τὴν ἀναφορὰν ἕξει· εἰ δὲ μὴ καθικνοῖτο τῆς μεγαλοφυοῦς θεωρίας ὁ ἡμέτερος λόγος, ὁ μὲν ἔξω τῆς τοιαύτης ἔσται κατηγορίας, τοῦ μὴ βούλεσθαι δοκεῖν τοῖς μαθηταῖς ἐγγενέσθαι τι δεξιὸν, ἐκφεύγων τὴν μέμψιν, ἡμεῖς δ' ἂν εἰκότως ὑπεύθυνοι δόξαιμεν τοῖς μωμοσκοποῦσιν, ὡς οὐ χωρήσαντες ἐν τῷ μικροφυεῖ τῆς καρδίας ἡμῶν τοῦ καθηγητοῦ τὴν σοφίαν. [3] *Ἔστι δὲ οὐ μικρὸς ὁ προκείμενος ἡμῖν εἰς* [128] *θεωρίαν σκοπὸς, οὐδέ τινος τῶν ἐν τῷ κόσμῳ θαυμάτων τὰ δεύτερα φερόμενος, τάχα δὲ καὶ μείζων ἑκάστου τῶν γινωσκομένων, διότι οὐδὲν ἕτερον Θεῷ ἐκ τῶν ὄντων ὡμοίωται, πλὴν τῆς κατὰ τὸν ἄνθρωπον κτίσεως. Ὥστε παρὰ τοῖς εὐγνώμοσι τῶν ἀκροατῶν πρόχειρον ἡμῖν τὴν ἐπὶ τοῖς λεγομένοις συγγνώμην εἶναι, κἂν πολὺ κατόπιν τῆς ἀξίας ὁ λόγος ἔλθοι· δεῖ γὰρ, οἶμαι, τῶν περὶ τὸν ἄνθρωπον ἁπάντων, τῶν τε προγεγενῆσθαι πεπιστευμένων, καὶ τῶν νῦν θεωρουμένων, καὶ τῶν εἰς ὕστερον ἐκβήσεσθαι προσδοκωμένων, μηδὲν παραλιπεῖν ἀνεξέταστον· ἦ γὰρ ἂν ἐλλιπεστέρα τοῦ ἐπαγγέλματος ἡ σπουδὴ διελέγχοιτο, εἰ τοῦ ἀνθρώπου προκειμένου τῇ θεωρίᾳ, παρεθείη τι τῶν συντεινόντων πρὸς τὴν ὑπόθεσιν· ἀλλὰ καὶ τὰ δοκοῦντα περὶ αὐτοῦ ἐναντίως ἔχειν, διὰ τὸ μὴ τὰ* [B] *αὐτὰ τοῖς ἐξ ἀρχῆς γεγενημένοις καὶ νῦν περὶ τὴν φύσιν ὁρᾶσθαι διά τινος ἀναγκαίας ἀκολουθίας ἔκ τε τῆς γραφικῆς ὑφηγήσεως καὶ ἐκ τῆς παρὰ τῶν λογισμῶν εὑρισκομένης συναρτῆσαι προσήκει, ὡς ἂν συμβαίνοι πᾶσα πρὸς ἑαυτὴν ἡ ὑπόθεσις εἱρμῷ καὶ τάξει τῶν ἐναντίως ἔχειν δοκούντων πρὸς ἓν καὶ τὸ αὐτὸ πέρας συμφερομένων, οὕτω τῆς θείας δυνάμεως ἐλπίδα τοῖς ὑπὲρ ἐλπίδα καὶ πόρον τοῖς ἀμηχάνοις ἐφευρισκούσης· σαφηνείας δὲ χάριν, καλῶς ἔχειν ᾠήθην, ἐπὶ κεφαλαίων σοι προθεῖναι τὸν λόγον, ὡς ἂν ἔχοις πάσης τῆς πραγματείας ἐν ὀλίγῳ τῶν καθέκαστον ἐπιχειρημάτων εἰδέναι τὴν δύναμιν.*

Α Ἐν ᾧ τίς ἐστι μερικὴ περὶ τοῦ κόσμου φυσιολογία, καί τις ἁβροτέρα διήγησις περὶ τῶν προγεγονότων τῆς τοῦ ἀνθρώπου γενέσεως.

Β Διὰ τί τελευταῖος μετὰ τὴν κτίσιν ὁ ἄνθρωπος.

27 *καθικνοῖτο*] *ita* Æ L N O P Q R V W X *Forb* : *καθίκνοιτο* B C G S : *καθίκνοῖτο* T : *καθικνοῖντο* M : *καθίκοιτο Ald Mign* 28 *ὁ ἡμέτερος λόγος om.* G L M P R^{eras} S T V W X *ἡμέτερος om.* I *λόγος*] *σκοπὸς* N (*et in mg ἐν ἄλλῳ οὐ κεῖται ὁ ἡμέτερος σκοπὸς*) 29 *γενέσθαι* B N *ἐκφεύγων*] *ita* C G N O P Q R S T V W X *Forb* : *ἐκφεῦγον* B : *ἐκφυγὼν Ald Mign* 30 *δόξαιμεν*] *ita* C G^{pc} I K L M N O P R^{pc} S T V W X *Forb* : *δόξωμεν Ald Mign* : *δόξαιμεν ἂν* Æ Q 31 *ἡμῶν om.* Æ I M Q T V W *δὲ*] *ita* Æ ß G K L M N O P Q R S V W X *Ald Forb* : *δ' Mign* 32 *ἐν τῷ κόσμῳ*] *ita* Æ B C I K N O Q R V W *Forb* : *τοῦ κόσμου* G L M P S T X : *ἐν κόσμῳ Ald Mign* 33 *δευτερεῖα* Æ B C K N Q *γινωσκομένων*] *ita* Æ B C G K L M N O P Q R S V X *Forb* : *γινομένων* I : *γιγνωσκομένων Ald Mign* 34 *ἐκ τῶν ὄντων θεῷ* N *ἐκ om.* B G L M P R S V X 36 *ὁ λόγος τῆς ἀξίας* N 37–8 *πεπιστευμένων—προσδοκωμένων*] *προσδοκωμένων καὶ τῶν νῦν θεωρουμένων* W *καὶ τῶν νῦν θεωρουμένων*] *ita* Æ B C G I K L M O P Q R S X *Forb* : *post προσδοκωμένων* (*l.* 38) V *Dion Eri Ald Mign* 38 *εἰς ὕστερον*] *ita* B C G K L M O Q R^{ac} V X *Forb* : *ἐσύστερον* I R^{2} : *εἰσύστερον Ald Mign* 39 *ἂν ἐλλιπεστέρα*] *ἀνελλιπεστέρα* B : *ἂν ἐλλειπεστέρα* G P Q T V W X 41 *αὐτοῦ*] *ita* Æ B C I K L N^{pc} O Q R S *Forb* : *αὐτὸν* V W X *Ald Mign* 42 *τινας* V 43 *ἀφηγήσεως* *εὑρισκομένης*] *ita* Æ B C G I K L O P Q R S T V W X *Forb* : *ἐπινοίας εὑρισκομένης* M *Ald* : *εὑρισκομένης ἐπινοίας Mign* (N *in mg ἐν ἑτέρῳ λείπει τὸ ἐπινοίας*) *συναρτίσαι* Æ C I K N O Q T V 43–4 *συναρτῆσαι—ὑπόθεσις*] pulchre omnem sibimet materiam conuenit adunare *Eri* 44 *πρὸς ἑαυτὴν om. Ald Mign* *ἑαυτὴν*] *αὐτὴν M* *ἡ om.* G 45 *οὕτω*] *ita* Æ B C G K L M N O P Q S R T^{eras} V W X *Forb* : *οὕτω καὶ Ald Mign* 46 *τοῖς ὑπὲρ ἐλπίδα om.* G *πόρον*] *πόνον* *ἐφευρισκούσης*] *εὑρισκομένης B* 47 *ᾠήθην*] *ὠήθημεν* N *προσθεῖναι* T W 48 *ἔχῃς* I *τῆς om.* R *ὀλίγοις* R *καθ' ἕκαστον* V X 49 *δύναμιν*] *ὑπόθεσιν Mign* 50–1 de perfectione et pulcritudine mundi et de discordia concordia 4 elementorum *Λ* 50 *ἐν*] *πρῶτον κεφάλαιον ἐν* Æ P G V X *Ald* : *κεφάλαιον πρῶτον ἐν* O *ἐν—κόσμου om.* N 51 *τοῦ om.* N 52 quod rationabiliter homo ultimus creaturarum creatus est *Λ* *διατί* G N *μετὰ τὴν κτίσιν τελευταῖος Ald*

upon the exposition of what was lacking, if anything should be found in our work not to be unworthy of his teaching, it will wholly be ascribed to the teacher, yet if our treatise does not ascend to his sublime contemplation, he will be free from this charge, avoiding the blame of seeming not to wish that his disciples become skilful, while we perhaps may seem to be blamed by the accusers, for being unable to contain in the smallness of our heart the wisdom of the instructor.[4] [**3**] The scope for contemplation proposed by us is not small, being second to none of the wonders of the world, perhaps even greater than any of those known, because no other existing thing is likened to God except the human creation.[5] As such, we shall find ready allowance for what we say by the well-disposed among our hearers, even if our treatise lags far behind the dignity of the subject. For it is necessary, I suppose, to leave unexamined nothing of all that concerns the human being—of what we believe to have taken place previously, of what we now contemplate, and of what we expect to transpire afterwards (for our effort would be convicted of failing its promise, if, when the human being is proposed for contemplation, anything contributing to the topic were to be omitted)—but it is also proper to fit together, from scriptural guidance and from that discovered by reasoning, the things concerning the human being that seem to be opposed (as what is now seen pertaining to nature by a kind of necessary sequence is not the same as those that occurred from the beginning) so that our whole subject may be consistent with itself in train of thought and order, with things seemingly contrary being brought together to one and the same end, and with the divine power finding a hope for things beyond hope and a means of accomplishing things unworkable.[6] For the sake of clarity, I think it well to set out the treatise for you by headings, that you may be able to know in brief the force of each of the arguments of the whole work.

1. In which is a partial physiological consideration of the nature of the world, and a more minute account of the things preceding the genesis of the human being.[7]
2. Why the human being is last, after the creation.[8]
3. That the nature of the human being is more honourable than all the visible creation.[9]

[4] Cf. Gregory of Nyssa, *Hex.* 28 (Drobner, 42.5–6).

[5] Cf. Gregory of Nyssa, *Cant.* 2 (Langerbeck, 68.1–11).

[6] Cf. Gregory of Nyssa, *Hex.* 6 (Drobner, 6.5–6).

[7] In the Latin translation of Dionysius Exiguus, as preserved in *Bodl. 238*, it is given as: 'Of the perfection and beauty of the world and of the harmonious discord of the four elements'.

[8] *Bodl. 238*: 'That it was reasonable that the human being should be created last of the creatures'.

[9] *Bodl. 238*: 'That God created the human being with great deliberation'.

Γ Ὅτι τιμιωτέρα πάσης τῆς φαινομένης κτίσεως ἡ τοῦ ἀνθρώπου φύσις.

Δ Ὅτι διὰ πάντων ἐπισημαίνει τὴν ἀρχικὴν ἐξουσίαν ἡ τοῦ ἀνθρώπου κατασκευή.

Ε Ὅτι ὁμοίωμα τῆς θείας βασιλείας ὁ ἄνθρωπος.

Ϛ Ἐξέτασις τῆς τοῦ νοῦ πρὸς τὴν φύσιν συγγενείας, ἐν ᾧ καὶ ἐκ παρόδου τὸ τῶν Ἀνομοίων διελέγχεται δόγμα.

Ζ Διὰ τί γυμνὸς τῶν ἐκ φύσεως ὅπλων τε καὶ προκαλυμμάτων ὁ ἄνθρωπος.

Η Διὰ τί ὄρθιον τοῦ ἀνθρώπου τὸ σχῆμα, καὶ ὅτι διὰ τὸν λόγον αἱ χεῖρες, ἐν ᾧ τις καὶ περὶ διαφορᾶς ψυχῶν φιλοσοφία.

Θ Ὅτι ὀργανικὸν κατεσκευάσθη τοῦ ἀνθρωποῦ τὸ σχῆμα πρὸς τὴν τοῦ λόγου χρείαν.

Ι Ὅτι διὰ τῶν αἰσθήσεων ὁ νοῦς ἐνεργεῖ.

ΙΑ Ὅτι ἀθεώρητος ἡ τοῦ νοῦ φύσις.

ΙΒ Ἐξέτασις ἐν τίνι τὸ ἡγεμονικὸν νομιστέον, ἐν ᾧ καὶ περὶ δακρύων καὶ περὶ γέλωτος φυσιολογία, καὶ θεώρημά τι φυσικὸν περὶ τῆς κατὰ τὴν ὕλην καὶ τὴν φύσιν καὶ τὸν νοῦν κοινωνίας.

ΙΓ Περὶ ὕπνου καὶ χάσμης καὶ ὀνείρων αἰτιολογία.

ΙΔ Ὅτι οὐκ ἐν μέρει τοῦ σώματος ὁ νοῦς· ἐν ᾧ καὶ διάκρισις τῶν τε σωματικῶν καὶ ψυχικῶν κινημάτων.

ΙΕ Ὅτι κυρίως ψυχή, ἡ λογικὴ καὶ ἔστι καὶ λέγεται· αἱ δ᾽ ἄλλαι ὁμωνύμως κατονομάζονται· ἐν ᾧ καὶ τό, διὰ παντὸς τοῦ σώματος διήκειν τὴν τοῦ νοῦ δύναμιν καταλλήλως ἑκάστου μέρους προσαπτομένην.

ΙϚ Θεωρία τοῦ θείου ῥητοῦ τοῦ εἰπόντος, **ποιήσωμεν ἄνθρωπον κατ᾽ εἰκόνα καὶ ὁμοίωσιν ἡμετέραν**· ἐν ᾧ ἐξετάζεται, τίς ὁ τῆς εἰκόνος λόγος, καὶ πῶς ὁμοιοῦται

53 quod cum magna deliberatione deus hominem creaverit *Λ* φύσις] κτίσις B G P X : conditio *Dion* 54–5 de regia dignitate humanae formae *Λ* 56 quomodo ad imaginem dei fact est humana anima *Λ* 57–8 quod deus non habet membra humana et quod una est imago patris et filii contra eunomianos *Λ* 58 ἀνομοίων] ἐναντίων Æ 59 cur homo non sit creatus cum cornibus et aliis munimentis sicut quaedam alia *Λ* καλυμμάτων N 60–1 de dignitate humanae formae et quare post alios creaturas homo creatus sit *Λ* 60 τὸ τοῦ ἀνθρωποῦ B N 61 καὶ *om.* B φιλοσοφία περὶ ψυχῶν διαφορᾶς B διαφορῶν Æ 62–3 quod forma humani corporis congruat rationalitate mentis *Λ* 62 τὸ τοῦ ἀνθρωποῦ N : τὸ ἀνθρωποῦ G P X σχῆμα] σῶμα Æ G O P X 64 de quinque sensibus corporis *Λ* 65 definitio mentis humanae *Λ* νοῦ] ἀνθρώπου *Ald* 66–8 quod principale hominis non solum [totum *Forb*] in cerebro sed in toto habitat corpore *Λ* 66 ἐν ᾧ *om.*N περί^{2} *om.* Æ G P V X 67 καί^{1} *om.* Æ N 67–8 θεώρημά—κοινωνίας *faciunt cap.* ιγ A B C I K N O Q R T *Σ Λ* contemplatio quaedam naturalis de materia et natura et mentis inspectione *Dion* : quod sicut a deo mens gubernatur ita a mente materialis uita corporis *Λ* 69 ιγ : ιδ A B C I K N Q R T *Dion Σ Λ* quod corpus nostrum semper sit in motu *Λ* 70 ιδ : ιε A B C I K N O Q R T *Dion Σ Λ* 70–1 quod aliquando mens seruit corpori et de tribus differentiis eius, uitali, spirituali et rationali *Λ* 71 καὶ] καὶ τῶν N 72 ιε : ις A B C I K N O Q R T *Dion Σ Λ* 72–4 quod utialis efficientiae irrationabilium non uere sed equivoce dicitur anima et de ineffabili communione corporis et animae *Λ* 72 ἡ] ἡ τοῦ ἀνθρώπου ἡ καὶ N καί^{1} *om.* G P X δὲ Æ G P V X 74 προσαπτομένην] ἐφαπτομένην N 75 ις : ιζ A B C I K N O Q R T *Dion Σ Λ* 75–8 quod excellentia hominis non in eo est quod iuxta philosophos ad imaginem mundi conditus est, sed in eo quod ad imaginem dei factus est et quomodo ad imaginem dei factus est *Λ* 75 θεώρημα N τοῦ] *ita* Æ N *Forb* : *om.* V X *Ald* 75–6 κατ᾽ εἰκόνα καὶ ὁμοίωσιν ἡμετέραν *om.* N^{ac} καὶ ὁμοίωσιν *om.* G N^{2} P V X καὶ ὁμοίωσιν ἡμετέραν] ἡμετέραν καὶ καθ᾽ ὁμοίωσιν Æ O 76 ᾧ] ᾧ καὶ N πῶς] *ita* G N^{pc} P X *Forb* : εἰ *Ald*

4. That the formation of the human being throughout signifies his sovereign authority.[10]
5. That the human being is a likeness of the divine royalty.[11]
6. An examination of the kinship of the intellect to nature; in which also, by way of digression, the doctrine of the Anomoeans is refuted.[12]
7. Why the human being is by nature destitute weapons and covering.[13]
8. Why the form of the human being is upright, and that the hands are on account of reason; in which also is a certain philosophical treatment regarding the difference of souls.[14]
9. That the form of the human being was fashioned as an instrument for the use of reason.[15]
10. That the intellect works by means of the senses.[16]
11. That the nature of the intellect is invisible.[17]
12. An examination concerning in which part the ruling principle should be considered to be; in which also is a physiological consideration of tears and laughter, and a physical theory regarding the association of matter, nature, and the intellect.[18]
13. Concerning the causality of sleep, yawning, and dreams.[19]
14. That the intellect is not in a part of the body; in which also is a distinction of the movements of body and soul.[20]
15. That the rational soul is and is called 'soul' properly, while the others are called so equivocally; in which also is this, that the power of the intellect extends throughout the whole body, touching appropriately every part.[21]
16. A contemplation of the divine word which says, *Let us make the human being in accordance with our image and likeness*;[22] in which is examined what the definition of the image is, and how the passible and mortal is likened to the blessed and impassible, and how the male and the female are in the image, these not being in the Prototype.[23]

[10] *Bodl. 238*: 'Of the kingly dignity of the human form'.

[11] *Bodl. 238*: 'How the human soul is made in the image of God'.

[12] *Bodl. 238*: 'That God does not have human limbs, and that the image of the Father and the Son is one, against the Eunomians'.

[13] *Bodl. 238*: 'Why the human was not created with horns and other defences like the other [animals]'.

[14] *Bodl. 238*: 'Of the dignity of the human form, and why the human was created after the other creatures'.

[15] *Bodl. 238*: 'That the form of the human body is congruent with the rationality of the mind'.

[16] *Bodl. 238*: 'Of the five bodily senses'.

[17] *Bodl. 238*: 'The definition of the human mind'.

[18] *Bodl. 238*: 'That the principle of the human being does not reside in the brain but in the whole body'; and, as Chap. 13 (at *De Imag.* 12.9): 'That as the mind is governed by God, so is the material life of the body by the mind'.

[19] *Bodl. 238* (as Chap. 14): 'That our body is always in motion'.

[20] *Bodl. 238* (as Chap. 15): 'That the mind is sometimes in servitude to the body, and of its three differences, vital, spiritual, and rational'.

[21] *Bodl. 238* (as Chap. 16): 'That the vital energy of the irrational creatures is not truly but equivocally called "soul" and of the unspeakable communion of body and mind'.

[22] Gen. 1:26.

[23] *Bodl. 238* (as Chap. 17): 'That the excellence of the human being does not consist in the fact that, according to the philosophers, he is made after the image of the world, but in the fact that he is made in the image of God and how he is made in the image of God'.

τῷ μακαρίῳ τε καὶ ἀπαθεῖ τὸ ἐμπαθὲς καὶ ἐπίκηρον, καὶ πῶς ἐν τῇ εἰκόνι τὸ ἄρρεν καὶ τὸ θῆλυ, ἐν τῷ πρωτοτύπῳ τούτων οὐκ ὄντων.

ΙΖ Τί χρὴ λέγειν πρὸς τοὺς ἐπαποροῦντας, εἰ μετὰ τὴν ἁμαρτίαν ἡ παιδοποιΐα, πῶς ἂν ἐγένοντο αἱ ψυχαὶ εἰ ἀναμάρτητοι διέμειναν οἱ ἐξ ἀρχῆς ἄνθρωποι.

ΙΗ Ὅτι τὰ ἄλογα ἐν ἡμῖν πάθη ἐκ τῆς πρὸς τὴν ἄλογον φύσιν συγγενείας τὰς ἀφορμὰς ἔχει.

ΙΘ Πρὸς τοὺς λέγοντας, πάλιν ἐν βρώσει καὶ πόσει εἶναι τῶν ἐλπιζομένων ἀγαθῶν τὴν ἀπόλαυσιν, διὰ τὸ ἐξ ἀρχῆς ἐν τῷ παραδείσῳ γεγράφθαι διὰ τούτων τὸν ἄνθρωπον ζῆν.

Κ Τίς ἡ ἐν τῷ παραδείσῳ ζωή, καὶ τί τὸ ἀπηγορευμένον ἐκεῖνο ξύλον;

ΚΑ Ὅτι ἡ ἀνάστασις οὐ τοσοῦτον ἐκ τοῦ κηρύγματος τοῦ γραφικοῦ, ὅσον ἐξ αὐτῆς τῆς ἀνάγκης τῶν πραγμάτων ἀκολούθως ἐλπίζεται.

ΚΒ Πρὸς τοὺς λέγοντας, Εἰ καλόν τι καὶ ἀγαθὸν ἡ ἀνάστασις, τί οὐχὶ ἤδη γέγονεν, ἀλλὰ χρόνων τισὶ περιόδοις ἐλπίζεται.

ΚΓ Ὅτι ὁ τὴν ἀρχὴν τῆς τοῦ κόσμου συστάσεως ὁμολογῶν, ἀναγκαίως καὶ περὶ τοῦ τέλους συνθήσεται.

ΚΔ Ἀντίρρησις πρὸς τοὺς λέγοντας, συναΐδιον εἶναι τῷ Θεῷ τὴν ὕλην.

ΚΕ Πῶς ἄν τις καὶ τῶν ἔξωθεν προσαχθείη πιστεῦσαι τῇ γραφῇ περὶ τῆς ἀναστάσεως διδασκούσῃ.

ΚϚ Ὅτι οὐκ ἔξω τοῦ εἰκότος ἡ ἀνάστασις.

ΚΖ Ὅτι δυνατόν ἐστιν εἰς τὰ τοῦ παντὸς στοιχεῖα τοῦ ἀνθρωπίνου σώματος ἀναλυθέντος, πάλιν ἐκ τοῦ κοινοῦ ἑκάστῳ τὸ ἴδιον ἀποσωθῆναι.

ΚΗ Πρὸς τοὺς λέγοντας, προϋφεστάναι τὰς ψυχὰς τῶν σωμάτων, ἢ τὸ ἔμπαλιν, πρὸ τῶν ψυχῶν διαπεπλᾶσθαι τὰ σώματα· εν ᾧ τις καὶ ἀνατροπὴ τῆς κατὰ τὰς μετεμψυχώσεις μυθοποιΐας.

ΚΘ Κατασκευὴ τοῦ μίαν καὶ τὴν αὐτὴν ψυχῇ τε καὶ σώματι τὴν αἰτίαν τῆς ὑπάρξεως εἶναι.

Λ Θεωρία τις ἰατρικωτέρα περὶ τῆς τοῦ σώματος ἡμῶν κατασκευῆς δι' ὀλίγων.

79 ιζ : ιη A B C I K N O Q R T *Dion Σ Λ* 79–80 contra eos qui dicunt peccatum utiliter introductum ad propagationem humani generis et quod per peccatum haec [haec *om. Forb*] animalem generationem meruit *Λ* 80 ἐξ] ἀπ' N 81 ιη : ιθ A B C I K N O Q R T *Dion Σ Λ* 81–2 quod ceterae quoque passiones nobis et irrationalibus animantibus communes sunt et quod per earum refrenationem similes deo dicimur *Λ* 83 ιθ : κ A B C I K N O Q R T *Dion Σ Λ* 83–5 cuiusmodi debeat intelligi esse cibus hominis quo uescebatur in paradise et a quo prohibitus est *Λ* 83 καὶ] *ita* Æ G N O P V X *Forb* : καὶ ἐν *Ald* εἶναι *post* ἀπόλαυσιν *(l. 84) pon.* Æ N O 84 παραδείσῳ *om.* V 86 κ : κα A B C I K N O Q R T *Dion Σ Λ* quare scriptura uocauerit arborem lignum scientiae boni et mali *Λ* ἐκεῖνο] *ita* Æ G N P X *Forb* : ἐκεῖ V : *om. Ald* 87 κα : κβ A B C I K N O Q R T *Dion Σ Λ* 87–8 quod divinum consilium non est mutabile *Λ* 87 ἡ *om.* P 88 τῶν πραγμάτων ἀνάγκης Æ G N O P V X 87 κβ : κγ A B C I K N O Q R T *Dion Σ Λ* 89–90 quod consummata generatione hominum tempus quoque deficiet *Λ* 89 οὐκ G P X 91 κγ : κδ A B C I K N O Q R T *Dion Σ Λ* 91–2 contra eos qui dicunt materiam deo coeternam *Λ* 93 κδ : κε A B C I K N O Q R T *Dion Σ Λ* quod omnis materia quibusdam quantitatibus subsistit *Λ* 94 κε : κς A B C I K N O Q R T *Dion Σ Λ* 94–5 de fide resurrectionis et de tribus mortuis quos dominus Iesus suscitauit *Λ* 94 καὶ] καὶ ἐκ N 96 κς : κζ A B C I K N O Q R T *Dion Σ Λ* quod quantumcunque absumptum fuerit corpus humanum facile illud colligat potentia diuina *Λ* ἀνάστασις] resurrectio mortuorum *Dion* 97 κζ : κη A B C I K N O Q R T *Dion Σ Λ* 97–8 quod quamuis communiter resurgant corpora proprias tamen animas recipient *Λ* 97 ἀνθρωπείου G P : ἀνθρωπίου X 98 τὸ ἴδιον ἑκάστῳ Æ G O P V X 99 κη : κθ A B C I K N O Q R T *Dion Σ Λ* 99–101 de diversis opinionibus originis animae *Λ* 100 διαπεπλάσθαι Æ N O V τις] τις ζήτησις G P V X 102 κθ : λ A B C I K N O Q R T *Dion Σ Λ* 102–3 quod deus pariter animam et corpus hominis fecerit *Λ* 103 εἶναι] esse uideatur *Dion* 104 λ : λα A B C I K N Q R T *Dion Σ Λ* : *om.* O de triplici natura corporis *Λ* τις *om.* G P V X

17. What we must answer to those who ask: 'If procreation comes after the sin, how would souls have come into being if human beings had remained sinless from the beginning?'[24]
18. That our irrational passions have their starting point from kinship with the irrational nature.[25]
19. To those who say: 'The enjoyment of the good things hoped for will again be in food and drink, because from the beginning in Paradise, it is written, the human being lived by these means.'[26]
20. What was the life in Paradise, and what was that forbidden tree?[27]
21. That the resurrection is consequentially hoped for not so much from the scriptural proclamation but as much from the very necessity of things.[28]
22. To those who say: 'If the resurrection is something beautiful and good, why has it not already happened, but is hoped for in some period of time?'[29]
23. That one who acknowledges the beginning of the world's constitution must necessarily agree also regarding its end.[30]
24. An argument against those who say that matter is co-eternal with God.[31]
25. How one, even of those outside, may be brought to believe the Scripture's teaching regarding the resurrection.[32]
26. That the resurrection is not beyond probability.[33]
27. That it is possible, when the human body is dissolved into the elements of the universe, for what belongs to each to be saved from the common [pool].[34]
28. To those who say 'souls pre-exist bodies', or the reverse, 'bodies were formed before souls'; in which is also a refutation of the myth-making concerning transmigrations of souls.[35]
29. An elaboration of the fact that the cause of existence for soul and body is one and the same.[36]
30. A brief, more medical, contemplation regarding the formation of our body.[37]

[24] *Bodl. 238* (as Chap. 18): 'Against those who say that sin was a useful introduction for the propagation of the human race; and that by sin it deserved animal generation'.

[25] *Bodl. 238* (as Chap. 19): 'That our other passions also are common to us and to the irrational animals, and that by the restraint of them we are said to be like God'.

[26] *Bodl. 238* (as Chap. 20): 'How the food ought to be understood with which the human was fed in paradise and from which he was prohibited'.

[27] *Bodl. 238* (as Chap. 21): 'Why Scripture called the tree "the tree of the knowledge of good and evil"'.

[28] *Bodl. 238* (as Chap. 22): 'That the divine counsel is immutable'.

[29] *Bodl. 238* (as Chap. 23): 'That when the generation of humans is finished, time also will come to an end'.

[30] *Bodl. 238* (as Chap. 24): 'Against those who say that matter is co-eternal with God'.

[31] *Bodl. 238* (as Chap. 25): 'That matter exists in certain quantities'.

[32] *Bodl. 238* (as Chap. 26): 'Of faith in the resurrection and of the three dead persons whom the Lord Jesus raised'.

[33] *Bodl. 238* (as Chap. 27): 'That however much the human body may have been consumed, the divine power can easily bring it together'.

[34] *Bodl. 238* (as Chap. 28): 'That although bodies rise together they will however receive their own souls'.

[35] *Bodl. 238* (as Chap. 29): 'On different views of the origin of the soul'.

[36] *Bodl. 238* (as Chap. 30): 'That God equally made the body and the soul of the human being'.

[37] *Bodl. 238* (as Chap. 31): 'Of the threefold nature of the body'.

Ἐν ᾧ τίς ἐστι μερικὴ περὶ τοῦ κόσμου φυσιολογία, καί τις ἁβροτέρα διήγησις περὶ τῶν προγεγονότων τῆς τοῦ ἀνθρώπου γενέσεως.

[1.1] ***Αὕτη ἡ βίβλος γενέσεως οὐρανοῦ καὶ γῆς***, *φησὶν ἡ γραφή· ὅτε συνετελέσθη πᾶν τὸ φαινόμενον, καὶ πρὸς τὴν οἰκείαν θέσιν ἕκαστον τῶν ὄντων ἀποκριθὲν ἀνεχώρησεν· ὅτε περιέσχεν ἐν κύκλῳ τὰ πάντα τὸ οὐράνιον σῶμα, τὴν δὲ μέσην τοῦ παντὸς ἀπέλαβε χώραν τὰ βαρέα καὶ κατωφερῆ τῶν σωμάτων, γῆ τε καὶ ὕδωρ, ἐν ἀλλήλοις διακρατούμενα· σύνδεσμος δέ τις καὶ βεβαιότης τῶν γεγενημένων ἡ θεία τέχνη καὶ δύναμις τῇ φύσει τῶν ὄντων ἐναπετέθη, διπλαῖς ἐνεργείαις ἡνιοχοῦσα τὰ πάντα· (στάσει γὰρ καὶ κινήσει τὴν γένεσιν τοῖς μὴ οὖσι καὶ τὴν διαμονὴν τοῖς οὖσιν* [D] *ἐμηχανήσατο) περὶ τὸ βαρύ τε καὶ ἀμετάθετον τῆς ἀκινήτου φύσεως, οἷον περί τινα πάγιον ἄξονα, τὴν ὀξυτάτην τοῦ πόλου κίνησιν, τροχοῦ δίκην, ἐν κύκλῳ περιελαύνουσα, καὶ δι' ἀλλήλων ἀμφοτέροις συντηροῦσα τὸ ἀδιάλυτον· τῆς τε κυκλοφορουμένης οὐσίας διὰ τῆς ὀξείας κινήσεως τὸ ναστὸν τῆς γῆς ἐν κύκλῳ περισφιγγούσης, τοῦ τε στερροῦ καὶ ἀνενδότου διὰ τῆς ἀμεταθέτου παγιότητος ἀδιαλείπτως ἐπιτείνοντος τῶν περὶ αὐτὴν κυκλουμένων τὴν δίνησιν· ἴση δὲ καθ' ἑκάτερον τῶν ταῖς ἐνεργείαις διεστηκότων ἡ ὑπερβολὴ ἐναπειργάσθη, τῇ τε στασίμῳ φύσει καὶ τῇ ἀστάτῳ περιφορᾷ· οὔτε γὰρ ἡ γῆ τῆς ἰδίας βάσεως μετατίθεται, οὔτε ὁ οὐρανός ποτε τὸ σφοδρὸν ἐνδίδωσι καὶ ὑποχαλᾷ τῆς κινήσεως.*

[1.2] *Ταῦτα δὲ καὶ πρῶτα* [129] *κατὰ τὴν τοῦ πεποιηκότος σοφίαν, οἱόν τις ἀρχὴ τοῦ παντὸς μηχανήματος προκατεσκευάσθη τῶν ὄντων, δεικνύντος οἶμαι τοῦ μεγάλου Μωϋσέως, διὰ τοῦ* ***ἐν ἀρχῇ τὸν οὐρανὸν καὶ τὴν γῆν*** *παρὰ τοῦ Θεοῦ γεγενῆσθαι εἰπεῖν, ὅτι κινήσεώς τε καὶ στάσεως ἔκγονα τὰ ἐν τῇ κτίσει φαινόμενα πάντα, κατὰ θεῖον βούλημα παραχθέντα εἰς γένεσιν· τοῦ τοίνυν οὐρανοῦ καὶ τῆς γῆς ἐκ διαμέτρου πρὸς ἄλληλα κατὰ τὸ ἐναντίον ταῖς ἐνεργείαις διεστηκότων, ἡ μεταξὺ*

1–2 *ἐν—γενέσεως*] de perfectione et pulcritudine mundi et de discordia concordia 4 elementorum *Λ* 1 *ἐν ᾧ—κόσμου om.* N *ἐν ᾧ—διήγησις om.* Æ *ἁβροτέρα*] clarior *Dion Eri* 2 *τοῦ om.* N *ἀνθρώπου*] *ἀνθρώπου κατασκευῆς καὶ* I 5 *περιέσχεν ἐν*] *περιέσχε* K R[ac] T *ἐν om.* O 6 *ἀπέλαβε*] *ἔλαβε* N 7 *ἐν ἀλλήλοις διακρατούμενα*] a se inuicem discreta sun *Eri* *δέ* X[pc2] 8 *ἐναπετέθη*] *ἐναπετελέθη* V 9 *τὴν*] *τὴν τε* G H K M N O P R T V W X 10 *ἐμηχανήσατο*] *ἐχαρίσατο* G H P[pc] *τε*] *ita* A B G H I K L M O P Q R S X *Forb* : *om.* V W *Ald Mign* *ἀεικινήτου* N 11 *τροχοῦ δίκην om.* G H M N P X 12 *συντηροῦσα*] *συνηγοροῦσα* N 13 *κυκλωφορουμένης* O *τὸ ναστὸν*] *τὸν ἄστατὸν* O 14 *τε om.* N 16 *ἐναπεργάσθη* P X : *ἐναπείργασται* B 18 *ὁ om.* B G L P S T X *καὶ* X[pc2] 19 *δὲ om.* T *καὶ om.* K O V[ac] (*add. 2ª man.*) *πρῶτα*] *πρῶτα καὶ* V *οἷόν*] *οἱ* V[ac] (*corr. 2ª man.*) 20 *μηχανήματος*] machinantis *Eri* *δεικνύντος*] *ita H K M* O R S V W X *Ald Mign* : *δεικνῦντος Forb* : N *accent. eras* 21 *μωσέως* V 21–2 *γεγενῆσθαι παρὰ τοῦ θεοῦ* B G L M N P S T X 21 *τοῦ om.* A 22 *γεγενῆσθαι*] *προγεγενῆσθαι* H : *πεποιῆσθαι* R *ἔγγονα* R 23 *πάντα*] *ita* A B G H I K L M O P S T W X *Forb* : *πάντα τὰ* V *Ald Mign* *κατὰ θεῖον βούλημα*] *τῷ θείῳ βουλήματι* A I K O Q *κατὰ*] *ita* B G H L M P R S[ac] T *Forb* : *κατὰ τὸ Ald Mign* *γένεσιν*] *γένεσιν ἐστιν* R 24 *τῆς ἐνεργείας Ald Mign*

In which is a partial physiological consideration of the nature of the world, and a more minute account of the things preceding the genesis of the human being.[1]

[**1.1**] *This is the book of the genesis of heaven and earth*, says the Scripture,[2] when everything that appears was completed and each separated being withdrew to its own place, when the body of heaven encompassed all things around, and those bodies that are heavy and borne downwards, earth and water, holding each other back, took the middle place of the universe, while the divine art and power was implanted in the nature of things as a sort of bond and stability for the things that came to be, guiding the universe by a twofold activity, for by rest and motion it devised the genesis of the things that were not and the continuance of the things that are, driving around in a circle—about the heavy and immutable element of the immovable nature, as around some fixed axle—the most rapid motion of the celestial sphere, like a wheel, and preserving the indissolubility of both by their mutual action, as the circling substance by its rapid motion compresses the solid body of the earth in a circle, while that which is firm and unyielding by its unchanging fixedness continually urges on the rotation of those things circling around it, and equal intensity is wrought in each of those which differ in their activities, that is, in the stationary nature and in the never-resting revolving vaults [of heaven], for neither is the earth moved from its own foundation nor does the heaven ever relax its fervour or slacken its motion.

[**1.2**] These, moreover, were formed first before others, according to the wisdom of the Maker, as a kind of beginning of the whole machine, as the great Moses indicated, I think, by saying that *the heaven and the earth* were made by God *in the beginning*,[3] so that all things appearing in the creation are the offspring of rest and motion, brought to genesis in accordance with the divine will. The heaven and the earth, then, being diametrically opposed to each other in their

[1] *Bodl. 238*: 'Of the perfection and beauty of the world and of the harmonious discord of the four elements'.

[2] Gen. 2:4. [3] Gen. 1:1.

τῶν ἐναντίων κτίσις ἐν μέρει τῶν παρακειμένων μετέχουσα, δι' ἑαυτῆς μεσιτεύει τοῖς ἄκροις, ὡς ἂν ἐπίδηλον γενέσθαι τὴν πρὸς ἄλληλα τῶν ἐναντίων διὰ τοῦ μέσου συνάφειαν· τὸ γὰρ ἀεικίνητον καὶ λεπτὸν τῆς πυρώδους οὐσίας μιμεῖται μέν πως ὁ ἀήρ, ἔν τε τῷ κούφῳ τῆς φύσεως καὶ τῷ πρὸς τὴν κίνησιν ἐπιτηδείως [B] ἔχειν· οὐ μὴν τοιοῦτός ἐστιν οἷος τῆς πρὸς τὰ πάγια συγγενείας ἀλλοτριοῦσθαι, οὔτε ἀεὶ μένων ἀκίνητος, οὔτε διαπαντὸς ῥέων καὶ σκεδαννύμενος· ἀλλὰ τῇ πρὸς ἑκάτερον οἰκειότητι οἷόν τι μεθόριον τῆς τῶν ἐνεργειῶν ἐναντιότητος γίνεται, μιγνὺς ἅμα καὶ διαιρῶν ἐν ἑαυτῷ τὰ διεστῶτα τῇ φύσει. [1.3] *Κατὰ τὸν αὐτὸν λόγον καὶ ἡ ὑγρὰ οὐσία διπλαῖς ποιότησι πρὸς ἑκάτερον τῶν ἐναντίων ἁρμόζεται· τῷ μὲν γὰρ βαρεῖά τε καὶ κατωφερὴς εἶναι, πολλὴν πρὸς τὸ γεῶδες τὴν συγγένειαν ἔχει· τῷ δὲ μετέχειν ῥοώδους τινὸς καὶ πορευτικῆς ἐνεργείας, οὐ πάντη τῆς κινουμένης ἠλλοτρίωται [C] φύσεως· ἀλλά τις ἐστὶ καὶ διὰ τούτου μίξις τῶν ἐναντίων καὶ σύνοδος, τῆς τε βαρύτητος εἰς κίνησιν μετατεθείσης, καὶ τῆς κινήσεως ἐν τῷ βάρει μὴ πεδηθείσης· ὥστε συμβαίνειν πρὸς ἄλληλα τὰ κατὰ τὸ ἀκρότατον τῇ φύσει διεστηκότα διὰ τῶν μεσιτευόντων ἀλλήλοις ἑνούμενα.*

[1.4] *Μᾶλλον δὲ κατὰ τὸν ἀκριβῆ λόγον, οὐδὲ αὐτὴ τῶν ἀντικειμένων ἡ φύσις ἀμίκτως πάντη πρὸς τὴν ἑτέραν τοῖς ἰδιώμασιν ἔχει, ὡς ἄν, οἶμαι, πάντα πρὸς ἄλληλα νεύοι τὰ κατὰ τὸν κόσμον φαινόμενα, καὶ συμπνέοι πρὸς ἑαυτὴν ἡ κτίσις ἐν τοῖς τῶν ἀντικειμένων ἰδιώμασιν εὑρισκομένη· τῆς γὰρ κινήσεως οὐ μόνον κατὰ τὴν τοπικὴν μετάστασιν νοουμένης, ἀλλὰ καὶ ἐν τροπῇ καὶ ἀλλοιώσει θεωρουμένης· πάλιν δ' αὖ τῆς ἀμεταθέτου φύσεως τὴν κατὰ τὸ ἀλλοιοῦσθαι κίνησιν [D] οὐ προσιεμένης· ἐναλλάξασα τὰς ἰδιότητας ἡ τοῦ Θεοῦ σοφία, τῷ μὲν ἀεικινήτῳ τὸ ἄτρεπτον, τῷ δὲ ἀκινήτῳ τὴν τροπὴν ἐνεποίησε· προμηθείᾳ τινὶ τάχα τὸ τοιοῦτον οἰκονομήσασα, ὡς ἂν μὴ τὸ τῆς φύσεως ἴδιον, ὅπερ ἐστὶ τὸ ἄτρεπτόν τε καὶ ἀμετάθετον, ἐπί τινος τῶν κατὰ τὴν κτίσιν βλεπόμενον, Θεὸν νομίζεσθαι τὸ κτίσμα ποιήσειεν· οὐ γὰρ ἔτι θεότητος ὑπόληψιν σχοίη, ὅπερ ἂν κινούμενον ἢ ἀλλοιούμενον τύχῃ. Διὰ τοῦτο ἡ μὲν γῆ στάσιμός ἐστι, καὶ οὐκ ἄτρεπτος· ὁ δὲ οὐρανὸς ἐκ τοῦ ἐναντίου τὸ τρεπτὸν οὐκ ἔχων, οὐδὲ τὸ στάσιμον ἔχει· ἵνα τῇ μὲν ἑστώσῃ φύσει τὴν τροπήν, τῇ δὲ μὴ τρεπομένῃ τὴν κίνησιν, ἡ θεία συμπλέξασα δύναμις, καὶ ἀλλήλαις ἀμφοτέρας τῇ ἐναλλάξει τῶν ἰδιωμάτων προσοικειώσῃ, καὶ τῆς περὶ τὸ θεῖον ὑπολήψεως ἀλλοτριώσῃ· [132] οὐθέτερον γὰρ ἂν τούτων, καθὼς εἴρηται, τῆς θειοτέρας φύσεως νομισθείη, οὔτε τὸ ἄστατον, οὔτε τὸ ἀλλοιούμενον.*

26 ἂν *om.* I 28 τῷ] τὸ K O Q R^{ac} : τοῦ L 30 ἑκάτερον] ἕτερον *Ald Mign* 31 μιγνύων R 32 διαιρῶν] *om. Eri* ἐν ἑαυτῷ] *om.* N : ἐν αὐτῷ *Ald Mign* ἡ *om.* M 34 τε X^{pc2} τῷ] τὸ O 35 πορευτικῆς] εὐπορευτικῆς *vel* ἀπορευτικῆς R^{ac} κινουμένης] νοουμένης K O 36 τούτουν X 37 καὶ τῆς κινήσεως ἐν τῷ βάρει μὴ πεδηθείσης *om.* O ἐν *om.* N μὴ] μὴ μὴ X παιδηθείσης V 38 διεστηκότα] προεστηκότα K O 42 φαινόμενα] φερόμενα A I K O συμπνέει B^{pc1} K L M : ξυμπνέοι *Mign* 44 τοπικὴν] typicam *Eri* ἀλλοιώσει] ἐν ἀλλοιώσει N 45–6 πάλιν—προσιεμένης] iterumque ipsa natura dum mouetur non immensurabiliter motum producit *Eri* 45 δ'αὐτῆς K L Q V X 46 προιεμένης K V 46–7 τῷ . . . τῷ] τὸ . . . τὸ O 48 φύσεως] θείας φύσεως A I K N O Q R S^{mg1} *Dion Eri* 49 βλεπόμενον] *ita* ß G H L O P Q R R S T V W X *Forb* : βλεπομένων *Ald Mign* 50 γὰρ] γὰρ ἂν A B N O Q R S^{pc} ἔτι *om.* A B 51 ἀλλοιούμενον] παλοιούμενον N 52 ἐκ *om. Ald Mign* τὸ *om. Ald Mign* ἔχει] *add.* eodem enim motu semper uoluitur *Eri* 53 φύσει ἑστώσῃ *Mign* 54 ἀλλήλας A B ἀμφοτέραις ß ἐπαλλάξει A I K N O 55 οὐθέτερον] *ita* A R S^{pc} *Ald Forb* : οὐθ' ἕτερον G H K L O P Q S^{ac} V W X : οὐδέτερον *Mign* ἂν *om.* B R 56 θειοτέρας] θείας L ἀλλοιούμενον] ἀλλοτριούμενον P

activities, the creation being between the opposites, having in part a share in what is adjacent to it, through itself mediates between the extremes, so that clearly the connection of the opposites comes to be through the mid-point: for air in a way imitates the perpetual motion and subtlety of the fiery substance, both in the lightness of nature and in its suitableness for motion, yet it is not such as to be alienated from kinship with the solid substance, for it neither remains continually immobile, not continuously flowing and being dispersed, but becomes, in its affinity to each, a kind of borderland in the opposition between activities, in itself at once mixing and dividing things distinct by nature. [**1.3**] In the same way, the liquid substance also is attached by twofold qualities to each of the opposites; on the one hand, as heavy and borne downwards it has close kinship to the earthy, but, on the other hand, as partaking of a certain fluid and mobile activity it is not altogether alien from the mobile nature; yet by means of this there is also a kind of mixture and concurrence of the opposites, weight being transferred to motion and motion not being hindered by weight, so that things most extremely opposite in nature combine with one another, being united by those mediating between them.

[**1.4**] Or rather, according to the accurate account, the very nature of contrary things is not entirely unmixed with properties of the other, so that, I think, everything that appears in the world mutually converges and the creation, though found in properties of contrary things, coheres with itself;[4] for as motion is not conceived merely as shifting in place, but is also contemplated in change and alteration, and again as the immovable nature does not accept the motion of alteration, the wisdom of God has transposed these properties, and produced unchangeableness in that which is ever-moving and change in that which is immovable,[5] arranging this perhaps with a certain provision, lest the property of nature, that is, immutability and immobility, when seen in anything of the creation would cause the creature to be thought God; for that which may happen to be moved or to undergo change would no longer be suspected of divinity. Therefore, the earth is stable yet not immutable, while the heaven, on the contrary, not having mutability yet neither has stability, so that the divine power, by interweaving change in the stable nature and motion in that not subject to change, might, by the interchange of attributes, assimilate both to each other and remove from them the supposition of being divine, for neither of these, as was said—neither that which is unstable nor that which is changeable—can be considered as being of the more divine nature.

[4] Cf. Gregory of Nyssa, *Eccl.* 7 (Alexander, 406.2–7; ET 121); *Cat. Or.* 6.3 (Mühlenberg, 21.16–22); Heraclitus Fr B 8, 10; Plotinus, *Enn.* 2.3.7.13–23; 2.3.12.24–32; 4.4.40.1–3; Chrysippus *SVF* 2.543 (=DL 7.140); Galen, *De nat. fac.* 1.13 (39).

[5] Cf. Gregory of Nyssa, *Hex.* 78 (Drobner, 78.16–22).

[1.5] *Ἤδη τοίνυν τὰ πάντα πρὸς τὸ ἴδιον ἔφθασε τέλος· **συνετελέσθη** γάρ, καθώς φησι Μωϋσῆς, **ὅ τε οὐρανὸς καὶ ἡ γῆ** καὶ τὰ διὰ μέσου πάντα, καὶ τῷ καταλλήλῳ κάλλει τὰ καθέκαστον διεκοσμήθη· ὁ οὐρανὸς μὲν ταῖς τῶν φωστήρων αὐγαῖς, θάλαττα δὲ καὶ ἀὴρ τοῖς νηκτοῖς τε καὶ ἐναερίοις τῶν ζώων, γῆ δὲ ταῖς παντοίαις τῶν φυτῶν τε καὶ βοσκημάτων διαφοραῖς, ἅπερ ἀθρόως ἅπαντα θείῳ βουλήματι δυναμωθεῖσα κατὰ ταὐτὸν ἀπεκύησε. Καὶ πλήρης μὲν ἦν τῶν ὡραίων ἡ γῆ, ὁμοῦ τοῖς ἄνθεσι τοὺς καρποὺς ἐκβλαστήσασα. Πλήρεις δὲ οἱ λειμῶνες τῶν ὅσα τοὺς λειμῶνας ἐπέρχεται· πᾶσαί τε ῥαχίαι καὶ ἀκρώρειαι καὶ πᾶν ὅσον πλάγιόν τε καὶ ὕπτιον καὶ ὅσον ἐν* [B] *κοίλοις, τῇ νεοθαλεῖ πόᾳ καὶ τῇ ποικίλῃ τῶν δένδρων ὥρᾳ κατεστεφάνωτο, ἄρτι μὲν τῆς γῆς ἀνασχόντων, εὐθὺς δὲ πρὸς τὸ τέλειον κάλλος ἀναδραμόντων· ἐγεγήθει δὲ πάντα κατὰ τὸ εἰκὸς καὶ διεσκίρτα τὰ τῷ προστάγματι τοῦ Θεοῦ ζωογονηθέντα βοτά, κατ' ἀγέλας τε καὶ κατὰ γένη ταῖς λόχμαις ἐνδιαθέοντα, ταῖς δὲ τῶν μουσικῶν ὀρνίθων ᾠδαῖς ἁπανταχῇ περιηχεῖτο πᾶν ὅσον κατηρεφές τε καὶ σύσκιον. Ἥτε κατὰ θάλατταν ὄψις, ὡς εἰκός, ἄλλη τοιαύτη τις ἦν, ἄρτι πρὸς ἡσυχίαν τε καὶ γαλήνην ἐν ταῖς συναγωγαῖς τῶν κοίλων καθισταμένη, καθ' ἣν ὅρμοι καὶ λιμένες θείᾳ βουλήσει ταῖς ἀκταῖς αὐτομάτως ἐγκοιλανθέντες, προσημέρουν τῇ ἠπείρῳ τὴν θάλατταν. Αἵ τε ἠρεμαῖαι τῶν κυμάτων κινήσεις τῷ κάλλει* [C] *τῶν λειμώνων ἀνθωραΐζοντο, ὑπὸ λεπταῖς τε καὶ ἀπήμοσιν αὔραις κατ' ἄκραν τὴν ἐπιφάνειαν γλαφυρῶς ἐπιφρίσσουσαι· καὶ ἅπας ὁ κατὰ τὴν κτίσιν πλοῦτος, κατὰ γῆν τε καὶ θάλατταν, ἕτοιμος ἦν, ἀλλ' ὁ μετέχων οὐκ ἦν.*

Διὰ τί τελευταῖος μετὰ τὴν κτίσιν ὁ ἄνθρωπος.

[2.1] *Οὔπω γὰρ τὸ μέγα τοῦτο καὶ τίμιον χρῆμα, ὁ ἄνθρωπος, τῷ κόσμῳ τῶν ὄντων ἐπεχωρίαζεν· οὐδὲ γὰρ ἦν εἰκός, τὸν ἄρχοντα πρὸ τῶν ἀρχομένων ἀναφανῆναι, ἀλλὰ τῆς ἀρχῆς πρότερον ἑτοιμασθείσης, ἀκόλουθον ἦν ἀναδειχθῆναι τὸν βασιλεύοντα.*

57 *τὰ om.* R 57–8 *καθώς— γῆ*] *ὁ οὐρανὸς καὶ ἡ γῆ καθώς φησι μωϋσῆς* A I K O Q 58 *μωϋσῆς*] *ὁ μωϋσῆς* N : *μωσῆς* V *ὅ τε οὐρανὸς καὶ ἡ γῆ om.* M *οὐρανὸς*] *ὁ οὐρανὸς* N 59 *κάλλει*] *κόσμῳ* V *ὁ om.* A G H I K N O Q R 60 *δὲ*] *τε* R *καὶ ἀὴρ—ζώων*] atque aer animantibus tam natatilibus quam uolatilibus mire tripudians *Dion* : aerque animalibus *Eri* *τοῖς παντοίοις* N 61 *διαφοραῖς* X^pc2 *ἅπαντα ἀθρόως* N *ἅπαντα*] *πάντα* A I K O Q : *om.* B *θείῳ*] *τῷ θείῳ* A I K O 62 *ἦν om.* N *τῶν ὡραίων ἡ γῆ*] speciebus universis *Dion* : montibus terra *Eri* 63 *ἐκβλαστήσασα*] *ἐβλάστησεν* N : *συμβλαστήσασα* A I K Q R *λειμῶνες*] *λειμῶνες καὶ* V 64 *τε*] *δὲ* A B I K N O Q R *ῥαχίαι*] *ῥαχείαι* N : *τραχείαι* P^pc : *τραχεῖαι* G H L P^ac R S T V W X *καὶ*[1]] *τε καὶ* A B I K N O Q R *πλάγιόν*] *πάγιόν* X : *πέλαγιόν* N *τε om.* V 65 *τῇ νεοθαλεῖ πόᾳ*] *τὴν εὐθαλῆ πόαν* K (*et ῇ . . . ῇ . . . ᾳ sup. l.*) R^ac 66 *ἀνασχόντων*] *ita* A B G H I K L M O P Q R S T V W X *Forb* : *ἀνισχόντων Ald Mign* 67–8 *ἐγεγήθει— βοτὰ*] humi autem omnia consequenter exultantia issu Dei fecunda pecora rident *Eri* 65 *γεγήθει* G N 67 *τὰ om.* B I K N Q 68 *ζωογονηθέντα βοτὰ*] *ζωογονηθέντα φυτὰ καὶ βοτὰ τὰ βοσκόμενα καὶ ἀγελιζόμενα εἰς τοὺς δρυμοὺς καὶ τὰ ὄρη ἐνέμοντο* R *βοτὰ*] *βοσκήματα* N *κατὰ om.* R 69 *ταῖς δὲ*] *ταῖς τε* N : *καὶ ταῖς* I : *ταῖς* A K O Q R *ἁπανταχῇ om.* N 70 *ἥτε*] *ἥτε καὶ* V *κατὰ* X^pc2 *θάλασσαν* N 72 *ὅρμοι*] *ὅρμοι τε* A I K N Q R *ἐγκοιλωθέντες* W : *ἐγκοιλαθέντες* K T : *ἐκκοιλαθέντες* I 73 *προσημεροῦσι* N *θάλασσαν* B I R 74 *ἀνθωραΐζοντο*] *ἀντ' ὡραΐζοντο* X 74–5 *ὑπὸ λεπταῖς—ἐπιφρίσσουσαι*] lenibus sollemnitur sonantes *Eri* 74 *τε*] *ita* A B G H I K N O P Q R S V^pc W X *Forb* : *om. Ald Mign* 75 *ἅπας*] *πας* Æ^ac N 76 *κατὰ om.* R *θάλατταν*] *κατὰ θάλατταν* V : *θάλασσαν* I

---

1 *διὰ—ἄνθρωπος*] quod rationabiliter homo ultimus creaturarum creatus est *Λ* *διατί* I K L M N O P R V *μετὰ τὴν κτίσιν τελευταῖος Ald Mign* Cur novissimus post creaturam factus sit homo *Dion* 2 *χρῆμα*] *κτῆμα* A I K N O Q 3 *εἰκὸς ἦν* N 4 *βασιλεύσοντα* S : *βασιλέα* B

[**1.5**] Now all things had arrived at their own end, for, as Moses says, *the heaven and the earth were finished*,[6] and all things in-between, and each thing was adorned with their corresponding beauty: the heaven with the rays of the stars, the sea and air with the living creatures that swim and fly, and the earth with every variety of plants and animals—to all of which the earth, empowered by the divine will, gave birth altogether. The earth was full of beautiful things, blossoming forth at the same time with flowers and fruits. The meadows were full of all that grows in the meadows; and all the mountain ridges and summits and every hillside and slope and hollow were crowned with young grass and with the varied produce of the trees, just risen from the ground, yet shot up at once into their perfect beauty; and all the animals that had come into life at God's command were likely rejoicing and skipping about, running about in the thickets in herds according to their kind, while every sheltered and shady spot was ringing with the chants of the songbirds. And at sea, most likely the sight to be seen was similar, as it had just settled to peace and calm in the gathering together of its depths, where havens and harbours, hollowed out by divine counsel on the coasts, brought sea into accord with land. The gentle motion of the waves vied in beauty with the meadows, rippling delicately with light and harmless breezes that skimmed the surface; and all the wealth of creation by land and sea was ready, but there was no one to share it.

Why the human being is last, after the creation.[7]

[**2.1**] For that great and honourable thing, the human being, had not yet occupied its place in the world of beings, as it was not reasonable for the ruler to appear before the ruled; but with the dominion first made ready, it was consistent for the king to be presented. When, then, the Maker of all had prepared beforehand a

[6] Gen. 2:1.

[7] *Bodl. 238*: 'That it was reasonable that the human being should be created last of the creatures'.

Ἐπειδὴ τοίνυν οἷόν τινα βασίλειον καταγωγὴν τῷ μέλλοντι βασιλεύειν ὁ τοῦ παντὸς ποιητὴς προηυτρέπισεν, αὕτη δὲ ἦν γῆ τε καὶ νῆσοι καὶ θάλαττα, καὶ οὐρανὸς ὑπὲρ τούτων ὀρόφου δίκην ἐπικυρτούμενος· πλοῦτος δὲ παντοδαπὸς τοῖς βασιλείοις τούτοις ἐναπετέθη· πλοῦτον δὲ λέγω πᾶσαν τὴν κτίσιν, ὅσον ἐν φυτοῖς καὶ βλαστήμασι καὶ ὅσον αἰσθητικόν τε καὶ ἔμπνουν καὶ ἔμψυχον· [133] εἰ δὲ χρὴ καὶ τὰς ὕλας εἰς πλοῦτον καταριθμήσασθαι, ὅσαι διά τινος εὐχροίας τίμιαι τοῖς ἀνθρωπίνοις ὀφθαλμοῖς ἐνομίσθησαν, οἷον χρυσίον τε καὶ ἀργύριον καὶ τῶν λίθων δὴ τούτων ἃς ἀγαπῶσιν οἱ ἄνθρωποι, καὶ τούτων πάντων τὴν ἀφθονίαν καθάπερ τισὶ βασιλικοῖς θησαυροῖς τοῖς τῆς γῆς κόλποις ἐγκατακρύψας—οὕτως ἀναδείκνυσιν ἐν τῷ κόσμῳ τὸν ἄνθρωπον, τῶν ἐν τούτῳ θαυμάτων, τῶν μὲν θεατὴν ἐσόμενον, τῶν δὲ κύριον· ὡς διὰ μὲν τῆς ἀπολαύσεως τὴν σύνεσιν τοῦ χορηγοῦντος ἔχειν, διὰ δὲ τοῦ κάλλους τε καὶ μεγέθους τῶν ὁρωμένων τὴν ἄρρητόν τε καὶ ὑπὲρ λόγον τοῦ πεποιηκότος δύναμιν ἀνιχνεύειν.

[2.2] Διὰ ταῦτα τελευταῖος μετὰ τὴν κτίσιν εἰσήχθη ὁ ἄνθρωπος, οὐχ ὡς ἀπόβλητος ἐν ἐσχάτοις ἀπορριφείς, ἀλλ᾽ ὡς ἅμα τῇ γενέσει βασιλεὺς εἶναι τῶν ὑποχειρίων προσήκων. Καὶ ὥσπερ τις ἀγαθὸς ἑστιάτωρ [B] οὐ πρὸ τῆς παρασκευῆς τῶν ἐδωδίμων τὸν ἑστιώμενον εἰσοικίζεται, ἀλλ᾽ εὐπρεπῆ τὰ πάντα παρασκευάσας, καὶ φαιδρύνας τοῖς καθήκουσι κόσμοις τὸν οἶκον, τὴν κλισίαν, τὴν τράπεζαν, ἐφ᾽ ἑτοίμοις ἤδη τοῖς πρὸς τὴν τροφὴν ἐπιτηδείοις ἐφέστιον ποιεῖται τὸν δαιτυμόνα· κατὰ τὸν αὐτὸν τρόπον ὁ πλούσιός τε καὶ πολυτελὴς τῆς φύσεως ἡμῶν ἑστιάτωρ παντοίοις κάλλεσι κατακοσμήσας τὴν οἴκησιν, καὶ τὴν μεγάλην ταύτην καὶ παντοδαπῆ πανδαισίαν ἑτοιμασάμενος, οὕτως εἰσάγει τὸν ἄνθρωπον, ἔργον αὐτῷ δοὺς οὐ τὴν κτῆσιν τῶν μὴ προσόντων ἀλλὰ τὴν ἀπόλαυσιν τῶν παρόντων· καὶ διὰ τοῦτο διπλᾶς αὐτῷ τῆς κατασκευῆς τὰς ἀφορμὰς καταβάλλεται, τῷ γηΐνῳ τὸ θεῖον ἐγκαταμίξας, ἵνα δι᾽ ἀμφοτέρων συγγενῶς τε καὶ οἰκείως πρὸς ἑκατέραν ἀπόλαυσιν ἔχῃ, τοῦ Θεοῦ μὲν διὰ τῆς θειοτέρας φύσεως, τῶν δὲ κατὰ τὴν γῆν ἀγαθῶν διὰ τῆς ὁμογενοῦς αἰσθήσεως ἀπολαύων.

5 *τινα βασίλειον καταγωγὴν*] *τι βασίλειον καταγώγιον* R *τοῦ μέλλοντος* N 6 *προευτρέπισεν* A I L *θάλασσαν* I 7 *παντοδαπὴς* N 8 *πᾶσαν τὴν κτίσιν*] *πᾶν τὸ ἐν τῇ κτίσει* N 11 *τε om.* G L M N P S V W X *ἄργυρον* B 11–12 *τῶν λίθων δὴ τούτων*] *λίθους* I 12 *ἃς*] *οὓς* B L R 13 *ἐγκατακρύψας*] *ἐνάποκρύψας* N 14 *τῶν—μὲν om.* N 17 *ἀνεξιχνεύειν* A C I K O : *ἀνεξιχνιάζειν* N 18 *μετὰ— ἄνθρωπος*] *εἰσήχθη μετὰ τὴν κτίσιν ὁ ἄνθρωπος* N R : *ὁ ἄνθρωπος μετὰ τὴν κτίσιν εἰσήχθη* A C I K O Q : in hunc mundum post creatum novissimus introductus est homo *Dion* 19 *ἐσχάτοις*] *τοῖς ἐσχάτοις* A C I K O Q *βασιλεὺς εἶναι*] *βασιλεύειν* N Q : esse rectorum *Dion* : rex fieret 20–1 *τῶν ἐδωδίμων*] delectabilium *Eri* 21 *ἑστιώμενον*] *δαιτυμῶμα* B *εἰσοικίζεται*] *παρ᾽ αὐτῷ εἰσοικίζεται* B *εὐπρεπῆ*] *εὐτρεπῆ* A B C N O R^{2} T V W *παρασκευάσας*] *κατασκευάσας* P 22 *κλησίαν* G^{ac} P^{ac} T V X : *ἐκκλησίαν* N R^{ac} S^{2} 23 *τρυφὴν* Æ O *δαιτυμόνα*] *φίλον* B 25 *κάλλεσι* R^{mg2} : *ἄνθεσι* R^{ac} *παντοδαπὴν* I M R S^{pc} 26 *ἑτοιμάσας* N *ἔργον αὐτῷ δοὺς*] dans ei opus eximium custodire mandatum *Dion* 26–7 *οὐ τὴν κτῆσιν τῶν μὴ προσόντων*] non ut ea quae non erant crearet *Eri* 27 *κτῆσιν*] *κτίσιν* $Æ^{ac}$ G K L O P R^{ac} W X *διὰ τοῦτο καὶ* A C I K L N O Q R *διπλὰς* G K N O P V 28 *καταμίξας* V 29 *ἔχῃ*] *ἔχει* V W X : *ἔχῃ τῶν* N 29–30 *μὲν Θεοῦ* R 30 *τὴν om.* A N Q

certain royal lodging, as it were, for the future king (this was the land, and islands, and sea, and the heaven arching over them like a roof) and when all kinds of wealth had been stored in this palace (and by wealth I mean the whole creation, whatever is in plants and offshoots, and whatever has sense and is breathing and is animated; and, if materials should also be counted as wealth, whatever for their beauty are reckoned precious in human eyes, such as gold, and silver, and such jewels as humans love—the abundance of all these concealed in the bosom of the earth as in a royal treasury), he thus presents the human being to the world, to be a beholder of some of the wonders therein and lord of others, so as to have, by his enjoyment, knowledge of the Benefactor and, through the beauty and majesty of the things seen, to search out the power, unspeakable and beyond language, of the Maker.

[2.2] For these reasons the human being was brought into the world last, after the creation, not being relegated to the end as worthless, but as one for whom it was fitting to be king over his subjects simultaneously with his genesis.[8] And just as a good host does not bring his guest to his house before the preparation of the feast, but, when he has put everything in good order, and decked his house, his couches, and his table with their fitting adornments, when things suitable for his refreshment are already prepared, he brings his guest home; in the same way the rich and munificent Host of our nature, when he had adorned the dwelling place with beauties of every kind and made ready this great and varied banquet, then introduces the human being, giving him as his work not the acquisition of things absent but the enjoyment of things present; and for this reason he establishes for him a twofold origin of formation, blending the divine with the earthy, so that by means of both he may, congenitally and appropriately, have enjoyment of each, enjoying God by means of the more divine nature and the good things of earth by the sense akin to them.

[8] Cf. Philo, *Opif.* 23, 77–8; Nemesius, *De nat. hom.* 1.4–5 (Morani, 4.45–5.1).

Ὅτι τιμιωτέρα πάσης τῆς φαινομένης κτίσεως ἡ τοῦ ἀνθρώπου φύσις.

[3.1] *Ἄξιον δὲ μηδὲ τοῦτο παριδεῖν ἀθεώρητον, ὅτι, τοῦ τηλικούτου κόσμου καὶ τῶν κατ' αὐτὸν μερῶν στοιχειωδῶς πρὸς τὴν τοῦ παντὸς σύστασιν ὑποβληθέντων, ἀποσχεδιάζεταί πως ἡ κτίσις ὑπὸ τῆς θείας δυνάμεως, ὁμοῦ τῷ προστάγματι ὑφισταμένη· τῆς δὲ τοῦ ἀνθρώπου κατασκευῆς βουλὴ προηγεῖται, καὶ προτυποῦται παρὰ τοῦ τεχνιτεύοντος διὰ τῆς τοῦ λόγου γραφῆς τὸ ἐσόμενον, καὶ οἷον εἶναι προσήκει, καὶ πρὸς ποῖον ἀρχέτυπον τὴν ὁμοιότητα φέρειν, καὶ ἐπὶ τίνι γενήσεται, καὶ τί ἐνεργήσει γενόμενον, καὶ τίνων ἡγεμονεύσει, πάντα προδιασκοπεῖται ὁ λόγος,* [D] *ὡς πρεσβυτέραν αὐτὸν τῆς γενέσεως τὴν ἀξίαν λαχεῖν, πρὶν παρελθεῖν εἰς τὸ εἶναι τὴν τῶν ὄντων ἡγεμονίαν κτησάμενον.* ***Εἶπε*** *γάρ, φησίν,* ***ὁ Θεός, ποιήσωμεν ἄνθρωπον κατ' εἰκόνα ἡμετέραν καὶ καθ' ὁμοίωσιν, καὶ ἀρχέτωσαν τῶν ἰχθύων τῆς θαλάσσης καὶ τῶν θηρίων τῆς γῆς καὶ τῶν πετεινῶν τοῦ οὐρανοῦ καὶ τῶν κτηνῶν καὶ πάσης τῆς γῆς.***

[3.2] *Ὢ τοῦ θαύματος· ἥλιος κατασκευάζεται, καὶ οὐδεμία προηγεῖται βουλή· οὐρανὸς ὡσαύτως, ὧν οὐδέν τι τῶν κατὰ τὴν κτίσιν ἴσόν ἐστι,* [136] *ῥήματι μόνῳ τὸ τοιοῦτον θαῦμα συνίσταται, οὔτε ὅθεν οὔτε ὅπως οὔτε ἄλλό τι τοιοῦτον παρασημηναμένου τοῦ λόγου· οὕτω καὶ τὰ καθ' ἕκαστον πάντα, αἰθήρ, ἀστέρες, ὁ διὰ μέσου ἀήρ, θάλαττα, γῆ, ζῶα, φυτά, πάντα λόγῳ πρὸς γένεσιν ἄγεται· μόνῃ δὲ τῇ τοῦ ἀνθρώπου κατασκευῇ περιεσκεμμένως πρόσεισιν ὁ τοῦ παντὸς ποιητής, ὡς καὶ ὕλην αὐτῷ τῆς συστάσεως προετοιμάσαι, καὶ ἀρχετύπῳ τινὶ κάλλει τὴν μορφὴν ὁμοιῶσαι, καὶ προθέντα τὸν σκοπόν, οὗ χάριν γενήσεται, κατάλληλον αὐτῷ καὶ οἰκείαν ταῖς ἐνεργείαις δημιουργῆσαι τὴν φύσιν, ἐπιτηδείως πρὸς τὸ προκείμενον ἔχουσαν.*

1 *ὅτι—φύσις*] quod cum magna deliberatione deus hominem creaverit *Λ* *φαινομένης om.* B *φύσις*] *κτίσις* G H O P T Z 2 *ὅτι τοῦ*] *ὅπως τοῦ μὲν* L 3 *αὐτοῦ* L *μερῶν*] *μερῶν τῶν* A C N O Q *σύστασιν*] *om. Dion Eri* *ὑποβληθέντων*] *προβληθέντων* A B C I K O Q S : *ὑποβληθέντων* E^{ac} (*προ sup. l.*) 4 *ἀποσχεδιάζεται*] *ὑποσχεδιάζεται* E : *αὐτοσχεδιάζεται* A C I K O *κτῆσις* N 5 *ὑφισταμένη*] *συνισταμένη* A B C I K L N O R S 6 *προτυποῦται*] *τυποῦται* M T V W 7 *φέρειν τὴν ὁμοιότητα* B *φέρει* R^{2} *τίνι* S^{pc} : *τι* B G H P S^{ac} X 8 *γινόμενον* B G H I K L M N P S V W X 9 *προδιασκοπεῖται*] *προδι' ἐσκόπησεν* N *αὐτὸν*] *αὐτῷ* M V W : *om.* N 10 *κτησάμενος* A $Æ^{ac}$: *δεξάμενον* R 11 *ὁ θεὸς φησὶν* A I K N O Q *καθ'*] *ita* A B E G H I K L N O P Q R S V W X *Forb* : *om. Ald Mign* 12 *καὶ τῶν θηρίων τῆς γῆς om.* N 12–13 *καὶ τῶν πετεινῶν—πάσης τῆς γῆς om.* M T V W 15 *οὐρανὸς*] *οὐρανὸς καὶ* B *οὐρανὸς—ἐστι*] caelum similiter in conditione aequale est *Eri* *ὧν*] *ᾧ* A I K M Q S^{pc} *οὐδέν om.* A I K N O Q R^{ac} *τὴν om.* A(?) G H *ἴσον*] *θαυμάτων* N *μόνον* N R 16 *τὸ om.* I K N R *τοιοῦτο*[1] G H P^{2} S V W : *τοσοῦτον* A I K N O Q R *τοιοῦτο*[2] L M V : *om.* H 17 *παρασημηναμένου τοῦ λόγου*] intimatur *Dion* : praeter significatiuum uerbum *Eri* *οὕτως* R : *ὅτε* Æ *καὶ om.* N *τὰ om.* H L M T W *καθέκαστον* Æ H I L X *πάντα*] creaturum *Dion* 17–18 *αἰθὴρ—ἀὴρ ante οὕτω* (*l. 17*) *pon.* N *θάλασσα* I 18–19 *μόνῃ δὲ τῇ τοῦ ἀνθρώπου κατασκευῇ*] *μόνη ἡ κατασκευὴ* G H P : *μόνη δὲ ἡ τοῦ ἀνθρώπου κατασκευὴ* V 19 *πρόεισιν* $Æ^{ac}$ I N P^{ac} V 21 *προσθέντα* X 22 *τὴν om.* A I K O Q

That the nature of the human being is more honourable than all the visible creation.[9]

[**3.1**] But it is right that we should not leave this point unconsidered, that while so great a world and its parts are laid down in an elementary fashion for the composition of the universe, the creation is, somehow, enacted offhand by the divine power, existing at once by his command, while counsel precedes the formation of the human being and what he will be is foreshadowed by the Artist through the writing of the account, and what kind of being it is fitting he should be, and to what archetype he should bear a likeness, and for what purpose he shall come into being, and, having come to be, what activity, and what he shall rule—all these things the account lays out beforehand, so that he has a rank assigned before his genesis, possessing rule over beings before his coming into being, for it says, *God said, 'Let us make the human being in accordance with our image and in accordance with our likeness, and let him have rule over the fish of the sea, and the beasts of the earth, and the birds of the heaven, and the cattle, and of all the earth'.*[10]

[**3.2**] What a wonder! A sun is fashioned, and no counsel precedes it; heaven likewise, and to these no single thing in creation is equal; so great a wonder is formed by a spoken word alone, with the account indicating neither when, nor how, nor any such detail. So too in every single case—the aether, the stars, the intermediate air, the sea, the earth, the animals, the plants—all are brought to genesis by a word;[11] while only to the formation of the human being does the Maker of all draw near with circumspection, so as to prepare beforehand for him material for his structure, and to liken his form to some archetypal beauty, and, setting before him the goal for which he will come to be, to craft for him the nature appropriate for him and proper for his activities, suitable to the project.

[9] *Bodl. 238*: 'That God created the human being with great deliberation'. For Chapter 3, see Philo, *Opif.* 72–5; Basil, *Hom. de creat. hom.* 1.3 (Hörner, 5–6).

[10] Gen. 1:26.

[11] Cf. Gregory of Nyssa, *Hex.* 9 (Drobner, 18.9–11).

Ὅτι διὰ πάντων ἐπισημαίνει τὴν ἀρχικὴν ἐξουσίαν ἡ τοῦ ἀνθρώπου κατασκευή.

[4] *Καθάπερ γὰρ ἐν τῷ βίῳ τούτῳ καταλλήλως τῇ χρείᾳ σχηματίζεται παρὰ τῶν τεχνιτευόντων τὸ ὄργανον· οὕτως οἷόν τι σκεῦος εἰς βασιλείας ἐνέργειαν ἐπιτήδειον τὴν ἡμετέραν φύσιν ὁ ἀριστοτέχνης ἐδημιούργησε, τοῖς τε κατὰ τὴν ψυχὴν προτερήμασι καὶ αὐτῷ τῷ τοῦ σώματος σχήματι τοιοῦτον εἶναι παρασκευάσας, οἷον ἐπιτηδείως πρὸς βασιλείαν ἔχειν· ἡ μὲν γὰρ ψυχὴ τὸ βασιλικόν τε καὶ ἐπηρμένον αὐτόθεν δείκνυσι, πόρρω τῆς ἰδιωτικῆς ταπεινότητος κεχωρισμένον, ἐκ τοῦ ἀδέσποτον αὐτὴν εἶναι καὶ αὐτεξούσιον,* [C] *ἰδίοις θελήμασιν αὐτοκρατορικῶς διοικουμένην· τίνος γὰρ ἄλλου τοῦτο καὶ οὐχὶ βασιλέως ἐστίν; καὶ ἔτι πρὸς τούτοις, τὸ τῆς δυναστευούσης τῶν πάντων φύσεως εἰκόνα γενέσθαι, οὐδὲν ἕτερόν ἐστιν ἢ εὐθὺς βασιλίδα δημιουργηθῆναι τὴν φύσιν. Ὥσπερ γὰρ κατὰ τὴν ἀνθρωπίνην συνήθειαν, οἱ τὰς εἰκόνας τῶν κρατούντων κατασκευάζοντες, τόν τε χαρακτῆρα τῆς μορφῆς ἀναμάσσονται, καὶ τῇ περιβολῇ τῆς πορφυρίδος τὴν βασιλικὴν ἀξίαν συμπαραγράφουσι, καὶ λέγεται κατὰ συνήθειαν καὶ ἡ εἰκών, βασιλεύς· οὕτω καὶ ἡ ἀνθρωπίνη φύσις, ἐπειδὴ πρὸς ἀρχὴν τῶν ἄλλων κατεσκευάζετο, διὰ τῆς πρὸς τὸν βασιλέα τοῦ παντὸς ὁμοιότητος, οἷόν τις ἔμψυχος εἰκὼν ἀνεστάθη, κοινωνοῦσα τῷ ἀρχετύπῳ καὶ τῆς ἀξίας καὶ τοῦ ὀνόματος· οὐ πορφυρίδα περικειμένη, οὐδὲ σκήπτρῳ καὶ διαδήματι τὴν ἀξίαν ἐπισημαίνουσα, οὐδὲ γὰρ τὸ ἀρχέτυπον ἐν τούτοις ἐστίν· ἀλλ᾽ ἀντὶ μὲν τῆς* [D] *ἁλουργίδος τὴν ἀρετὴν ἠμφιεσμένη, ὃ δὴ πάντων βασιλικώτατον ἐσθημάτων ἐστίν· ἀντὶ δὲ τοῦ σκήπτρου τῇ μακαριότητι τῆς ἀθανασίας ἐρειδομένη· ἀντὶ δὲ τοῦ βασιλικοῦ διαδήματος, τῷ τῆς δικαιοσύνης στεφάνῳ κεκοσμημένη· ὥστε διὰ πάντων ἐν τῷ τῆς βασιλείας ἀξιώματι δείκνυσθαι δι᾽ ἀκριβείας πρὸς τὸ ἀρχέτυπον κάλλος ὁμοιωθεῖσαν.*

4.6–9 (*ἡ μὲν γὰρ ψυχὴ—διοικουμένην*): *Doctrina Patrum de Incarnatione Verbi* 19.VII (Diekamp, 122.14–15) 4.6–11 (*ἡ μὲν γὰρ ψυχὴ—φύσιν*): John (of Damascus) *Sacra Parallela* II^{1}98/K cap. A 2, 20 (Thum, 117.3–9) 4.11–17 (*ὥσπερ—ὀνόματος*): John of Damascus, *Imag.* 1.49/2.45 (Kotter, 3.153.4–11) 4.11–5.3 (*ὥσπερ—θεωρεῖται*): John (of Damascus) *Sacra Parallela* II^{1}38/K cap. A 1, 38 (Thum, 67.11–68.5)

1 *ὅτι—κατασκευή*] de regia dignitate humanae formae *Λ* 4 *τὴν om.* I W 5 *προτερήμασι*] observationibus *Eri* 6 *μὲν γὰρ om. SP* 7 *ταπεινώσεως* N 8 *θελήμασιν*] *θελήμασιν καὶ* A I K N Q : *θελήμασι καὶ* O 8–9 *αὐτοκρατορικοῖς διοικουμένη* N 9 *ἄλλου*] alius *Eri* : *om. SP* *ἐστίν*] *ἔσται* A K Q *ἔτι*] *ἔστιν SP* 10 *τῶν πάντων om. SP* *εἰκόνα φύσεως* M *οὐδὲν*] *ὅπερ οὐδὲν SP* 11 *ἢ εὐθὺς SP* *βασιλίδα*] *βασιλέα* Æ *γὰρ om. Dam. SP* 12 *συνήθειαν* X^{mg2} *οἱ om.* N 14 *συμπεριγράφουσι* L N V *κατὰ*] *κατὰ τὴν* Æ *ἡ om.* B I P^{ac} *βασιλεύς*] *καὶ βασιλεύς Dam* *οὕτως* Æ R O 15 *ἀρχὴν τῶν*] *τὴν ἀρχὴν Mign* *κατεσκευάζεται* R^{ac} 15–16 *διὰ τῆς—ὁμοιότητος om. Dam* 16 *ἔμψυχος om.* N 17 *οὐδὲ*] *οὔτε* N V 18 *τὴν*] *τὴν βασιλικὴν SP* *οὐδὲ*] *οὔτε* V 19 *τοιούτοις* R *ἀλουργίδος* G N P R X 20 *ἐσθημάτων*] *τῶν ἐσθημάτων* I *τοῦ om.* N 21 *τῷ τῆς om.* M T W 22 *κοσμουμένη* M : *κεκοσμημένος* Æ : *κοσμημένη* W : *κατεστρεμμένη* V *δείκνυσθαι*] *παραδείκνυσθαι* Æ 23 *ὁμοιωθεῖσα* L R

That the formation of the human being throughout signifies his sovereign authority.[12]

[4] Just as in this life a tool appropriate to its use is fashioned by artists, so also the best Artist[13] crafted our nature as it were a vessel fit for the exercise of royalty, preparing it both with the superior advantages of soul and by the very form of the body to be such as to be adapted for royalty; for the soul immediately shows its royal and exalted character, far removed as it is from subordinate lowliness, in that it is without lord and is self-governed, swayed autocratically by its own will. For to whom else does this belong, other than to a king? And further, besides these points, that it has come to be as the image of that Nature which rules over all means nothing else than that our nature was crafted to be immediately royal. Just as in human customs, those who fashion images of rulers both mould the figure of their form and represent the royal rank by the purple robe, and even the image is customarily called a king, so also human nature, since it was fashioned to rule the rest, on account of its likeness to the King of all, was established as it were as a living image, sharing with the Archetype in both rank and name, not robed in purple, nor indicating rank by sceptre and diadem (for neither is Archetype arrayed in these), but, instead of the purple robe, clothed in virtue, which is the most royal of all raiments, and in place of the sceptre, leaning on the blessedness of immortality, and instead of the royal diadem, adorned with the crown of righteousness, so that in everything that belongs to the dignity of royalty it is shown to be precisely assimilated to the beauty of the archetype.

[12] *Bodl. 238*: 'Of the kingly dignity of the human form'.

[13] Cf. Clement of Alexandria, *Protrep.* 10.98.3; Pindar, Frag. 57 (Snell).

Ὅτι ὁμοίωμα τῆς θείας βασιλείας ὁ ἄνθρωπος.

[5.1] *Τὸ δὲ δὴ θεῖον κάλλος οὐ σχήματί τινι καὶ μορφῆς εὐμοιρίᾳ, διά τινος εὐχροίας ἐναγλαΐζεται, ἀλλ' ἐν ἀφράστῳ μακαριότητι κατ' ἀρετὴν θεωρεῖται. Ὥσπερ τοίνυν τὰς ἀνθρωπίνας μορφὰς διὰ χρωμάτων τινῶν ἐπὶ τοὺς πίνακας οἱ γραφεῖς μεταφέρουσι, τὰς οἰκείας τε καὶ καταλλήλους βαφὰς ἐπαλείφοντες τῷ μιμήματι, ὡς ἂν δι' ἀκριβείας τὸ ἀρχέτυπον κάλλος μετενεχθείη πρὸς τὸ ὁμοίωμα· οὕτω μοι νόει καὶ τὸν ἡμέτερον πλάστην, οἷόν τισι βαφαῖς τῇ τῶν ἀρετῶν ἐπιβολῇ πρὸς τὸ ἴδιον κάλλος τὴν εἰκόνα περιανθίσαντα, ἐν ἡμῖν δεῖξαι τὴν ἰδίαν ἀρχήν· πολυειδῆ δὲ καὶ ποικίλα τὰ οἱονεὶ χρώματα τῆς εἰκόνος, δι' ὧν ἡ ἀληθινὴ ἀναζωγραφεῖται μορφή· οὐκ ἐρύθημα καὶ λαμπρότης* [B] *καὶ ἡ ποιὰ τούτων πρὸς ἄλληλα μίξις, οὐδέ τινος μέλανος ὑπογραφὴ ὀφρῦν τε καὶ ὀφθαλμὸν ὑπαλείφουσα, καὶ κατά τινα κρᾶσιν τὰ κοῖλα τοῦ χαρακτῆρος ὑποσκιάζουσα, καὶ ὅσα τοιαῦτα ζωγράφων χεῖρες ἐπετεχνήσαντο,· ἀλλ' ἀντὶ τούτων καθαρότης, ἀπάθεια, μακαριότης, κακοῦ παντὸς ἀλλοτρίωσις, καὶ ὅσα τοῦ τοιούτου γένους ἐστὶ, δι' ὧν μορφοῦται τοῖς ἀνθρώποις ἡ πρὸς τὸ θεῖον ὁμοίωσις· τοιούτοις ἄνθεσιν ὁ δημιουργὸς τῆς ἰδίας εἰκόνος τὴν ἡμετέραν διεχάραξε φύσιν.*

[5.2] *Εἰ δὲ καὶ τὰ ἄλλα συνεξετάζοις, δι' ὧν τὸ θεῖον κάλλος χαρακτηρίζεται, εὑρήσεις καὶ πρὸς ἐκεῖνα δι' ἀκριβείας σωζομένην ἐν τῇ καθ' ἡμᾶς εἰκόνι τὴν ὁμοιότητα. Νοῦς καὶ λόγος ἡ θειότης ἐστίν·* ***ἐν ἀρχῇ*** *τε γὰρ* ***ἦν ὁ Λόγος****, καὶ οἱ κατὰ Παῦλον* ***νοῦν Χριστοῦ ἔχουσι*** *τὸν ἐν αὐτοῖς* ***λαλοῦντα****·* [C] *οὐ πόρρω τούτων καὶ τὸ ἀνθρώπινον· ὁρᾷς ἐν σεαυτῷ καὶ τὸν λόγον καὶ τὴν διάνοιαν, μίμημα τοῦ ὄντως νοῦ τε καὶ λόγου.* ***Ἀγάπη*** *πάλιν* ***ὁ Θεὸς****, καὶ ἀγάπης πηγή· τοῦτο γάρ φησιν Ἰωάννης ὁ μέγας, ὅτι* ***ἡ ἀγάπη ἐκ τοῦ Θεοῦ ἐστιν*** *καί,* ***ὁ Θεὸς ἀγάπη ἐστί·*** *τοῦτο καὶ ἡμέτερον πεποίηται πρόσωπον ὁ τῆς φύσεως πλάστης·* ***ἐν τούτῳ*** *γὰρ, φησὶ,* ***γνώσονται πάντες, ὅτι μαθηταί μου ἐστὲ, ἐὰν ἀγαπᾶτε ἀλλήλους.*** *Οὐκοῦν μὴ παρούσης ταύτης, ἅπας ὁ χαρακτὴρ τῆς εἰκόνος μεταπεποίηται. Πάντα ἐπιβλέπει καὶ πάντα ἐπακούει τὸ θεῖον, καὶ πάντα διερευνᾶται· ἔχεις καὶ σὺ τὴν δι' ὄψεως καὶ ἀκοῆς τῶν ὄντων ἀντίληψιν, καὶ τὴν ζητητικήν τε καὶ διερευνητικὴν τῶν ὄντων διάνοιαν.*

5.2–6 (*Τὸ δὲ—τὸ ὁμοίωμα*): John of Damascus, *Imag.* 1.50/2.46 (Kotter, 3.154.3–9)

1 *ὅτι—ἄνθρωπος*] quomodo ad imaginem dei facta est humana anima *Λ* 2 *δὴ*] *ita* A E G I L M N O P Q R S T V W X *Forb* : *om. Dam SP Ald Mign* 3 *ἐναγλαΐζεται*] *ita codd. Dam Forb* : *ἀναγλαΐζεται* I : *ἐπαγλαΐζεται* R[ac] : *ἐναγκαλίζεται* K : *ἀγλαΐζεται Ald Mign* 4 *διὰ χρωμάτων τινῶν post γραφεῖς pon.* R *μεταμορφοῦσι* Æ 5 *τε om.* N *καὶ om.* V *ἐπαλείφοντες*] *ita codd. Dam Forb* : *ἀπαλείφοντες Ald Mign* 6 *μετενεχθῇ* R 8 *περιανθήσαντα* E G I K N O P Q T W X *ἰδίαν*] *οἰκείαν* I : *θείαν* K O *τὰ om.* N 9 *ἀναζωγραφεῖται*] *διαζωγραφεῖται* A B K O Q R T : *ζωγραφεῖται* I *ἐρύθημα*] *ita* Æ ß G I K L M N O P Q R S V W X *Ald Forb* : *ἐρύθρημα Mign* 10 *μίξεως* V 11–12 *ὀφθαλμὸν—ὑποσκιάζουσα*] oculumque subscribit *Eri* 11 *ὀφθαλμὸν*] *ita* A B I K M N O R V W *Forb* : *ὀφθαλμοὺς* X *Ald Mign* *κράσιν* ß I : *τάξιν* E G M P V W X : *κρᾶσιν καὶ τάξιν* L 12 *ἐπετεχνάσαντο* A B K O Q R S[pc] V : *ἐτεχνάσαντο* N : *ἐπιτεχνάζονται* I : *ἀπετεχνήσαντο* T 14 *τοιούτοις*] *τοῖς τοιούτοις* A B I K N O Q R[ac] T V 16 *συνεξετάζεις* M 17 *ἐκεῖνο* E G I K L M O P Q S T V W X 18 *θεότης* B E I K L M N O R S *οἱ*] *οἱ προφῆται Mign* 19 *ἔχουσιν* N V *τὸν om.* N *αὐτοῖς*] *ἑαυτοῖς* R *πόρρω*] *πόρρω δὲ* B *ὁρᾷς*] *ὁρᾷς γὰρ* I 20 *μιμήματα* N T *ὄντος* A B K N O P 21 *ἡ om. Mign* 21–2 *ἐστιν ἐκ τοῦ Θεοῦ* K 22 *ἐστιν*] *ἐστι* A B I K N O Q R X : *om.* V W *Ald Mign* 22 *τοῦτο*] *τοιοῦτο* I *ἡμέτερον*] *τὸ ἡμέτερον* I 23 *πλάστης*] *λόγος* X *φησὶ om.* V W *μαθηταί μου*] *ἐμοὶ μαθηταί* E 24–5 *οὐκοῦν—μεταπεποίηται*] nempe igitur dum haec praesens sit omnis character imaginis perficitur 25 *πάντων* B E 27 *ζητηκήν* V : *ζωτικήν* I N W

That the human being is a likeness of the divine royalty.[14]

[5.1] The divine beauty is not in being adorned with a certain shape or excellent form, but is contemplated in unspeakable blessedness in accordance with virtue. Just as painters convey human forms in their pictures by means of certain colours, applying to their copy the appropriate and corresponding tints, so that the beauty of the archetype may be accurately transferred to the likeness, so also, as I understand it, our Fashioner also, painting the image to resemble his own beauty by the addition of virtues, as it were with colours, shows in us his own sovereignty; manifold and varied are the colours, as it were, by which his true form is portrayed—not red, or white, or some kind of mixture of these with each other, nor a touch of black that paints the eyebrow and the eye, and shades, by some combination, the hollows in the figure, and all such things which the hands of painters contrive—but instead of these, purity, freedom from passion, blessedness, estrangement from all evil, and whatever of such a kind through which the likeness to the divine is formed in human beings. With such lustres did the Craftsman of his own image mark our nature.

[5.2] And if you were to examine also the other points by which the divine beauty is characterized, you will find that to them too the likeness in our image is accurately preserved.[15] The divinity is intellect and word: for *in the beginning was the Word*,[16] and those, according to Paul, who *have the intellect of Christ* have it *speaking* in them.[17] Humankind too is not far removed from these: you see in yourself word and mind, an imitation of the very Intellect and Word. Again, *God is love*, and the source of love; for this the great John declares, that *love is of God*, and *God is love*.[18] The Fashioner of our nature has made this to be our character also; for, he says, by *this shall all know that you are my disciples, if you love one another*.[19] Therefore, if this be absent, the whole stamp of the image is transformed. The Divine beholds all things and hears all things, and searches out all things; you too have the ability of apprehending things by means of sight and hearing and the mind that enquires into beings and searches them out.[20]

[14] *Bodl. 238*: 'How the human soul is made in the image of God'.
[15] Cf. Gregory of Nyssa, *An. et res.* 3.11–12 (Spira, 34.4–8).
[16] John 1:1.
[17] 1 Cor. 2:16; 2 Cor. 13:3.
[18] 1 John 4:7, 8.
[19] John 13:35.
[20] Cf. Gregory of Nyssa, *An. et res.* 3.34 (Spira, 39.11–16).

Ἐξέτασις τῆς τοῦ νοῦ πρὸς τὴν φύσιν συγγενείας, ἐν ᾧ καὶ ἐκ παρόδου τὸ τῶν ἀνομοίων διελέγχεται δόγμα.

[6.1] *Καί με μηδεὶς οἴεσθω καθ' ὁμοιότητα τῆς ἀνθρωπίνης ἐνεργείας ἐν διαφόροις δυνάμεσι τὸ θεῖον λέγειν τῶν ὄντων ἐφάπτεσθαι. Οὐ γάρ ἐστι δυνατὸν ἐν τῇ ἁπλότητι τῆς θειότητος τὸ ποικίλον τε καὶ πολυειδὲς τῆς ἀντιληπτικῆς ἐνεργείας κατανοῆσαι· οὐδὲ γὰρ παρ' ἡμῖν πολλαί τινές εἰσὶν αἱ ἀντιληπτικαὶ τῶν πραγμάτων δυνάμεις, εἰ καὶ πολυτρόπως διὰ τῶν αἰσθήσεων* [140] *τῶν κατὰ τὴν ζωὴν ἐφαπτόμεθα· μία γάρ τις ἐστι δύναμις, αὐτὸς ὁ ἐγκείμενος νοῦς, ὁ δι' ἑκάστου τῶν αἰσθητηρίων διεξιὼν καὶ τῶν ὄντων ἐπιδρασσόμενος· οὗτος θεωρεῖ διὰ τῶν ὀφθαλμῶν τὸ φαινόμενον· οὗτος συνίησι διὰ τῆς ἀκοῆς τὸ λεγόμενον, ἀγαπᾷ τε τὸ καταθύμιον, καὶ τὸ μὴ καθ' ἡδονὴν ἀποστρέφεται, καὶ τῇ χειρὶ χρῆται πρὸς ὅ, τι βούλεται, κρατῶν τε δι' αὐτῆς καὶ ἀπωθούμενος, καθ' ὅπερ ἂν λυσιτελεῖν κρίνῃ τῇ τοῦ ὀργάνου συνεργίᾳ εἰς τοῦτο συγχρώμενος.*

[6.2] *Εἰ τοίνυν ἐν τῷ ἀνθρώπῳ, κἂν διάφορα τύχῃ τὰ πρὸς αἴσθησιν κατεσκευασμένα παρὰ τῆς φύσεως ὄργανα, ὁ διὰ πάντων ἐνεργῶν καὶ κινούμενος καὶ καταλλήλως ἑκάστῳ πρὸς τὸ προκείμενον κεχρημένος, εἷς ἐστι καὶ ὁ αὐτὸς, ταῖς διαφοραῖς τῶν ἐνεργειῶν οὐ συνεξαλλάσσων τὴν φύσιν· πῶς ἄν τις ἐπὶ τοῦ Θεοῦ διὰ* [B] *τῶν ποικίλων δυνάμεων τὸ πολυμερὲς τῆς οὐσίας καθυποπτεύσειεν;* ***ὁ*** *γὰρ* ***πλάσας τὸν ὀφθαλμὸν****, καθώς φησιν ὁ προφήτης, καὶ* ***ὁ φυτεύσας τὸ οὖς****, πρὸς τὰ ἐν αὐτῷ παραδείγματα τὰς ἐνεργείας ταύτας οἱόν τινας γνωριστικοὺς χαρακτῆρας τῇ φύσει τῶν ἀνθρώπων ἐνεσημήνατο·* ***ποιήσωμεν*** *γὰρ, φησὶν,* ***ἄνθρωπον κατ' εἰκόνα ἡμετέραν.***

[6.3] *Ἀλλὰ ποῦ μοι τῶν Ἀνομοίων ἡ αἵρεσις; τί πρὸς τὴν τοιαύτην ἐροῦσι φωνήν; πῶς διασώσουσιν ἐν τοῖς εἰρημένοις τοῦ δόγματος αὐτῶν τὴν κενότητα; ἆρα δυνατὸν εἶναι φήσουσι, μίαν εἰκόνα διαφόροις ὁμοιωθῆναι μορφαῖς; εἰ ἀνόμοιος κατὰ τὴν φύσιν τῷ Πατρὶ ὁ Υἱὸς, πῶς μίαν κατασκευάζει τῶν διαφόρων φύσεων τὴν εἰκόνα; ὁ γὰρ* ***ποιήσωμεν κατ' εἰκόνα ἡμετέραν*** *εἰπὼν, καὶ διὰ τῆς πληθυντικῆς σημασίας τὴν*

1–2 *ἐξέτασις—δόγμα*] quod deus non habet membra humana et quod una est imago patris et filii contra eunomianos *Λ* 1 *ἐκ παρόδου*] *ἐν παρόδῳ* M 2 *διελέγχει* R 3 *ἐν*] *ἐν ταῖς* R 4 *οὐ*] *οὐ δὲ* R *ἐστι* *om.* R 5 *θεότητος* A B E H I K L N O R V *ποικίλον*] receptionem *Eri* *πολυειδὲς*] *πθεοειδὲς* X 6 *παρ'*] *ita* A B E I K L N O Q R S T *Forb* : *om.* V W X *Ald Mign* *παρ' ἡμῖν*] apud nos *Eri* *αἱ* *om.* Æ G H K P[pc] 7 *τὴν* *om.* *Ald Mign* 8 *ἐφαπτώμεθα* V *Ald Mign* *δύναμις* *om.* B 9 *διεξιὼν*] *ἐξιὼν* B *ἐπιδρασσόμενος*] transcurrit *Eri* 10 *φαινόμενον*] *βλεπόμενον* R *συνίησι*] *ita* A B E I K L N O R S T *Forb* : *συννοεῖ* G H P X : *συνιεῖ* V W *Ald Mign* *διὰ τῆς*] *δι'* L 11 *κατευθύμιον* *Ald Mign* *χρᾶται* R *πρὸς*] *ita* A B E K L N O Q R S T *Forb* : *πρὸς τὸ* V W *Ald Mign* 12 *τε*] *δὲ* M W *Ald* : *om.* *Mign* *αὐτῆς*] *ἑαυτῆς* Æ H P *ἀπωθούμενος*] *ἀπωθούμενος καὶ* B *καθ'ὅπερ*] *ita* A B E I L Q S *Forb* : *καθ' ἅπερ* P : *καθάπερ* G H K M O R T V W X : *ἅπερ* *Ald Mign* *κρίνοι* I 13 *εἰς* *om.* G H M P V W X *τούτῳ* H M 15 *κατασκευασμένα* G H 16 *καὶ*[1] *om.* H M 17 *διαφόροις* R S *τοῦ* *om.* A B I K N O Q T 18 *καθυποπτεύσειεν*] *ita* A B E I K L N O S T *Forb* : *κατοπτεύσειεν* V W X *Ald Mign* 19 *ὁ* *om.* G H M P R S V W X 20 *αὐτῷ*] *ita* Æ ß G H K L M N O R S V W *Forb Mign* : *αὐτῶ* P : *ἑαυτῷ* Q : *αὑτῷ* *Ald* *γνωστικοὺς* Æ T 21 *φησὶν* *om.* V W 22 *ἡμετέραν*] *ἡμετέραν καὶ καθ' ὁμοίωσιν* A B E I K L O Q R : et similitudinem nostram *Dion* 23 *μοι* *om.* R *τί*] *ἢ τί* A B K O Q 24 *ἐν*] *ἐν τούτοις* N *καινότητα* M T : novitatem *Dion Eri* 25–6 *τῷ πατρὶ κατὰ τὴν φύσιν* N 26 *ὁ υἱὸς τῷ πατρὶ* L 27 *ποιήσωμεν*] *ita* A B E G H I K M N O P Q R S V W X *Forb* : *ποιήσωμεν ἄνθρωπον* *Ald Mign* *κατ' εἰκόνα* *om.* N *πληνθυτικῆς* V

An examination of the kinship of the intellect to nature; in which also, by way of digression, the doctrine of the Anomoeans is refuted.[21]

[6.1] And let no one suppose me to say that the divine is in touch with beings in a similar way to human activity, by means of different faculties. For it is not possible to comprehend in the simplicity of the divinity the varied and diverse apprehending activity; for neither in our own case are the faculties which apprehend things many, although we are in touch in many ways, through the senses, with those things pertaining to life; for there is one faculty, the implanted intellect itself, which passes through each of the organs of sense and grasps the beings beyond: this, by means of the eyes, contemplates what appears; this, by means of the hearing, understands what is said; loves what is to its taste and turns from what is not pleasant, and uses the hand for whatever it wills, holding or rejecting with it, using the help of this instrument for whatever it deems to be advantageous.

[6.2] If, then, in the human being, even though the organs formed by nature for perception may be different, that which works and moves through them all, and uses each appropriately for the object before it, is one and the same, not changing its nature by the differences of the activities, how could anyone suppose there to be a multiplicity of essence in regard to God on the ground of his varied faculties? For *he that fashioned the eye*, as the prophet says, and *that planted the ear*,[22] stamped on the nature of human beings these activities to be as it were indicative characteristics, with reference to their paradigms in himself; for he says, *Let us make the human being in accordance with our image.*[23]

[6.3] But where, for me, is the heresy of the Anomoeans? What will they say to such an utterance? How will they defend the vanity of their doctrine in view of the words cited? Will they say that it is possible that one image should be made like to different forms? If the Son is by nature unlike the Father, how does he form one image of the different natures? For he who said, *Let us make in accordance our*

[21] *Bodl. 238*: 'That God does not have human limbs, and that the image of the Father and the Son is one, against the Eunomians'.
[22] Ps. 93:9. [23] Gen. 1:26.

ἁγίαν Τριάδα [C] *δηλώσας, οὐκ ἂν τῆς εἰκόνος μοναδικῶς ἐπεμνήσθη, εἴπερ ἀνομοίως εἶχε πρὸς ἄλληλα τὰ ἀρχέτυπα· οὐδὲ γὰρ ἦν δυνατὸν τῶν ἀλλήλοις μὴ συμβαινόντων ἓν ἀναδειχθῆναι ὁμοίωμα· ἀλλ' εἰ διάφοροι ἦσαν αἱ φύσεις, διαφόρους ἂν πάντως καὶ τὰς εἰκόνας αὐτῶν ἐνεστήσατο, τὴν κατάλληλον ἑκάστῃ δημιουργήσας· ἀλλ' ἐπειδὴ μία μὲν ἡ εἰκών, οὐχ ἓν δὲ τὸ τῆς εἰκόνος ἀρχέτυπον· τίς οὕτως ἔξω διανοίας ἐστὶν ὡς ἀγνοεῖν, ὅτι τὰ τῷ ἑνὶ ὁμοιούμενα καὶ πρὸς ἄλληλα πάντως ὁμοίως ἔχει; διὰ τοῦτό φησι· (τάχα τὴν κακίαν ταύτην ἐν τῇ κατασκευῇ τῆς ἀνθρωπίνης ζωῆς ὁ λόγος ὑποτεμνόμενος)* ***ποιήσωμεν ἄνθρωπον κατ' εἰκόνα καὶ ὁμοίωσιν ἡμετέραν.***

Διατί γυμνὸς τῶν ἐκ φύσεως ὅπλων τε καὶ προκαλυμμάτων ὁ ἄνθρωπος.

[7.1] *Ἀλλὰ τί βούλεται τὸ τοῦ σχήματος ὄρθιον; τί δὲ οὐχὶ συμφυεῖς εἰσιν αἱ πρὸς τὸν βίον δυνάμεις τῷ σώματι, ἀλλὰ γυμνὸς μὲν τῶν φυσικῶν σκεπασμάτων, ἄοπλος δέ τις καὶ πένης ὁ ἄνθρωπος καὶ τῶν πρὸς τὴν χρείαν ἐνδεὴς ἁπάντων, ἐπὶ τὸν βίον παράγεται, ἐλεεῖσθαι μᾶλλον ἢ μακαρίζεσθαι κατὰ τὸ φαινόμενον ἄξιος, οὐ προβολαῖς κεράτων καθωπλισμένος, οὐκ ὀνύχων ἀκμαῖς, οὐχ ὁπλαῖς ἢ ὀδοῦσιν ἤ τινι κέντρῳ θανατηφόρον ἰὸν ἐκ φύσεως ἔχοντι, οἷα δὴ τὰ* [141] *πολλὰ τῶν ζώων ἐν ἑαυτοῖς πρὸς τὴν τῶν λυπούντων ἄμυναν κέκτηται, οὐ τῇ τῶν τριχῶν περιβολῇ τὸ σῶμα κεκάλυπται, καίτοιγε ἴσως τὸν εἰς ἀρχὴν τῶν ἄλλων προτεταγμένον οἰκείοις ὅπλοις ἔδει περιπεφράχθαι παρὰ τῆς φύσεως, ὡς ἂν μὴ τῆς παρ' ἑτέρων ἐπικουρίας πρὸς τὴν ἰδίαν ἀσφάλειαν δέοιτο· νυνὶ δὲ λέων μὲν καὶ σῦς καὶ τίγρις καὶ πάρδαλις καὶ εἴ τι τοιοῦτον ἕτερον, ἀρκοῦσαν ἔχει πρὸς σωτηρίαν τὴν ἐκ φύσεως δύναμιν· καὶ τῷ ταύρῳ μὲν τὸ κέρας, καὶ τῷ λαγωῷ τὸ τάχος, καὶ τῇ δορκάδι τὸ πήδημα καὶ τὸ κατὰ τὸν ὀφθαλμὸν ἀσφαλές, καὶ ἄλλῳ τινὶ ζώῳ τὸ μέγεθος, καὶ ἑτέροις ἡ προνομαία, καὶ τοῖς πετεινοῖς τὸ πτερὸν, καὶ τῇ μελίσσῃ τὸ κέντρον, καὶ πᾶσι πάντως ἕν τι εἰς σωτηρίαν παρὰ τῆς φύσεως ἐμπέφυκε· μόνος δὲ πάντων ὁ ἄνθρωπος, τῶν μὲν ταχυδρομούντων* [B] *ἀργότερος, τῶν δὲ πολυσαρκούντων βραχύτερος, τῶν δὲ τοῖς συμφύτοις ὅπλοις ἠσφαλισμένων εὐαλωτότερος· καὶ πῶς, ἐρεῖ τις, ὁ τοιοῦτος τὴν ἀρχὴν τὴν κατὰ πάντων κεκλήρωται;*

28 *ἐπεμνήσθη*] *ἐμνημόνευσεν* A B I K N O Q R 29 *εἶχε*] *ita* A B E I K L N O Q R T *Forb* : *ἔχει* G H M P V W X : *ἔχοι Ald Mign* *οὐδὲ*] *οὔτε* N : *οὐ Ald Mign* 30 *ἓν*] *om.* T : *εἰς ἓν Ald Mign* 31 *ἂν om. Ald Mign* *πάντως καὶ τὰς*] *πάντας* Q *ἐνεστήσαντο* V : *ἀνεστήσατο* A B I K N O T : *ἀνεστήσαντο* E *ἑκάστῳ* N 32 *ἡ om.* I Q R 33 *οὕτω* R 34 *ὁμοίως ἔχει*] *ὁμοίως ἔχει τὴν ὁμοιότητα* V : *ἔχει τὴν ὁμοιότητα* A B I K N O R 35–36 *ἡμετέραν καὶ ὁμοίωσιν* R 36 *ὁμοίωσιν*] *καθ' ὁμοίωσιν* Q

1 *διατί—ἄνθρωπος*] cur homo non sit creatus cum cornibus uel aliis munimentis sicut quaedam alia *Λ* *φύσεως*] *τῆς φύσεως* N *καλυμμάτων* R 2 *οὐχὶ*] *οὐχὶ καὶ* N V 3 *ἄνοπλος* H N R T V W 4 *ἐνδεεῖς* X *βίον*] *βίον πορεύεται καὶ* B 5 *παράγεται*] *παραγίνεται* N *κατὰ τὸ φαινόμενον*] *om.* Q : esse videatur *Dion* : quantum apparet *Eri* *ἄξιος κατὰ τὸ φαινόμενον* B *κατὰ*] *πρὸς* R 7 *θανατηφόρῳ* K M N V : moritfero *Eri* *τὰ om.* N 8 *κέκτηνται* V 9 *κεκάλυπται*] *περικεκάλυπται* R : *καλύπτεται Ald Mign* *καίτοιγε*] *καίτοιγε εἴποι τις ἂν* B E L R S *οἰκείοις*] *ὡς οἰκείοις* B 10 *περιπεφράχθαι*] *πεφράχθαι* A I K N O Q T : perfici *Eri* 11 *σῦς*] *ὗς* Æ G I K M N O P Q V W X : *σὺς Ald* 12 *ἐκ*] *ἐκ τῆς* N R V 13 *μὲν om.* Æ I K N O Q T *καὶ τῷ λαγωῷ*] *τῷ δὲ λαγωῷ* B 13–14 *καὶ τὸ κατὰ τὸν ὀφθαλμὸν ἀσφαλὲς om.* N 14 *κατὰ τὸν*] *ita* A B E G I K M P Q R S T *Forb* : *κατ'* V *Ald Mign* 15 *προνομαία*] catulorum rapina *Eri* *καὶ τῇ μελίσσῃ τὸ κέντρον om.* Q *ταῖς μελίσσαις* Æ I K N O R T 16 *εἰς σωτηρίαν*] *τῆς σωτηρίας* G M P R W X *παρὰ τῆς φύσεως εἰς σωτηρίαν* A B E I K N O Q T V *πάντων*] *τῶν πάντων* N R T V 18 *συμφύτοις*] *ἐμφύτοις* L *ἠμφεισμένων* R[2mg] 19 *τὴν*[2] *om.* Æ L

image, and by the plural signification revealed the Holy Trinity, would not, if the archetypes were unlike one another, have mentioned the image in the singular: for it would not be possible for there to be displayed one likeness of things which do not concur with each other.[24] Rather, if the natures were different he would assuredly have presented different images of them also, making the appropriate one for each; but if the image is one, while the archetype of the image is not one, who is so mindless as not to know that things resembling one thing surely resemble each other also? Therefore he says (the account perhaps cutting short this wickedness at the very formation of human life), *Let us make the human being in accordance with our image and likeness.*

Why the human being is by nature destitute weapons and covering.[25]

[7.1] But what does the uprightness of his figure mean? And why is it that those means supporting life are not connatural with the body? Instead, the human being is brought into life bare of natural covering, an unarmed and poor being, deficient in all things useful, according to appearances worthy of being pitied rather than being admired, not armed with prominent horns, nor sharp claws, nor hoofs, nor teeth, nor possessing by nature any deadly venom in a sting—things such as most animals have in themselves for defence against those who do them harm—nor is his body protected with a covering of hair; and yet perhaps it was necessary that the one positioned for rule over the others should be defended by nature with arms of his own, so that he might not need assistance from others for his own safety.[26] But, as it is, the lion, the boar, the tiger, the leopard, and all the like have by nature the means sufficient for their safety: the bull has his horn, the hare his speed, the deer his leap and unerring sight, and another animal has size, others a proboscis, the birds their wings, and the bee its sting, and in absolutely everything there is something implanted by nature for safety. Alone of all, the human being is slower than those swift of foot, smaller than those of great bulk, more defenceless than those that are protected by natural arms; and how, one will say, has such a being obtained the sovereignty over all things?

[24] Cf. Basil, *Hom. de creat. hom.* 1.4 (Hörner, 6.15–8.10); Basil, *Hex.* 9.6; Philo, *Opif.* 72–5.

[25] *Bodl. 238*: 'Why the human was not created with horns and other defences like the other [animals]'.

[26] Cf. Philo, *Opif.* 83; Galen, *De usu part.* 1.4 (Helmreich, 1, 5–6; ET 1, 71); Origen, *Cels.* 4.76; Nemesius, *De nat. hom.* 1.50 (Morani, 8.15–23).

[7.2] Ἀλλ' οὐδὲν οἶμαι χαλεπὸν δεῖξαι, ὅτι τὸ δοκοῦν ἐπιδεὲς τῆς φύσεως ἡμῶν, ἀφορμὴ πρὸς τὸ κρατεῖν τῶν ὑποχειρίων ἐστίν· εἰ γὰρ οὕτω δυνάμεως εἶχεν ὁ ἄνθρωπος ὡς τῇ μὲν ὠκύτητι παρατρέχειν τὸν ἵππον, ἄτριπτον δὲ ὑπὸ στερρότητος ἔχειν τὸν πόδα, ὁπλαῖς τισιν ἢ χηλαῖς ἐρειδόμενον, κέρατα δὲ καὶ κέντρα καὶ ὄνυχας ἐν ἑαυτῷ φέρειν· πρῶτον μὲν θηριώδης τις ἂν ἦν καὶ δυσάντητος, τοιούτων αὐτοῦ τῷ σώματι συμπεφυκότων· ἔπειτα δὲ παρεῖδεν ἂν τὴν τῶν ἄλλων ἀρχὴν, οὐδὲν τῆς συνεργίας τῶν ὑποχειρίων δεόμενος· [C] νυνὶ δὲ τούτου χάριν ἐφ' ἕκαστον τῶν ὑπεζευγμένων ἡμῖν αἱ τοῦ βίου χρεῖαι κατεμερίσθησαν, ὡς ἀναγκαίαν ποιεῖν τὴν κατ' ἐκείνων ἀρχήν.

[7.3] Τὸ μὲν γὰρ βραδὺ τοῦ σώματος ἡμῶν καὶ δυσκίνητον, τὸν ἵππον τῇ χρείᾳ προσήγαγέ τε καὶ ἐδαμάσατο· ἡ δὲ τῆς σαρκὸς γυμνότης ἀναγκαίαν τὴν τῶν προβάτων ἐπιστασίαν ἐποίησεν, ἐκ τῆς ἐτησίου τῶν ἐρίων φορᾶς τῆς ἡμετέρας φύσεως ἀναπληροῦσαν τὸ λεῖπον· τὸ δὲ τὰς ἀφορμὰς ἡμῖν τὰς πρὸς τὸν βίον καὶ ἐξ ἑτέρων εἰσάγεσθαι, τὰ ἀχθοφόρα τῶν ζώων ταῖς τοιαύταις ὑπηρεσίαις ὑπέζευξεν· ἀλλὰ μὴν τὸ μὴ δύνασθαι καθ' ὁμοιότητα τῶν βοσκημάτων ποηφαγεῖν, ὑποχείριον τῷ βίῳ τὸν βοῦν ἀπειργάσατο, τοῖς ἰδίοις πόνοις τὴν ζωὴν ἡμῖν ἐξευμαρίζοντα· ἐπεὶ δὲ καὶ ὀδόντων καὶ δήγματος ἦν ἡμῖν χρεία πρὸς τὸ καταγωνίζεσθαί τινα τῶν [D] ἄλλων ζώων διὰ τῆς τῶν ὀδόντων λαβῆς, πάρεσχεν ὁ κύων μετὰ τοῦ τάχους τὴν ἰδίαν γένυν τῇ ἡμετέρᾳ χρείᾳ, οἷόν τις ἔμψυχος μάχαιρα τῷ ἀνθρώπῳ γινόμενος· κεράτων δὲ προβολῆς καὶ ὀνύχων ἀκμῆς ἰσχυρότερός τε καὶ τομώτερος ἐπινενόηται τοῖς ἀνθρώποις ὁ σίδηρος, οὐκ ἀεὶ συμπεφυκὼς ἡμῖν, ὥσπερ τοῖς θηρίοις ἐκεῖνα, ἀλλ' ἐπὶ καιροῦ συμμαχήσας, τὸ λοιπὸν ἐφ' ἑαυτοῦ μένει· καὶ ἀντὶ τῆς κροκοδείλου φολίδος, ἔστι μὲν καὶ αὐτὸν ἐκεῖνον ὅπλον ποιήσασθαι, κατὰ καιρὸν τὴν δορὰν περιθέμενον· εἰ δὲ μὴ, σχηματίζεται καὶ πρὸς τοῦτο παρὰ τῆς τέχνης ὁ σίδηρος, ὃς ἐπὶ καιροῦ πρὸς τὸν πόλεμον ὑπηρετήσας, πάλιν ἐλεύθερον τοῦ ἄχθος ἐπ' εἰρήνης τὸν ὁπλίτην κατέλιπεν· ὑπηρετεῖ δὲ τῷ βίῳ καὶ τὸ πτερὸν τῶν ὀρνέων, ὡς μηδὲ τοῦ πτηνοῦ τάχους δι' ἐπινοίας [144] ἡμᾶς ἀπολείπεσθαι· τὰ μὲν γὰρ ἐξ αὐτῶν τιθασσὰ γίνεται, καὶ συνεργεῖ τοῖς θηρεύουσι· τὰ δὲ δι' ἐκείνων ταῖς χρείαις ἡμῶν δι' ἐπινοίας ὑπάγεται· ἀλλὰ καὶ πτερόεντας ἡμῖν τοὺς ὀϊστοὺς ἡ τέχνη δι' ἐπινοίας ποιησαμένη, τὸ πτηνὸν τάχος ταῖς ἡμετέραις χρείαις διὰ τοῦ τόξου χαρίζεται· τὸ δὲ εὐπαθεῖς καὶ εὐτρίπτους ἡμῖν πρὸς τὴν πορείαν εἶναι τὰς βάσεις, ἀναγκαίαν ποιεῖ τὴν ἐκ τῶν ὑποχειρίων συνεργίαν· ἐκεῖθεν γάρ ἐστι τοῖς ποσὶ περιαρμόσαι τὰ πέδιλα.

20 *ἀλλ' οὐδὲν om.* K O *τῆς φύσεως ἡμῶν ἐπιδεὲς* R 22 *ὀξύτητι* A B K N O Q *ἄτρεπτον* Æ P[2] T 26 *τῶν*] *κατὰ τῶν* A B I K N O Q T V *συνεργείας* X 27 *ὑποζευγμένων* N O Q R V 29 *γὰρ om. Ald Mign* *βραδὺ*] *βραχὺ* M V *ἡμῶν καὶ om. Ald Mign* *τὸν om.* N 30 *ἐδαμάσατο*] *ὠνομάσατο* K 31 *ἐρίφων* W 32 *ἀναπληροῦσα* B G N O P Q R S V W X *τὰς πρὸς*] *πρὸς τὰς* V (*τὰς ante πρὸς supr. l. 2[a] man.*) 33 *ταῖς om.* N *ὑπέζευξεν*] *συνέζευξε* B 34 *ἀλλὰ μὴν*] *σὺν τούτοις δὲ* B 35 *ζωὴν*] *γῆν* N *ἡμῖν*] *ἡμῶν* R : *om.* K M O W *ἐξευμαρίζοντα*] copulat *Eri* 36 *ἦν om.* E G I L M P R S X *ἡμῖν om.* W *Mign* 37 *τῶν ἄλλων ζώων τινα* N *λαβῆς*] *βλάβης* V *Mign* 38 *γινόμενος*] *ita* Æ G I L M N P Q R S V W X *Forb* : *γενόμενος Ald Mign* 39 *ἀμῆς* V *τε om.* N 39–40 *καὶ τομώτερος—οὐκ ἀεὶ*] *ἐπινενόηται τῶν ἀνθρωπῶν ὁ σίδηρος καὶ τομώτερος οὐκ εἰς* N 39 *τομώτερος*] robustius *Eri* *ἐπινενόηται*] distribuitur *Eri* 41 *τῆς*] *ita* A B E G I K L M N P Q S V W X *Forb* : *τῆς τοῦ Ald Mign* 42 *φολίδος*] *ita* A B E K L M N P[2] Q R S *Forb* : *φωλίδος* V W X *Ald Mign* 43 *εἰ δὲ μὴ*] vide nempe *Eri* *καὶ πρὸς τοῦτο σχηματίζεται* Æ I K N O Q R T 44 *ἐπὶ καιροῦ*] *ἐνὶ καιρῷ* M *ἄχθους* V W X *Ald Mign* *ἐπ'*] *ἐπὶ* O 45 *κατέλειπεν* O 46 *πτηναίου* Æ B K O Q : *πτήναι* A : *τῶν πτηνῶν* R *τιθασὰ* R S T 47 *τὰ*] *τὸ* T *τὰς χρείας* N *δι' ἐπινοίας ἡμῶν* G M P R V W X 48 *ὑπάγεται*] *ἐπάγεται* N : *ἄγεται* Q *καὶ*] *καὶ ἐκ τῶν χηνῶν αἱ στρωμναί· καὶ ἐκ τῶν γυπῶν* R 49 *πτηνῶν* M 50 *εὐτρέπτους* N T[ac] *πρὸς τὴν πορείαν ἡμῖν* N *πορείαν*] *πορείαν ἡμῶν* R

[7.2] But I think it would not be difficult to show that the apparent deficiency of our nature is an occasion for dominion over the subjects. For if the human being had such means as to be able to outrun the horse in swiftness, and to have a foot that, from its solidity, could not be worn out, supported by hoofs or claws of some kind, and to bear upon himself horns and stings and talons, he would, first, with such things growing on his body, be a wild-looking and formidable creature; then, moreover, he would have neglected his rule over the others, not needing the cooperation of his subjects; but as it is, for this reason the needs of life are divided among each of those subjugated to us, to make our rule over them necessary.

[7.3] It was the slowness and difficult movement of our body that brought the horse to supply the need and tamed him; it was the nakedness of flesh that made necessary the tending of sheep, which compensates for the deficiency of our nature by its annual produce of wool; it was importing from others the supplies of life that subjugated beasts of burden to such services; moreover, it was not being able to eat grass like cattle that caused the ox to be subjected to our life, making life easy for us by its proper labour; since we needed teeth and a bite to fight against some of the other animals by the grip of the teeth, the dog gave, along with his speed, his own jaw for our use, becoming like a living sword for the human being; stronger and more penetrating than prominent horns or sharp claws is the iron discovered by human beings, which doesn't constantly grow with us, as they do with the animals, but allies itself with us for a period and is left aside afterwards; and instead of the crocodile's scaly hide, that very hide can be made into armour, putting it upon the skin for a time; and if not that, iron is shaped by craft for this purpose also, which, having served its purpose for a period during a battle, leaves the armed soldier once again free from the burden during peace; the wing of the birds also serves our life, so that by inventiveness we are not left behind even by the speed of wings, for some of them become tame and cooperate with hunters, while others by contrivance are brought to our needs; moreover, craft, through inventiveness, makes our arrows feathered and by means of the bow supplies the speed of wings for our needs; that our feet are easily hurt and worn in travelling makes necessary the aid from the subjected animals, for from them are the shoes we fit on our feet.

Διατί ὄρθιον τοῦ ἀνθρώπου τὸ σχῆμα, καὶ ὅτι διὰ τὸν λόγον αἱ χεῖρες, ἐν ᾧ τις καὶ περὶ διαφορᾶς ψυχῶν φιλοσοφία.

[**8.1**] *Ὄρθιον δὲ τῷ ἀνθρώπῳ τὸ σχῆμα καὶ πρὸς τὸν* [B] *οὐρανὸν ἀνατείνεται καὶ ἄνω βλέπει· ἀρχικὰ καὶ ταῦτα καὶ τὴν βασιλικὴν ἀξίαν ἀποσημαίνονται· τὸ γὰρ μόνον ἐν τοῖς οὖσι τοιοῦτον εἶναι τὸν ἄνθρωπον, τοῖς δ' ἄλλοις ἅπασι πρὸς τὸ κάτω νενευκέναι τὰ σώματα, σαφῶς δείκνυσι τὴν τῆς ἀξίας διαφοράν, τῶν τε ὑποκυπτόντων τῇ δυναστείᾳ καὶ τῆς ὑπερανεστώσης αὐτῶν ἐξουσίας· τοῖς μὲν γὰρ ἄλλοις ἅπασι τὰ ἔμπροσθεν κῶλα τοῦ σώματος πόδες εἰσί, διότι τὸ κεκυφὸς ἐδεῖτο πάντως τοῦ ὑπερείδοντος· ἐπὶ δὲ τῆς τοῦ ἀνθρώπου κατασκευῆς χεῖρες τὰ κῶλα ἐγένοντο· τοῦ γὰρ ὀρθίου σχήματος αὐτάρκης ἦν πρὸς τὴν χρείαν μία βάσις, διπλοῖς ποσὶν ἐν ἀσφαλείᾳ τὴν στάσιν ἐρείδουσα.*

[**8.2**] *Ἄλλως δὲ καὶ τῇ τοῦ λόγου χρείᾳ συνεργός ἐστιν ἡ τῶν χειρῶν ὑπουργία· καί τις ἴδιον τῆς λογικῆς φύσεως τὴν τῶν χειρῶν ὑπηρεσίαν εἰπών,* [C] *οὐ τοῦ παντὸς ἁμαρτήσεται· οὐ μόνον πρὸς τὸ κοινὸν τοῦτο καὶ πρόχειρον ἀποτρέχων τῇ διανοίᾳ, ὅτι γράμμασι τὸν λόγον διὰ τῆς τῶν χειρῶν εὐφυΐας ἐνσημαινόμεθα· ἔστι μὲν γὰρ οὐδὲ τοῦτο λογικῆς χάριτος ἄμοιρον, τὸ φθέγγεσθαι διὰ γραμμάτων ἡμᾶς, καὶ τρόπον τινὰ διὰ χειρὸς διαλέγεσθαι, τοῖς τῶν στοιχείων χαρακτῆρσι τὰς φωνὰς διασώζοντας· ἀλλ' ἐγὼ πρὸς ἕτερον βλέπων, συνεργεῖν φημι τὰς χεῖρας τῇ ἐκφωνήσει τοῦ λόγου.*

[**8.3**] *Μᾶλλον δὲ πρὶν περὶ τούτου διεξετάσαι, τὸν παρεθέντα λόγον κατανοήσωμεν· μικροῦ γὰρ ἡμᾶς τὸ κατὰ τὴν τάξιν τῶν γεγονότων διέλαθεν—τίνος χάριν προηγεῖται μὲν ἡ βλάστη τῶν ἐκ τῆς γῆς φυομένων, ἐπιγίνεται δὲ τὰ ἄλογα τῶν ζώων, καὶ οὕτω μετὰ τὴν κατασκευὴν τούτων ὁ ἄνθρωπος·* [D] *τάχα γὰρ οὐ μόνον τὸ ἐκ τοῦ προχείρου νοούμενον διὰ τούτων μανθάνομεν, ὅτι τῶν ζώων ἕνεκεν ἡ πόα χρήσιμος ἐφάνη τῷ κτίσαντι, διὰ δὲ τὸν ἄνθρωπον τὰ βοτά· οὗ χάριν πρὸ μὲν τῶν βοσκημάτων ἡ ἐκείνων τροφή, πρὸ δὲ τοῦ ἀνθρώπου τὸ ὑπηρετεῖν μέλλον τῇ ἀνθρωπίνῃ ζωῇ.* [**8.4**] *Ἀλλ' ἐμοὶ δοκεῖ δόγμα τι τῶν κεκρυμμένων παραδηλοῦν διὰ τούτων ὁ Μωϋσῆς, καὶ τὴν περὶ ψυχῆς φιλοσοφίαν δι' ἀπορρήτων παραδιδόναι, ἣν ἐφαντάσθη μὲν καὶ ἡ ἔξωθεν παίδευσις, οὐ μὴν τηλαυγῶς*

1–2 *διατί—φιλοσοφία*] de dignitate humanae formae et quare post alios creaturas homo creatus sit 1 *διατί* I K L M N O P R V W : *ὅτι* Æ *ὄρθιον*] *ὄρθιον δὲ* B Q *σχῆμα*] *σχῆμα καὶ πρὸς τὸν οὐρανὸν ἀνατείνεται B* 1–2 *ἐν ᾧ—φιλοσοφία*] *καὶ περὶ διαφορᾶς ἐν ᾧ τις ψυχῶν φιλοσοφία* W 1 *τις om.* B D 3 *τοῦ ἀνθρώπου* B 3 *καί*[2]] *ἔνθε καὶ* V 4 *ἀξίαν*] *ἀρχὴν* B *ἀποσημαίνονται*] *ita* G K L O P Q S T X *Forb* : *ὑποσημαίνοντα* B E I R : *ἐπισημαίνοντα* Æ M N V W : *ἐπισημαίνονται Ald Forb* 5 *δ'*] *ita* Æ ß G K M P Q R S W X *Forb* : *δὲ* V *Ald Mign* *πᾶσι* A B E I K L N O Q T *τὸ*] *τὰ* N 6 *τῆς om.* V 8 *πᾶσι* A B I K N O Q R T V *κυφὸς* W 9 *ἐπερείδοντος* V *ἐπεὶ* V *τοῦ ἀνθρώπου*] *ἀνθρώπου* R V W : *ἀνθρωπίνης* G L M P S T X *χεῖρες τὰ*] *αἱ χεῖρες* N V 10 *τοῦ γὰρ ὀρθίου*] *τῳ γὰρ ὀρθίῳ τοῦ* A B I K N O Q R V *αὔταρκες* R 12 *συνεργόν* N 13 *ἴδιαν* T 14 *τοῦτο om.* K O 15 *εὐφυΐας*] administratione *Dion* : ingenia *Eri* *μὲν om.* N 16 *χάριτος om.* I 18 *διασώζοντας*] *ἐναρμόζοντας* A B I K N O Q R[ac] T *πρὸς*] *καὶ πρὸς* Æ R *ἕτερα* N R : *ἑτέρους* Æ 20 *περὶ τούτου*] *τοῦτο* N *τούτου*] *ita* A B E G L M O P Q R S T V W X *Forb* : *τούτων Ald Mign* *διεξετάσαι*] *κατ' ἐξετάσαι* N *παρεθέντα*] *παροθέντα* T[ac] : *παροφέντα* T[pc] : *παρατεθέντα* Æ *κατανοήσωμεν*] *διεξετάσωμεν* I 21 *διέλαθεν*] *παρέλαθε* R 22 *τῆς om.* R 24 *τούτων*] *ita* A B E G I K M N O P Q R T V W X *Forb* : *τοῦτο* L : *τούτου Ald Mign* *μανθάνομεν*] *καταμανθάνομεν* N *ζώων*] *μὲν ζώων* A B E I K N O Q R T V *ἕνεκα* N 26 *ἡ om. Ald Mign* 27 *ἀλλά μοὶ* A B I K N O Q R *δόγμα δοκεῖ* N *τῶν κεκρυμμένων*] *κεκρυμμένον* N 28 *μωσῆς* V *περὶ om.* N *ψυχῆς*] *τῆς ψυχῆς* N R 29 *παραδιδόναι*] *παραδοῦναι* V : *ἀποδιδόναι* N : *παραδιδόναι ἡμῖν* R *ἔξωθεν*] *ἔξω* I N R

Why the form of the human being is upright, and that the hands are on account of reason; in which also is a certain philosophical treatment regarding the difference of souls.[27]

[**8.1**] The human form is upright, and extends aloft towards heaven, and looks upwards: these things are marks of sovereignty and indicate the royal dignity.[28] That the human being alone among beings is such as this, while all others incline their bodies downwards, clearly indicates the difference of dignity between those who stoop beneath his dominion and that authority which rises above them: for all of them, the foremost limbs of their bodies are feet, because that which stoops assuredly needs that which supports it. But in the formation of the human being these limbs are hands; for the upright form one base was sufficient for its needs, supporting its posture securely on two feet.

[**8.2**] The service of the hands cooperates in other ways with the needs of reason.[29] Indeed, if one were to say that the ministry of the hands is a particular property of the rational nature, he would not be entirely wrong, not only jumping in thought to the common and ordinary point that we indicate our reasoning, through the dexterity of the hands, in written letters. That we speak by writing and, in a certain way, converse by the hand, preserving the sounds by the characters of the alphabet, is not without a share in the rational gift; but I am referring to something else when I say that the hands cooperate with bidding of reason.

[**8.3**] Before discussing this point, however, let us consider the subject passed over, for the subject of the order of the things that came to be almost escaped us: for what reason does the growth of things sprouting up from the earth take precedence, and the irrational animals come next, and then, after the fashioning of these, the human being? Perhaps we may learn from these things not only the obvious thought, that the grass appeared to the Creator useful for the sake of the animals, while the beasts were on account of the human being, and that for this reason, before the cattle there was their food, and before the human being that which was to minister to human life. [**8.4**] But it seems to me that by these points Moses reveals a certain doctrine about hidden things, and secretly delivers the philosophy concerning the soul, which outside learning also imagined but did not

[27] *Bodl. 238*: 'Of the dignity of the human form, and why the human was created after the other creatures'.

[28] Cf. Plato, *Tim.* 90a, 91e–92a; Xenophon, *Mem.* 1.4.11; Aristotle, *De part. an.* 4.10 (686a.27); Basil, *Hom. de creat. hom.* 2.15 (Hörner, 66–7); Basil, *Hex.* 9.2.

[29] Cf. Aristotle, *De part. an.* 4.10 (687a7–18), referring also to Anaxagoras; Xenophon, *Mem.* 1.4.11; Galen, *De usu part.* 1.3 (Helmreich, 1, 3–5; ET 1, 69–71).

κατενόησε· διδάσκει γὰρ ἡμᾶς διὰ τούτων ὁ λόγος, ἐν τρισὶ διαφοραῖς τὴν ζωτικὴν καὶ ψυχικὴν δύναμιν θεωρεῖσθαι· ἡ μὲν γάρ τις ἐστὶν αὐξητική τε μόνον καὶ θρεπτική, τὸ κατάλληλον εἰς προσθήκην τῶν τρεφομένων προσάγουσα, ἣν φυτική τε λέγεται καὶ περὶ τὰ φυτὰ θεωρεῖται· ἔστι γὰρ καὶ ἐν τοῖς φυομένοις ζωτικήν τινα δύναμιν [145] *αἰσθήσεως ἄμοιρον κατανοῆσαι· ἕτερον δὲ παρὰ τοῦτο ζωῆς εἶδός ἐστιν, ὃ καὶ τοῦτο ἔχει καὶ τὸ κατ᾽ αἴσθησιν οἰκονομῆσαι προσείληφεν, ὅπερ ἐν τῇ φύσει τῶν ἀλόγων ἐστίν· οὐ γὰρ μόνον τρέφεται καὶ αὔξεται, ἀλλὰ καὶ τὴν αἰσθητικὴν ἐνέργειάν τε καὶ ἀντίληψιν ἔχει· ἡ δὲ τελεία ἐν σώματι ζωὴ ἐν τῇ λογικῇ, τῇ ἀνθρωπίνῃ λέγω, καθορᾶται φύσει, καὶ τρεφομένη καὶ αἰσθανομένη καὶ λόγου μετέχουσα καὶ νῷ διοικουμένη.*

[8.5] *Γένοιτο δ᾽ ἂν ἡμῖν τοιαύτη τις ἡ τοῦ λόγου διαίρεσις· τῶν ὄντων τὸ μέν τι νοητόν, τὸ δὲ σωματικὸν πάντως ἐστίν· ἀλλὰ τοῦ μὲν νοητοῦ παρείσθω νῦν ἡ πρὸς τὰ οἰκεῖα τομή· οὐ γὰρ τούτων ὁ λόγος·* [B] *τοῦ δὲ σωματικοῦ, τὸ μὲν ἄμοιρον καθόλου ζωῆς, τὸ δὲ μετέχει ζωτικῆς ἐνεργείας· πάλιν τοῦ ζωτικοῦ σώματος, τὸ μὲν αἰσθήσει συζῇ, τὸ δὲ ἀμοιρεῖ τῆς αἰσθήσεως· εἶτα τὸ αἰσθητικὸν τέμνεται πάλιν εἰς λογικόν τε καὶ ἄλογον· διὰ τοῦτο πρῶτον μετὰ τὴν ἄψυχον ὕλην οἷον ὑποβάθραν τινὰ τῆς τῶν ἐμψύχων ἰδέας τὴν φυτικὴν ταύτην ζωὴν συστῆναι λέγει ὁ νομοθέτης, ἐν τῇ τῶν φυτῶν βλάστῃ προϋποστᾶσαν· εἶθ᾽ οὕτως ἐπάγει τῶν κατ᾽ αἴσθησιν διοικουμένων τὴν γένεσιν· καὶ ἐπειδὴ κατὰ τὴν αὐτὴν ἀκολουθίαν, τῶν διὰ σαρκὸς τὴν ζωὴν εἰληχότων, τὰ μὲν αἰσθητικὰ καὶ δίχα τῆς νοερᾶς φύσεως ἐφ᾽ ἑαυτῶν εἶναι δύναται, τὸ δὲ λογικὸν οὐκ ἂν ἑτέρως γένοιτο ἐν σώματι, εἰ μὴ τῷ αἰσθητῷ συγκραθείη· διὰ τοῦτο τελευταῖος μετὰ τὰ βλαστήματα καὶ τὰ βοτὰ κατεσκευάσθη ὁ ἄνθρωπος, ὁδῷ τινι πρὸς τὸ τέλειον ἀκολούθως* [C] *προϊούσης τῆς φύσεως.*

30 *ἡμᾶς*] *οἶμαι* A B I K N O Q R T : ut arbitror *Dion Eri* : *οἶμαι ἡμᾶς* V *ζωτικὴν*] *ζωτικήν τε* B I K N O Q R V 31 *καὶ ψυχικὴν*] *καὶ ἔμψυχον* R : *om.* A L *ἡ μὲν γάρ τις ἐστὶν*] herbarum siquidem natura *Dion* *αὐξητική τις ἐστὶν* I 31–2 *αὐξητική τε μόνον καὶ θρεπτικὴ*] quae solummodo incrementum dat et nutrit et uocatur auctiua et nutritoria *Eri* 31 *τε om.* I N *μόνον om.* I 32 *προσθήκας* B *προσάγουσα*] *εἰσάγουσα* W *φυτικὴ*] *ita* A ß E I K L O R S *Wils* : germinabilis *Dion* : germinalis *Eri* : *φυσικὴ* B T V W X *Ald Mign Forb* 33 *τε*] *ita* Æ ß G I K L N O P Q R S T V X *Forb* : *om. Ald Mign* 34 *κατανοῆσαι αἰσθήσεως ἄμοιρον* R *εἶδός ζωῆς* R 35 *οἰκονομεῖσθαι* A B E I K N O Q R S² V 36 *μόνον γὰρ* B *τρέφεται*] *τρέφεταί τε* A B I K Q *καὶ αὔξεται om.* M *αὐξάνεται* W 37 *τε om.* N 38 *καθορᾶται λέγω* R *καὶ τρεφομένη*] *τρεφομένη τε Ald Mign* 40 *δ᾽ ἂν*] *δὲ* R *μέν τι*] *μέντοι* B K : *τι expunct.* R² 41 *μὲν om.* A B I K N O Q R^ac T *νῦν*] *μὲν* L 42 *τούτων*] *περὶ τούτων* A B I K L N O Q R S T V 44 *αἰσθήσει*] *ἐν αἰσθήσει* N *συζῇ*] coniungitur *Eri* *εἶτα*] *εἴ* X 45 *τε om.* M *ἄψυχον om.* M *οἷον*] *οἱονεὶ* A B E I K N O 46 *φυτικὴν*] *ita* Æ I K O Q R *Wils* : germinalem *Dion* : *ψυχικὴν* N : *φυσικὴν* V W X *Ald Mign Forb* : naturalem *Eri* 47 *βλαστήσει* A B E K N O Q 48 *αὐτὴν om.* Æ K 49 *εἰληχότων*] *εἰληφότων* A B I K O Q R V : acceperunt *Eri* : *ἀνειληφότων* N : sortita sunt *Dion* *ἐπ᾽ αὐτῶν* M : *ἀφ᾽ ἑαυτῶν* T 49–50 *δύναται εἶναι* R 50 *δύνανται* N *ἑτέρως γένοιτο ἐν σώματι*] *ἐν ἑτέρῳ σώματι γένοιτο* A B : *ἑτέρῳ σώματι γένοιτο* I K N O Q : *ἐν ἑτερῳ γένοιτο σώματι* R T : *ἑτέρως γένοιτο σώματι* E *αἰσθητῷ*] *αἰσθητικῷ* A B R^ac (*αἰσθητῷ* R^pc) : *αἰσθητῷ ᾧ* T² 51 *τὰ*¹ *om.* Q R I *τὰ*² *om.* N 52 *προϊούσης ἀκολούθως* Æ I K N O Q R T

clearly comprehend. Through these things, the account teaches us that the vital and animating power is contemplated in three divisions.[30] One is simply growth and nutrition, supplying what is suitable for the increase of those being nourished, which is called 'vegetative' and is contemplated in plants, for one can perceive in growing plants a certain power of life without a share in sense-perception.[31] There is another form of life besides this, which has both that one and adds regulation by sense-perception, as is in the nature of irrational animals, for not only are they nourished and grow, but they also have the activity of sense-perception and apprehension. The perfect embodied life is seen in the rational, I mean the human, nature, which both is nourished and endowed with sense-perception and partakes of reason and is ordered by intellect.

[8.5] We might make a division of our subject in some such way: of existing things, there is the intellectual and there is certainly the bodily.[32] But let the appropriate division of the intellectual be left aside for now, for our argument is not concerned with these. Of the bodily, some are entirely without a share in life and some share in vital energy; again, of living bodies, some live with sense-perception and some without sense-perception; then, that which has sense-perception is again divided into rational and irrational. For this reason the lawgiver says that after inanimate matter, as a sort of foundation for the form of animated things, first this vegetative life was constituted, existing formerly in the growth of plants; then he proceeds to introduce the genesis of those beings ordered by sense-perception; and since, following the same sequence, of those who have received life through the flesh, those with sense-perception are able of themselves to exist, even without the intellectual nature, while the rational aspect could not otherwise be embodied except as blended with the sense-perceptive. For this reason, the human being was fashioned last, after the plants and animals, nature advancing in a certain way sequentially to perfection.

[30] Cf. Gregory of Nyssa, *An. et res.* 3.37–43 (Spira, 40.11–42.4). The threefold distinction goes back to Aristotle, *De an.* 2.3 (413a23–415a13), and is extensively treated by Alexander of Aphrodisias in his *De Anima* (cf. esp. Bruns, 8.25–11.5; 29.1–30.17; 80.16–24) and *Mantissa* §1 (Bruns 105.3–106.5); cf. Posidonius, Frag. 33 (Kidd, 1, 52; = Galen, *Hipp. et Plat.* 5.6.37–8, De Lacy, 1, 334); Philo, *Opif.* 65–6; Origen, *Princ.* 2.8.1; see also Porphyry, *Isag.* 3 (Busse, 10.3–18; ET 10).

[31] The mss vary between calling this soul φυτικός ('vegetative') or φυσική ('natural'). Aristotle refers to it as φυτικός ('vegetative') in *Eth. nic.* 1.13.18 (1102b29) and as θρεπτικός ('nutritive') in *De an.* 2.3 (414b2); Alexander of Aphrodisias uses φυτικός (*De an.*, Bruns, 35.24, 38.13, 75.31, 96.9).

[32] Cf. Gregory of Nyssa, *Eccl.* 6 (Alexander, 373.21–374.1; ET 100).

Διὰ πάσης γὰρ ἰδέας τῶν ψυχῶν κατακιρνᾶται τὸ λογικὸν τοῦτο ζῶον ὁ ἄνθρωπος· τρέφεται μὲν γὰρ κατὰ τὸ φυτικὸν τῆς ψυχῆς εἶδος· τῇ δὲ αὐξητικῇ δυνάμει ἡ αἰσθητικὴ προσεφύη, μέσως ἔχουσα κατὰ τὴν ἰδίαν φύσιν τῆς τε νοερᾶς καὶ τῆς ὑλωδεστέρας οὐσίας· τοσούτῳ παχυμερεστέρα ταύτης ὅσῳ καθαρωτέρα ἐκείνης· εἶτά τις γίνεται πρὸς τὸ λεπτὸν καὶ φωτοειδὲς τῆς αἰσθητικῆς φύσεως ἡ τῆς νοερᾶς οὐσίας οἰκείωσίς τε καὶ ἀνάκρασις· ὡς ἐν τρισὶ τούτοις τὸν ἄνθρωπον τὴν σύστασιν ἔχειν· καθὼς καὶ παρὰ τοῦ ἀποστόλου τὸ τοιοῦτον ἐμάθομεν, ἐν οἷς πρὸς τοὺς Ἐφεσίους ἔφη, ἐπευχόμενος αὐτοῖς τὴν **ὁλοτελῆ** χάριν **τοῦ σώματος καὶ τῆς ψυχῆς καὶ τοῦ πνεύματος ἐν τῇ παρουσίᾳ τοῦ Κυρίου** φυλαχθῆναι· ἀντὶ τοῦ θρεπτικοῦ [D] μέρους **τὸ σῶμα** λέγων, τὸ δὲ αἰσθητικὸν **τῇ ψυχῇ** διασημαίνων, τὸ νοερὸν δὲ **τῷ πνεύματι**· ὡσαύτως καὶ τὸν γραμματέα διὰ τοῦ εὐαγγελίου παιδεύει ὁ Κύριος, πάσης ἐντολῆς προτιθέναι τὴν εἰς Θεὸν ἀγάπην τὴν ἐξ ὅλης **καρδίας καὶ ψυχῆς καὶ διανοίας** ἐνεργουμένην· καὶ γὰρ ἐνταῦθα τὴν αὐτὴν δοκεῖ μοι διαφορὰν ἑρμηνεύειν ὁ λόγος, τὴν μὲν σωματικωτέραν κατάστασιν **καρδίαν** εἰπών, **ψυχὴν** δὲ τὴν μέσην, **διάνοιαν** δὲ τὴν ὑψηλοτέραν φύσιν, τὴν [148] νοεράν τε καὶ διανοητικὴν δύναμιν.

[8.6] Ὅθεν καὶ τρεῖς διαφορὰς προαιρέσεων ὁ ἀπόστολος οἶδε, τὴν μὲν **σαρκικὴν** κατονομάζων, ἣ περὶ γαστέρα καὶ τὰς περὶ ταύτην ἡδυπαθείας ἠσχόληται· τὴν δὲ **ψυχικήν**, ἣ μέσως πρὸς ἀρετὴν καὶ κακίαν ἔχει, τῆς μὲν ὑπερανεστῶσα, τῆς δὲ καθαρῶς οὐ μετέχουσα· τὴν δὲ **πνευματικήν**, ἣ τὸ τέλειον ἐνθεωρεῖ τῆς κατὰ Θεὸν πολιτείας· διό φησι πρὸς Κορινθίους, τὸ ἀπολαυστικὸν αὐτῶν καὶ ἐμπαθὲς ὀνειδίζων, ὅτι **σάρκινοί** ἐστε καὶ τῶν τελειοτέρων δογμάτων ἀχώρητοι· ἑτέρωθι δὲ σύγκρισίν τινα τοῦ μέσου πρὸς τὸ τέλειον ποιούμενος, λέγει· **ψυχικὸς δὲ ἄνθρωπος οὐ δέχεται τὰ τοῦ πνεύματος· μωρία γὰρ αὐτῷ ἐστιν· ὁ δὲ πνευματικὸς ἀνακρίνει μὲν πάντα, αὐτὸς δὲ ὑπ᾽ οὐδενὸς ἀνακρίνεται**· ὡς οὖν ἀναβέβηκεν **ὁ ψυχικὸς τὸν** [B] **σαρκικόν**, κατὰ τὴν αὐτὴν ἀναλογίαν καὶ **ὁ πνευματικὸς** τούτου ὑπερανέστηκεν. [8.7] Εἰ οὖν

54 ψυχῶν] ἐμψύχων N : ψυχικῶν R   κατακίρναται I K L O   ζῶον] *ita* A B E G N O P Q R S V W X *Forb Mign* : ζῶν *Ald*   ὁ ἄνθρωπος] *om. Eri*   55 φυτικὸν] *ita* A B E I K N O Q R T *Wils* : germinalem *Dion Eri* : φυσικὸν V W X *Ald Forb Mign*   57 τοσοῦτον N T   ὅσον T   58–9 εἶτά τις—ἀνάκρασις] deinde quaedam fit societas atque concretio sensualis naturae ad subtile ac lucidum intellectualis essentia *Eri*   58 αἰσθητικῆς] αἰσθητῆς A B I K O Q T   αἰσθητικῆς ... νοερᾶς] νοερᾶς ... αἰσθητῆς N   59 οὐσίας *om.* N   τρισὶ] τοῖς τρισὶ R   60 τὸ] *ita* Æ ß N O P R S V W X *Forb Mign* : τὸν *Ald*   61 ἐφεσίους] θεσσαλονικεῖς K O *Dion*   ἔφη] φησὶν Æ I K N O Q R T : *om.* B   ἐπευχόμενος] προσευχόμενος V W *Ald Mign*   ὁλοτελῆ] τελεοτελῆ I   63 τῇ ψυχῇ διασημαίνων] διὰ τῆς ψυχῆς σημαίνων R   δὲ τῷ] *ita* Æ ß G N O P R S V W X *Forb* : τῷ L : τῷ δὲ *Ald Mign*   65 πάσης ἐντολῆς] πάντων B   ψυχῆς καὶ καρδίας V   66 τὴν αὐτὴν δοκεῖ μοι διαφορὰν] δοκεῖ τὴν αὐτὴν μοι διαφορὰν R : δοκεῖ μοι τὴν διαφορὰν τὴν αὐτὴν N   68 διανοητικὴν] ποιητικὴν V W *Ald Mign*   69 καὶ *om.* W   προαιρέσεως *Ald Mign*   σαρκίνην M V W   70 περὶ[1]] τὰς περὶ L   περὶ ταύτην] μετ᾽ αὐτὴν N : μετὰ ταύτην T   72 ἣ] ἣν X   ἐνθεωρεῖ] ἣ ἐνθεωρεῖται L N R   73 τὸ ἀπολαυστικὸν αὐτῶν καὶ ἐμπαθὲς] eis studium uoluptariae uitae atque passibilis *Dion* : passibilem eorum usum *Eri*   74 ὅτι] λέγει ὅτι N   τελεωτέρων R : τελείων N   δογμάτων] διδαγμάτων A B E I K N O Q R T   75 πρὸς τὸ τέλειον τοῦ μέσου B I K N O Q R   τοῦ μέσου *om.* A   ἄνθρωπος] ὁ ἄνθρωπος L   76 πάντα] τὰ πάντα A B I N O Q R T   77 οὖν] γοῦν R : δὲ N : γὰρ A B I K O Q   ἀναβέβηκεν] ὑπεραναβέβηκεν I R   σάρκινον M W   78 τοῦτον N

This rational animal, the human being, is blended of every form of soul: he is nourished by the vegetative kind of soul; and to the power of growth was added that of sense-perception, which stands midway according to its own nature between the intellectual and the more material essence, being as much denser than the one as it is more refined than the other; then takes place a certain appropriation and commixture of the intellectual essence with the subtle and enlightened element of the sense-perceptive nature, so that the human being is composed of these three, just as we are taught such a thing by the apostle in what he says to the Ephesians,[33] praying for them that the *complete* grace of *the body and the soul and the spirit* may be preserved at the coming of the Lord, using the word *body* for the nutritive part, denoting the sense-perceptive by the word *soul*, and the intellectual by *spirit*. Likewise the Lord also instructs the scribe in the Gospel that he should set before every commandment the love of God exercised *with all the heart and soul and mind*,[34] for here also it seems to me that the report indicates the same difference, calling the more corporeal state *heart*, the intermediate *soul*, and the higher nature, the intellectual and reasoning faculty, *mind*.

[**8.6**] Hence also the apostle recognizes three different dispositions, naming one *carnal*, which is busied with the belly and the pleasures connected with it, another *animated*, which holds a middle position with regard to virtue and vice, rising above the one but without pure participation in the other, and another *spiritual*, which perceives the perfection of citizenship according to God: he thus says to the Corinthians, reproaching their devotion to pleasure and passion, *You are carnal*[35] and incapable of receiving the more perfect teaching; while elsewhere, making a comparison of the middle kind with the perfect, he says, *but the animated human does not receive the things of the Spirit, for they are foolishness to him; however, he that is spiritual judges all things, but himself is judged of no one.*[36] As, then, *the animated* is higher than *the carnal*, by the same proportion also *the spiritual* rises above *the animated*. [**8.7**] If, therefore,

[33] 1 Thess. 5:23. The Greek manuscripts and Eriugena mention 'Ephesians'; Dionysius Exiguus alone corrects the error and gives full verse.

[34] Mark 12:30. [35] Cf. 1 Cor. 3:3. [36] Cf. 1 Cor. 2:14–15.

τελευταῖον μετὰ πᾶν ἔμψυχον ἡ γραφὴ γεγενῆσθαι λέγει τὸν ἄνθρωπον, οὐδὲν ἕτερον ἢ φιλοσοφεῖ τὰ περὶ ψυχῆς ἡμῖν ὁ νομοθέτης, ἐπ᾽ ἀναγκαίᾳ τινὶ τῇ τῆς τάξεως ἀκολουθίᾳ τὸ τέλειον ἐν τελευταίοις βλέπων· ἐν μὲν γὰρ τῷ λογικῷ καὶ τὰ λοιπὰ περιείληπται, ἐν δὲ τῷ αἰσθητικῷ καὶ τὸ φυτικὸν εἶδος πάντως ἐστίν, ἐκεῖνο δὲ περὶ τὸ ὑλικὸν θεωρεῖται μόνον· οὐκοῦν εἰκότως καθάπερ διὰ βαθμῶν ἡ φύσις, τῶν τῆς ζωῆς λέγω ἰδιωμάτων, ἀπὸ τῶν μικροτέρων [C] ἐπὶ τὸ τέλειον ποιεῖται τὴν ἄνοδον.

[8.8] Ἐπειδὴ τοίνυν λογικόν τι ζῶόν ἐστιν ὁ ἄνθρωπος, κατάλληλον ἔδει τῇ χρείᾳ τοῦ λόγου κατασκευασθῆναι τὸ τοῦ σώματος ὄργανον· καθάπερ τοὺς μουσικοὺς ἔστιν ἰδεῖν πρὸς τὸ τῶν ὀργάνων εἶδος τὴν μουσικὴν ἐκπονοῦντας, καὶ οὔτε διὰ βαρβίτων αὐλοῦντας οὔτε ἐν αὐλοῖς κιθαρίζοντας· κατὰ τὸν αὐτὸν τρόπον ἔδει τῷ λόγῳ κατάλληλον εἶναι τὴν τῶν ὀργάνων κατασκευήν, ὡς ἂν προσφυῶς ἐνηχοίη πρὸς τὴν τῶν ῥημάτων χρείαν ὑπὸ τῶν φωνητικῶν μορίων τυπούμενος· διὰ τοῦτο συνηρτήθησαν αἱ χεῖρες τῷ σώματι· εἰ γὰρ καὶ μυρίας ἐστὶν ἀπαριθμήσασθαι τὰς κατὰ τὸν βίον χρείας πρὸς ἃς τὰ εὐμήχανα ταῦτα καὶ πολυαρκῆ τῶν χειρῶν ὄργανα χρησίμως ἔχει, πρὸς πᾶσαν τέχνην καὶ [D] πᾶσαν ἐνέργειαν, τὸν κατὰ πόλεμόν τε καὶ εἰρήνην, εὐαφῶς μετιόντα· ἀλλά γε πρὸ τῶν ἄλλων διαφερόντως τοῦ λόγου χάριν προσέθηκεν αὐτὰς ἡ φύσις τῷ σώματι· εἰ γὰρ ἄμοιρος τῶν χειρῶν ὁ ἄνθρωπος ἦν, πάντως ἂν αὐτῷ καθ᾽ ὁμοιότητα τῶν τετραπόδων καταλλήλως τῇ τῆς τροφῆς χρείᾳ διεσκεύαστο τοῦ προσώπου τὰ μόρια· ὥστε προμήκη τε τὴν μορφὴν εἶναι καὶ ἐπὶ μυκτῆρας ἀπολεπτύνεσθαι, καὶ προβεβλῆσθαι τὰ χείλη τοῦ στόματος τυλώδη καὶ σταθερὰ καὶ παχέα, πρὸς τὴν ἀναίρεσιν τῆς πόας ἐπιτηδείως ἔχοντα· ἐγκεῖσθαι δὲ τοῖς ὀδοῦσι τὴν γλῶτταν, ἄλλην τινὰ τοιαύτην, πολύσαρκον καὶ ἀντιτυπῆ καὶ τραχεῖαν καὶ συγκατεργαζομένην τοῖς ὀδοῦσι τὸ ὑπ᾽ ὀδόντα γινόμενον· ἢ ὑγράν τε καὶ [149] διακεχυμένην κατὰ τὰ πλάγια, οἷα ἡ τῶν κυνῶν τε καὶ τῶν λοιπῶν τῶν ὠμοβόρων ἐστί, τῷ καρχάρῳ τῶν ὀδόντων μεταξὺ τῶν διαστημάτων ἐνδιαρρέουσα·

79 πᾶν] τὴν N   80 φιλοσοφεῖν R T   νομοθέτης] νομοθέτης παραδέδωκεν R   ἐν ἀναγκαίᾳ Æ I K O R : ἐναναγκαίᾳ B : ἀναγκαίᾳ N T   τῇ *om.* Æ S   τῆς *om. Ald Mign*   81 γὰρ *om.* N   82 φυτικὸν] *ita* A B E G I K L M O P R S V W X *Wils* : germinalem *Dion* : φυσικὸν *Ald Mign Forb* : naturalis *Eri*   περὶ] πάντως περὶ N   83 οὐκοῦν] non ergo *Eri*   διὰ] ὡς διὰ N   85 *ante* ἐπειδὴ *inc. cap. 9 Dion Eri* : *Λ habet inscr.* quod forma humani corporis congruat rationalitate mentis   ἐστιν *om.* B   86 λόγου] σώματος I   τοὺς] γὰρ τοὺς Æ I L R S   88 βαρβίτων] βαλβίδων G M O P T V W X   κατὰ *om.* N R   88–9 κατάλληλον εἶναι τῷ λόγῳ I   τῷ λόγῳ *om.* N   90 πρὸς—τυπούμενος] ad eam sonaret in ipsis particularis uerborum uocibus coaptatis formata *Eri*   διὰ] διὰ τοι R   91 συνήρτησαν N   92 πολυαρκῆ] principalia *Eri*   93 πρὸς *om.* N R^{ac} T V W   τὸν] τῶν Æ ß G N O P Q S V   τε *om.* N   94 εὐφυῶς N   γε] *ita* Æ ß G I K L N O P Q R S T W X *Forb* : *om.* V W *Ald Mign*   πρὸ] *ita* Æ ß G I K M N O P Q R^{ac} T V W *Forb* : καὶ πρὸ *Ald Mign*   96 καταλλήλως] καταλλήλως αὐτῷ E   97 διεσκέδαστο A : διεσκεύαστω V : κατεσκευάσατο T   τε *om.* N R   98 τυλλώδη *Ald*   99 σταθηρὰ G R   παχεῖα V X   δὲ] τε N   100 γλῶτταν] *ita* Æ ß C D E F G I K L M O P R S V W *Forb Mign* : γλῶσσαν X *Ald*   ἄλλην τινὰ τοιαύτην πολύσαρκον] ἀλλ᾽ οὐ τοιαύτην πολύσαρκον δέ τινα A   τινὰ] *om.* Q R^{ac} : *post* πολύσαρκον *pon.* B C I K N O   πολύσαρκον] πολύσαρκον τινὰ T   ἀντίτυπον E M R : ἀντιτυπεῖαν L   100–101 τραχεῖαν καὶ ἀντιτυπῆ R   101 ὑπ᾽] ὑπὸ τὸν W *Ald Mign*   ὀδόντας R   τε *om.* B   102 οἷα Æ D E F S^{pc} *Mign* : οἵους A   τῶν λοιπῶν *om.* M W   τῶν^{3} *om.* D R S V   103 ὠμοβόρων] αἱμοβόρων D R S T V W   ἐστὶ] ἐστὶ ἐν τῷ ἐσθίειν N

Scripture says that the human being came into being last, after every animated being, the lawgiver is doing nothing other than teaching us matters regarding the soul, seeing that by a certain necessary sequence of order the perfect comes last: for the others are included in the rational also, while in the sense-perceptive there is also surely the vegetative form, and that in turn is only contemplated in material beings. Thus, reasonably, nature makes the ascent, as it were by steps, I mean the properties of life, from the lower to the perfect.[37]

[8.8][38] Since, then, the human being is a kind of rational animal, the instrument of the body must be fashioned to be appropriate for the use of reason. Just as one may see musicians producing music according to the form of the instruments, and not piping with harps nor harping upon flutes, in the same way it is necessary that the formation of these instruments be appropriate for reason, so that when struck by the vocal organs it might resound fittingly for expressing words.[39] On this account the hands were attached to the body; for though there can be enumerated very many uses in daily life for which these skilfully contrived and helpful instruments, the hands—that easily follow every art and every activity, alike in war and peace—are serviceable, yet, before every other [cause], nature added them to our body pre-eminently for the sake of reason. For if the human being were without hands, the various parts of his face would certainly have been arranged like those of the quadrupeds, appropriate for the purpose of feeding, so that its form would have been lengthened and pointed towards the nostrils, and his lips would have projected from his mouth, lumpy and stiff and thick, adapted for pulling up grass, and the tongue would either have lain between the teeth, of a kind with the lips—fleshy and hard and rough, assisting his teeth in dealing with what comes under them—or it would have been moist and hanging out at the side like that of dogs and other carnivorous beasts, projecting through the gaps in his jagged row of teeth. If, then,

[37] Cf. Aristotle, *Hist. an.* 7(8).1 (588b4–50): 'Nature proceeds from the inanimate to the animals by such small steps....' (*οὕτω δ' ἐκ τῶν ἀψύχων εἰς τὰ ζῷα μεταβαίνει κατὰ μικρὸν ἡ φύσις*); Philo, *Opif.* 65–6.

[38] Both Dionysius Exiguus and Eriugena begin Chapter 9 here. *Bodl. 238* has the heading: 'That the form of the human body is congruent with the rationality of the mind'.

[39] Cf. Galen, *De usu part.* 1.3 (Helmreich, 1, 4.7–9; ET 1, 69–70).

εἰ οὖν μὴ παρῆσαν αἱ χεῖρες τῷ σώματι, πῶς ἂν ἔναρθρος τούτῳ ἐνετυπώθη φωνὴ, τῆς κατασκευῆς τῶν κατὰ τὸ στόμα μορίων οὐ συνδιασχηματιζομένης πρὸς τὴν χρείαν τοῦ φθόγγου; ὡς ἐπάναγκες εἶναι ἢ βληχᾶσθαι πάντως ἢ μηκάζειν ἢ ὑλακτεῖν ἢ χρεμετίζειν τὸν ἄνθρωπον, ἢ βουσὶν ἢ ὄνοις βοᾷν παραπλήσιον, ἤ τινα θηριώδη μυκηθμὸν ἀφιέναι· νυνὶ δὲ, τῆς χειρὸς ἐντεθείσης τῷ σώματι, εὔσχολόν ἐστι τὸ στόμα τῇ ὑπηρεσίᾳ τοῦ λόγου· οὐκοῦν ἴδιον τῆς λογικῆς φύσεως αἱ χεῖρες ἀναπεφήνασιν, οὕτω τοῦ πλάστου διὰ τούτων ἐπινοήσαντος τῷ λόγῳ τὴν εὐκολίαν.

Ὅτι ὀργανικὸν κατεσκευάσθη τοῦ ἀνθρωποῦ τὸ σχῆμα πρὸς τὴν τοῦ λόγου χρείαν.

[9.1] Ἐπειδὴ τοίνυν θεοειδῆ τινὰ χάριν τῷ πλάσματι ἡμῶν ὁ ποιήσας δεδώρηται, τῶν ἰδίων ἀγαθῶν ἐνθεὶς τῇ εἰκόνι τὰς ὁμοιότητας· διὰ τοῦτο τὰ μὲν λοιπὰ τῶν ἀγαθῶν ἔδωκεν ἐκ φιλοτιμίας τῇ ἀνθρωπίνῃ φύσει· νοῦ δὲ καὶ φρονήσεως οὐκ ἔστι κυρίως εἰπεῖν ὅτι δέδωκεν, ἀλλ' ὅτι μετέδωκε, τὸν ἴδιον αὐτοῦ τῆς φύσεως κόσμον ἐπιβαλὼν τῇ εἰκόνι. Ἐπεὶ οὖν νοερόν τι χρῆμα καὶ ἀσώματόν ἐστιν ὁ νοῦς, ἀκοινώνητον ἂν ἔσχε τὴν χάριν καὶ ἄμικτον, μὴ διά τινος ἐπινοίας φανερουμένης αὐτοῦ τῆς κινήσεως· τούτου χάριν τῆς ὀργανικῆς ταύτης προσεδεήθη κατασκευῆς, ἵνα πλήκτρου δίκην τῶν φωνητικῶν μορίων ἁπτόμενος, διὰ τῆς ποιᾶς [C] τῶν φθόγγων τυπώσεως ἑρμηνεύσῃ τὴν ἔνδοθεν κίνησιν. [9.2] Καὶ ὥσπερ τις μουσικῆς ἔμπειρος ὢν, ἰδίαν ἐκ πάθους μὴ ἔχοι φωνὴν, βουλόμενος δὲ φανερὰν ποιῆσαι τὴν ἐπιστήμην, ἀλλοτρίαις ἐμμελωδοίη φωναῖς, δι' αὐλῶν ἢ λύρας δημοσιεύων τὴν τέχνην· οὕτω καὶ ὁ ἀνθρώπινος νοῦς, παντοδαπῶν νοημάτων εὑρετὴς ὢν, τῷ μὴ δύνασθαι τοῖς διὰ σωματικῶν αἰσθήσεων ἐπαΐουσι γυμνῇ τῇ ψυχῇ δεικνύειν τὰς τῆς διανοίας ὁρμὰς, καθάπερ τις ἁρμοστὴς ἔντεχνος, τῶν ἐμψύχων τούτων ὀργάνων ἁπτόμενος, διὰ τῆς ἐν τούτοις ἠχῆς φανερὰ ποιεῖ τὰ κεκρυμμένα νοήματα.

[9.3] Σύμμικτος δέ τις ἡ μουσικὴ περὶ τὸ ἀνθρώπινον ὄργανον αὐλοῦ καὶ λύρας, ὥσπερ ἐν συνῳδίᾳ τινὶ κατὰ ταὐτὸν ἀλλήλοις συμφθεγγομένων· τὸ μὲν γὰρ πνεῦμα

104 αἱ χεῖρες] τὰ χείλη T ἐνετυπώθη τούτῳ A B C I K N O Q R : formata in eo fieret *Eri* ἐτυπώθη D φωνῇ C D^{ac} G^{ac} K N^{ac} 105 τὸ *om.* F G I L M P S V X στόμα] σῶμα N V συνδιασχηματιζομένη M 106 ἢ[1] *om.* A B C I K N O Q R T βληχάζειν A μηκάζειν] μυκάζειν A C D^{ac} K N O S^{ac} W : μυκίζειν G P X : μυκᾶσθαι L 108 μυκηθμὸν] βρυχηθμὸν A B C K N O Q R : βρυχθμὸν I 108–9 εὔσχολον ἐστι τὸ στόμα τῇ *om.* T 108 εὔσχολον] εὔκολον R : εὔσχημον L 109 στόμα] στωμα R^{ac} : σῶμα G M P V W X οὐκοῦν] non ero *Eri* 110 ἐναπεφήνασιν M τῷ λόγῳ τὴν εὐκολίαν] τὴν εὐκολίαν τοῦ λόγου N τοῦ λόγου R^{ac} T

1 κατεσκευάσθη *post* χρειάν *pon.* N τοῦ ἀνθρωποῦ τοῦ ἀνθρωποῦ X τὸ τοῦ ἀνθρώπου M σχῆμα] σῶμα A B E I K O 3 ὁμοιότητας] ἰδιότητας E I M V W 4 ἔδωκεν] δέδωκεν R 5 δέδωκεν] ἔδωκεν A B I K N O Q T ἀλλ' ὅτι μετέδωκε *om.* X αὐτοῦ τῆς φύσεως κόσμον] κόσμον τῆς αὐτοῦ φύσεως I : κόσμον τῆς φύσεως E 6 ἐπειδὴ R 7 ἂν *om.* D 7–8 μὴ—κινήσεως] dum per nullum organum intelligentiae sua motus manifestaretur *Eri* 7 φανερουμένης] φερομένης ß 8 τῆς ὀργανικῆς *om.* B προσεδεείθη X : adiecta est *Eri* 9 μορίων] ὀργάνων N 10 ὥσπερ] ὥσπερ εἴ A B D^2 I K M N O Q R S^2 T 11 ὢν] *ita* A B D F G I K L M O P Q R S T V W X *Forb* : *om.* N : ὢν ἂν *Ald Mign* ἰδίαν] ἠδείαν G R^{ac} X : ἠδεῖαν F L P V ἐκ πάθους *om.* ß ἐκ] ἐκ τοῦ D πάθους] βάθους B ἔχοι] ἔχῃ F^{ac} : ἔχει B^{ac} I : ἔχων N T 12 ἐπιστήμην] musicam *Eri* ἀλλοτρίοις Q ἐμμελωδοίη] μελωδοίη A B I K N O Q : ἐμμελωδοίη S : ἐμμελῳδοίη *Ald Mign* φωνὴν ß δι' *om.* V ἢ] καὶ B^{ac} (ἢ *sup. l.*) : καὶ ß 13 ὁ νοῦς ὁ ἀνθρώπινος A B I K N O Q T 14 τῷ] τὸ A B C D E F K O τοῖς] τοῖς μὴ X : *om. Ald Mign* ἐπανΐουσιν X ἐπαΐουσι γυμνῇ] ἐπαϊούσῃ *Ald Mign* 15 ψυχῇ] *add.* dicit quia anima per se ipsam dum sit incorporea sine corpore dictiones habere sensibiles non potest *Eri* καθάπερ—ἔντεχνος] quasi per modulationem quandam haec artificiosius *Dion* : ueluti quidam coaptatus in arte *Eri* ἐναρμοστὴς A B I K O Q ἐντέχνως I P^2 : ἐντέχνῃ B T : ἐν τέχνῃ K O Q 16 τούτων *om.* N φανερὰ ποιεῖ] φανεροποιεῖ N ποιεῖ] ποιεῖται D I L R^2 S 19 συνοδίᾳ ß G K L *Ald* : ᾠδῇ I : συνῳδίᾳ *Mign* ταὐτὸν] κατ' αὐτὸν D^{ac} Q V

our body had no hands, how could articulate sound have been formed in it, seeing that the formation of the parts of the mouth would not been configured for the use of speech, so that the human being must of necessity have either bleated, or baaed, or barked, or neighed, or bellowed like oxen or asses, or uttered some bestial bellowing? But as it is, with the hand being part of the body, the mouth is at leisure for the service of the reason. Therefore, the hands are shown to be proper to the rational nature, the Fashioner having thus devised by their means a facility for reason.

That the human form was fashioned as an instrument for the use of reason.

[**9.1**] Since, then, our Maker has bestowed upon our moulded figure a certain godlike grace, by implanting in the image the likenesses of his own good gifts, for this reason he gave, of his munificence, the other good gifts to human nature; yet it is not strictly right to say that he 'gave' of intellect and practical wisdom, but that he 'gave a share' of them, adding to the image the proper adornment of his own nature. Since, then, the intellect is a thing intelligible and incorporeal, its grace would have been incommunicable and isolated, without its movement being manifest by some contrivance. For this reason, there was need of this instrumental formation, that, by touching like a plectrum the vocal organs, it might indicate, by the quality of the sounds struck, the movement within. [**9.2**] And just as some experienced musician, who lost his own voice by some illness, yet wanting to make his skill known, might make melody with the voices of others, so making public his art through aid of flutes or the lyre, so also the human intellect—an inventor of all sorts of conceptions, being unable to show, by the naked soul, the impulses of its mind to those who hear by bodily senses—touches, like some skilful composer, these animated instruments to make manifest its hidden thoughts by the sounds produced upon them.

[**9.3**] The music of the human instrument is a sort of combination of flute and lyre, sounding together in combination with the others as in a kind of concert.[40]

[40] Cf. Gregory of Nyssa, *Inscr.* 1.3.22 (McDonough, 33.1–6; ET 91).

διὰ τῆς ἀρτηρίας ἀπὸ τῶν πνευματοδόχων ἀγγείων ἀνωθούμενον, ὅταν ἡ ὁρμὴ τοῦ φθεγγομένου πρὸς φωνὴν τονώσῃ τὸ μέλος, ταῖς ἔνδοθεν προσαρασσόμενον προσβολαῖς, αἳ κυκλοτερῶς τὸν αὐλοειδῆ τοῦτον διειλήφασι πόρον, μιμεῖταί πως τὴν διὰ τοῦ αὐλοῦ γινομένην φωνήν, ταῖς ὑμενώδεσιν ἐξοχαῖς ἐν κύκλῳ περιδονούμενον· ὑπερῷα δὲ τὸν κάτωθεν φθόγγον ἐκδέχεται τῷ κατ' αὐτὴν κενώματι, διδύμοις αὐλοῖς τοῖς ἐπὶ τοὺς μυκτῆρας διήκουσι, καὶ οἷον λεπίδων τισὶν ἐξοχαῖς τοῖς περὶ τὸν ἠθμὸν χόνδροις τὴν φωνὴν περισχίζουσα, γεγωνοτέραν τὴν ἠχὴν ἀπεργάζεται· παρειὰ δὲ καὶ γλῶττα καὶ ἡ περὶ τὸν φάρυγγα διασκευή, καθ' ἣν ὁ ἀνθερεὼν ὑποχαλᾶται κοιλαινόμενος, καὶ ὀξυτονῶν ἐπιτείνεται—[152] *ταῦτα πάντα τὴν ἐν ταῖς νευραῖς τοῦ πλήκτρου κίνησιν ὑποκρίνεται ποικίλως καὶ πολυτρόπως, ἐπὶ καιροῦ σὺν πολλῷ τῷ τάχει μεθαρμόζοντα πρὸς τὴν χρείαν τοὺς τόνους· χειλέων δὲ διαστολὴ καὶ ἐπίμυσις ταὐτὸν ποιεῖ τοῖς διὰ τῶν δακτύλων ἐπιλαμβάνουσι τοῦ αὐλοῦ τὸ πνεῦμα κατὰ τὴν ἁρμονίαν τοῦ μέλους.*

Ὅτι διὰ τῶν αἰσθήσεων ὁ νοῦς ἐνεργεῖ.

[10.1] *Οὕτω τοίνυν τοῦ νοῦ διὰ τῆς ὀργανικῆς ταύτης* [B] *κατασκευῆς ἐν ἡμῖν μουσουργοῦντος τὸν λόγον, λογικοὶ γεγόναμεν, οὐκ ἂν (ὡς οἶμαι) ἔχοντες τὴν τοῦ λόγου χάριν εἰ τὸ βαρύ τε καὶ ἐπίπονον τῆς κατὰ τὴν βρῶσιν λατρείας χείλεσι τὴν χρείαν τοῦ σώματος ἐπορίζομεν· νυνὶ δὲ τὴν τοιαύτην λειτουργίαν αἱ χεῖρες εἰς ἑαυτὰς μετενέγκασαι, εὔθετον τῇ ὑπηρεσίᾳ τοῦ λόγου τὸ στόμα κατέλιπον.* **[10.2]** *Διπλῆ δὲ περὶ τὸ ὄργανον ἡ ἐνέργεια· ἡ μὲν πρὸς ἐργασίαν ἠχῆς, ἡ δὲ πρὸς ὑποδοχὴν τῶν ἔξωθεν νοημάτων· καὶ οὐκ ἐπιμίγνυται πρὸς τὴν ἑτέραν ἡ ἄλλη, ἀλλὰ παραμένει τῇ ἐνεργείᾳ ἐφ' ᾗ ἐτάχθη παρὰ τῆς φύσεως, οὐκ ἐνοχλοῦσα τῇ γείτονι, οὔτε τῆς ἀκοῆς λαλούσης, οὔτε τῆς φωνῆς ἀκουούσης· ἡ μὲν γὰρ ἀεί τι πάντως προΐεται, ἡ δὲ ἀκοὴ δεχομένη διηνεκῶς οὐκ ἐμπίπλαται, καθώς φησί που ὁ Σολομών.*

[10.3] *Ὅ μοι δοκεῖ καὶ* [C] *μάλιστα τῶν ἐν ἡμῖν ἄξιον εἶναι καὶ θαυμάζεσθαι, τί τὸ πλάτος ἐκείνου τοῦ ἔνδοθεν χωρήματος, εἰς ὃ πάντα συρρεῖ τὰ διὰ τῆς ἀκοῆς εἰσχεόμενα; τίνες οἱ ὑπομνηματογράφοι τῶν εἰσαγομένων ἐν αὐτῇ λόγων; καὶ ποῖα*

20 *ἀνωρούμενον* V : *ἀνεωρούμενον* W 21 *φθεγγομένου*] sonantis arteriam *Eri* *μέλος*] *μέρος* V W *Ald Mign* 21–2 *ταῖς—προσβολαῖς*] interiores ordines eleuans *Eri* 21 *προσρασσόμενον* V W 22 *προβολαῖς* M² N P R² T *διειλήφασι*] pertranat *Eri* *πως*] omnino *Eri* 23 *γενομένην* E *ἐν om.* N R^ac 24 *ὑπερώα* Æ L M R² : *ὑπερῷα* S *Mign* 26 *ἠθμὸν*] *ἰθμὸν* B F² : *ἴθμον* T : *ἰσθμὸν* I N V : *λαιμὸν* E (*in mg γρ. ἰσθμὸν*) *γεγονωτέραν* W X 27 *ἠχὴν*] *ἰσχὺν* K *παρειαὶ* R *γλῶσσαι* R W *τὸν*] *τὴν* A Æ B C D E F Q 28 *ὑποχαλᾶται*] *καὶ ὑποχαλᾶται* N T *ὀξυτονῶν* V^pc2 (*ξυ add. 2^a man*) 29 *καὶ* V^pc2 30 *τῷ om.* N 32 *κατὰ*] *καὶ Ald Mign*

1 *ἐνεργεῖται* N Q T : operatur *Eri* 2 *οὕτως* N *διὰ τῆς*] *δι'* G P X : *om.* F *ταύτης om.* G M P V W X 3 *τοῦ λόγου* L *ὡς om.* D *ἔχοντες*] *σχόντες* T 4 *βαρύ*] *βαρύτεροι* F M *τε om.* A B C F K M N O Q *τὴν*¹ *om.* B *χείλεσι*] *ita* A B C G I K M N O P Q T V W X *Forb* : *τοῖς χείλεσι Ald Mign* *τὴν*²] *ita* A B C D E F G L M N P Q R S T V W X *Ald Forb* : *πρὸς τὴν Mign* 5 *τῇ χρείᾳ* A B C I K N O Q T *νῦν* C K O *τὴν om.* T *λειπτουργίαν* G P V X 5–6 *εἰς ἑαυτὰς αἱ χεῖρες* N 6 *μετενεγκοῦσαι* A B C I K N O Q R T 7 *ante διπλῆ inc. cap. 10* D E F G H I L M P S V W X *Dion Eri* : *Λ habet inscr.* de quinque sensibus corporis 9 *παραμένει*] *παραμένει ἑκάστη* R *ᾗ*] *ἧς* A B C I K M N O Q T 10 *ἀκουούσης οὔτε τῆς φωνῆς λαλούσης* B 10–11 *ἡ—προΐεται*] uox enim semper et omnino auditui procedit *Eri* 10 *γὰρ ἀεί*] *γὰρ ἕδρα εἴ* V : *ἕδρα εἴ* F G H P W X *γὰρ*] *γὰρ φωνὴ* R 11 *προσΐεται* F^mg G P V^ac X : *προσεΐεται* V^pc : *προσοίσεται* H *ἐμπίπλαται*] *ita* B C D E H I K M N O R S V W X *Forb* : *ἐμπίπλανται* A : *ἐμπίμπλαται* F^pc *Ald Mign* *που φησί* R *που*] *καὶ* I *ὁ*] *ita* A B C E G I K N O P Q R T X *Forb* : *om.* V W *Ald Mign* *σολομῶν* ß H I N P 12 *ὅ om.* V W *καὶ*¹ *om.* R *τῶν ἐν ἡμῖν καὶ μάλιστα* T *τῶν*] *τὸ* V *ἄξιον εἶναι καὶ θαυμάζεσθαι*] admiratione dignissimum *Dion* : mirandum *Eri* *καὶ*² *om.* A B C E I K N O Q T 13 *ἐκεῖνο* A B C E I K N O Q R : illa *Dion Eri* *ἔνδον* A B C I K N O Q *τὰ om.* N 14 *οἱ om.* N T

For the breath, as it is forced up from the lungs through the windpipe when the impulse of the speaker attunes the member to sound, striking against the internal protuberances which divide this flute-like passage in a circular manner, imitates in a way the sound produced by a flute, being driven round in a circle by the membranous projections; while the palate receives the sound from below its own cavity, dividing the sound by the two passages that lead to the nostrils, and by the cartilages about the perforated bone, as it were by some scaly protuberance, makes its resonance louder; and the cheek and tongue and the construction of the pharynx—by which the chin is relaxed when drawn in and tightened when extended—all these answer, in varied and manifold ways, to the movement of the plectrum on the strings, at the right time with great rapidity harmonizing the tones as required; while the opening and closing of the lips has the same effect as when they halt the wind of the flute with the fingers according to the harmony of the melody.

That the intellect works by means of the senses.

[10.1] Since, then, the intellect produces the music of reason by means of this instrumental construction within us, we have become rational, but would not, as I suppose, have the grace of reason if we used our lips to supply the needs of the body, the heavy and burdensome part of the business of providing food. As it is, however, the hands, appropriating this ministry to themselves, leave the mouth well-adapted for the service of reason. **[10.2]**[41] The activity of the instrument, however, is twofold: one for the production of sound, the other for the reception of concepts from without; and the one operation does not blend with the other, but remains in the activity for which it was appointed by nature, not interfering with its neighbour, either by the hearing speaking or by speech hearing; for the one is surely always uttering something, while the hearing is continuously receiving but not filled, as Solomon says somewhere.[42]

[10.3] The thing about our internal faculties that seems to me both to be especially noteworthy and wondered at is: what is the breadth of that inner receptacle into which flows everything that is poured in through the hearing?

[41] Some Greek mss, together with Dionysius Exiguus and Eriugena, begin Chapter 10 here. *Bodl. 238* has the heading: 'Of the five bodily senses'.

[42] Cf. Eccl. 1:8.

δοχεῖα τῶν ἐντιθεμένων τῇ ἀκοῇ νοημάτων; καὶ πῶς, πολλῶν τε καὶ παντοδαπῶν ἀλλήλοις ἐπεμβαλλομένων, σύγχυσις καὶ πλάνη κατὰ τὴν ἐπάλληλον θέσιν τῶν ἐγκειμένων οὐ γίνεται; τὸ ἴσον δ' ἄν τις καὶ ἐπὶ τῆς τῶν ὄψεων ἐνεργείας θαυμάσειεν· ὁμοίως γὰρ καὶ διὰ τούτων ὁ νοῦς τῶν ἔξω τοῦ σώματος ἐπιδράσσεται, καὶ πρὸς ἑαυτὸν ἕλκει τῶν φαινομένων τὰ εἴδωλα, τοὺς χαρακτῆρας τῶν ὁρατῶν ἐν ἑαυτῷ καταγράφων. [10.4] Καὶ ὥσπερ εἴ τις πολύχωρος εἴη πόλις ἐκ διαφόρων εἰσόδων τοὺς πρὸς αὐτὴν συμφοιτῶντας εἰσδεχομένη, οὐκ ἐπὶ τὸ αὐτὸ κατά τι τῶν ἐν τῇ πόλει συνδραμοῦνται οἱ πάντες, [D] ἀλλ' οἱ μὲν κατὰ τὴν ἀγοράν, οἱ δὲ κατὰ τὰς οἰκήσεις, ἄλλοι δὲ κατὰ τὰς ἐκκλησίας ἢ τὰς πλατείας ἢ τοὺς στενωποὺς ἢ τὰ θέατρα, κατὰ τὴν ἰδίαν ἕκαστος γνώμην μεταχωρήσουσι· τοιαύτην τινὰ βλέπω καὶ τὴν τοῦ νοῦ πόλιν τὴν ἔνδοθεν ἐν ἡμῖν συνῳκισμένην, ἣν διάφοροι μὲν αἱ διὰ τῶν αἰσθήσεων εἴσοδοι καταπληροῦσιν· ἕκαστον δὲ τῶν εἰσιόντων φυλοκρινῶν τε καὶ διεξετάζων ὁ νοῦς, τοῖς καταλλήλοις τῆς γνώσεως τόποις ἐναποτίθεται.

[10.5] Καὶ ὥσπερ ἐπὶ τοῦ κατὰ τὴν πόλιν ὑποδείγματος, ἔστι πολλάκις ὁμοφύλους τινὰς ὄντας καὶ συγγενεῖς μὴ διὰ τῆς αὐτῆς πύλης ἐντὸς γενέσθαι, ἄλλου κατ' ἄλλην εἴσοδον κατὰ τὸ συμβὰν εἰσδραμόντος, οὐδὲν δὲ ἧττον ἐντὸς τῆς περιβολῆς τοῦ τείχους γενόμενοι, πάλιν μετ' ἀλλήλων εἰσί, [153] πρὸς ἀλλήλους οἰκείως ἔχοντες· καὶ τὸ ἔμπαλίν ἐστιν εὑρεῖν γινόμενον· οἱ γὰρ ἀπεξενωμένοι τε καὶ ἄγνωστοι ἀλλήλων μιᾷ χρῶνται πρὸς τὴν πόλιν εἰσόδῳ πολλάκις, ἀλλ' οὐ συνάπτει τούτους ἀλλήλοις ἡ κατὰ τὴν εἴσοδον κοινωνία· δύνανται γὰρ καὶ ἐντὸς γενόμενοι διακριθῆναι πρὸς τὸ ὁμόφυλον· τοιοῦτόν τι βλέπω καὶ ἐπὶ τῆς κατὰ τὸν νοῦν εὐρυχωρίας· πολλάκις γὰρ καὶ ἐκ διαφόρων τῶν αἰσθητηρίων μία γνῶσις ἡμῖν συναγείρεται, τοῦ αὐτοῦ πράγματος πολυμερῶς πρὸς τὰς αἰσθήσεις μεριζομένου· πάλιν δ' αὖ τὸ ἐναντίον, ἔστιν ἐκ μιᾶς τινος τῶν αἰσθήσεων πολλὰ καὶ ποικίλα μαθεῖν, οὐδὲν ἀλλήλοις κατὰ τὴν φύσιν συμβαίνοντα·

15 τε *om.* V W *Ald Mign* 16 ἄλλοις T ἐπιλαμβομένων E κατὰ] *om.* F : τῶν κατὰ T : τῶν κα V 17 τῆς . . . ἐνεργείας] ταῖς . . . ἐνεργείαις A C I K O Q T 18 ἔξωθεν R 19 ἐπιδράσσεται] peragit *Eri* 21 αὐτὸ] αὐτὸ δὲ E 22 ἐν *om.* N συνδραμοῦνται] *ita* A B C D E^{pc} F I K L M N O Q R S T *Forb* : συνδραμόντες V W *Ald Mign* κατὰ τὴν] κατ' A B C I K N O Q T 23 τὰς *om. Mign* ἄλλοι δὲ] *ita* A B D E F I L O Q R S T *Forb* : ἄλλοι μὲν C : ἄλλ' οἱ μὲν K : ἢ N : ἄλλοι V W X *Ald Mign* κατὰ *om.* N τὰς ἐκκλησίας *om.* B 24 μεταχωρήσουσι] χωρήσουσι Æ : μεταχωροῦσι *Ald Mign* 25 νοῦ] ἀνθρώπου N ἐν *om.* B R ἣν *om.* T 26 αἱ *om.* B διὰ *om.* R 27 φυλοκρινῶν] *ita* A B C D E F^{pc} G H K O R S V X *Forb* : φυλοκρίνῶν T : φυλοκρίνων P : φιλοκρινῶν ß F^{ac} M W *Ald Mign* : φυλοκρινεῖ N^{ac} : φιλοκρινεῖ N^{pc2} τε καὶ *om.* N τοῖς] καὶ τοῖς N 29 κατὰ τὴν] κατ' αὐτὴν L πολλάκις] πολλάκις ἰδεῖν N R 30 μὴ διὰ] μηδὲ *Ald Mign* αὐτῆς] αὐτῆς αὐτῆς W : *om.* Æ πύλης] ciuitatem *Eri* 31 δὲ *om.* F τῆς περιβολῆς ἐντὸς E ἐντὸς] ἐκτὸς T περιβολῆς] περιβολῆς καὶ D E 32 γινόμενοι I εἰσὶ] εἰσὶ οἱ Æ B I K M N O Q T 33 γινόμενον εὑρεῖν D E F G H L M P S V W X γενόμενον N ἀπαξεγνωσμένοι V ἄγνωστοι 34 ἀλλήλων] ἀγνοοῦντες ἀλλήλους A B I K N O Q R T χρῶνται] χρῶν τε καὶ V 35 δυνατὸν R γενομένους R 36 πρὸς τὸ ὁμόφυλον διακριθῆναι E 37 γὰρ καὶ ἐκ] ἐν X καὶ *om.* A ß G H I K M O P Q W τῶν *om. Mign* 38 συνεγείρεται A B C D E F K συναγείρεται τοῦ αὐτοῦ πράγματος] eiusdem re congeritur *Eri* 40 συμβαίνοντα] accedentia *Eri*

Who are the note-takers of the words that are brought in by it? And what kind of containers are there for the concepts inserted by the hearing? And how is it that, with many and various kinds pressing one upon another, there doesn't occur a confusion and error in the respective places of things laid up there? One may well wonder equally regarding the activity of the eyes, for by them also in a similar manner the intellect apprehends things external to the body and draws to itself images of things that appear, marking in itself the impression of things which are seen. **[10.4]** And just as if there were some large city receiving those coming in by different entrances, all will not congregate at the same spot in some place in the city, but some will go to the market, some to the houses, others to the churches, or the streets, or lanes, or the theatres, each according to his own inclination, I see some such city of our intellect also established in us, which the different entrances through the senses fill up, while the intellect, distinguishing and examining each of the things that enters, stores them in their proper departments of knowledge.

[10.5] And, as in the example of the city, it may often happen that those of the same race and kin do not enter by the same gate, coming in by different entrances, as it may happen, but nonetheless, having come within the boundary of the wall, are brought together again, being akin with each other; and one may find the reverse happening, for those who are strangers and unknown to each other often use the same entrance to the city, but their sharing an entry does not bind them together, for even when within they can be separated to join their kin. Something of the same kind I see in the open spaces of the intellect, for often the knowledge we gather from the different organs of sense is one, as the same object is divided in many ways in relation to the senses, and again, on the contrary, one may learn from one of the senses many and varied things not relating to each other by nature.[43]

[43] Cf. Alexander of Aphrodisias, *De an.* (Bruns, 61.8–19).

[10.6] *Οἷον κρεῖττον γὰρ ἐν ὑποδείγματι διασαφηνίσαι τὸν λόγον· προκείσθω ζητεῖσθαί τι περὶ χυμῶν ἰδιότητος, τί μὲν ἡδὺ πρὸς τὴν αἴσθησιν,* [B] *τί δὲ φευκτὸν τοῖς γευομένοις ἐστίν· οὐκοῦν εὑρέθη διὰ τῆς πείρας ἥτε τῆς χολῆς πικρότης καὶ τὸ προσηνὲς τῆς κατὰ τὸ μέλι ποιότητος· φανερῶν δὲ ὄντων τούτων, μίαν εἰσάγει γνῶσιν· τὸ αὐτὸ πρᾶγμα πολυμερῶς τῇ διανοίᾳ εἰσοικιζόμενον (ἡ γεῦσις, ἡ ὄσφρησις, ἡ ἀκοή, πολλάκις δὲ καὶ ἡ ἀφὴ καὶ ἡ ὄψις)· καὶ γὰρ ἰδών τις τὸ μέλι, καὶ τοῦ ὀνόματος ἀκούσας, καὶ τῇ γεύσει λαβών, καὶ τὸν ἀτμὸν διὰ τῆς ὀσφρήσεως ἐπιγνούς, καὶ τῇ ἀφῇ δοκιμάσας, τὸ αὐτὸ πρᾶγμα δι᾽ ἑκάστου τῶν αἰσθητηρίων ἐγνώρισε.* [10.7] *Ποικίλα δὲ πάλιν καὶ πολυειδῆ διὰ μιᾶς τινος αἰσθήσεως διδασκόμεθα· τῆς τε ἀκοῆς παντοίας δεχομένης φωνάς, τῆς τε διὰ τῶν ὀφθαλμῶν ἀντιλήψεως ἀδιάκριτον ἐχούσης τὴν ἐνέργειαν ἐπὶ τῆς τῶν* [C] *ἑτερογενῶν θεωρίας· ὁμοίως γὰρ λευκῷ τε προσπίπτει καὶ μέλανι καὶ πᾶσι τοῖς κατὰ τὸ ἐναντίον διεστῶσι τῷ χρώματι· οὕτως ἡ γεῦσις, οὕτως ἡ ὄσφρησις, οὕτως ἡ διὰ τῆς ἀφῆς κατανόησις, παντοδαπῶν πραγμάτων ἑκάστη διὰ τῆς οἰκείας ἀντιλήψεως τὴν γνῶσιν ἐντίθησιν.*

Ὅτι ἀθεώρητος ἡ τοῦ νοῦ φύσις.

[11.1] *Τί τοίνυν ἐστὶ κατὰ τὴν ἑαυτοῦ φύσιν ὁ νοῦς, ὁ ταῖς αἰσθητικαῖς δυνάμεσιν ἑαυτὸν ἐπιμερίζων, καὶ δι᾽ ἑκάστης καταλλήλως τὴν τῶν ὄντων γνῶσιν ἀναλαμβάνων; ὅτι γὰρ ἄλλο τι παρὰ τὰς αἰσθήσεις ἐστίν,* [D] *οὐκ ἂν οἶμαί τινα τῶν ἐμφρόνων ἀμφιβάλλειν· εἰ γὰρ ταὐτὸν ἦν τῇ αἰσθήσει, πρὸς ἓν πάντως εἶχε τῶν κατ᾽ αἴσθησιν ἐνεργουμένων τὴν οἰκειότητα, διὰ τὸ ἁπλοῦν μὲν αὐτὸν εἶναι, μηδὲν δὲ ποικίλον ἐν τῷ ἁπλῷ θεωρεῖσθαι· νυνὶ δὲ πάντων συντιθεμένων, ἄλλο μέν τι τὴν ἀφὴν εἶναι, ἄλλο δὲ τὴν ὄσφρησιν, καὶ τῶν ἄλλων ὡσαύτως ἀκοινωνήτως τε καὶ ἀμίκτως πρὸς ἄλληλα διακειμένων, ἐπειδὴ κατὰ τὸ ἴσον ἑκάστῃ καταλλήλως πάρεστιν, ἕτερόν τινα χρὴ πάντως αὐτὸν παρὰ τὴν αἰσθητικὴν ὑποτίθεσθαι φύσιν, ὡς ἂν μή τις ποικιλία τῷ νοητῷ συμμιχθείη.*

41 *διασαφῆσαι* A ß I K N O Q T : *σαφηνίσαι* L 42 *ζητῆσαι* K *τι ζητεῖσθαί* N 43 *γευομένοις*] *γενομέμοις* G L P^{ac} : *γεγευμένοις* E R^{pc} : *γεγευσμένοις* D R^{ac} : *λεγευομένοις* Q *οὐκοῦν*] nonne ergo *Eri* *εὑρεθῆ* V W X : *ηὑρέθη* N *τῆς*^{1} *om.* N T *ἥτε*] *ἢ* N : *ἦτε* Æ 44 *τὸ om.* P *φανερῶν*] *διαφόρων Ald Mign* 45–6 *ἡ γεῦσις*] *ἡ πεῦσις* B : *ἢ γεύσει Mign* 46 *ἡ ὄσφρησις*] *ita* D E F G H L N P R S T V W X *Forb Ald* : *ἡ ὄψις* A B C I K M O Q *Dion Eri* : *ἢ ὀσφρήσει Mign* 46 *ἡ ἀκοή*] *ἢ ἀκοῇ Mign* *πολλάκις δὲ καὶ ἡ ἀφὴ καὶ ἡ ὄψις*] odoratum, etiam frequenter et tactum *Dion* *ἡ ἀφὴ*] *ἀφὴ* L N : *τῇ ἀφῇ Mign* *ἡ ὄψις*] *ita* D F G H L P S T V X *Forb Ald* : *ἡ ὅρασις* E N R : *ἡ ὄσφρησις* A B C I K M O Q : olfactus *Eri* : *τῇ ὄψει Mign* *ἰδών*] *καὶ ἰδών* A ß C K N O Q 48 *τῇ*^{1} *om.* N 49 *αἰσθητηρίων*] *αἰσθήσεων* G H *πάλιν om.* N T *πολυειδῆ*] *πολυσχιδῆ* N 50 *διδασκώμεθα* O^{ac} *δεχομένης*] *εἰσδεχομένης* E *διὰ*] *διὰ τῆς* I 52 *τε γὰρ λευκῷ* H *τε om.* N 53 *οὕτως ἡ γεῦσις, οὕτως ἡ ὄσφρησις*] sic odoratus, sic gustus *Dion* *οὕτως ἡ ὄσφρησις om.* I 53–4 *οὕτως ἡ διὰ τῆς ἀφῆς κατανόησις om. Eri*

---

1 *νοῦ*] *ἀνθρώπου Ald Mign* : definitio mentis humanae *Λ* 2 *ὁ*^{2} *om.* ß L *ὁ ταῖς*] *ita codd. Forb* : *ὅταν* V W *Ald* : *ὁ ἐν Mign* 5 *ἐμφρόνων*] *εὐφρονούντων* F *ἓν*] *ἓν ἂν* A B C I K M N O Q R T 6 *ἁπλοῦς* A B C O T *μὲν αὐτὸν*] *μὲν αὐτὸς* A B C K O T : *αὐτὸν μὲν* H *αὐτὸν om.* Q 7 *νῦν* N *πάντων*] *πάντως* C O 7–8 *εἶναι τὴν ἀφὴν* R 8 *δὲ*] *δὲ τι* N 8–9 *ἀκοινωνήτως τε καὶ ἀμίκτως*] absque communione *Eri* 9 *ἴσον Ald Mign* 10 *τινα*] *τι* Æ I N T *πάντως αὐτὸν χρὴ Ald Mign* *παρὰ—φύσιν*] praeter sensum substituere naturam *Eri* *αἰσθητὴν* I R^{ac} V *Ald Mign* *ὑποθεσθαι* P^{ac} : *ὑποθέσθαι* N T 11 *ποικίλα* N *τῶν νοητῶν* H : *τῷ νῷ* R : *τῶν ὄντων* Æ

[**10.6**] For instance—for it is better to make our argument clear by illustration—let us suppose an enquiry is made into the property of tastes, regarding what is sweet to the sense and what is to be avoided by those tasting. By experience, then, both the bitterness of gall and the pleasantness of the quality of honey are discovered. These things being known, yet the knowledge brought about is one, the same thing being introduced to our mind in many ways (taste, smell, hearing, and frequently touch and sight). For when one sees honey, and hears its name, and receives it by taste, and recognizes its odour by smell, and tests it by touch, he recognizes the same thing by means of each of the senses. [**10.7**] On the other hand, we are instructed about varied and multiform points by each single sense, with hearing receiving all sorts of sounds, and apprehension through the eyes exercising its activity by the vision of things of different kinds—for it falls alike on white and black, and all things that are distinguished by contrariety of colour—so with taste, so with smell, so with comprehension by touch: each implants in us by means of its own perception the knowledge of things of every kind.

That the nature of the intellect is invisible.[44]

[**11.1**] What then, in its own nature, is this intellect that distributes itself into the sense-perceptive powers, and accordingly receives, through each, the knowledge of beings? That it is something else besides the senses I suppose no reasonable person doubts, for if it were identical with sense-perception, it would certainly reduce the proper character of the activities carried out by sense-perception to one, on the one hand because it itself is simple, and on the other because no diversity is contemplated in what is simple. Now, however, as all agree that touch is one thing and smell another, and as the rest of the senses are similarly so disposed to each other as to exclude communion or mixture, it must surely be supposed, since the intellect is appropriately present in each equally, that it is something other than sense-perceptive nature, so that no diversity may be attached to the intelligible.

[44] *Bodl. 238*: 'The definition of the human mind'.

[11.2] ***Τίς ἔγνω νοῦν Κυρίου;*** *φησὶν ὁ ἀπόστολος· ἐγὼ δὲ παρὰ τοῦτό φημι, τίς τὸν ἴδιον νοῦν κατενόησεν; εἰπάτωσαν οἱ τοῦ Θεοῦ τὴν φύσιν ἐντὸς ποιούμενοι τῆς ἑαυτῶν* [156] *καταλήψεως, εἰ ἑαυτοὺς κατενόησαν; εἰ τοῦ ἰδίου νοῦ τὴν φύσιν ἐπέγνωσαν; πολυμερής τίς ἐστι καὶ πολυσύνθετος; καὶ πῶς τὸ νοητὸν ἐν συνθέσει; ἢ τίς ὁ τῆς τῶν ἑτερογενῶν ἀνακράσεως τρόπος; ἀλλ' ἁπλοῦς καὶ ἀσύνθετος; καὶ πῶς εἰς τὴν πολυμέρειαν τὴν αἰσθητικὴν διασπείρεται; πῶς ἐν μονότητι τὸ ποικίλον; πῶς ἐν ποικιλίᾳ τὸ ἕν;*

[11.3] *Ἀλλ' ἔγνων τῶν ἠπορημένων τὴν λύσιν, ἐπ' αὐτὴν ἀναδραμὼν τοῦ Θεοῦ τὴν φωνήν·* ***Ποιήσωμεν*** *γάρ, φησίν,* ***ἄνθρωπον κατ' εἰκόνα καὶ καθ' ὁμοίωσιν ἡμετέραν.*** *Ἡ γὰρ εἰκὼν ἕως ἂν ἐν μηδενὶ λείπηται τῶν κατὰ τὸ ἀρχέτυπον νοουμένων, κυρίως ἐστὶν εἰκών· καθ' ὃ δ' ἂν διαπέσῃ τῆς πρὸς τὸ πρωτότυπον ὁμοιότητος, κατ' ἐκεῖνο τὸ μέρος εἰκὼν οὐκ ἔστιν· οὐκοῦν ἐπειδὴ ἓν τῶν περὶ τὴν θείαν φύσιν θεωρουμένων* [B] *ἐστὶ τὸ ἀκατάληπτον τῆς οὐσίας· ἀνάγκη πᾶσα καὶ τούτῳ τὴν εἰκόνα πρὸς τὸ ἀρχέτυπον ἔχειν τὴν μίμησιν.* [11.4] *Εἰ γὰρ ἡ μὲν τῆς εἰκόνος φύσις κατελαμβάνετο, τὸ δὲ πρωτότυπον ὑπὲρ κατάληψιν ἦν· ἡ ἐναντιότης τῶν ἐπιθεωρουμένων τὸ διημαρτημένον τῆς εἰκόνος διήλεγχεν· ἐπειδὴ δὲ διαφεύγει τὴν γνῶσιν ἡ κατὰ τὸν νοῦν τὸν ἡμέτερον φύσις, ὅς ἐστι κατ' εἰκόνα τοῦ κτίσαντος, ἀκριβῆ πρὸς τὸ ὑπερκείμενον ἔχει τὴν ὁμοιότητα, τῷ καθ' ἑαυτὸν ἀγνώστῳ χαρακτηρίζων τὴν ἀκατάληπτον φύσιν.*

Ἐξέτασις ἐν τίνι τὸ ἡγεμονικὸν νομιστέον, ἐν ᾧ καὶ περὶ δακρύων καὶ γέλωτος φυσιολογία, καὶ θεώρημά τι φυσικὸν περὶ τῆς κατὰ τὴν ὕλην καὶ τὴν φύσιν καὶ τὸν νοῦν κοινωνίας.

[12.1] *Σιγάτω τοίνυν πᾶσα στοχαστικὴ ματαιολογία τῶν μορίοις τισὶ σωματικοῖς τὴν νοητὴν ἐναποκλειόντων ἐνέργειαν· ὧν οἱ μὲν ἐν καρδίᾳ τὸ ἡγεμονικὸν εἶναι τίθενται, οἱ δὲ τῷ ἐγκεφάλῳ τὸν νοῦν ἐνδιαιτᾶσθαί φασιν, ἐπιπολαίοις τισὶ πιθανότησι τὰς τοιαύτας ἐπινοίας κρατοῦντες. Ὁ μὲν γὰρ τῇ καρδίᾳ προστιθεὶς τὴν ἡγεμονίαν, τὴν κατὰ τόπον αὐτῆς θέσιν ποιεῖται τοῦ λόγου τεκμήριον, διὰ τὸ δοκεῖν πως τὴν μέσην τοῦ παντὸς σώματος ἐπέχειν χώραν αὐτήν, ὡς τῆς* [D] *προαιρετικῆς κινήσεως εὐκόλως ἐκ τοῦ μέσου πρὸς ἅπαν μεριζομένης τὸ σῶμα,*

12 *τίς*] *τίς γὰρ* E *φησὶν ὁ ἀπόστολος*] *ὡς ὁ παῦλος φησιν* E 15 *ἔγνωσαν* N *συνθέσει*] *συναισθήσει* H 16 *ὁ τῆς om.* T 19–20 *τὴν φωνήν τοῦ θεοῦ* E 19 *θεοῦ*] *θεοῦ εἰ* V 20 *γὰρ om.* B L Q *φησὶν om.* A B C K L O Q *ἄνθρωπον φησὶν* I T *ἄνθρωπον om.* D *καὶ καθ' ὁμοίωσιν ἡμετέραν*] *ἡμετέραν καὶ καθ' ὁμοίωσιν* B I N R : *ἡμετέραν καὶ ὁμοίωσιν* E : nostram et similitudinem *Eri* 21 *ἐν om.* C G I K N O R 22 *ὁμοιότητος*] *ὁμοιώσεως* *E N* R 23 *οὐκ ἔστιν εἰκὼν* B *οὐκοῦν*] non ergo *Eri* *ἐπειδὴ* X^{mg} *ἓν*] in *Eri* 24 *τούτῳ*] *ita* A B C G H I K M P Q R^{ac} S V X *Forb* : *τοῦτο* D F^{ac} L : *τούτου* Æ E F^{2} R^{2} T : *τούτο* W : *ἐν τούτῳ* *Ald Mign* 25 *μίμησιν*] *ὁμοιότητα* I 26–7 *τὸ διημαρτημένον*] quod oportet peccatum *Eri* 27 *ἐπεὶ* A C I M N O Q R V W *τὸν om.* N

Cap. 12 in Munich, BSB, *Cod. graec. 562*, 113^{v}–117^{r} (sigla J)

1–3 *ἐξέτασις—κοινωνίας*] quod principale hominis non solum [totum *Forb*] in cerebro sed in toto habitat corpore *Λ* 1 *τὸ ἡγεμονικὸν*] corporis principale animi *Eri* *ἐν ᾧ om.* N *γέλωτος*] *περὶ γέλωτος* *Ald Mign* 2–3 *καὶ θεώρημα—κοινωνίας om.* A B C I K N O Q T *Dion Eri* 5 *νοητικὴν* R^{2} : *διανοητικὴν* J *ἀποκλειόντων* J 6–7 *ἐπιπολαίοις—ἐπινοίας*] in quibusdam ciuitatibus suasione tales opiniones *Eri* 7 *ἐπινοίας*] *ὑπονοίας* A B C I K N O Q R^{ac} T *κρατύνοντες* A B C D I J^{pc2} K L M O Q R S T *προτιθεὶς* E L : *προσθεὶς* N 8 *τὴν κατὰ τόπον αὐτῆς θέσιν*] *τὴν καθ' ὑπόθεσιν αὐτῆς* I *θέσιν αὐτῆς* A B C K N O Q T 9 *ἐπέχειν*] *περιέχειν* J 10 *κινήσεως*] *δυνάμεως* L *τὸ om.* *Mign*

[11.2] *Who has known the intellect of the Lord?* asks the apostle;[45] and I ask further, who has understood his own intellect? Let them tell us, those who make the nature of God to be within their comprehension, whether they understand themselves! Whether they know the nature of their own intellect? Is it something manifold and much compounded? But how can the intelligible be composite? Or what is the mode of mixture of things that differ in kind? Or is it simple and incomposite? But how then is it dispersed into the manifold divisions of the senses? How is there diversity in singularity? How is the one in diversity?

[11.3] But I find the solution of these difficulties in returning to the very utterance of God: for he says, *Let us make the human being in accordance with our image and in accordance with our likeness.*[46] The image is properly an image so long as it lacks nothing of what is conceived in the archetype; but where it falls from its likeness to the prototype, in that respect it is not an image. Therefore, since one of the things contemplated regarding the divine nature is incomprehensibility of essence, it is wholly necessary that in this point also the image should have the imitation of the archetype. [11.4] For if the nature of the image were comprehended, while the prototype is above comprehension, the contrariety of the things contemplated would prove the defect of the image. But since the nature of our intellect, which is *in accordance with the image* of the Creator, evades knowledge, it has an accurate likeness to the transcendent one, figuring by its own unknowability the incomprehensible nature.[47]

An examination concerning in which part the ruling principle should be considered to be; in which also is a physiological consideration of tears and laughter, and a physical theory regarding the association of matter, nature, and the intellect.[48]

[12.1] Be silent, then, all the conjectural idle talk of those who confine the intellectual activity to certain bodily parts, some of whom place the governing principle in the heart, while others say that the intellect resides in the brain, strengthening such opinions by some plausible superficialities! For the one who attributes the governing authority to the heart makes its spatial position evidence of his argument, because it seems somehow to occupy the middle position of the whole body, since the deliberative movement is easily distributed from the middle to the whole body, and thus proceeds to activity; and he makes the troublesome

[45] Rom. 11:34. [46] Gen. 1:26. [47] Cf. Philo, *Opif.* 69–70.

[48] Several of the Greek mss, together with the Latin versions of Dionysius Exiguus and Eriugena, have only 12.1–8 as Chapter 12, and here only have the first part of the heading: 'An examination of which part we should consider the ruling principle to be; in which also is an inquiry concerning tears and laughter'; *Bodl. 238*: 'That the principle of the human being does not reside in the brain but in the whole body'.

καὶ οὕτως εἰς ἐνέργειαν προϊούσης· καὶ μαρτύριον ποιεῖται τοῦ λόγου τὴν λυπηράν τε καὶ θυμώδη τοῦ ἀνθρώπου διάθεσιν, ὅτι δοκεῖ πως τὰ τοιαῦτα πάθη συγκινεῖν τὸ μέρος τοῦτο πρὸς τὴν συμπάθειαν. Οἱ δὲ τὸν ἐγκέφαλον ἀφιεροῦντες τῷ λογισμῷ, ὥσπερ ἀκρόπολίν τινα τοῦ παντὸς σώματος τὴν κεφαλὴν δεδομῆσθαι παρὰ τῆς φύσεως λέγουσιν· ἐνοικεῖν δὲ ταύτῃ καθάπερ τινὰ βασιλέα τὸν νοῦν, οἷόν τισιν ἀγγελοφόροις ἢ ὑπασπισταῖς, τοῖς αἰσθητηρίοις ἐν κύκλῳ δορυφορούμενον· σημεῖον δὲ καὶ οὗτοι τῆς τοιαύτης ὑπονοίας ποιοῦνται, τὸ παράγεσθαι τοῦ καθεστηκότος τὸν λογισμὸν τῶν κεκακωμένων τὰς μήνιγγας, καὶ τὸ ἐν ἀγνοίᾳ τοῦ πρέποντος [157] γίνεσθαι τοὺς ἐν μέθῃ καρηβαρήσαντας.

[**12.2**] Προστιθέασι δὲ καί τινας φυσικωτέρας αἰτίας τῆς τοιαύτης περὶ τὸ ἡγεμονικὸν ὑπονοίας ἑκάτερος τῶν ταύταις ταῖς δόξαις παρισταμένων. Ὁ μὲν γὰρ πρὸς τὸ πυρῶδες συγγενῶς ἔχειν τὴν ἐκ τῆς διανοίας κίνησιν λέγει, διὰ τὸ ἀεικίνητον εἶναι καὶ τὸ πῦρ καὶ τὴν διάνοιαν· καὶ ἐπειδὴ πηγάζειν ἐν τῷ μορίῳ τῆς καρδίας ἡ θερμότης ὁμολογεῖται, διὰ τοῦτο τῷ εὐκινήτῳ τῆς θερμότητος τὴν τοῦ νοῦ κίνησιν ἀνακεκρᾶσθαι λέγων, δοχεῖον τῆς νοερᾶς φύσεως τὴν καρδίαν εἶναί φησιν, ἐν ᾗ τὸ θερμὸν περιείληπται. Ὁ δὲ ἕτερος πᾶσι τοῖς αἰσθητηρίοις οἷον ὑποβάθραν τινὰ καὶ ῥίζαν εἶναι λέγει τὴν μήνιγγα (οὕτω γὰρ ὀνομάζουσι τὸν περιεκτικὸν τοῦ ἐγκεφάλου ὑμένα) καὶ τούτῳ πιστοῦται τὸν ἴδιον λόγον· ὡς οὐχ ἑτέρωθι τῆς [B] νοητικῆς ἐνεργείας καθιδρυμένης, εἰ μὴ κατ' ἐκεῖνο τὸ μέρος, ᾧ καὶ τὸ οὖς ἐφηρμοσμένον τὰς ἐμπιπτούσας αὐτῷ φωνὰς προσαράσσει· καὶ ἡ ὄψις κατὰ τὸν πυθμένα τῆς τῶν ὀφθαλμῶν ἕδρας συμπεφυκυῖα, διὰ τῶν ἐμπιπτόντων ταῖς κόραις εἰδώλων πρὸς τὸ ἔσω ποιεῖται τὴν τύπωσιν· καὶ τῶν ἀτμῶν αἱ ποιότητες διὰ τῆς τῶν ὀσφρήσεων ὁλκῆς ἐν αὐτῷ διακρίνονται· καὶ ἡ κατὰ τὴν γεῦσιν αἴσθησις τῇ ἐπικρίσει τῆς μήνιγγος δοκιμάζεται, ἐκ τοῦ σύνεγγυς ἐκφύσεις τινὰς νευρώδεις ἀφ' ἑαυτῆς αἰσθητικὰς διὰ τῶν αὐχενίων σπονδύλων ἐπὶ τὸν ἰσθμοειδῆ πόρον κατὰ τοὺς αὐτόθι μύας ἐγκαταμιξάσης.

11 ποιοῦνται N τοῦ λόγου ποιεῖται A B C I K O Q R 12–13 τοιαῦτα πάθη—Οἱ δὲ] τοιαῦτα ἀπάθειαν· οἱ δὲ K 13 συμπάθειαν] πάθειαν C ἀφαιροῦντες V W 14 δεδωρῆσθαι A B C I K O Q 16 ἀγγελοφόροις] *ita* F G H J P V W X *Forb* : ἀγγελιαφόροις A[2] R S *Ald Mign* : ἀγγελαφόροις A[ac] : ἀγγελιφόροις M : ἀγγελιοφόροις Æ L : ἀγγεληφόροις B C I K N O Q 17 οὗτοι] αὐτοὶ A B C I K O Q τοιαύτης] αὐτῆς E ὑπονοίας] ἐπινοίας J τὸ] τοῦ G H J P V W X παραγενέσθαι ß 18 καθεστῶτος *Ald Mign* κεκαμένων D[ac] : κεκαυμένων N 20 προστίθησι Æ J N R T W αἰτίας φυσικωτέρας N 21 ἑκάτερος] ἕκαστος N προϊσταμένων D R S : περιϊσταμένων M : προσισταμένων J 22 ἔχειν συγγενῶς I ἀεικίνητον] εὐκίνητον J : incommunicabilis *Eri* 23 καὶ[1] *om.* J 24 ἡ θερμότης *om.* N *Dion Eri* ὡμολόγηται E L M 25 ἀνακρᾶσθαι W 26 δ' I J P X 28 τούτῳ] τοῦτο ß I J Q πιστοῦται] *ita* C[2] G H I J K N O P V W X *Forb* : πιστοῦνται *Ald Mign* 29 ᾧ] ἐν ᾧ Æ : ὡς V W 31 διὰ] διαπέμπει A B C I K M N O Q T ἐκπιπτόντων M 32 ἔσω] εἴσω A B C I K N O Q : aequaliter *Eri* ποιεῖται *om.* A B C I K M N O Q T 33 ἐν αὐτῷ] ἐν ἑαυτῷ D R[ac] : *om.* J τὴν *om.* L αἴσθησις *om.* N 34 δοκιμάζεται ἐκ τοῦ σύνεγγυς *om.* E ἀφ'] ἐφ' N T 35 σπονδύλων] *ita* ß D G H I L M P R S T V W X *Ald Forb Mign* : σφονδύλων A C N O Q : σφενδύλων K : σπονδήλων J ἰσθμοειδῆ] A B C D K L M N R T *Forb* : ἰσθοειδῆ ß : ἠσθμοειδῆ S[ac] : ἠσθμοειδὴ V W : ἰθμοϊειδῆ G : ἰθμοειδῆ P[ac] Q X : ἠθμοειδῆ *Ald Mign* κατὰ] καὶ N O Q T *Eri* 36 αὐτόθεν Q : inde *Eri* μυίας H R[2] ἐγκαταμίξασα A B C I K M N O Q T

and fierce disposition of a human being a testimony for his argument, because such affections seem somehow to move this part towards the same affection. Those, on the other hand, who consecrate the brain to the deliberating faculty, say that the head has been constructed by nature as a kind of citadel of the whole body, and that in it the intellect dwells like a king, with a bodyguard of sense organs surrounding it like messengers and shield-bearers.[49] And they produce as a sign of such a supposition the fact that the deliberating faculty of those who have suffered injury to the cerebral membranes is abnormally distorted and that those intoxicated with strong drink become ignorant of what is seemly.

[**12.2**] Each of those who propound these views also puts forward some more physical reasons regarding the governing principle on behalf of such positions. One says that the movement which proceeds from the mind is akin to the fiery nature, because both the fire and the mind are perpetually moving; and since heat is acknowledged to arise in the region of the heart, claiming on this basis that the movement of intellect is compounded with the mobility of heat, he asserts that the heart, in which heat is enclosed, is the receptacle of the intellectual nature.[50] The other declares that the cerebral membranes (for so they call the tissue that surrounds the brain) is as it were a foundation or root of all the senses,[51] and by this makes his own argument trustworthy, on the grounds that the intellectual activity cannot be seated anywhere else apart from that part where the ear, connected with it, registers the sounds that fall upon it; and the sight, naturally belonging to the hollow of the seat of the eyes, produces the internal impressions from the images that fall upon the pupils; and in it, by the drawing in of smells, are discerned the qualities of scents; and the sense of taste is tried by the test of the cerebral membranes, mixing certain neural sensations from itself—from the similar outgrowth, through the vertebrae of the neck, to the ethmoidal passage—with the muscles there.

[49] The image of the citadel occurs in Plato, Philo, Galen, Alexander of Aphrodisias, and Calcidius; the image of bodyguards or spear-bearers in Philo, Alcinous, Galen, and Nemesius. Cf. Plato, *Tim.* 45ab, 70ab; *Resp.* 8.560b8; Philo, *Opif.* 139; *Spec.* 3.111, 4.93, 4.123; Alcinous, *Epi.* 17.4; Galen, *Hipp. et Plat.* 2.4.17 (De Lacy 120.1–7); *De usu part.* 8.2. (Helmreich, 1, 445.14–17; ET 1, 387); *De foet. form.* 3.26 (Nickel, 76.5); Alexander of Aphrodisias, *De an.* (Bruns, 97.20–3); Nemesius *De nat. hom.* 6.177 (Morani, 57.8); Calcidius, *Pl. Tim.* 2.213, 2.220, 2.224, 2.231.

[50] Cf. Galen, *De usu part.* 6.7 (Helmreich, 1, 318.15–19; ET 1, 292); Calcidius, *Pl. Tim.* 2.224; Alexander of Aphrodisias, *De an.* (Bruns, 39.21–40.3; 98.24–99.6).

[51] Cf. Galen, *De usu part.* 8.4 (Helmreich, 1, 453.10–16, ET 1, 393); *Hipp. et Plat.* 6.3.4 (De Lacy, 372.27–32).

[12.3] *Ἐγὼ δὲ τὸ μὲν ἐπιταράσσεσθαι πολλάκις πρὸς τὰς τῶν παθημάτων ἐπικρατήσεις τὸ διανοητικὸν τῆς ψυχῆς, καὶ ἀμβλύνεσθαι* [C] *τῆς κατὰ φύσιν ἐνεργείας τὸν λογισμὸν ἔκ τινος σωματικῆς περιστάσεως, ἀληθὲς εἶναι φημί· καὶ πηγήν τινα τοῦ κατὰ τὸ σῶμα πυρώδους τὴν καρδίαν εἶναι, πρὸς τὰς θυμώδεις ὁρμὰς συγκινουμένην· καὶ ἔτι πρὸς τούτοις, τὸ ὑποβεβλῆσθαι τοῖς αἰσθητηρίοις τὴν μήνιγγα, κατὰ τὸν λόγον τῶν τὰ τοιαῦτα φυσιολογούντων, περιπτυσσομένην ἐν ἑαυτῇ τὸν ἐγκέφαλον καὶ τοῖς ἐκεῖθεν ἀτμοῖς ὑπαλειφομένην, τῶν ταῖς ἀνατομικαῖς θεωρίαις ἐσχολακότων τὸ τοιοῦτον ἀκούων, οὐκ ἀθετῶ τὸ λεγόμενον·* [D] *οὐ μὴν ἀπόδειξιν ποιοῦμαι ταύτην τοῦ τοπικαῖς τισι περιγραφαῖς ἐμπεριειλῆφθαι τὴν ἀσώματον φύσιν.*

[12.4] *Τάς τε γὰρ παραφορὰς οὐκ ἐκ μόνης καρηβαρίας γίνεσθαι μεμαθήκαμεν, ἀλλὰ καὶ τῶν τὰς πλευρὰς ὑπεζωκότων ὑμένων ἐμπαθῶς διατεθέντων ὁμοίως ἀρρωστεῖν τὸ διανοητικὸν διορίζονται οἱ τῆς ἰατρικῆς ἐπιστήμονες, φρενίτιν τὸ πάθος καλοῦντες, ἐπειδὴ φρένες τοῖς ὑμέσι τούτοις ἐστὶ τὸ ὄνομα. Καὶ ἡ ἀπὸ τῆς λύπης ἐπὶ τὴν καρδίαν γινομένη συναίσθησις ἐσφαλμένως ὑπονοεῖται· οὐ γὰρ τῆς καρδίας ἀλλὰ τοῦ στόματος τῆς κοιλίας δριμυσσομένου, εἰς τὴν καρδίαν τὸ πάθος ὑπ' ἀπειρίας ἀνάγουσι. Τοιοῦτον δέ τι φασὶν οἱ ἐπεσκεμμένοι δι' ἀκριβείας τὰ πάθη, ὅτι συμπτώσεως τῶν πόρων καὶ μύσεως ἐν ταῖς λυπηραῖς διαθέσεσι φυσικῶς περὶ ἅπαν γινομένης* [160] *τὸ σῶμα, πρὸς τὰς ἐν τῷ βάθει κοιλότητας συνωθεῖται πᾶν τὸ πρὸς τὴν διαπνοὴν κωλυόμενον· ὅθεν καὶ τῶν ἀναπνευστικῶν σπλάγχνων στενοχωρουμένων τῷ περιέχοντι, βιαιοτέρα πολλάκις ἡ ὁλκὴ τοῦ πνεύματος ὑπὸ τῆς φύσεως γίνεται, πρὸς τὴν τῶν συμπεπτωκότων διαστολὴν τὸ στενωθὲν εὐρυνούσης· τὸ δὲ τοιοῦτον ἄσθμα σύμπτωμα λύπης ποιούμεθα, στεναγμὸν αὐτὸ καὶ ἀναποτνιασμὸν ὀνομάζοντες. Ἀλλὰ καὶ τὸ δοκοῦν ὑποθλίβειν τὸ περικάρδιον μέρος, οὐ τῆς καρδίας, ἀλλὰ τοῦ στόματός ἐστι τῆς γαστρὸς ἀηδία, διὰ τῆς αὐτῆς αἰτίας, λέγω δή, τῆς κατὰ τὴν σύμπτωσιν τῶν πόρων, τοῦ χοληδόχου ἀγγείου τὸν δριμὺν ἐκεῖνον καὶ δακνώδη χυμὸν ὑπὸ στενοχωρίας ἐπὶ τὸ στόμα τῆς γαστρὸς παρεγχέοντος· ἀπόδειξις δὲ τούτου τὸ ὕπωχρον γίνεσθαι καὶ ἰκτερώδη τοῖς* [B] *λυπουμένοις τὴν ἐπιφάνειαν, ἀπὸ τῆς ἄγαν συνοχῆς ἐπὶ τὰς φλέβας τὸν ἴδιον χυμὸν τῆς χολῆς ἐπισπειρούσης.*

37 *ἐπιταράττεσθαι* R 38 *τῆς κατὰ φύσιν*] *τὰς φύσεως* N *φύσιν*] *τὴν φύσιν* *E* 39 *σωματικῆς* *om.* N *ἀληθῶς* N 40 *τὴν καρδίαν εἶναι* *post* *ὁρμὰς* *pon.* N *θυμοειδεῖς* F T 41 *κινουμένην* T 42 *φυσιολογούντων*] *φιλοσοφούντων* H J : naturali disputatione pertractant *Dion* : philosophantium de natura *Eri* *ἐν* *om.* Q 44 *τὸ τοιοῦτον* *om.* N *τὸ τοιοῦτον ἀκούων* *om.* R^{ac} 45 *ἀπόδειξιν*] *ἀπόδειξιν εἰς τὸ τοιοῦτον* R *ταύτην*] talem *Eri* 45–6 *τοῦ τοπικαῖς—φύσιν*] localibus puniri circumscriptionibus incomprehensibilem incorporealemque naturam *Eri* 47 *ἐκ μόνης καρηβαρίας*] ex capitis *Dion* : ex solo corde *Eri* *καρηβαρίας*] *ita* A B C D G H M N P O Q R S V W *Forb* : *καρηβαρείας* X *Ald Mign* *μεμαθήκαμεν γίνεσθαι* A B C I K O Q 48 *ἀλλὰ*] *καὶ γὰρ* N *διατιθέντων* L : *διατιθεμένων* H 49 *φρενίτιν*] *ita* ß H K L M N O Q R S V W *Ald Forb* : *φρενῖτιν* X *Mign* 51 *γιγνομένη* C I K N *συναίσθησις*] *om. Dion* : combustionem *Eri* 52 *στόματος*] *αἵματος* V W *πάθος*] *βάθος* C K O *ὑπὸ* Æ I K O 53 *ἄγουσι* M *τοιοῦτο* Æ N *δι'*] *μετὰ* N 54 *μυώσεως* N : *μυστικῶς* L *φυσικῶς* *om.* N 55 *γιγνωμένης* N *τὸ*^{2}] *τὸ διὰ* V 56 *τὴν* *om.* G H P R W X *κολυώμενον* W 57 *ὑπὸ* *om.* T 59 *εὐρυνούσης*] *ita* Æ ß G H I L M O P R S T V W X *Forb* : *εὐρυνούσης* *Ald Mign* *τοιοῦτο* N *ἄσθμα*] *ita* Æ G H I K L M N O P R S V W X *Forb* : *ἆσθμα* *Mign* *αὐτὸ* *om.* T 60 *ἀναποτιναγμὸν* V 61 *ἀηδία*] *ἡ ἀηδία* D R^{ac} S 62 *δὴ*] *δὲ* N T *τοῦ πόρου* I N *χολοδόχου* L 64 *παρεκχέοντος* Q : *παραχέοντος* N *ἰκτεριώδη* A C N O R^2 66 *ἐπισπειρούσης*] *ἐνσπειρούσης* A B C I K O Q

[**12.3**] I admit it to be true that the discursive faculty of the soul is often disturbed with respect to being seized by the passions, and that the calculating faculty is blunted in its natural activity by some bodily accident; and that the heart is a sort of source of the fiery element in the body, and is moved with the fierce impulses; and, in addition to this, hearing the same account from those who devote their time to anatomical research, I do not reject the statement that the cerebral membranes form a foundation for the senses, according to the argument of those who investigate natural phenomena, enfolding in itself the brain and being steeped in the vapours arising from it. Yet I do not hold this to be a proof that the incorporeal nature is itself bounded by any spatial limitations.[52]

[**12.4**] We know that mental aberrations do not occur from heaviness of head alone, but those skilled in the healing art declare that the discursive faculty is also similarly weakened when the membranes undergirding the sides are affected by disease, calling the disease 'frenzy', since the name given to those parts is 'wits'.[53] And the sensation resulting from sorrow is mistakenly supposed to arise in the heart; for while it is not the heart, but the entrance of the belly that is pained, people ignorantly refer the affection to the heart. Those who have accurately studied the affections give some such account as this: by a compression and closing of the pores, which naturally happens around the whole body in a state of grief, everything hindered in its passage is driven to the cavities in the depth of the body, and therefore, with the respiratory organs also constricted by what surrounds them, the drawing of breath often becomes more violent under the influence of nature trying to widen what has been contracted so as to dilate the compressed passages; such breath we hold to be a symptom of grief, and call it a groan or a shriek. And that, as well, which appears to oppress the region of the heart is a nausea not of the heart but of the entrance to the stomach, arising from the same cause (I mean, that of the compression of the pores), as the vessel containing bile by contraction pours that bitter and pungent juice upon the entrance of the stomach; a proof of this is that the complexion of those grieving becomes sallow and jaundiced, as the bile pours its own juice into the veins because of the excessive pressure.

[52] Cf. Gregory of Nyssa, *An. et res.* 2.53; 4.10 (Spira, 30.1–2; 49.16–19).

[53] A word play in Greek, in which 'wits' is *frenes*.

[12.5] Ἀλλὰ καὶ τὸ ἐξ ἐναντίου γινόμενον πάθος, τὸ κατὰ τὴν εὐφροσύνην φημὶ καὶ τὸν γέλωτα, μᾶλλον τὸν λόγον συνίστησι. Διαχέονται γάρ πως καὶ λύονται δι' ἡδονῆς οἱ τοῦ σώματος πόροι τῶν ἔκ τινος ἀκοῆς ἡδείας διαχεθέντων. Ὡς γὰρ ἐκεῖ διὰ τῆς λύπης μύουσιν αἱ λεπταί τε καὶ ἄδηλοι τῶν πόρων διαπνοαί, καὶ διασφίγξασαι [C] τὴν ἔνδοθεν τῶν σπλάγχνων διάθεσιν, ἐπὶ τὴν κεφαλὴν καὶ τὰς μήνιγγας τὸν νοτερὸν ἀτμὸν ἀναθλίβουσιν, ὃς πολὺς ἐναποληφθεὶς ταῖς τοῦ ἐγκεφάλου κοιλότησι, διὰ τῶν κατὰ τὴν βάσιν πόρων ἐπὶ τοὺς ὀφθαλμοὺς ἐξωθεῖται, τῆς τῶν ὀφρύων συμπτώσεως ἐφελκομένης διὰ σταγόνων τὴν ὑγρασίαν· ἡ δὲ σταγὼν δάκρυον λέγεται· οὕτω μοι νόησον, ἐκ τῆς ἐναντίας διαθέσεως πλέον τοῦ συνήθους εὐρυνομένων τῶν πόρων, εἰσέλκεσθαί τι πνεῦμα δι' αὐτῶν ἐπὶ τὸ βάθος, κἀκεῖθεν πάλιν ἐξωθεῖσθαι παρὰ τῆς φύσεως διὰ τοῦ κατὰ τὸ στόμα πόρου, πάντων τῶν σπλάγχνων (καὶ μάλιστά γε τοῦ ἥπατος, ὥς φασι) διά τινος κλόνου καὶ βρασμώδους κινήσεως τὸ τοιοῦτον πνεῦμα συνεξωθούντων· ὅθεν εὐκολίαν τινὰ τῇ διεξόδῳ τοῦ πνεύματος μηχανωμένη ἡ φύσις, ἀνευρύνει τὸν περὶ τὸ στόμα πόρον, ἑκατέρωθεν περὶ τὸ ἄσθμα τὰς παρειὰς διαστέλλουσα· ὄνομα δὲ τῷ [D] γινομένῳ γέλως ἐστίν.

[12.6] Οὔτε οὖν διὰ τοῦτο τῷ ἥπατι τὸ ἡγεμονικὸν λογιστέον, οὔτε διὰ τὴν περικάρδιον ζέσιν τοῦ αἵματος ἐν ταῖς θυμικαῖς διαθέσεσιν ἐν καρδίᾳ νομιστέον εἶναι τοῦ νοῦ τὴν καθίδρυσιν· ἀλλὰ ταῦτα μὲν εἰς τὰς ποιὰς τῶν σωμάτων κατασκευὰς ἀνακτέον, τὸν δὲ νοῦν ὁμοτίμως ἑκάστῳ τῶν μορίων κατὰ τὸν ἄφραστον τῆς ἀνακράσεως λόγον ἐφάπτεσθαι νομιστέον. [12.7] Κἂν τὴν γραφήν τινες ἡμῖν πρὸς τοῦτο προτείνωνται, τῇ καρδίᾳ τὸ ἡγεμονικὸν μαρτυροῦσαν, οὐκ ἀνεξετάστως τὸν λόγον δεξόμεθα· ὁ γὰρ καρδίας μνησθεὶς, καὶ νεφρῶν ἐμνημόνευσεν, εἰπών· **ἐτάζων καρδίας καὶ νεφροὺς ὁ Θεός**· ὥστε ἢ ἀμφοτέροις ἢ οὐθετέρῳ τὸ νοερὸν κατακλείουσιν.

[12.8] Ἀμβλύνεσθαι δὲ τὰς νοητικὰς ἐνεργείας ἢ καὶ παντάπασιν ἀπρακτεῖν ἐν τῇ ποιᾷ διαθέσει τοῦ σώματος [161] διδαχθεὶς, οὐχ ἱκανὸν ποιοῦμαι τοῦτο τεκμήριον τοῦ τόπῳ τινὶ τὴν δύναμιν τοῦ νοῦ περιείργεσθαι, ὡς ταῖς ἐπιγινομέναις τοῖς μέρεσι φλεγμοναῖς τῆς οἰκείας εὐρυχωρίας ἐξειργόμενον· σωματικὴ γὰρ ἡ τοιαύτη δόξα, τὸ

67 *ἐναντίας* Æ R 67–8 *καὶ τὸν γέλωτα, μᾶλλον*] magis autem risus *Eri* 68 *συνίστημι* X *λύονται*] *ita* A B C G H I K M P O Q T V W X *Forb* : *διαλύονται Ald Mign* 69 *οἱ om.* I *διαχυθέντων* D T (*sup. l.*) 69–70 *μύουσιν διὰ τῆς λύπης* N T 70 *τε om.* R *διαπνοαὶ*] *ἀναπνοαὶ* Q 71 *ἔνδον* N *τὰς μήνιγγας τὸν νοτερὸν*] meniggas (hoc est membranulas cerebri) austeriorem (id est umidiorem) *Eri* *τὸν νοτερὸν*] *τὸ νώτερον* V *νοτερὸν*] *νοερὸν* N : *νοτιαῖον* R 72–3 *διὰ τῶν κατὰ τὴν βάσιν πόρων*] per naturales poros *Eri* 74 *ἐφελκομένης*] *ita* A B C D G H I K L M O P R S V W X *Forb* : *ἐξελκομένης Ald Mign* *ὑγρασίαν*] *ὑγρὰν οὐσίαν* N 75 *εὐρυνομένων* G N R 76 *τι*] *τὸ* N *ἐπὶ*] *εἰς* N *πάλιν*] *πᾶσα* A² 77 *τὸ om.* T *καὶ om.* R *γε*] *τε* N 78 *τινος om.* I 79 *διεξόδου* I : *ἐξόδῳ* H M *τοῦ πνεύματος*] *τούτο* N 80 *τὸ*¹ *om.* G H M W X *περὶ τὸ ἄσθμα*] *τῇ περὶ τὸ ἄσωμα εὐκολιᾳ* N T V *ἄσθμα*] *ita* Æ H I L N O P S T V W X *Forb* : *ἆσθμα Ald Mign* 82 *τῷ*] *ἐν τῷ* A B C D I K L M N O Q R S 83 *τοῦ αἵματος om.* N 84 *ποιὰς om.* I 85 *ὁμοτίμως*] *om. Eri* *ἑκάστῳ τῶν μορίων om.* C K O *ἑκάστοῦ* A B Q R T 86 *ἄφραστον*] *ἄρατον* L 87 *ἡμῖν τινες* N T *πρὸς*] *εἰς* R *προτείνονται* Æ^ac J N *ἡγεμονικὸν*] *ἡγεμονικὸν ἐνοικεῖν* I 88 *τὸν om.* W *δεξώμεθα* L T *καρδίαν* ß *Ald Mign* 89 *ὁ Θεός om.* K 90 *οὐθετέρῳ*] *ita* A B C D G I M R S^pc V *Ald Forb* : *οὐθ' ἑτέρῳ* H K L N O P Q S^ac : *οὐθ' ἑτέρως* J : *οὐδετέρῳ Mign* 91 *ἢ om.* X 92 *διδαχθεὶς*] doces *Eri* *τοῦτο om.* A ß I K N O Q T 93 *τοῦ νοῦ om.* L *περιείργασθαι* I *ἐπιγιγνομέναις* N 94 *ἐξειργόμενον*] *ita* Æ ß C I K O Q *Forb* : *ἐξειργομένη* T^ac (*ου sup. l.*) : *ἐξειργομένην* N : *ἐξειργομ...* S^eras : *ἐξειργασμένης* L : *ἐξειργομένης* V W X *Ald Mign* *τὸ*] *τοῦ* T

[12.5] Moreover, the opposite affection, I mean that of gladness and laughter, contributes further to the argument. For the pores of the body of those who are dissolved [in levity] by hearing something pleasant are also somehow dissolved and relaxed through pleasure. Just as in the former case, the slight and imperceptible exhalations of the pores are constrained by grief, and, tightly binding the internal arrangement of the inner organs, they force up towards the head and the cerebral membranes the humid vapour which, being retained in excess in the cavities of the brain, is driven out through the pores at its base towards the eyes, while the closing of the eyelids expels the moisture as drops, and the drop is called a tear; so also, I would have you understand that, when the pores, from the contrary condition, are unusually widened, some air is drawn in through them into the interior, and thence expelled again by nature through the passage of the mouth, while all the inner organs (and especially, they say, the liver) together expel this air by a certain turmoil and agitated movement, from which nature, contriving to give facility for the exit of the air, widens the passage of the mouth, extending the cheeks on either side round about the breath, and the result is called laughter.[54]

[12.6] Therefore, we must neither ascribe the governing principle to the liver nor think that the seat of the intellect is in the heart, because of the boiling blood around the heart in those of a wrathful disposition; but we must refer these things to the character of the formation of our bodies, and must consider that the intellect equally touches each of the parts according to an inexpressible principle of mixing.[55] **[12.7]** And if regarding this point someone should bring forward the Scripture, which testifies that the governing principle is in the heart, we will not receive the statement unexamined; for he who made mention of the heart also mentioned the kidneys, saying, *God tests the heart and the kidneys*,[56] so that they must confine the intellectual principle either to both together or to neither.

[12.8] Although I know that intellectual activities are blunted, or even made altogether ineffective in a certain condition of the body, I do not hold this as sufficient evidence for limiting the faculty of the intellect to any particular place, so that it would be forced out of its proper space by inflammations arising in nearby

[54] Cf. Gregory of Nyssa, *Eccl.* 2 (Alexander, 310.6–311.2; ET 56); Aristotle, *Probl.* 35.6 (965a14).

[55] Cf. Gregory of Nyssa, *An. et res.* 2.46 (Spira, 27.23–28.5); Gregory of Nazianzus, *Ep.* 101.37–9; Alexander of Aphrodisias, *De an.* (Bruns, 13.9–17.8).

[56] Ps. 7:10.

μὴ δύνασθαι προκατειλημμένου τοῦ ἀγγείου διά τινος τῶν ἐμβεβλημένων, ἕτερόν τι ἐν αὐτῷ χώραν εὑρεῖν· ἡ γὰρ νοητὴ φύσις οὔτε ταῖς κενώσεσιν ἐμφιλοχωρεῖ τῶν σωμάτων οὔτε τῷ πλεονάζοντι τῆς σαρκὸς ἐξωθεῖται· ἀλλ' ἐπειδὴ καθάπερ τι μουσικὸν ὄργανον ἅπαν τὸ σῶμα δεδημιούργηται, ὥσπερ συμβαίνει πολλάκις ἐπὶ τῶν μελῳδεῖν μὲν ἐπισταμένων, ἀδυνατούντων δὲ δεῖξαι τὴν ἐπιστήμην, τῆς τῶν ὀργάνων ἀχρηστίας οὐ παραδεχομένης τὴν τέχνην (τὸ γὰρ ἢ χρόνῳ διαφθαρὲν ἢ παρερρηγμένον ἐκ καταπτώσεως ἢ ὑπό τινος ἰοῦ καὶ εὐρῶτος ἠχρειωμένον, [B] *ἄφθογγον μένει καὶ ἀνενέργητον, κἂν ὑπὸ τοῦ προέχειν δοκοῦντος κατὰ τὴν αὐλητικὴν τέχνην ἐμπνέηται) οὕτω καὶ ὁ νοῦς δι' ὅλου τοῦ ὀργάνου διήκων καὶ καταλλήλως ταῖς νοητικαῖς ἐνεργείαις, καθ' ὃ πέφυκεν, ἑκάστου τῶν μερῶν προσαπτόμενος, ἐπὶ μὲν τῶν κατὰ φύσιν διακειμένων τὸ οἰκεῖον ἐνήργησεν, ἐπὶ δὲ τῶν ἀσθενούντων δέξασθαι τὴν τεχνικὴν αὐτοῦ κίνησιν, ἄπρακτός τε καὶ ἀνενέργητος ἔμεινε· πέφυκε γάρ πως ὁ νοῦς πρὸς μὲν τὸ κατὰ φύσιν διακείμενον οἰκείως ἔχειν· πρὸς δὲ τὸ παρενεχθὲν ἀπὸ ταύτης ἀλλοτριοῦσθαι.*

[12.9] [C] *Καί μοι δοκεῖ φυσικώτερον εἶναί τι κατὰ τὸ μέρος τοῦτο θεώρημα, δι' οὗ μαθεῖν ἔστι τι τῶν ἀστειοτέρων δογμάτων· ἐπειδὴ γὰρ τὸ κάλλιστον πάντων καὶ ἐξοχώτατον ἀγαθὸν αὐτὸ τὸ θεῖόν ἐστι, πρὸς ὃ πάντα νένευκεν ὅσα τοῦ καλοῦ τὴν ἔφεσιν ἔχει, διὰ τοῦτό φαμεν καὶ τὸν νοῦν, ἅτε κατ' εἰκόνα τοῦ καλλίστου γενόμενον, ἕως ἂν μετέχῃ τῆς πρὸς τὸ ἀρχέτυπον ὁμοιότητος καθόσον ἐνδέχεται, καὶ αὐτὸν ἐν τῷ καλῷ διαμένειν· εἰ δέ πως ἔξω γένοιτο τούτου, γυμνοῦσθαι τοῦ κάλλους ἐν ᾧ ἦν· ὥσπερ δὲ ἔφαμεν τῇ ὁμοιώσει τοῦ πρωτοτύπου κάλλους τοῦ κατακοσμεῖσθαι τὸν νοῦν, οἷόν τι κάτοπτρον τῷ χαρακτῆρι τοῦ ἐμφαινομένου μορφούμενον· κατὰ τὴν αὐτὴν ἀναλογίαν, καὶ τὴν οἰκονομουμένην ὑπ' αὐτοῦ φύσιν ἔχεσθαι τοῦ νοῦ λογιζόμεθα, καὶ τῷ παρ' ἐκείνου κάλλει καὶ αὐτὴν κοσμεῖσθαι, οἷόν* [D] *τι κατόπτρου κάτοπτρον γινομένην· κρατεῖσθαι δὲ ὑπὸ ταύτης καὶ συνέχεσθαι τὸ ὑλικὸν τῆς ὑποστάσεως, περὶ ἣν θεωρεῖται ἡ φύσις.*

95 *ἐμβεβλημένων*] inspiciuntur *Eri* 96 *χώραν ἐν αὐτῷ* L *νοητική* N *οὔτε*] *οὐ* A B C O Q *κενώσεσιν*] *κοιλότησιν* A B C D I K L N O Q R S T 98 *ὥσπερ*] *ἅπερ* A C I K O : *ὅπερ* B T 99 *μὲν om.* J T 100 *διαφθαρὲν*] *ita* D G H L P S V X *Forb* : *διεφθορὸς* A B C I K N O Q R T : *φθαρὲν* W *Ald Mign* 101 *καταπτώσεως*] *πτώσεως* J : *καταπαύσεως* I 102 *κατὰ om.* N 103 *αὐλητικὴν om.* G H P W X *ἐμπνέοντος* L : *ἐμπεπονεῖται* J 104 *καθ' ὃ*] *ita* A B C G H I J K L M N O P V W X *Forb* : *καθὸ Ald Mign* *καθ' ὃ πέφυκεν post μερῶν pon.* A B C I K N O Q T *ἑκάστῳ Mign* 105–7 *ἐπὶ δὲ—ἔμεινε*] in his uero quae infirmantur artificalem sui motum inactuosus et piger manet accipere *Eri* 106 *τεχνικὴν*] *φυσικὴν* N 107 *ἀνενέργητον* C 108 *παραχθὲν* I *ἀπὸ ταύτης*] *ἀπ' αὐτῆς* N *ἀπὸ om.* T 109 *ante καί inc. cap. 13 cum inscr. θεώρημά τι φυσικὸν περὶ τῆς κατὰ τὴν ὕλην καὶ τὴν φύσιν καὶ τὸν νοῦν κοινωνίας* A B C I K N O Q R T : speculatio quaedam de materiae et naturae et animi theoria *Eri* : quod sicut a deo mens gubernatur ita a mente materialis uita corporis *Λ* *δοκεῖ*] *δοκεῖ καὶ* A B C I K M O Q T *τι*] *τὸ* N *τοῦτο*] *τοῦτο τὸ* W 110 *τι om.* N 111 *ἀγαθὸν*] *τῶν ἀγαθῶν* D : *πάντων τῶν ἀγαθῶν* N 113–14 *ἕως ἂν—διαμένειν*] quatenus ad principale exemplum bonum similitudinem participarit, quantum quidem ipsum in bono licit permanere *Eri* 113 *μετέχει* L : *μετέχοι* M : *μετέχεται* C K *τῆς—ἐνδέξεται om.* C K *ὁμοιότητος*] *ὁμοιώσεως* N *καθόσον*] *καθ' ὅσον* I L M R : *καθόσον μὲν* N 114 *γένηται* R *κάλλους*] *κάλλους τοῦ* O V W X 115 *τοῦ*[2] *om.* O V W X *Ald Mign* 116 *τῷ om.* C 118 *παρ' ἐκείνου*] *παρακειμένῳ* V W *Ald Mign* *καὶ αὐτὴν om.* N *κατακοσμεῖσθαι* C G H K O P X : *διακοσμεῖσθαι* R 119 *κατόπτρου*] *om.* N R[ac] : *κατόπτρῳ* T *post κρατεῖσθαι* V *def. ad* [ἀσώμα]*τόν; πῶς* (*cap. 16, l. 21*) *δὲ om.* L N *ὑπὸ ταύτης*] *ὑπ' αὐτῆς* P R

parts (for such an opinion—that when a vessel is already occupied by something placed in it, nothing else is able to find a place there—is corporeal). For the intelligible nature does not dwell in the empty spaces of bodies nor is it forced out by the encroachment of the flesh; but since the whole body has been made like some musical instrument, as often happens in the case of those who know how to play but are unable to demonstrate their prowess because the uselessness of the instrument does not admit their art (for that which is destroyed by time, or broken by a fall, or made useless by some rust or rot, is mute and inoperable, even if it be breathed upon by one considered preeminent in flute playing), so also the intellect, passing throughout the instrument and touching each of the parts in a manner appropriate to its intellectual activities, according to its nature, produces its proper effect on those parts disposed according to nature, but upon those parts too weak to accept the movement of its art it remains ineffective and inactive; for the intellect is naturally somehow familiar with that which is disposed according to nature, but to be alien from that which is removed from it.[57]

[12.9][58] I also think there is a contemplation of this particular point, closer to nature, by which one may learn something of the more refined teachings. For since the most beautiful and supreme good of all is the divinity itself, to which incline all things that have the desire for the beautiful, we therefore say that the intellect, as being in accordance with the image of the most beautiful, as long as it partakes so far as possible in the likeness to the archetype, also remains in the beautiful; but if it were somehow to be outside this, it will be stripped bare of the beauty in which it was. And just as we said that the intellect was adorned by the likeness of the archetypal beauty, being formed, as though it were a mirror, by the figure of that which appears in it, so we consider that the nature administered by the intellect possesses something of the intellect in the same proportion and that it is adorned by the beauty issuing from the intellect, such that it becomes, as it were, a mirror of a mirror; by it, the material element of existence, in which nature is contemplated, is ruled and sustained.[59]

[57] Cf. Gregory of Nyssa, *An. et res.* 2.53; 4.10 (Spira, 30.1–2; 49.16–19).

[58] Several of the Greek mss, together with the Latin versions of Dionysius Exiguus and Eriugena, begin Chapter 13 here, with the heading: 'A natural theory regarding the association of matter, nature, and intellect'; *Bodl. 238* has: 'That as the mind is governed by God, so is the material life of the body by the mind'. Hereafter, those mss which divide the work into 31 chapters increase the numeration of the chapters by one.

[59] Cf. Gregory of Nazianzus, *Or.* 2.17.

[12.10] Ἕως ἂν οὖν ἔχηται τοῦ ἑτέρου τὸ ἕτερον, διὰ πάντων ἀναλόγως ἡ τοῦ ὄντως κάλλους κοινωνία διέξεισι, διὰ τοῦ ὑπερκειμένου τὸ προσεχὲς καλλωπίζουσα· ἐπειδὰν δέ τις γένηται τῆς ἀγαθῆς ταύτης συμφυΐας διασπασμὸς, ἢ καὶ πρὸς τὸ ἔμπαλιν, ἀντακολουθῇ τῷ ὑποβεβηκότι τὸ ὑπερέχον, τότε αὐτῆς τε τῆς ὕλης, ὅταν μονωθῇ τῆς φύσεως, διηλέγχθη τὸ ἄσχημον (ἄμορφον γάρ τι καθ' ἑαυτὴν ἡ ὕλη καὶ ἀκατάσκευον) καὶ τῇ ἀμορφίᾳ ταύτης συνδιεφθάρη τὸ κάλλος τῆς φύσεως, ὃ διὰ τοῦ νοῦ καλλωπίζεται· καὶ οὕτως ἐπ' αὐτὸν τὸν νοῦν τοῦ κατὰ τὴν ὕλην [164] αἴσχους διὰ τῆς φύσεως ἡ διάδοσις γίνεται, ὡς μηκέτι τοῦ Θεοῦ τὴν εἰκόνα ἐν τῷ χαρακτῆρι καθορᾶσθαι τοῦ πλάσματος· οἷον γάρ τι κάτοπτρον κατὰ νώτου τὴν τῶν ἀγαθῶν ἰδέαν ὁ νοῦς ποιησάμενος, ἐκβάλλει μὲν τῆς ἐλλάμψεως τοῦ ἀγαθοῦ τὰς ἐμφάσεις, τῆς δὲ ὕλης τὴν ἀμορφίαν εἰς ἑαυτὸν ἀναμάσσεται.

[12.11] Καὶ τούτῳ γίνεται τῷ τρόπῳ τοῦ κακοῦ ἡ γένεσις, διὰ τῆς ὑπεξαιρέσεως τοῦ καλοῦ παρυφισταμένη· καλὸν δὲ πᾶν, ὅπερ ἂν τύχῃ πρὸς τὸ πρῶτον ἀγαθὸν οἰκείως ἔχον· ὅ τι δ' ἂν ἔξω γένηται τῆς πρὸς τοῦτο σχέσεώς τε καὶ ὁμοιώσεως, ἄμοιρον τοῦ καλοῦ πάντως ἐστίν. Εἰ οὖν ἓν μὲν κατὰ τὸν θεωρηθέντα λόγον τὸ ὄντως ἀγαθόν· ὁ δὲ νοῦς τῷ κατ' εἰκόνα τοῦ καλοῦ γεγενῆσθαι, καὶ αὐτὸς ἔχει τὸ καλὸς εἶναι· ἡ δὲ φύσις ἡ ὑπὸ τοῦ νοῦ συνεχομένη, καθάπερ τὶς εἰκὼν εἰκόνος ἐστί· [B]—δείκνυται διὰ τούτων ὅτι τὸ ὑλικὸν ἡμῶν συνέστηκε μὲν καὶ περικρατεῖται ὅταν οἰκονομῆται ὑπὸ τῆς φύσεως· λύεται δὲ καὶ διαπίπτει πάλιν, ὅταν χωρισθῇ τοῦ περικρατοῦντος τε καὶ συνέχοντος καὶ διασπασθῇ τῆς πρὸς τὸ καλὸν συμφυΐας. [12.12] Τὸ δὲ τοιοῦτον οὐκ ἄλλως γίνεται ἢ ὅταν τῆς φύσεως πρὸς τὸ ἔμπαλιν γένηται ἡ ἐπιστροφὴ, μὴ πρὸς τὸ καλὸν τῆς ἐπιθυμίας νευούσης, ἀλλὰ πρὸς τὸ χρῇζον τοῦ καλλωπίζοντος· ἀνάγκη γὰρ πᾶσα τῇ πτωχευούσῃ τῆς ἰδίας μορφῆς ὕλῃ κατὰ τὸ ἄσχημόν τε καὶ ἀκαλλὲς συμμεταμορφοῦσθαι τὸ ὁμοιούμενον.

[12.13] Ἀλλὰ ταῦτα μὲν ἡμῖν ἐξ ἀκολουθίας τινὸς παρεξητάσθη, διὰ τῆς εἰς τὸ προκείμενον θεωρίας ἐπεισελθόντα· τὸ γὰρ ζητούμενον ἦν, εἰ ἐν μέρει τινὶ τῶν ἐν ἡμῖν ἡ νοερὰ καθίδρυται [C] δύναμις, ἢ διὰ πάντων κατὰ τὸ ἦσον διήκει· τῶν γὰρ τοπικοῖς μέρεσι περιειργόντων τὸν νοῦν καὶ εἰς σύστασιν τῆς τοιαύτης αὐτῶν

121 οὖν ἂν R οὖν *om.* H οὖν ἔχηται] συνέχηται T 121–2 ἡ τοῦ ὄντως κάλλους κοινωνία] illius summi et ueri participatio *Dion* : ipsa ueri boni societas *Eri* ὄντος καλοῦ N 123 γίνηται M 124 ἀντακολουθεῖ G H P R^{ac} W X : ἀντακολουθεῖν L : ἀντακολουθήσῃ A B C I K M O Q : ἀντακολουθήσει T : ἐπακολουθήσει N τῷ ὑποβεβηκότι τὸ ὑπερέχον] supereminenti supereminens *Eri* τε *om.* D R 125 διηλέγχθη] *ita* A C D N O P Q R S T W X *Forb* : διηλέχθη G H L M : διηλλέχθη B : διηνέχθη *Ald Mign* ἄμορφον γάρ] ἀμόρφονταί X τι] τι χρῆμα A C I K M N O Q R T *Dion Eri* 126 ταύτῃ A C K N R συνδιεφθάρη] συνεφθάρη Q : συνδιεφθάρει O : συνδιαφθείρεται N ὃ] *ita* D H L P^{2} R T W *Dion Ald Forb* : ᾧ A B C G I K M N O P^{ac} Q S X : in qua *Eri* : ᾗ *Mign* 128 διάδοσις] μετάδοσις R τὴν τοῦ Θεοῦ L 129 καθορᾶσθαι] καθ' ὁμοιοῦσθαι N τι *om.* T 130 ἐκλάμψεως W *Mign* 131 τὴν δὲ τῆς ὕλης A B C I K N Q R T ἀναμάττεται L 132 ἡ τοῦ κακοῦ I N ὑφεξαιρέσεως ß K : ὑφ' ἐξαιρέσεως G P X : ὑφαιξερέσεως C O 133 παρυφισταμένη] συνισταμένη L ὅπερ] ὅτι περ A ß C D I K L M N O Q S 134 τε καὶ ὁμοιώσεως *om.* M T W 135 ἄμοιρον] ἄμοιρον πῶς N 136 κάλλους Q γενέσθαι L 137 ἡ^{2} *om.* Q εἰκὼν *om.* C K 139 οἰκονομειται D^{ac} (η *sup. l.*) : οἰκονομεῖται N P^{ac} W 140 περικρατοῦντος] κρατοῦντος C K O 142 γενήσεται D : γίνηται M ἐπιστροφὴ] ἀποστροφὴ M μὴ] τῆς T : καὶ μὴ X 143 χρῇζον *Mign* πτωχευούσῃ] πτωχευούσῃ τῇ I 144 ὁμοιούμενον] ὁμοούσιον N 145 παρεξετάσθη ß G P R^{2} X 146 ὑπεισελθόντα R^{2mg} : *om.* G H P R^{ac} W X ἐν *om.* M W 147 ἶσον O X *Mign* 148 καὶ *om.* M N Q T W

[**12.10**] Thus, so long as one holds to the other, the communication of the true beauty extends proportionally through the whole series, beautifying by the superior that which comes next; but whenever a certain interruption of this beneficial connection occurs, or when, on the contrary the superior comes to follow the inferior, then the unseemliness of matter itself is exposed, when it is isolated from nature (for in itself matter is something formless and unwrought), and by its formlessness is also destroyed the beauty of the nature which was beautified by the intellect; and in this way the transmission of the ugliness of matter reaches back through the nature to the intellect itself, so that the image of God is no longer beheld in the figure of that which was moulded; for the intellect, setting the idea of the Good like a mirror behind its back, deflects the lustrous rays of the good, and receives into itself the shapelessness of matter.[60]

[**12.11**] And in this way the genesis of evil occurs, arising through the withdrawal of the good. Everything is good that is related to the First Good; but that which comes to be outside its relation and likeness to this, is certainly devoid of the Good. If, then, according to the argument being considered, that which is truly good is one, and the intellect, as having come to be in accordance with the image of the Good, also has the possibility to be good, while the nature, sustained by the intellect, is like an image of an image, then it is shown that our material part holds together, and is upheld, when it is administered by nature; but, on the other hand, it is dissolved and falls apart again when it is separated from that which upholds and sustains it, and is severed from its connection to the good. [**12.12**] Such a condition as this does not arise except when an overturning of nature to the opposite state occurs, in which desire does not incline towards the good but towards that which is in need of being beautified; for it is absolutely necessary that that being made like to matter, which is destitute of its own form, should be conformed to it in respect of its unseemliness and absence of beauty.

[**12.13**] But we have discussed these points by following a certain line of argument, since they were introduced by our contemplation of the point before us; for the subject of enquiry was whether the intellectual faculty has its seat in any of the parts within us or extends equally over them all. For those who enclose the

[60] Cf. Plotinus, *Enn.* 1.6.5.39–58; 1.8; 3.6.11.

ὑπολήψεως προφερόντων, τὸ μὴ εὐοδοῦσθαι τὴν διάνοιαν ἐπὶ τῶν παρὰ φύσιν διακειμένων τὰς μήνιγγας· ἀπέδειξεν ὁ λόγος, ὅτι κατὰ πᾶν μέρος τοῦ ἀνθρωπίνου συγκρίματος, καθ' ὃ πέφυκεν ἕκαστος ἐνεργεῖν, ἴσως ἡ τῆς ψυχῆς δύναμις ἀνενέργητος μένει, μὴ διαμένοντος ἐν τῇ φύσει τοῦ μέρους· καὶ διὰ τούτων ἐξ ἀκολουθίας τὸ προτεθὲν παρενέπεσε τῷ λόγῳ θεώρημα, δι' οὗ μανθάνομεν, ἐν τῷ ἀνθρωπίνῳ συγκρίματι ὑπὸ Θεοῦ μὲν διοικεῖσθαι τὸν νοῦν, ὑπ' ἐκείνου δὲ τὴν ὑλικὴν ἡμῶν ζωήν, ὅταν ἐν τῇ φύσει μένῃ· εἰ δὲ παρατραπείη τῆς φύσεως, καὶ τῆς κατὰ τὸν νοῦν ἐνεργείας ἀλλοτριοῦσθαι. [12.14] *Ἀλλ' ἐπανέλθωμεν πάλιν ὅθεν ἐξέβημεν, ὅτι* [D] *ἐπὶ τῶν μὴ παρατραπέντων ἐκ πάθους τινὸς τῆς φυσικῆς καταστάσεως, τὴν οἰκείαν δύναμιν ὁ νοῦς ἐνεργεῖ, καὶ ἔρρωται μὲν ἐπὶ τῶν συνεστώτων, ἀδυνατεῖ δὲ πάλιν ἐπὶ τῶν μὴ χωρούντων αὐτοῦ τὴν ἐνέργειαν· ἔστι γὰρ καὶ δι' ἑτέρων τὸ περὶ τούτων δόγμα πιστώσασθαι· καὶ εἰ μὴ βαρὺ τῇ ἀκοῇ τῶν προκεκμηκότων ἤδη τῷ λόγῳ, καὶ περὶ τούτων, ὡς ἂν οἷοί τε ὦμεν, δι' ὀλίγων διαληψόμεθα.*

Περὶ ὕπνου καὶ χάσμης καὶ ὀνείρων αἰτιολογία.

[13.1] *Ἡ ὑλικὴ καὶ ῥοώδης αὕτη τῶν σωμάτων ζωή, πάντοτε διὰ κινήσεως προϊοῦσα, ἐν τούτῳ ἔχει τοῦ εἶναι τὴν δύναμιν, ἐν τῷ μὴ στῆναί ποτε τῆς κινήσεως. Καθάπερ δέ τις ποταμὸς κατὰ τὴν ἰδίαν ῥέων ὁρμήν, πλήρη μὲν δείκνυσι τὴν κοιλότητα, δι' ἧς ἂν τύχῃ φερόμενος, οὐ μὴν ἐν τῷ αὐτῷ ὕδατι περὶ τὸν αὐτὸν ἀεὶ τόπον ὁρᾶται, ἀλλὰ τὸ μὲν ὑπέδραμεν αὐτοῦ, τὸ δὲ ἐπερρύη· οὕτω καὶ τὸ ὑλικὸν τῆς τῇδε ζωῆς διά τινος κινήσεως καὶ ῥοῆς τῇ συνεχείᾳ τῆς τῶν ἐναντίων διαδοχῆς ἀμείβεται, ὡς ἂν μηδέποτε στῆναι δύνασθαι τῆς μεταβολῆς, ἀλλὰ τῇ ἀδυναμίᾳ τοῦ ἀτρεμεῖν ἄπαυστον ἔχειν διὰ τῶν ὁμοίων ἐναμειβομένην τὴν κίνησιν· εἰ δέ ποτε κινούμενον παύσαιτο,* [B] *καὶ τοῦ εἶναι πάντως τὴν παῦλαν ἕξει.*

[13.2] *Οἷον διεδέξατο τὸ πλῆρες ἡ κένωσις, καὶ πάλιν ἀντεισῆλθεν ἡ πλήρωσις τῇ κενότητι· ὕπνος τὸ σύντονον τῆς ἐγρηγόρσεως ὑπεχάλασεν, εἶτα ἐγρήγορσις τὸ*

150 *διακειμένων*] *παρακειμένων* Q 151 *καθ' ὃ*] *καθὰ* Q : *καθὸ* H R S : *καθὼς* T *ἕκαστον* Æ B C G H M N O P Q S W X 162 *ἀνενέργητος*] efficientiam *Dion* : efficax *Eri* *καὶ* *om.* M *τούτων*] *τοῦτο* W *Mign* 153 *παρενέπεσε τὸ προτεθὲν* N *προτεθὲν*] *πρότερον* M *δι' οὗ*] *διὰ τοῦτο οὖν* I *ἐν* *om.* I W 155 *παρατραποίει* G P X *τὸν* *om.* H T 159–60 *δι' ἑτέρων τὸ περὶ τούτων δόγμα*] per aliam doctrinam quae de talibus *Eri* *περὶ τούτων*] *τοιοῦτο* T 160 *τῇ ἀκοῇ* *om.* C I K O Q *Eri* *τοῖς προκεκμηκόσιν* I : *τῷ προκεκμηκότι* Q *Eri* 160–1 *τοῦ λόγου* M 161 *τούτου* M Q *οἷον* G N P *δι' ὀλίγων ὡς ἂν οἷοί τε ὦμεν* A B C I K M O T *διαληψόμεθα δι' ὀλίγων* L *δι' ὀλίγων* *om.* Q *διαληψώμεθα* *Mign*

Cap. 14 Æ ß I K O N Q R T *Dion Eri om.* L

13.12–25 (*ὕπνος— ἄνεσις*): John (of Damascus) *Sacra Parallela* II^{1}2122/K cap. *Υ* 3, 8 (Thum, 1122.3–19)

1 *περὶ—αἰτιολογία*] quod corpus nostrum semper sit in motu *Λ* 4 *κατὰ* *om.* B 6 *τόπον ὁρᾶται ἀεὶ* N *ἐπέδραμεν* M *ἐπερρύη*] *ita* Æ ß B^{ac} G H M P^2 T *Forb* : *ὑπερρύη* I K N O Q : *ἐπιρρύη* L : *ἐπερρύει* B^{pc} P^{ac} W X : *ἐπιρρέει* D E R S : *ὑπερρέει* *Ald Mign* *οὕτως* Æ N 7 *ῥοῆς*] *ἐπιρροῆς* Q 8 *ἀμείβεται*] *ἐναμείβεται* Æ B E I K M N O Q T *ἂν* *om.* Æ B I K M N O Q *μεταβολῆς*] *καταβολῆς* ß 9 *ἀδυναμίᾳ*] *ita* Æ B I K M N O Q R *Forb* : *δυνάμει* W X *Ald Mign* : in potentia *Eri* *ἔχει* K : *ἔχοι* R^2 10 *παύσηται* T : *παύσοιτο* W *Ald Mign* *ἕξει*] *add.* hoc est omnino etiam cessabit *Eri* 11 *οἷον*] ueluti *Eri* *καὶ* *om.* N T *ἀντεισῆλθεν*] *ἐπεισῆλθεν* N 12 *κενότητι*] *κενώσει* Æ B E I K O Q *ἐγρηγορίσεως* W *εἶτα*] *εἶτα ἡ* Q

intellect in spatial parts of the body and who offer, for the support of this supposition of theirs, the fact that the mind does not have free rein in the case of those whose cerebral membranes are in an unnatural condition, our argument showed that in every part of the human compound, each having a natural activity, the power of the soul remains equally ineffective if that part does not continue in its natural condition; and thus our argument, by following its sequence, came upon the theory just mentioned, by which we learn that in the human compound the intellect is to be ordered by God, and that by it our material life is governed, provided that it remains in its natural state, but that if it is perverted from nature, it is also alienated from the activity of the intellect. **[12.14]** But let us return again to the point from which we started, that in those who are not perverted from their natural condition by some affection, the intellect exercises its own power and is vigorous in those who stand firm but, on the contrary, it is powerless to those who do not give space to its activity. We may confirm our doctrine about these things by yet other arguments, and, if it is not tedious to hear for those who are already wearied by our treatise, we shall discuss these matters also, so far as we are able, in a few words.

A rationale of sleep, yawning, and dreams.[61]

[13.1] The very life of our bodies, material and subject to flux, always advancing by way of movement, has the faculty of being in this, that it never rests from movement. Just as some river, flowing on by its own impulse, keeps the channel in which it runs filled, yet is not seen in the same water always at the same place, but part of it flows away while another part flows in,[62] so also the material element of our life here undergoes change in the continuity of the succession of opposites by way of a kind of movement and flux, so that it can never cease from change but, in the inability to keep still, has its ceaseless alternating movement through similar things, and if it should ever cease moving, it will assuredly have the cessation also of being.

[13.2] For instance, emptying succeeds fullness, and again in reverse after emptiness comes a filling-up; sleep relaxes the strain of wakefulness, then waking

[61] *Bodl. 238* (as Chap. 14): 'That our body is always in motion'.
[62] Cf. Heraclitus, A6 (DK; Plato, *Crat.* 402a8–10).

ἀνειμένον ἐτόνωσε· καὶ οὐδέτερον τούτων ἐν τῷ διηνεκεῖ συμμένει, ἀλλ' ὑποχωρεῖ ταῖς παρουσίαις ἀλλήλων ἀμφότερα· οὕτω τῆς φύσεως ἑαυτὴν ταῖς ὑπαλλαγαῖς ἀνακαινιζούσης, ὡς ἑκατέρων ἐν τῷ μέρει μεταλαγχάνουσαν, ἀδιασπάστως ἀπὸ τοῦ ἑτέρου μεταβαίνειν ἐπὶ τὸ ἕτερον. Τό τε γὰρ διαπαντὸς συντετάσθαι ταῖς ἐνεργείαις τὸ ζῷον, ῥῆξίν τινα καὶ διασπασμὸν τῶν ὑπερτεινομένων ποιεῖται μερῶν· ἥτε διηνεκὴς τοῦ σώματος ἄνεσις διάπτωσίν τινα τοῦ συνεστῶτος καὶ λύσιν ἐργάζεται· τὸ δὲ κατὰ καιρὸν μετρίως ἑκατέρων ἐπιθιγγάνειν, δύναμις πρὸς διαμονήν ἐστι τῆς φύσεως, [C] διὰ τῆς διηνεκοῦς πρὸς τὰ ἀντικείμενα μεταβάσεως ἐν ἑκατέροις ἑαυτὴν ἀπὸ τῶν ἑτέρων ἀναπαυούσης. Οὕτω τοίνυν τετονωμένον διὰ τῆς ἐγρηγόρσεως τὸ σῶμα λαβοῦσα, λύσιν ἐπινοεῖ διὰ τοῦ ὕπνου τῷ τόνῳ, τὰς αἰσθητικὰς δυνάμεις πρὸς καιρὸν ἐκ τῶν ἐνεργειῶν ἀναπαύσασα, οἷόν τινας ἵππους μετὰ τοὺς ἀγῶνας τῶν ἁρμάτων ἐκλύουσα.

[**13.3**] Ἀναγκαία δὲ τῇ συστάσει τοῦ σώματος ἡ εὔκαιρος ἄνεσις, ὡς ἂν ἀκωλύτως ἐφ' ἅπαν τὸ σῶμα διὰ τῶν ἐν αὐτῷ πόρων ἡ τροφὴ διαχέοιτο, μηδενὸς τόνου τῇ διόδῳ παρεμποδίζοντος· καθάπερ γὰρ ἐκ τῆς διαβρόχου γῆς, ὅταν ἐπιθάλψῃ θερμοτέραις ἀκτῖσιν ὁ ἥλιος, ἀτμοί τινες ὁμιχλώδεις ἀπὸ τοῦ βάθους ἀνέλκονται· ὅμοιόν τι γίνεται καὶ ἐν τῇ καθ' ἡμᾶς γῇ, τῆς τροφῆς ἔσωθεν ὑπὸ τῆς φυσικῆς θερμότητος ἀναζεούσης· [D] ἀνωφερεῖς δὲ ὄντες οἱ ἀτμοὶ κατὰ φύσιν καὶ ἀερώδεις καὶ πρὸς τὸ ὑπερκείμενον ἀναπνέοντες, ἐν τοῖς κατὰ τὴν κεφαλὴν γίνονται χωρίοις, οἷόν τις καπνὸς εἰς ἁρμονίαν τοίχου διαδυόμενος· εἶτα ἐντεῦθεν ἐπὶ τοὺς τῶν αἰσθητηρίων πόρους ἐξατμιζόμενοι διαφοροῦνται, δι' ὧν ἀργεῖ κατ' ἀνάγκην ἡ αἴσθησις, τῇ παρόδῳ τῶν ἀτμῶν ἐκείνων ὑπεξιοῦσα. Αἱ μὲν γὰρ ὄψεις τοῖς βλεφάροις ἐπιλαμβάνονται, οἷόν τινος μηχανικῆς μολυβδίνης, τοῦ τοιούτου λέγω βάρους, τοῖς ὀφθαλμοῖς ἐπιχαλώσης τὸ βλέφαρον· παχυνθεῖσα δὲ τοῖς αὐτοῖς τούτοις ἀτμοῖς ἡ ἀκοή, καθάπερ θύρας τινὸς τοῖς ἀκουστικοῖς μορίοις ἐπιτεθείσης, ἡσυχίαν ἀπὸ τῆς κατὰ φύσιν ἐνεργείας ἄγει· καὶ τὸ τοιοῦτον πάθος ὕπνος ἐστὶν, ἀτρεμούσης

13 *οὐδ' ἕτερον* G H P : *οὔθ' ἕτερον* K O Q : *οὐθέτερον* Æ B I M N R *SP*   *συμμένει*] *συμβαίνει* H K M P R   *ὑποχωροῦσιν* B   14 *ἀλλήλων ταῖς παρουσίαις* B   *ἀλλήλων*] *ἀλλήλοις* I   *ἀμφότερα ἀλλήλων* Æ K N O T   *οὕτω*] *οὗ* O   *ταῖς ὑπαλλαγαῖς om.* Q   15 *τῷ om.* M Q   *ἀδιαπαύστως* D L : *ἀπαύστως* M N Q R T W : *ἀσπάστως* (uel *ἀσπασίως, ἀσπαστῶς*) *SP*   16 *τό τε*] *τοῦ τε* H P W X : *τού τε* G   *συντετᾶσθαι* ß N O P R W   17 *διασπασμὸν*] *διαμερισμὸν* Q   *τῶν om.* W   18–19 *διάπτωσίν τινα τοῦ συνεστῶτος καὶ λύσιν*] casum quendam atque solutionem consistens *Eri*   *καὶ λύσιν τοῦ συνεστῶτος* M N   19 *λῦσιν* L : *διάλυσιν* M   *μετρίως*] mensurate *Eri*   *ἑκατέρων*] *ἑκατέρωθεν* D (*transp. post ἐπιθιγγάνειν*) E S W : *om. SP*   *ἐπιθιγγάνειν*] *ἐπιτυγχάνειν* *Mign*   21 *ἑτέρων*] *ἑκατέρων* N   21–2 *διὰ τῆς ἐγρηγόρσεως τετονωμένον* N   *τετονωμένον—σῶμα*] uegetatum corpus per uigilias natura *Eri*   22 *λῦσιν* L M   *ἐπινοεῖ*] *ἐμποιεῖ* *Mign*   *τοῦ τόνου* B   23 *ἐκ*] *διὰ* R   *ἀναπαύουσα* D E G H L P S   *ἵππους*] *πόλους* Q : *πώλους SP* : pullos *Eri*   24 *ἁρμάτων*] *ἀλμάτων* R : *ἁμάτων* N   *ἐκλύσασα* *Ald Mign*   25 *σώματος*] *σώματος καὶ* M   26 *τόνου*] *πόρου* W   26–7 *τῇ διόδῳ om.* M   27 *παρεμποδίζοντος*] *ita* W *Ald Mign Forb* : *παραποδίζοντος* Æ[ac] B D E G[pc] H K N O P Q S X   *γῆς διαβρόχου* N   *ἐπιθάλψῃ*] *ita* Æ B E G H I K M O P X *Forb* : *ἐπιθάλπῃ* Q : *ἐπιλάμψῃ* W *Ald Mign*   28 *ἀνέλκονται* P : *ἐξέλκονται* Æ B I K M N O Q R[ac] T   29 *τι om.* Q   *τροφῆς ἔσωθεν ὑπὸ τῆς om.* O   30 *δὲ*] *τε* Q   *κατὰ φύσιν om.* L   *καὶ*] *τε* T   32 *τοίχου*] *τύχου* O W   *διαδυόμενος*] *δυαλυόμενος* M N T : solutus *Eri*   33 *διαφυροῦνται* *Ald*   *κατὰ* Æ L M R   34 *παρόδῳ*] *παραδόξῳ* M   *γὰρ om.* B   35 *μηχανικῆς*] B D E G H I M N O P Q S T W X *Forb* : *μηχανῆς* *Mign*   *μολυβδένης* Q : *μολιβδίνης* Æ[2] ß H I M N P[2] R X : *μολυβδείνης* G P[ac] : *μολυβδαίνης* W   *τοῦ om.* D   *λέγω om.* Q   36 *βάρους λέγω* N T   *τοῖς ὀφθαλμοῖς om.* D   *τούτοις om.* N T   37 *ἀτμοῖς τούτοις* K O   *ἐπιτεθείσης*] *ἀποτεθείσης* B : *ἐναποτεθείης* ß   38 *κατὰ*] *κατὰ τὴν* N   *ἄγει*] *εἰσάγει* Q   *τοιοῦτο* Æ L

braces up what had become relaxed; and neither of these remains continually, but both give way, each at the other's coming; thus by their interchange nature renews herself by partaking of each in turn, passing uninterruptedly from one to the other. For the living creature to be always exerting itself in its activities produces a certain rupture and tearing of its overstrained parts, while continual relaxing of the body effects a certain failure and loosening of its constitution; but to be in touch with each of these at the proper time in a moderate degree is a staying power of nature, by the continual transference to the opposite state giving herself in each of them rest from the other. Thus, finding the body strained through wakefulness, she devises relaxation for the strain by means of sleep, giving to the faculties of sense-perception rest from their activities at the appropriate time, loosening them like horses from the chariots after the race.

[**13.3**] Rest at proper times is necessary for the constitution of the body, that the nourishment may be dispersed unhindered to the whole body through the passages in it, without any strain to hinder its progress. Just as from the sodden earth, when the sun heats it up with its warm rays, certain misty vapours are drawn up from its depths, so also a similar thing happens in the earth that is us, when the nourishment within is heated up by natural warmth, and the vapours, being naturally upwards-borne and air-like and aspiring to what is above, come to be in the regions of the head, like smoke penetrating the joints of a wall; then, from there they are dispersed, being exhaled to the pores of the organs of sense-perception, and by them the senses are necessarily rendered inactive, giving way to the passing of these vapours. For the eyes are pressed upon by the eyelids when some, as it were, leaden contrivance (I mean a weight of this kind) lets down the eyelid upon the eyes; and the hearing, dulled by these same vapours, as some kind of door being placed upon the acoustic organs, brings peace from its natural activities; and such an affection is sleep, with sense-perception being at rest in the

ἐν τῷ σώματι τῆς αἰσθήσεως, [167] *καὶ παντάπασιν ἐκ τῆς κατὰ φύσιν κινήσεως ἀπρακτούσης, ὡς ἂν εὐπόρευτοι γένωνται τῆς τροφῆς αἱ ἀναδόσεις, δι' ἑκάστου τῶν πόρων τοῖς ἀτμοῖς συνδιεξιοῦσαι.*

[13.4] *Καὶ τούτου χάριν εἰ στενοχωροῖτο μὲν ὑπὸ τῆς ἔνδοθεν ἀναθυμιάσεως ἡ περὶ τὰ αἰσθητήρια διασκευή, κωλύοιτο δὲ κατά τινα χρείαν ὁ ὕπνος· πλῆρες γενόμενον τῶν ἀτμῶν τὸ νευρῶδες, αὐτὸ ὑφ' ἑαυτοῦ φυσικῶς διατείνεται, ὡς διὰ τῆς ἐκτάσεως τὸ παχυνθὲν ὑπὸ τῶν ἀτμῶν μέρος ἐκλεπτυνθῆναι· οἷόν τι ποιοῦσιν οἱ διὰ τῆς σφοδροτέρας στρεβλώσεως τὸ ὕδωρ τῶν ἱματίων ἐκθλίβοντες. Καὶ ἐπειδὴ κυκλοτερῆ τὰ περὶ τὸν φάρυγγα μέρη, πλεονάζει δὲ τὸ νευρῶδες ἐν τούτοις· ὅταν καὶ ἀπὸ τούτων ἐξωσθῆναι δέῃ τὴν τῶν ἀτμῶν παχυμέρειαν, ἐπειδὴ ἀμήχανόν ἐστι δι' εὐθείας ἀποκριθῆναι τὸ κυκλοειδὲς μέρος, εἰ μὴ κατὰ τὸ περιφερὲς σχῆμα διαταθείη· τούτου χάριν ἀποληφθέντος ἐν τῇ χάσμῃ τοῦ πνεύματος, ὅ τε ὁ ἀνθερεὼν ἐπὶ τὸ κάτω τοῖς γαργαρεῶσιν ὑποκοιλαίνεται, καὶ* [B] *τῶν ἐντὸς πάντων εἰς κύκλου σχῆμα διαταθέντων, ἡ λιγνυώδης ἐκείνη παχύτης ἡ ἐναπειλημμένη τοῖς μέρεσι συνδιαπνεῖται τῇ διεξόδῳ τοῦ πνεύματος. Πολλάκις δὲ, καὶ μετὰ τὸν ὕπνον οἶδε τὸ τοιοῦτον συμβαίνειν, ὅταν τι τῶν ἀτμῶν ἐκείνων περιλειφθείη τοῖς τόποις ἄπεπτόν τε καὶ ἀδιάπνευστον.*

[13.5] *Ἐκ τούτων τοίνυν ὁ ἀνθρώπινος νοῦς δείκνυσιν ἐναργῶς, ὅτι τῆς φύσεως ἔχεται, συνεστώσης μὲν καὶ ἐγρηγορυίας, καὶ αὐτὸς συνεργῶν καὶ κινούμενος· παρεθείσης δὲ τῷ ὕπνῳ, μένων ἀκίνητος·—εἰ μή τις ἄρα τὴν ὀνειρώδη φαντασίαν νοῦ κίνησιν ὑπολάβοι κατὰ τὸν ὕπνον ἐνεργουμένην· ἡμεῖς δέ φαμεν, μόνην δεῖν τὴν ἔμφρονά τε καὶ συνεστῶσαν τῆς διανοίας ἐνέργειαν ἐπὶ τὸν νοῦν ἀναφέρειν· τὰς δὲ κατὰ τὸν ὕπνον φαντασιώδεις* [C] *φλυαρίας, ἰνδάλματά τινα τῆς κατὰ τὸν νοῦν ἐνεργείας οἰόμεθα τῷ ἀλογωτέρῳ τῆς ψυχῆς εἴδει κατὰ τὸ συμβὰν διαπλάττεσθαι· τῶν γὰρ αἰσθήσεων τὴν ψυχὴν ἀπολυθεῖσαν διὰ τοῦ ὕπνου, καὶ τῶν κατὰ τὸν νοῦν ἐνεργειῶν ἐκτὸς εἶναι κατ' ἀνάγκην συμβαίνει· διὰ γὰρ τούτων πρὸς τὸν ἄνθρωπον ἡ τοῦ νοῦ συνανάκρασις γίνεται· τῶν οὖν αἰσθήσεων παυσαμένων, ἀργεῖν ἀνάγκη καὶ*

40 *εὐπόρευτοι*] *εὔποροί τε* N *γίνωνται* Æ B O : *γένοιντο* M N Q R T 41 *συνδιεξιοῦσαι*] *ita* Æ B I M N O Q T *Forb Ald* : *συνδιεξιοῦται* K : *συνεξιοῦσαι* D E G H P R S X : *συνεξιοῦσα* L : *συνδιεξιούσης* *Mign* 42 *εἰ στενοχωροῖτο*] sciendi sunt loci *Eri* *στενοχωρεῖτο* K M[ac] 43 *κωλύοιτο*] *λύοιτο* I *πλήρης* T 44 *φυσικῶς*] *ἐφεστηκὸς* B *ἐκστάσεως* M : *ἐνστάσεως* T 45 *ἐκπλατυνθῆναι* N 46 *σφοδροτέρας*] *λεπτοτέρας* M 47 *τὸν*] *τὴν* L Q 48 *δέῃ*] *δέοι* R W *Ald Mign* *τὴν*] *τὴν ἀπὸ* D E 49 *ἀποκριθῆναι*] *ita* A B C G H I K N O P T X *Forb* : *ἀποτείνεσθαι* E : *ἀποτεῖναι* W *Ald Mign* *μέρος*] *μέρος καὶ ἀποτεῖναι* N 50 *διατεθείη* H M N R T[ac] *ἀπολειφθέντος* B E L R[ac] 50–1 *ὅ τε—ὑποκοιλαίνεται*] quando infra mentum (in eo enim subsistit) subcollocatur *Eri* 50 *ὅ τε*] *ita codd. Forb* : *ὅτε Ald Mign* *ὁ om.* O W 51 *γαργαλεῶσιν* G H P[ac] W *ἐπικοιλαίνεται* N T 52 *πάντως* T *διατεθέντων* B H I M N O Q T *ἰλυγνιώδης* R : *ἀτμώδης* M *ἢ*[2] *om.* T 53 *διεξόδῳ*] *ἐξόδῳ* B W 54 *τοιοῦτο* Æ H N Q W 55 *περιληφθείη* Æ[ac] B K P[2] : *περιληφθῇ* M Q : *περιφθείη* I *ἄπεμπτον* H *Ald Mign* 56 *τούτου* M *τοίνυν*] *οὖν* I 57 *ἐγρηγορουμένης* R *συνεργῶν*] *ἐνεργῶν* Æ B E I K M N O Q R T W 58 *παρεθείσης—ἀκίνητος om.* W *ἆρα* G N P Q X 59 *ὑπολάβῃ* L *δεῖ* K O : *om.* N 60 *εὔφρονα* I L 61 *φαντασιώδεις φλυαρίας*] phantasias…in superfluitates *Eri* 62 *ἐνεργείας*] *ἐνεργείας ἡμῶν* R *συμβαῖνον* R *διαπλάσσεσθαι* N R : *διαπλάττεσσθαι* *Forb* 63 *ἀπολυθεῖσαν*] *διαλυθεῖσαν* T : *διαλειπουσῶν* N *τὸν om.* O *Ald Mign* 64 *τούτων*] *τούτο* I 65 *συνανάκρασις*] *σύγκρασις* N *οὖν*] *δ' οὖν* H : *γοῦν* N

body and altogether ceasing from its natural movement, so that the digestive processes of nourishment may have free course for the passing of the vapours through each of the pores.

[13.4] And for this reason if the apparatus of the organs of sense-perception are constricted by the rising vapours within and sleep hindered by some occupation, the nervous system, becoming filled with the vapours, is naturally and spontaneously extended so that the part thickened by the vapours is rarefied by the extension, like those do who squeeze water out of clothes by violent wringing. And, since the parts around the pharynx are circular, and the nervous tissue abounds there, when there is need for the thickness of the vapours to be expelled from those parts, since it is impossible for the circular part to be separated directly, but only by being distended in the outline of the circumference, for this reason, by checking the breath in a yawn, which, with the chin moved downwards, forms a hollow to the uvula, and all the interior parts being stretched into the figure of a circle, that smoky thickness which had been detained in the neighbouring parts is emitted together with the passage of the breath. Frequently the like may happen even after sleep, when anything of those vapours remains in the regions spoken of undigested and unexhaled.

[13.5] Hence, then, the human intellect clearly shows its natural condition, itself cooperating and moving [with nature] when braced and awake, yet remaining unmoved when abandoned to sleep, unless anyone supposes that the phantasy of dreams is a movement of the intellect exercised in sleep. We would say that only the conscious and sound activity of the mind should be referred to the intellect; as to the fantastic nonsense that occurs in sleep, we suppose that some appearances of the activity of the intellect are accidentally fashioned by the less rational form of the soul; for the soul, being released by sleep from the senses, also by necessity comes to be outside the activities of the intellect, as it is through the senses that the mixing together of the intellect with the human being takes place. Therefore, when

τὴν διάνοιαν· τεκμήριον δὲ τὸ καὶ ἐν ἀτόποις τε καὶ ἐν ἀμηχάνοις πολλάκις δοκεῖν εἶναι τὸν φανταζόμενον· ὅπερ οὐκ ἂν ἐγένετο, λογισμῷ καὶ διανοίᾳ τῆς ψυχῆς τηνικαῦτα διοικουμένης. [13.6] *Ἀλλά μοι δοκεῖ ταῖς προτιμοτέραις τῶν δυνάμεων τῆς ψυχῆς ἠρεμούσης (φημὶ δὲ ταῖς κατὰ τὸν νοῦν καὶ τὴν αἴσθησιν ἐνεργείαις·) μόνον τὸ θρεπτικὸν αὐτῆς μέρος ἐνεργὸν κατὰ τὸν ὕπνον εἶναι· ἐν δὲ τούτῳ τῶν* [D] *καθ' ὕπαρ γινομένων εἴδωλά τινα καὶ ἀπηχήματα τῶν τε κατ' αἴσθησιν καὶ τῶν κατὰ διάνοιαν ἐνεργουμένων, ἅπερ αὐτῇ διὰ τοῦ μνημονικοῦ τῆς ψυχῆς εἴδους ἐνετυπώθη, ταῦτα καθὼς ἔτυχεν ἀναζωγραφεῖσθαι, ἀπηχήματός τινος μνημονικοῦ τῷ τοιούτῳ εἴδει τῆς ψυχῆς παραμείναντος.*

[13.7] *Ἐν τούτοις οὖν φαντασιοῦται ὁ ἄνθρωπος, οὐχ εἱρμῷ τινι πρὸς τὴν τῶν φαινομένων ὁμιλίαν ἀγόμενος, ἀλλὰ πεφυρμέναις τισὶ καὶ ἀνακολούθοις ἀπάταις περιπλανώμενος. Καθάπερ δὲ κατὰ τὰς σωματικὰς ἐνεργείας, ἑκάστου* [169] *τῶν μερῶν ἰδιαζόντως τι κατὰ τὴν ἐγκειμένην αὐτῷ φυσικῶς δύναμιν ἐνεργοῦντος, γίνεταί τις καὶ τοῦ ἠρεμοῦντος μέλους πρὸς τὸ κινούμενον συνδιάθεσις· ἀναλόγως καὶ ἐπὶ τῆς ψυχῆς, κἂν τὸ μὲν αὐτῆς ἠρεμοῦν, τὸ δὲ κινούμενον τύχῃ, τὸ ὅλον τῷ μέρει συνδιατίθεται· οὐδὲ γὰρ ἐνδέχεται συνδιασπασθῆναι πάντη τὴν κατὰ φύσιν ἑνότητα, κρατούσης ἐν μέρει τινὸς τῶν κατ' αὐτὴν δυνάμεων διὰ τῆς ἐνεργείας. Ἀλλ' ὥσπερ ἐγρηγορότων τε καὶ σπουδαζόντων ἐπικρατεῖ μὲν ὁ νοῦς, ὑπηρετεῖ δὲ ἡ αἴσθησις, οὐκ ἀπολείπεται δὲ τούτων ἡ διοικητικὴ τοῦ σώματος δύναμις· (ὁ μὲν γὰρ νοῦς πορίζει τὴν τροφὴν τῇ χρείᾳ, ἡ δὲ αἴσθησις τὸ πορισθὲν ὑπεδέξατο, ἡ δὲ θρεπτικὴ τοῦ σώματος δύναμις ἑαυτῇ τὸ δοθὲν προσῳκείωσεν·) οὕτω καὶ κατὰ τὸν ὕπνον ἀντιμεθίσταταί πως ἐν ἡμῖν ἡ* [B] *τῶν δυνάμεων τούτων ἡγεμονία, καὶ κρατοῦντος τοῦ ἀλογωτέρου, παύεται μὲν ἡ τῶν ἑτέρων ἐνέργεια, οὐ μὴν παντελῶς ἀποσβέννυται· ἐπειγομένης δὲ τηνικαῦτα διὰ τοῦ ὕπνου πρὸς τὴν πέψιν τῆς θρεπτικῆς δυνάμεως, καὶ πᾶσαν τὴν φύσιν πρὸς ἑαυτὴν ἀσχολούσης, οὔτε παντελῶς διασπᾶται ταύτης ἡ κατ' αἴσθησιν δύναμις (οὐ γὰρ ἐνδέχεται τὸ ἅπαξ συμπεφυκὸς διατέμνεσθαι) οὔτε ἀναλάμπειν αὐτῆς ἡ ἐνέργεια δύναται, τῇ τῶν*

66 *καί*[1] *om.* K O W *ἀτόποις*] *τόποις* E *Ald* : *ἀπόροις* M *τε om. Mign* *ἐν om.* Æ B D I K L Q W *Ald* *δοκεῖν*] *ἀργὸν* M 67 *τὸν*] *τὸ* L M T *ἐγίνετο* Æ B E I K M N O R : *ἐγίγνετο* T 68 *ἀλλὰ*] *καὶ* R 69 *ἠρεμούσης* R *δὲ*] *δὴ* B H R 71 *γινομένων*] *ita* Æ B D E G H O P R S W X *Forb* : *γινομένῳ* Q : *γενομένων Ald Mign* *ἀπηχήματα*] *ἀπηχήματα συμβαίνειν* N *τε om.* K 72 *αὐτῇ*] *ita* Æ B D E G I K L M N P S T W X *Dion Forb* : *αὐτὴ* H O Q R *Ald Eri* : *αὐτῷ Mign* *μνημονικοῦ*] *ita* Æ ß G H I K M N O P Q W X *Ald Forb* : *μνημονευτικοῦ Mign* *τῆς ψυχῆς om.* W 73 *ταῦτα*] *ταῦτα μὴ* N *ἐτύγχανε ζωγραφεῖσθαι* D E G H L N P R S X *μνημονικοῦ*] *μνημονικοῦ τῆς ψυχῆς* G H P X 74 *τῆς ψυχῆς τῷ τοιούτῳ εἴδει* E P *τῆς ψυχῆς εἴδει* B 75 *οὖν φαντασιοῦται*] coimaginatur *Eri* 76 *πεφορημέναις* G H M P^{ac} W^{ac} X *Ald* : *πεφωρημέναις* W^{pc} 77 *περιπλανώμενος*] *ἐπιπλανώμενος* Æ B I K M N O T *δὲ*] *γὰρ* D E G H L M P X *ἑκάστου om. Mign* 79 *ἠρεμοῦντος*] *ita* Æ H K L M N O P S W X *Forb Mign* : *ἠρεμοῦντος* R *Ald* *μέλους*] *μέρους* R W *Dion Eri Ald Mign* *κεινούμενον* W *συνδιάθεσις*] *διάθεσις* Æ H 80 *ψυχῆς*] *γῆς* K *ἠρεμοῦν*] *ita* Æ H L M N O S W X *Forb Mign* : *ἠρεμοῦντο* K : *ἠρεμοῦν Ald* 81 *συνδιατίθεται*] coaffectari consequitur *Eri* *διασπασθῆναι* Æ B I K M N O W *πάντη om.* B 83 *τε*] *μὲν* L 84 *διοικητὴ* N 86 *θρεπτικὴ*] *ποριστικὴ* M *προσοικείωσεν* K N O P^{ac} W X *οὕτως* Æ N W *καὶ om.* M N R^{ac} 87 *ἀντιμεθίσταται*] participatur *Eri* *ἐν om.* T 89 *ἐπιγινομένης* H : *ἐπιγενομένης* M *πέμψιν* K 90 *θρεπτικῆς*] threptica (id est nutritiua) *Eri* 91 *οὐ*] *οὐδὲ* H M 92 *συμπεφυκὸς*] *ἐμπεφυκὸς* P *ἡ αὐτῆς Mign*

the senses are at rest, the mind also must be inactive; and a proof of this is that the dreamer often seems to be in absurd and impossible situations, which would not happen if the soul were regulated by the calculating faculty and mind. [**13.6**] But it seems to me that when the soul is resting with respect to its more excellent faculties (I mean the activities of the intellect and sense-perception), only the nutritive part of it is active during sleep, and in it some shadows and echoes of things which happened while awake (of activities of both sense-perception and mind) are impressed upon it by the aspect of the soul concerned with memory; these are pictured haphazardly, as some echo of a memory still lingering in this aspect of the soul.

[**13.7**] With these, then, the human being is beguiled, not led to acquaintance with things that appear by any train of thought, but wandering among confused and inconsequential delusions. But just as in bodily activities, while each of the parts individually acts in some particular way according to the faculty which naturally resides in it, there also arises in the limb at rest a shared state with that which is in motion, similarly in the case of the soul, even if one part is at rest and another in motion, the whole is co-affected with the part; for it is not possible that the natural unity should in any way be severed, even though one of the faculties in it holds sway in virtue of its activity. But just as, when human beings are awake and busy, the intellect prevails, and sense-perception serves it, yet the faculty which regulates the body is not dissociated from them (for the intellect furnishes the food for its wants, sense-perception receives what is furnished, and the nutritive faculty of the body appropriates to itself what is given to it), so also in sleep the governing of these faculties is in some way reversed in us, and while the less rational aspect prevails, the activity of the others ceases, yet it is not completely extinguished; but while the nutritive faculty is busied with digestion during sleep, and occupies all our nature with itself, the faculty of sense-perception is neither completely severed from it (for that which has once been naturally joined together cannot be torn asunder), nor can its activity be revived, as it is hindered by the inactivity of the organs of sense-perception during sleep; and, by the same

αἰσθητηρίων ἀργίᾳ κατὰ τὸν ὕπνον ἐμπεδηθεῖσα· κατὰ τὸν αὐτὸν δὲ λόγον καὶ τοῦ νοῦ πρὸς τὸ αἰσθητικὸν εἶδος τῆς ψυχῆς οἰκειουμένου, ἀκόλουθον ἂν εἴη καὶ κινουμένου τούτου, συγκινεῖσθαι λέγειν αὐτὸν, καὶ ἠρεμοῦντι συγκαταπαύεσθαι.

[13.8] *Οἷον δέ τι περὶ τὸ πῦρ γίνεσθαι πέφυκεν, ὅταν μὲν ὑποκρυφθῇ τοῖς ἀχύροις ἁπανταχόθεν,* [C] *μηδεμιᾶς ἀναπνοῆς ἀναρριπιζούσης τὴν φλόγα, οὔτε τὰ προσπαρακείμενα νέμεται οὔτε παντελῶς κατασβέννυται, ἀλλ' ἀντὶ φλογὸς ἀτμός τις διὰ τῶν ἀχύρων ἐπὶ τὸν ἀέρα διέξεισιν· εἰ δέ τινος λάβοιτο διαπνοῆς, φλόγα τὸν καπνὸν ἀπεργάζεται· τὸν αὐτὸν τρόπον καὶ ὁ νοῦς τῇ ἀπραξίᾳ τῶν αἰσθήσεων κατὰ τὸν ὕπνον συγκαλυφθεὶς, οὔτε ἐκλάμπειν δι' αὐτῶν δυνατῶς ἔχει οὔτε μὴν παντελῶς κατασβέννυται, ἀλλ' οἷον καπνοειδῶς κινεῖται, τὸ μέν τι ἐνεργῶν, τὸ δὲ οὐ δυνάμενος.*

[13.9] *Καὶ ὥσπερ τις μουσικὸς κεχαλασμέναις ταῖς χορδαῖς τῆς λύρας ἐμβαλὼν τὸ πλῆκτρον, οὐ κατὰ ῥυθμὸν προάγει τὸ μέλος (οὐ γὰρ ἂν τὸ μὴ συντεταμένον ἠχήσειεν) ἀλλ' ἡ μὲν χεὶρ τεχνικῶς πολλάκις κινεῖται, πρὸς τὴν τοπικὴν θέσιν* [D] *τῶν τόνων τὸ πλῆκτρον ἄγουσα, τὸ δὲ ἠχοῦν οὐκ ἔστιν, εἰ μὴ ὅσον ἄσημόν τινα καὶ ἀσύντακτον ἐν τῇ κινήσει τῶν χορδῶν ὑπηχεῖ τὸν βόμβον· οὕτω διὰ τοῦ ὕπνου τῆς ὀργανικῆς τῶν αἰσθητηρίων κατασκευῆς χαλασθείσης, ἢ καθόλου ἠρεμεῖ ὁ τεχνίτης, εἴπερ τελείαν λύσιν ἐκ πληθώρας τινὸς καὶ βάρους πάθοι τὸ ὄργανον· ἢ ἀτόνως τε καὶ ἀμυδρῶς ἐνεργήσει, οὐχ ὑποδεχομένου τοῦ αἰσθητικοῦ ὀργάνου δι' ἀκριβείας τὴν τέχνην.*

[13.10] *Διὰ τοῦτο ἥ τε μνήμη συγκεχυμένη καὶ ἡ πρόγνωσις προκαλύμμασί τισιν ἀμφιβόλοις ἐπιδιστάζουσα, ἐν εἰδώλοις τῶν καθ' ὕπαρ σπουδαζομένων φαντασιοῦται, καί τι τῶν ἐκβαινόντων πολλάκις ἐμήνυσε· τῷ γὰρ λεπτῷ τῆς φύσεως ἔχει τι πλέον παρὰ τὴν σωματικὴν παχυμέρειαν εἰς τὸ καθορᾶν τι τῶν ὄντων δύνασθαι· οὐ μὴν δι' εὐθείας τινὸς δύναται* [172] *διασαφεῖν τὸ λεγόμενον, ὡς τηλαυγῆ τε καὶ πρόδηλον εἶναι τὴν τῶν προκειμένων διδασκαλίαν, ἀλλὰ λοξὴ καὶ ἀμφίβολος τοῦ μέλλοντος ἡ δήλωσις γίνεται, ὅπερ αἴνιγμα λέγουσιν οἱ τὰ τοιαῦτα ὑποκρινόμενοι.*

93 *ἐμπεδηθείσης* K *δὲ*] *δὴ* N R : *om.* D G H L P S X 94 *τῆς ψυχῆς εἶδος* Æ B E M N Q R T *τῆς ψυχῆς om.* D I K L O S *οἰκειωμένου* K O : *ὠκειωμένου* Æ B I : *ἐνοικειουμένου* T 95 *ἠρεμοῦντι*] *ita* Æ D E G H K L M O P S T W X *Forb* : *ἠρεμοῦντι* I R : *ἠρεμοῦντος Ald Mign* 96 *γενέσθαι* G P X *πέφυκεν om.* ß *μὲν om.* A *ὑπὸκρυφῇ* K O : *ὑποκρυβῇ* L 97 *πανταχόθεν* G H L M N P X *ἀναπνοῆς*] *διαπνοῆς* Q : *πνοῆς* B R 97–8 *τὰ προσπαρακείμενα*] *τὰ πρὸς παρακείμενα* L : *πρὸς τὰ παρακείμενα* Æ B E K M O : *τὰ παρακείμενα* I T 98 *ἀλλὰ* M *ἀτμός*] *καπνὸς* N Q : fumus *Dion Eri* 99 *τις om.* T *τὸν ἀέρα*] *τῶν ἀχύρων* B *δέ τινος*] *δέ τι* T : *δ' ἔτι* T^{pc} *διαπνοῆς*] *ἀναπνοῆς* L 101 *δι' αὐτῶν*] *διαυγῶς* G H P S^{mg} W X : *om.* B *δυνατὸς* Q 102 *κατασβέννυται*] *ἀποσβέννυται* K L 103 *ταῖς om.* D G H L P S X *ἐμβάλλων* Æ Q 104 *οὐ κατὰ ῥυθμὸν*] *οὐκ εὔρυθμον* R : *οὐ κατ' ἀριθμὸν Ald* *ἂν om.* T *μὴ om.* I *μὴ συντεταμένον*] *συγκεχαυνωμένον* T : *μὴ συντεταμένον ἢ τὸ κεχαυνωμένον* A B C I K O 105 *ἠχήσειεν· ἀλλ' ἡ μὲν χεὶρ*] *ἠχήσει· ἐν ἄλλῃ μὲν χειρὶ* T *πολλάκις τεχνικῶς* N 106 *ἄσημον*] confusus *Dion* : ignobilem *Eri* *τινά ἄσημον* X 107 *ὑπηχεῖν* A B C I K M N O R^{ac} T : *ὑφηχεῖν* Q : *ἀπηχεῖ* E : subsonare *Eri* 108 *κατασκευῆς om.* D 109 *λύσιν* X^{mg2} *πληθώρας*] *πληθούρας* G P Q W X : umiditate *Eri* 110 *οὐκ ἐπιδεχομένου* K O 113 *ἐπιδιστάζουσα*] *ita* A B C I K M N O Q R (*νυ sup. l.*) T *Wils* : *ἐπινυστάζουσα* F (*δι sup. l.*) W X *Ald Mign Forb* : obruta *Dion* : dubitans *Eri* 114 *ἐμβαινόντων* I *ἐμήνυσε*] *ἐμνημόνευσεν* N : *ἐμήνοισεν* W 115 *καθορᾷν Mign* 116 *ὡς*] *ὥστε* Q 117 *προκειμένων*] *λεγομένων* M^{ac} R W 118 *ἡ δήλωσις τοῦ μέλλοντος* T

reasoning, the intellect also being appropriated to the sense-perceptive form of the soul, it would follow that we should say that the intellect is moved with the latter when it is moving and rests with it when it is at rest.

[**13.8**] As naturally happens with fire when it is covered all over with chaff and no breath fans the flame, it neither consumes what lies beside it, nor is entirely quenched, but instead of flame it rises to the air through the chaff as vapour; yet if it should obtain any breath of air, it turns the smoke to flame. In the same way, the intellect, when hidden by the inactivity of the senses during sleep, is neither able to shine out through them nor is it completely extinguished, but has, as it were, a smouldering movement, operating in some respects, yet unable in others.

[**13.9**] And just as a musician plucking the slackened strings of a lyre with the plectrum produces no rhythmic melody (for that which is not stretched will not sound), and although his hand frequently moves skilfully, bringing the plectrum to the position set for the notes, yet there is no sound, except in so far as there is a sort of indistinct and irregular hum from the movement of the strings, so also in sleep, with the instrumental structures of the organs of sense-perception being relaxed, the artist is either entirely at rest, if the instrument is affected by a complete relaxation through a certain satiety or heaviness, or will act slackly or faintly, if the instrument of sense-perception does not accurately receive its art.

[**13.10**] For this reason memory is confused, and foreknowledge, though rendered doubtful by certain ambiguous veils, is represented in images of our waking pursuits, and often discloses something of what is going to happen; for by its subtlety of nature [the intellect] has some advantage—to be able to see things—over corporeal density; but it is not able to make its meaning clear by direct methods so that the information regarding the matter in hand should be clear and evident, but its declaration of what is to come is indirect and ambiguous, what those who interpret such matters call an 'enigma'.

[13.11] *Οὕτως ὁ οἰνοχόος ἐκθλίβει τὴν βότρυν τῇ κύλικι τοῦ Φαραώ· οὕτω κανηφορεῖν ὁ σιτοποιὸς ἐφαντάσθη· ἐν οἷς καθ' ὕπαρ ἑκάτερος τὴν σπουδὴν εἶχεν, ἐν τούτοις εἶναι καὶ διὰ τῶν ὀνείρων οἰόμενος· τῶν γὰρ συνήθων αὐτοῖς ἐπιτηδευμάτων τὰ εἴδωλα τῷ προγνωστικῷ τῆς ψυχῆς ἐντυπωθέντα, παρέσχεν ἐπὶ καιροῦ τῶν ἐκβησομένων διὰ τῆς τοιαύτης τοῦ νοῦ προφητείας καταμαντεύσασθαι.*

[13.12] [B] *Εἰ δὲ Δανιὴλ καὶ Ἰωσὴφ καὶ οἱ κατ' ἐκείνους θείᾳ δυνάμει, μηδεμιᾶς αὐτοὺς ἐπιθολούσης αἰσθήσεως, τὴν τῶν μελλόντων γνῶσιν προεπαιδεύοντο, οὐδὲν τοῦτο πρὸς τὸν προκείμενον λόγον· οὐ γὰρ ἄν τις ταῦτα τῇ δυνάμει τῶν ἐνυπνίων λογίσαιτο, ἐπεὶ πάντως ἐκ τοῦ ἀκολούθου καὶ τὰς καθ' ὕπαρ γινομένας θεοφανείας, οὐκ ὀπτασίαν ἀλλὰ φύσεως ἀκολουθίαν κατὰ τὸ αὐτόματον ἐνεργουμένην οἰήσεται. Ὥσπερ τοίνυν πάντων ἀνθρώπων κατὰ τὸν ἴδιον νοῦν διοικουμένων, ὀλίγοι τινές εἰσιν οἱ τῆς θείας ὁμιλίας ἐκ τοῦ ἐμφανοῦς ἀξιούμενοι· οὕτω κοινῶς πᾶσι καὶ ὁμοτίμως τῆς ἐν ὕπνοις φαντασίας κατὰ φύσιν ἐγγινομένης, μετέχουσί τινες, οὐχὶ πάντες, θειοτέρας τινὸς διὰ τῶν ὀνείρων τῆς ἐμφανείας· τοῖς δ' ἄλλοις πᾶσι, κἂν γένηταί τις ἐξ ἐνυπνίων περί τι πρόγνωσις, κατὰ τὸν εἰρημένον* [C] *γίνεται τρόπον.*

[13.13] *Εἰ δὲ καὶ ὁ Αἰγύπτιος καὶ ὁ Ἀσσύριος τύραννος θεόθεν πρὸς τὴν τῶν μελλόντων ὡδηγοῦντο γνῶσιν, ἕτερόν ἐστι τὸ διὰ τούτων οἰκονομούμενον· φανερωθῆναι γὰρ ἔδει κεκρυμμένην τὴν τῶν ἁγίων σοφίαν, ὡς ἂν μὴ ἄχρηστος τῷ κοινῷ παραδράμῃ τὸν βίον. Πῶς γὰρ ἐγνώσθη τοιοῦτος ὢν Δανιήλ, μὴ τῶν ἐπαοιδῶν καὶ μάγων πρὸς τὴν εὕρεσιν τῆς φαντασίας ἀτονησάντων; πῶς δ' ἂν περιεσώθη τὸ Αἰγύπτιον, ἐν δεσμωτηρίῳ καθειργμένου τοῦ Ἰωσήφ, εἰ μὴ παρήγαγεν εἰς μέσον αὐτὸν ἡ τοῦ ἐνυπνίου κρίσις; οὐκοῦν ἄλλο τι ταῦτα καὶ οὐχὶ κατὰ τὰς κοινὰς φαντασίας λογίζεσθαι χρή.*

120 *ἐκθλίβει*] *ἐν θλίψει* B E : *ἐνθλίβει* Æ W *τὴν*] *τὸν* W X *τοῦ*] *τῷ* M 122 *καὶ* om. I *οἰόμενοι* B N Q O 123 *τὰ εἴδωλα* om. M *παρέχει* K : praestiterunt *Dion Eri* 125 *καταμαντεύσασθαι*] *μαντεύσασθαι* D G H L P S X : *καταμαντεύεσθαι* Æ 126 *εἰ*] *οἱ* B *καὶ οἱ κατ' ἐκείνους θείᾳ δυνάμει*] ipsa quae in illis erat diuina uirtus *Eri* *ἐκείνους*] *αὐτοὺς* M 127 *αὐτοὺς*] *αὐτοῖς* Æ ß E I K R O : *αὐταῖς* M *ἐπιθηλούσης* B : *ἐπιθλιβούσης* N 128 *τοῦτο*] *τούτων* B *οὐ*] *οὐδὲ* *Ald Mign* 129 *λογίσαιτο*] *καταλογίσαιτο* I *γιγνομένας* N : *γενομένας* K R 130 *οὐχ ὀπτασίαν* G O P W X : *οὐχ ὀπτασίας* N *ἐνεργουμένας* N *οἰήσεται*] *ποιήσεται* P 132 *οἱ τῆς θείας ὁμιλίας* om. B *ἐμφανοῦς*] *ἀφανοῦς* I K M O *οὕτως* W 133 *γιγνομένης* N : *γινομένης* T 134 *διά τινος τῶν ὀνείρων θειοτέρας* N *τῆς* om. D F G H L N P R S W X *ἐμφανείας*] *θεοφανείας* D F G H L P S W X : *φανερώσεως* N : *προγνώσεως* R *δ'*] *δὲ* Æ ß K M O Q 135 *ἐγγένηται* Æ E I K M O Q T : *ἐγγίνηται* N : *ἐπιγένηται* B *ἐξ ἐνυπνίων*] *ἐξυπνίων* W 137 *ὁδηγοῦντο* G P X : *ὁδηγοῦνται* A B C I K M N O Q W 138 *τὴν τῶν ἁγίων κεκρυμμένην* M *ἄχρηστον* M T : *ἄπιστος* Æ 139 *παραδράμοι* Æ I N O Q R : *παραδράμειν* T *γὰρ*] *γὰρ ἂν* Æ B I K M N O Q R T *ἐγνωρίσθη* D E F G H L P S X *δανιὴλ τοιοῦτος ὢν* M *μὴ* om. N 140 *εὕρεσιν*] *ἐρεύνησιν* G H P R W X 141 *αἰγύπτιον*] *αἰγύπτιον ἔθνος* *Mign* : aegyptus *Dion Eri* *καθειργμένου* X[pc] (*γ supr. l. 2[a] man.*) 142 *παρεισήγαγεν* N *αὐτὸν εἰς μέσον* R T *μέσους* *Ald Mign* *οὐχὶ*] *οὐ* B N 143 *λογίζεσθαι*] *ἡγεῖσθαι* Æ B I K M N Q R T : duci *Eri*

[13.11] As such, the cupbearer presses the cluster for Pharaoh's cup; in this way the baker seemed to carry his baskets: each supposing himself in a dream to be engaged in those things in which he was busied when awake[63]; for the images of their customary occupations imprinted on the prescient element of the soul provided them for a time the ability to foretell, by this sort of prophecy on the part of the intellect, what should come to pass.

[13.12] But if Daniel and Joseph and others like them were instructed in advance by divine power, without any confusion of sense-perception, in the knowledge of things to come, this counts for nothing for the present argument; for no one would ascribe this to the power of dreams, since he would then fully suppose, by consequence, that those theophanies also which took place in wakefulness were not a vision but a consequence of nature effected spontaneously. Just as, then, while human beings are guided by their own intellects, there are some few who are deemed worthy of evident divine company, so also while the phantasies arising in sleep occur in a common and similar manner for all, some, not all, participate by means of their dreams in some more divine manifestation; but to all others, even if a foreknowledge of anything does occur from dreams, it occurs in the manner spoken of.

[13.13] And again, if the Egyptian and the Assyrian kings were divinely guided to the knowledge of things to come, the effect arranged by their means is a different thing; for it was necessary that the hidden wisdom of the saints should be revealed, that each might not pass his life without benefit for the state. For how could Daniel have been known for what he was, if the soothsayers and magicians had not been unequal to the task of discovering the dream? And how could the Egyptian people have been preserved, with Joseph shut up in prison, if his discernment of the dream had not brought him into the midst of them? Accordingly, these are something else, and must not be counted with the common phantasies.

[63] Cf. Gen. 40.

[13.14] Ἡ δὲ συνήθης αὕτη τῶν ὀνείρων ὄψις κοινὴ πάντων ἐστὶ, πολυτρόπως καὶ πολυειδῶς ταῖς φαντασίαις [D] ἐγγινομένη· ἢ γὰρ παραμένει, καθὼς εἴρηται, τῷ μνημονικῷ τῆς ψυχῆς τῶν μεθημερινῶν ἐπιτηδευμάτων τὰ ἀπηχήματα· ἢ πολλάκις καὶ πρὸς τὰς ποιὰς τοῦ σώματος διαθέσεις ἡ τῶν ἐνυπνίων κατάστασις ἀνατυποῦται. Οὕτω γὰρ ὁ διψώδης ἐν πηγαῖς εἶναι δοκεῖ, καὶ ἐν εὐωχίαις ὁ τροφῆς προσδεόμενος, καὶ ὁ νέος σφριγώσης αὐτῷ τῆς ἡλικίας καταλλήλως τῷ πάθει φαντασιοῦται.

[13.15] Ἔγνων δὲ καὶ ἄλλην ἐγὼ τῶν καθ' ὕπνον γινομένων αἰτίαν, θεραπεύων τινὰ τῶν ἐπιτηδείων ἑαλωκότα φρενίτιδι, ὃς βαρούμενος τῇ τροφῇ πλείονι τῆς δυνάμεως αὐτῷ προσενεχθείσῃ, ἐβόα, τοὺς περιεστῶτας μεμφόμενος ὅτι ἔντερα κόπρου πληρώσαντες εἶεν ἐπιτεθεικότες αὐτῷ· [173] καὶ ἤδη τοῦ σώματος αὐτῷ πρὸς ἱδρῶτα σπεύδοντος, ᾐτιᾶτο τοὺς παρόντας ὕδωρ ἔχειν ἡτοιμασμένον, ἐφ' ᾧ τε καταβρέξαι κείμενον· καὶ οὐκ ἐνεδίδου βοῶν, ἕως ἡ ἔκβασις, τῶν τοιούτων μέμψεων τὰς αἰτίας ἡρμήνευσεν· ἀθρόως γὰρ ἱδρώς τε πολὺς ἐπερρύη τῷ σώματι, καὶ ἡ γαστὴρ ὑποφθαρεῖσα τὴν ἐν τοῖς ἐντέροις βαρύτητα διεσήμανεν. Ὅπερ τοίνυν ἀμβλυνθείσης ὑπὸ τῆς νόσου τῆς νήψεως ἔπασχεν ἡ φύσις συνδιατιθεμένη τῷ πάθει τοῦ σώματος, τοῦ μὲν ὀχλοῦντος οὐκ ἀναισθήτως ἔχουσα, διασαφῆσαι δὲ τὸ λυποῦν ἐναργῶς, διὰ τὴν ἐκ τῆς νόσου παραφορὰν, οὐκ ἰσχύουσα· τοῦτο κατὰ τὸ εἰκὸς, εἰ, μὴ ἐξ ἀρρωστίας ἀλλὰ τῷ κατὰ φύσιν ὕπνῳ, τὸ διανοητικὸν τῆς ψυχῆς κατηυνάσθη, ἐνύπνιον ἂν τῷ οὕτως διακειμένῳ ἐγίνετο, ὕδατι μὲν τῆς τοῦ ἱδρῶτος ἐπιρροῆς, [B] ἐντέρων δὲ βάρει τῆς κατὰ τὴν τροφὴν ἀχθηδόνος σημαινομένης.

[13.16] Τοῦτο καὶ πολλοῖς τῶν τὴν ἰατρικὴν πεπαιδευμένων δοκεῖ,—παρὰ τὰς τῶν παθημάτων διαφορὰς, καὶ τὰς τῶν ἐνυπνίων ὄψεις τοῖς κάμνουσι γίνεσθαι· ἄλλας μὲν τῶν στομαχούντων, ἑτέρας δὲ τῶν κεκακωμένων τὰς μήνιγγας, καὶ τῶν ἐν πυρετοῖς πάλιν ἑτέρας, τῶν τε κατὰ χολὴν καὶ τῶν ἐν φλέγματι κακουμένων οὐ τὰς αὐτὰς, καὶ τῶν πληθωρικῶν καὶ τῶν ἐκτετηκότων πάλιν ἄλλας· ἐξ ὧν ἔστιν ἰδεῖν, ὅτι ἡ θρεπτική τε καὶ αὐξητικὴ δύναμις τῆς ψυχῆς ἔχει τι καὶ τοῦ νοεροῦ συγκατεσπαρμένον αὐτῇ διὰ τῆς ἀνακράσεως, ὃ τῇ ποιᾷ διαθέσει τοῦ σώματος τρόπον τινὰ ἐξομοιοῦται, κατὰ τὸ ἐπικρατοῦν πάθος ταῖς φαντασίαις μεθαρμοζόμενον.

144 *ὀνειράτων* I K O *πολυτρόπως καὶ om.* N 145 *παραμένη* O *καθὼς εἴρηται om.* N 146 *ἐπιτηδευμάτων*] oportun<it>atum *Eri* 148 *τροφῆς*] *τρῆφυς* B G H 149 *καὶ ὁ νέος—φαντασιοῦται om.* G H P X *καταλλήλως*] *ita* Æ B D E I K L M N Q R S T *Ald Forb* : *καταλλήλῳ Mign* 150 *ὕπνον*] *ita* A C D E F G H L M N O Q R S X *Ald Forb* : *ὕπνων* ß W : *ὕπνους* I K : *ὕπνου Mign* *γινομένων*] *ita* D G P S W X *Forb* : *γενομένην* F : *γινομένην* H : *αἰνιγμάτων* A B C E I K M N O Q R T *Dion Eri* : *γενομένων Ald Mign* 150–1 *θεραπεύων—φρενίτιδι*] nam quidam de necessariis captus phrenesi *Dion* : curans quendam captum frenesi his quibus oportebat curari *Eri* 151 *βαρυνόμενος* A B C E N O R T 152 *αὐτῷ*] *αὐτοῦ Ald Mign* *προσενεχθείσης* K M N O Q W X 153 *πληρώσαντες*] *πλήσαντες* N R T *ἤδη*] *δὴ* N 154 *ἱδρῶτας* ß G H R S X : *ἱδρώτας* P *ᾧ τε*] *ὥπερ τούτου* B 155 *οὐκ*] *οὐδ'* X *ἔκβασις*] *ἔκστασις* I 156 *τε γὰρ ἱδρὼς* B *τε om.* I *ἐπερρύη*] *ἐπερρύει* B (*non* ß) F P$^{ac?}$ P *ἐπερρύη τε* N 157 *ἐν τοῖς om.* N *διεσήμαινεν* G L P W X : *διεσήμηνεν* I : *ὑπεσήμηνεν* M : *ὑπεσήμανεν* B *ὅπερ*] *ὥσπερ* M 158 *ἀμβλυθείσης* H P R^{ac} T : *ἀμβληθείσης* I *νύψεως*] *φύσεως* L *συνδιατιθεμένη*] *νῦν διατιθεμένη* Q 159 *ὀχλοῦντος*] *ἐνοχλοῦντος* Æ B C E I M P Q *οὐκ ἀναισθήτως*] non etiam sensibiliter *Eri* *διασαφηνίσασα* M *δὲ om.* M 160 *ἰσχύσασα* N 161 *τῆς ψυχῆς om.* D *κατευνάσθη* Æ Q : *κατηυγάσθη* D E F G H K M P R^{2} S 162 *οὕτω* Æ I N R : *τοιούτῳ* K O *τῆς*] *τοὺς* W 163 *δὲ*] *τὲ* W *τῆς om.* T *κατὰ τὴν τροφὴν*] *τῶν ἐντέρων* D *διασημαινομένης* Æ B I K O 164 *τοῖς* . . . *πεπαιδευμένοις* Æ I K N O 166 *πυρετῷ* N 167 *φλέγματι*] *πνεύματι* Æ B D E^{mg} *κεκακωμένων* M T *καὶ*^{2} *om.* M 168 *πληθουρικῶν* W *ἄλλας*] *ἄλλο* N 169 *τῆς ψυχῆς δύναμις* Æ I M N Q R T *Eri* *τῆς ψυχῆς om.* K O *ἔχῃ Ald Mign* 170 *τοῦ σώματος διαθέσι* M 171*συνεξομοιοῦται* Æ B I K M N O Q R T *κατὰ*] *καὶ Mign*

[**13.14**] But this usual seeing of dreams is common to all, arising in our phantasies in different modes and forms. For either there remain, as we have said, in the aspect of the soul concerned with memory, the echoes of daily occupations, or, frequently, the constitution of dreams is characterized with regard to a particular condition of the body. Thus, the thirsty person seems to be among springs, the one in need of food to be amidst festivities, and the youth, his time of life bursting with desire, is beset with images corresponding to his passion.

[**13.15**] I also know another cause of the things that happen in sleep. When attending one of my close friends seized by frenzy, being indignant at the food being given to him in too great quantity for his strength, he kept crying out, finding fault with those who were about him for filling intestines with dung and putting them upon him; and when his body was already hastening towards a sweat, he blamed those with him for having water ready to soak him as he lay. And he did not cease crying out until the outcome revealed the causes of these complaints, for all at once a copious sweat broke out over his body and the loosening of his bowels explained the weight in the intestines. The same condition, then, which, while his sobriety was dulled by disease, his nature suffered, being co-affected by the passion of the body—not being imperceptive of what was amiss, but not being strong enough to express clearly its pain due to the distraction resulting from the disease—this, if the discursive faculty of the soul were put to rest, not from infirmity but from natural sleep, would perhaps appear as a dream to one so disposed, with the streams of sweat expressed by the water and the vexation of the food by the weight of the intestines.

[**13.16**] This view is also held by many of those trained in medicine, that the visions of the dreams had by the patients accord with the differences of diseases: the visions of those with a weak stomach are of one kind, another are those of persons suffering from injury to the cerebral membranes, and those of persons in fevers are yet another, those of people suffering from bilious and from phlegmatic affections are not the same, and again those of plethoric persons and persons with wasting disease are different—from which one may see that the faculty of the soul pertaining to nutrition and growth has something of the intellectual aspect sown together in it through commixture, which in some manner is assimilated to the particular state of the body, by being adapted in its phantasies to the disease which has seized it.

[13.17] Ἔτι δὲ καὶ πρὸς τὰς τῶν ἠθῶν καταστάσεις τυποῦται τοῖς πολλοῖς [C] τὰ ἐνύπνια· ἄλλα τοῦ ἀνδρείου καὶ ἄλλα τοῦ δειλοῦ τὰ φαντάσματα· ἄλλοι τοῦ ἀκολάστου ὄνειροι, καὶ ἄλλοι τοῦ σώφρονος· ἐν ἑτέροις ὁ μεταδοτικὸς, καὶ ἐν ἑτέροις φαντασιοῦται ὁ ἄπληστος· οὐδαμοῦ τῆς διανοίας ἀλλὰ τῆς ἀλογωτέρας διαθέσεως ἐν τῇ ψυχῇ τὰς τοιαύτας φαντασίας ἀνατυπούσης—οἷς προειθίσθη διὰ τῆς καθ' ὕπαρ μελέτης, τούτων τὰς εἰκόνας καὶ ἐν τοῖς ἐνυπνίοις ἀναπλαττούσης.

Ὅτι οὐκ ἐν μέρει τοῦ σώματος ὁ νοῦς· ἐν ᾧ καὶ διάκρησις τῶν τε σωματικῶν καὶ ψυχικῶν κινημάτων.

[14.1] Ἀλλὰ πολὺ τῶν προκειμένων ἀπεπλανήθημεν· δεῖξαι γὰρ ἡμῖν ὁ λόγος προέθετο τὸ, μὴ μέρει τινὶ τοῦ σώματος ἐνδεδέσθαι τὸν νοῦν, ἀλλὰ παντὸς κατὰ τὸ ἶσον ἐφάπτεσθαι, καταλλήλως τῇ φύσει τοῦ ὑποκειμένου μέρους ἐνεργοῦντα τὴν κίνησιν· ἔστι δὲ ὅπου καὶ ἐπακολουθεῖ ταῖς φυσικαῖς ὁρμαῖς ὁ νοῦς, οἷον ὑπηρέτης γινόμενος· καθηγεῖται γὰρ πολλάκις ἡ τοῦ σώματος φύσις, καὶ τοῦ λυποῦντος αἴσθησιν ἐντιθεῖσα καὶ τοῦ εὐφραίνοντος ἐπιθυμίαν· ὥστε ταύτην μὲν τὰς πρώτας παρέχειν ἀρχὰς, ἢ βρώσεως ὄρεξιν ἤ τινος ὅλως τῶν καθ' ἡδονὴν τὴν ὁρμὴν ἐμποιοῦσαν· τὸν δὲ νοῦν ἐκδεχόμενον τὰς τοιαύτας ὁρμὰς, ταῖς οἰκείαις περινοίαις τὰς πρὸς τὸ [176] ποθούμενον ἀφορμὰς συνεκπορίζειν τῷ σώματι· τὸ δὲ τοιοῦτον οὐκ ἐπὶ πάντων ἐστὶν, ἀλλὰ μόνων τῶν ἀνδραποδωδέστερον διακειμένων, οἳ δουλώσαντες τὸν λόγον ταῖς ὁρμαῖς τῆς φύσεως, διὰ τῆς τοῦ νοῦ συμμαχίας τὸ κατὰ τὰς αἰσθήσεις ἡδὺ δουλοπρεπῶς κολακεύουσιν· ἐπὶ δὲ τῶν τελειοτέρων οὐχ οὕτως γίνεται· καθηγεῖται γὰρ ὁ νοῦς, λόγῳ καὶ οὐχὶ πάθει τὸ λυσιτελὲς προαιρούμενος, ἡ δὲ φύσις κατ' ἴχνος ἕπεται τῷ προκαθηγουμένῳ.

[14.2] Ἐπειδὴ δὲ τρεῖς κατὰ τὴν ζωτικὴν δύναμιν διαφορὰς ὁ λόγος εὗρε, τὴν μὲν τρεφομένην χωρὶς αἰσθήσεως, τὴν δὲ τρεφομένην μὲν καὶ αἰσθανομένην, ἀμοιροῦσαν δὲ τῆς λογικῆς ἐνεργείας, τὴν δὲ λογικὴν καὶ τελείαν διὰ πάσης διήκουσαν τῆς δυνάμεως, ὡς καὶ ἐν ἐκείναις εἶναι καὶ τῆς νοερᾶς τὸ πλέον ἔχειν· [B] μηδεὶς διὰ τούτων ὑπονοείτω τρεῖς συγκεκροτῆσθαι ψυχὰς ἐν τῷ ἀνθρωπίνῳ συγκρίματι, ἐν ἰδίαις περιγραφαῖς θεωρουμένας, ὥστε συγκρότημά τι πολλῶν ψυχῶν τὴν ἀνθρωπίνην φύσιν εἶναι νομίζειν. Ἀλλ' ἡ μὲν ἀληθής τε καὶ τελεία ψυχὴ μία τῇ

173 *τυποῦνται* T *τοῖς om. Mign* 175 *ὄνειροι*] *οἱ ὄνειροι* I N T 176 *διανοίας*] *διανοίας ἱσταμένης* H *ἀλογωτέρας*] altero *Eri* 177 *ἐν τῇ ψυχῇ διαθέσεως* Æ B I K M N O Q R T *τῇ om* R *προηθίσθη* G N P[ac] W X : *προσειθίσθη* Æ I M R : *προσεθίσθη* Q : *προσεθισθῇ* ß : *πρὸς ἐθισθεῖ* K O : *προσεθιάθη* B 178 *καὶ ἐν*] *κὰν* N : *κᾂν* T : *καὶ* Æ *ἀναπλασσούσης* Q

Cap. 15 Æ ß I K N O Q R T *Dion Eri*

1–2 *ὅτι—κινημάτων*] quod aliquando mens seruit corpori et de tribus differentiis eius, uitali seu spirituali rationali *Λ* 4 *τὸ*[1]] *ὡς* N : *om.* D *ἐνδεδέσθαι*] *ἐνδέχεσθαι* K *πάντως* T 5 *ἴσον* O X *Ald Mign* *μέρους*] *μέλους* D G H P R S W X *ἐνεργοῦντος* D L M R 6 *καὶ ὅπου* G H L N P R[2] S T X *καὶ om.* Æ B I K O R[ac] 7 *γινόμενος*] *ita* Æ B D G I K L M O P R S T W X *Ald Forb* : *γενόμενος Mign* *καθηγεῖσθαι* G H P X 9 *ἀρχὰς*] *ὁρμὰς* M R *βρώσεως*] *βρώσεως ἢ πόσεως* T *τῶν om.* K *τῶν καθ' ἡδονὴν ὅλως* B 12 *μόνον* Æ D[ac] G H L N O P S W X : *om.* M *ἀνδραποδωδεστέρως* R 14 *τελεωτέρων* M 15 *οὕτω* H O R S W 15–16 *καθηγεῖται—προαιρούμενος*] certum est apod quos mens praecedit in omnibus et ratione potius quam passione id quod oportet exequitur *Dion* : imperat enim animus rationi et non patitur quod utile est eligens *Eri* 17 *δὲ om.* L *τρεῖς post δύναμιν pon.* L 18 *μὲν*] *om.* I M W : *τε* N *αἰσθανομένην*] *αὐξανομένην Mign* 19 *διὰ πάσης*] *δι' ἁπάσης Ald Mign* 20 *ὡς om.* N Q *καὶ ὡς* T *καὶ om.* K *τῇ νοερᾷ* Æ B I K M O T : *ἐν τῇ νοερᾷ* N *πλεῖον* T 21 *ὑπονοείτω*] *ἔχειν ὑπονοείτω* M : *ἐπινοείτω* Q : *ὑπολαμβανέτω* N *συγκεκροτεῖσθαι* G N P W X *ἐν om.* M 22 *περιγραφαῖς*] *συγγραφαῖς* D *συγκρότημά τι*] *συγκρίματι* T : conflatum *Dion* : conformatione *Eri* 23 *φύσιν om.* Q *Dion Eri* *εἶναι φύσιν* N *τε om.* M

[13.17] Moreover, most peoples' dreams are conformed to the state of their character: the phantasms of the brave are one kind, the coward's another; the dreams of the incontinent of one kind, those of the continent another; the liberal and the avaricious are subject to different phantasies—in no case are these phantasies framed by the mind, but by the less rational disposition in the soul, which fashions images, even in dreams, of those things to which each is accustomed by his daily occupation.

That the intellect is not in a part of the body; in which also is a distinction of the movements of body and soul.[64]

[14.1] But we have wandered far from our subject, for the argument set out to show that the intellect is not restricted to any part of the body but is equally in touch with the whole, producing its movement according to the nature of the part under its influence. There are cases, however, in which the intellect follows the natural impulses, becoming, as it were, their servant; for often the nature of the body takes the lead by introducing either the sensation of that which gives pain or the desire for that which gives pleasure, so that it may be said to furnish the first beginnings, by producing in us the desire for food or, generally, the impulse towards some pleasant thing; while the intellect, receiving such impulses, helps supply the body by its own deliberations with the means for attaining the desired object. Such is not the case for all, but only those of a more abject disposition, who enslave the reason to the impulses of nature and slavishly flatter the pleasures of the senses by the alliance of their intellect; but in the case of the more perfect this does not happen, for the intellect takes the lead, choosing the expedient course by reason and not by passion, while their nature follows in the tracks of its leader.

[14.2] Given that our argument discovered three different forms regarding the vital faculty—one which is nourished without sense-perception, another which is both nourished and is capable of sense-perception, but is without share in the reasoning activity, and, third, the rational and perfect, pervading the whole faculty, so that amongst these forms the advantage belongs to the intellectual—let no one suppose, because of this, that in the human compound there are three souls welded together, each contemplated within its own limits, so as to think that

[64] *Bodl. 238* (as Chap. 15): 'That the mind is sometimes in servitude to the body, and of its three differences, vital, spiritual, and rational'.

φύσει ἐστίν, ἡ νοερά τε καὶ ἄϋλος, ἡ διὰ τῶν αἰσθήσεων τῇ ὑλικῇ καταμιγνυμένη φύσει· τὸ δὲ ὑλῶδες ἅπαν ἐν τροπῇ τε καὶ ἀλλοιώσει κείμενον, εἰ μὲν μετέχοι τῆς ψυχούσης δυνάμεως, κατὰ αὔξησιν κινηθήσεται· εἰ δὲ ἀποπέσοι τῆς ζωτικῆς ἐνεργείας, εἰς φθορὰν ἀναλύσει τὴν κίνησιν. **[14.3]** *Οὔτε οὖν αἴσθησις χωρὶς ὑλικῆς οὐσίας, οὔτε τῆς νοερᾶς δυνάμεως χωρὶς αἰσθήσεως ἐνέργεια γίνεται.*

Ὅτι κυρίως ψυχὴ ἡ λογικὴ καὶ ἔστι καὶ λέγεται, αἱ δὲ ἄλλαι ὁμωνύμος κατονομάζονται· ἐν ᾧ καὶ τὸ διὰ παντὸς τοῦ σώματος δίηκειν τὴν τοῦ νοῦ δύναμιν, καταλλήλως ἑκάστοῦ μέρους προσαπτομένην.

[15.1] *Εἰ δέ τινα τῆς κτίσεως τὴν θρεπτικὴν ἐνέργειαν ἔχει, ἢ πάλιν ἕτερα τῇ αἰσθητικῇ διοικεῖται δυνάμει μήτε ἐκεῖνα αἰσθήσεως μήτε ταῦτα τῆς νοερᾶς μετέχοντα φύσεως, καὶ διὰ τοῦτό τις ψυχῶν πλῆθος καθυποπτεύει—οὐ κατὰ τὸν διαιροῦντα λόγον ὁ τοιοῦτος τὴν τῶν ψυχῶν διαφορὰν δογματίσει· διότι πᾶν τὸ ἐν τοῖς οὖσι νοούμενον, εἰ μὲν τελείως εἴη ὅπερ ἐστὶ, κυρίως καὶ ὀνομάζεται ὅπερ λέγεται· τὸ δὲ μὴ διὰ πάντων ὂν ἐκεῖνο ὃ κατωνόμασται, ματαίαν καὶ τὴν προσηγορίαν ἔχει. Οἷον εἴ τις τὸν ἀληθῆ δείξειεν* [D] *ἄρτον, φαμὲν τὸν τοιοῦτον κυρίως ἐπιλέγειν τῷ ὑποκειμένῳ τὸ ὄνομα· εἰ δέ τις τὸν ἀπὸ λίθου τεχνηθέντα τῷ κατὰ φύσιν ἀντιπαραδείξειεν, ᾧ σχῆμα μὲν τὸ αὐτὸ καὶ τὸ μέγεθος ἴσον καὶ ἡ τοῦ χρώματος ὁμοιότης, ὥστε διὰ τῶν πλείστων τὸν αὐτὸν εἶναι τῷ πρωτοτύπῳ δοκεῖν, ἐπιλείπει δὲ αὐτῷ τὸ καὶ τροφὴν δύνασθαι εἶναι· παρὰ τοῦτο οὐ κυρίως ἀλλ' ἐκ καταχρήσεως τῆς ἐπωνυμίας τοῦ ἄρτου τετυχηκέναι τὸν λίθον λέγομεν· καὶ πάντα τὰ κατὰ τὸν αὐτὸν λόγον, ἃ μὴ δι' ὅλων ἐστὶν ὅπερ λέγεται, ἐκ καταχρήσεως ἔχει τὴν κλῆσιν.*

24 ἡ^{2}] ᾗ Æ B D G H K L O P S X καταμίγνυται Æ B D G H K L P S X : καταμίγνοιται O : συγκαταμιγνυμένη M 25 μετέχει B G^{ac} I M 26 ψυχούσης] ἐμψυχούσης D L M P S W X : ἐμψύχου G H : ψυχικῆς N κατὰ] κατὰ τὴν I M : κατ' G H L P S X ἀποπέσει H$^{?}$ R$^{2?}$: ἀποπέση R$^{ac?}$ 27 ἀναλύει G H N P T X οὖν] *om.* ß : οὖν ἡ G H P W X

Cap. 16 Æ ß N Q R T *Dion Eri*

15.7–10 (πᾶν τὸ—προσηγορίαν ἔχει): *Doctrina Patrum de Incarnatione Verbi* 22.XI (Diekamp, 140.13–18) 15.16–17 (ἃ μὴ—τὴν κλῆσιν): *Doctrina Patrum de Incarnatione Verbi* 22.XII (Diekamp, 141.1–2)

1–3 ὅτι—προσαπτομένην] quod uitalis efficientiae irrationabilium non uere sed equiuoce dicitur anima et de ineffabili communione corporis et animae *Λ* 1 ἡ ψυχὴ N ἡ *om.* B K T δὲ] *ita* Æ G I K N O P Q R S *Forb* : δ' *Ald Mign* 2–3 ἐν ᾧ—προσαπτομένην *om.* W 2 ἐν ᾧ *om.* N διήκειν τοῦ σώματος D R τοῦ] τοῦ παντὸς N 3 ἑκάστῳ μέρει M 4 ἔχει ἐνέργειαν D G H L P S X ἑτέρᾳ P 5 μήτ' G H L P S X τῆς *om.* N 6 τις] τί N καθυπτοπεύῃ H : καθυποπτεύσει M : καθ' ὑποπτεύει X 7 διαιροῦντα] αἱροῦντα D G H M S T^{pc} W X^{ac} : αἰροῦντα L P X^{pc} : αιροῦντα N : ἐροῦντα T^{ac} : excelsam *Eri* πᾶν—πάλιν (*cap. 21, l. 18*) *foliis (post 129^{v}) pluribus avulsis* R 9 ὂν] ὢν W 10 ἀληθινὸν B ἄρτον δείξειεν D G H L P S X 12 ἀντιπαραδείξειεν] ὑποδείξειεν L ᾧ] ὃ D^{ac} S : ὡς T : *om.* G H M P X τὸ αὐτὸ] τοιοῦτον N 12 τὸ *om.* N ἴσον X ἡ *om.* N T 13 τὸν αὐτὸν] ταυτὸν N : αὐτὸν G H P X 14 ἐπιλείπει δὲ] ἐπεὶ δὲ λείπει B G H I K N O P T X : ἐπειδὴ δὲ λείπει M W : ἐπειδὴ λείπει Æ αὐτῷ] αὐτὸ K : *om.* L εἶναι] δούναι W 15 τὸ λίθον τετυχηκέναι N τὸν λίθον *om.* K O λέγωμεν *Mign* 15–16 καὶ πάντα—λόγον *om.* I 16 τὰ *om.* Æ B G H M N P T W X μὴ δι' ὅλων] μὴ δι' ὅλως G : μὴ δὲ ὅλως N : μηδόλως K ὅπερ] ἅπερ Æ B I K N O ἔχειν N

human nature is a sort of conglomeration of several souls. The true and perfect soul is one by nature, the intellectual and immaterial, which mingles with the material nature through the senses.[65] Everything material, being subject to change and alteration, will, if it participates in the animating faculty, move in accordance with growth; if, however, it falls away from the life-giving activity, it will dissolve its movement into corruption. [**14.3**] Therefore, neither is there sense-perception without material substance nor is there activity of sense-perception without the intellectual faculty.

That the rational soul is and is called 'soul' properly, while the others are called so equivocally; in which also is this, that the power of the intellect extends throughout the whole body, touching appropriately every part.[66]

[**15.1**] If some things in creation possess the nutritive activity, and others again are regulated by the sense-perceptive faculty, the former having no share in the senses nor the latter in the intellectual nature, and if, for this reason, anyone suspects that there is a plurality of souls, such a one will be positing the difference of souls not in accordance with their distinguishing definition. For everything we think of among beings, if it be perfectly what it is, is also properly called by what it is named; but of that which is not completely what it is named, the appellation is also in vain. For instance, if someone were to show us true bread, we say that he properly applies the name to the subject; but if someone were to show us instead something made out of stone to resemble the natural bread—which had the same shape and equal size and similarity of colour, so as to appear in most points to be the same as the prototype, but which lacks the ability of being food—on this account we say that the stone has the name of 'bread' not properly but by a misuse of language, and that all things which fall under the same description, that are not wholly what they are called, have their name from a misuse of terms.

[65] Cf. Gregory of Nyssa, *An. et res.* 3.1 (Spira, 31.18–32.1); Alexander of Aphrodisias, *De an.* (Bruns, 94.1–6).

[66] *Bodl. 238* (as Chap. 16): 'That the vital energy of the irrational creatures is not truly but equivocally called "soul" and of the unspeakable communion of body and mind'.

[15.2] *Οὕτω τοίνυν καὶ τῆς ψυχῆς ἐν τῷ νοερῷ τε καὶ λογικῷ τὸ τέλειον* [177] *ἐχούσης, πᾶν ὃ μὴ τοῦτό ἐστιν ὁμώνυμον μὲν εἶναι δύναται τῇ ψυχῇ, οὐ μὴν καὶ ὄντως ψυχή, ἀλλά τις ἐνέργεια ζωτική, τῇ τῆς ψυχῆς κλήσει συγκεκριμένη· διὸ καὶ τὴν τῶν ἀλόγων φύσιν, ὡς οὐ πόρρω τῆς φυτικῆς ταύτης ζωῆς κειμένην, ὁμοίως ἔδωκε τῇ χρήσει τοῦ ἀνθρώπου ὁ τὰ καθ' ἕκαστον νομοθετήσας, ὡς ἀντὶ λαχάνου τοῖς μετέχουσιν εἶναι·* **πάντα** *γάρ, φησί,* **τὰ κρέα φάγεσθε, ὡς λάχανα χόρτου**· *μικρὸν γάρ τι πλεονεκτεῖν δοκεῖ τῇ αἰσθητικῇ ἐνεργείᾳ τοῦ δίχα ταύτης τρεφομένου τε καὶ αὐξανομένου· παιδευσάτω τοῦτο τοὺς φιλοσάρκους μὴ πολὺ τοῖς κατ' αἴσθησιν φαινομένοις προσδεσμεῖν τὴν διάνοιαν, ἀλλ' ἐν τοῖς ψυχικοῖς προτερήμασι προσασχολεῖσθαι, ὡς τῆς ἀληθοῦς ψυχῆς ἐν τούτοις θεωρουμένης, τῆς δὲ αἰσθήσεως καὶ ἐν τοῖς ἀλόγοις τὸ ἴσον ἐχούσης.*

[15.3] [B] *Ἀλλ' ἐφ' ἕτερον ἡ ἀκολουθία παρηνέχθη τοῦ λόγου· οὐ γὰρ τοῦτο τῇ θεωρίᾳ προέκειτο, ὅτι προτιμότερον τῶν ἐν τῷ ἀνθρώπῳ νοουμένων ἐστὶν ἡ κατὰ τὸν νοῦν ἐνέργεια ἢ τὸ ὑλικὸν τῆς ὑποστάσεως· ἀλλ' ὅτι οὐχὶ μέρει τινὶ τῶν ἐν ἡμῖν ὁ νοῦς περιέχεται, ἀλλ' ἐπίσης ἐν πᾶσι καὶ διὰ πάντων ἐστίν. Οὔτε ἔξωθεν περιλαμβάνων οὔτε ἔνδοθεν ἐγκρατούμενος· ταῦτα γὰρ ἐπὶ κάδων ἢ ἄλλων τινῶν σωμάτων ἀλλήλοις ἐντιθεμένων κυρίως λέγεται· ἡ δὲ τοῦ νοητοῦ πρὸς τὸ σωματικὸν κοινωνία, ἄφραστόν τε καὶ ἀνεπινόητον τὴν συνάφειαν ἔχει, οὔτε ἐντὸς οὖσα (οὔτε γὰρ ἐγκρατεῖται σώματι τὸ ἀσώματον) οὔτε ἐκτὸς περιέχουσα· οὐ γὰρ περιλαμβάνεται τὰ ἀσώματα, ἀλλὰ κατά τινα τρόπον ἀμήχανόν τε καὶ ἀκατανόητον ἐγγίζων ὁ νοῦς τῇ φύσει καὶ προσαπτόμενος, καὶ ἐν* [C] *αὐτῇ καὶ περὶ αὐτὴν θεωρεῖται· οὔτε ἐγκαθήμενος οὔτε περιπτυσσόμενος, ἀλλ' ὡς οὐκ ἔστιν εἰπεῖν οὔτε νοῆσαι· πλὴν ὅτι κατὰ τὸν ἴδιον αὐτῆς εἱρμὸν εὐοδουμένης τῆς φύσεως, καὶ ὁ νοῦς ἐνεργὸς γίνεται· εἰ δέ τι πλημμέλημα περὶ ταύτην συμπέσοι, σκάζει κατ' ἐκεῖνο καὶ τῆς διανοίας ἡ κίνησις.*

18 *οὕτως* N *καὶ om.* T *λογικῷ τε καὶ νοερῷ* M 19 *τοῦτό*] *τοιοῦτον* K N *δύναται εἶναι* L *εἶναι om.* N *καὶ om.* G H I P X 19–20 *οὐ μὴν καὶ ὄντως ψυχὴ om.* O 20 *ὄντως*] *κυρίως* I *τῇ τῆς ψυχῆς κλήσει συγκεκριμένη*] quae per abusionem anima nuncupatur *Dion* : uocatione animae coutens *Eri* *συγκεχρημένη* Æ B D E I K L N O Q S T 21 *φυτικῆς*] *ita* Æ ß G O *Wils* : *ψυχικῆς* N : *φυσικῆς* W X *Ald Forb Mign* : seminali *Dion* : *om. Eri* 22 *χρήσει*] *χρήσει ταύτῃ* Æ 23 *φάγεσθε, ὡς λάχανα χόρτου*] *ὡς λάχανα φάγεσθε* W *φάγεσθαι* G^{ac} Q : *φάγεσαι* Æ B 23–4 *μικρὸν γὰρ*] *ὃ καὶ μικρὸν* N : *ὃ κἂν μικρὸν* P^{2} T 24 *δίχα ταύτης*] per eandem *Eri* 25 *αὐξομένου* I O^{pc} T W *παιδευσάτω*] *παιδευοῦσα τὸ* Q : discant *Eri* *τοῦτο*] *τοίνυν* Æ B K O : *om.* G H M N P Q T X 26 *προσδεσμεῖν*] *προσδραμεῖν Ald Mign* 27 *προσενασχολεῖσθαι* E : *προσαπασχολεῖσθαι* N T : *ἀπασχολεῖσθαι* D *ὡς*] *ὡς μὴ* T *τούτοις*] *τοῖς τοιούτοις* Æ B I K O 28 *ἴσον* X *Ald Mign* 30 *προύκειτο* Æ I K O Q *ὅτι*] *τι* W *προτιμότερον*] *ita* Æ B D H I K L M O P^{2} S T W *Forb* : *προτιμώτερον* X *Ald Mign* *τῷ om.* M *νοουμένων*] *θεωρουμένων* D L 31 *τὸν om.* O *Ald Mign* *ἢ*] *ἤπερ* N 32–3 *οὔτ'… οὔτ'* G H P S X 33 *ἐγκρατούμενος*] *κρατούμενος Ald Mign* 34 *σωμάτων ἀλλήλοις ἐντιθεμένων om.* W *νοητοῦ*] *ita* Æ B D G H I K L M O P S T W X *Forb* : *νοῦ Ald Mign* 35 *τὴν om.* N *οὔτε*[1]] *οὔτ'* G P S X *οὔτε*[2]] *οὐδὲ* N : *οὐ* Æ B I K O Q 36 *ἐγκρατεῖται*] *κρατεῖται* D G H L P S X *οὔτε*] *οὔτ'* G P S X *οὐ*] *οὐδὲ* Æ B K N O : *οὔτε* T 37 *περιλαμβάνεται*] *περιλαμβάνει* Æ : *περιλαμβάνει τι Mign* *τὸ ἀσώματον* Q *ἀμήχανόν*] inuisibili *Dion* : superrationabilem *Eri* 39 *οὔτε*[1]] *οὔτ'* G H : *om.* B : *οὔτε γὰρ* W *ἀλλ' ὡς*] *ita* Æ G H K M N O P^{ac} S W X *Ald Forb* : *ἄλλως* I L P^{2} : *ἀλλ'* Q : *ἀλλὰ ὡς Mign* 40 *οὔτε*] *ita* G H P S^{pc} X *Forb* : *οὐδὲ* Æ B I K M N O Q T W : *ἢ Ald Mign* *νοῆσαι*] *ἐννοῆσαι* I K *αὐτῆς*] *ἑαυτῆς* Q W 41 *γίγνεται* W *πλημμελήματα* X *ταύτην*] *αὐτὴν* Æ B I K N O T *ἐμπέσοι* D G H I K L N O P S : *ἐκπέσοι* M

[15.2] Therefore, just as the soul has its perfection in that which is intellectual and rational, everything that is not so may indeed have the homonym of 'soul', yet is not really soul, but a certain vital energy associated with the appellation of 'soul'. Thus, also he who gave laws on every matter, likewise gave the nature of animals, as not far removed from this vegetative life, to the use of the human being, for them to partake of it instead of vegetables, for he says: *You shall eat all kinds of flesh just as green vegetables*. For the sense-perceptive activity seems to have but a slight advantage over that which is nourished and grows without it. Let this teach the lovers of the flesh not to bind their mind too closely to what appears to the senses, but rather to busy themselves with the advantages that pertain to the soul, as the true soul is contemplated in these, while sense-perception is equally amongst the animals.

[15.3] The course of our argument, however, has diverged to yet another point, for the subject of our contemplation was not that the activity of the intellect is of more dignity among the things conceived of in the human being than the material element of the concrete being, but that the intellect is not confined to any one part of us, but is equally in all and through all. It neither surrounds anything from the outside nor is enclosed within anything, for these phrases are properly applied to casks or other bodies placed one inside the other. The communion of the intellectual with the bodily is a conjunction unspeakable and inconceivable, neither being within it (for the incorporeal is not enclosed in a body) nor yet surrounding it from outside (for things incorporeal do not surround [something else]), but the intellect, approaching our nature in some inexplicable and incomprehensible way and coming to touch it, is to be thought of as both in it and around it, neither seated in it nor enfolded with it, but in a way which we cannot speak or think,[67] except this: that while nature prospers according to its own order, the intellect is also active; but if any misfortune befalls the former, the movement of the mind halts correspondingly.

[67] Cf. Gregory of Nyssa, *An. et res.* 2.46 (Spira, 27.23–28.5); Gregory of Nazianzus, *Ep.* 101.37–9; Alexander of Aphrodisias, *De an.* (Bruns, 13.9–17.8).

Θεωρία τοῦ θείου ῥητοῦ τοῦ εἰπόντος, ποιήσωμεν ἄνθρωπον κατ' εἰκόνα ἡμετέραν καὶ ὁμοίωσιν· ἐν ᾧ ἐξετάζεται, τίς ὁ τῆς εἰκόνος λόγος, καὶ πῶς ὁμοιοῦται τῷ μακαρίῳ τε καὶ ἀπαθεῖ τὸ ἐμπαθὲς καὶ ἐπίκηρον· καὶ πῶς ἐν τῇ εἰκόνι τὸ ἄρρεν καὶ τὸ θῆλυ, ἐν τῷ πρωτοτύπῳ τούτων οὐκ ὄντων.

[16.1] Ἀλλ' ἐπαναλάβωμεν πάλιν τὴν θείαν φωνὴν, **ποιήσωμεν ἄνθρωπον κατ' εἰκόνα καὶ ὁμοίωσιν ἡμετέραν.** Ὡς μικρά τε καὶ ἀνάξια τῆς τοῦ ἀνθρώπου μεγαλοφυΐας τῶν ἔξωθέν τινες ἐφαντάσθησαν, τῇ πρὸς τὸν κόσμον τοῦτον συγκρίσει μεγαλύνοντες, ὡς ᾤοντο, τὸ ἀνθρώπινον· φασὶ γὰρ μικρὸν εἶναι κόσμον τὸν ἄνθρωπον, ἐκ τῶν αὐτῶν τῷ παντὶ στοιχείων συνεστηκότα. Οἱ γὰρ τῷ κόμπῳ τοῦ ὀνόματος [180] τοιοῦτον ἔπαινον τῇ ἀνθρωπίνῃ χαριζόμενοι φύσει, λελήθασιν ἑαυτοὺς τοῖς περὶ τὸν κώνωπα καὶ τὸν μῦν ἰδιώμασι σεμνοποιοῦντες τὸν ἄνθρωπον· καὶ γὰρ κἀκείνοις ἐκ τῶν τεσσάρων τούτων ἡ κρᾶσίς ἐστι, διότι πάντως ἑκάστου τῶν ὄντων ἢ πλείων ἢ ἐλάττων τις μοῖρα περὶ τὸ ἔμψυχον θεωρεῖται, ὧν ἄνευ συστῆναί τι τῶν αἰσθήσεως μετεχόντων, φύσιν οὐκ ἔχει. Τί οὖν μέγα, κόσμου χαρακτῆρα καὶ ὁμοίωμα νομισθῆναι τὸν ἄνθρωπον; οὐρανοῦ τοῦ παρερχομένου, γῆς τῆς ἀλλοιουμένης, πάντων τῶν ἐν τούτοις περικρατουμένων τῇ παρόδῳ τοῦ περιέχοντος συμπαρερχομένων; [16.2] Ἀλλ' ἐν τίνι κατὰ τὸν ἐκκλησιαστικὸν λόγον τὸ ἀνθρώπινον μέγεθος; Οὐκ ἐν τῇ πρὸς τὸν κτιστὸν κόσμον ὁμοιότητι, ἀλλ' ἐν τῷ **κατ' εἰκόνα** γενέσθαι τῆς τοῦ κτίσαντος φύσεως.

[16.3] Τίς οὖν [B] ὁ τῆς εἰκόνος λόγος; ἴσως ἐρεῖς· πῶς ὡμοίωται τῷ σώματι τὸ ἀσώματον; πῶς τῷ ἀϊδίῳ τὸ πρόσκαιρον; τῷ ἀναλλοιώτῳ τὸ διὰ τροπῆς ἀλλοιούμενον; τῷ ἀπαθεῖ τε καὶ ἀφθάρτῳ τὸ ἐμπαθὲς καὶ φθειρόμενον; τῷ ἀμιγεῖ

Cap. 17 Æ ß I K N O Q T *Dion Eri, et caput hoc inc. ad verba* ὡς μικρά (*l.* 6) *in* D E F G L M P S X

16.62–17.2 (πρῶτον—ἄνθρωποι): Paris, BN, *grec. 1356*, fragments (sigla Z) 16.89–98 (ἐπεὶ δὲ—τὴν γνώμην): John (of Damascus) *Sacra Parallela* II[1]99 / K cap. A 2, 21 (Thum, 117.12–118.5)

1–4 θεωρία—ὄντων] quod excellentia hominis non in eo est quod iuxta philosophos ad imaginem mundi conditus est, sed in eo quod ad imaginem dei factus est et quomodo ad imaginem dei factus est *Λ* 1 θεώρημα T 1–3 τοῦ θείου—ἐπίκηρον· καὶ *om.* W 1 τοῦ[2]] *ita* H M Q T S[pc] *Forb* : *om.* O *Ald Mign* εἰπόντος] λέγοντες M 1–2 κατ' εἰκόνα ἡμετέραν καὶ ὁμοίωσιν] *ita Forb* : κατ' εἰκόνα καὶ ὁμοίωσιν ἡμετέραν *Ald Mign* καὶ ὁμοίωσιν] *om.* Æ B G H I K N O P Q *Dion Eri* : καὶ καθ' ὁμοίωσιν D L S 2 ᾧ] ᾗ M λόγος *om.* O πῶς] *ita* D G H L P S *Forb* : εἰ O *Mign* 4 καὶ τὸ] τε καὶ M τούτων] τούτῳ K *Ald* 6 καὶ ὁμοίωσιν ἡμετέραν] καὶ καθ' ὁμοίωσιν ἡμετέραν Q : ἡμετέραν καὶ καθ' ὁμοίωσιν L N ἡμετέραν] ἡμετέραν φησιν I 7 τινες τῶν ἔξωθεν G L P S X : ex his quae extra sunt *Eri* τινες *om.* D 8 ὡς ᾤοντο] quasi in ipso existeret *Eri* τὸ ἀνθρώπινον] τὸν ἄνθρωπον Æ B N O κόσμον εἶναι Æ B I K O 9 τῷ[1]] τὸ O τῷ κόμπῳ] ornamento *Eri* 11 τὴν μυίαν T 12 τῶν *om.* T τεσσάρων] τεττάρων B : τεσσάρων στοιχείων N πάντων Æ ἑκάστῳ I 13 πλείω ἢ ἐλάττω G P X 14 αἰσθήσεων T μέγα] post *Eri* 15 περιερχομένου *Ald Mign* 16 παρακρατουμένων B 17 συμπεριεχομένων P ἀλλ' ἐν τίνι] ἀλλὰ N 18 κτιστὸν] κτισθέντα D (κτισθε *in ras 2[a] m.*) 19 γεγενῆσθαι B C I K M N O Q T κτίσαντος] κτίσεως B : κτίστου ß 20 τίς—ἐρεῖς] fortassis ergo quae sit imaginis ratio quaeras *Dion* εἰκόνος] φύσεως I ἴσως] οὗτος N ἐρεῖς *om.* B τῷ *om.* D G P S X 20–1 σώματι τὸ ἀσώματον] ἀσωμάτῳ τὸ ἐν σώματι I : ἀσωμάτῳ τὸ ἐνσώματον N : incorporeo corporale *Dion Eri* 21 πῶς *om.* N

A contemplation of the divine word which says, Let us make the human being in accordance with our image and likeness. In which is examined what the definition of the image is, and how the passible and mortal is likened to the blessed and impassible, and how the male and the female are in the image, these not being in the Prototype.[1]

[**16.1**] But let us now take up again the divine saying, *Let us make the human being in accordance with our image and likeness.* How mean and how unworthy of the majesty of the human being are the fancies of some of those outside, who magnify humankind, as they supposed, by comparing it to this world. For they say that the human being is a little cosmos, composed from the same elements as the universe.[2] Those who bestow such praise on human nature by a pompous name, forget that they are dignifying the human being with the properties of the gnat and the mouse! They also are a blend of these four elements, for assuredly there is seen in the animated nature of each being some part, either more or less, of those elements without which any being with sense-perception would not, by nature, exist. What great thing is it, then, for the human being to be accounted as a figure and likeness of the world—of the heaven that passes away, of the earth that changes, of all the things which are contained in them, which pass away with the turning of what contains them? [**16.2**] But in what is the human greatness according to the ecclesiastical teaching? Not in the likeness to the created world, but in coming to be *in accordance with the image* of the nature of the Creator.

[**16.3**] What, then, you may ask, is the definition of the image? How is the incorporeal likened to the body? How the temporal to the eternal? That which is altered by change to the unalterable? That which is subject to passion and

[1] *Bodl. 238* (as Chap. 17): 'That the excellence of the human being does not consist in the fact that, according to the philosophers, he is made after the image of the world, but in the fact that he is made in the image of God and how he is made in the image of God'.

[2] Cf. Plato, *Tim.* 30a–31a; Aristotle *Phys.* (8.2.252b26–7); Philo, *Quis rer. div. haer.* 155; Clement of Alexandria, *Protrep.* 1.5.3; Methodius, *De res.* 2.10.2 (Bonwetsch, 350.9–351.2); Nemesius, *De nat. hom.* 1.63–4 (Morani, 15.3–6); Basil, *Hom. de creat. hom.* 2.14 (Hörner, 65.11–15); Gregory of Nazianzus, *Or.* 28.22; 38.11.

πάσης κακίας τὸ πάντοτε συνοικοῦν ταύτῃ καὶ συντρεφόμενον; πολὺ γὰρ τὸ μέσον ἐστὶ, τοῦ τε κατὰ τὸ ἀρχέτυπον νοουμένου, καὶ τοῦ κατ' εἰκόνα γεγενημένου· ἡ γὰρ εἰκὼν, εἰ μὲν ἔχει τὴν πρὸς τὸ πρωτότυπον ὁμοιότητα, κυρίως τοῦτο κατονομάζεται· εἰ δὲ παρενεχθείη τοῦ προκειμένου ἡ μίμησις, ἄλλό τι καὶ οὐκ εἰκὼν ἐκείνου τὸ τοιοῦτόν ἐστι.

[16.4] *Πῶς οὖν ὁ ἄνθρωπος, τὸ θνητὸν τοῦτο καὶ ἐμπαθὲς καὶ ὠκύμορον, τῆς ἀκηράτου καὶ καθαρᾶς καὶ ἀεὶ οὔσης φύσεώς ἐστιν εἰκών; Ἀλλὰ τὸν μὲν ἀληθῆ περὶ τούτου λόγον μόνη ἂν εἰδείη σαφῶς ἡ* [C] *ὄντως ἀλήθεια· ἡμεῖς δὲ καθ' ὅσον χωροῦμεν, στοχασμοῖς τισι καὶ ὑπονοίαις τὸ ἀληθὲς ἀνιχνεύοντες, ταῦτα περὶ τῶν ζητουμένων ὑπολαμβάνομεν. Οὔτε ὁ θεῖος ψεύδεται λόγος,* **κατ' εἰκόνα** *Θεοῦ εἰπὼν γεγενῆσθαι τὸν ἄνθρωπον, οὔτε ἡ ἐλεεινὴ τῆς ἀνθρωπίνης φύσεως ταλαιπωρία τῇ μακαριότητι τῆς ἀπαθοῦς ζωῆς καθωμοίωται· ἀνάγκη γὰρ τῶν δύο τὸ ἕτερον ὁμολογεῖσθαι, εἴ τις συγκρίνοι τῷ Θεῷ τὸ ἡμέτερον, ἢ παθητὸν εἶναι τὸ θεῖον ἢ ἀπαθὲς τὸ ἀνθρώπινον, ὡς ἂν διὰ τῶν ἴσων ὁ τῆς ὁμοιότητος λόγος ἐπ' ἀμφοτέρους καταλαμβάνοιτο· εἰ δὲ οὔτε τὸ θεῖον ἐμπαθὲς οὔτε τὸ καθ' ἡμᾶς ἔξω πάθους ἐστὶν, ἄρα τις ἕτερος ὑπολέλειπται λόγος, καθ' ὃν ἀληθεύειν φαμὲν τὴν θείαν φωνὴν, τὴν ἐν εἰκόνι Θεοῦ γεγενῆσθαι τὸν* [D] *ἄνθρωπον λέγουσαν.*

[16.5] *Οὐκοῦν αὐτὴν ἐπαναληπτέον ἡμῖν τὴν θείαν γραφὴν, εἴ τις ἄρα γένοιτο διὰ τῶν γεγραμμένων πρὸς τὸ ζητούμενον ἡμῖν χειραγωγία. Μετὰ τὸ εἰπεῖν, ὅτι* **ποιήσωμεν ἄνθρωπον κατ' εἰκόνα**, *καὶ ἐπὶ τίσι* **ποιήσωμεν**, *ἐπάγει τοῦτον τὸν λόγον, ὅτι* **καὶ ἐποίησεν ὁ Θεὸς τὸν ἄνθρωπον κατ' εἰκόνα Θεοῦ ἐποίησεν αὐτόν· ἄρσεν καὶ θῆλυ ἐποίησεν αὐτούς**· *εἴρηται μὲν οὖν ἤδη καὶ ἐν τοῖς ἔμπροσθεν, ὅτι πρὸς καθαίρεσιν τῆς αἱρετικῆς ἀσεβείας ὁ τοιοῦτος προαναπεφώνηται λόγος, ἵνα διδαχθέντες ὅτι* **ἐποίησε τὸν ἄνθρωπον** *ὁ μονογενὴς Θεὸς* **κατ' εἰκόνα Θεοῦ**, *μηδενὶ λόγῳ τὴν θεότητα τοῦ Πατρὸς καὶ τοῦ Υἱοῦ διακρίνωμεν, ἐπίσης τῆς ἁγίας γραφῆς Θεὸν ἑκάτερον ὀνομαζούσης, τόν τε πεποιηκότα τὸν ἄνθρωπον καὶ οὗ κατ' εἰκόνα ἐγένετο.*

23 *ταύτῃ*] *αὐτῇ* N *συντρεφόμενον*] conuertitut *Eri* 24 *ἡ*] *εἰ* V 25 *εἰ μὲν ἔχει*] quippe si seruet *Dion* : siquidem si habuerit *Eri* *μὲν om.* I *ἔχοι* Æ D G K L N O P Q S X *κυρίως*] *κυρίως ἂν* N T *κατονομάζεται*] *καὶ ὀνομάζεται* Q X *Eri* : *κατονομάζοιτο* N T 26 *προκειμένου*] *πρωτοτύπου* N 28 *τούτον* W 29 *ἀκηράτου*] *ἀφθάρτου* L : *ἀκηράτου καὶ ἀφθόρου* Æ B I K O 31 *ἐνιχνεύοντες* I : *ἐξιχνεύοντες* N T 32 *οὔτε*] *οὐδὲ γὰρ* G P W X : *οὔτε γὰρ* D L M S *εἰπὼν θεοῦ* W 32–3 *γεγενῆσθαι εἰπὼν* Æ B G I K O P Q S V X 33 *τὸν ἄνθρωπον*] *τὸ ἀνθρώπινον* G P Q V X *ἀνθρωπίνης om.* M 34 *καθωμοίωται*] *κατηξίωται* D 35 *συγκρίνει* T 36 *ἀνθρώπινον*] *ἡμέτερον* B *ἐπ' ἀμφοτέροις* G M P S V X : *ἐν ἀμφοφτέροις* Æ B I K N O T 37 *ἐμπαθὲς*] *ἐν πάθει* Æ B C K M N O T *πάθους*] *τοῦ πάθους* T 38 *ἆρα* G I P X *ὑπολείπεται* Æ B C I K O Q T 40 *Οὐκοῦν*] non ergo *Eri* *αὐτὴν om.* L *ἡμῖν om.* P Q X *θείαν*] *ἁγίαν* Æ B G I K L M O P Q T V X : *om.* D *εἴ τις*] *ἥτις* M T *Ald* *γένηται* T 41 *ἡμῖν om.* *Ald* *Mign* 42 *κατ' εἰκόνα om.* Æ B I K M N O Q T *Dion Eri* 43 *ὅτι om.* D G L P Q S X *ἄνθρωπον*] *ἄνθρωπον καὶ* *Mign* 44 *ἄρρεν* W *ἤδη om.* V *ἐν τοῖς ἔμπροσθεν*] quae coram sunt *Eri* 45 *καθαίρεσιν*] *κατάλυσιν* Q V W *Eri* *προαναφωνεῖται* Q 46 *ἐποίησε*] *ἐποίησε ὁ θεὸς* M *θεὸς*] *υἱὸς* Q *θεοῦ om.* Æ 47 *ἐπίσης*] fideli *Eri* *ἁγίας om.* B 48 *τε om.* Æ B N *ἄνθρωπον*] *οὐρανὸν* B 49 *γεγένηται* Æ B I N O T

corruption to that which is impassible and incorruptible?[3] That which constantly dwells with evil and grows up with it to that which unmixed with any evil? For great is the span[4] between that which is conceived regarding the archetype and that which has come to be in accordance with the image; for the image is properly so named if it keeps the likeness to the prototype, but if the imitation is removed from the subject, then it is something else and not its image.

[**16.4**] How then is the human being, this mortal being, subject to the passions and short-lived, an image of that undefiled and pure and everlasting nature? But, perhaps, only the very Truth clearly knows the true account regarding this; yet we, so far as we are able, tracking down the truth by guesses and suspicions, apprehend these things regarding those that are sought. Neither does the divine word lie in saying that the human being came to be *in accordance with the image* of God, nor is the pitiable wretchedness of human nature[5] likened to the blessedness of the impassible life. For if anyone were to compare that which is ours to God, it would be necessary to confess one of two things: either that the divine is subject to passion or that humankind is impassible—as long as the definition of likeness is to be understood equally in both cases. If, then, the divine is not subject to passion nor is our state beyond passion, what other account remains whereby we may say that the divine voice speaks the truth saying that the human being came to be in the image of God?

[**16.5**] Let us, then, take up again the divine Scripture, for perhaps there may be some guidance from what is written about that which we seek. After saying, *Let us make the human being in accordance with the image*,[6] besides saying *Let us make*, it adds this statement, *and God made the human being, in accordance with the image of God made he him; male and female made he them*.[7] It has already been said, in the above, that this statement was uttered beforehand for the purging of heretical impiety, in order that being instructed that the Only-begotten God *made the human being in accordance with the image of God*, we should not in any way distinguish the divinity of the Father and the Son, since Holy Scripture names each of them equally 'God', the one who made the human being and in accordance with whose image he came to be.

[3] Cf. Basil, *Hom. de creat. hom.* 1.6 (Hörner, 11.6–8).

[4] The word translated here as 'span' is *τὸ μέσον*, which a little later (*De hom.* 16.9) Gregory uses to describe the human being; the word is usually translated as 'mid-point' or 'middle', indicating not so much something (a third thing) between two separate points or beings, but as that which also touches and so includes both, hence I have opted for 'span'.

[5] Cf. Gregory of Nyssa, *An. et res.* 10.70 (Spira, 113.2–3).

[6] Gen. 1:26.

[7] Gen. 1:27.

[16.6] [181] *Ἀλλ᾽ ὁ μὲν περὶ τούτων λόγος ἀφείσθω. Πρὸς δὲ τὸ προκείμενον ἐπιστρεπτέον τὴν ζήτησιν—πῶς καὶ τὸ θεῖον μακάριον καὶ ἐλεεινὸν τὸ ἀνθρώπινον, καὶ ὅμοιον ἐκείνῳ τοῦτο παρὰ τῆς γραφῆς ὀνομάζεται.* [16.7] *Οὐκοῦν ἐξεταστέον μετ᾽ ἀκριβείας τὰ ῥήματα· εὑρίσκομεν γὰρ, ὅτι ἕτερον μέν τι τὸ* ***κατ᾽ εἰκόνα*** *γενόμενον, ἕτερον δὲ τὸ νῦν ἐν ταλαιπωρίᾳ δεικνύμενον·* ***ἐποίησεν ὁ Θεὸς,*** *φησὶ,* ***τὸν ἄνθρωπον, κατ᾽ εἰκόνα Θεοῦ ἐποίησεν αὐτόν.*** *Τέλος ἔχει ἡ τοῦ κατ᾽ εἰκόνα γεγενημένου κτίσις· εἶτα ἐπανάληψιν ποιεῖται τοῦ κατὰ τὴν κατασκευὴν λόγου, καί φησιν,* ***ἄρσεν καὶ θῆλυ ἐποίησεν αὐτούς.*** *Παντὶ γὰρ οἶμαι γνώριμον εἶναι, ὅτι ἔξω τοῦτο τοῦ πρωτοτύπου νοεῖται·* ***ἐν γὰρ Χριστῷ Ἰησοῦ,*** *καθώς φησιν ὁ ἀπόστολος,* ***οὔτε ἄρρεν οὔτε θῆλύ ἐστιν·*** *ἀλλὰ μὴν εἰς ταῦτα* [B] *διῃρῆσθαι ὁ λόγος φησὶ τὸν ἄνθρωπον.* [16.8] *Οὐκοῦν διπλῆ τίς ἐστιν ἡ τῆς φύσεως ἡμῶν κατασκευή, ἥτε πρὸς τὸ θεῖον ὡμοιωμένη, ἥτε πρὸς τὴν διαφορὰν ταύτην διῃρημένη· τοιοῦτον γάρ τι ὁ λόγος ἐκ τῆς συντάξεως τῶν γεγραμμένων αἰνίττεται, πρῶτον μὲν εἰπὼν ὅτι,* ***ἐποίησεν ὁ Θεὸς τὸν ἄνθρωπον, κατ᾽ εἰκόνα Θεοῦ ἐποίησεν αὐτόν·*** *πάλιν δὲ τοῖς εἰρημένοις ἐπαγαγὼν, ὅτι* ***ἄρσεν καὶ θῆλυ ἐποίησεν αὐτοὺς,*** *ὅπερ ἀλλότριον τῶν περὶ Θεοῦ νοουμένων ἐστίν.*

[16.9] *Οἶμαι γὰρ ἐγὼ δόγμα τι μέγα καὶ ὑψηλὸν διὰ τῶν εἰρημένων ὑπὸ τῆς ἁγίας γραφῆς παραδίδοσθαι· τὸ δὲ δόγμα τοιοῦτόν ἐστι. Δύο τινῶν κατὰ τὸ ἀκρότατον πρὸς ἄλληλα διεστηκότων, μέσον ἐστὶ τὸ ἀνθρώπινον, τῆς τε θείας καὶ ἀσωμάτου φύσεως καὶ τῆς ἀλόγου καὶ κτηνώδους* [C] *ζωῆς· ἔξεστι γὰρ ἑκατέρου τῶν εἰρημένων ἐν τῷ ἀνθρωπίνῳ συγκρίματι θεωρῆσαι τὴν μοῖραν—τοῦ μὲν θείου τὸ λογικόν τε καὶ διανοητικὸν, ὃ τὴν κατὰ τὸ ἄρρεν καὶ θῆλυ διαφορὰν οὐ προσίεται· τοῦ δὲ ἀλόγου τὴν σωματικὴν κατασκευὴν καὶ διάπλασιν εἰς ἄρρεν τε καὶ θῆλυ μεμερισμένην· ἑκάτερον γὰρ τούτων ἐστὶ πάντως ἐν παντὶ τῷ μετέχοντι τῆς ἀνθρωπίνης ζωῆς· ἀλλὰ προτερεύειν τὸ νοερὸν, καθὼς παρὰ τοῦ τὴν ἀνθρωπογονίαν ἐν τάξει διεξελθόντος ἐμάθομεν· ἐπιγεννηματικὴν δὲ εἶναι τῷ*

50 *τούτου* B I 51–2 *πῶς—ὀνομάζεται*] quomodo diuinum et beatum et miserum et simile illi hoc a sancta scriptura nominatur? *Eri* 52 *ἐκείνῳ τοῦτο*] *τοῦτο ἐκείνῳ* D G L P S V X : *ἐκείνῳ τούτῳ* K O : *ἐκείνῳ* B *οὐκοῦν*] non itaque *Eri* 53 *ἐξεταστέον*] ordinanda sunt *Eri* *μετὰ ἀκριβείας* Æ ß I K N O W : *δι᾽ ἀκριβείας* G L M P Q S V X : *om.* D *εὑρήσομεν Mign* *μὲν om.* D 54 *δὲ*] *δέ τι* B *ἐποίησεν*] *ἐποίησεν οὖν* N 54–5 *φησὶν ὁ θεὸς* N 55–63 *τέλος—ἐποίησεν αὐτὸν om.* N 56 *ἐπανάληψιν*] adiungitur uelut *Dion* : *ΕΠΑΝΑΛΗΜΨΙΝ* (id est adiectionem) *Eri* 57 *ἄρρεν* Æ B I K O Q W 59 *ἄρσεν* D G L M P S X *φησὶ διῃρῆσθαι ὁ λόγος* Æ B I K O W : *φησὶ ὁ λόγος διῃρῆσθαι* M *διῃρῆσθαι*] *διαιρεῖσθαι* T : *διηρεῖσθαι* G P[ac] V X : *διῃρῆσθαι Ald Mign* 60 *οὐκοῦν*] non itaque *Eri* 61 *διῃρημένη Ald Mign* *τοιοῦτο* Æ K L O 62 *αἰνίσσεται* Æ B K M O *αἰνίττεται—μορφή (cap. 18.8, l. 71)* def. V 64 *ἐπάγων* Æ B C I K O Q T *ἄρρεν* Æ B I K O Q W 65 *νοουμένων*] *νόμῳ* B 66 *ἁγίας*] *ita* Æ B G I K L M O P Q S X *Forb* : *θείας* W *Ald Mign* 67 *δύο*] *δύο γὰρ* Æ B G I K M N O P Q T X 68 *ἀνθρώπινον*] humanam … naturam *Dion* *τε om.* N *θείας τε* D G L P Q S X 69 *φύσεως om. Dion* *ζωῆς*] naturam *Dion* *ἑκατέρας* Q 70 *τῷ ἀνθρωπίνῳ συγκρίματι*] humana comparatione *Eri* 71 *διανοητικόν τε καὶ λογικὸν* L *τὴν om.* G P X *θῆλυ*] *τὸ θῆλυ* Æ I K N O *διαφορὰν—θῆλυ om.* Z 72 *διάπλασιν*] duplicationem *Eri* *εἰς*] *τὸ κατὰ* N *ἄρρεν*] *τὸ ἄρρεν* N T *τε om.* N Q *θῆλυ*] *τὸ θῆλυ* N 73 *μεμερισμένον* Z *γὰρ τούτων ἐστὶ*] *πάρεστι τούτων* T 74 *ζωῆς*] substantia *Dion* *ἀλλὰ*] *ἀλλὰ καὶ* D S : *ἀλλὰ καὶ τὸ* L *τῷ νοερῷ* M T 74–5 *καθὼς—ἐμάθομεν*] ei rei quam humanae propagationi seruire uidemus ordine ipso conditionis exsequente didicimus *Dion* 74 *καθὼς om.* Æ ß I K N O Q T *Eri* *παρὰ om.* Z 75 *ἐν τάξει παρὰ τοῦ τὴν ἀνθρωπογονίαν* Q *ἀνθρωπογένειαν* Æ : *ἀνωπολυγονίαν* ß : humanam generationem *Eri* *τάξει*] *τῇ τάξει* N Q 75–6 *ἐπιγεννηματικὴν—συγγένειαν*] ad effectum quippe generationis quaedam est hominis cum irrationabilibus innata coniunctio *Dion* 75 *ἐπιγενηματικὴν* Æ ß G L M O P S W X : *ἐπιγενητὴν* N : supergenitiuam *Eri* *δὲ om.* W 75–6 *τῷ ἀνθρώπῳ εἶναι* M

[**16.6**] However, let the argument about these matters be left aside. Let the enquiry be turned to the question before us: how, the divine being blessed and humankind pitiable, is the latter called 'like' the former by Scripture? [**16.7**] The words must be examined with precision. For we find that what came to be *in accordance with the image* is one, and what is now manifest in wretchedness is another. *God made*, it says, *the human being, in accordance with the image of God he made it.* The creation of that which came to be *in accordance with the image* has an end; then it makes a repetition[8] of the account regarding the formation, and says, *male and female he made them.* I think it is known to everyone that this is understood to be outside the Prototype, *for in Christ Jesus*, as the apostle says, *there is neither male nor female,*[9] but the account says that the human being is indeed divided into these. [**16.8**] Therefore, the formation of our nature is in a sense twofold, that being likened to the divine [and] that being divided according to this difference; for something like this the account hints at by the syntax of what is written, first saying, *God made the human being, in accordance with the image of God he made it*, and then, adding to what has been said, *male and female he made them*, something that is foreign to what is conceived about God.[10]

[**16.9**] I think that by these words, Holy Scripture conveys to us a great and lofty doctrine; and the doctrine is this. While two [elements]—the divine and incorporeal nature, and the irrational and animal life—are separated from each other as extremes, the human is the span.[11] For there is to be beheld in the human compound a share of each of those mentioned—of the divine, the rational and intelligent, which does not admit the difference of male and female; of the irrational, the bodily formation and construction, divided into male and female—for each of them is certainly in all that partakes of human life. But the

[8] 'Repetition' translates the word ἐπανάληψιν which can mean either a 'resumption' or 'repetition' (cf. LSJ); Dionysius Exiguus takes it as indicating an addition (*adiungitur uelut*), as does Eriugena in his translation of the work (*ΕΠΑΝΑΛΗΜΨΙΝ id est adiectionem*), although in the *Periphyseon* (4.795a) he takes it as 'repetition' (*ΕΠΑΝΑΛΗΜΨΙΝ id est repetitionem*).

[9] Gal. 3:38.

[10] Cf. Gregory of Nyssa, *Cant.* 7 (Langerbeck, 213.2–6).

[11] On μέσον as 'span' see footnote 4 above (at chap. 16.3). Cf. Gregory of Nyssa, *An. et res.* 3.35 (Spira, 39.17–18); Philo, *Opif.* 135; Plotinus, *Enn.* 4.8.4.32; Nemesius, *De hom. nat.* 1.39 (Morani, 2.21–3.5). In the Greek, Gregory places the clause about the human being as the mid-point in the middle of the sentence.

ἀνθρώπῳ τὴν πρὸς τὸ ἄλογον κοινωνίαν τε καὶ συγγένειαν· πρῶτον μὲν γάρ φησιν, ὅτι **ἐποίησεν ὁ Θεὸς κατ' εἰκόνα** Θεοῦ **τὸν ἄνθρωπον**, δεικνὺς διὰ τῶν εἰρημένων, καθὼς φησιν ὁ ἀπόστολος, ὅτι ἐν τῷ [D] τοιούτῳ **ἄρρεν καὶ θῆλυ οὐκ ἔστιν**· εἶτα ἐπάγει τῆς ἀνθρωπίνης φύσεως τὰ ἰδιώματα, ὅτι **ἄρρεν καὶ θῆλυ ἐποίησεν αὐτούς**.

[16.10] Τί οὖν διὰ τούτου μανθάνομεν; Καί μοι μηδεὶς νεμεσάτω, πόρρωθεν [184] προσάγοντι τὸν λόγον τῷ προκειμένῳ νοήματι. Θεὸς τῇ ἑαυτοῦ φύσει πᾶν ὅτι πέρ ἐστι κατ' ἔννοιαν λαβεῖν ἀγαθὸν, ἐκεῖνό ἐστι—μᾶλλον δὲ, παντὸς ἀγαθοῦ τοῦ νοουμένου τε καὶ καταλαμβανομένου ἐπέκεινα ὢν, οὐ δι' ἄλλό τι κτίζει τὴν ἀνθρωπίνην ζωὴν ἢ διὰ τὸ ἀγαθὸς εἶναι· τοιοῦτος δὲ ὢν, καὶ διὰ τοῦτο πρὸς τὴν δημιουργίαν τῆς ἡμετέρας φύσεως ὁρμήσας, οὐκ ἂν ἡμιτελῆ τὴν τῆς ἀγαθότητος ἐνεδείξατο δύναμιν, τὸ μέν τι δοὺς ἐκ τῶν προσόντων αὐτῷ, τοῦ δὲ φθονήσας τῆς μετουσίας· ἀλλὰ τὸ τέλειον τῆς ἀγαθότητος εἶδος ἐν τούτῳ ἐστὶν, ἐκ τοῦ καὶ παραγαγεῖν τὸν ἄνθρωπον ἐκ τοῦ μὴ ὄντος εἰς γένεσιν, καὶ ἀνενδεᾶ τῶν ἀγαθῶν ἀπεργάσασθαι· ἐπεὶ δὲ πολὺς τῶν καθ' ἕκαστον ἀγαθῶν ὁ κατάλογος, οὐ μὲν οὖν ἔστιν ἀριθμῷ ῥᾳδίως τοῦτον διαλαβεῖν. Διὰ τοῦτο [B] περιληπτικῇ τινι φωνῇ τὰ πάντα συλλαβὼν ὁ λόγος ἐσήμανεν, ἐν τῷ εἰπεῖν, **κατ' εἰκόνα** Θεοῦ γεγενῆσθαι τὸν ἄνθρωπον· ἴσον γάρ ἐστι τοῦτο τῷ εἰπεῖν, ὅτι παντὸς ἀγαθοῦ μέτοχον τὴν ἀνθρωπίνην φύσιν ἐποίησεν· εἰ γὰρ πλήρωμα μὲν ἀγαθῶν τὸ θεῖον, ἐκείνου δὲ τοῦτο εἰκών· ἄρα ἐν τῷ πλῆρες εἶναι παντὸς ἀγαθοῦ, πρὸς τὸ ἀρχέτυπον ἡ εἰκὼν ἔχει τὴν ὁμοιότητα. **[16.11]** Οὐκοῦν ἐστιν ἐν ἡμῖν παντὸς μὲν καλοῦ ἰδέα, πᾶσα δὲ ἀρετὴ καὶ σοφία καὶ πᾶν ὅτι πέρ ἐστι πρὸς τὸ κρεῖττον νοούμενον· ἓν δὲ τῶν πάντων καὶ τὸ ἐλεύθερον ἀνάγκης εἶναι, καὶ μὴ ὑπεζεῦχθαί τινι φυσικῇ δυναστείᾳ, ἀλλ'

76 τὰ ἄλογα N τε *om.* T μὲν *om.* Æ B G I K M O P T X 77 θεοῦ] αὐτοῦ D L : τοῦ θεοῦ W *Ald Mign* τὸν ἄνθρώπον κατ' εἰκόνα θεοῦ D G L P S X 78 ἄρσεν D G L P S X 79 φύσεως] φύσεως ὁρμήσας G M P W X : φύσεως ἑρμηνεύσας S^{pcmg} ἄρσεν D L S 80 τούτων G M P S X νεμεσσάτω B : νομισάτω T^{ac} : νεμεσησάτω T^{pc} : νεμισάτω Z : μωμησάτων D E L S^{ac} 81 τὸν λόγον προσάγοντι I θεὸς] ὁ θεὸς Q τὴν ἑαυτοῦ φύσιν Z 81–2 πέρ ἐστι] πάρεστι G M 82 τοῦ *om.* N 83 τε καὶ *om.* B τε καὶ καταλαμβανομένου *om.* T ἐπέκεινα ὢν] praestantior *Dion* : summitas existens *Eri* ὢν] ὧν Z : πλὴν T 84 ἀγαθὸν Æ N τοιοῦτος δὲ ὢν, καὶ διὰ τοῦτο] ac per hoc *Eri* 85 ἡμετέρας] ἀνθρωπίνης *Ald Mign* ἡμιτελῆ] εἰ μη τελεῖ W Z 86 μέν τι] μέντοι T τοῦ] τὸ G P X φθονείσας W 87 καὶ *om.* G K O P X 88 παράγειν T ὄντως K O^{pc} ἀνενδεῆ *Mign* 89 ἐπειδὴ *SP* ἀγαθῶν *om.* *SP* 90 ἔστιν ἀριθμῷ ῥᾳδίως τοῦτον] ἔστιν τοῦτον ἀριθμῷ ῥᾳδίως W ἐστι τοῦτο ραδίως Z ῥᾳδίως] *Ald Mign* : ῥαδίως *Forb* τοῦτον ῥᾳδίως Æ I K M N O Q τοῦτον διαλαβεῖν ῥᾳδίως B *SP* τινι] *ita* Æ B I K M N O *Forb* : τῇ W *Ald Mign* : *om.* D G L P S T X 90–1 τὰ πάντα] *ita* D G L M P^2 Q S T *Forb* : πάντα Æ B K O P^{ac} : ἅπαντα *Ald Mign* 91 ἐσήμηνε I ἐν τῷ] τῷ Æ I : τὸ K O 91–2 κατ' εἰκόνα—τῷ εἰπεῖν *om.* O X 92 ὅτι *om.* *SP* μέτεχον L : μετέχειν G P : μετέχουσαν N Q 92–3 τὴν ἀνθρωπείαν φύσιν μέτοχον *SP* 93 εἰ γὰρ *om.* T 93–4 ἐκείνου δὲ τοῦτο] ἐκεῖνο δὲ τούτου D G I M N P Q S^{ac} X : huius homo *Dion* : illius autem hoc id est homo *Eri* 94 ἄρα ἐν τῷ πλῆρες] ἄρρεν τὸ πλῆρες Z ἄρα] *ita* G L M N P Q S *Forb* : ἆρα K X : ἄρ' W *SP Ald Mign* πλήρης Æ Q *SP* : πλήρη T 95 οὐκοῦν] non igitur *Eri* ἐστιν ἐν ἡμῖν] ἐν ἡμῖν ἐστι Æ B I K O : ἔστι μὲν ἡμῖν N : ἔστι μὲν ἐν ἡμῖν *SP* ἡμῖν *om.* T μὲν] δὲ W : *om.* M T *SP* καλοῦ] ἀγαθοῦ T *SP* 96 ὅτι] ὅ G N P T X ἐστι] ἂν ἐστι T 96–7 ἓν δὲ—εἶναι] prae omnibus uero quod ab omni necessitate liberi sumus *Dion* : in eo item quod sit omnium necessitate liberum *Eri* 96 πάντων] πάντων ἐστιν T 97 δυναστείᾳ φυσικῇ M : naturali (hoc est materiali) potentiae *Eri*

intellectual takes precedence, as we have learnt from one who gives in detail an ordered account of the origin of the human being,[12] participation and kinship with the irrational is concomitant to being human,[13] for he first says that *God made the human being in accordance with the image* of God, showing by what was said, just as the Apostle says, that in such a one *there is not male and female*, then he adds the particularities of human nature, that *male and female he made them*.[14]

[16.10] What, then, do we learn from this? Let no one be indignant with me if I bring from afar an explanation of the present matter. God, in his own nature, is everything that can be conceived of as good; or rather, being beyond any good that can be conceived or comprehended, he creates the human being for no other reason than that he is good. And being such, and for this reason setting upon the construction of our nature, he would not demonstrate the power of his goodness halfway, giving some of his own attributes, yet grudging participation in others; but the perfect form of goodness is in this, both in leading the human being out of non-being into genesis, and in his being made lacking no good gift.[15] Since the catalogue of the individual goods is extensive, it cannot easily be numbered. Therefore, the account indicated them all, summarizing them in a comprehensive phrase, by saying that the human being came to be *in accordance with the image* of God, for this is the same as to say that he made human nature participate in all good, for if the divine is the plenitude of good gifts, and this is the image of that, then the image has its likeness to the archetype in being filled with every good.[16] **[16.11]** Thus, there is in us a form of every beauty, all virtue and wisdom, and every higher thing that can be conceived. Of all these, one is to be free from

[12] The phrase 'the origin of the human being' translates Gregory's single word 'anthropogony'. The image of Moses providing an 'anthropogony' is used again at the end of the treatise, in 30.33, and earlier in Josephus, *C. Ap.* 1.8; Clement of Alexandria, *Strom.* 4.13.90.4; Eusebius, *Hist. eccl.* 1.2.4, 6; *Praep. Ev.* 11.4.4, 11.28.7. Dionysius Exiguus took the word in a different sense, as referring to sexual procreation, translating this clause as 'But from one who speaks about the very order of creation we have learnt that what is intellectual in us takes precedence before that which we see serves for the propagation of the human race'.

[13] 'Concomitant' translates the word ἐπιγεννηματικὴν, for which LSJ gives 'of the nature of an ἐπιγέννημα, resulting, consequential'. In philosophy, ἐπιγέννημα seems to be have been used primarily by the Stoics, for whom joy, cheerfulness, and the like are 'by-products' of virtue; cf. *SVF* 3.19.29 and 3.43.11 (=DL 7.95, 85–6) and Cicero, *Fin.* 3.9.32: 'But in the other arts when we speak of an "artistic" performance, this quality must be considered as in a sense subsequent to and a result of the action, it is what the Stoics call ἐπιγεννηματικόν.' In medical terms, ἐπιγέννημα can be used to describe a symptom accompanying a disease (cf. Galen, *Def.*, ed. Kühn, 19.395). It was translated with this sense by Eriugena ('supergenitiuam'). Dionysius Exiguus, in a similar manner to the way he translated 'anthropogony' in the previous clause, renders this clause as 'for in fact there is some kind of innate conjunction of the human with irrational things for the accomplishing of generation', and he was followed by Wilson: 'his community and kindred with the irrational is for man a provision for reproduction'. The verbal form of the word is used in this treatise 30.33, where the subject is again Moses' 'anthropogony'.

[14] Cf. Philo, *Opif.* 76: 'And when Moses had called the genus "human", quite admirably did he distinguish its species, adding that it had been created "male and female", and this though its individual members had not yet taken shape.'

[15] Cf. Plato, *Tim.* 29d–30a; Gregory of Nyssa, *Or. Cat.* 5.3–10 (Mühlenberg, 16.16–20.5); Gregory of Nyssa, *An. et res.* 7.24 (Spira, 78.6–11).

[16] Cf. Gregory of Nyssa, *An. et res.* 6.22 (Spira, 68.9–14).

αὐτεξούσιον πρὸς τὸ δοκοῦν ἔχειν τὴν γνώμην· ἀδέσποτον γάρ τι χρῆμα ἡ ἀρετὴ καὶ ἑκούσιον, τὸ δὲ κατηναγκασμένον καὶ βεβιασμένον [C] ἀρετὴ εἶναι οὐ δύναται.

[**16.12**] Ἐν πᾶσι τοίνυν τῆς εἰκόνος τοῦ πρωτοτύπου κάλλους τὸν χαρακτῆρα φερούσης, εἰ μὴ κατά τι τὴν διαφορὰν ἔχοι, οὐκέτ' ἂν εἴη πάντως ὁμοίωμα ἀλλὰ ταὐτὸν ἐκείνῳ διὰ πάντων ἀναδειχθήσεται τὸ ἐν παντὶ ἀπαράλλακτον. Τίνα τοίνυν αὐτοῦ τε τοῦ θείου καὶ τοῦ πρὸς τὸ θεῖον ὡμοιωμένου τὴν διαφορὰν καθορῶμεν; ἐν τῷ, τὸ μὲν ἀκτίστως εἶναι, τὸ δὲ διὰ κτίσεως ὑποστῆναι· ἡ δὲ τῆς τοιαύτης ἰδιότητος διαφορὰ πάλιν ἑτέρων ἰδιωμάτων ἀκολουθίαν ἐποίησε· συνομολογεῖται γὰρ πάντη τε καὶ πάντως, τὴν μὲν ἄκτιστον φύσιν καὶ ἄτρεπτον εἶναι, καὶ ἀεὶ ὡσαύτως ἔχειν· τὴν δὲ κτιστὴν ἀδύνατον ἄνευ ἀλλοιώσεως συστῆναι· αὐτὴ γὰρ ἡ ἐκ τοῦ μὴ ὄντος εἰς τὸ εἶναι πάροδος, κίνησίς τις ἐστὶ καὶ ἀλλοίωσις τοῦ μὴ ὄντος εἰς τὸ εἶναι, κατὰ τὸ [D] θεῖον βούλημα μεθισταμένου. [**16.13**] Καὶ ὥσπερ τὸν ἐπὶ τοῦ χαλκοῦ χαρακτῆρα ***Καίσαρος εἰκόνα*** λέγει τὸ εὐαγγέλιον, δι' οὗ μανθάνομεν κατὰ μὲν τὸ πρόσχημα τὴν ὁμοίωσιν εἶναι τοῦ μεμορφωμένου πρὸς Καίσαρα ἐν δὲ τῷ ὑποκειμένῳ τὴν διαφορὰν ἔχειν· οὕτω καὶ κατὰ τὸν παρόντα λόγον, ἀντὶ χαρακτήρων τὰ ἐπιθεωρούμενα τῇ τε θείᾳ φύσει καὶ τῇ ἀνθρωπίνῃ κατανοήσαντες ἐν οἷς ἡ ὁμοιότης ἐστὶν· ἐν τῷ ὑποκειμένῳ τὴν διαφορὰν ἐξευρίσκομεν, ἥτις ἐν τῷ ἀκτίστῳ καὶ τῷ κτιστῷ καθορᾶται.

[**16.14**] Ἐπειδὴ τοίνυν τὸ μὲν ὡσαύτως ἔχει ἀεὶ, τὸ δὲ διὰ κτίσεως γεγενημένον ἀπὸ ἀλλοιώσεως τοῦ εἶναι ἤρξατο καὶ συγγενῶς πρὸς τὴν τοιαύτην ἔχει τροπήν· διὰ [185] τοῦτο ***ὁ εἰδὼς τὰ πάντα πρὶν γενέσεως αὐτῶν***, καθώς φησιν ἡ προφητεία, ἐπακολουθήσας, μᾶλλον δὲ προκατανοήσας, τῇ προγνωστικῇ δυνάμει πρὸς ὅ τι ῥέπει κατὰ τὸ αὐτοκρατές τε καὶ αὐτεξούσιον τῆς ἀνθρωπίνης προαιρέσεως ἡ κίνησις, ἐπειδὴ τὸ ἐσόμενον εἶδεν· ἐπιτεχνᾶται τῇ εἰκόνι τὴν κατὰ τὸ ἄρρεν καὶ θῆλυ διαφοράν, ἥτις οὐκέτι πρὸς τὸ θεῖον ἀρχέτυπον βλέπει, ἀλλά, καθὼς εἴρηται, τῇ ἀλογωτέρᾳ προσῳκείωται φύσει. [**16.15**] Τὴν δὲ αἰτίαν τῆς τοιαύτης ἐπιτεχνήσεως μόνοι μὲν ἂν εἰδεῖεν οἱ τῆς ἀληθείας ***αὐτόπται καὶ ὑπηρέται τοῦ λόγου***· ἡμεῖς δὲ,

98 ἔχει N   ἀδέσποτον] ἀδέσποτον μὲν Æ B I N W   ἡ ἀρετὴ χρῆμα L   ἡ *om.* T   99 καὶ βεβιασμένον ἀρετὴ] ἀρετῆς Z   101 τι *om.* Z   ἔχοι] *ita* Æ B D G K L M O P S T X *Forb* : ἔχει I N : ἔχῃ *Ald* : ἔχῃ *Mign*   οὐκέτ'] *ita* Æ G K L O P Q S X *Forb* : οὐκ D : οὐκέτι W *Ald Mign*   102 ταὐτὸν] ipsum atque aequale *Dion* : hoc *Eri*   ἐκείνῳ] ἐκεῖνο *Ald Mign*   διὰ πάντων] πάντως N   103 ὁμοιωμένου N : ὡμοιωμένου B[ac] (*ω post οι in ου a 1*[a] *man. mutatum*) : ὁμοιουμένου D G L M P S T W : ὁμοιουμένου καὶ X   ἐν *om.* Q   104 τὸ[1] : τὸν Z   ἄκτιστον Q : increata *Dion* : non creatum *Eri*   105 πάλιν ἑτέρων] παλαιοτέρων Z   συνωμολόγηται M T : ἐνομολογεῖται G   τε *om.* Æ B I K N O   106 καὶ[1] *om.* Q   εἶναι καὶ ἄτρεπτον φύσιν D G L P S X   καὶ[2] *om.* I   107 κτιστὴν] κτίσιν Z   ἀδύνατον] μὴ N Q   συστῆναι *om.* T   108 ἐστὶ τις W   τὸ[2] *om.* B N   109 μεθισταμένη N   τὸν ἐπὶ τοῦ χαλκοῦ] impressam in aere *Dion* : in aere *Eri*   τοῦ *om.* T   110 εἰκόνα] εἰκόνα εἶναι T   κατὰ μὲν τὸ πρόσχημα] τὸ σχῆμα Z   πρόσχημα] σχῆμα Æ B I K M N O Q T   112 ἀντὶ χαρακτήρων] imaginationem quae *Eri*   τε *om.* G N P Q X   114 ἐξευρίσκομεν, ἥτις] ἐξευρισκομένου· τίς Z   τῷ *om.* D G I N P   116 ἐπειδὴ] ἐπεὶ T   ἔχει] ἔχει καὶ *Ald Mign*   ἀπὸ] *ita* G L M N P S X *Forb* : ἀπ' O W *Ald Mign*   117 συγγενῶν W   ἔχει] ἔχει πρὸ W   118 φησι τῇ προφητείᾳ T   119 ἀπακολουθήσας I   προκατανοήσας] κατανοήσας N   120 τὸ αὐτοκρατές τε καὶ αὐτεξούσιον] suam uirtutem suamque potentiam *Eri*   ἡ τῆς ἀνθρωπίνης προαιρέσεως D G L M P Q S T X   121 εἶδεν] οἶδεν I T : ἴδεν Q   κατὰ] *ita* Æ B D I K L M P Q S T X *Forb* : πρὸς N : περὶ κατὰ W : περὶ *Ald Mign*   ἄρσεν D   καὶ] καὶ τὸ L M N O Q   122–3 τῇ ἀλογωτέρᾳ προσῳκείωται] in mutabiliori possidet *Eri*   123 προσοικείωται N P[ac] W   ἐπιτεχνάσεως I : ἐπιτεχνίσεως K O : τεχνήσεως D : artificis *Dion* : supermachinationis *Eri*   124 μὲν *om.* B K O

necessity, and not in bondage to any natural domination, but to have self-determining deliberation regarding what we resolve. For virtue is something free and voluntary; what is constrained and forced cannot be virtue.[17]

[**16.12**] Now as the image bears in all points the stamp of the prototypical beauty, if it did not have a difference in some respect it would assuredly no longer be a likeness but, being without divergence in any point, it will be shown to be identical to it in every way.[18] What difference then do we discern between the divine itself and that which is likened to the divine? We find it in the fact that one exists uncreatedly, the other subsists through creation, and the difference of this property produces further a sequence of other properties. For it is certainly and universally confessed that the uncreated nature is also immutable, and always remains as it is; while the created nature cannot subsist without alteration, for its very passage from non-being into being is a kind of movement and alteration of the non-existent being changed by the divine purpose into being.[19] [**16.13**] And just as the Gospel calls the stamp upon the coin *the image of Caesar*,[20] from which we learn that in regard to outward appearance there was a likeness in that which was modelled on Caesar but a difference in the substratum, so also in the present account, when, instead of the outward forms, we consider the [attributes] contemplated in the divine nature and the human, in which there is the likeness, we find that the difference beheld between the uncreated and the created lies in the substratum.[21]

[**16.14**] Since, then, the one always remains as it is, while the other, having come into being though creation, began to exist from alteration and has kinship with such change, on this account *he who knows all things before their genesis*, as the prophecy says,[22] following, or rather knowing beforehand, by his power of foreknowledge towards what the movement of human choice inclines, in accordance with its independence and self-determination—since he knows what is to be, he devised for the image the difference according to male and female, which no longer looks to the divine archetype but, as was said, assimilates to the less rational nature. [**16.15**] The reason for such a device only those who were *eyewitnesses* of the truth *and ministers of the Word* can know;[23] but we, as far as is possible, by

[17] Cf. Gregory of Nyssa, *An. et res.* 7.17 (Spira, 76.11–13); *Cant.* 5 (Langerbeck, 160.17–161.1); cf. Plato, *Resp.* 10.617e.

[18] Cf. Gregory of Nyssa, *An. et res.* 2.41 (Spira, 26.10–18); Plato, *Crat.* 432b.

[19] Cf. Gregory of Nyssa, *Or. Cat.* 6.7, 21.1–3 (Mühlenberg, 24.1–6, 55.4–56.10); Origen, *Princ.* 2.9.2; 4.4.8.

[20] Matt. 22:21.

[21] Cf. Methodius, *De res.* 2.24 (Bonwetsch, 379–80).

[22] Sus. (*Θ*) 42; cf. *Hex.* 9 (Drobner, 18.12–14).

[23] Luke 1:2.

καθώς ἐστι δυνατόν, διὰ στοχασμῶν τινων καὶ εἰκόνων φαντασθέντες τὴν ἀλήθειαν, τὸ ἐπὶ νοῦν ἐλθὸν οὐκ ἀποφαντικῶς ἐκτιθέμεθα, ἀλλ' ὡς ἐν γυμνασίας εἴδει τοῖς εὐγνώμοσι τῶν ἀκροωμένων προσθήσομεν.

[16.16] *Τί τοίνυν ἐστὶν* [B] *ὃ περὶ τούτων διενοήθημεν; Εἰπὼν ὁ λόγος ὅτι* ***ἐποίησεν ὁ Θεὸς τὸν ἄνθρωπον****, τῷ ἀορίστῳ τῆς σημασίας ἅπαν ἐνδείκνυται τὸ ἀνθρώπινον· οὐ γὰρ συνωνομάσθη τῷ κτίσματι νῦν ὁ Ἀδάμ, καθὼς ἐν τοῖς ἐφεξῆς ἡ ἱστορία φησίν· ἀλλ' ὄνομα τῷ κτισθέντι ἀνθρώπῳ οὐχ ὁ τὶς ἀλλ' ὁ καθόλου ἐστίν· οὐκοῦν τῇ καθολικῇ τῆς φύσεως κλήσει τοιοῦτόν τι ὑπονοεῖν ἐναγόμεθα, ὅτι τῇ θείᾳ προγνώσει τε καὶ δυνάμει πᾶσα ἡ ἀνθρωπότης ἐν τῇ πρώτῃ κατασκευῇ περιείληπται· χρὴ γὰρ Θεῷ μηδὲν ἀόριστον ἐν τοῖς γεγενημένοις παρ' αὐτοῦ νομίζειν, ἀλλ' ἑκάστου τῶν ὄντων εἶναί τι πέρας καὶ μέτρον, τῇ τοῦ πεποιηκότος σοφίᾳ περιμετρούμενον.*

[16.17] *Ὥσπερ τοίνυν ὁ τὶς ἄνθρωπος τῷ κατὰ τὸ σῶμα ποσῷ περιείργεται, καὶ μέτρον αὐτῷ τῆς ὑποστάσεως ἡ πηλικότης ἐστίν, ἡ συναπαρτιζομένη* [C] *τῇ ἐπιφανείᾳ τοῦ σώματος· οὕτως οἶμαι καθάπερ ἐν ἑνὶ σώματι ὅλον τὸ τῆς ἀνθρωπότητος πλήρωμα τῇ προγνωστικῇ δυνάμει παρὰ τοῦ Θεοῦ τῶν ὅλων περισχεθῆναι, καὶ τοῦτο διδάσκειν τὸν λόγον τὸν εἰπόντα, ὅτι* ***καὶ ἐποίησεν ὁ Θεὸς τὸν ἄνθρωπον, κατ' εἰκόνα*** *Θεοῦ* ***ἐποίησεν αὐτόν****· οὐ γὰρ ἐν μέρει τῆς φύσεως ἡ εἰκών, οὐδὲ ἔν τινι τῶν κατ' αὐτὴν θεωρουμένων ἡ χάρις· ἀλλ' ἐφ' ἅπαν τὸ γένος ἐπίσης ἡ τοιαύτη διήκει δύναμις· σημεῖον δέ, πᾶσιν ὡσαύτως ὁ νοῦς ἐγκαθίδρυται· πάντες τοῦ διανοεῖσθαι καὶ προβουλεύειν τὴν δύναμιν ἔχουσι, καὶ τὰ ἄλλα πάντα δι' ὧν ἡ θεία φύσις ἐν τῷ κατ' αὐτὴν γεγονότι ἀπεικονίζεται. Ὁμοίως ἔχει ὅ τε τῇ πρώτῃ τοῦ κόσμου κατασκευῇ συναναδειχθεὶς ἄνθρωπος καὶ ὁ μετὰ τὴν τοῦ παντὸς συντέλειαν γενησόμενος,* [D] *ἐπίσης ἐφ' ἑαυτῶν φέρουσι τὴν θείαν εἰκόνα.* [16.18] *Διὰ τοῦτο εἷς ἄνθρωπος κατωνομάσθη τὸ πᾶν, ὅτι τῇ δυνάμει τοῦ Θεοῦ οὔτε τι παρῴχηκεν οὔτε μέλλει, ἀλλὰ καὶ τὸ προσδοκώμενον ἐπίσης τῷ παρόντι τῇ περιεκτικῇ τοῦ παντὸς ἐνεργείᾳ περικρατεῖται. Πᾶσα τοίνυν ἡ φύσις ἡ ἀπὸ τῶν πρώτων μέχρι τῶν ἐσχάτων διήκουσα, μία τις τοῦ ὄντος ἐστὶν εἰκών· ἡ δὲ πρὸς τὸ ἄρρεν καὶ θῆλυ τοῦ γένους διαφορὰ προσκατεσκευάσθη τελευταῖον τῷ πλάσματι, διὰ τὴν αἰτίαν, ὡς οἶμαι, ταύτην.*

125 *εἰκόνων*] *εἰκότων* B O T : indiciis *Dion* : consequentiis *Eri* *φαντασθέντες*] *φθάσαντες* N : *φράσαντες* Q W : uestigia persquentes *Dion* : silentes *Eri* 126 *ἐλθὸν*] *ἐλθὼν* O W : *ἐλθεῖν* Z *ἀποφατικῶς* M N W *εἴδει*] si oportet *Eri* 127 *προθήσομεν* B I T : *προθήσωμεν* Q : *προ θήσομεν* N 129 *ἀορίστῳ*] *ἀοράτῳ* L : *ἀρίστω* Z *ἐπιδείκνυται* N 130 *συνωνομάσθη τῷ κτίσματι*] in conditione nominatus est *Dion* *κτίσματι*] *κτίσαντι* Z *ὁ om.* Q 131 *ὃ τὶς ἀλλ' ὃ* H N *ὁ τὶς*] *ὅτι* Z *τίς* ß I K L M P S *καθόλου*] *καθόλον* L *οὐκοῦν*] non igitur *Eri* 131–2 *τῇ καθολικῇ*] *τῆς καθολικῆς τῇ* Z 132 *τοιοῦτο* Æ 132–3 *τε προγνώσει* Æ B K O 135 *περιμετρούμενον*] *καταμετρούμενον* D 136 *τίς* Æ G H I K L M O P S X : *om.* B 137 *συναπαρτιζομένη*] *ἀπαρτιζομένη* D : *συναρπαζομένη* L 138 *ἐν om.* B D L *ἑνὶ*] *ἑνὶ τινι* Æ B I K M O Q 138–9 *ὅλον τὸ . . . πλήρωμα τῇ*] *ὅλῳ τῷ . . . πληρώματι* T 139 *τῷ θεῷ* D G H L P S X 140 *περὶενσχεθῆναι* N *τοῦτον* D G H P X *διδάσκει* D *ὅτι om.* N *καί*[2] *om.* K M O W 141 *κατ'*] *καὶ κατ' Mign* 142 *οὐδ'* D G H I L P S X *κατ' αὐτὴν*] *καθ' ἑαυτὴν* B : *καθ' αὐτὸν Mign* : *om.* Z 143 *διήκει*] *ἦλθε* W *δὲ*] *δὲ ὅτι Mign* *πᾶσιν ὡσαύτως*] *πάλιν ὡς αὐτὸς* T 144 *πάντες*] *πάντες γὰρ* I M *καὶ*[1]] *καὶ τοῦ* T *τὰ ἄλλα*] *τἄλλα* Æ B D G H I L P S X 145 *καθ' αὐτὴν* M : *καθ' ἑαυτὴν* Æ B H *ὅ τε*] *ὅτι* I : *ὃ* L 146 *κατασκευῇ τοῦ κόσμου* N *τοῦ κόσμου om.* D G H L P S[ac] (*corr. in marg.*) X *μετὰ*] *κατὰ Ald Mign* 147 *γενησόμενος*] *γεγενημένος* M : *ἡγησόμενος* K O 149 *οὔτε*] *οὔτε τι* D L M 151 *τοῦ ὄντος*] substantiae *Dion* : uere existentis *Eri* *ἐστὶ τοῦ ὄντος* I 152 *καὶ*] *καὶ τὸ* D G H I M P S W X *διαφορὰ τοῦ γένους* B *προκατεσκευάσθη* D M P X : *προκατασκευάσθη* H *πλάσματι*] *πλάσαντι* Z

means of some guesses and images picturing the truth, do not set forth categorically what comes to mind, but add it in a form of an exercise for our well-disposed hearers.[24]

[16.16] What is it then that we think concerning these matters? When the account says that *God made the human being*, all humankind is indicated by the indefinite character of the term; for the creature was not here also called 'Adam', as the narrative that follows relates, but the name given to the created human is not the particular but of the universal.[25] Thus, we are led by the universal name of the nature to suppose something such as this, that by divine foreknowledge and power all humanity is included in the first formation. For it is fitting for God not to think of any of the things that had come to be by him as indeterminate, but that for each being there should be some limit and measure marked out by the wisdom of the Maker.

[16.17] Now just as any particular human being is encompassed by his bodily dimensions, and his magnitude, commensurate with the appearance of his body, is the measure of his subsistence, so also, I think, that the entire plenitude of humanity was included by the God of all, by the power of his foreknowledge, as in one body, and that this is what the account teaches, saying that *And God made the human being, in accordance with the image* of God *made he him*. For the image is not in part of our nature, nor is the grace in any one of the things contemplated regarding it, but this power extends equally to the whole genus; a sign of this is that the intellect is seated in all alike. For all have the power of understanding and deliberating,[26] and all the other attributes through which the divine nature is reflected in that which came to be in accordance with it. The human being manifested together with the first formation of the world, and he who shall come to be after consummation of all, both likewise have this: they equally bear in themselves the divine image. **[16.18]** For this reason the whole was called one human being, because to the power of God nothing has either passed or is to come, but even that which is looked for is embraced equally with the present by his all-embracing activity. The whole nature, then, extending from the first to the last, is a kind of single image of He Who Is. But the difference between male and female was additionally fashioned last for that which is moulded, I suppose, for this reason.

[24] 'As an exercise': cf. Gregory of Nyssa, *Hex.* 6 (Drobner, 13.17–18); *An. et res.* 3.36 (Spira, 40.6), where it is also in reference to characteristics not found in the archetype but which are concomitant (ἐπιγεγενῆσθαι, 3.35; Spira, 40.3); *Trid. spat.* (Gebhardt, 286.15–16).

[25] Cf. Gregory of Nyssa, *Hex.* 31 (Drobner, 44.8).

[26] Cf. Gregory of Nyssa, *Hex.* 7 (Drobner, 15.3–5).

Τί χρὴ λέγειν πρὸς τοὺς ἐπαποροῦντας, εἰ μετὰ τὴν ἁμαρτίαν ἡ παιδοποιΐα, πῶς ἂν ἐγένοντο αἱ ψυχαὶ εἰ ἀναμάρτητοι διέμειναν οἱ ἐξ ἀρχῆς ἄνθρωποι.

[17.1] Μᾶλλον δέ, πρὶν τὸ προκείμενον διερευνῆσαι, κρεῖττον ἴσως τοῦ προφερομένου παρὰ τῶν μαχομένων ἡμῖν ἐπιζητῆσαι τὴν λύσιν· λέγουσι γάρ, πρὸ τῆς ἁμαρτίας μήτε τόκον ἱστορεῖσθαι μήτε ὠδῖνα μήτε τὴν πρὸς παιδοποιΐαν ὁρμήν· ἀποικισθέντων δὲ τοῦ παραδείσου μετὰ τὴν ἁμαρτίαν, καὶ τῆς γυναικὸς τῇ τιμωρίᾳ τῶν ὠδίνων κατακριθείσης, οὕτως ἐλθεῖν τὸν Ἀδὰμ εἰς τὸ γνῶναι γαμικῶς τὴν ὁμόζυγον, καὶ τότε τῆς παιδοποιΐας τὴν ἀρχὴν γενέσθαι· εἰ οὖν [B] γάμος ἐν τῷ παραδείσῳ οὐκ ἦν οὔτε ὠδὶς οὔτε τόκος, ἀνάγκην εἶναί φασιν ἐκ τοῦ ἀκολούθου λογίζεσθαι, μὴ ἂν ἐν πλήθει γενέσθαι τὰς τῶν ἀνθρώπων ψυχάς, εἰ μὴ πρὸς τὸ θνητὸν ἡ τῆς ἀθανασίας χάρις μετέπεσε καὶ ὁ γάμος διὰ τῶν ἐπιγινομένων συνετήρει τὴν φύσιν, ἀντὶ τῶν ὑπεξιόντων τοὺς ἐξ αὐτῶν ἀντεισάγων· ὥστε λυσιτελῆσαι τρόπον τινὰ τὴν ἁμαρτίαν ἐπεισελθοῦσαν τῇ ζωῇ τῶν ἀνθρώπων· ἔμεινε γὰρ ἂν ἐν τῇ τῶν πρωτοπλάστων δυάδι τὸ ἀνθρώπινον γένος, μὴ τοῦ κατὰ τὸν θάνατον φόβου πρὸς διαδοχὴν τὴν φύσιν ἀνακινήσαντος.

[17.2] Ἀλλ' ἐν τούτοις πάλιν ὁ μὲν ἀληθὴς λόγος, ὅστις ποτὲ ὢν τυγχάνει, μόνοις ἂν εἴη δῆλος τοῖς κατὰ Παῦλον τὰ τοῦ παραδείσου μυηθεῖσιν ἀπόρρητα· ὁ δὲ ἡμέτερος τοιοῦτός ἐστιν. Ἀντιλεγόντων ποτὲ τῶν Σαδδουκαίων τῷ κατὰ [C] τὴν ἀνάστασιν λόγῳ, καὶ τὴν πολύγαμον ἐκείνην γυναῖκα, τὴν τοῖς ἑπτὰ γενομένην ἀδελφοῖς, εἰς σύστασιν τοῦ καθ' ἑαυτοὺς δόγματος προφερόντων, εἶτα τίνος μετὰ τὴν ἀνάστασιν ἔσται πυνθανομένων, ἀποκρίνεται πρὸς τὸν λόγον ὁ Κύριος, οὐ μόνον τοὺς Σαδδουκαίους παιδεύων ἀλλὰ καὶ πᾶσι τοῖς μετὰ ταῦτα τῆς ἐν τῇ ἀναστάσει ζωῆς φανερῶν τὸ μυστήριον. **Ἐν γὰρ τῇ ἀναστάσει,** φησίν, **οὔτε γαμοῦσιν οὔτε γαμίσκονται, οὔτε γὰρ ἀποθανεῖν ἔτι δύνανται· ἰσάγγελοι γάρ εἰσι, καὶ υἱοὶ Θεοῦ εἰσι, τῆς ἀναστάσεως υἱοὶ ὄντες·** ἡ δὲ τῆς ἀναστάσεως χάρις οὐδὲν ἕτερον ἡμῖν ἐπαγγέλλεται ἢ τὴν εἰς τὸ ἀρχαῖον τῶν πεπτωκότων ἀποκατάστασιν· ἐπάνοδος γάρ τις ἐστὶν ἐπὶ τὴν πρώτην ζωὴν ἡ προσδοκωμένη χάρις, τὸν ἀποβληθέντα τοῦ παραδείσου πάλιν εἰς αὐτὸν [D] ἐπανάγουσα· εἰ τοίνυν ἡ τῶν ἀποκαθισταμένων ζωὴ πρὸς τὴν τῶν ἀγγέλων οἰκείως ἔχει, δῆλον ὅτι ὁ πρὸ τῆς παραβάσεως βίος

Cap. 18 Æ I K N O Q T *Dion Eri*

1–2 *τί—ἄνθρωποι*] contra eos qui dicunt peccatum utiliter introductum ad propagationem humani generis et quod per peccatum haec animalem generationem meruit *Λ* *πῶς ἂν—ἄνθρωποι om.* W 2 *αἱ ψυχαὶ*] *οἱ ἄν(θρωπ)οι* Z *ἐξ ἀρχῆς οἱ* Q 4 *γὰρ om.* N T 5 *τόκον*] *γάμον* D E F G L P S W X *τὴν om.* D G P X 6 *τῇ om.* B Q 8 *τῷ om.* D G L P S X 9 *ὠδὶν* Æ D K N O P T S[ac] (*s sup. l.*) X : *ὠδῖν* G : *ὠδίνη* L 11–12 *ὁ γάμος—ἀντεισάγων*] nuptiae per superuenientes est pro oboedientibus reductos naturam conseruarent *Eri* 12 *ἐξ*] *ἀντ'* Æ B I K O 15 *ἀνακαινίσαντος* I K M O W 16 *πάλιν*] *πᾶσιν* N *μὲν*] *μὴν* *Mign* *μόνος* M 17 *εἴη δῆλος*] *ἐπίδολος* N *δῆλον* X *τοῦ om.* Q *δὲ*] *δ'* M 19 *ἐκείνην om.* N *γυναῖκα ἐκείνην* M *γεγενημένην* N T : *γεγαμημένην* A B 20 *κατ' αὐτοὺς* I 20–1 *ἔσται μετὰ τὴν ἀνάστασιν* D G L P S X 22 *σαδδικαίους* W *τοῖς μετὰ ταῦτα τῆς ἐν τῇ ἀναστάσει*] *τῆς μετὰ τὴν ἀνάστασιν* Æ B I K M O Q T *Dion Eri* *ταῦτα*] *ταύτης* D[2] : *om.* D[ac] G P *ἐν τῇ om.* X 24 *γαμίζονται* B L N : *ἐκγαμίζονται* I : ducent uxores *Dion* *οὔτε*] *οὐδὲ* B I K N O 24–5 *εἰσι θεοῦ* Æ B K M O Q 25 *εἰσι om.* I 26 *ἀρχαῖον*] *ἀρχέτυπον* N 27 *ἐπὶ τὴν πρώτην ἐστὶν* M Q *ἐστιν om.* D G L P S X 28 *εἰς*] *ἐπ'* M T : *πρὸς* N *αὐτὸν*] *ἑαυτὸν* X 29 *δῆλον ὅτι*] *δηλονότι* *Ald Mign* *παραβάσεως*] *καταπτώσεως* M Q : ruinam *Dion Eri* *βίος*] *ἄνθρωπος* M *Dion* : *ὡς* Q : *om.* *Eri*

What we must answer to those who ask: 'If procreation comes after the sin, how would souls have come into being if human beings had remained sinless from the beginning?'[27]

[17.1] It is better, perhaps, before investigating the matter, rather to enquire into the solution brought forward by our opponents; for they say that before the sin there is no account of childbirth or of travail or of the impulse towards procreation; but that when they were banished from Paradise after the sin, and the woman was condemned with the punishment of travail, then Adam entered into marital knowledge with his partner, and then there was the beginning of procreation. If, then, marriage did not exist in Paradise, nor travail nor childbirth, they say that, by necessary consequence, it must be supposed that human souls would not have existed in plurality if the grace of immortality had not fallen away to mortality and marriage preserved our nature by means of descendants, introducing the offspring of those departing to take their place, so that the sin that entered in, in a certain way, benefitted the life of human beings, for the human race would have remained in the pair of the first-formed, had not the fear of death impelled their nature to provide succession.

[17.2] But in these matters, again, the true account, whatever it may be, can be clear only to those, like Paul, who are initiated into the ineffable things of Paradise;[28] but our answer is this. When the Sadducees at one time argued against the account of the resurrection, and, to establish their own doctrine, brought forward that polygamous woman, who had been wife to seven brothers, and then enquired whose she will be after the resurrection, the Lord answered their argument, not only instructing the Sadducees, but also revealing to all who come after them the mystery of the life in the resurrection: *For in the resurrection*, he says, *they neither marry nor are given in marriage, neither can they die any more; for they are equal to the angels, and are children of God, being the children of the resurrection.*[29] Now the grace of the resurrection promises us nothing other than the restoration of the fallen to the primordial state; for the grace looked for is a kind of ascent to the first life, bringing back again to Paradise him who was cast

[27] *Bodl. 238* (as Chap. 18): 'Against those who say that sin was a useful introduction for the propagation of the human race; and that by sin it deserved animal generation'.

[28] Cf. 2 Cor. 12:4.

[29] Luke 20:35–6; cf. Gregory of Nyssa, *An. et res.* 10.58 (Spira, 110.16–20); Methodius, *De res.* 1, 51.2 (Bonwetsch, 305.6–13).

ἀγγελικός τις ἦν· διὸ καὶ ἡ πρὸς τὸ ἀρχαῖον τῆς ζωῆς ἡμῶν ἐπάνοδος τοῖς ἀγγέλοις ὡμοίωται· ἀλλὰ μήν, καθὼς εἴρηται, γάμου [189] παρ᾽ αὐτοῖς οὐκ ὄντος, ἐν μυριάσιν ἀπείροις αἱ στρατιαὶ τῶν ἀγγέλων εἰσίν, οὕτω γὰρ ἐν ταῖς ὀπτασίαις ὁ Δανιὴλ διηγήσατο· οὐκοῦν, κατὰ τὸν αὐτὸν τρόπον, εἴπερ μηδεμία παρατροπή τε καὶ ἔκστασις ἀπὸ τῆς ἀγγελικῆς ὁμοτιμίας ἐξ ἁμαρτίας ἡμῖν ἐγένετο, οὐκ ἂν οὐδὲ ἡμεῖς τοῦ γάμου πρὸς τὸν πληθυσμὸν ἐδεήθημεν· ἀλλ᾽ ὅστις ἐστὶν ἐν τῇ φύσει τῶν ἀγγέλων τοῦ πλεονασμοῦ τρόπος (ἄρρητος μὲν καὶ ἀνεπινόητος στοχασμοῖς ἀνθρωπίνοις, πλὴν ἀλλὰ πάντως ἐστίν) οὗτος ἂν καὶ ἐπὶ τῶν **βραχύ τι παρ᾽ ἀγγέλους ἠλαττωμένων** ἀνθρώπων ἐνήργησεν, εἰς τὸ ὡρισμένον ὑπὸ τῆς βουλῆς τοῦ πεποιηκότος μέτρον τὸ ἀνθρώπινον αὔξων. [17.3] Εἰ δὲ στενοχωρεῖταί τις, ἐπιζητῶν τὸν τῆς γενέσεως τῶν ψυχῶν τρόπον, εἰ μὴ προσεδεήθη τῆς διὰ τοῦ γάμου συνεργίας ὁ ἄνθρωπος, ἀντερωτήσομεν [B] καὶ ἡμεῖς τὸν τῆς ἀγγελικῆς ὑποστάσεως τρόπον, πῶς ἐν ἀπείροις μυριάσιν ἐκεῖνοι, καὶ μία οὐσία ὄντες καὶ ἐν πολλοῖς ἀριθμούμενοι· τοῦτο γὰρ προσφόρως ἀποκρινούμεθα τῷ προφέροντι, πῶς ἂν ἦν δίχα τοῦ γάμου ὁ ἄνθρωπος; εἰπόντες, ὅτι καθώς εἰσι χωρὶς γάμου οἱ ἄγγελοι· τὸ γὰρ ὁμοίως ἐκείνοις τὸν ἄνθρωπον εἶναι πρὸ τῆς παραβάσεως, δείκνυσιν ἡ εἰς ἐκεῖνο πάλιν ἀποκατάστασις.

[17.4] Τούτων οὖν ἡμῖν οὑτωσὶ διευκρινηθέντων, ἐπανιτέον ἐπὶ τὸν πρότερον λόγον—πῶς μετὰ τὴν κατασκευὴν τῆς εἰκόνος, τὴν [C] κατὰ τὸ ἄρρεν καὶ θῆλυ διαφορὰν ὁ Θεὸς ἐπιτεχνᾶται τῷ πλάσματι· πρὸς τοῦτο γάρ φημι χρήσιμον εἶναι τὸ προδιηνυσμένον ἡμῖν θεώρημα· ὁ γὰρ τὰ πάντα παραγαγὼν εἰς τὸ εἶναι, καὶ ὅλον ἐν τῷ ἰδίῳ θελήματι τὸν ἄνθρωπον πρὸς τὴν θείαν εἰκόνα διαμορφώσας, οὐ ταῖς κατ᾽ ὀλίγον προσθήκαις τῶν ἐπιγινομένων ἀνέμεινεν ἰδεῖν ἐπὶ τὸ ἴδιον πλήρωμα τὸν ἀριθμὸν τῶν ψυχῶν τελειούμενον· ἀλλ᾽ ἀθρόως αὐτῷ πληρώματι πᾶσαν τὴν ἀνθρωπίνην φύσιν διὰ τῆς προγνωστικῆς ἐνεργείας κατανοήσας, καὶ τῇ ὑψηλῇ τε καὶ ἰσαγγέλῳ λήξει τιμήσας, ἐπειδὴ προεῖδε τῇ ὁρατικῇ δυνάμει μὴ εὐθυποροῦσαν πρὸς τὸ καλὸν τὴν προαίρεσιν, καὶ διὰ τοῦτο τῆς ἀγγελικῆς ζωῆς ἀποπίπτουσαν—ὡς

30 ἀγγελικός] ἄγγελος Q *Dion Eri* τοῖς *om.* N 31 μὴν *om.* M καθὼς εἴρεται *om.* N 32 ἀπείροις] ἀπόροις M : ἄπειροι T οὕτως W 33 οὐκοῦν] non igitur *Eri* κατὰ τὸν αὐτὸν τρόπον] per eundem hominem *Eri* αὐτὸν] αὐτὸν ἂν Æ B^{pc} G I L M Q S W 34 ὁμοτιμίας] πολιτείας I ἐξεγένετο I : γέγονεν D G L P S X 33 οὐδ᾽ G I P S X : οὔτε N 35 ἐδεήθημεν] alligaremur *Eri* ἀλλ᾽ ὅστις] alius quidam *Eri* 36 ἀγγέλων] ἀγγέλων ὁ D G L M^{2} P S W X ἀνεπινόητος] ἀνενόητος I : ἀπερινόητος T 37 ἐστιν *om.* N οὕτως Æ G K M O P Q W X 38 ἀνθρώπων *om.* M N Q T W *Dion Eri* 39 εἰ] ἐὰν A B I K O στενοχωρῆται Æ ß^{pc} B^{pc} : σταναχωρῆται I : στενοχωρεῖ G L M N P S (ται *sup. l.*) X *Dion Eri* 40 ψυχῶν] *ita* Æ B D G I L O M P S W X *Dion Eri Forb* : ἀνθρώπων *Ald Mign* προσεδέθη Q : alligaretur *Eri* διὰ *om.* D G L P S X 41 συνεργείας D L P Q T W X : κοινωνίας K O ἀντερωτήσωμεν G K L O P Q W X τῆς ὑποστάσεως τῆς ἀγγελικῆς N 42 μυριάσιν *om.* B καὶ^{1}] καὶ ἐν B μιᾷ ß I K M O P *Dion* οὐσία] ὑποστάσει M 43 προσφέροντι D^{ac} N ἦν *om.* X 44 ἐπειπόντες B χωρὶς γάμου] *ita* D G I K L M P Q S X *Forb* : γάμου χωρὶς W *Ald Mign* χωρὶς] δίχα τοῦ K O 45 ὁμοίως] ὅμοιον *Mign* ἐκεῖνα T 47 οὖν *om.* O ἡμῖν οὑτωσὶ] οὕτως ἡμῖν Æ B I K N O οὑτωσὶ] *ita* D G L P S W *Forb* : οὕτως Æ B I K M N O Q : οὕτω *Ald Mign* 48 θῆλυ καὶ ἄρρεν M Q θῆλυ] τὸ θῆλυ I N 49 διαφορὰν *om.* M ἐπιτεχνᾶται τῷ πλάσματι] suo dignatus sit excogitare figmento *Dion* : supermachinatus est . . . formationi *Eri* 49–50 τὸ προδιηνυσμένον ἡμῖν θεώρημα] superiorem hanc inspectionem quae a nobis exprompta est *Dion* : prius perfectam a nobis theoriam *Eri* 50 προδιηνυσμένον] προδιηνισμένον O : διηνυμένον K : προδεικνυσμένον F^{ac} : προδεδεικνυμένον F^{pc} : προδεικνυόμενον B : προδεδειγμένον M *Dion* ἡμῖν *om.* D πάντα] πάντα ἡμῖν T 51 θείαν] ἰδίαν M N διαμορφώσας] μεταμορφώσας K M O 52 τὸν] τῷ O 53 ψυχῶν] ἀνθρώπων T αὐτῷ] ἐν τῷ P : αὐτῷ τῷ Æ B I K O 54 τε *om.* D G L P S X 55 προΐδε P Q X διορατικῇ N μὴ *om.* D 56 καλὸν] κακὸν G ἀγγελικῆς] εὐαγγελικῆς M

out from it.[30] If then the life of those restored is akin to that of the angels, it is clear that the mode of life before the transgression was something angelic, and hence our ascent to the primordial condition of life is likened to the angels. Yet, as has been said, while there is no marriage among them, the armies of the angels are in countless myriads, for so Daniel declared in his visions; therefore, in the same way, if there had not come upon us as the result of sin a turning away and a displacement from equality of honour with the angels, neither should we have needed marriage for multiplying, but whatever the mode of increase is in the nature of the angels (unspeakable and inconceivable by human guesses, except that it assuredly exists), it would have operated also in the case of human beings, *made a little lower than the angels*,[31] increasing humankind to the measure determined by the will of the Maker. [17.3] But if anyone is perplexed, when enquiring about the mode of the genesis of souls had the human being not needed the assistance of marriage, we shall ask him in turn about the mode of the angelic subsistence: how they exist in countless myriads, being one essence and at the same time numerically many. For we will give a suitable answer to one who raises the question, how would the human being have been without marriage, if we say, just as the angels are without marriage; for the restoration again to that state shows that the human being was like them before the transgression.

[17.4] Now that we have thus cleared up these matters, let us return to the former point: how it was that after the formation of the image, God contrived for that which is moulded the difference of male and female. The reflection we have completed is, I say, useful for this one. He who brought all things into being, and modelled the human being as a whole by his own will into the divine image, did not wait to see the number of souls made complete in its proper plenitude by the gradual addition of those subsequently coming to be, but considering the human nature as a whole, in its plenitude, by the activity of foreknowledge, and honouring it with an allocation exalted and equal to the angels, since he foresaw by his visionary power the [human] will not keeping a straight course towards the good and, because of this, falling away from the angelic life, in order that the

[30] Cf. Gregory of Nyssa, *An. et res.* 10.69–70 (Spira, 112.19–113.4); *Eccl.* 1 (Alexander, 296.16–18; ET 45); *Virg.* 12 (Cavarnos, 302.5–9).

[31] Ps. 8:6.

ἂν μὴ κολοβωθείη τὸ τῶν ψυχῶν τῶν ἀνθρωπίνων πλῆθος, ἐκπεσὸν ἐκείνου τοῦ τρόπου καθ' ὃν [D] οἱ ἄγγελοι πρὸς πλῆθος ηὐξήθησαν· διὰ τοῦτο τὴν κατάλληλον τοῖς εἰς ἁμαρτίαν κατολισθήσασι τῆς αὐξήσεως ἐπίνοιαν ἐγκατασκευάζει τῇ φύσει, ἀντὶ τῆς ἀγγελικῆς μεγαλοφυΐας τὸν κτηνώδη τε καὶ ἄλογον τῆς ἐξ ἀλλήλων διαδοχῆς τρόπον ἐμφυτεύσας τῇ ἀνθρωπότητι. [17.5] Ἐντεῦθέν μοι δοκεῖ καὶ ὁ μέγας Δαυὶδ, κατοικτιζόμενος τοῦ ἀνθρώπου τὴν ἀθλιότητα, τοιούτοις λόγοις καταθρηνῆσαι τὴν φύσιν, ὅτι **ἄνθρωπος ἐν τιμῇ ὢν οὐ συνῆκε** (**τιμὴν** λέγων τὴν πρὸς τοὺς ἀγγέλους ὁμοτιμίαν) διὰ τοῦτο, φησὶ, **παρασυνεβλήθη τοῖς κτήνεσι τοῖς ἀνοήτοις καὶ ὡμοιώθη αὐτοῖς**· ὄντως γὰρ κτηνώδης ἐγένετο ὁ τὴν ῥοώδη [192] ταύτην γένεσιν τῇ φύσει παραδεξάμενος διὰ τὴν πρὸς τὸ ὑλῶδες ῥοπήν.

Ὅτι τὰ ἄλογα ἐν ἡμῖν πάθη ἐκ τῆς πρὸς τὴν ἄλογον φύσιν συγγενείας τὰς ἀφορμὰς ἔχει.

[18.1] *Οἶμαι γὰρ ἐκ τῆς ἀρχῆς ταύτης καὶ τὰ καθ' ἕκαστον πάθη οἷον ἔκ τινος πηγῆς συνδοθέντα πλημμυρεῖν ἐν τῇ ἀνθρωπίνῃ ζωῇ· τεκμήριον δὲ τῶν λόγων, ἡ τῶν παθημάτων συγγένεια, κατὰ τὸ ἶσον ἡμῖν τε καὶ τοῖς ἀλόγοις ἐμφαινομένη· οὐ γὰρ δὴ θέμις τῇ ἀνθρωπίνῃ φύσει τῇ κατὰ τὸ θεῖον εἶδος μεμορφωμένῃ,* [B] *τῆς ἐμπαθοῦς διαθέσεως προσμαρτυρεῖν τὰς πρώτας ἀρχάς· ἀλλ' ἐπειδὴ προεισῆλθεν εἰς τὸν κόσμον τοῦτον ἡ τῶν ἀλόγων ζωὴ, ἔσχε δέ τι διὰ τὴν εἰρημένην αἰτίαν τῆς ἐκεῖθεν φύσεως καὶ ὁ ἄνθρωπος, (τὸ κατὰ τὴν γένεσιν λέγω) συμμετέσχε διὰ τούτου καὶ τῶν λοιπῶν τῶν ἐν ἐκείνῃ θεωρουμένων τῇ φύσει· οὐ γὰρ κατὰ τὸν θυμόν ἐστι τοῦ ἀνθρώπου ἡ πρὸς τὸ θεῖον ὁμοίωσις, οὔτε διὰ τῆς ἡδονῆς ἡ ὑπερέχουσα χαρακτηρίζεται φύσις· δειλία τε καὶ θράσος καὶ ἡ τοῦ πλείονος ἔφεσις καὶ τὸ πρὸς τὸ ἐλαττοῦσθαι μῖσος καὶ πάντα τὰ τοιαῦτα, πόρρω τοῦ θεοπρεποῦς χαρακτῆρός ἐστι.* [18.2] *Ταῦτα τοίνυν ἐκ τοῦ ἀλόγου μέρους ἡ ἀνθρωπίνη φύσις πρὸς ἑαυτὴν ἐφειλκύσατο. Οἷς γὰρ ἡ ἄλογος ζωὴ πρὸς συντήρησιν ἑαυτῆς ἠσφαλίσθη, ταῦτα πρὸς τὸν ἀνθρώπινον μετενεχθέντα βίον, πάθη* [C] *ἐγένετο· θυμῷ μὲν γὰρ συντηρεῖται τὰ ὠμοβόρα, φιληδονίᾳ δὲ τὰ πολυγονοῦντα τῶν ζώων· σώζει τὸν*

57 κολοβωθῇ T : κολοβωθήειη Q ψυχῶν τῶν ἀνθωπίνων] ἀνθρώπων ψυχῶν B ἐκπεσὼν ß Q 58 πρὸς] εἰς T : πρὸς τὸ *Ald Mign* τὴν *om.* N 59 κατασκευάζει N 60 μεγαλοφυΐας] συμφυΐας G P^2 61 ἐμοὶ Æ B I K O T 62 δαυίδ] *ita Forb* : δαβίδ *Ald Mign* 63 καταθρινῆσαι O 64 τοὺς *om.* Æ B I K M O Q T W φησὶ *om.* D G L P S X παρασυνεβλήθη φησὶ M Q παρασυνεβλήθη] παρ' ἐσυνεβλήθη N P^{ac} W : παρὰ ἐσυνεβλήθη Q 65 καὶ ὡμοιώθη αὐτοῖς] *om. Eri* 65–6 κτηνώδης ἐγένετο ὁ . . . παραδεξάμενος] κτηνώδεις ἐγένοντο οἱ [ὡς Æ : ἡ I] . . . παραδεξάμενοι Æ B I K N O T 65 ὁ *om.* D G L S W X ῥοώδη] ζωώδη P S^{ac} (ῥο *sup. l.*) W X *Dion Eri* 66 ῥοπήν] τροπὴν $P^{ac?}$ Q

Cap. 19 Æ ß K N O Q *Dion Eri*

1–2 ὅτι—ἔχει] quod ceterae quoque passiones nobis et irrationalibus animatibus communes sunt et quod per earum refrenationem similes deo dicimur *Λ* 3 καὶ *om.* T 4 συναναδοθέντα B πλημμύρειν N ζωῇ] conuersatione *Dion* τεκμήριον δὲ τῶν λόγων] τεκμηριοῖ δὲ τὸν λόγον Æ B F^{pc} I K M N O Q T : confirmat autem rationem *Eri* 5 ἴσον I K M N O S W X τε *om.* N 6 δὴ] μὴ T φύσει *om.* K O τὸ *om.* M N 7 πρώτας *om.* Q *Dion Eri* προσῆλθεν D^{ac} I L M : προῆλθεν D^{pc2} K N O 8 δέ *om.* N 8–9 τῆς ἐκεῖθεν φύσεως] ex eadem formatione *Dion* : ex uita quae ibi est *Eri* 9 φύσεως] φύσεως γένεσιν L καὶ *om.* B τὸ κατὰ τὴν γένεσιν λέγω] iuxta generandi de coitu rationem *Dion* τὸ . . . λέγω] τῷ . . . λόγῳ I N O συμμετέσχε] μετέσχε L S : συμμετέχει γὰρ N τοῦτο G L P Q S X 10 ἐν ἐκείνῃ] ἐκεῖθεν Q 12 καὶ θράσος *om.* I 13 ἐλαττούμενον N ἅπαντα Æ B I K O T 15 ἐφελκύσατο G P W X ἑαυτῆς] αὐτῆς D G L P S W X 16 ἐγένοντο M μὲν *om.* K 17 ὠμοβόρα] αἱμοβόρα T φιληδονίᾳ] S *Forb* : φιληδονία W X *Ald Mign* *punctis post* σώζει *Ald Mign* τὸν] τὴν N

multitude of human souls should not be cut short, by falling from that mode by which the angels increased to a multitude, for this reason he formed in our nature that device for increase appropriate to those who had slipped into sin, implanting in humanity, instead of the angelic nobility, the animal and irrational mode of succession from one another. [**17.5**] Hence also, it seems to me, the great David, lamenting the misery of the human being, mourns over his nature with such words as these, that, *the human being in honour knew it not* (meaning by *honour* the equality of honour with the angels), [and] therefore, he says, *he was compared to senseless beasts, and made like them.*[32] For the one who received in his nature this genesis subject to flux on account of his inclination to things material truly became like a beast.

That our irrational passions have their starting point from kinship with the irrational nature.[33]

[**18.1**] For I think that from this beginning the passions of each one issue as from a spring, to flow over in human life. Proof of my words is the kinship of passions manifest alike in ourselves and in the irrational animals; for it is not right to ascribe the first beginnings of the impassioned disposition to that human nature modelled in accordance with the divine form; but as the life of the irrational animals entered into this world first, and the human being, for the reason already mentioned, has something of their nature (I mean regarding genesis), he therefore also partook of the other [attributes] contemplated in that nature.[34] For the likeness of the human being towards the divine is not by virtue of anger, nor is the superior nature characterized by pleasure; cowardice also, and rashness, and the desire of gain, and the hatred of loss, and all the like, are far removed from the divinely-fitting character. [**18.2**] These, then, human nature drew to itself from the irrational side. For these things, with which the irrational life was armed for self-preservation, when transferred to the human mode of life became passions: for the carnivorous animals are sustained by anger,

[32] Ps. 48:13.

[33] *Bodl. 238* (as Chap. 19): 'That our other passions also are common to us and to the irrational animals, and that by the restraint of them we are said to be like God'.

[34] Cf. Gregory of Nyssa, *An. et res.* 3.12 (Spira, 34.7–11).

ἄναλκιν ἡ δειλία, καὶ τὸν εὐάλωτον τοῖς ἰσχυροτέροις ὁ φόβος, τὸν δὲ πολύσαρκον ἡ λαιμαργία· καὶ τὸ διαμαρτεῖν οὐτινοσοῦν τῶν καθ᾽ ἡδονὴν, λύπης ὑπόθεσις ἐν τοῖς ἀλόγοις ἐστί· ταῦτα πάντα καὶ τὰ τοιαῦτα διὰ τῆς κτηνώδους γενέσεως συνεισῆλθε τῇ τοῦ ἀνθρώπου κατασκευῇ.

[18.3] *Καί μοι συγκεχωρήσθω κατά τινα πλαστικὴν θαυματοποιΐαν διαγράψαι τῷ λόγῳ τὴν ἀνθρωπίνην εἰκόνα.* Καθάπερ γὰρ ἔστιν ἰδεῖν ἐν τοῖς πλάσμασι τὰς διαγλύφους μορφὰς ἃς μηχανῶνται πρὸς ἔκπληξιν τῶν ἐντυγχανόντων οἱ τὰ τοιαῦτα φιλοτεχνοῦντες, μιᾷ κεφαλῇ δύο μορφὰς προσώπων ὑποχαράσσοντες· οὕτω μοι δοκεῖ διπλῆν [D] φέρειν ὁ ἄνθρωπος πρὸς τὰ ἐναντία τὴν ὁμοιότητα— τῷ μὲν θεοειδεῖ τῆς διανοίας πρὸς τὸ θεῖον κάλλος μεμορφωμένος, ταῖς δὲ κατὰ πάθος ἐγγινομέναις ὁρμαῖς πρὸς τὸ κτηνῶδες φέρων τὴν οἰκειότητα· πολλάκις δὲ καὶ ὁ λόγος ἀποκτηνοῦται, διὰ τῆς πρὸς τὸ ἄλογον ῥοπῆς τε καὶ διαθέσεως συγκαλύπτων τὸ κρεῖττον τῷ χείρονι· ἐπειδὰν γάρ τις πρὸς ταῦτα τὴν διανοητικὴν ἐνέργειαν καθελκύσῃ, καὶ ὑπηρέτην τῶν παθῶν γενέσθαι τὸν λογισμὸν ἐκβιάσηται, παρατροπή τις γίνεται τοῦ ἀγαθοῦ χαρακτῆρος πρὸς τὴν ἄλογον εἰκόνα, πάσης πρὸς τοῦτο μεταχαρασσομένης τῆς φύσεως, καθάπερ γεωργοῦντος τοῦ λογισμοῦ τὰς τῶν παθημάτων ἀρχὰς καὶ δι᾽ ὀλίγων εἰς πλῆθος ἐπαύξοντος· τὴν γὰρ παρ᾽ ἑαυτοῦ συνεργίαν χρήσας τῷ πάθει, πολύχουν καὶ ἀμφιλαφῆ τὴν τῶν [193] ἀτόπων γένεσιν ἀπειργάσατο.

[18.4] *Οὕτως ἡ φιληδονία τὴν μὲν ἀρχὴν ἔσχεν ἐκ τῆς πρὸς τὸ ἄλογον ὁμοιώσεως, ἀλλ᾽ ἐν τοῖς ἀνθρωπίνοις πλημμελήμασι προσηυξήθη,* τοσαύτας διαφορὰς τῶν κατὰ τὴν ἡδονὴν ἁμαρτανομένων γεννήσασα, ὅσας ἐν τοῖς ἀλόγοις οὐκ ἔστιν εὑρεῖν. Οὕτως ἡ πρὸς τὸν θυμὸν διανάστασις συγγενὴς μέν ἐστι τῇ τῶν ἀλόγων ὁρμῇ, αὔξεται δὲ τῇ τῶν λογισμῶν συμμαχίᾳ· ἐκεῖθεν γὰρ ἡ μῆνις, ὁ φθόνος, τὸ ψεῦδος, ἡ ἐπιβουλὴ, ἡ ὑπόκρισις· [B] ταῦτα πάντα τῆς πονηρᾶς τοῦ νοῦ γεωργίας ἐστίν· εἰ γὰρ γυμνωθείη τῆς ἐκ τῶν λογισμῶν συμμαχίας τὸ πάθος, ὠκύμορός τις καὶ ἄτονος ὁ θυμὸς καταλείπεται, πομφόλυγος δίκην, ὁμοῦ τε γινόμενος καὶ εὐθὺς ἀπολλύμενος. Οὕτως ἡ τῶν συῶν λαιμαργία τὴν πλεονεξίαν εἰσήνεγκε, καὶ τὸ τοῦ ἵππου γαῦρον γέγονε τῆς ὑπερηφανίας ἀρχή· καὶ τὰ καθ᾽ ἕκαστον πάντα τῆς κτηνώδους ἀλογίας

19 ἐν *om.* N Q T 20 πάντα ταῦτα T 22 συγκεχωρείσθω G N O P : συγκεχωρίσθω B Q X πλαστικὴν] πλασμευτικὴν B : πλασματικὴν Æ θαυμαστοποιΐαν P 24 διγλύφους *Mign* 25 ὑποχαράττοντες L M 26 οὕτως M μοι *om.* K O τὰ ἐναντία] τἀναντία Æ B D G N O P X 27 πρὸς τὸ θεῖον *om.* I K O 28 πάθος] τὸ πάθος D G L N P S X γινομέναις N 29 ὁ λόγος] ὅλος Æ C F[ac] I K M N O : ὅλως B Q : pene *Dion* 30 τοῦτο N 31 καὶ *om.* M γενέσθαι τῶν παθῶν W *Ald Mign* παθημάτων M Q 32 ἐκβιάσεται K O 33 μεταχαττομένης L : χαρασσομένης D[ac] P G X : παραχαρασσομένης D[pc2] 34 λογισμοῦ] νοῦ O ὀλίγον N 35 συνέργειαν G P[ac] W X : ἐνέργειαν N 38 ἀλλ᾽ ἐν] ἐν δὲ Æ B I K O προσηυξήθη] ἐπηυξήθη M 38–9 κατὰ τὴν] καθ᾽ T 39 ἁμαρτημάτων D N ὅσας] οἵας N 40 τῆς . . . ὁρμῆς N T 41 συμμαχίᾳ] συμπαθείᾳ M ὁ φθόνος *post* τὸ ψεῦδος *pon.* B : *post* ὑπόκρισις (*l.* 42) *pon.* A D E F G L P S X 42 ὑπόκρισις] ὑπόκρισις ὁ δόλος, ἡ ὑπουλία, ἡ ἀπιστία, ἡ κακοήθεια, τὸ θράσος, ἡ κακηγορία, Æ B C I K (*om.* ὁ δόλος) O γεωργίας] ἐνεγείας T : operationis *Eri* γὰρ *om.* I 43 ἐκ *om.* Q συμμαχίας] συνεργίας B ὠκιμότερος G P[ac] X : ὠκυμοτώτερος P[2] 44 καταλιμπάνεται T 45 συῶν] κυνῶν D E[mg] εἰσήνεγκε] εἰσήγαγεν I 46 ὑπερηφανείας W τὰ *om.* L Q X καθ᾽ ἕκαστον πάντα τὰ D G P S X

and those animals that breed prolifically, by their love of pleasure; cowardice preserves the weak, fear what is easily taken by the more powerful, and greediness those of great bulk; and to miss anything that tends towards pleasure is for the animals a matter of pain. All these and suchlike entered the human formation through the animal-like genesis.

[18.3][35] Allow me to describe the human image by comparison with some wonderful piece of modelling. For just as one may see those carved shapes in moulded figures, which craftsmen of such things contrive for the astonishment of observers, tracing out two forms of faces on a single head, so also, it seems to me, that the human being bears a twofold likeness to opposite things, being formed, in the divine aspect of the mind, in accordance with the divine beauty, but also bearing, in the passionate impulses that arise in him, a relationship to the animal-like [form]. For frequently even his reason is made animal-like through his inclination and disposition to the irrational, obscuring the better by the worse. For whenever someone drags down his discursive activity towards these, and forces his calculating faculty to become the servant of the passions, a sort of turning away occurs, from the good stamp towards the irrational image, his whole nature being traced out anew in accord with this, as his calculating faculty cultivates the beginnings of the passions and gradually causes them to grow into a multitude; furnishing passion with its own cooperation, it effects the genesis, plenteous and abundant, of evils.

[18.4] Thus, the love of pleasure had its beginning from the likeness to the irrational animal, but was increased by human transgressions, begetting such varieties of sinning for pleasure as is not to be found among the irrational animals. Thus, the rising of anger is indeed akin to the impulse of the irrational animals, but it grows by the alliance of the calculating faculty. For thence come malignity, envy, deceit, treachery, hypocrisy: all these are the result of the evil husbandry of the intellect. For if the passion were stripped of the alliance with calculating thoughts, the anger that is left behind is short-lived and weak, like a bubble, bursting as soon as it comes into being. Thus, the greediness of pigs introduces covetousness, and the high spirit of the horse becomes the origin of pride; and all

[35] For the following paragraphs (18.3–5), see Gregory of Nyssa, *An. et res.* 3.39–50 and 6.9–10 (Spira, 41–3; 65.9–66.2); and Chapter 12 above.

ἀφορμηθέντα διὰ τῆς πονηρᾶς τοῦ νοῦ χρήσεως κακία ἐγένετο, **[18.5]** Ὥσπερ οὖν καὶ τὸ ἔμπαλιν, εἴπερ ὁ λογισμὸς τῶν τοιούτων κινημάτων ἀντιμεταλάβοι τὸ κράτος, εἰς ἀρετῆς εἶδος ἕκαστον τούτων ἀντιμεθίσταται· ποιεῖ γὰρ ὁ μὲν θυμὸς τὴν ἀνδρίαν, τὸ δὲ δειλὸν τὴν ἀσφάλειαν, καὶ ὁ φόβος τὴν εὐπείθειαν, τὸ μῖσος δὲ τὴν τῆς κακίας ἀποστροφήν, ἡ δὲ ἀγαπητικὴ δύναμις τὴν πρὸς τὸ ἀληθῶς καλὸν [C] ἐπιθυμίαν· τὸ δὲ γαῦρον τοῦ ἤθους ὑπεραίρει τῶν παθημάτων καὶ ἀδούλωτον ὑπὸ τοῦ κακοῦ διαφυλάσσει τὸ φρόνημα. Ἐπαινεῖ δὲ τὸ τοιοῦτον τῆς ἐπάρσεως εἶδος καὶ ὁ μέγας ἀπόστολος, συνεχῶς ἐγκελευόμενος **τὰ ἄνω φρονεῖν**· καὶ οὕτως ἐστὶν εὑρεῖν, ὅτι πᾶν τὸ τοιοῦτον κίνημα τῷ ὑψηλῷ τῆς διανοίας συνεπαιρόμενον, τῷ κατὰ τὴν θείαν εἰκόνα κάλλει συσχηματίζεται.

[18.6] Ἀλλ᾽ ἐπειδὴ βαρεῖά τις ἐστὶ καὶ κατωφερὴς ἡ τῆς ἁμαρτίας ῥοπή, πλεῖον τὸ ἕτερον γίνεται· μᾶλλον γὰρ τῷ βάρει τῆς ἀλόγου φύσεως συγκατασπᾶται τὸ ἡγεμονικὸν τῆς ψυχῆς, ἤπερ τῷ ὕψει τῆς διανοίας τὸ βαρύ τε καὶ χοϊκὸν ἀνυψοῦται· διὰ τοῦτο πολλάκις ἀγνοεῖσθαι ποιεῖ τὸ θεῖον δῶρον ἡ περὶ ἡμᾶς ἀθλιότης, οἷον προσωπεῖον εἰδεχθὲς τῷ κατὰ τὴν εἰκόνα κάλλει τὰ πάθη τῆς [D] σαρκὸς ἐπιπλάσσουσα. **[18.7]** Οὐκοῦν συγγνωστοί πως εἰσὶν οἱ πρὸς τὰ τοιαῦτα βλέποντες, εἶτα τὴν θείαν μορφὴν ἐν τούτοις εἶναι οὐκ εὐχερῶς συντιθέμενοι· ἀλλὰ διὰ τῶν κατωρθωκότων τὸν βίον, ἔξεστι τὴν θείαν ἐν τοῖς ἀνθρώποις εἰκόνα βλέπειν· εἰ γὰρ ἐμπαθής τις καὶ σάρκινος ὢν ἀπιστεῖσθαι ποιεῖ τὸν ἄνθρωπον ὡς θείῳ κάλλει κεκοσμημένον· ὁ ὑψηλὸς πάντως τὴν ἀρετὴν καὶ καθαρεύων ἐκ μολυσμάτων βεβαιώσει σοι τὴν πρὸς τὸ κρεῖττον ἐπὶ τῶν ἀνθρώπων ὑπόληψιν. **[18.8]** Οἷον κρεῖττον γὰρ ἐν ὑποδείγματι δεῖξαι τὸν λόγον· ἀπήλειψε τῷ τῆς πονηρίας μολύσματι τὸ τῆς φύσεως κάλλος τὶς τῶν ἐπὶ κακίᾳ γνωρίμων, Ἰεχονίας τυχὸν ἢ εἴ τις ἕτερος ἐπὶ κακῷ μνημονεύεται· ἀλλ᾽ ἐν Μωϋσῇ καὶ τοῖς κατ᾽ ἐκεῖνον καθαρὰ διεφυλάχθη ἡ [196] τῆς εἰκόνος μορφή. Ἐν οἷς τοίνυν οὐκ ἠμαυρώθη τὸ κάλλος, ἐν

47 ἐγίνετο G P X 48 ἀντιμεταλαμβάνοι T : ἀντιλαμβάνοιτο N : ἀντιλάβοιτο M : ἀντιμεταβάλοι D : ἀντιμεταβάλλοι G L P S τὸ² *om.* N 49 ποιεῖ] ποιεῖ μὲν B Q μὲν *om.* B 50 ἀνδρείαν B G K M O P W : ἀνδρείαν S^ac (ϊ *sup. l.*) καὶ *om.* M μίσος N 51 τῆς κακίας *om.* M ἀποστροφὴν] ἀποτροπὴν Q : reditum *Eri* 52 ὑπὲραίρεται N ὑπὸ] ἀπὸ Æ B I K O T 53 διαφυλάττει D L : φυλάσσει B τὸ τοιοῦτο Æ N Q : τῷ τοιούτῳ K O τῆς ἐπάρσεως τὸ τοιοῦτον L 54 συνεχῶς *om.* Q : assidue *Eri* 55 πᾶν—συνεπαιρόμενον] semper altitudo intelligentiae per ipsam mota confinitatem *Eri* τοιοῦτο Æ Q S W τὴν *om.* T 57 ἀλλ᾽ ἐπειδὴ] ἐπεὶ δὲ D G L P S X πλέον D G L P S X 57–8 τὸ ἕτερον] τὸ ἔργον Æ T : τῆς ἁμαρτίας B (*sed exp. a 1^a man.*) : *om.* ß 58–60 μᾶλλον—ἀνυψοῦται *om.* W 59 ἤπερ] ἤπερN : εἴπερ G I L P : ἤπερ X^pc2 60 ἀνυψοῦται] ἀνοχλεῖται T 61 κατὰ τὴν] κατ᾽ N πάθη] παθήματα Æ ß M N O Q T W 62 ἐπιπλάττουσα B I L M οὐκοῦν] non ergo *Eri* 64 εἰκόνα ἐν τοῖς ἀνθρώποις D G L P X 66–7 ὁ ὑψηλὸς—βεβαιώσει] si excelsus omnino uirtute firmabit *Eri* 66 καὶ *om.* D G P X ἐκ *om.* M 68 ἀπήλειψε] ἐπήλειψε M Q : ἐπέκρυψε N τῷ] τὸ O 69 τις *post* τῶν *pon.* Æ B M Q : *post* γνωρίμων L O 70 ἕτερος εἴ τις N 71 μορφή] ἀρχή W

the particular forms originating from the irrationality of the animals become vices by the evil use of the intellect.[36] **[18.5]** So also, therefore, on the contrary, if the calculating faculty instead assumes control over these movements, each of them is transposed to a form of virtue. For anger produces courage, cowardice caution, fear obedience, hatred aversion from vice, the faculty of love the desire of the truly beautiful; high spirit in character raises thought above the passions and guards it from bondage to evil. The great Apostle also praises such a form of elevation, urging us always *to think about those things that are above*.[37] And so one finds that every such movement, when elevated by the loftiness of mind, is conformed to the beauty of the divine image.

[18.6] But since the tendency to sin is heavy and bears downward, the opposite more often happens. For the governing principle of the soul is dragged downwards by the weight of the irrational nature much more than is the heavy and earthy element raised up by the loftiness of mind. Therefore, our wretchedness often causes the divine gift to be unknown, spreading the passions of the flesh, like some ugly mask, over the beauty of the image. **[18.7]** Those, therefore, are in some sense excusable, who do not readily admit, when they look upon such cases, that the divine form is in them. But it is possible to see the divine image in human beings through those who have correctly ordered their mode of life. For if one who is impassioned and fleshly makes it unbelievable [to think that] the human being has been adorned as it were, with divine beauty, surely one of lofty virtue and pure from pollution will confirm for you the better conception of human beings. **[18.8]** For instance (for it is better to explain our argument by an example), one of those noted for evil—Jechoniah, perhaps, or some other remembered for evil—has expunged the beauty of his nature by the pollution of wickedness, but in Moses, and those like him, the form of the image was kept pure.[38] In those, then, where the beauty has not been obscured, there is

[36] Cf. Philo, *Opif.* 73. [37] Col. 3:2.

[38] Cf. Gregory of Nyssa, *An. et res.* 3.22–3 (Spira, 36.9–17); *Vit. Moys.* 2.318–19 (Musurillo, 143.14–144.3).

τούτοις ἐναργὴς ἡ τῶν λεγομένων πίστις ἐστὶν, ὅτι ἄνθρωπος τοῦ Θεοῦ μίμημα γέγονεν.

[18.9] Ἀλλ' ἐπαισχύνεταί τις τυχὸν, τῷ διὰ βρώσεως ἡμῖν καθ' ὁμοιότητα τῶν ἀλόγων τὴν ζωὴν συνεστᾶναι, καὶ διὰ τοῦτο ἀνάξιον ἡγεῖται τὸν ἄνθρωπον τοῦ κατ' εἰκόνα Θεοῦ πεπλᾶσθαι δοκεῖν· ἀλλ' ἐλπιζέτω τῆς λειτουργείας ταύτης ἀτέλειαν δοθήσεσθαι τῇ φύσει ποτὲ, κατὰ τὴν προσδοκωμένην ζωήν. **Οὐ γάρ ἐστι**, καθώς φησιν ὁ ἀπόστολος, **ἡ βασιλεία τοῦ Θεοῦ βρῶσις καὶ πόσις, οὐδὲ ἐπ' ἄρτῳ ζήσεσθαι μόνῳ τὸν ἄνθρωπον**, ὁ Κύριος προηγόρευσεν, ἀλλ' ἐν **παντὶ ῥήματι ἐκπορευομένῳ διὰ στόματος Θεοῦ**. Ἀλλὰ καὶ τῆς ἀναστάσεως ἰσάγγελον ἡμῖν ὑποδεικνυούσης τὸν βίον, βρώσεως δὲ παρὰ τοῖς ἀγγέλοις οὐκ οὔσης, ἱκανὴ [B] πίστις τοῦ ἀπαλλαγήσεσθαι τῆς τοιαύτης λειτουργίας τὸν ἄνθρωπον, τὸν καθ' ὁμοιότητα τῶν ἀγγέλων ζησόμενον.

Πρὸς τοὺς λέγοντας, πάλιν ἐν βρώσει καὶ πόσει εἶναι τῶν ἐλπιζομένων ἀγαθῶν τὴν ἀπόλαυσιν, διὰ τὸ ἐξ ἀρχῆς ἐν τῷ παραδείσῳ γεγράφθαι διὰ τούτων τὸν ἄνθρωπον ζῆν.

[19.1] [C] Ἀλλ' ἴσως τις οὐκ εἰς τὸ αὐτὸ πάλιν τῆς ζωῆς εἶδος ἐπανελεύσεσθαι λέγει τὸν ἄνθρωπον, εἴγε πρότερον μὲν ἐν τῷ ἐσθίειν ἦμεν, μετὰ ταῦτα δὲ τῆς τοιαύτης λειτουργίας ἀφεθησόμεθα. Ἀλλ' ἐγὼ, τῆς ἁγίας ἀκούων γραφῆς, οὐ μόνον σωματικὴν ἐπίσταμαι βρῶσιν, οὐδὲ τὴν διὰ σαρκὸς εὐφροσύνην· ἀλλά τινα καὶ ἑτέραν οἶδα τροφὴν, ἀναλογίαν τινὰ πρὸς τὴν τοῦ σώματος ἔχουσαν, ἧς ἡ ἀπόλαυσις ἐπὶ μόνην τὴν ψυχὴν διαβαίνει· **φάγετε τῶν ἐμῶν ἄρτων**, ἡ σοφία τοῖς πεινῶσι διακελεύεται· καὶ μακαρίζει τοὺς τὴν τοιαύτην βρῶσιν **πεινῶντας** ὁ Κύριος· καὶ **εἴ τις διψᾷ**, φησὶν, **ἐρχέσθω πρός με καὶ πινέτω**· καὶ ὁ μέγας Ἡσαΐας **πίετε εὐφροσύνην** τοῖς δυνατοῖς [D] ἐπαΐειν τῆς μεγαλοφυΐας αὐτοῦ ἐγκελεύεται· ἔστι δέ τις καὶ ἀπειλὴ προφητικὴ κατὰ τῶν τιμωρίας ἀξίων, ὡς **λιμῷ** κολασθησομένων· ὁ δὲ **λιμὸς**, οὐκ ἄρτου τίς ἐστιν ἀπορία καὶ ὕδατος, ἀλλὰ λόγου ἐπίλειψις· **οὐ λιμὸν** γὰρ **ἄρτου**, φησὶν, ἢ **δίψαν ὕδατος**, ἀλλὰ **λιμὸν τοῦ ἀκοῦσαι λόγον Κυρίου**.

72 ἐνεργὴς Q : ἀληθὴς M   ὅτι] ὅτι ὁ K M N O S   74 ἐπαισχύναιτέ W   τῷ] τὸ B N O P^2 Q T   ἡμῖν *om.* Æ   75 συνεστάναι Æ I K M S T W *Ald Mign* : καθεστάναι X   76 πεπλάσθαι Æ I K M O S V X *Mign*   δοκεῖν πεπλᾶσθαι D   λειτουργίας ß G P W X   77 δοθείσεσθαι W   τῇ φύσει δοθήσεσθαι M   καθὼς *om.* D G L P S V X   78 οὐδ' G I P X   78–9 ζήσεσθαι μόνῳ] *ita* Æ B D G L P Q S V X *Forb* : μόνῳ ζήσεσθαι O W *Ald Mign*   78 ζήσεται D   79 τὸν ἄνθρωπον] ἄνθρωπος D   προσηγόρευσεν B D^{ac} G N O P^{pc} V W   80 ὑποδεικνυούσης] ἀποκεικνυούσης C

Cap. 20 Æ I N O Q *Dion Eri*

19.25–21.16 (διορατικωτέροις—ἀλλ'ἀναγκαίοις): Paris, BN, *grec. 1356*, fragments (sigla Z) *Cap. 19–29 desunt* K

1–3 πρὸς—ζῆν] cuiusmodi debeat intelligi esse cibus hominis quo uescebatur in paradise et a quo prohibitus est *Λ*   1 καὶ πόσει *om.* N   πόσει] *ita* Æ B D G I L M P Q S *Forb* : ἐν πόσει *Ald Mign*   εἶναι] *post* ἀπόλαυσιν *(l. 2) pon.* Æ B I M N O Q *Dion Eri*: *om.* W   2–3 διὰ τὸ—ζῆν *om.* W   2 ἐξ ἀρχῆς *om.* I   τῷ om. D I   4 ἀλλ' *om.* Q   τις *om.* I   πάλιν *om.* M   5 μετὰ] μετὰ δὲ M   7 καὶ ἑτέραν τινὰ B   καὶ *om.* N Q   7–8 τροφὴν οἶδα B   7 οἶδα] οἶμαι N   8 ἡ *om.* Q   9 τὴν *om.* M Q   φάγετε] φάγετε γὰρ I τὸν ἐμὸν ἄρτον Æ B D I O P^2 Q T V   διακελεύεται] παρακελεύεται M N T   9–12 καὶ μακαρίζει—ἐγκελεύεται *om.* X   10 τοιαύτην] αὐτὴν B   φησὶν *om.* D G L N O P S T   11 πρός με] *ita* Æ G I L M N P S V W *Ald Forb* : πρὸς μὲ *Mign*   12 ἐπαΐειν] *ita* Æ ß G I L N P Q S V : ἐπαείειν W : ἐπακούειν M : ἐπὶ T   13 τιμωρίας ἀξίων] τιμωρηθησομένων T   λιμῷ] λιμῷ καὶ δίψει N   τίς ἐστιν] τινός ἐστιν M T : μόνον D   14 ἢ] καὶ Æ B I O T : οὐδὲ N   15 λόγων *Ald Mign*

made clear the faithfulness of what was said, that the human being has come to be as an imitation of God.

[18.9] But it may be that someone is ashamed that our life, in accordance with the likeness of the irrational animals, is sustained by food, and for this reason considers the human being unworthy of being supposed to have been moulded in the image of God. But it may be hoped that exemption from this function will one day be given to our nature, in the life that is looked for. *The Kingdom of God is not food and drink*, as the apostle says;[39] *neither does the human being live by bread alone*, the Lord declared, but *by every word that proceeds from the mouth of God.*[40] Moreover, as the resurrection indicates to us a mode of life equal to the angels, and with the angels there is no food, there is sufficient grounds for believing that the human being, who will live in likeness to the angels, will be delivered from such a function.

To those who say: 'The enjoyment of the good things hoped for will again be in food and drink, because from the beginning in Paradise, it is written, the human being lived by these means.'[41]

[19.1] But perhaps someone will say that the human being will not return again to the same form of life, if we formerly existed by eating but hereafter will be released from such a function. I, however, when I hear the Holy Scripture, do not understand only bodily food or the cheerfulness of the flesh; but I know another kind of food also, having some sort of analogy to that of the body, the enjoyment of which extends to the soul alone: *Eat of my bread*, is the bidding of Wisdom to the hungry; and the Lord blesses those who *hunger* for such food, and says, *If anyone thirst, let him come unto Me, and drink*: and *drink joy*, the great Isaiah charges those able to hear his sublimity.[42] There is a prophetic threatening also against those worthy of vengeance, that they shall be punished with *famine*; but the *famine* is not a lack of bread and water, but a lack of a word: *not a famine of bread*, he says, *nor a thirst for water*, but *a famine of hearing a word of the Lord.*[43]

[39] Rom. 14:17. [40] Matt. 4:4.

[41] *Bodl. 238* (as Chap. 20): 'How the food ought to be understood with which the human was fed in paradise and from which he was prohibited'.

[42] Prov. 9:5; Matt. 5:6; John 7:37; cf. Isa. 12:3. [43] Amos 8:11.

[19.2] *Οὐκοῦν τῆς τοῦ Θεοῦ φυτείας τῆς ἐν Ἐδὲμ (τρυφὴ δὲ ἡ Ἐδὲμ ἑρμηνεύεται) ἄξιόν τινα προσήκει τὸν καρπὸν ἐννοῆσαι, καὶ τρέφεσθαι διὰ τούτου μὴ ἀμφιβάλλειν τὸν ἄνθρωπον· καὶ μὴ πάντως τὴν παροδικὴν καὶ ἀπόρρυτον ταύτην τροφὴν ἐπὶ τῆς τοῦ παραδείσου διαγωγῆς ἐννοεῖν·* ***ἀπὸ παντὸς***, *φησί,* ***ξύλου τοῦ ἐν τῷ παραδείσῳ βρώσει φάγῃ***. [19.3] *Τίς δώσει τῷ ὑγιεινῶς πεινῶντι τὸ ξύλον ἐκεῖνο, τὸ ἐν τῷ παραδείσῳ, τὸ παντὸς ἀγαθοῦ περιληπτικόν, ᾧ ὄνομά ἐστι τὸ πᾶν,* [197] *οὗ χαρίζεται τῷ ἀνθρώπῳ τὴν μετουσίαν ὁ λόγος; τῷ γὰρ γενικῷ τε καὶ ὑπερκειμένῳ λόγῳ πᾶσα τῶν ἀγαθῶν ἰδέα πρὸς ἑαυτὴν συμφυῶς ἔχει, καὶ ἕν τι τὸ ὅλον ἐστί. Τίς δέ με τῆς συμμιγοῦς τε καὶ ἐπαμφοτεριζούσης τοῦ ξύλου γεύσεως ἀποστήσει; πάντως γὰρ οὐκ ἄδηλον τοῖς διορατικωτέροις, τί τὸ πᾶν ἐκεῖνο οὗ καρπὸς ἡ ζωή, καὶ πάλιν, τί τὸ ἐπίμικτον τοῦτο οὗ πέρας ὁ θάνατος· ὁ γὰρ τοῦ παντὸς τὴν ἀπόλαυσιν ἀφθόνως προθείς, λόγῳ τινὶ πάντως καὶ προμηθείᾳ τῆς τῶν ἐπικοίνων μετουσίας ἀπείργει τὸν ἄνθρωπον.*

[19.4] *Καί μοι δοκεῖ τὸν μέγαν Δαυὶδ καὶ τὸν σοφὸν Σολομῶντα διδασκάλους τῆς τοῦ λόγου τούτου παραλαβεῖν ἐξηγήσεως· ἀμφότεροι γὰρ τῆς συγκεχωρημένης τρυφῆς μίαν ἡγοῦνται τὴν χάριν, αὐτὸ τὸ ὄντως ἀγαθόν, ὃ δὴ καὶ πᾶν ἐστιν ἀγαθόν· Δαυὶδ* [B] *μὲν λέγων,* ***Κατατρύφησον τοῦ Κυρίου***· *Σολομὼν δὲ τὴν σοφίαν αὐτήν, ἥ τις ἐστὶν ὁ Κύριος,* ***ξύλον ζωῆς*** *ὀνομάζων.* [19.5] *Οὐκοῦν ταὐτόν ἐστι* ***τῷ τῆς ζωῆς ξύλῳ τὸ πᾶν ξύλον***, *οὗ τὴν βρῶσιν τῷ κατὰ Θεὸν πλασθέντι ὁ λόγος δίδωσιν· ἀντιδιαιρεῖται δὲ τῷ ξύλῳ τούτῳ ἕτερον ξύλον, οὗ ἡ βρῶσις* ***καλοῦ καὶ κακοῦ γνῶσίς*** *ἐστιν, οὐκ ἰδιαζόντως ἑκάτερον τῶν κατὰ τὸ ἐναντίον σημαινομένων ἐν μέρει καρποφοροῦντος, ἀλλά τινα συγκεχυμένον καὶ σύμμικτον καρπὸν ἐξανθοῦντος ταῖς ἐναντίαις συγκεκραμένον ποιότησιν· οὗ κωλύει μὲν τὴν βρῶσιν ὁ ἀρχηγὸς τῆς ζωῆς, συμβουλεύει δὲ ὁ ὄφις, ἵνα τῷ θανάτῳ κατασκευάσῃ τὴν εἴσοδον· καὶ πιθανὸς γίνεται συμβουλεύσας, εὐχροίᾳ*

16 *οὐκοῦν*] numquid *Eri* *τοῦ θεοῦ om.* T 17 *τὸν καρπὸν ἐννοῆσαι προσήκει* W *Ald Mign* 18 *τὴν om.* Q *ταύτην καὶ ἀπόρρυτον* M *ἀπόρρητον* B L *τρυφὴν Dion* 19 *τοῦ*[1] *om.* I *διαγωγῆς ἐννοεῖν*] *τρυφῆς ἐννοῆσαι* V W *ἐννοῆσαι* D G L P S X *παντὸς*] *παντὸς γὰρ* M *φησι om.* O Q T *ξύλου φησι* Æ B I M N W 20 *φάγῃ*] *φαγῇ* G P T V : *φάγῇ* S[ac] *ὑγεεινῶς Forb* *τὸ*[2]] *τῷ* V 22 *τῷ ἀνθρώπῳ*] *τοῦ ἀνθρώπου* : *om.* B *τῷ ἀνθρώπῳ τὴν μετουσίαν*] *τὴν μετουσίαν τῷ ἀνθρώπῳ* D *μετουσίαν*] *περιουσίαν* V W *λόγος*] *νόμος* Æ B I M N O Q *Dion Eri* 23 *συμφυῶς πρὸς ἑαυτὴν* D *ἑαυτὴν*] *αὑτὴν* D G L P S *τι om.* M N Q T *Dion Eri* 24 *τε om.* D G P X 25 *ἀπιστήσει* O *τι om.* N *τὸ om.* Z *πᾶν*] *πᾶν εἴη* T *οὗ*] *ᾧ* M 26 *τι om.* N *οὗ πέρας ὁ θάνατος om.* N T V W Z *Eri* 27 *προσθεὶς* G N P 28 *ἐπικοίνων*] *κοινῶν* N 29 *κἀμοὶ* T *post* *μέγαν* reliqua desunt V *δαυίδ* (*et l.* 32)] *ita Forb* : *δαβίδ Ald Mign* *σοφὸν*] sapientissimum *Dion* *διδάσκαλον* Æ B D G I M O P X *Eri* : *om. Dion* 30 *λόγου*] *νόμου* Æ M O Q *Dion Eri* 31 *συγκεχωρισμένης* B *τροφῆς* G L P Q S X *Dion Eri* *τὴν om.* D L *ὄντως*] *ὄντως ὂν* Æ B N O T W : *ὄντως ὃν* Q 31–2 *ὃ δὴ καὶ πᾶν ἐστιν ἀγαθὸν om.* I M Q T 32 *πᾶν*] *πᾶσιν* X 33 *σολομῶν* Æ *ὁ κύριος ἐστὶν* N 34 *οὐκοῦν*] non ergo *Eri* *ξύλῳ τὸ πᾶν ξύλον*] *ξύλον τῷ παντὶ ξύλῳ* I 35 *λόγος*] *νόμος* Æ B I M O Q *Dion Eri* *ἀντιδιαιρεῖ* M T *ξύλον ἕτερον* M 36 *ἡ om.* T *καλοῦ*] *καλοῦ τε* D L Q *ἑκατέρου* N 37 *καὶ om.* D 38 *ταῖς om.* N 40 *γέγονε* Æ I M N O Q T W *Dion* : *om.* B *σύμβουλος* N

[19.2] Therefore, one should understand the fruit in Eden (and Eden means 'delight') as something worthy of God's planting and not doubt whether the human being was nourished by it. And one should certainly not, with respect to the course of life in Paradise, understand transitory and perishable nourishment: *of every tree for food in Paradise,* he says, *you may eat.*[44] **[19.3]** Who will give to one with a wholesome hunger that tree that is in Paradise, which includes all good, the name of which is 'the all';[45] of which the account bestows a share to the human being? For in the generic and transcendent word [i.e. 'all'], every form of good is in harmony with itself, and the whole is one. And who will keep me back from the mixed and doubled tasting of the tree? For surely it is not unclear to the more perceptive what 'the all' is whose fruit is life, and again, what the mixed is whose limit is death; for he who ungrudgingly holds out the enjoyment of 'the all' debars, surely for some reason and forethought, the human being from participation in things that are common.

[19.4] It seems to me that I may take the great David and the wise Solomon as my teachers in the interpretation of this passage: for both understand the grace of the permitted delight to be one, the truly good itself, which is indeed also 'all' good: David, when he says, *Delight in the Lord*, and Solomon, when he names Wisdom herself, which is the Lord, *a tree of life.*[46] **[19.5]** Thus, the *all tree*, which the account gives as food to the one moulded by God, is the same as *the tree of life.*[47] There is opposed to this tree another tree, the food of which is *the knowledge of good and evil,*[48] not as if bearing as fruit, individually in turn, each of these things signified as opposites, but in that it produces some kind of blended and mixed fruit, compounded of opposite qualities, of which the Prince of life forbids eating, but the serpent counsels, so that he might prepare an entrance for death. And his counsel was persuasive, covering over the fruit with a certain

[44] Gen. 2:16.

[45] Gregory is playing here on the words used in Gen. 2:16, *ἀπὸ παντὸς ξύλου*, 'from every tree' (as RSV): the word usually translated as 'every' means 'all', and as such can be taken as the designation of the (singular) tree, i.e. 'the all tree'.

[46] Ps. 36:4; Prov. 3:18. [47] Gen. 2:9. [48] Gen. 2:9, 17.

τινὶ καὶ ἡδονῇ τὸν καρπὸν περιχρώσας, ὡς ἂν ὀφθείη τε ἡδέως καὶ τὴν ὄρεξιν πρὸς τὴν γεῦσιν ὑπερεθίσειεν.

Τίς ἡ ἐν τῷ παραδείσῳ ζωὴ, καὶ τί τὸ ἀπηγορευμένον ἐκεῖνο ξύλον;

[20.1] *Τί οὖν ἐκεῖνό ἐστιν ὃ καλοῦ τε καὶ κακοῦ συγκεκραμένην ἔχει τὴν γνῶσιν, ταῖς δι' αἰσθήσεως ἡδοναῖς ἐπηνθισμένον; ἆρα μὴ πόρρω τῆς ἀληθείας παραστοχάζομαι, τῇ τοῦ γνωστοῦ διανοίᾳ εἰς ἀφορμὴν τῆς θεωρίας συγχρώμενος. Οἶμαι γὰρ οὐκ ἐπιστήμην ἐνταῦθα παρὰ τῆς γραφῆς νοεῖσθαι τὴν γνῶσιν, ἀλλά τινα διαφορὰν ἐκ τῆς γραφικῆς συνηθείας εὑρίσκω, γνώσεώς τε καὶ διακρίσεως· τὸ μὲν γὰρ* ***διακρίνειν*** *ἐπιστημόνως* ***τὸ καλὸν ἐκ τοῦ κακοῦ****, τελειοτέρας ἕξεως εἶναί φησιν ὁ ἀπόστολος, καὶ* ***γεγυμνασμένων αἰσθητηρίων****· διὸ καὶ πρόσταγμα ποιεῖται* ***πάντα δοκιμάζειν****, καὶ* ***τοῦ πνευματικοῦ τὸ διακρίνειν*** *ἴδιον* [D] *εἶναι φησίν· ἡ δὲ γνῶσις οὐ πανταχοῦ τὴν ἐπιστήμην τε καὶ τὴν εἴδησιν ὑφηγεῖται κατὰ τὸ σημαινόμενον, ἀλλὰ τὴν πρὸς τὸ κεχαρισμένον διάθεσιν· ὡς,* ***ἔγνω Κύριος τοὺς ὄντας αὐτοῦ****, καὶ πρὸς τὸν Μωϋσέα φησὶν, ὅτι* ***ἔγνων σε παρὰ πάντας****· περὶ δὲ τῶν ἐν κακίᾳ κατεγνωσμένων λέγει ὁ τὰ πάντα εἰδὼς, ὅτι* ***οὐδέποτε ἔγνων ὑμᾶς****.*

[20.2] *Οὐκοῦν τὸ ξύλον, ἀφ' οὗ* [200] *ἡ σύμμικτος γνῶσις καρποφορεῖται, τῶν ἀπηγορευμένων ἐστί· μέμικται δὲ διὰ τῶν ἐναντίων ὁ καρπὸς ἐκεῖνος, ὁ συνήγορον ἔχων ἑαυτοῦ τὸν ὄφιν, τάχα κατὰ τὸν λόγον τοῦτον, ὅτι οὐ γυμνὸν πρόκειται τὸ κακὸν, αὐτὸ ἐφ' ἑαυτοῦ κατὰ τὴν ἰδίαν φύσιν φαινόμενον· ἦ γὰρ ἂν ἄπρακτος ἦν ἡ κακία, μηδενὶ προσκεχρωσμένη καλῷ τῷ πρὸς ἐπιθυμίαν αὐτῆς ἐφελκομένῳ τὸν ἀπατώμενον· νυνὶ δὲ σύμμικτός πως ἐστὶν ἡ τοῦ κακοῦ φύσις, ἐν μὲν τῷ βάθει τὸν ὄλεθρον οἷόν τινα δόλον ἐγκεκρυμμένον ἔχουσα, ἐν δὲ τῇ κατὰ τὸ φαινόμενον ἀπάτῃ καλοῦ τινα φαντασίαν παραδεικνύουσα. Καλὸν δοκεῖ τοῖς φιλαργύροις ἡ τῆς ὕλης εὔχροια· ἀλλὰ* ***ῥίζα πάντων τῶν κακῶν ἡ φιλαργυρία*** *γίνεται. Τίς δ' ἂν ἐπὶ τὸν δυσώδη βόρβορον τῆς ἀκολασίας κατώλισθεν, εἰ μὴ τὴν ἡδονὴν καλόν τε καὶ αἱρετὸν* [B] *ᾤετο ὁ τῷ δελέατι τούτῳ πρὸς τὸ πάθος κατασυρόμενος; οὕτω καὶ τὰ λοιπὰ τῶν*

41 *πρὸς*] *ὑπὲρ* N 42 *ὑπερεθίσειεν*] *ὑπερθίσειεν* L : *ὑπερθήσειεν* G P (*ε sup. ή*) X : *ὑπερκινήσειεν* N

Cap. 21 Æ ß I N O Q T *Dion Eri*

1 *τίς—ξύλον*] quare scriptura uocauerit illa arborem lignum scientia boni et mali *Λ* *ἐκεῖνο*] *ita* Æ B D G H I M N O P Q T *Forb* : *om. Ald Mig* *ξύλον ἐκεῖνο* W 2 *ὃ*] *ὃ καὶ* T *τε om.* M N T 3 *αἰσήσεων* M T *ἐπηνθισμένον*] insitum *Eri* 4 *παραστοχάζομαι*] *ita* Æ B D G I L N O P Q S T X *Ald Forb* : *στοχάζομαι* M : *παραστοχάσομαι Mign* *τῆς om.* M 5 *γνῶσιν*] *γνῶ* Z 6 *εὑρίσκων* L *τε καὶ διακρίσεως om.* L 7 *ἐπιστημόνως*] *ἐπιστηομινκῶς* N : *ἐπιστημόνως ὡς* L *τελεωτέρας* Æ 8 *αἰσθητηρίων*] *τὰ αἰσητήρια* M *προστάγματα* Q 9 *τὸ om.* Æ P *ἡ*] *εἰ* O 10 *τε om.* T *κατὰ τὸ σημαινόμενον ὑφηγεῖται* Æ B I M N O Q T W *Dion* : *καὶ το σημαινόμενον ὑφηγεῖται* Z *ὑφηγεῖται*] *om. Eri* 11 *ὡς*] *ὡς τὸ* I 12 *ὅτι om.* N O Q *Dion* *δὲ om.* B *Dion* *κατεγνωσμένων*] *διεγνωσμένων* D G P X : *κατεγνωσμένον* S[ac] (*διε sup. l.*) 13 *τὰ om.* Æ B I N O Q T W 14 *οὐκοῦν*] non ergo *Eri* 15 *μέμικται*] *ἐνμέμικται* B *ὁ*] *ὡς* T : *om.* N 16 *λόγον τοῦτον*] *ἑαυτοῦ λόγον* Q 17 *ἐφ'*] *ἀφ'* N *ἦ*] *ἢ* G L : *εἰ* P W X 18 *προσκεχρημένη* H : *προσκεχωρισμένη* O : *συνκεχρωσμένη* T 19 *νυνὶ*] *νοῦν·εἰ* T *ἡ τοῦ κακοῦ φύσις ἐστὶν* Æ B I M O Q T W *Dion Eri* *μὲν*] *μένων* W 20 *δόλον*] *δοκὸν* ß : *λόχον* Æ N O T W : *λόγον* I M 21 *παραδεικνύουσα*] *παραδεικνύσα* O : *παραδεικνύουσαν* Z : *παραδεικνύουσα ὥσπερ ἡ φιλαργυρία καὶ ἄλλα τοιαῦτά τινα· καὶ γὰρ* H 22 *φιλαργυρία*] *φιλαρία* Z 23 *ἀκολασίας*] *πορνείας ἢ φιληδονίας* N *κατωλίσθησεν* T *τε*] *τι Mign* *αἱρετὸν*] *ἀγαθὸν* N 24 *ὁ om.* Æ ß I O *Dion* *δελέατι*] *δελεάματι* Æ[ac] D

attractiveness and delight, so that it might appear pleasant and stimulate the appetite for a taste.

What was the life in Paradise, and what was that forbidden tree?[49]

[**20.1**] What then is that which has the knowledge of good and evil blended together, and is decked with the pleasures of sense?[50] I am not aiming wide of the truth in employing, as a starting point for my contemplation, the meaning of 'knowable'.[51] It is not, I think, 'science' which Scripture here means by 'knowledge'; for I find a certain distinction, from customary scriptural use, between 'knowledge' and 'discernment'. For to *discern* skilfully *the good from the evil*, the Apostle says is of a more perfect condition and *of exercised senses*;[52] on which account he also gives the injunction *test all things*,[53] and says that *discernment* belongs to the *spiritual*.[54] But 'knowledge' does not always indicate, by its signification, 'science' and 'intelligence', but the disposition towards what is pleasing, as in, *The Lord knows those that are his*,[55] and as he says to Moses, *I knew you above all*,[56] while of those condemned in their wickedness, the one who knows all things says, *I never knew you*.[57]

[**20.2**] The tree, therefore, from which is borne the fruit of mixed knowledge, is among those things which are forbidden; and that fruit, which has the serpent as its own advocate, is mixed of opposites, perhaps so that evil is not proposed nakedly, itself appearing in its own nature. For evil would be unsuccessful if did not avail itself of beauty, enticing the one deceived to a desire of it; but as it is, the nature of evil is mixed in some way, keeping destruction, like some bait, hidden in its depth, but displaying some illusion of good in the deceit of appearances. The attractiveness of the matter seems good to those who love money, yet, *the love of money is a root of all evil*.[58] Who would sink into the stinking mire of licentiousness, were it not that he, whom this bait drags into passion, thinks pleasure a good and acceptable thing? Thus also, the other sins keep their destruction hidden, and

[49] *Bodl. 238* (as Chap. 21): 'Why Scripture called the tree "the tree of the knowledge of good and evil"'.

[50] Cf. Gregory of Nyssa, *Or. Cat.* 21.4–5 (Mühlenberg, 56.10–57.6).

[51] Cf. Gen. 2:9, where the tree is called 'the tree of the knowable [γνωστὸν] of good and evil'.

[52] Heb. 5:14. [53] 1 Thess. 5:21. [54] 1 Cor. 2:15. [55] Num. 16:5; 2 Tim. 2:19.

[56] Exod. 33:12. [57] Matt. 7:23. [58] 1 Tim. 6:10.

ἁμαρτημάτων ἐγκεκρυμμένην ἔχοντα τὴν διαφθορὰν, αἱρετὰ παρὰ τὴν πρώτην δοκεῖ, διά τινος ἀπάτης τοῖς ἀνεπισκέπτοις ἀντ' ἀγαθοῦ σπουδαζόμενα.

[20.3] *Ἐπειδὴ τοίνυν οἱ πολλοὶ τὸ καλὸν ἐν τῷ τὰς αἰσθήσεις εὐφραίνοντι κρίνουσι, καί τις ἐστὶν ὁμωνυμία τοῦ τε ὄντος καὶ τοῦ δοκοῦντος εἶναι καλοῦ· τούτου χάριν ἡ πρὸς τὸ κακὸν ὡς πρὸς τὸ ἀγαθὸν γινομένη ἐπιθυμία,* **καλοῦ καὶ κακοῦ γνῶσις** *ὑπὸ τῆς γραφῆς ὠνομάσθη, συνδιάθεσίν τινα καὶ ἀνάκρασιν ἑρμηνευούσης τῆς γνώσεως. Οὔτε ἀπολύτως κακὸν, διότι περιήνθισται τῷ καλῷ, οὔτε καθαρῶς ἀγαθὸν, διότι ὑποκέκρυπται τὸ κακόν, ἀλλὰ σύμμικτον δι' ἑκατέρων τοῦ ἀπηγορευμένου ξύλου τὸν καρπὸν εἶναί φησιν, οὗ τὴν γεῦσιν εἰς θάνατον ἄγειν* [C] *εἶπε τοὺς ἁψαμένους· μονονουχὶ φανερῶς τὸ δόγμα βοῶν, ὅτι τὸ ὄντως ὂν ἀγαθὸν ἁπλοῦν καὶ μονοειδές ἐστι τῇ φύσει, πάσης διπλόης καὶ τῆς πρὸς τὸ ἐναντίον συζυγίας ἀλλότριον· τὸ δὲ κακὸν ποικίλον τε καὶ κατεσχηματισμένον ἐστὶν, ἄλλό τι νομιζόμενον, καὶ ἕτερον διὰ τῆς πείρας ἀναφαινόμενον· οὗ τὴν γνῶσιν, τουτέστι τὴν διὰ τῆς πείρας ἀνάληψιν, θανάτου καὶ διαφθορᾶς ἀρχήν τε καὶ ὑπόθεσιν γίνεσθαι.*

[20.4] *Διὰ τοῦτο προδείκνυσιν ὁ ὄφις τὸν πονηρὸν τῆς ἁμαρτίας καρπὸν, οὐχ ὡς εἶχε φύσεως τὸ κακὸν ἐκ τοῦ προφανοῦς ἐπιδείξας (οὐ γὰρ ἂν ἠπατήθη ὁ ἄνθρωπος τῷ προδήλῳ κακῷ) ἀλλὰ, διά τινος ὥρας τὸ φαινόμενον ἀγλαΐσας καί τινα κατὰ τὴν αἴσθησιν ἡδονὴν ἐγγοητεύσας τῇ γεύσει, πιθανὸς ἐφάνη τῇ γυναικὶ, καθώς* [D] *φησιν ἡ γραφή·* **καὶ εἶδε** *γάρ φησιν* **ἡ γυνή ὅτι καλὸν τὸ ξύλον εἰς βρῶσιν καὶ ὅτι ἀρεστὸν τοῖς ὀφθαλμοῖς ἰδεῖν, καὶ ὡραῖόν ἐστι τοῦ κατανοῆσαι· καὶ λαβοῦσα τοῦ καρποῦ αὐτοῦ ἔφαγεν·** *ἡ δὲ βρῶσις ἐκείνη θανάτου μήτηρ τοῖς ἀνθρώποις γέγονεν· αὕτη τοίνυν ἡ σύμμικτός ἐστι καρποφορία, σαφῶς τοῦ λόγου τὸν νοῦν ἑρμηνεύοντος, καθ' ὃν* **καλοῦ τε καὶ κακοῦ γνωστὸν** *ὠνομάσθη τὸ ξύλον ἐκεῖνο· ὅτι κατὰ τὴν τῶν δηλητηρίων κακίαν τῶν παραρτυθέντων τῷ μέλιτι, καθὸ μὲν καταγλυκαίνει τὴν αἴσθησιν, καλὸν εἶναι δοκεῖ· καθὸ δὲ φθείρει τὸν προσαπτόμενον, κακοῦ παντὸς ἔσχατον γίνεται. Ἐπεὶ οὖν ἐνήργησε κατὰ τῆς τοῦ ἀνθρώπου ζωῆς τὸ πονηρὸν*

25 *διαφθορὰν*] *διαφορὰν* I P[ac] (*corr. 1[a] man.*) *Dion Eri* *πρώτην*] *πρώτην γνῶσιν* N : primam delectationem 26 *ἀντὶ* N *ἀγαθῶν* M 27 *κρίνονται* H 28 *καὶ*] *καὶ μία* Q 27 *τις om.* Æ B I O *ὁμωνυμία*] *ἐπωνυμία* Q *εἶναι om.* Æ B I M N O T W 29 *τὸ om.* Æ B M Q *γενομένη* Q *καλοῦ*] *καλοῦ τε* M 29–30 *ὑπὸ τῆς γραφῆς om.* D 30 *ἀνάκρασιν*] *συνανάκρασιν* Æ B I O 32 *τοῦ*] *τῶν τοῦ* Z 33 *εἶπε εἰς θάνατον ἄγειν* Æ B I M N O Q T W *ἀγαγεῖν* T *εἶπε ἄγειν* L *ἁψαμένους*] *γευσαμένους* N 34 *μονονουχὶ*] *μόνον· οὐχὶ* Z : solummodo non *Eri* *φανερῶς om.* D *ὂν*] *ὃν* Q : *ὢν* B (*sed non* ß) : *om. Ald Mign* 35 *τὴν φύσιν* M 36 *καταισχηματισμένον* O *ἐστὶν om.* T *ἄλλό τι νομιζόμενον*] alicui commixtum *Eri* 37 *ἀναφενόμενον* N : *φαινόμενον* M : apparens *Eri* *τὴν*[2] *om.* D G H P X *διὰ τῆς πείρας*] *τῆς διαπείρας* D (*eras. διὰ*) 38 *καὶ*[1] *om.* M *διαφθορᾶς*] *διαφορᾶς* P[ac] : *φθορᾶς* D I L O *γενέσθαι* I O 39–40 *οὐχ ὡς—ἐπιδείξας*] sic ex propatulo malum non habere naturam ostendens *Eri* 40 *προφανῶς* Q : *περιφανοῦς* M *ἐπιδείξας*] *ὑποδείξας* B N 41 *ὥρας om.* N *ἀγλαΐσας* N 42 *γεύσει*] *γεύσει καὶ* D 43 *καὶ*[1] *om.* B P[2] *γὰρ om.* M *ἡ γυνή φησιν* W *Ald Mign* *φησιν om.* M 44 *ἰδεῖν*] *τοῦ ἰδεῖν* O *ἐστι post ἀρεστὸν* (*l. 43*) *pon.* M : *om.* B 45 *αὐτοῦ om.* M *γέγονεν τοῖς ἀνθρώποις* Æ B O : *γέγονε προδήλως τοῖς ἀνθρώποις* I *γέγονεν*] *ἐγίνετο* D : *γίνεται* M 46 *ἡ om.* D G P W X *ἑρμηνεύσαντος* Æ B I M O Q T 47 *ἐκεῖνο om.* M 48 *τῶν παραρτυθέντων τῷ μέλιτι*] quae in melle fiunt *Eri* *παρατυθέντων τῷ μέλιτι*] *τῷ μέλι κεκραμμένων* Q 49 *προσαψάμενον* Æ B I M N O Q T 50 *ἔσχατον*] *αἴσχιον* N *ἐνήργησε*] *ἐνείργησε* W : *ἐνήργησαν* Z

seem at the first sight acceptable, making themselves, by some deceit, eagerly sought after by the unwary instead of what is good.

[**20.3**] Therefore, since the majority judge the good to be in that which gratifies the senses, and there is a certain homonymy between that which is and that which appears to be 'good', for this reason the desire arising towards evil, as though towards the good, is named by Scripture *the knowledge of good and evil*, 'knowledge', as we have said, expressing a certain mixed disposition.[59] It means that the fruit of the forbidden tree is not absolutely evil, for it is decked with good, nor purely good, for evil is hidden within it, but as compounded of both; [Scripture] said that tasting of it leads those who touch it to death, almost proclaiming aloud the doctrine that the truly existing good is in its nature simple and single in form, alien from all duplicity and from conjunction with its opposite, while evil is varied and fairly adorned, reckoned to be one thing but shown by experience to be another, the knowledge of which, that is, its reception by experience, is the beginning and ground of death and destruction.

[**20.4**] Therefore, the serpent points out the evil fruit of sin, not showing the evil in its own nature clearly (for the human being would not have been deceived by manifest evil) but, through some radiance beautifying what appears and enchanting the taste by a certain sensual pleasure, he presents it to the woman winningly, just as the Scripture says: *and the woman*, it says, *saw that the tree was good for food and that it was pleasing to the eyes to see and beautiful to perceive, and, taking the fruit of it, she ate*:[60] this eating became the mother of death to human beings. This, then, is the compounded fruit-bearing; the account clearly expresses the meaning that that tree was called *of the knowledge of good and evil* because, like the evil of poisons prepared with honey, it appears to be good, insofar as it produces a sense of sweetness in the senses, but is the worst of all evil, insofar as it destroys the one who touches it.[61] When, then, the evil poison worked its effect upon the life of the human being, then *the human being*—that noble thing and name, the copy of

[59] Cf. Gregory of Nyssa, *Cant.* 12 (Langerbeck, 348.12–352.5).

[60] Gen. 3:6.

[61] Cf. Gregory of Nyssa, *Or. Cat.* 7.3 (Mühlenberg, 29.13–16).

δηλητήριον, τότε **ὁ** [201] **ἄνθρωπος**, *τὸ μέγα καὶ πρᾶγμα καὶ ὄνομα, τὸ τῆς θείας φύσεως ἀπεικόνισμα,* **τῇ ματαιότητι**, *καθώς φησιν ὁ προφήτης,* **ὡμοιώθη**. [20.5] *Οὐκοῦν ἡ μὲν εἰκὼν πρὸς τὸ κρεῖττον τῶν ἐν ἡμῖν νοουμένων ᾠκείωται· τὰ δὲ ὅσα περὶ τὸν βίον λυπηρά τε καὶ ἄθλια, πόρρω τῆς πρὸς τὸ θεῖόν ἐστιν ὁμοιώσεως.*

Ὅτι ἡ ἀνάστασις οὐ τοσοῦτον ἐκ τοῦ κηρύγματος τοῦ γραφικοῦ, ὅσον ἐξ αὐτῆς τῆς τῶν πραγμάτων ἀνάγκης ἀκολούθως ἐλπίζεται.

[21.1] *Ἀλλ' οὐχ οὕτως ἐστὶν ἰσχυρὸν ἡ κακία ὡς τῆς* [B] *ἀγαθῆς ὑπερισχύσαι δυνάμεως· οὐδὲ κρείττων καὶ μονιμωτέρα τῆς τοῦ Θεοῦ σοφίας ἡ τῆς φύσεως ἡμῶν ἀβουλία· οὐδὲ γάρ ἐστι δυνατὸν, τὸ τρεπόμενόν τε καὶ ἀλλοιούμενον τοῦ ἀεὶ ὡσαύτως ἔχοντος καὶ ἐν τῷ ἀγαθῷ πεπηγότος ἐπικρατέστερόν τε καὶ μονιμώτερον εἶναι· ἀλλ' ἡ μὲν θεία βουλὴ πάντη τε καὶ πάντως τὸ ἀμετάθετον ἔχει· τὸ δὲ τρεπτὸν τῆς φύσεως ἡμῶν οὐδὲ ἐν τῷ κακῷ πάγιον μένει.* [21.2] *Τὸ γὰρ ἀεὶ πάντως κινούμενον, εἰ μὲν πρὸς τὸ καλὸν ἔχοι τὴν πρόοδον, διὰ τὸ ἀόριστον τοῦ διεξοδευομένου πράγματος οὐδέποτε λήξει τῆς ἐπὶ τὰ πρόσω φορᾶς· οὐδὲ γὰρ εὑρήσει τοῦ ζητουμένου πέρας οὐδὲν, οὗ δραξάμενον στήσεταί ποτε τῆς κινήσεως· εἰ δὲ πρὸς τὸ ἐναντίον τὴν ῥοπὴν σχοίη, ἐπειδὰν διανύσῃ τῆς κακίας τὸν* [C] *δρόμον, καὶ ἐπὶ τὸ ἀκρότατον τοῦ κακοῦ μέτρον ἀφίκηται, τότε τὸ ἀεικίνητον τῆς ὁρμῆς οὐδεμίαν ἐκ φύσεως στάσιν εὑρίσκον, ἐπειδὰν διαδράμῃ τὸ ἐν κακίᾳ διάστημα, κατ' ἀνάγκην ἐπὶ τὸ ἀγαθὸν τρέπει τὴν κίνησιν· μὴ γὰρ προϊούσης κακίας πρὸς τὸ ἀόριστον, ἀλλ' ἀναγκαίοις πέρασι κατειλημμένης, ἀκολούθως ἡ τοῦ ἀγαθοῦ διαδοχὴ τὸ πέρας τῆς κακίας ἐκδέχεται· καὶ οὕτω, καθὼς εἴρηται, τὸ ἀεικίνητον ἡμῶν τῆς φύσεως πάλιν ὕστατον ἐπὶ τὴν ἀγαθὴν ἀνατρέχει πορείαν, τῇ μνήμῃ τῶν προδεδυστυχημένων πρὸς τὸ μὴ πάλιν ἐν τοῖς ἴσοις γενέσθαι σωφρονιζόμενον.*

52 *ἀπεικόνισμα*] *ἀπεικονίσματι* Z *τῇ ματαιότητι post ὡμοιώθη* (*l.* 52) *pon.* B *ὁ προφήτης φησὶν* M Q 53 *ἡ μὲν*] *ἡμῖν* Z *ᾠκείωται*] *οἰκείωται* N Q W 54 *δὲ*] *δ'* G I L S X *ὅσα*] *ὅσα τῶν* Æ L M N S T W *ἄθλια*] *ἄθλια καὶ* D G P^{ac} S X *ὁμοιώσεως*] *οἰκειώσεως* D G L P S X

Cap. 22 Æ ß I N O Q T *Dion Eri*

1–2 *ὅτι—ἐλπίζεται*] quod divinum consilium non est mutabile *Λ* 1 *τοσοῦτον*] *τοιοῦτον* D 1–2 *ἐξ αὐτῆς—ἐλπίζεται*] ex ipsa rerum necessitate speratur *Dion* 2 *ἀνάγκης τῶν πραγμάτων* W *Ald Mign* *ἀκολούθως om.* N W *ἐλπίζεται om. D* 4 *κρείττω* D^{ac} G P S X : *κρεῖττον* N W : *κρείττον* Q *τοῦ om. Ald Mign* 5 *οὐδὲ*] *οὔτε* Æ B M T : *οὐ* I *δυνατὸν om.* I O *τε om.* D G P X 7 *τε om.* G H M Q T 8 *οὐδ'* I *τῷ om.* N *κακῷ*] *κατ'αὐτὴν* I 9 *ἔχει* Æ H I M N T *ἀόριστον*] eximietatem *Eri* 10 *πράγματος*] *πνεύματος* Æ B I O *τὰ*] *τὸ* Æ ß I M N O Q W 11 *τοῦ om. Mign* *οὗ δραξάμενον*] *οὐδ' ἀρξάμενον* M W *στήσεται*] *στήσαι τέ* B $ß^{ac}$ *ποτε om.* N 12 *εἰ δὲ—σχοίη*] *om. Eri* *τὸ ἐναντίον*] *τοὐναντίον* I *ῥοπὴν*] *τροπὴν* T *σχοίει* G P *ἐπειδὰν*] *ἢ ἐπειδὰν* Z *διανύσει* B (*sed non* ß) : *διανοίσει* G P 13 *τὸ*[2]] *τε* I *τῆς ὁρμῆς τὸ ἀεικίνητον* W : *τὸ τῆς ὁρμῆς ἀεικίνητον Ald Mign* 14 *φύσεως στάσιν*] *στάσεως φύσιν* M *διαδράμῃ*] *ἐκδράμῃ* N T 15 *προϊούσης*] *προϊούσης τῆς* Æ B D I M N O Q *πρὸς*] *ita* Æ ß G I L N O P Q S T W X *Forb* : *ἐπὶ Ald Mign* 16 *ἀλλὰ* N *πέρασι*] *πέρμασι* $N^{ac?}$: *τέρμασι* N^{pc2} *κατειλημμένης*] *προειλημμένης* N T 17 *ἐκδέχεται*] *ἐκχεῖται* T *οὕτως* O W 18 *τῆς φύσεως ἡμῶν* I *πάλιν ὕστατον*] *παλίσυρτον* M : *πάλιν συντόνως* Æ B I O : *πάλιν εἰς ἑαυτὸ* Q : *πάλιν* N R^{ac} T : iterum firmiter *Eri* *ἀνατρέχει*] *ἀνατρέπει* O : *ἐπανατρέχει* M Q R W *πορείαν*] *πορείαν ὕστερον* R 19 *προδεδυστηχημένων* O *ἐν*] *ἐναλῶναι* Q *Ald Mign* *γενέσθαι*] *ἐγγενέσθαι* D : *om.* Q *Ald Mign*

the divine nature—*was likened*, as the prophet says, *to vanity*.[62] [**20.5**] The image, therefore, is appropriated to the better part of those aspects conceived about ourselves; but all that which is painful and wretched in our mode of life is far removed from the likeness to the divine.

That the resurrection is consequentially hoped for not so much from the scriptural proclamation but as much from the very necessity of things.[63]

[**21.1**] But wickedness is not so strong as to prevail over the power of good, nor is the thoughtlessness of our nature stronger and more abiding than the wisdom of God; for it is impossible that that which is mutable and alterable should be stronger and more abiding than that which is always as it is and established in the good. But the divine counsel certainly and absolutely possesses immutability, while the changeability of our nature does not remain steadfast even in evil. [**21.2**] That which is always in motion, if its progress is towards the good, will never cease, because of the infinity of the course to be traversed, from moving towards what lies ahead; for it will not find any limit of that which it seeks, such that when it has grasped it, it will then bring rest from movement.[64] But if its tendency is in the opposite direction, whenever it has traversed the course of wickedness and reached the extreme limit of evil, then that which is ever-moving, finding no resting point for its natural impulse, since it has run through the interval in wickedness, by necessity turns its movement towards the good. For as evil does not extend to infinity, but is bounded by necessary limits, the accession of the good consequently succeeds the limit of evil, and thus, as we have said, the ever-moving character of our nature runs its journey once more at last towards the good, chastened by the memory of its former misfortunes so that it will never again be in the same circumstances.[65]

[62] Ps. 143:4. [63] *Bodl. 238* (as Chap. 22): 'That the divine counsel is immutable'.
[64] Cf. Gregory of Nyssa, *Or. Cat.* 21.2–3 (Mühlenberg, 55.21–56.10).
[65] Cf. Irenaeus, *Haer.* 3.20.1–2; Origen, *Princ.* 3.4.3.

[21.3] *Οὐκοῦν ἔσται πάλιν ἐν καλοῖς ὁ δρόμος ἡμῖν, διὰ τὸ πέρασιν ἀναγκαίοις περιωρίσθαι τῆς κακίας τὴν φύσιν. Καθάπερ γὰρ οἱ δεινοὶ τὰ μετέωρα, τοῦ μὲν φωτὸς πάντα λέγουσι τὸν κόσμον εἶναι κατάπλεων,* [D] *τὸ δὲ σκότος τῇ ἀντιφράξει τοῦ κατὰ τὴν γῆν σώματος ἀποσκιαζόμενον γίνεσθαι· ἀλλὰ τοῦτο μὲν κατὰ τὸ σχῆμα τοῦ σφαιροειδοῦς σώματος, κατὰ νώτου, τῆς ἡλιακῆς ἀκτῖνος κωνοειδῶς κατακλείεσθαι· τὸν δὲ ἥλιον, πολλαπλασίονι τῷ μεγέθει τὴν γῆν ὑπερβάλλοντα, πανταχόθεν αὐτὴν ταῖς ἀκτῖσιν ἐν κύκλῳ περιπτυσσόμενον, συνάπτειν κατὰ τὸ πέρας τοῦ κώνου τὰς τοῦ φωτὸς συμβολάς· ὥστε (καθ' ὑπόθεσιν) εἰ γένοιτό τινι δύναμις διαβῆναι τὸ μέτρον, εἰς ὅσον ἐκτείνεται ἡ σκιά, πάντως ἂν ἐν φωτὶ γενέσθαι μὴ διακοπτομένῳ ὑπὸ τοῦ σκότους· οὕτως οἶμαι δεῖν καὶ περὶ ἡμῶν διανοεῖσθαι, ὅτι διεξελθόντες τὸν τῆς κακίας ὅρον, ἐπειδὰν ἐν τῷ ἄκρῳ γενώμεθα τῆς* [204] *κατὰ τὴν ἁμαρτίαν σκιᾶς, πάλιν ἐν φωτὶ βιοτεύσομεν, κατὰ τὸ ἀπειροπλάσιον ὡς πρὸς τὸ τῆς κακίας μέτρον τῆς τῶν ἀγαθῶν φύσεως περιττευούσης.* **[21.4]** *Πάλιν οὖν ὁ παράδεισος, πάλιν τὸ ξύλον ἐκεῖνο, ὃ δὴ καὶ ζωῆς ἐστι ξύλον· πάλιν τῆς εἰκόνος ἡ χάρις καὶ ἡ τῆς ἀρχῆς ἀξία. Οὔ μοι δοκεῖ τούτων ὅσα νῦν πρὸς τὴν τοῦ βίου χρείαν παρὰ τοῦ Θεοῦ τοῖς ἀνθρώποις ὑπέζευκται, ἀλλ' ἑτέρας τινὸς βασιλείας ἐστὶν ἡ ἐλπίς, ἧς ὁ λόγος ἐν ἀπορρήτοις μένει.*

Πρὸς τοὺς λέγοντας, Εἰ καλόν τι καὶ ἀγαθὸν ἡ ἀνάστασις, τί οὐχὶ ἤδη γέγονεν, ἀλλὰ χρόνων τισὶ περιόδοις ἐλπίζεται.

[22.1] *Ἀλλὰ τῆς ἀκολουθίας τῶν ἐξητασμένων ἐχώμεθα· ἴσως γάρ τις πρὸς τὸ γλυκὺ τῆς ἐλπίδος πτερωθεὶς τὴν διάνοιαν, ἄχθος ἡγεῖται καὶ ζημίαν, τὸ μὴ θᾶττον ἐν τοῖς ἀγαθοῖς ἐκείνοις γενέσθαι, ἃ ὑπὲρ αἴσθησίν τε καὶ γνῶσιν ἀνθρωπίνην ἐστί, καὶ δεινὴν ποιεῖται τὴν διὰ μέσου πρὸς τὸ ποθούμενον τοῦ χρόνου παράτασιν· ἀλλὰ μὴ στενοχωρείσθω καθάπερ τις τῶν νηπίων, τὴν πρὸς ὀλίγον ἀναβολὴν τῶν καθ' ἡδονὴν δυσχεραίνων· ἐπειδὴ γὰρ ὑπὸ λόγου καὶ σοφίας τὰ πάντα οἰκονομεῖται, ἀνάγκη πᾶσα μηδὲν ἄμοιρον ἡγεῖσθαι τῶν γινομένων αὐτοῦ τε τοῦ λόγου καὶ τῆς ἐν αὐτῷ σοφίας.* **[22.2]** *Ἐρεῖς οὖν, Τίς οὗτος ὁ λόγος ἐστί,* [C] *καθ' ὃν οὐκ εὐθὺς ἐπὶ*

20 *οὐκοῦν*] non ergo *Eri* *ἐν*] *ἐν τοῖς* T *ἡμῖν*] *ἡμῶν* N R 21 *γὰρ om.* N 22 *λέγουσι om.* N *κατάπλεον* B (*sed non* ß) : *κατάπλεω* N : *ἀνάπλεω* M : *καὶ πλείω* D G L P S[ac] X 23 *ἀποσκιαζόμενον*] *σκιαζόμενον* M 24 *κατὰ νώτου*] considero *Eri* *κωνοειδῶς*] *καινοειδοῦς* B 25 *πολλαπλασίως* N : *πολλαπλάσιον* T *ὑπερβάλλεσθαι* X 26 *ἐν κύκλῳ ταῖς ἀκτῖσιν* N R W 25 *ἐν om.* N *συνάπτει* L *κατὰ om.* I 27 *συμβουλὰς* R *ὥστε*] *ὡς οὔ* R[ac] *εἰ καθ' ὑπόθεσιν* I *ὑπόθεσιν*] materiam *Eri* 28 *εἰς om.* B D G P X *ἂν om.* N T 29 *δεῖν*] *δεῖ* T : *om.* B (*sed non* ß) *ἡμῶν*] *ἡμῶν αὐτῶν* R 30 *διεξελθόντες*] *ἐξελθόντες* D M *ἐν om.* T *γενόμεθα* O 31 *ἐν*] *ἐν τῷ* Æ B N O R *ὡς κατὰ τὸ ἀπειροπλάσιον Mign* 32 *κακίας*] *σκίας* R *Dion* 33 *τὸ*] *τὸ πᾶν* Q R *Dion Eri* *ὃ δὴ καὶ*] *τῆς* T 34 *ἡ om.* M *τούτων*] *τούτων οὐδὲν* Q *Ald Mign* 35–6 *ἀλλ' ἑτέρας—μένει*] spes irrationabilis sed in alterius cuiusdam uitae ineffabilibus manere *Eri* 35 *βασιλείας om.* Q *Dion* *ἐστὶν om.* G L P Q S X *ἡ om* B G L M P S X

Cap. 23 Æ I N O Q R T : *cap. inc. inferius ἐχώμεθα* (*l.* 3) Q *Dion* : *def. Eri*

1–2 *πρὸς—ἐλπίζεται*] quod consummata generatione hominum tempus quoque deficiet *Λ* 1 *τι*] *τε* N Q : *ἐστι* L *τί*] *διατί* D G P Q X : *om.* W *οὐκ* D G I L O P R S X 2 *χρόνοις* Æ B I N O T W *τισὶν* W *περιόδοις*] *καὶ περιόδοις* Æ B I N O T 3 *ἐχόμεθα* L P[2] Q T 3–54 *ἴσως—τὸ ἀνθρώπινον*] *def. Eri* 4 *ἡγήσεται* I 5 *γίνεσθαι* N *ἃ om.* G P X *τε om.* Q T 6 *διὰ*] *διὰ τοῦ* R 7 *τὴν om.* D G P X *ὀλίγην* D E 7–8 *καθ' ἡδονὴν*] *κακῶν* D E R[2mg] 8 *ὑπὸ*] *διὰ* M 10 *οὖν*] *οὖν μοι* O *τίς*] *τί* W : *τί καὶ* B *οὗτος om.* R *εὐθὺς οὐκ* W

[**21.3**] Our course, therefore, will again be in what is good, because the nature of evil is bounded by necessary limits. Just as experts in astronomical phenomena say that the whole cosmos is full of light, and that darkness casts its shadow by the interposition of the body of the earth, but that, according to the figure of the spherical body, behind it this darkness is shut off from the rays of the sun in the shape of a cone, while the sun, being larger than the earth many times in size, enfolding it all round on all sides with its rays, unites at the limit of the cone the streams of light, so that, by hypothesis, if anyone had the power to surpass the measure to which the shadow extends, he would certainly be in light unbroken by darkness[66]—so also, I think, we ought to understand this regarding ourselves that, passing through the boundary of evil, whenever we have come to the furthest point of the shadow of sin we shall again live in light, as the nature of the good is infinitely more abundant than the measure of wickedness. [**21.4**] Therefore again Paradise; again that tree, which is indeed the tree of life; again the grace of the image and the dignity of sovereignty. It does not seem to me that the hope is for those things that are now subjugated by God to human beings for the needs of our mode of life, but for another kingdom, the account of which abides in unspeakable mysteries.

To those who say: 'If the resurrection is something beautiful and good, why has it not already happened, but is hoped for in some period of time?'[67]

[**22.1**] Let us give our attention, however, to the next point of our discussion. It may be that someone, giving his mind wings to soar towards the sweetness of our hope,[68] considers it a burden and a loss that we do not more speedily come to be in those good things which are above human sense-perception and knowledge, and [so] makes the extension of time intervening until that which is desired a cause for complaint. But do not be anxious, like children annoyed at the brief delay of something pleasurable; for since all things are administered by reason and wisdom, it must not be supposed that anything that happens is bereft of reason itself and the wisdom in it. [**22.2**] You will say then: What is this reason, in accordance

[66] Cf. Gregory of Nyssa, *Hex.* 32 (Drobner, 45.14–20); *An. et res.* 2.10–18 (Spira, 16.15–18.19); Basil, *Hex.* 9.1. Aristotle, *Meteor.* 1.8 (345b1–9); Pliny *Nat. hist.* 2.49–52; Alexander of Aphrodisias, *Meteor.* A8 (Hayduck, 38.7–13).

[67] *Bodl. 238* (as Chap. 23): 'That when the generation of humans is finished, time also will come to an end'.

[68] Cf. Ps. 54:7; Plato, *Phaedr.* 249c4–6.

τὸ ποθούμενον ἡ τοῦ λυπηροῦ βίου μετάστασις γίνεται, ἀλλ' εἰς χρόνους τινὰς ὡρισμένους ἡ βαρεῖα καὶ σωματώδης αὕτη παραταθεῖσα ζωὴ, ἀναμένει τὸ πέρας τῆς τοῦ παντὸς συμπληρώσεως, ἵνα τὸ τηνικαῦτα καθάπερ χαλινοῦ τινος ἐλευθερωθεῖσα ἡ ἀνθρωπίνη ζωὴ, πάλιν ἄνετός τε καὶ ἐλευθέρα πρὸς τὸν μακάριον καὶ ἀπαθῆ βίον ἐπαναδράμοι;

[22.3] *Ἀλλ' εἰ μὲν ἐγγίζει τῇ ἀληθείᾳ τῶν ζητουμένων ὁ λόγος, αὐτὴ ἂν εἰδείη σαφῶς ἡ ἀλήθεια· ὃ δ' οὖν ἐπὶ τὴν ἡμετέραν ἦλθε διάνοιαν, τοιοῦτον ἐστί. Λέγω δὴ, τὸν πρῶτον πάλιν ἐπαναλαβὼν λόγον·* ***ποιήσωμεν****, φησὶν ὁ Θεὸς,* ***ἄνθρωπον κατ' εἰκόνα καὶ ὁμοίωσιν ἡμετέραν· καὶ ἐποίησεν ὁ Θεὸς τὸν ἄνθρωπον, κατ' εἰκόνα Θεοῦ ἐποίησεν αὐτόν****· ἡ μὲν οὖν εἰκὼν τοῦ Θεοῦ, ἡ ἐν πάσῃ τῇ ἀνθρωπίνῃ φύσει θεωρουμένη,* [D] *τὸ τέλος ἔσχεν· ὁ δὲ Ἀδὰμ οὔπω ἐγένετο· τὸ γὰρ γήϊνον πλάσμα κατά τινα ἐτυμολογικὴν ὀνομασίαν Ἀδὰμ λέγεται, καθώς φασιν οἱ τῆς Ἑβραίων φωνῆς ἐπιΐστορες· διὸ καὶ ὁ ἀπόστολος, διαφερόντως τὴν πάτριον τῶν Ἰσραηλιτῶν πεπαιδευμένος φωνήν, τὸν ἐκ γῆς ἄνθρωπον* ***χοϊκὸν*** *ὀνομάζει, οἱονεὶ μεταβαλὼν τὴν τοῦ Ἀδὰμ κλῆσιν εἰς τὴν Ἑλλάδα φωνήν.*

[22.4] *Γέγονεν οὖν κατ' εἰκόνα ὁ ἄνθρωπος, ἡ καθόλου φύσις, τὸ θεοείκελον χρῆμα· γέγονε δὲ τῇ παντοδυνάμῳ σοφίᾳ οὐχὶ μέρος τοῦ ὅλου ἀλλ' ἅπαν ἀθρόως τὸ τῆς φύσεως πλήρωμα. Εἶδεν ὁ πάντων τῶν περάτων περιδεδραγμένος, καθώς φησιν ἡ γραφὴ ἡ λέγουσα,* ***ἐν τῇ χειρὶ αὐτοῦ τὰ πέρατα τῆς γῆς****· εἶδεν* ***ὁ εἰδὼς τὰ πάντα καὶ πρὶν γενέσεως αὐτῶν****, ἐμπεριλαβὼν* [205] *τῇ γνώσει ὅσον κατ' ἀριθμὸν ἐν τοῖς καθ' ἕκαστον ἔσται τὸ ἀνθρώπινον. Ἐπεὶ δὲ κατενόησεν ἐν τῷ πλάσματι ἡμῶν τὴν πρὸς τὸ χεῖρον ῥοπὴν, καὶ ὅτι, τῆς πρὸς τοὺς ἀγγέλους ὁμοτιμίας ἑκουσίως ἀπορρυὲν, τὴν πρὸς τὸ ταπεινὸν κοινωνίαν προσοικειώσεται· διὰ ταῦτα κατέμιξέ τι καὶ τοῦ ἀλόγου τῇ ἰδίᾳ εἰκόνι· οὐ γάρ ἐστιν ἐν τῇ θείᾳ τε καὶ μακαρίᾳ φύσει ἡ κατὰ τὸ ἄρρεν καὶ θῆλυ διαφορά· ἀλλὰ, τῆς ἀλόγου κατασκευῆς ἐπὶ τὸν ἄνθρωπον μετενεγκὼν τὸ ἰδίωμα, οὐ κατὰ τὸ ὑψηλὸν τῆς κτίσεως ἡμῶν τὸν πλεονασμὸν τῷ γένει χαρίζεται· οὐ γὰρ ὅτε τὸ κατ' εἰκόνα ἐποίησε, τότε τὴν τοῦ αὐξάνεσθαι καὶ πληθύνεσθαι δύναμιν τῷ ἀνθρώπῳ προσέθηκεν, ἀλλ' ὅτε διέκρινε τῇ κατὰ τὸ*

11 *μετάστασις*] *κατάστασις* S 12 *βαρεία* N *ἀναμένῃ* I 13 *τὸ* om. M Q 14 *πάλιν* om. L *μακάριον*] *μακάριον τε* M 15 *ἐπαναδράμῃ* D G P² T X : *ἐπαναδράμοιεν* M : *ἐπαναδράμει* P^ac 16 *τῆς ἀληθείας* N *αὕτη* L : *αὐτὴ δ'* N 17 *τοιοῦτο* Æ : *τοῦτο* I O *δὴ*] *δὲ* Æ B I M N O Q R T W X 18 *ἐπαναλαβὼν*] *ἐπαναδραμὼν* L *ὁ θεὸς* om. R 19 *ἡμετέραν καὶ ὁμοίωσιν* D Q R : *ἡμετέραν καὶ καθ' ὁμοίωσιν* L N 20 *οὖν* om. N *ἡ*² om. G L N *τῇ* om. M 21 *τὸ*² om. D 22 *ἐτοιμολογικὴν* O W X *λέγεται ἀδὰμ* W *Ald Mign* 24 *ἐκ* om. T *μεταβάλλων* T 26 *γέγονεν οὖν*] *γέγονε τοίνυν* D G L P S X *εἰκόνα*] *εἰκόνα θεοῦ* N R *ὁ ἄνθρωπος* om. N 27 *γέγονε δὲ* om. M *ἀλλ' ἅπαν*] *ἀλλ' ἅμα ἅπαν* Æ B I O : *ἀλλὰ πᾶν* N R^ac T *ἀθρόως*] *εὐθέως* D G L P S X *τὸ* om. W 28 *ἡ* om. R *λέγουσα*] *λέγουσα ὅτι* M *αὐτοῦ*] *σου* T : *αὐτοῦ εἶναι* Æ B I O Q *τῆς*] *ἐπὶ τῆς* M : *εἶναι τῆς* W *καὶ* om. Æ B I M N O Q R T W 30 *γενέσεως αὐτῶν*] *γενέσθαι* D G L P S X *ἐμπεριλαβὼν*] *ἐκπεριλαβὼν* ß G O P T W X : *καὶ περιλαβὼν* R *τὴν γνῶσιν* T *κατ'*] *κατὰ* G L P S X 30–1 *καθ' ἕκαστον*] *ἕκαστον* *Ald* : *καθέκαστον* ß I 31 *ἔσται*] *ἐστι* M N Q R T W *ἐπεὶ δὲ*] *ἐπειδὴ* Æ B M R^ac W : *ἐπειδὴ δὲ* I T *ἐν* om. N 33 *τῆς . . . κοινωνίας* L *προσῳκειώσατο* M *ταῦτα*] *τοῦτο* Æ B I M N O Q R T W *καὶ* om. D 34 *τε* om. N 35 *καὶ*] *ἢ* R *ἀλόγου*] *τοῦ λόγου* B *μετενεγκὼν*] *ἐπενεγκὼν* L 37 *τὸ*] *τὸν* T : om. Æ B I M N O Q R^ac W *τότε*] *τότε καὶ* D L *τοῦ*] *τοῦ θεοῦ* W 37–8 *αὐξάνεσθε καὶ πληθύνεσθε* B G² L² P² S^ac X *καὶ πληθύνεσθαι* om. I 38–9 *τὴν . . . διαφορὰν* N Q T

with which the transference of our painful mode of life to that which is desired does not take place immediately, but that this heavy and corporeal life itself waits, extended to some determined time, for the limit of the consummation of all things, in order that then the human life may be set free, as it were from the bridle, ascending again, released and free, to the blessed and impassible mode of life?

[22.3] Well, whether our answer is near the truth of what is sought, the Truth itself may clearly know; but what comes to our mind is this. Taking up again the first text, I say: *Let us make*, says God, *the human being in accordance to our image and likeness; and God made the human being, in accordance with the image of God he made him.*[69] The image of God, then, that which is contemplated in the universal human nature, had its end; but as yet, Adam was not.[70] For the earthy moulded figure, by an etymological designation, is called 'Adam', as those acquainted with the Hebrew language say; therefore, the Apostle, who was especially learned in his native Israelite language, names the human being from the earth *earthy*, as though translating the name Adam into the Greek language.[71]

[22.4] In accordance with the image, then, the human being came to be, that is, the universal nature, the godlike thing; by the omnipotent wisdom not a part of the whole, but the plenitude of nature as a whole came to be. He who holds all limits in his grasp saw, as the Scripture says, *all the ends of the earth in his hands*, he, *who knows all things even before their genesis*, saw, embracing in his knowledge, how many in number humanity will be in its individuals.[72] Since he perceived in our moulded figure the inclination towards the worse, and that, voluntarily falling from equality of honour with the angels, it would appropriate fellowship with the lowly nature, he mingled, for this reason, an element of the irrational with his own image, for the distinction between male and female is not in the divine and blessed nature; but, when transferring the property of the irrational formation to the human being, he bestowed upon our race the power of multiplying, not according to the lofty character of our creation, for it was not when he made that which is in accordance with the image that he added the power to increase and multiply, but when he divided it by the distinction between male

[69] Gen. 1:26–7. [70] Cf. Philo, *Opif.* 76. [71] 1 Cor. 15:47.
[72] Ps. 94:4; Sus. (Θ) 42; cf. Gregory of Nyssa, *Hex.* 9 (Drobner, 18.13–16).

ἄρρεν καὶ θῆλυ διαφορᾷ, τότε φησίν, ***αὐξάνεσθε καὶ πληθύνεσθε καὶ πληρώσατε τὴν γῆν·*** [B] *τὸ γὰρ τοιοῦτον οὐ τῆς θείας φύσεως ἴδιον ἀλλὰ τῆς ἀλόγου ἐστί, καθὼς ἡ ἱστορία παρασημαίνεται, πρότερον ἐπὶ τῶν ἀλόγων εἰρῆσθαι ταῦτα παρὰ τοῦ Θεοῦ διηγησαμένη· ὡς, εἴ γε πρὸ τοῦ ἐπιβαλεῖν τῇ φύσει τὴν κατὰ τὸ ἄρρεν καὶ θῆλυ διαφορὰν τὴν διὰ τῆς φωνῆς ταύτης δύναμιν εἰς τὸ* ***αὐξάνεσθαι*** *τῷ ἀνθρώπῳ προσέθηκεν, οὐκ ἂν τοῦ τοιούτου τῆς γεννήσεως εἴδους προσεδεήθημεν, δι' οὗ γεννᾶται τὰ ἄλογα.*

[22.5] *Τοῦ τοίνυν προκατανοηθέντος διὰ τῆς προγνωστικῆς ἐνεργείας πληρώματος τῶν ἀνθρώπων διὰ τῆς ζωωδεστέρας γενέσεως ἐπὶ τὴν ζωὴν μέλλοντος παριέναι, ὁ τάξει τινὶ καὶ εἱρμῷ διακυβερνῶν τὰ πάντα* [C] *Θεός, ἐπειδὴ ὅλως τὸ τοιοῦτον τῇ ἀνθρωπότητι τῆς γεννήσεως εἶδος ἀναγκαῖον ἐποίησεν ἡ πρὸς τὸ ταπεινὸν τῆς φύσεως ἡμῶν ἐπίκλισις, ἣν εἶδε πρὶν γενέσθαι ὁ ἐπίσης τῷ ἐνεστῶτι τὸ μέλλον βλέπων, διὰ τοῦτο καὶ τὸν σύμμετρον τῇ κατασκευῇ τῶν ἀνθρώπων χρόνον προκατενόησεν· ὥστε τῇ παρόδῳ τῶν προορισθεισῶν ψυχῶν συναπαρτισθῆναι τὴν τοῦ χρόνου παράτασιν, καὶ τότε στῆναι τὴν ῥοώδη τοῦ χρόνου κίνησιν, ὅταν μηκέτι φύηται δι' αὐτοῦ τὸ ἀνθρώπινον· τελεσθείσης δὲ τῆς τῶν ἀνθρώπων γενέσεως, τῷ τέλει ταύτης συγκαταλῆξαι τὸν χρόνον, καὶ οὕτω τὴν τοῦ παντὸς ἀναστοιχείωσιν γενέσθαι, καὶ τῇ μεταβολῇ τοῦ ὅλου συναμειφθῆναι καὶ τὸ ἀνθρώπινον, ἀπὸ τοῦ φθαρτοῦ καὶ γεώδους ἐπὶ τὸ ἀπαθὲς καὶ ἀΐδιον.*

[22.6] *Ὅ μοι δοκεῖ καὶ ὁ θεῖος ἀπόστολος κατανοήσας, προειπεῖν διὰ* [D] *τῆς πρὸς Κορινθίους ἐπιστολῆς τὴν αἰφνίδιον τοῦ χρόνου στάσιν καὶ τὴν εἰς τὸ ἔμπαλιν τῶν κινουμένων ἀνάλυσιν, ἐν οἷς φησιν·* ***ἰδοὺ μυστήριον ὑμῖν λέγω· πάντες μὲν οὐ κοιμηθησόμεθα, πάντες δὲ ἀλλαγησόμεθα, ἐν ἀτόμῳ, ἐν ῥιπῇ ὀφθαλμοῦ, ἐν τῇ ἐσχάτῃ σάλπιγγι·*** *τοῦ γὰρ πληρώματος, ὡς οἶμαι, τῆς ἀνθρωπίνης φύσεως κατὰ τὸ προγνωσθὲν μέτρον εἰς πέρας ἐλθόντος, διὰ τὸ μηκέτι λείπειν τῷ τῶν ψυχῶν ἀριθμῷ μηδὲν εἰς ἐπαύξησιν, ἐν ἀκαρεῖ τοῦ χρόνου γενήσεσθαι τὴν ἐναλλαγὴν τῶν ὄντων ἐδίδαξεν (****ἄτομον*** *ὀνομάσας καὶ* ***ῥιπὴν ὀφθαλμοῦ*** *τὸ ἀμερὲς ἐκεῖνο* [208] *τοῦ χρόνου καὶ ἀδιάστατον πέρας·) ὡς μηκέτι δυνατὸν εἶναι τῷ κατὰ τὸ ἔσχατόν τε καὶ ἀκρότατον τῆς ἀκμῆς ἐπιβάντι τοῦ χρόνου, διὰ τὸ μηδὲν ὑπολείπεσθαι τῇ ἀκρότητι μέρος, τὴν περιοδικὴν ταύτην διὰ θανάτου μεταβολὴν κτήσασθαι, ἀλλ' εἰ μόνον*

39 *θῆλυ*] *τὸ θῆλυ* N T 42 *ἐπιβάλλειν* T 44 *τοῦ om.* N *γενέσεως* Æ ß O Q R T *προσεδέθημεν* T 46 *τοῦ*] *ita* Æ B I M N O R[ac] T W *Forb* : *τούτου Ald Mign* : *om.* D G P R[pc] X *προκατανοηθέντος*] *κατανοηθέντος* T *ἐνεργείας*] *ἐνεργείας τοῦ* D G P S W X 47 *γεννήσεως* Q 48 *θεὸς om.* M *τοιοῦτο* Æ 49 *εἶδος τῆς γεννήσεως* T *γενέσεως* Æ ß I N O R[ac] *εἶδος om.* D G L P S X 50 *τὸ μέλλον*] *μᾶλλον* Q 51 *τῆς κατασκευῆς* N R T *χρόνον τῶν ἀνθρώπων* T 52 *προορισθεισῶν*] *ita* Æ D G N O P R S T *Forb* : *περιορισθεισῶν Ald Mign* *συναπαρτισθῆναι*] *ἀπαρτισθῆναι* N 55 *οὕτως* W 55–6 *γενέσθαι ἀναστοιχείωσιν* N 56 *συναμειφθῆναι*] *συναναμιχθῆναι* W 58 *κατανοήσας*] *προκατανοήσας* I O P[ac] 59 *τὴν*[2] *om.* T 60 *λέγω ὑμῖν* I 62 *τοῦ*] *τοῦ τε* M *ὡς om.* R 63 *μηκέτι*] *μηκέτι λοιπὸν* D R[2] 64 *ἐν*] *ἐν τῷ* T *ἀκαρεῖ*] *ἀκαριαίῳ* N R *τοῦ om.* N *γενέσθαι* D P[ac] T *ἐναλλαγὴν*] *ἀλλαγὴν* Æ B I O Q 65 *ἐκείνου* Æ ß I M O 65–6 *τοῦ χρόνου om.* N 66 *δυνατὸν*] *δυνάμενον* T *τῷ*] *τῷ* X[pc2] : *τὸ* G H N O Q 66 *post διὰ* N *def. ad cap. 23 (l. 4)* *διὰ τὸ μηδὲν ὑπολείπεσθαι*] non deest *Eri* *μηδὲν*] *μὴ* T 68 *τὴν*] *τι* T *κτίσασθαι* P

and female that he then said, *Increase and multiply and fill the earth.*[73] For such is not a property of the divine nature, but of the irrational, as the narrative indicates, when it narrates that this was first said by God in the case of the irrational animals;[74] since if, before putting upon our nature the distinction between male and female, he had added the power for *increase* expressed by this utterance, we should not have needed this form of birth, by which the irrational animals are born.

[22.5] With the plenitude of human beings, then, preconceived by the activity of foreknowledge, coming into life by means of this more animal form of birth, God, who guides all things in a certain order and sequence—since the inclination of our nature to what is lowly (which he who beholds, equally with the present, what is to be before it happens) made this form of birth absolutely necessary for humanity—therefore also foreknew the time coextensive with the formation of human beings, so that the extent of time should be adapted for the entrance of the predetermined souls, and that the flowing movement of time should then halt, when humanity is no longer produced by it. And when the genesis of human beings is completed, time should stop together with the end of it, and then should take place the reconstitution of all, and with the changing of the whole, humanity should also be changed, from the corruptible and earthy to the impassible and eternal.[75]

[22.6] This, it seems to me, is what the divine Apostle was considering when he foretold, in his epistle to the Corinthians, the sudden stoppage of time and the deliverance of moving things into the opposite state, when he says, *Behold, I tell you a mystery: we shall not all sleep, but we shall all be changed, in a moment, in the twinkling of an eye, at the last trumpet.*[76] For when, I suppose, the plenitude of human nature has arrived at the limit, in accordance with the foreknown measure, because there is no longer anything wanting in terms of growth in the number of souls, he taught that the change of beings will take place in an instant of time (calling that limit of time which has no parts or extension *a moment* and *the twinkling of an eye*); so that it will no longer be possible for one who has set foot upon the last and extreme edge of time (for nothing is lacking from that extremity) to obtain this circling change by death, but only when the trumpet of the

[73] Gen. 1:28. [74] Cf. Gen. 1:22.
[75] Cf. Gregory of Nyssa, *An. et res.* 9.20–3 (Spira, 96.17–97.15).
[76] 1 Cor. 15:51–2; cf. Gregory of Nyssa, *An. et res.* 10.29 (Spira, 104.1–5).

ἠχήσειεν ἡ τῆς ἀναστάσεως σάλπιγξ, ἡ τὸ τεθνηκὸς ἀφυπνίζουσα καὶ τοὺς ἐν τῇ ζωῇ καταλειφθέντας καθ' ὁμοιότητα τῶν ἐξ ἀναστάσεως ἀλλοιουμένων πρὸς ἀφθαρσίαν ἀθρόως μεταβάλλουσα, ὡς μηκέτι τὸ βάρος τῆς σαρκὸς ἐπὶ τὸ κάτω βρίθειν καὶ τῇ γῇ παρακατέχειν τὸν ὄγκον, ἀλλὰ μετάρσιον δι' ἀέρος φοιτᾷν· **ἁρπαγησόμεθα** γάρ, φησίν, **ἐν νεφέλαις εἰς ἀπάντησιν τοῦ Κυρίου εἰς ἀέρα, καὶ οὕτως πάντοτε σὺν Κυρίῳ ἐσόμεθα.**

[22.7] Οὐκοῦν ἀναμεινάτω τὸν χρόνον τὸν ἀναγκαίως τῇ ἀνθρωπίνῃ αὐξήσει συμπαρατείνοντα· [B] καὶ γὰρ οἱ περὶ τὸν Ἀβραὰμ πατριάρχαι, τοῦ μὲν ἰδεῖν τὰ ἀγαθὰ τὴν ἐπιθυμίαν ἔσχον, καὶ οὐκ ἀνῆκαν ἐπιζητοῦντες τὴν ἐπουράνιον πατρίδα, καθώς φησιν ὁ ἀπόστολος· ἀλλ' ὅμως ἐν τῷ ἐλπίζειν ἔτι τὴν χάριν εἰσί, **τοῦ Θεοῦ κρεῖττόν τι περὶ ἡμῶν προβλεψαμένου**, κατὰ τὴν τοῦ Παύλου φωνήν, **ἵνα μή**, φησί, **χωρὶς ἡμῶν τελειωθῶσιν**· εἰ οὖν ἐκεῖνοι φέρουσι τὴν ἀναβολὴν **οἱ πόρρωθεν** διὰ μόνης πίστεως καὶ τῆς ἐλπίδος **ἰδόντες** τὰ ἀγαθά, καὶ **ἀσπασάμενοι**, καθὼς μαρτυρεῖ ὁ ἀπόστολος, τὸ ἀσφαλὲς τῆς τῶν ἐλπισθέντων ἀπολαύσεως ἐν **τῷ πιστὸν ἡγήσασθαι τὸν ἐπαγγειλάμενον** θέμενοι· τί χρὴ πράττειν τοὺς πολλοὺς ἡμᾶς, οἷς τυχὸν οὐδὲ ἡ πρὸς τὸ κρεῖττον ἐλπὶς ἐκ τῶν βεβιωμένων ἐστίν; ἐξέλιπε δι' ἐπιθυμίας καὶ ἡ τοῦ προφήτου ψυχή, καὶ ὁμολογεῖ διὰ τῆς ψαλμῳδίας τὸ ἐρωτικὸν τοῦτο πάθος, **ἐπιποθεῖν** λέγων **καὶ ἐκλείπειν αὐτοῦ τὴν ψυχὴν ἐν ταῖς αὐλαῖς τοῦ Κυρίου γενέσθαι**, κἂν ἐν τοῖς ἐσχάτοις δέῃ **παραρριπτεῖσθαι**· ὡς μεῖζον ὂν καὶ προτιμότερον τὸ ἐν ἐκείνοις ἔσχατον εἶναι, τοῦ πρωτεύειν ἐν τοῖς ἁμαρτωλοῖς τοῦ βίου σκηνώμασιν· ἀλλ' ὅμως ἠνείχετο τῆς ἀναβολῆς, μακαρίζων μὲν τὴν ἐκεῖ διαγωγήν, καὶ τὴν ἐν βραχεῖ μετουσίαν **χιλιάδων** χρόνου προτιμοτέραν ποιούμενος· **κρεῖσσον**, γάρ φησιν, **ἡμέρα μία ἐν ταῖς αὐλαῖς σου ὑπὲρ χιλιάδας**· ἀλλ' οὐκ ἐδυσχέραινε [D] τῇ ἀναγκαίᾳ περὶ τῶν ὄντων οἰκονομίᾳ, ἱκανόν τε εἰς μακαρισμὸν ᾤετο τοῖς ἀνθρώποις καὶ τὸ δι' ἐλπίδος ἔχειν τὰ ἀγαθά· διό φησιν ἐπὶ τέλει τῆς ψαλμῳδίας· **Κύριε τῶν δυνάμεων, μακάριος ἄνθρωπος ὁ ἐλπίζων ἐπὶ σέ.**

69 τοὺς τεθνηκότας M 70 καταληφθέντας Æ D L O S^{ac} 71 ἀθρόως] ἀχρόνως T : repente *Eri* μεταβληθήσεσθε C O : μεταβληθήσεσθαι Æ B L R T 73 ἐν νεφέλαις *om.* T εἰς ἀπάντησιν] obuiam *Dion Eri* εἰς ἀέρα] *om. Eri* οὕτω Æ I W 75–109 οὐκοῦν—προεμπορεύεσθαι *def. Eri* 77 ἀνῆκαν] ἂν T ἐπιζητοῦντες] ζητοῦντες Æ 78 ἐν τῷ] ἐπὶ τὸ I ἔτι] ἐπὶ L T 79 περὶ ἡμῶν κρεῖττον τι Æ B I M O Q R T W κατὰ τὴν τοῦ παύλου φωνήν] καθὼς ὁ παῦλός φησιν D : *post* τελειωθῶσιν *(l. 80) pon.* I τοῦ *om.* Æ B O φησὶ *om.* Æ B D I L O R S T 81 ἀσπασάμενοι] διασπασάμενοι B μαρτυρεῖ] *om.* T : μαρτυρεῖ φησι ß R T 82 ἀπολαύσεως *om.* X ἐν τῷ πιστὸν ἡγήσασθαι *om.* M ἡγεῖσθαι L 82–3 ἡγήσασθαι τὸν] ἡγ σ W (*lit. eras.*) 84 ἐξέλιπε] ἐξέλιπε δὲ R 85 ψυχὴ] φωνὴ B πάθος] τοῦ πάθους D L Q R 86 λέγων] λέγειν D P : λέγει G 87 δέῃ] δέοι B I M O R παραρίπεσθαι W : παραριπτεῖσθαι G P S^{ac} X : παραρρίπτεσθαι M R : παραρίπτείσθαι Q ὂν *om.* D T 88 ἐν^2 *om.* T 89 ἠνέσχετο T 90 βραχεῖ] βραχεῖ ταύτης I 91 κρείσσων Æ I O R γὰρ *om. Mign* 92 ἐδυσχέραινε] ἐδυσχέρανε M : ἐδυσχέραινε ἐν Æ B τε] δὲ Æ B I M O Q R T W 94 κύριε] κύριε ὁ θεὸς W *Ald Mign* ἄνθρωπος] ὁ ἄνθρωπος Æ σέ] σοι D G L P T S^{pc} X

resurrection sounds, awakening the dead and transforming those who remain in life, according to the likeness of those who have undergone the change through resurrection, at once to incorruptibility, so that the weight of the flesh no longer weighs downwards nor does its burden hold them to the earth, but they arise aloft through the air, for *we shall all be caught up*, he says, *in the clouds to meet the Lord in the air, and so we shall be ever with the Lord.*[77]

[**22.7**] Therefore, let him wait the time necessarily co-extensive with human increase. For even the Patriarchs with Abraham, while they had the desire to see the good things and did not cease seeking the heavenly homeland, as the Apostle says, yet nevertheless are still in the state of hoping for that grace, *God having foreseen something better for us*, according to the saying of Paul, *that without us they would not be made perfect.*[78] If, then, those—who, by faith only and hope, *saw* the good things *afar off* and *embraced them*, as the apostle bears witness, placing their certainty of the enjoyment of the things hoped for in the fact that they *considered him faithful who has promised*[79]—bear the delay, what ought most of us to do, for whom, perhaps, from the passage of our life there is no hope of better things? Even the prophet's soul fainted with desire, and in psalmody he confesses this passionate love, saying his *soul longs, even faints to be in the courts of the Lord*, even if he must be *rejected* to a place among the last, as it is a greater and more honourable thing to be among the last than to be first among the sinful tabernacles of this mode of life; yet he was nevertheless patient of the delay, considering the life there blessed and accounting a brief participation in it more honourable than *thousands* of time, for, he says, *one day in the courts is better than thousands*; but he was not annoyed at the necessary economy concerning beings and thought it sufficient blessedness for human beings to have those good things even by way of hope; on which account he says at the end of the psalmody, *O Lord of hosts, blessed is the human being hoping in you.*[80]

[77] 1 Thess. 4:17. [78] Heb. 11:40. [79] Heb. 11:13. [80] Ps. 83:3, 11, 13.

[22.8] *Οὐ τοίνυν οὐδὲ ἡμᾶς στενοχωρεῖσθαι χρὴ περὶ τὴν ἐν βραχεῖ τῶν ἐλπιζομένων ἀναβολῆν, ἀλλ' ὅπως ἂν μὴ ἀπόβλητοι τῶν ἐλπιζομένων γενοίμεθα τὴν σπουδὴν ἔχειν· ὥσπερ γὰρ εἴ τις προείποι τινὶ τῶν ἀπειροτέρων, ὅτι κατὰ τὸν καιρὸν τοῦ θέρους ἡ τῶν καρπῶν γενήσεται συλλογή, καὶ πλήρεις μὲν αἱ ἀποθῆκαι, μεστὴ δὲ τῶν ἐδωδίμων ἡ τράπεζα τῷ τῆς εὐθηνίας ἔσται καιρῷ, μάταιος ἂν εἴη ὁ ἐπισπεύδων τοῦ καιροῦ τὴν παρουσίαν,* [209] *δέον σπέρματα καταβάλλειν καὶ δι' ἐπιμελείας ἑαυτῷ τοὺς καρποὺς ἑτοιμάζεσθαι· ὁ μὲν γὰρ καιρὸς, καὶ βουλομένου καὶ μή, πάντως κατὰ τὸν τεταγμένον ἐπιστήσεται χρόνον· οὐχ ὁμοίως δὲ αὐτὸν ὄψονται, ὅ τε προετοιμάσας ἑαυτῷ τὴν τῶν καρπῶν ἀφθονίαν, καὶ ὁ πάσης παρασκευῆς ἔρημος καταληφθεὶς ὑπὸ τῆς ὥρας· οὕτως οἶμαι δεῖν, προδήλου πᾶσι διὰ τοῦ θείου κηρύγματος ὄντος ὅτι ἐνστήσεται τῆς ἐναλλαγῆς ὁ καιρὸς, μὴ χρόνους πολυπραγμονεῖν (**οὐ** γὰρ ἡμῶν εἶπεν **εἶναι τὸ καιροὺς γνῶναι καὶ χρόνους**) μηδὲ λογισμούς τινας ἀναζητεῖν, δι' ὧν σαθρώσει τὴν ψυχὴν περὶ τὴν ἐλπίδα τῆς ἀναστάσεως· ἀλλὰ τῇ πίστει τῶν προσδοκωμένων ἐπερειδόμενον, διὰ τῆς ἀγαθῆς πολιτείας τὴν μέλλουσαν χάριν προεμπορεύεσθαι.*

Ὅτι ὁ τὴν ἀρχὴν τῆς τοῦ κόσμου συστάσεως ὁμολογῶν, ἀναγκαίως καὶ περὶ τοῦ τέλους συνθήσεται.

[23.1] *Εἰ δέ τις, τὴν νῦν τοῦ κόσμου φορὰν εἱρμῷ τινι διεξαγομένην βλέπων, δι' ἧς τὸ χρονικὸν θεωρεῖται διάστημα, μὴ ἐνδέχεσθαι λέγοι τὴν προαγγελθεῖσαν τῶν κινουμένων στάσιν γενήσεσθαι· δῆλος ὁ τοιοῦτός ἐστι, μηδὲ ἐν ἀρχῇ γεγενῆσθαι παρὰ τοῦ Θεοῦ τὸν οὐρανὸν καὶ τὴν γῆν πιστεύων· ὁ γὰρ ἀρχὴν τῇ κινήσει διδοὺς, οὐκ ἀμφιβάλλει πάντως καὶ περὶ τοῦ τέλους· καὶ ὁ τὸ τέλος μὴ προσδεχόμενος, οὐδὲ τὴν ἀρχὴν παρεδέξατο· ἀλλ' ὥσπερ* ***κατηρτίσθαι τοὺς αἰῶνας τῷ ῥήματι νοοῦμεν τοῦ Θεοῦ****, πιστεύοντες (καθώς φησιν ὁ ἀπόστολος)* ***εἰς τὸ μὴ ἐκ φαινομένων*** [C] ***τὰ βλεπόμενα γεγονέναι****· τῇ αὐτῇ πίστει χρησόμεθα περὶ τὸ ῥῆμα τοῦ Θεοῦ, τοῦ τὴν*

95 *περὶ τὴν ἐν βραχεῖ*] *τῇ* I *τὴν*] *τῶν* O 95–6 *τὴν . . . ἀναβολῆν*] *ita* Æ B D G M P R T W X *Forb* : *τῆς . . . ἀναβολῆς Ald Mign* 96 *ἐλπιζομένων*] *προσδοκωμένων* Æ B I M O Q R T W *γενοίμεθα*] *γενώμεθα* Q R T 98 *πλήρις* O 99 *τῷ*] *τὸ* O 100 *καταβαλεῖν* D G L P R S^{ac} W X : *βάλλειν* Æ 101 *ἐμμελείας* M *ἑτοιμάσασθαι* ß *μὲν om.* T 101–2 *καὶ βουλομένου καὶ μή, πάντως*] *πάντως καὶ μὴ βουλομένου* R 102 *ἐπιστήσεται*] *ἐπιστῶ* D : *ἐπείγεται* T 103 *τῶν καρπῶν τὴν* D 104 *ἔρημος*] *ἄμοιρος* R *καταληφθεὶς*] *ita* Æ B D G L M O P Q R^{pc} S T^{pc} W X *Dion Forb* : *καταλειφθεὶς Ald Mign* *δεῖν*] *δεῖ* I : *δὴ* B : *om.* Æ O 105 *ὄντος—καιρὸς om.* T *ὄντως* M *ἐναλλαγῆς*] *ἀλλαγῆς* Æ B I M O Q W 106 *οὐ*] *οὐδὲ Ald Mign* *γνῶναι*] *εἶναι* X *χρόνους*] *τοὺς χρόνους* T 107 *σαθρώσει*] *σαθρώσει τις Ald Mign* 108 *ἀναστάσεως*] *ἀναστάσεως γίνεσθαι* R 109 *προσεμπορεύεσθαι* T

Cap. 24 Æ ß I O Q R T *Dion Eri*

23.6–7 (*ὁ γὰρ—τέλους*): John (of Damascus) *Sacra Parallela* II[1]52 / K cap. A 1, 52 (Thum, 86, 10).

1–2 *ὅτι—συνθήσεται*] contra eos qui dicunt materiam deo coeternam *Λ* 1 *ὅτι—ὁμολογῶν*] *κόσμου συστάσεως ὁμολογῶν τὴν ἀρχὴν* O 2 *τέλους*] *τέλους κόσμου* T 3 *διεξαγομένην*] *ἐξαγομένη* Æ B 4 *προσαγγελθεῖσαν* T 5 *γενέσθαι* Æ B I O : *γεγενῆσθαι* M Q : *γίνεσθαι* T *ἐστι ὁ τοιοῦτος* I *μηδ'* I L 6 *τῷ θεῷ* B *γὰρ*] *γὰρ τὴν* R^{2} : *om. SP* *τῆς κινήσεως* M *δοὺς* Æ B Q R T *SP* 7 *ἀμφιβάλλοι* L *πάντως om. SP* *καὶ*^{1} *om.* Æ B I L M N O R T W *Dion SP* *τοῦ*] *ita* Æ ß G I L M N P R S W X *Ald Forb* : *om. Mign* 8 *παρὰδέξαιτο* N 8–9 *τῷ ῥήματι νοοῦμεν τοῦ Θεοῦ*] *νοοῦμεν ῥήματι Θεοῦ* Æ B C I O T : *νοοῦμεν τῷ ῥήματι τοῦ Θεοῦ* Q R W : *τῷ ῥήματι τοῦ Θεοῦ* M *τοῦ Θεοῦ πιστεύοντες νοοῦμεν* N 9 *εἰς τὸ*] *ita* Æ B D G L M O P Q R S T W X *Ald Forb* : *ἀπὸ τῶν* I : *ἐν τῷ* N : *ἐκ τῶν Mign* *ἐκ φαινομένων*] *ita* Æ ß G L M O P R S W X *Ald Forb* : *ἐκφαινομένων* D N^{ac} : *ἐκφαινομένῳ* N^{2} : *ἐκφαινόμενον* Q T : *φαινομένων Mign* 9–10 *τὸ βλεπόμενον* N T : *τὰ μὴ βλεπόμενα* L 10 *χρησώμεθα* Æ B D^{ac} N O P S T *τοῦ ῥήματος* I N Q R^{2} : *τῷ ῥήματι* R^{ac} *τοῦ*^{2}] *τοῦ καὶ* M : *τὸ* D G P^{pc} X

[22.8] Neither, then, should we be troubled at the brief delay of the things hoped for, but give diligence that we may not be cast out of the things hoped for. Just as, if one were to tell some inexperienced person beforehand that the gathering of the crops will take place in the season of the summer and the stores will be filled and the table be abundantly supplied with food in the time of plenty, it would be a foolish person who would hasten the coming of the season when he [instead] ought to sow seeds and prepare the crops for himself by diligent care; for the season will surely come, whether he wills it or not, at the appointed time; and it will be seen differently by the one who has prepared for himself an abundance of fruits and by him who, at that hour, is found destitute of any preparation. So also I think it is necessary, as by the divine proclamation it is clear to all that the time of change will come, not to trouble oneself about dates (for, he said, *it is not for* us *to know times and dates*[81]), nor to seek calculations, by which one will sap the soul of hope in the resurrection, but to rest upon faith in the things expected, purchasing in advance, through good citizenship, the grace that is to come.

That one who acknowledges the beginning of the world's constitution must necessarily agree also regarding its end.[82]

[23.1] But if someone, seeing the present course of the world carrying on in a certain sequence, by which temporal extension is contemplated, should say that it is not possible that the predicted cessation of moving things should happen, neither, clearly, does such a one believe that the heaven and the earth came to be in the beginning by God; for one who grants a beginning of movement surely does not doubt regarding its end, and one not accepting the end, neither admits the beginning. But just as it is by believing that *we understand that the ages were framed by the Word of God*, as the Apostle says, *so that things which are seen came to be from those that do not appear*,[83] we use the same faith regarding the word of

[81] Acts 1:7.

[82] *Bodl. 238* (as Chap. 24): 'Against those who say that matter is co-eternal with God'. For chapters 23–4, cf. Gregory of Nyssa, *An. et res.* 9.2–13 (Spira, 91.19–94.16); *Hex.* 7 (Drobner, 14.13–16.11); Origen, *Princ.* 4.4.7–8; Basil, *Hex.* 2.2.

[83] Heb. 11:3.

ἀναγκαίαν τῶν ὄντων στάσιν προαγορεύσαντος. [23.2] *Τὸ δὲ πῶς ἐξαιρετέον τῆς πολυπραγμοσύνης· καὶ γὰρ κἀκεῖ* ***πίστει κατηρτίσθαι τὸ βλεπόμενον ἐκ τῶν μηδέπω φαινομένων*** *κατεδεξάμεθα, παραδραμόντες τῶν ἀνεφίκτων τὴν ζήτησιν· καίτοι περὶ πολλῶν ἡμῖν ὁ λόγος ἀπορεῖν ὑπετίθετο, οὐ μικρὰς παρέχων τὰς ἀφορμὰς πρὸς τὴν τῶν πεπιστευμένων ἀμφιβολίαν.*

[23.3] *Ἐξῆν γὰρ κἀκεῖ τοῖς ἐριστικοῖς, ἐκ τῶν εὐλόγων κατὰ τὸ ἀκόλουθον ἀνατρέπειν τὴν πίστιν, πρὸς τὸ μὴ νομίζειν ἀληθῆ τὸν περὶ τῆς ὑλικῆς κτίσεως εἶναι λόγον, ὃν ἡ ἁγία πρεσβεύει γραφή, πάντων τῶν ὄντων ἐκ τοῦ Θεοῦ εἶναι διαβεβαιουμένη τὴν γένεσιν· οἱ γὰρ τῷ ἐναντίῳ παριστάμενοι λόγῳ, συναΐδιον εἶναι τῷ Θεῷ* [D] *τὴν ὕλην κατασκευάζουσι, τοιούτοις ἐπιχειρήμασι πρὸς τὸ δόγμα χρώμενοι—εἰ ἁπλοῦς ὁ Θεὸς τῇ φύσει καὶ ἄϋλος, ἄποιός τε καὶ ἀμεγέθης καὶ ἀσύνθετος καὶ τῆς κατὰ τὸ σχῆμα περιγραφῆς ἀλλοτρίως ἔχων· πᾶσα δὲ ὕλη ἐν διαστηματικῇ παρατάσει καταλαμβάνεται, καὶ τὰς διὰ τῶν αἰσθητηρίων καταλήψεις οὐ διαπέφευγεν, ἐν χρώματι καὶ σχήματι καὶ ὄγκῳ καὶ πηλικότητι καὶ ἀντιτυπίᾳ καὶ τοῖς λοιποῖς τοῖς περὶ αὐτὴν θεωρουμένοις γινωσκομένη, ὧν οὐδὲν ἐν τῇ θείᾳ* [212] *φύσει δυνατόν ἐστι κατανοῆσαι· τίς μηχανὴ ἐκ τοῦ ἀΰλου τὴν ὕλην ἀποτεχθῆναι; ἐκ τοῦ ἀδιαστάτου τὴν διαστηματικὴν φύσιν; εἰ γὰρ ἐκεῖθεν ὑποστῆναι ταῦτα πιστεύεται, δῆλον ὅτι ἐν αὐτῷ ὄντα κατὰ τὸν ἄρρητον λόγον, οὕτω προῆλθεν εἰς γένεσιν· εἰ δὲ ἐν ἐκείνῳ τὸ ὑλῶδες ἦν, πῶς ἄϋλος ὁ ἐν ἑαυτῷ τὴν ὕλην ἔχων; ὡσαύτως δὲ καὶ τὰ ἄλλα πάντα δι' ὧν ἡ ὑλικὴ φύσις χαρακτηρίζεται· εἰ ἐν τῷ Θεῷ ἡ ποσότης, πῶς ἄποσος ὁ Θεός; εἰ ἐν ἐκείνῳ τὸ σύνθετον, πῶς ἁπλοῦς καὶ ἀμερὴς καὶ ἀσύνθετος; ὥστε ἢ ὑλικὸν εἶναι κατ' ἀνάγκην αὐτὸν διὰ τὸ ἐκεῖθεν ὑποστῆναι τὴν ὕλην, ὁ λόγος βιάζεται· ἢ εἰ τοῦτό τις φεύγοι, ἔξωθεν ἐπεισενεχθῆναι τὴν ὕλην αὐτῷ πρὸς τὴν κατασκευὴν τοῦ παντὸς ὑπολαμβάνειν ἐπάναγκες.*

[23.4] *Εἰ οὖν ἔξω τοῦ Θεοῦ ἦν, ἄλλό τι* [B] *παρὰ τὸν Θεὸν πάντως ἦν, συνεπινοούμενον κατὰ τὸν τῆς ἀϊδιότητος λόγον τῷ ἀγεννήτως ὄντι· ὥστε δύο*

11 *προαγορεύοντος* N R : *προαγορεῦσαν* D E G P X : *προσαγορεύσαντος* S T   11–12 *ἐξαιρετέον τῆς πολυπραγμοσύνης*] curiosi est quaerere *Dion*   11 *ἐξαίρετον* D G P X : eximium est *Eri*   12 *κἀκεῖ*] *ἐκεῖ* Æ B I M N O R[ac] W : *καὶ ἐκεῖ* R[2]   *τὰ βλεπόμενα* Q *Dion*   13 *μηδέπω*] *οὐδέπω* D E : *μήπω* Æ B I : *μὴ* M Q R   *φαινομένων*] *βλεπομένων* D E G I L P S T X   14 *πολλῶν*] *πολλῶν καὶ* R   *ὑποτίθεται* L   *παρέχων*] *ἔχων* Æ   *τὰς*] *ita* Æ B G I L M N O P R S T W X *Ald Forb* : *om. Mign*   15 *πρὸς*] *εἰς* D E G L P S X   *πιστευομένων* I L   18–19 *διαβεβαιουμένη ἐκ τοῦ θεοῦ εἶναι* N   19 *περιϊστάμενοι* Q : *παριστάμενον* W : praestant *Eri*   20 *τὴν ὕλην τῷ θεῷ* N R T   *ἐπιχειρήμασι*] rethoricis conclusionibus *Eri*   21 *δόγμασι* B   *ἄποιος*] *ἄποσος* Æ B C M N O Q R T *Dion*   22 *κατὰ*] *πρὸς* N   *ἐν om.* D G L P S X   23 *διαστηματικὴ* G P X   *παραστάσει* N : *διατάσει* B   *καταλαμβάνονται* R[ac]   24 *διαπέφυγεν* W   24–5 *ἐν χρώματι—ἀντιτυπίᾳ*] in colore et figura, mole quoque et qualitate et impressionne uel duritia *Dion* : in re atque tumore et quantitate et solidate *Eri*   24 *καὶ*[1]] *καὶ ἐν* Q   25 *τοῖς*] *τῆς* W   26 *τις μηχανὴ*] *τῇ μηχανῇ* T : *τὶς μηχανικὴ* B   27 *ἀποτεχθῆναι*] *ἀποτεχθῆναι καὶ* B I   *διαστατικὴν* D E F G P S X   *φύσιν*] *ὕλην* M   28 *πιστεύεται*] *ita* Æ B D G L M N O P Q S W X *Forb* : *τίς πιστεύσειε* R : *πεπίστευεται Ald Mign*   *δῆλον ὅτι*] *ita* B G L N O P R S W X *Forb* : *δηλονότι Ald Mign*   *οὕτως* X   29 *ἑαυτῷ*] *ita* Æ D G I L M O P Q S W X *Forb* : *αὑτῷ* B *Mign* : *αὐτῷ* ß *Ald*   30 *τ' ἄλλα* L : *τἆλλα* Æ R   32 *κατὰ* O   *τὸ*] *τοῦ* Æ B G M O P Q R S W X   33 *φεύγει* I L   *ἐπεισηνεχθῆναι* W   34 *τὴν om.* D G L P S X   35 *ἔξω*] *ἔξωθεν* B M R   *ἦν om.* Q   36 *τῷ ἀγγήτως ὄντι κατὰ τὸν τῆς ἀϊδιότητος λόγον* R   *ἀγεννήτως*] *ἀγενήτως* G P S : *ἀγεννήτῳ* L

God foretelling the necessary cessation of beings. [**23.2**] The question of how must be put beyond curiosity; for even in the case mentioned, it was *by faith* that we accepted that *things which are seen were framed from those that do not* yet *appear*, passing by the search into things beyond reach. And yet our reason suggests difficulties on many points, presenting no slight occasions for doubt regarding things believed.

[**23.3**] For in that case, too, it is possible for those prone to arguing to overturn the faith by reasonable argumentation, so that we should not think true the statement conveyed by Holy Scripture regarding material creation, confirming that all beings have their genesis from God. Those who stand by the opposite view, holding matter to be co-eternal with God, use arguments such as these to support their own doctrine: if by nature God is simple and immaterial, without quantity and without size and without combination, and is otherwise than having circumscription by figure, while all matter is apprehended in extension measured by intervals and does not escape apprehension by the senses, but is known in colour and figure and bulk and magnitude and resistance, and the other things contemplated regarding it, none of which it is possible to conceive in the divine nature—what mechanism is there for matter to be constructed from the immaterial? Or for nature that is extended [to come] from the non-extended? If these things are believed to have existence from that source, it is clear that, being in him in accordance with some inexpressible principle, it thus comes to genesis; but if that which is material was in him, how can he be immaterial while having matter in himself? Similarly with all the other marks by which material nature is characterized: if there is quantity in God, how is God without quantity? If that which is compound is in him, how is he simple and without parts and without combination? So, the argument compels the conclusion that either, by necessity, he is himself material because matter exists from him, or, if one avoids this, that it is necessary to suppose that matter was imported by him from outside for the construction of the universe.

[**23.4**] If, then, it was external to God, there surely was something else besides God, conceived, in accordance with the principle of eternity, together with him

ἄναρχα καὶ ἀγέννητα κατὰ ταὐτὸν ἀλλήλοις τῷ λόγῳ συγκαταλαμβάνεσθαι, τοῦ τεχνικῶς ἐνεργοῦντος καὶ τοῦ δεχομένου τὴν ἐπιστημονικὴν ταύτην ἐνέργειαν· καὶ εἴ τις ἐκ τῆς ἀνάγκης ταύτης ἀΐδιον ὑποτίθοιτο τῷ Δημιουργῷ τῶν πάντων ὑποκεῖσθαι τὴν ὕλην, ὅσην ὁ Μανιχαῖος εὑρήσει τῶν ἰδίων δογμάτων τὴν συνηγορίαν, ὃς τὴν ὑλικὴν οὐσίαν κατὰ τὸ ἀγέννητον ἀντιπαρεξάγει τῇ ἀγαθῇ φύσει; ἀλλὰ μὴν καὶ ἐκ τοῦ Θεοῦ τὰ πάντα, τῆς γραφῆς λεγούσης ἀκούοντες, πεπιστεύκαμεν· καὶ τὸ ὅπως ἦν ἐν τῷ Θεῷ, τὸ ὑπὲρ τὸν ἡμέτερον λόγον, οὐκ ἀξιοῦμεν περιεργάζεσθαι, πάντα τῇ θείᾳ δυνάμει χωρητὰ πεπιστευκότες—καὶ τὸ μὴ ὂν ὑποστήσεσθαι, καὶ τῷ ὄντι πρὸς τὸ [C] *δοκοῦν ἐπιβαλεῖν τὰς ποιότητας.*

[23.5] *Οὐκοῦν ἀκολούθως, ὡς ἀρκεῖν ἡγούμεθα τοῖς οὖσι πρὸς τὴν ἐκ τοῦ μὴ ὄντος ὑπόστασιν, τὴν τοῦ θείου θελήματος δύναμιν· οὕτω καὶ τὴν ἀναστοιχείωσιν τῶν συνεστώτων εἰς τὴν αὐτὴν ἀνάγοντες δύναμιν, εἰς οὐδὲν ἔξω τοῦ εἰκότος τὴν πίστιν παραληψόμεθα· καίτοιγε δυνατὸν ἴσως ἦν, εὑρεσιλογίᾳ τινὶ τοὺς περὶ τῆς ὕλης ἐρεσχελοῦντας πεῖσαι, μὴ δοκεῖν ἐρήμην κατατρέχειν τοῦ λόγου.*

Ἀντίρρησις πρὸς τοὺς λέγοντας, συναΐδιον εἶναι τῷ Θεῷ τὴν ὕλην.

[24.1] *Οὐδὲ γὰρ ἔξω τῶν κατὰ τὸ ἀκόλουθον εὑρισκομένων ἡ περὶ τῆς ὕλης ὑπόληψις φέρεται, ἡ ἐκ τοῦ νοητοῦ τε καὶ ἀΰλου ταύτην ὑποστῆναι πρεσβεύουσα· πᾶσαν γὰρ εὑρήσομεν ἐκ ποιοτήτων τινῶν συνεστῶσαν τὴν ὕλην, ὧν εἰ γυμνωθείη καθ' ἑαυτὴν οὐδαμοῦ τῷ λόγῳ καταληφθήσεται· ἀλλὰ μὴν ἕκαστον ποιότητος εἶδος λόγῳ τοῦ ὑποκειμένου χωρίζεται· ὁ δὲ λόγος νοητή τίς ἐστι, καὶ οὐχὶ σωματικὴ θεωρία· οἷον προκειμένου ζώου τινὸς ἢ ξύλου τῇ θεωρίᾳ ἤ τινος ἄλλου τῶν ὑλικὴν ἐχόντων τὴν σύστασιν, πολλὰ περὶ τὸ ὑποκείμενον τῇ κατ' ἐπίνοιαν διαιρέσει κατενοήσαμεν, ὧν ἑκάστου πρὸς τὸ συνθεωρούμενον* [213] *ἀμίκτως ὁ λόγος ἔχει· ἕτερος γὰρ ὁ τοῦ χρώματος καὶ ἕτερος τοῦ βάρους ὁ λόγος, ὁ τῆς ποσότητος πάλιν*

37 *ἄναρχα*] anarcha (hoc est principio carentia) *Eri* *ἀγέννητα καὶ ἄναρχα* D E F G L P S X *ἀγέννητα*] *ἀγένητα* Æ G I L M P S X 34–5 *κατὰ ταὐτὸν*] *κατ' αὐτὸν* G Q *τῷ λόγῳ om.* T *συγκαταλαμβάνεσθαι*] *καταλαμβάνεσθαι* N : *συμπαραλαμβάνεσθαι* D E *τοῦ*] *τοῦ τε* B W 38 *τεχνικῶς*] *τεχνίτου* I 39 *ἀΐδιον*] *συναΐδον* Æ B E I N O *πάντων*] *ita* Æ B D G I L M O P R S T W X *Forb* : *ἁπάντων Ald Mign* *ὑποκεῖσθαι om.* N T 40 *ὕλην*] *ὕλην πλείστην* L S T *εὑρήσοι* A (*sed non* Æ) D G² P S *τῶν ἰδίων δογμάτων εὑρήσει* N *τὴν*¹ *om.* O *τὴν*² *om.* Æ ß N Q R 41 *οὐσίαν*] *ita* B D E F G L M P R² S X *Forb* : *αἰτίαν* O W *Dion Eri Ald Mign* *ἀγένητον* Æ G I L M O P S² *ἀντιπαρεξάγει*] *παρεξάγει* D E F G P X : *ἀντεπεξάγει* M : *ἀντιπαρέξει* R *καὶ om.* I 42 *ἀκούοντες λεγούσης* D G L P S X *ἀκούοντες*] *ἀκούειν* M *ὅπως*] *πῶς* Æ B N O T 43 *τὸ*] *τῷ* Æ : *om.* Q R² *ἡμέτερον*] *ἡμέτερον ὂν* Q *περιεργάσασθαι* R 43–4 *πάντα—πεπιστευκότες*] diuinam naturam creatricem credentes esse cunctorum *Dion* 44 *χωρητὰ*] plena *Eri* *ὑποστήσεσθαι*] *ita* Æ B D G I L O P R² S T W X *Ald Forb* : *ὑποστήσασθαι Mign* *τοῦ ὄντος* I 45 *ἐπιβάλλειν* M Q R T : *ὑποβάλλειν* Æ B I O : *om.* N *τὰς ποιότητας*] *περὶ τὰς ποιότητας χρήσασθαι* N 46 *οὐκοῦν*] non ergo *Eri* *ἀκολούθως om.* D G P X *ὡς ἀκολούθως* I *ὡς om.* N Q T *ἡγούμεθα*] *ἡ γύνη* B : *ἡ γυνὴ* ß 47 *οὕτως* G M P R S W X 48 *συνεστηκότων* R *ἀνάγοντες*] *ἐναγόντες* I : *om.* M *πίστιν*] *ἐπιστείμην* Q : disciplinae *Dion* : disciplinam *Eri* 49 *καίτοιγε inc. novum cap.* R *ἦν om.* M *εὑρεσιλογίᾳ τινὶ*] *εὑρεσιλογίαις τισὶ* B *τινὶ om.* N 50 *ἐρεσχηλοῦντας* Q : *ἐρεσχολοῦντας* I

Cap. 25 Æ ß I N O Q R T *Dion* : *def. Eri*

1 *ἀντίρρησις—ὕλην*] quod omnis materia quibusdam quantitatibus subsistit *Λ* 3 *φέρεται*] *φαίνεται* S *Ald Mign* *τε om.* N *ὑποστῆναι*] *εἶναι* D G H P S X 4 *γὰρ om.* T *εὑρίσκομεν* D G H L P S X *συνεστῶσαν*] *ὑφεστῶσαν* M 5 *τοῦ λογοῦ* N *ἕκαστος* B 6 *λόγῳ*] *λόγῳ τε* T *οὐχὶ*] *οὐ* Æ B D I L N O R T 7 *προκειμένου om.* T *τινὸς ζώου* I N O 8 *τοῦ ὑποκειμένου* N 9 *ἕκαστος* B M : *ἕκαστον* Æ I O *θεωρούμενον* W 10 *ὁ*¹ *om.* D G H L P Q R S X *ὁ τοῦ βάρους λόγος* W *λόγος*] *λόγος καὶ* D *πάλιν*] *πάλιν ἕτερος* S²ᵐᵍ

who exists ingenerately, so that two unoriginate and ingenerate principles, each identical with the other, are presupposed by the argument: the one operating constructively and that receiving this skilful operation. And if anyone, by the necessity of this argument, should suppose an eternal matter as the substratum for the Creator of all, how great a support the Manichaean (who opposes material essence, by virtue of ingenerateness, to the good nature) will find for his particular teachings. Yet we do indeed believe that all things are of God, as we hear the Scripture saying; and as to the question of how it was in God, a question beyond our reason, we do not seek to pry, believing that all things are contained by the divine power, both to give existence to what is not and to overlay qualities to the being for appearance.

[**23.5**] Consequently, then, just as we suppose the power of the divine will sufficient to bring beings into subsistence from non-being, so also we will not base our belief on anything beyond probability in referring the reconstitution of what is assembled to the same power. Moreover, it might perhaps be possible, by some skilful use of words, to persuade those who speak frivolously about matter not to appear to inveigh against our argument!

An argument against those who say that matter is co-eternal with God.[84]

[**24.1**] The notion representing matter as subsisting from the intelligible and immaterial is not outside the bounds of what we find to be consistent. For we will find that all matter is composed of certain qualities; if it were stripped of these it, in itself, could in no way be grasped by idea.[85] Moreover, in idea, each kind of quality is separated from the substratum; and the idea is an intellectual and not bodily contemplation. For instance, if some animal or tree is presented for contemplation, or any other thing having material constitution, in the division of it by aspect we perceive many things about the substratum, and the idea of each of them is not confused with that which we also contemplate: for the idea of colour is one and of weight another, and again that of quantity and the particularity of the quality of touch: for 'softness' and 'two cubits long', and the rest of the things

[84] *Bodl. 238* (as Chap. 25): 'That matter exists in certain quantities'.

[85] The method of 'abstraction' that follows goes back to Aristotle, *Metaph. Z* 7.3.3–6 (1029a8–34); it was used as a method of arriving at the One (cf. Alcinous, *Epi.* 10.5; Clement, *Strom.* 5.11.71.2); for its application to matter, see Origen, *Princ.* 4.4.7; *Cels.* 3.41, 4.57.

καὶ ὁ τῆς ποιᾶς κατὰ τὴν ἁφὴν ἰδιότητος· ἥτε γὰρ μαλακότης καὶ τὸ δίπηχυ καὶ τὰ λοιπὰ τῶν εἰρημένων, οὔτε ἀλλήλοις οὔτε τῷ σώματι κατὰ τὸν λόγον συμφέρεται· ἑκάστου γὰρ τούτων ἴδιος, καθό ἐστιν, ὁ ἑρμηνευτικὸς ὅρος ἐπινοεῖται, οὐδὲν ἐπικοινωνῶν ἄλλῃ τινὶ τῶν περὶ τὸ ὑποκείμενον θεωρουμένων ποιότητι.

[**24.2**] *Εἰ τοίνυν νοητὸν μὲν τὸ χρῶμα, νοητὴ δὲ καὶ ἡ ἀντιτυπία καὶ ἡ ποσότης καὶ τὰ λοιπὰ τῶν τοιούτων ἰδιωμάτων, ἕκαστον δὲ τούτων εἰ ὑφαιρεθείη τοῦ ὑποκειμένου, πᾶς ὁ τοῦ σώματος συνδιαλύεται λόγος· ἀκόλουθον ἂν εἴη, ὧν τὴν ἀπουσίαν τῆς τοῦ σώματος λύσεως αἰτίαν εὕρομεν, τούτων τὴν συνδρομὴν ἀποτίκτειν τὴν ὑλικὴν φύσιν* [B] *ὑπολαμβάνειν· ὡς γὰρ οὐκ ἔστι σῶμα, ᾧ τὸ χρῶμα καὶ τὸ σχῆμα καὶ ἡ ἀντιτυπία καὶ ἡ διάστασις καὶ τὸ βάρος καὶ τὰ λοιπὰ τῶν ἰδιωμάτων οὐ πρόσεστιν, ἕκαστον δὲ τούτων σῶμα οὐκ ἔστιν ἀλλ' ἕτερόν τι παρὰ τὸ σῶμα κατὰ τὸ ἰδιάζον εὑρίσκεται· οὕτω κατὰ τὸ ἀντίστροφον, ὅπου δ' ἂν συνδράμῃ τὰ εἰρημένα, τὴν σωματικὴν ὑπόστασιν ἀπεργάζεται· ἀλλὰ μὴν εἰ νοητὴ τῶν ἰδιωμάτων τούτων ἡ κατανόησις, νοητὸν δὲ τῇ φύσει τὸ θεῖον· οὐδὲν ἀπεικὸς, ἐκ τῆς ἀσωμάτου φύσεως τὰς νοερὰς ταύτας ἀφορμὰς πρὸς τὴν τῶν σωμάτων γένεσιν ὑποστῆναι, τῆς μὲν νοητῆς φύσεως τὰς νοητὰς ὑφιστώσης δυνάμεις, τῆς δὲ τούτων πρὸς ἄλληλα συνδρομῆς τὴν ὑλώδη φύσιν παραγούσης εἰς γένεσιν.* [**24.3**] *Ἀλλὰ ταῦτα μὲν κατὰ τὸ πάρεργον ἡμῖν παρεξητάσθω· ἡμῖν δὲ πάλιν ἐπὶ τὴν* [C] *πίστιν ἐπανακτέον τὸν λόγον, δι' ἧς ἔκ τε τοῦ μὴ ὄντος ὑποστῆναι τὸ πᾶν ἐδεξάμεθα, καὶ πάλιν εἰς ἄλλην τινὰ μεταστοιχειοῦσθαι κατάστασιν παρὰ τῆς γραφῆς διδαχθέντες, οὐκ ἀμφιβάλλομεν.*

Πῶς ἄν τις καὶ τῶν ἔξωθεν προσαχθείη πιστεῦσαι τῇ γραφῇ περὶ τῆς ἀναστάσεως διδασκούσῃ.

[**25.1**] *Ἀλλ' ἴσως τις πρὸς τὰ διαλυθέντα σώματα βλέπων, καὶ πρὸς τὸ μέτρον τῆς ἰδίας δυνάμεως τὸ θεῖον κρίνων, τὸν τῆς ἀναστάσεως λόγον ἀδύνατον εἶναί φησι, καὶ στήσεσθαι τὰ νῦν κινούμενα καὶ ἀναστήσεσθαι τὰ νῦν μὴ κινούμενα μὴ ἐνδέχεσθαι λέγων.* [**25.2**] *Ἀλλ' ὁ τοιοῦτος πρῶτον μὲν καὶ μέγιστον ποιείσθω τεκμήριον* [D]

11 *ποιᾶς*] *ποιότητος* N 12 *εἰρημένων*] *προειρημένων* T *συμφύρεται* N 13 *ἑκάτῳ* Q *καθό ἐστιν ἴδιος* I *καθὸ*] *ita* Æ B H L N P R S *Forb* : *καθὼς I M* : *καθ' ὃ* O W X *Ald Mign* *ὅρος*] *λόγος* D N Q R^{2} : ration *Dion* : causa *Eri* 14 *ἄλλῳ* W *ποιοτήτων* T 15 *ποσότης*] *ποιότης* N 16 *δὲ om.* M 17 *πᾶς om.* N *ἀκούλουθον* W *ἂν*] *δ' ἂν* N 18 *ἀπουσίαν*] *ὑφαίρεσιν* R T *εὕρωμεν* H : *ηὕραμεν* P^{ac} X : *εὕραμεν* G : *εὑρίσκομεν* N 19 *ὡς γὰρ*] *ὥσπερ* T 20 *χρῶμα*] res (*ΟΥΣΙΑ*) *Eri* *καὶ τὸ βάρος*] *post σχῆμα* (*l. 20*) *pon.* N : *om.* D G H P X : *τὸ βάρος τε* I 21 *τῶν*] *τῶν τοιούτων* R *πρόσεστιν*] *πρόεστιν* G P X 22 *τὸ ἀντίστροφον*] *τὸν ἀντίστροφον λόγον* B *δ' om.* I 23 *συνδράμοι* M *κατεργάζεται* N T *ἀλλὰ μὴν εἰ*] *ἀλλ' εἰ μὲν* I M *εἰ om.* Æ B N O R^{ac} T : *ἡ* W *νοητὴ*] *νοητὴ μὲν* R 24 *τούτων om.* Q *τῇ φύσει om.* I *οὐδὲν*] *οὐδὲν ἆρα* N 26 *ὑφεστώσης* ß H M R 27 *ἀλλήλας* B 28 *παρεξητάσθη* ß G H N P^{ac} : *ἐξητάσθη* N : *συνεξετάσθω* R^{ac} (*παρε sup. l.*) : *ἐξητάσθω* R^{2} S *ἡμῖν δὲ πάλιν ἐπὶ τὴν πίστιν*] *ἐπὶ τὴν πίστιν δὲ πάλιν* I 29 *ἀνακτέον* T 30 *τινὰ om.* M *κατάστασιν*] *στάσιν* D

Cap. 26 Æ I N Q R T *Dion* : *def. Eri*

1–2 *πῶς—διδασκούσῃ*] de fide resurrectionis et de tribus mortuis quos dominus Iesus suscitauit *Λ* 1 *καὶ*] *καὶ ἐκ* N *τῶν ἔξωθεν om.* I *προαχθείη* D^{pc} O T : *προσαχθῇ* Q *τῇ γραφῷ πιστεῦσαι* R 2 *διδασκούσης* N : *om.* T W 4 *ἰδίας*] *οἰκείας* B 5 *νῦν om.* A (*sed non* Æ) D L *καὶ ἀναστήσεσθαι τὰ νῦν μὴ κινούμενα om.* D^{ac} I N *μὴ*[1] X^{pc2} (*post κινούμενα* X *add. καὶ ἀναστήσεσθαι τὰ νῦν κινούμενα sed exp.*) *μὴ*[2]] *μὴ δὲ* D R T 6 *λέγοι* W *καὶ om.* N *ποιείσθω om.* D G P X *τεκμήριον ποιείσθω* E

spoken of, are not conflated with each other in idea nor with the body; the explanatory definition conceived for each of these is particular, according to what it is, having nothing in common with any other quality of those aspects contemplated about the substratum.

[**24.2**] If, then, colour is something intellectual, and resistance also is intellectual, and so with quantity and the other such properties, [so that] if each of these should be withdrawn from the substratum the whole idea of the body is dissolved, it would be consistent to suppose that the concurrence of those things, the absence of which we found to be a cause of the dissolution of the body, generates material nature. For as that is not a body which has not colour and figure and resistance and extension and weight and the rest of the properties, while each of these, in its particularity, is found to be not the body but something else besides the body, so also conversely, whenever the things spoken of are in concurrence they effect bodily existence. Moreover, if the perception of these properties is intellectual, and the divinity is also intellectual in nature, there is nothing unreasonable [in supposing that] these intellectual occasions for the genesis of bodies subsist from the incorporeal nature, the intellectual nature on the one hand giving subsistence to the intellectual potentialities, and the mutual concurrence of these bringing material nature to genesis. [**24.3**] But let us put aside such matters, as being a digression; we must direct our treatise, once again, to the faith by which we accept that the universe subsists from non-being, and do not doubt when we are taught by the Scripture that it will again be changed into some other state.

How one, even of those outside, may be brought to believe the Scripture's teaching regarding the resurrection.[86]

[**25.1**] Perhaps someone, looking at the dissolution of bodies, and assessing the divine by the measure of his own power, asserts that the idea of the resurrection is impossible, saying that it cannot be that those things which now move should become stationary and that those which are now not moving should be raised again. [**25.2**] Let such a one, however, take as the first and greatest evidence of the

[86] *Bodl. 238* (as Chap. 26): 'Of faith in the resurrection and of the three dead persons whom the Lord Jesus raised'.

τῆς κατὰ τὴν ἀνάστασιν ἀληθείας τὸ τοῦ κήρυκος αὐτῆς ἀξιόπιστον· ἡ δὲ τῶν λεγομένων πίστις ἐκ τῆς τῶν λοιπῶν τῶν προρρηθέντων ἐκβάσεως τὸ ἀσφαλὲς ἔχει· ἐπειδὴ γὰρ πολλούς τε καὶ παντοδαποὺς παρέθετο λόγους ἡ θεία γραφὴ, δυνατόν ἐστιν ὅπως ἂν ἔχῃ ψεύδους ἢ ἀληθείας τὰ λοιπὰ τῶν εἰρημένων θεασαμένους, δι᾽ ἐκείνων καὶ τὸ περὶ τῆς ἀναστάσεως δόγμα κατανοῆσαι. Εἰ μὲν γὰρ ἐν τοῖς ἄλλοις ψευδεῖς οἱ λόγοι καὶ διεσφαλμένοι τῆς ἀληθείας ἐλέγχονται, οὐδὲ τοῦτο πάντως ἐκτὸς ψεύδους ἐστίν· εἰ δὲ τὰ ἄλλα πάντα μαρτυροῦσαν ἔχει τῇ ἀληθείᾳ τὴν πεῖραν, ἀκόλουθον ἂν εἴη δι᾽ ἐκείνων καὶ τὴν περὶ τῆς ἀναστάσεως πρόρρησιν ἀληθῆ νομίσαι. Οὐκοῦν [216] *ἐπιμνησθῶμεν ἑνὸς ἢ δυοῖν τῶν προκατηγγελμένων, καὶ ἀντιπαραθῶμεν τοῖς προρρηθεῖσι τὴν ἔκβασιν, ὥστε γνῶναι δι᾽ αὐτῶν εἰ πρὸς τὴν ἀλήθειαν ὁ λόγος βλέπει.*

[25.3] *Τίς οὐκ οἶδεν ὅπως ἤνθει κατὰ τὸ ἀρχαῖον ὁ Ἰσραηλίτης λαὸς, πάσαις ταῖς κατὰ τὴν οἰκουμένην δυναστείαις ἀντεγειρόμενος; οἷα ἦν τὰ βασίλεια κατὰ τὴν τῶν Ἱεροσολύμων πόλιν; οἷα τὰ τείχη, οἱ πύργοι, ἡ τοῦ ἱεροῦ μεγαλουργία; ἅπερ καὶ τοῖς μαθηταῖς τοῦ Κυρίου ἄξια θαύματος ἐνομίσθη, καὶ κατανοεῖν ἀξιοῦσι τὸν Κύριον, θαυμαστικῶς περὶ τὰ φαινόμενα διατεθέντες, ὡς ἡ τοῦ εὐαγγελίου ἱστορία δηλοῖ, λέγοντες πρὸς αὐτόν,* ***ποταπὰ τὰ ἔργα καὶ ποταπαὶ αἱ οἰκοδομαί·*** *ὁ δὲ τὴν ἐσομένην περὶ τὸν τόπον ἐρήμωσιν καὶ τὸν ἀφανισμὸν τοῦ κάλλους ἐκείνου πρὸς τοὺς τὸ παρὸν θαυμάζοντας ὑποδείκνυσι, λέγων μηδὲν* [B] *τῶν φαινομένων μετ᾽ ὀλίγον ὑπολειφθήσεσθαι. Ἀλλὰ καὶ παρὰ τὸν τοῦ πάθους καιρὸν, αἱ μὲν γυναῖκες ἐπηκολούθουν θρηνοῦσαι τὴν ἄδικον ἐπ᾽ αὐτῷ ψῆφον (οὔπω γὰρ εἰς τὴν τῶν γινομένων οἰκονομίαν ἀπέβλεπον) ὁ δὲ συμβουλεύει τὰ μὲν περὶ αὐτὸν γινόμενα σιωπᾶν· μηδὲ γὰρ εἶναι δακρύων ἄξια· ὑπερθέσθαι δὲ τὸν ὀδυρμὸν καὶ τὸν θρῆνον εἰς τὸν ἀληθῆ τῶν δακρύων καιρὸν, ὅταν περισχεθῇ τοῖς πολιορκοῦσιν ἡ πόλις καὶ εἰς τοσοῦτον συνοχῆς ἔλθῃ τὰ πάθη ὡς μακαριστὸν ἡγεῖσθαι τὸν μὴ γενόμενον· ἐν οἷς καὶ τὸ περὶ τὴν τεκνοφάγον προεμήνυσεν ἄγος, εἰπὼν μακαρισθήσεσθαι κατὰ τὰς*

7 *ἀνάστασιν*] *διάστασιν* A (*sed non* Æ) G P X *κήρυκος*] *κηρύγματος* W *Eri Ald Mign* 8 *τῶν λοιπῶν om.* R *ἀσφαλὲς*] *ἀληθὲς* R 9 *τε om.* Æ B I M N O Q R W *παρέθετο*] *παρέχεται* Q *λόγους παρέθετο* M 10 *ὅπως ἂν ἔχῃ ψεύδους ἢ ἀληθείας*] ut ueritas sustineat mendaces *Eri* *ἔχῃ*] *ἔχει* Q W : *ἔχοι* Æ L M N : *post* *ἀληθείας* (*l. 10*) *pon.* N 11 *περὶ om.* M 12 *ψευδεῖς—ἀληθείας*] mendaces sermones ueritates et deceptores *Eri* 13 *ἐκτὸς*] *ἐκτὸς τοῦ* Æ B I N O Q R T W *τὰ ἄλλα*] *τἄλλα* I L : *τᾶλλα* R 13 *ἔχει*] *ἔχουσι* M 13–14 *τῆς ἀληθείας* N 14 *τὴν*] *τὸν* O 15 *νομίζειν* B *νομισθῆναι* D E I : *νοῆσαι* L W *οὐκοῦν*] non igitur *Eri* *δυοῖν*] *δύο* Æ B I O : *δευτέρου* N 17 *δι᾽ αὐτῶν*] utrum *Dion* : eorum *Eri* 18 *ἤνθει*] interponebatur *Eri* 19 *τῶν om.* Æ N R 20 *ἱεροσολυμιτῶν* Æ B I M N O Q W *Eri* 22 *περὶ τὰ φαινόμενα θαυματστικῶς* T W 23 *πρὸς αὐτὸν om.* Q *Eri* *ποδαπὰ ἔργα καὶ ποδαπαὶ οἰκοδομαί* N 25 *ὑποδεικνύει* N 26 *παρὰ*] *περὶ* Q *καιρὸν τοῦ πάθους* D G L P S X 27 *ἐπ᾽ αὐτῷ ἄδικον* N 28 *μὲν om.* B *αὐτοῦ* N 29 *ὑπερθέσθαι δὲ*] *ὑπὲρ ἑαυτῶν δὲ θέσθαι* M 31 *τοσοῦτο* M Q *ἔλθοι* G L P S X *μακαρισμὸν* I : *μακάριον* M *ἡγεῖσθαι*] *εἶναι* N *γενόμενον*] *ita* Æ B D G I M N O P S T W X *Ald Forb* : *γεννώμενον* R *Mign* 32 *τεκνοφαγίαν* O Q *προεμύνησεν* B (*non* ß) : *ἐμήνυσεν* N *ἄγος*] *ἄγονος* L : *ἄγονον* M *μακαρισθήσεται* L : *μακαρίζεσθαι* Æ

truth regarding the resurrection the trustworthiness of the herald of this. Now the faith in what is said derives its certainty from the outcomes of the other things predicted. Since the Holy Scripture delivers many and various statements, it is possible, by reviewing how the rest of the utterances stand regarding falsehood and truth, to understand, in the light of them, the doctrine concerning the resurrection. For if in other matters the statements are proved to be false and to have failed being true, then certainly neither is this outside falsehood; but if all the others have experience to vouch for their truth, it would be consistent to deem as true, on their account, the prediction concerning the resurrection also. Therefore, let us recall one or two of the other predictions made and compare the outcome with the things foretold, so that we may know, through them, whether the idea of the resurrection points to the truth.

[**25.3**] Who does not know how the people of Israel flourished of old, raised up against all the power of the world? Or of what kind were the palaces in the city of Jerusalem? Of what kind were the walls, the towers, the majestic structure of the Temple? Things deemed worthy of admiration even by the disciples of the Lord, so that they expected the Lord to take notice of them, being disposed to wonder at what was seen, as the Gospel narrative clearly shows, when they said to him: *What works and what buildings!*[87] But he indicates to those who wondered at the present state of things the future desolation of the place and the disappearance of that beauty, saying that after a little while nothing of what was seen would be left. And again, at the time of the Passion, the women following him lamented the unjust sentence against him (for they could not yet see the economy of what was happening); but he bids them to be silent regarding the things done to him, for it does not deserve their tears, but to reserve their wailing and lamentations for the true time of tears, when the city should be compassed by besiegers, and their suffering reach so great a strait that they should consider him blessed who had not come into existence; in this he also denounced beforehand the abomination of eating children, saying that in those days the womb should be blessed which never bore.[88] Where then are those palaces? Where is the Temple? Where are the walls? Where are the defences of the towers? Where is the power of the Israelites? Were

[87] Cf. Mark 13:1. [88] Cf. Luke 23:27–9.

ἡμέρας ἐκείνας τὴν γαστέρα τὴν ἄγονον. Ποῦ τοίνυν ἐκεῖνα τὰ βασίλεια; ποῦ τὸ ἱερόν; ποῦ τὰ τείχη; ποῦ τῶν πύργων αἱ προβολαί; ποῦ δὲ ἡ τῶν Ἰσραηλιτῶν δυναστεία; [C] *οὐχ οἱ μὲν κατὰ πᾶσαν μικροῦ δεῖν τὴν οἰκουμένην ἄλλος ἀλλαχῇ διεσπάρησαν; τῇ δὲ τούτων καταστροφῇ συνηρειπώθη καὶ τὰ βασίλεια;* **[25.4]** *Δοκεῖ γάρ μοι ταῦτα καὶ τὰ τοιαῦτα προμηνῦσαι ὁ Κύριος, οὐ τῶν πραγμάτων χάριν—τί γὰρ τοσοῦτον ἦν τοῖς ἀκούουσι κέρδος τῶν πάντως ἐκβησομένων ἡ πρόρρησις; ἔγνωσαν γὰρ ἂν τῇ πείρᾳ, καὶ μὴ προμαθόντες τὸ γενησόμενον—ἀλλ᾽ ὥστε διὰ τούτων αὐτοῖς καὶ τὴν περὶ τῶν μειζόνων πίστιν εἰς ἀκολουθίαν ἐλθεῖν· ἡ γὰρ ἐν τούτοις διὰ τῶν ἔργων μαρτυρία, καὶ τῆς ἐν ἐκείνοις ἀληθείας ἐστὶν ἀπόδειξις.*

[25.5] [D] *Ὥσπερ γὰρ εἴ τινος γεωργοῦ τὴν τῶν σπερμάτων ὑφηγουμένου δύναμιν, ἀπιστεῖν συμβῇ τὸν γεωργίας ἀπείρατον, αὐτάρκης ἂν εἰς ἀπόδειξιν τῆς ἀληθείας ἦν τῷ γεηπόνῳ ἐν ἑνὶ σπέρματι τῶν ἐν τῷ μεδίμνῳ κειμένων δείξαντι τὴν δύναμιν, καὶ περὶ τῶν λοιπῶν ἐγγυᾶσθαι· ὁ γὰρ ἰδὼν τὸν ἕνα πυρὸν ἢ τὴν κριθὴν ἢ ὅ τι περ ἂν ἐν τῷ πληρώματι τοῦ μεδίμνου τύχῃ, μετὰ τὸ καταβληθῆναι τῇ βώλῳ στάχυν γενόμενον, οὐκέτ᾽ ἂν διὰ τοῦ ἑνὸς οὐδὲ περὶ τῶν λοιπῶν ἀπιστήσειεν· οὕτως ἱκανή μοι δοκεῖ πρὸς μαρτυρίαν εἶναι τοῦ κατὰ τὴν ἀνάστασιν μυστηρίου, ἡ τοῖς λοιποῖς τῶν εἰρημένων συνομολογουμένη ἀλήθεια.* **[25.6]** *Μᾶλλον δὲ καὶ αὐτῆς τῆς ἀναστάσεως ἡ* [217] *πεῖρα, ἣν οὐ διὰ λόγων τοσοῦτον ὅσον δι᾽ αὐτῶν τῶν ἔργων ἐδιδάχθημεν. Ἐπειδὴ γὰρ μέγα καὶ ὑπὲρ πίστιν ἦν τὸ κατὰ τὴν ἀνάστασιν θαῦμα, διὰ τῶν κατωτέρων τῆς θαυματοποιΐας ἀρξάμενος ἠρέμα πως τὴν πίστιν ἡμῶν προσεθίζει τοῖς μείζοσι.*

[25.7] *Καθάπερ γάρ τις μήτηρ καταλλήλως τιθηνουμένη τὸ νήπιον, τέως μὲν ἁπαλῷ τε καὶ ὑγρῷ τῷ στόματι τὸ γάλα διὰ τῆς θηλῆς ἐντίθησιν· ὀδοντοφυοῦντι*

34 *προβολαί*] *περιβολαὶ* N *δὲ om.* B N *τῶν ἰσραηλιτῶν ἡ* M N 35 *οἱ*] *ὁ* N *μικροῦ om.* N *δεῖν om.* B N *ἀλλαχοῦ* M 36 *καταστροφῇ*] *καταστροφῇ μικροῦ* I *συνηριπώθη* B D L O S^{pc} T : *συνηρηπώθη* N : *συνηρριπώθη* R^{pc2} : *συνηρρειπώθη* S^{ac} : *συνερριπώθη* G P S^{mg} W X : *συνεριπώθη* Q S^{2mg} : *συνερρυπώθη* M *καὶ om.* N 37 *μοι γὰρ* N R 38 *τοσοῦτον om.* I O *τοῖς ἀκούουσι ἦν* I O *πάντων* X 39 *ἐκβησομένων*] *ἐκβήσεσθαι μελλόντων* N *γὰρ om.* I W *προμαθόντες*] *μαθόντες* R 40 *γεννησόμενον* Q : *ἐκβησόμενον* B *ἀλλ᾽ ὥστε*] *ἄλλως τε* L *καὶ διὰ τούτων αὐτοῖς* N *αὐτοῖς*] *αὐτοὺς* I *τὴν περὶ τῶν μειζόνων πίστιν εἰς*] *εἰς τὴν περὶ τῆς τῶν μειζόνων πίστεως* I *πίστιν om.* M 41 *ἐλθεῖν*] *ἐλθεῖν ἀλήθειαν* M *διὰ τῶν ἔργων om.* M 42 *ἀληθείας*] *ἀκολουθίας* D E R^{2mg} 44 *συμβῇ*] *συμβαίη* M : *συνέβη* Q S^{ac} *τὸν*] *τὸν τῆς Mign* *ἀπείραστον* M : *ἀπείρητον* B *αὔταρκες* Æ B I L M N O Q S *ἂν*] *γὰρ* I : *ἂν ἦν* L : *ἦν* N *τῆς ἀληθείας ἀπόδειξιν* N *τῆς om.* M N *ἦν*] *ἂν* N : *om.* L 45 *ἐν*[1] *om.* N S *κειμένων*] *ἐγκειμένων* N *δείξαντι om.* D G P X 46 *πυρὸν*] *πυρὸν καὶ τὴν ὀλύραν* T *τὴν*] *ita* Æ B D G I M N O P Q R T X *Forb* : *τὴν μίαν* S W *Ald Mign* *περ*] *ὅπερ* Æ B I T : *οὗπερ* N 47 *τύχῃ*] *τύχοι* L M P R *καταβληθῆναι*] *ita* Æ B D G I M N O P R T W X *Forb* : *ἐγκαταβληθῆναι* S *Ald Mign* *βόλῳ* G N^{ac} (*ω sup. l.*) P^{ac} Q W : culmo *Eri* 48 *γινόμενον* I *οὐκέτ᾽*] *ita* Æ B D I L M O P Q R S X *Forb* : *οὐκ* G : *οὐκέτι* W *Ald Mign* 49 *μυστηρίου*] *μαρτυρίου* R 50 *συνομολογουμένη om.* B 51 *ἣν*] *ἦν* G L P X *διὰ τῶν ἔργων αὐτῶν* Æ B I M N O Q R T W 53 *κατωτέρω* G L P S X 53–4 *προσεθίζει τὴν πίστιν ἡμῶν* D G L P S X 54 *προσερεθίζει* M : *προεθίζει* T : nutribat *Eri* 55 *καθάπερ*] *καὶ καθάπερ* Æ *γάρ om.* Æ B N *τιθηνουμένη*] lactans *Dion Eri* *τέως*] *ἕως* B L 56 *τε om.* D *τὸ om.* D[2] *ἐντίθησιν*] *ἐνίησιν* Q

they not scattered in different places over almost all the world; and in their overthrow the palaces also brought to ruin? [25.4] For it seems to me that the Lord forewarned these things and others like them not for the sake of the matters themselves—for what great advantage to the hearers was the prediction of what was certainly going to happen? They would have known by experience, even if they had not previously learnt of what would come—but in order that by these means faith might also follow concerning more important matters; for the testimony through events in the former cases is also a proof of the truth in the latter.

[25.5] For just as if a farmer were explaining the power of seeds and it were to happen that someone inexperienced in farming should disbelieve him, it would be sufficient for proof of the truth of the matter for the agriculturist to show him the power in one seed of those lying in the bushel and give this as a pledge for the rest. For one who saw the single grain of wheat or barley, or whatever should be in the plenitude of the bushel, after being cast into the clod of earth, become an ear, by means of the one would no longer disbelieve concerning the others.[89] So also, the truth acknowledged regarding the other statements seems to me to be sufficient for evidence of the mystery of the resurrection. [25.6] Still more is this the case with the experience of resurrection itself, which we have been taught not so much by words as by events themselves. Since the marvel of resurrection was great and beyond belief, beginning gradually by lesser instances of his miraculous power, he accustoms our faith, as it were, for the greater instances.

[25.7] Just as a mother, nursing her babe appropriately, supplies milk by her breast to its mouth while still tender and soft; and when it begins to have teeth and to grow she introduces bread, not hard or such as it cannot chew, so that the tender and unpractised gums may not be chafed by rough food, but softening it with her own teeth, she makes it commensurate to and appropriate for the ability of the eater; and then as its ability increases by growth she gradually leads on the

[89] Cf. Gregory of Nyssa, *An. et res.* 10.102–6 (Spira, 120.2–121.4).

δὲ ἤδη καὶ αὐξανομένῳ προσάγει τὸν ἄρτον, οὐ τραχύν τε καὶ ἀκατέργαστον, ὡς ἂν μὴ περιξανθείη τῷ σκληρῷ τῆς τροφῆς τὸ τῶν οὔλων ἁπαλόν τε καὶ ἀγύμναστον, ἀλλὰ τοῖς ἰδίοις ὀδοῦσι καταλεάνασα, σύμμετρόν τε καὶ κατάλληλον τῇ δυνάμει τοῦ προσφερομένου ἐποίησεν· εἶτα κατὰ προσθήκην τῆς δυνάμεως ἐπιδιδούσης, προσεθισθὲν τοῖς ἁπαλωτέροις ἠρέμα τὸ νήπιον [B] προσάγει τῇ στερεωτέρᾳ τροφῇ· οὕτω τὴν ἀνθρωπίνην μικροψυχίαν ὁ Κύριος, οἱόν τι νήπιον ἀτελὲς διὰ τῶν θαυμάτων τρέφων καὶ τιθηνούμενος, πρῶτον μὲν ἐν ἀπεγνωσμένῃ νόσῳ τὴν τῆς ἀναστάσεως προοιμιάζεται δύναμιν, ὃ μέγα μὲν ἦν τῷ κατορθώματι, οὐ μὴν τοιοῦτον οἷον ἀπιστεῖσθαι λεγόμενον· **ἐπιτιμήσας** γὰρ **τῷ πυρετῷ** σφοδρῶς **τὴν πενθερὰν τοῦ Σίμωνος** καταφλέγοντι, τοσαύτην ἐποίησε τοῦ κακοῦ τὴν μετάστασιν, ὡς πρὸς τὸ **διακονεῖν** τοῖς παροῦσιν ἐνισχύσαι τὴν ἤδη τεθνήξεσθαι προσδοκωμένην.

[25.8] Εἶτα μικρόν τι τῇ δυνάμει προστίθησι, καὶ τοῦ βασιλικοῦ τὸν υἱὸν ἐν ὁμολογουμένῳ κινδύνῳ κείμενον (οὕτω γάρ φησιν ἡ ἱστορία, ὅτι ἤμελλε τελευτᾶν, τοῦ πατρὸς βοῶντος, **κατάβηθι πρὶν ἀποθανεῖν τὸ παιδίον**) ἐνεργεῖ πάλιν τοῦ τεθνήξεσθαι πεπιστευμένου [C] τὴν ἀνάστασιν· ἐν μείζονι τῇ δυνάμει τὸ θαῦμα κατεργασάμενος, τῷ μηδὲ πλησιάσαι τῷ τόπῳ, ἀλλὰ πόρρωθεν τῇ τοῦ προστάγματος ἰσχύϊ τὴν ζωὴν ἀποστεῖλαι.

[25.9] Πάλιν δι’ ἀκολουθίας τοῖς ὑψηλοτέροις ἐπαναβαίνει θαύμασι. Πρὸς γὰρ τὴν παῖδα τοῦ ἀρχισυναγώγου ὁρμήσας, ἑκὼν ἔδωκε τῇ ὁδοιπορίᾳ σχολήν, τὴν ἴασιν τῆς αἱμορροΐας δημοσιεύων λαθοῦσαν, ὡς ἂν ἐν τῷ χρόνῳ τούτῳ κατακρατήσειε τῆς νοσούσης ὁ θάνατος. Ἄρτι τοίνυν τῆς ψυχῆς χωρισθείσης τοῦ σώματος, καὶ θορυβουμένων ἐν τῇ γοερᾷ κραυγῇ τῶν ἐπικωκυόντων τῷ πάθει, καθάπερ ἐξ ὕπνου τῷ προστακτικῷ λόγῳ διανίστησι πάλιν πρὸς τὴν ζωὴν τὸ κοράσιον, ὁδῷ τινι καὶ ἀκολουθίᾳ πρὸς τὸ μεῖζον ἀναλαμβάνων τὴν ἀνθρωπίνην ἀσθένειαν.

[25.10] [D] Εἶτ’ ἐπὶ τούτοις ὑπερβαίνει τῷ θαύματι, καὶ δι’ ὑψηλοτέρας δυνάμεως ὁδοποιεῖ τοῖς ἀνθρώποις τὴν περὶ τῆς ἀναστάσεως πίστιν. Ναῒν τινὰ πόλιν κατὰ τὴν

57 ἤδη *om.* D G L P S X τε *om.* Æ B N Q R 59–60 τοῦ προσφερομένου] τὸν προσφερόμενον I : parvuli cibum *Dion* : oblati (uidelicet panis) *Eri* 60 εἶτα] εἶτα καὶ T προσθήκην] τὴν προσθήκην N 61 προσεθισθὲν] προεθισθὲν Æ : προσεθισθὲν τι I : additum *Eri* 61–2 τῷ νιπίῳ προσάγει τὴν στερεωτέραν τροφὴν I 61 στερροτέρᾳ D M 62 οὕτως Æ M W μακροψυχίαν W 63 καὶ τιθηνούμενος] lactansque *Eri* 63–4 ἐν—δύναμιν] in incognitam resurrectionis paulisper praecedit uirtutem *Eri* 63 ἐν *om.* Æ ἀπεγνωσμένῳ νοσήματι M 64 ἦν τῷ κατορθώματι] ἐν τῷ κατορθώματι ἦν N 65 οἷον] ὥστε R 67 διακονῆσαι I ἐνισχῦσαι G M P R W : ἐνίσχυσε T 67–8 προσδοκωμένην τεθνήξεσθαι *Ald Mign* 68 προσδοκωμένην *om.* R[ac] 69 προστίθησι *om.* B υἱὸν] υἱὸν ἰασάμενος N Q 70 κείμενον] κείμενον σώζει Q *Dion* οὕτως Æ G P X ἤμελλε] *ita* Æ ß D G M N P T W X *Forb* : ἔμελλε O S *Ald Mign* 71 βοῶντος] καταβοῶντος N παιδίον] παιδίον μου D G L P S W X 71–3 ἐνεργεῖ—κατεργασάμενος] operatur iterum in credito quod moriturus esset maiori resurrectionis miraculum perficiens *Eri* 72 πεπιστευμένου] πιστευομένου I : προσδοκωμένου D M (επιστευ *sup. l.*) : πιστευομένου προσδοκωμένου L 73 κατεργαζόμενος N T 74 πράγματος X 75 δι’] διὰ B ἐπαναβαίνει] ἐπιβαίνει D G L P R[2] S X : προσβαίνει O 76 ἀρχισυναγώγου] ἀρχισυναγώγου αὐτὸς Q : principis *Dion* : centurionis *Eri* 77 αἱμορρούσης N R[ac?] : αἱμορροούσης Q λαθοῦσαν] λανθάνουσαν Æ B I N O R T W 78 ἄρτι—σώματος *om.* W τῆς ψυχῆς *om.* N 79 ἐν] ἐπὶ S ἐπικωκυόντων] prohibentibus *Eri* 80 προσταγματικῷ I N O R[ac] τὴν *om.* D 82 εἶτα Æ G I L N O P S X δι’] διὰ W 83 ναεὶν M : ναΐμ G P κατὰ] κατὰ τὰ N

babe, accustomed to tender food, to more solid nourishment; so also the Lord, fostering and nursing through miracles the human weakness of soul, as some babe not fully grown, first makes a prelude of the power of the resurrection by the case of a desperate disease, which prelude, though great in achievement, yet was not such that the report of it would be disbelieved: for by *rebuking the fever* which was fiercely consuming *the mother-in-law of Simon*, he effected such a great removal of the evil so as to enable her, who was already expecting to approach death, to *minister* to those present.[90]

[**25.8**] Next he makes a slight addition to the power, and when the nobleman's son lay in acknowledged danger (for so the narrative says, that he was about to die, as his father cried, *come down, before the child dies*[91]), he again effects the resurrection of one believed about to die; accomplishing the miracle with greater power in that he did not even approach the place, but sent life from afar off by the force of his command.

[**25.9**] Again, in what follows he ascends to higher wonders. For having set out to the daughter of the ruler of the synagogue, he voluntarily made a pause on the journey, making public the hidden cure of the woman with an issue of blood, that in this period death might overcome the sick girl. When, then, her soul had been separated from the body, and those lamenting over the sickness were making a tumult with their mournful cries, he raises the maiden to life again, as if from sleep, by his word of command, leading on human weakness, by a sort of path and sequence, towards greater things.

[**25.10**] Next, he surpasses these acts with a miracle, and by a more exalted act of power he guides human beings to faith in the resurrection. Scripture tells of a

[90] Luke 4:38–9. For Chapter 25.7–12, see Gregory of Nyssa, *An. et res.* 10.30–3 (Spira, 104.7–105.2).

[91] John 4:49.

Ἰουδαίαν ἱστορεῖ ἡ γραφή· παῖς ἦν ἐν ταύτῃ μονογενὴς χήρᾳ τινὶ, οὐκέτι τοιοῦτος παῖς οἷος ἐν μειρακίοις εἶναι, ἀλλ᾽ ἤδη ἐκ παίδων εἰς ἄνδρας τελῶν. **Νεανίαν** αὐτὸν ὀνομάζει ὁ λόγος. Πολλὰ δι᾽ ὀλίγων διηγεῖται ἡ ἱστορία· θρῆνος ἄντικρύς ἐστι τὸ διήγημα· **χήρα**, φησὶν, ἦν τοῦ τεθνηκότος ἡ μήτηρ· ὁρᾷς τὸ βάρος τῆς συμφορᾶς, πῶς ἐν ὀλίγῳ τὸ πάθος ὁ λόγος ἐξετραγῴδησε; [220] τί γάρ ἐστι τὸ λεγόμενον; ὅτι οὐκ ἦν αὐτῇ παιδοποιΐας ἐλπὶς, τὴν ἐπὶ τῷ ἐκλείποντι συμφορὰν θεραπεύουσα· χήρα γὰρ ἡ γυνή· οὐκ εἶχε πρὸς ἕτερον ἀντὶ τοῦ κατοιχομένου βλέπειν· μονογενὴς γὰρ ὁ τόκος· ὅσον δὲ τὸ ἐπὶ τούτῳ κακὸν, παντὶ ῥᾴδιον συνιδεῖν τῷ μὴ ἀπεξενωμένῳ τῆς φύσεως· μόνον ἐν ὠδῖσιν ἐκεῖνον ἐγνώρισε, μόνον ταῖς θηλαῖς ἐτιθηνήσατο· μόνος αὐτῇ φαιδρὰν ἐποίει τὴν τράπεζαν, μόνος ἦν τῆς κατὰ τὸν οἶκον φαιδρότητος ὑπόθεσις, παίζων, σπουδάζων, ἀσκούμενος, φαιδρυνόμενος, ἐν προόδοις, ἐν παλαίστραις, ἐν συλλόγοις νεότητος· πᾶν ὅ τι μητρὸς ὀφθαλμοῖς γλυκύ τε καὶ τίμιον μόνος ἐκεῖνος ἦν, ἤδη τοῦ γάμου τὴν ὥραν ἄγων, ὁ τοῦ γένους ὅρπηξ, ὁ τῆς διαδοχῆς κλάδος, ἡ βακτηρία τοῦ γήρως. Ἀλλὰ καὶ ἡ τῆς ἡλικίας προσθήκη [B] ἄλλος θρῆνος ἦν· ὁ γὰρ **νεανίαν** εἰπὼν, τὸ ἄνθος εἶπε τῆς μαρανθείσης ὥρας, ἄρτι τοῖς ἰούλοις ὑποχλοάζοντα, οὔπω τοῦ πώγωνος διὰ βάθους ὑποπιμπλάμενον, ἔτι τῷ κάλλει τῶν παρειῶν ὑποστίλβοντα. Τί τοίνυν πάσχειν εἰκὸς ἐπ᾽ αὐτῷ τὴν μητέρα; οἱονεὶ πυρὶ τοῖς σπλάγχνοις ἐγκαταφλέγεσθαι; ὡς πικρῶς ἐπ᾽ αὐτῷ παρατείνειν τὸν θρῆνον, περιπλεκομένην προκειμένῳ τῷ πτώματι, ὡς μὴ ἂν ἐπισπεῦσαι τῷ νεκρῷ τὴν κηδείαν ἀλλ᾽ ἐμφορεῖσθαι τοῦ πάθους, ἐπιπλεῖστον αὐτῷ τοὺς ὀδυρμοὺς παρατείνουσαν· οὐδὲ τοῦτο παρῆκεν ὁ λόγος· **ἰδὼν γὰρ αὐτὴν** ὁ Ἰησοῦς, φησὶν, **ἐσπλαγχνίσθη, καὶ προσελθὼν ἥψατο τῆς σοροῦ, οἱ δὲ βαστάζοντες ἔστησαν·** καὶ λέγει τῷ νεκρῷ, **νεανίσκε, σοὶ λέγω, ἐγέρθητι,** [C] **καὶ παρέδωκεν αὐτὸν τῇ μητρὶ αὐτοῦ ζῶντα.** Ἤδη τοίνυν οὐκ ἐν ὀλίγῳ διαστήματι τοῦ νεκροῦ γεγενημένου, καὶ ὅσον οὐδέπω ἐναποτεθέντος τῷ τάφῳ, γίνεται παρὰ τοῦ Κυρίου τὸ μὲν θαῦμα μεῖζον, τὸ δὲ πρόσταγμα ἶσον.

84 ἐν ταύτῃ] ἐν αὐτῇ Q R : ἐνταῦθα N T   τινὶ] τινὶ ὢν D G P T X : τινὶ ὤν Q   85 παῖς *om.* N   οἷος] ὡς M   ἄνδρα D G L P S X   αὐτὸν] γὰρ αὐτὸν O : τὸν τοιοῦτον M   86 ἄντικρύς] oppositus *Eri*   87 ἡ *om.* Q   88 ὁ λόγος *om.* M N Q R *Dion Eri*   ἐτραγῴδησε R   λεγόμενον] dicitur unicus *Eri*   89 παιδοποιείας N   ἐκλείποντι] λείποντι M Q   θεραπεύουσαν B   γὰρ] γὰρ ἦν Æ B R T   90 κατοιχομένου] κατοιχουμένου W : ἀποιχομένου L   ὁ τόκος] ipse *Eri*   91 ῥᾳδίως Q   ἀποξενομένῳ G P X : ἀπεξενομένῳ Q   92 ὠδίσιν P R X   ἐγνώρισε ἐκεῖνον B   μόνον] μόνον ἐν L   ἐτιθηνάσατο W   93 ἐποίει τὴν X[pc2]   ἐποιεῖτο Æ B O : ἐποιεῖ I   τὴν οἰκίαν R   ὑπόθεσις] *ita* Æ B D G I L P S X *Forb* : ἡ ὑπόθεσις O W *Ald Mign*   94 σπουδάζων παίζων T   σπουδάζων] σπεύδων N   φαιδρυνόμενος *om.* N   παλλίστραις N   95 τι] τι ἐν N   ὀφθαλμοῖν *Ald Mign*   96 τῆς διαδοχῆς ὁ N   97 γήρως] γήρους *Ald Mign*   ἡλικίας] ἀληθείας M   ἦν] ἐστιν I M N O : ἐστὶν Æ B R T   98 εἶπε] εἶπε τῆς ἡλικίας οὔπω T[2]   99 ὑποχνοάζοντα Æ B C S[mg]   διὰ βάθους *om.* D   ὑποπιπλάμενον D[2] : ὑποπιμπλάμενου N[2]   100 παριῶν N Q   πάσχειν] *post* εἰκὸς *pon.* M : *post* μητέρα L   εἰκὸς] εἰκὸς ἦν *Ald Mign*   οἱονεὶ] οἵῳ Æ B I M N O Q R T W   101 τοῖς σπλάγχνοις] τὰ τῶν σπλάγχνῶν W   ἐγκαταφλέγεσθαι] ἐγκατακαίεσθαι M   102 θρῆνον] θρῆνον καὶ R   περιπλεκομένην] περιτηκομένον Æ B C I M N Q R[ac] T *Dion* : περιτηκομένην O   ἂν] ἐὰν B : ἐᾶν Æ ß I M R S T   ἐπισπεῦσαι] πιστεῦσαι T   103 αὐτῷ] αὐτῇ N   104 παρατείνουσαν] ἐπιτείνουσαν L   παρῆκεν ὁ λόγος] πεποίηκεν ὁ λέγων B[2]   αὐτὴν ὁ ἰησοῦς φησὶν] αὐτὴν φησὶν ὁ ἰησοῦς D G I L P O R S X : φησὶν αὐτὴν ὁ κύριος Æ : αὐτὴν φησὶν M : αὐτὴν φησὶν ὁ κύριος ἰησοῦς Q : αὐτὴν φησιν ὁ κύριος *Dion*   φησὶν *om.* B   105 βαστάσαντες *Ald Mign*   106 νεανίσκε] νεανία W *Ald Mign*   σοι λέγω νεανίσκε B D G L P S X   106–7 αὐτοῦ ζῶντα τῇ μητρὶ N   107 αὐτοῦ *om.* Æ B M N R T W   τοῦ νεκροῦ οὐκ ἐν ὀλίγῳ διαστήματι B   ἐν *om.* N   νεκροῦ *om.* T   γενομένου T   108 οὔπω Æ M N   παρὰ τοῦ] παρ᾽ αὐτοῦ *Ald Mign*   109 πρόσταγμα] πρᾶγμα S[pcmg]   ἴσον I M N P S X

certain city called Nain in Judaea; a certain widow there had an only child, no longer such a child as to be among boys but already passing from childhood to adulthood: the narrative calls him *a young man*.[92] The story describes a lot through a few words: the tale is a clear lamentation. It says the mother of the dead man was a *widow*. Do you see the weight of her misfortune, how the text sets out in a few words the tragedy of her suffering? For what does the word mean? That she had no more hope of childbearing, to heal the misfortune of his passing; for the woman was a widow, not able to look to another instead of him who had departed, for he was her only child. And how great an evil is this anyone may easily see who is not utterly estranged from nature. Him alone she had known in travail; him alone she had nursed at her breast; he alone made her table cheerful; he alone was the reason for brightness in her home, playing, studying, learning, beaming, in processions, in sports, in gatherings of youths; he alone was everything that is sweet and precious in a mother's eyes; now, arriving at the age of marriage, he was the scion of her stock, the shoot of its succession, the staff of her old age. Moreover, even the additional details of his time of life are another lament. Describing him as a *young man*, speaks of the flower of his faded beauty, as just producing the first growth of a beard, not yet with a full, thick beard, but still shining with the beauty of his cheeks. What, then, did his mother likely suffer for him? How would her heart be consumed, as it were, with fire? How bitterly would she prolong her lament over him, embracing the corpse lying before her, extending her lamentation for him as far as possible, so as not to hasten the funeral of the dead, but to be filled with sorrow! Nor does the narrative pass this by: for Jesus *seeing her*, it says, *had compassion; and he came and touched the bier; and the bearers stood still;* and he said to the one dead *'Young man, I say to you arise', and he delivered him alive to his mother*. There was not then but a short time since he had become dead, but was rather all but laid in the tomb; the miracle wrought by the Lord is greater, but the command the same.

[92] Cf. Luke 7:11–17.

[25.11] Ἔτι πρὸς τὸ ὑψηλότερον ἡ θαυματοποιΐα προέρχεται, ὡς ἂν μᾶλλον προσεγγίσειε τὰ φαινόμενα τῷ ἀπιστουμένῳ περὶ τὴν ἀνάστασιν θαύματι. [D] Ἀσθενεῖ τις τῶν συνήθων τῷ Κυρίῳ καὶ φίλων· Λάζαρος ὄνομα τῷ ἀσθενοῦντι· καὶ παραιτεῖται ὁ Κύριος τὴν τοῦ φίλου ἐπίσκεψιν, πόρρω τοῦ νοσοῦντος γενόμενος, ὡς ἂν εὕροι χώραν καὶ δύναμιν ἐν τῇ τῆς Ζωῆς ἀπουσίᾳ τὸ ἴδιον ἐργάσασθαι διὰ τῆς νόσου ὁ θάνατος· μηνύει τοῖς μαθηταῖς ὁ Κύριος κατὰ τὴν Γαλιλαίαν τὸ περὶ τὸν Λάζαρον πάθος· ἀλλὰ καὶ τὴν πρὸς αὐτὸν ὁρμὴν, ἐφ' ᾧ τε διαναστῆσαι τὸν κείμενον· περιδεεῖς δὲ ἦσαν ἐκεῖνοι διὰ τὴν τῶν Ἰουδαίων ὠμότητα, χαλεπὸν καὶ κινδυνῶδες ποιούμενοι τὸ πάλιν ἐπὶ τῆς Ἰουδαίας ἐν μέσῳ τῶν φονώντων γενέσθαι· καὶ διὰ τοῦτο μέλλοντες καὶ ἀναβαλλόμενοι, χρόνῳ ποιοῦνται τὴν ἀπὸ τῆς Γαλιλαίας ἐπάνοδον· κατεκράτει γὰρ ἡ ἐξουσία, καὶ ἤγοντο παρὰ τοῦ Κυρίου οἱ μαθηταὶ, οἱονεὶ τὰ προτέλεια τῆς καθολικῆς ἀναστάσεως ἐν Βηθανίᾳ μυηθησόμενοι. Τέσσαρες ἦσαν ἤδη μετὰ τὸ πάθος αἱ [221] ἡμέραι· πάντα πεπλήρωτο τῷ κατοιχομένῳ τὰ νομιζόμενα· τάφῳ κατεκρύβη τὸ σῶμα· ἐξῳδήκει κατὰ τὸ εἰκὸς ἤδη καὶ πρὸς διαφθορὰν διελύετο, μυδῶντος ἐν τῷ εὐρῶτι τῆς γῆς καὶ διαπίπτοντος ὑπ' ἀνάγκης τοῦ σώματος· φευκτὸν ἦν τὸ πρᾶγμα, βιαζομένης τῆς φύσεως τὸ διαλυθὲν εἰς δυσωδίαν ἀποδιδόναι πάλιν τῷ ζῆν. Τότε τὸ ἀπιστούμενον τῆς καθολικῆς ἀναστάσεως ἔργον δι' ἐναργεστέρου τοῦ θαύματος εἰς ἀπόδειξιν ἄγεται· οὐδὲ γὰρ ἐκ νόσου τις ἀνίσταται χαλεπῆς, οὐδὲ πρὸς ταῖς τελευταίαις ὢν ἀναπνοαῖς εἰς τὴν ζωὴν ἐπανάγεται, οὐδὲ παιδίον ἀρτιθανὲς ζωοποιεῖται, οὐδὲ μέλλων τῷ τάφῳ προσάγεσθαι νεανίας πάλιν ἐκ τῆς σοροῦ ἀναλύεται· ἀλλ' ἀνὴρ τῶν ἐξώρων, νεκρὸς, ἕωλος, ἐξῳδηκὼς, ἤδη καὶ λελυμένος, ὡς μηδὲ τοῖς ἐπιτηδείοις ἀνεκτὸν εἶναι τὸ προσεγγίσαι [B] τῷ τάφῳ τὸν Κύριον διὰ τὴν ἐγκειμένην ἀηδίαν τοῦ διαπεπτωκότος σώματος, μιᾷ κλήσει ζωοποιηθεὶς πιστοῦται τὸ κήρυγμα τῆς ἀναστάσεως, τουτέστι

111 *προσεγγίζοιεν* W   112 *ἀσθενεῖ*] *ἡ ἀσθενεί* Q : *ἠσθένει* *Ald Mign*   *συνήθει* B   *τοῦ κυρίου* D G P X   *καὶ om.* D G L P S X   114 *εὕρῃ* M   *ἀπὲργάσεσθαι* O : *ἐργάζεσθαι* W *Ald Mign*   115 *γαλιλαῖαν* N   116 *ὁρμὴν*] *ὁρμὴν ποιεῖται* R   *τε om.* I   *διαναστῆναι* B   117 *περιδεεῖς δὲ ἦσαν ἐκεῖνοι*] undique uero illi conuenerant *Eri*   *δὲ om.* B D G M P Q X   118 *ποιούμενοι*] *ἡγούμενοι* R   *ἐπὶ τῆς ἰουδαίας om.* N   *φονειτῶν* W : *φονευτῶν* M R$^{ac?}$ 119 *τοῦτο*] *τούτων* W   *ἀναβαλλόμενοι*] *ἀναβαλλόμενοι οὐ* R^{2} T   *χρόνῳ ποιοῦντα*] *ita* R^{2} W *Ald Mign Forb* : *χρονοποιοῦνται* B D G I O P R^{mg} X : *χρονοποιοῦσι* M   120 *κατεκράτει*] *ita* Æ B D G I L P Q R S T W X *Ald Forb* : *κατ' ἐκράτει* N : *κατεκρατήθη* M : *κατεκράθη* *Mign*   *παρὰ*] *ὑπὸ* M R   *οἱ μαθηταὶ παρὰ τοῦ κυρίου* R   121 *πρωτόλεια* I P^{2} R^{ac} : *πρωτέλεια* R^{2} *μυηθησόμενοι*] disciturі *Eri*   122 *ἤδη ἦσαν* R   *ἤδη om.* B T   *αἱ om.* D L R   *πεπλήρωτο*] *ἀπεπλήρωτο* D G P X : *πεπλήρωται* M   123 *τὸ σῶμα om.* B   *ἐξῳδήκει κατὰ τὸ εἰκὸς*] exterius quantum consequens erat apparet *Eri*   124 *πρὸς*] *εἰς* B   *διαφθορὰν*] *φθορὰν* D G I L O P S X   *διελέλυτο* G P S X   125 *ὑπ'*] *ὑπὸ* Æ ß N R W : *ὑπὸ τῆς* M   *φευκτέον* Æ B O Q T   126 *ἀποδιδόναι πάλιν τῷ ζῆν*] *ἀποδοῦναι* M : *om.* Æ B N Q R^{ac} T W *Dion Eri*   *τῷ*] *τὸ* G L X   127 *ἐνεργεστέρου* ß G M P S T W X *Ald*   128 *οὐδὲ*] *οὐ* Æ B I M N O Q R T W   *τις*] *τινὸς* N   *ἀνίσταται*] *ἀπανίσταται* Æ B I O   *χαλαιπῆς* W   129 *μέλλων*] *ὁ μέλλων* B   130–1 *ἀνὴρ—ἐξῳδηκὼς*] uir praematurus putrescens atque defluens *Dion* : uir extra quod consequens erat transiens *Eri*   130 *τῶν ἐξώρων*] *ἔξωρος* I   *νεκρὸς om.* M   131 *ἕωλος*] *αἴολος* N : *om.* M   *ἐξοιδηκὼς* G N R^{ac} X : *ἐξωδικὼς* Q   *ἤδη καὶ λελυμένος om.* I   *λελυμένος*] *διαλελυμένος* Æ   *εἶναι*] *εἶναι συγχωρῆσαι* Æ R   131–2 *τὸ προσεγγίσαι*] *ita* Æ B I M N O Q R S^{2} T W *Forb* : *πρὸς τὸ ἐγγίσαι* G L P S^{ac} X : *προσεγγίσαι* *Ald Mign*

[**25.11**] His wonder-working proceeds to a still more exalted act, that the phenomena may more closely approach the doubted miracle concerning the resurrection. One of the Lord's companions and friends is ill; Lazarus is the sick man's name; and the Lord declines visiting his friend, being far away from the sick man, that in the absence of the Life, death might find room and power to do his own work through the disease.[93] In Galilee the Lord informs his disciples of the suffering of Lazarus, but also of his own setting out to him, to raise up the one laid low. They were very afraid on account of the cruelty of the Jews, thinking it a difficult and dangerous matter to be again in Judaea, in the midst of those seeking to kill him. And thus, tarrying and delaying, they in time made their return from Galilee, for his authority prevailed; and the disciples were led by the Lord to be initiated in Bethany in the preliminary mysteries, as it were, of the general resurrection. Four days had already passed since the calamity; all the customary rites had been performed for the departed; the body was hidden in the tomb—it was probably already swollen and dissolving into corruption, as the body mouldered in the dank earth and necessarily decomposed. It would be a repulsive thing were nature compelled to bring back to life what was already dissolving into a foul smell. Then the doubted work of the general resurrection is brought to proof by a more manifest miracle: someone is not raised from severe sickness, nor brought back to life when at the very last breath, nor is a child just dead brought to life, nor a young man about to be taken to the tomb released from his bier, but a man past the prime of life—a corpse, rotten, swollen, and already decomposed, so that not even his close friends could bear for the Lord to draw near the tomb because of the odiousness of the body lying there—being brought to life by a single call: this

[93] Cf. John 11.

τὸ ἐπὶ τοῦ κοινοῦ προσδοκώμενον, ὃ ἐπὶ μέρους τῇ πείρᾳ ἐμάθομεν· καθάπερ γὰρ ἐν τῇ τοῦ παντὸς ἀναστοιχειώσει, φησὶν ὁ ἀπόστολος, **αὐτὸν καταβήσεσθαι τὸν Κύριον ἐν κελεύσματι, ἐν φωνῇ ἀρχαγγέλου**, καὶ διὰ σάλπιγγος εἰς ἀφθαρσίαν τοὺς νεκροὺς διαναστήσειν· οὕτω καὶ νῦν οἷόν τινα ὕπνον τὸν θάνατον τῇ φωνῇ τοῦ προστάγματος ὁ ἐν τῷ τάφῳ ἀποσεισάμενος, καὶ ἀποτινάξας ἑαυτοῦ τὴν ἐπιγενομένην διαφθορὰν τῇ νεκρότητι, ἄρτιος καὶ σῶος τοῦ τάφου ἐξάλλεται, μηδὲ τῷ δεσμῷ τῶν περὶ τοὺς πόδας καὶ τὰς χεῖρας κειριῶν κωλυθεὶς πρὸς τὴν ἔξοδον.

[25.12] [C] Ἆρα μικρὰ ταῦτα πρὸς πίστιν τῆς τῶν νεκρῶν ἀναστάσεως; ἢ ζητεῖς καὶ δι᾽ ἑτέρων βεβαιωθῆναί σοι τὴν περὶ τούτου κρίσιν; ἀλλά μοι δοκεῖ μὴ μάτην τοῖς κατὰ Καπερναοὺμ εἰρηκέναι, ὡς ἐκ προσώπου τῶν ἀνθρώπων ὁ Κύριος τοῦτο πρὸς ἑαυτὸν λέγων· **πάντως ἐρεῖτέ μοι τὴν παραβολὴν ταύτην, ἰατρέ, θεράπευσον σεαυτόν·** ἔδει γὰρ ἐν ἑτέροις σώμασι προσεθίσαντα τοὺς ἀνθρώπους τῷ κατὰ τὴν ἀνάστασιν θαύματι, ἐν τῷ καθ᾽ ἑαυτὸν ἀνθρώπῳ βεβαιῶσαι τὸν λόγον. Εἶδες ἐν ἑτέροις ἐνεργὸν τὸ κήρυγμα—τοὺς τεθνήξεσθαι μέλλοντας, τὸ παιδίον τὸ τοῦ ζῆν ἄρτι παυσάμενον, τὸν πρὸς τῷ τάφῳ νεανίαν, τὸν διεφθορότα νεκρόν, πάντας κατὰ τὸ ἶσον ἑνὶ προστάγματι πρὸς τὴν ζωὴν ἀναλύοντας. Ζητεῖς καὶ τοὺς διὰ τραυμάτων καὶ αἵματος ἐν τῷ θανάτῳ γεγονότας, μή τις ἐπὶ τούτων ἀτονία τῆς [D] ζωοποιοῦ δυνάμεως κωλύει τὴν χάριν; ἴδε τὸν ἐν ἥλοις διαπερονηθέντα τὰς χεῖρας· ἴδε τὸν τὴν πλευρὰν λόγχῃ διαπαρέντα· διένεγκε τοὺς δακτύλους σου διὰ τοῦ τύπου τῶν ἥλων· ἔμβαλε τὴν χεῖρά σου τῷ ἐκ τῆς λόγχης τραύματι· στοχάζῃ πάντως ἐπὶ πόσον εἰκὸς ἦν εἰς τὸ ἐντὸς τὴν αἰχμὴν διαδῦναι, διὰ τοῦ πλάτους τῆς ὠτειλῆς τὴν ἐπὶ τὸ ἔσω πάροδον λογιζόμενος· ἡ γὰρ εἴσοδον χειρὸς ἀνθρωπίνης χωρήσασα πληγή, πόσον ἐντὸς τοῦ βάθους γενέσθαι τὸν σίδηρον ὑποδείκνυσιν. Εἰ οὖν οὗτος ἐγήγερται, [224] εὔκολον ἂν εἴη τὸ ἀποστολικὸν ἐπιφθέγξασθαι, **πῶς λέγουσί τινες ὅτι ἀνάστασις νεκρῶν οὐκ ἔστιν;**

134 τοῦ *om.* R τῆς πείρας Æ B I M O Q R^{ac} T : διὰ τῆς πείρας N 136 ἀρχαγγέλου] ἀγγέλου Q τοὺς νεκροὺς εἰς ἀφθαρσίαν D G L M P Q S X 137 διαναστῆσαι M : διανίστησιν Æ I N O : ἀναστήσεσθαι B 138 ἀποτεινάξας G I Q X : ἀποτιναξάμενος L ἐπιγενομένην] *ita* Æ D G I L N O P Q R S X *Forb* : ἐπιγινομένην W *Ald Mign* 139 σῶος] σῶος ἐκ Q τῶν δεσμῶν D G P R^{2} S W X 139–40 τῶν … κειριῶν] τῷ … περικειμένῳ M 140 τὰς χεῖρας καὶ τοὺς πόδας B M κειριῶν] κειρίων Æ ß G^{mg} I L R^{2} : τενίων Q : ταινιῶν N$^{2?}$ P^{ac} R^{pc} : τενείων G X : ταινικως R$^{ac?}$ κωλυθεὶς] κωλυόντων D G L P S X 141 ταῦτα] ταῦτα τὰ B : ταῦτα ἐστιν N ἢ] *ita* Æ B D I L M N O P R S T W X *Forb* : εἰ *Eri Mign* 142 τούτου] τούτων L M μὴ] μηδέ D G L P S X 143 καπερναοὺμ] *ita* ß I L M N O P Q R S T^{2} X *Forb* : καπαρναοὺμ G : φαρναοὺμ Æ *Ald* : καφαρναοὺμ W *Mign* 143–4 πρὸς ἑαυτον τοῦτο D G L P S X 144 ἑαυτὸν] σὲ αὐτὸν L 145 προεθίσαντα M : προσεθίσαντας Q : propagantem *Eri* 146 θαύματι *om.* W τῷ καθ᾽ ἑαυτὸν ἀνθρώπῳ] τῇ ἰδίᾳ σαρκὶ καθ᾽ ἑαυτὸν Æ B I O ἀνθρώπῳ] ὑποδείγματι D E G L P R^{pc} X : ὑποδείγματι ἀνθρώπῳ W : ἀνθρώπῳ ὑποδείγματι T 146–7 εἶδες—κήρυγμα] multis specierum modis praedicationem *Dion* ἐνεργὸν ἐν ἑτέροις R 147 ἐνεργῶν L : ἐνεργὼν G : ἔργον Q τοῦ … μέλλοντος N T τεθνήξασθαι D τὸ^{2} *om.* R 148 τὸν πρὸς τῷ τάφῳ] πρὸς τὸν τάφον W διαφθαρέντα D G P T X πάντα D 149 ἴσον I M N P S X ἑνὶ] ἐν D G P X ἀναλύοντος D P : ἀναλύσαντας Æ B I R^{2} 150 τούτων] τούτῳ B 151 κωλύει] *ita* Æ B D G I L M O P Q R S T W X *Forb* : κωλύσῃ N : λύῃ *Ald Mign* ἴδε] *ita* Æ B D G I L M O P Q R S W X *Forb* : *om.* N : εἶδε *Ald Mign* ἐν *om.* T ἴδε] *ita* Æ B D G I L M N O P Q R S W X *Forb* : εἶδε *Ald Mign* 151–2 τῇ πλευρᾷ R 152 λόγχῃ] τῇ λόγχῃ T τοῦ τύπου] *ita* Æ B D G I M N O P Q R X *Forb* : τῶν τύπων S W *Ald Mign* 153 τῷ] τῷ ἐκ τῷ B (*non* ß) τῆς *om.* D G P X στοχάζει W πόσον] *ita* Æ B D G M N O P Q R S X *Forb Ald* : πόσων *Mign* 154 διαδύναι B L R O : διάδοῦναι N τὴν *om.* T 155 ἀνθρωπίνης χειρὸς N O χωρίσασα P πληγῇ N 156 τοῦ βάθους *om.* M γενέσθαι τοῦ βάθους N βάθους *om.* T γενέσθαι] γεγενῆσθαι *Ald Mign* τὸν σίδηρον γενέσθαι D I L οὖν *om.* N οὗτος] αὐτὸς O 157 εὔκολον] εὔραιρον Æ B E^{mg} N Q R^{pc} T W εὔκολον—ἐπιφθέγξασθαι *om.* I O εὐποφθέγξασθαι W

confirms the proclamation of the resurrection, that is, that which is expected as general, which we learn by the experience of a part. For just as in the reconstitution of all things, the Apostle says that *the Lord himself will descend with a shout, with the voice of the archangel,*[94] and by a trumpet raise up the dead to incorruptibility, so too now the one in the tomb shakes off death at the voice of the command, as if it were a sleep, shaking off from himself the corruption that had come upon him by the process of death, leaping out from the tomb whole and sound, not hindered in his departure by the bonds of the grave-cloths round his feet and hands.

[25.12] Are these things too small for faith in the resurrection of the dead? Or do you seek that your determination about this should be confirmed by yet other proofs? But it seems to me that the Lord did not speak in vain to those in Capernaum, when, as in the person of human beings, he said to himself, *You will surely say to me this proverb: Physician heal yourself.*[95] For it was right, after accustoming humans to the miracle of the resurrection in other bodies, to confirm the word in the human being that is himself. You saw the proclamation effective in others—those about to die, the child who had just ceased to live, the young man near the grave, the putrefying corpse, all alike released to life by one command. Do you seek for those who have come to death by wounds and bloodshed, in case any feebleness of the life-giving power hinders the grace? Behold him whose hands were pierced with nails; behold him whose side was transfixed with a spear; pass your fingers through the print of the nails; thrust your hand into the wound from the spear[96]—you can surely guess how far within it is likely the point would reach, if you reckon the passage inwards by the breadth of the wound, for the wound that grants entry to a human hand indicates to what depth the iron entered. If, then, he has been raised, well may the Apostle's words be exclaimed: *How say some that there is no resurrection of the dead?*[97]

[94] 1 Thess. 4:16. [95] Luke 4:23. [96] Cf. John 20:27. [97] 1 Cor. 15:12.

[25.13] *Ἐπειδὴ τοίνυν πᾶσα μὲν πρόρρησις τοῦ Κυρίου διὰ τῆς τῶν γεγονότων μαρτυρίας ἀληθὴς ἐπιδείκνυται, τοῦτο δὲ οὐ λόγῳ μεμαθήκαμεν μόνον ἀλλ' ἐξ αὐτῶν τῶν ἐπὶ τὴν ζωὴν ἐξ ἀναστάσεως ἐπανελθόντων, ἔργῳ τὴν ἀπόδειξιν τῆς ἐπαγγελίας ἐλάβομεν· τίς ὑπολείπεται τοῖς μὴ πιστεύουσιν ἀφορμή; οὐκ ἐρρῶσθαι φράσαντες τοῖς* ***διὰ τῆς φιλοσοφίας καὶ κενῆς ἀπάτης*** *παρακρουομένοις τὴν ἀκατάσκευον πίστιν, ψιλῆς ἑξόμεθα τῆς ὁμολογίας, μαθόντες ἐν ὀλίγῳ διὰ τοῦ προφήτου τὸν τρόπον τῆς χάριτος, δι' ὧν φησιν·* ***ἀντανελεῖς τὸ πνεῦμα αὐτῶν, καὶ ἐκλείψουσι, καὶ εἰς τὸν χοῦν αὐτῶν ἐπιστρέψουσιν· ἐξαποστελεῖς τὸ Πνεῦμά σου, καὶ κτισθήσονται,*** [B] ***καὶ ἀνακαινιεῖς τὸ πρόσωπον τῆς γῆς·*** *ὅτε καὶ* ***εὐφραίνεσθαι τὸν Κύριον ἐπὶ τοῖς ἔργοις αὐτοῦ*** *λέγει,* ***ἐκλειπόντων τῶν ἁμαρτωλῶν ἀπὸ τῆς γῆς·*** *πῶς γάρ τις ἐξ ἁμαρτίας ὀνομασθήσεται, τῆς ἁμαρτίας οὐκ οὔσης;*

Ὅτι οὐκ ἔξω τοῦ εἰκότος ἡ ἀνάστασις.

[26.1] *Ἀλλ' εἰσί τινες οἳ διὰ τὴν τῶν ἀνθρωπίνων λογισμῶν ἀτονίαν πρὸς τὰ ἡμέτερα μέτρα τὴν θείαν δύναμιν κρίνοντες, τὸ ἡμῖν ἀχώρητον οὐδὲ Θεῷ δυνατὸν* [C] *εἶναι κατασκευάζουσι. Δεικνύουσι γὰρ τῶν τε ἀρχαίων νεκρῶν τὸν ἀφανισμόν, τῶν τε διὰ πυρὸς ἀποτεφρωθέντων τὰ λείψανα, καὶ ἔτι πρὸς τούτοις τὰ σαρκοβόρα τῶν ζώων τῷ λόγῳ προφέρουσι, καὶ τὸν ἰχθὺν τῷ ἰδίῳ σώματι τὴν σάρκα τοῦ ναυαγήσαντος ἀναλαβόντα, καὶ τοῦτον πάλιν τροφὴν ἀνθρώπων γενόμενον καὶ εἰς τὸν τοῦ βεβρωκότος ὄγκον μετακεχωρηκότα διὰ τῆς πέψεως· καὶ πολλὰ τοιαῦτα μικροπρεπῆ καὶ τῆς μεγάλης τοῦ Θεοῦ δυνάμεως καὶ ἐξουσίας ἀνάξια ἐπ' ἀνατροπῇ τοῦ δόγματος διεξέρχονται, ὡς οὐ δυναμένου τοῦ Θεοῦ διὰ τῶν αὐτῶν πάλιν ὁδῶν δι' ἀναλύσεως ἀποκαταστῆσαι τῷ ἀνθρώπῳ τὸ ἴδιον.* [26.2] *Ἀλλ' ἡμεῖς ἐν ὀλίγῳ τὰς μακρὰς αὐτῶν τῆς λογικῆς ματαιότητος περιδρομὰς ὑποτεμνόμεθα,* [D] *ὁμολογοῦντες τὴν μὲν διάλυσιν τοῦ σώματος εἰς τὰ ἐξ ὧν συνέστηκε, γίνεσθαι, καὶ οὐ μόνον τὴν γῆν κατὰ τὸν θεῖον λόγον εἰς τὴν γῆν ἀναλύεσθαι, ἀλλὰ καὶ τὸν ἀέρα καὶ τὸ ὑγρὸν προσχωρεῖν τῷ ὁμοφύλῳ, καὶ ἑκάστου τῶν ἐν ἡμῖν πρὸς τὸ συγγενὲς τὴν μεταχώρησιν γίνεσθαι, κἂν τοῖς σαρκοβόροις ὀρνέοις, κἂν τοῖς ὠμοτάτοις θηρίοις*

159 *μὲν om.* I 160 *ἀλλ'*] *ita* Æ B D G I N O P Q R T W X *Forb* : *ἀλλὰ καὶ* S *Ald Mign* 161 *ἐπαγγελίας*] *ἀληθείας* N 162 *λάβωμεν* R[ac] *πιστεύσασιν* N *οὐκ*] *οἷς* S *ἐρρῶσθαι*] *ita codd. Ald Forb* : *ἐρρῶσθαι οὖν* I : *ἔρρωσθε Mign* *φράσασι* M 163 *τοῖς om.* B *τῆς om.* L S *ἀκατάσκευον*] simplicitatem *Dion* : imperfectam *Eri* 164 *πίστιν*] *πίστιν ἀγαπήσωμεν καὶ* Q *ψιλῆς*] purissimam *Dion* : nudam *Eri* *ἑξώμεθα* I : *δεξώμεθα* R[ac] 165 *ὧν*] *οὗ* M 166 *αὐτῶν*] *αὐτὸν* M 168 *ἐκλιπόντων* M *τῶν om.* B M

Cap. 27 Æ ß I N O Q R T *Dion* : *def. Eri*

1 *ὅτι—ἀνάστασις*] quod quantumcunque absumptum fuerit corpus humanum facile illud colligat potentia diuina *Λ* 2 *οἳ*] *οἱ Mign* *ἀτονίαν*] *ἀσθένειαν ἀτονεῖν* M 3 *κρίνοντες δύναμιν* R *ἡμῖν*] *ἡμῖν ὂν* R *ἀχώρητον*] *ἀδύνατον* M 4 *δείκνυσι* Q *τε om.* L 5 *πυρὸς*] *τοῦ πυρὸς* Q *ἀποτεφρωθέντων*] *τεφρωθέντων* D G L P S X 6 *τῷ λόγῳ om.* N *προσφέρουσι* Æ[ac] D I O Q R[ac] *τῷ*] *ἐν τῷ* R *ἰδίῳ*] *οἰκείῳ* D G L M P Q S X 7 *ἀναλαμβάνοντα* Æ ß I O : *ἀπολαβόντα* R 8 *βεβρωκότος*] *πεπτωκότος* G P 9 *σμικροπρεπῆ* B I *καὶ ἐξουσίας om.* B 10 *διεξέρχονται*] *ἐξέρχονται* B *πάλιν διὰ τῶν αὐτῶν* W *Ald Mign* 11 *ἀποκαταστῆναι* B *τὸ om.* Æ *ἐν ὀλίγῳ*] *ἑνὶ λόγῳ* B I O T 12 *μικρὰς* M R[ac] *τῆς λογικῆς αὐτῶν* I *λογικῆς*] *πιθανῆς* Æ B I O *ὑποτεμνώμεθα Mign* 13 *ὁμολογοῦμεν* I *μὲν om.* I *γενέσθαι* ß Q 16 *γενέσθαι* N Q : *γίγνεσθαι Ald Mign* *κἂν*[1]] *καὶ* N *ὠμοτάτοις*] *ὠμοῖς* R

[**25.13**] Since, then, every prediction of the Lord is shown to be true by the testimony of events, while we have not only learnt this by word, but also received, from those very people who have returned to life by resurrection, the proof of the promise in deed, what occasion is left to those who disbelieve? Shall we not bid farewell to those who, *by philosophy and vain deceit*,[98] pervert the unartificial faith, and hold fast the simple confession,[99] learning in brief from the prophet the mode of the grace through what he says: *You take away their breath, and they die, and return to the earth; you send forth your Spirit and they will be created, and you will renew the face of the earth*, at which time, he says, *the Lord rejoices in his works, sinners having perished from the earth*;[100] for how will anyone be called by the name of sin, when sin does not exist?

That the resurrection is not beyond probability.[101]

[**26.1**] There are, however, some who, through the feebleness of human reasoning, assessing the divine power by our own measure, maintain that what is beyond our capacity is not possible even to God.[102] They point to the disappearance of the dead of old, and to the remains of those reduced to ashes by fire; and further, besides these, they bring forward in idea the carnivorous beasts, and the fish that takes into its own body the flesh of one shipwrecked, while this again becomes food for human beings and passes, by digestion, into the bulk of the one who eats it. And they rehearse many such petty things, unworthy of the great power and authority of God, to overthrow of the doctrine, as though God were not able, once again by the same means, to restore to the human being his own. [**26.2**] But we briefly cut short their long convolutions of logical folly by acknowledging that the dissolution of the body into its component parts does take place, and not only does the earth, according to the divine Word, depart to the earth,[103] but the air and the moisture also revert to their kind, and there takes place the withdrawal of each element in us to its kind; and even if the human body becomes mingled with the

[98] Col. 2:8. [99] Cf. Heb. 10:23. [100] Ps. 103.29–30, 31, 35.

[101] *Bodl. 238* (as Chap. 27): 'That however much the human body may have been consumed, the divine power can easily bring it together'. For this chapter, cf. Athenagoras, *De res.* 3–8.

[102] Cf. Methodius, *De res.* 2.29 (Bonwetsch, 386). [103] Cf. Gen. 3:19.

ἀναμιχθῇ τὸ ἀνθρώπινον σῶμα διὰ τῆς βρώσεως, κἂν ὑπὸ τὸν ὀδόντα τῶν ἰχθύων ἔλθῃ, κἂν εἰς ἀτμοὺς καὶ κόνιν μεταβληθῇ τῷ πυρί· ὅπου δ' ἄν τις καθ' ὑπόθεσιν περιενέγκῃ τῷ λόγῳ τὸν ἄνθρωπον, ἐντὸς τοῦ κόσμου πάντως ἐστί· τοῦτον δὲ τῇ χειρὶ τοῦ Θεοῦ περικρατεῖσθαι ἡ θεόπνευστος διδάσκει φωνή· εἰ οὖν σύ τι τῶν ἐν τῇ σῇ παλάμῃ οὐκ ἀγνοεῖς, ἆρ' οἴει τῆς σῆς δυνάμεως [225] *ἀτονωτέραν εἶναι τὴν τοῦ Θεοῦ γνῶσιν, ὡς μὴ ἂν ἐξευρεῖν τῶν ἐμπεριεχομένων ὑπὸ τῆς θείας σπιθαμῆς τὴν ἀκρίβειαν;*

Ὅτι δυνατόν ἐστιν εἰς τὰ τοῦ παντὸς στοιχεῖα τοῦ ἀνθρωπίνου σώματος ἀναλυθέντος, πάλιν ἐκ τοῦ κοινοῦ τὸ ἴδιον ἑκάστῳ ἀποσωθῆναι.

[27.1] *Ἀλλὰ τυχὸν πρὸς τὰ στοιχεῖα τοῦ παντὸς βλέπων, δύσκολον οἴει, τοῦ ἐν ἡμῖν ἀέρος πρὸς τὸ συγγενὲς στοιχεῖον ἀναχεθέντος, καὶ τοῦ θερμοῦ τε καὶ ὑγροῦ καὶ τοῦ γεώδους ὡσαύτως τοῖς ὁμοφύλοις ἐγκαταμιχθέντων, πάλιν ἐκ τοῦ κοινοῦ τὸ οἰκεῖον ἐπὶ τὸ ἴδιον* [B] *ἀναδραμεῖν.* [27.2] *Εἶτα οὐ λογίζῃ διὰ τῶν ἀνθρωπίνων ὑποδειγμάτων, τὸ μηδὲ τοῦτο τῆς θείας δυνάμεως ὑπερβαίνειν τοὺς ὅρους; εἶδές που πάντως ἐν ταῖς ἀνθρωπίναις οἰκήσεσι κοινὴν ἀγέλην ζώων τινῶν, ἐκ κοινοῦ συνισταμένην· ἀλλ' ὅταν πάλιν πρὸς τοὺς κεκτημένους αὐτὴ καταμερίζηται, ἥτε πρὸς τοὺς οἰκείους συνήθεια καὶ τὰ ἐπικείμενα σημεῖα τὸ ἴδιον ἑκάστῳ ἀποκαθίστησι· τοιοῦτόν τι καὶ περὶ σεαυτὸν ἐννοῶν, οὐχ ἁμαρτήσεις τοῦ πρέποντος· φυσικῇ γάρ τινι σχέσει καὶ στοργῇ πρὸς τὸ συνοικῆσαν σῶμα τῆς ψυχῆς διακειμένης, ἐστί τις κατὰ τὸ λεληθὸς αὐτῇ διὰ τῆς συνανακράσεως τοῦ οἰκείου σχέσις τε καὶ ἐπίγνωσις, οἷον σημείων τινῶν παρὰ τῆς φύσεως ἐπικειμένων δι' ὧν ἡ κοινότης* [C] *ἀσύγχυτος μένει, διακρινομένη τοῖς ἰδιάζουσι· τῆς τοίνυν ψυχῆς τὸ συγγενές τε καὶ ἴδιον ἐφ' ἑαυτὴν πάλιν ἑλκούσης, τίς πόνος, εἰπέ μοι, τῇ θείᾳ δυνάμει κωλῦσαι τῶν οἰκείων τὴν συνδρομήν, ἀρρήτῳ τινὶ τῇ τῆς φύσεως ὁλκῇ πρὸς τὸ ἴδιον ἐπειγομένων; τὸ γὰρ ἐπιδιαμένειν τινὰ τῇ ψυχῇ, καὶ μετὰ τὴν διάλυσιν, σημεῖα τοῦ ἡμετέρου συγκρίματος δείκνυσιν ὁ κατὰ τὸν ᾄδην*

17 *διὰ τῆς—ἰχθύων*] *κἂν διὰ τῆς βρώσεως τῶν ἰχθύων ὑπὸ τὸν ὀδόντα* D L P S X : *κἂν διὰ τῆς κέφαλος* G *τῶν ὀδόντων* Q *ἰχθύων*] *θηρίων* T 18 *δ'*] *γὰρ* N Q 19 *τῷ λόγῳ* *om.* O *τοῦτο* M *τῇ*] *ἐν τῇ* M 20 *φωνή*] *γραφή* D E O[ac] P R S X 21 *ἆρα* Æ I N O : *ἄρα* R 21–2 *τοῦ θεοῦ τὴν* I

Cap. 28 Æ I N O Q R *Dion* : *def. Eri*

1–2 *ὅτι—ἀποσωθῆναι*] quod quamuis communiter resurgant corpora proprias tamen animas recipient *Λ* 1 *δυνατόν*] *ἀδύνατον* W X *ἐστιν om.* Q *ἀνθρωπείου* D E L P S X 2 *ἑκάστῳ τὸ ἴδιον Ald Mign* *ἀνασωθῆναι* L : *σωθῆναι* M 3 *ἀλλὰ—καθ' ὑπτίου* (*l.* 48) *def.* N, *folio avulso* *ἀποβλέπων* I 4 *ἀναχθέντος* B D E[ac] (*ε sup. l.*) I R W : *ἀνενεχθέντος* L : *ἀναλυθέντος* M *τε om.* T *τοῦ om.* R 5 *ἐκ τοῦ κοινοῦ πάλιν* Æ ß I O R 5–6 *τὸ ἴδιον ἐπὶ τὸ οἰκεῖον* Æ B I M Q R T 7 *τὸ om.* X 8 *οἰκήσεσι* X[pc] *ζώων τινῶν om.* M *Dion Eri* 9 *πρὸς τοὺς κεκτημένους πάλιν* D E *αὐτὴ πρὸς τοὺς κεκτημένους πάλιν* L P S X *αὐτὴ*] *αὐτὴν* M : *αὕτη* ß I L P S X : *αὐτῇ* R[ac] (*corr. a pr. m*) : *om.* D E *καταμερίζεται* Æ Q R[ac] (*corr. a pr. m*) : *καταμερίζῃ* L : *ἀναμερίζηται* M 10 *οἰκείους*] *ita* Æ B D E M O P Q R S T X *Forb* : *οἴκους Ald Mign* *συνήθεις* B : *συγγένεια* W *ἑκάστῳ*] *ἑκάστῳ* 11 *ἀποκαθίστω* T *τοιοῦτό* Æ L O *περὶ*] *τὸ περὶ* B *σαυτὸν* D L P X : *σαὐτὸν* S : *ἑαυτὸν* B *ἁμαρτήσῃ* Æ I O Q T 12 *τινι*] *τι* B *σχέσει*] uinculo *Dion* : coniunctione *Eri* 13 *τις*] *τι* O *συνανακράσεως*] *νῦν ἀνακράσεως* B I M Q T *Dion Eri* 14 *τινῶν σημείων* D E L P S X *Dion Eri* *παρὰ*] *περὶ* B 16 *ἐφ'*] *πρὸς* B *ἑαυτὴν*] *αὐτὴν* Q : *ἑαυτῆς* D E T *πάλιν om.* O 17 *δυνάμει*] *δυνάμει μὴ* Æ B I R T *Dion Eri* *κωλῦσαι* I P R : *κωλύσας* L *οἰκείων*] *οἰκείων ἁπάντων* I *τῇ*[2] *om.* Æ D E I L M O R[2] S T *τῆς om.* L S 18–19 *τῇ ψυχῇ σημεῖα τινα καὶ μετὰ τὴν διάλυσιν* I

carnivorous birds or with the most savage beasts by becoming their food, and even if it passes through the teeth of fish, and even if it be changed by fire into vapour and dust, wherever one may by hypothesis carry off in idea the human being, he surely remains in the world, and the world, the inspired voice teaches, is held in the hand of God. If, then, you are not ignorant of any of the things in the palm of your hand, do you think that the knowledge of God is feebler than your own power, that it should not discover the most minuscule of things encompassed by the divine span?

That it is possible, when the human body is dissolved into the elements of the universe, for what belongs to each to be saved from the common [pool].[104]

[27.1] But perhaps, looking at the elements of the universe, you think it a difficult thing, once the air in us has been dispersed into its kindred element, and the warmth, and the moisture, and the earthy have similarly been mingled with their own kind, that from the common source there should return to the particular what is proper to it. [27.2] Do you not reckon, then, that, from human examples, even this does not surpass the limits of divine power? You have surely seen somewhere among human habitations a common herd of some animals, collected from every quarter; but when it is divided again among its owners, familiarity with their homes and the marks put upon them restores to each his own. If you understand yourself also as something like this, you will not stray from what is fitting; for as the soul is disposed by a certain natural relation and care for the body wedded to it, there is hidden in it, by virtue of their commixture, a certain relation to and recognition of its own, as though some marks had been placed upon it by nature, by means of which the commonality remains unconfused, separated by the identifying signs. As, then, the soul attracts again to itself what is its kin and its own, what toil, tell me, for the divine power would hinder the concurrence of kindred things, when they are urged on to their own by a certain ineffable attraction of nature? For that some signs of our compound remain in the souls

[104] *Bodl. 238* (as Chap. 28): 'That although bodies rise together they will however receive their own souls'. For Chapter 27, see Gregory of Nyssa, *An et. res.* 1.8–10; 5.4–23 (Spira, 7.11–20; 52.20–57.20).

διάλογος, τῶν μὲν σωμάτων τῷ τάφῳ παραδοθέντων, γνωρίσματος δέ τινος σωματικοῦ ταῖς ψυχαῖς παραμείναντος, δι' οὗ καὶ ὁ Λάζαρος ἐγνωρίζετο καὶ οὐκ ἠγνοεῖτο ὁ πλούσιος.

[27.3] Οὐκοῦν οὐδὲν ἔξω τοῦ εἰκότος ἐστὶ, πάλιν πιστεύειν ἐκ τοῦ κοινοῦ πρὸς τὸ ἴδιον τὴν ἀνάλυσιν γίνεσθαι τῶν ἀνισταμένων σωμάτων, καὶ μάλιστά γε τῷ φιλοπονώτερον τὴν φύσιν ἡμῶν κατεξετάζοντι. [D] Οὔτε γὰρ δι' ὅλου ἐν ῥύσει καὶ μεταβολῇ τὸ ἡμέτερον—ἦ γὰρ ἂν ἄληπτον ἦν καθόλου τὸ μηδεμίαν στάσιν ἔχον ἐκ φύσεως—ἀλλὰ κατὰ τὸν ἀκριβέστερον λόγον, τὸ μέν τι ἕστηκε τῶν ἐν ἡμῖν, τὸ δὲ δι' ἀλλοιώσεως πρόεισιν· ἀλλοιοῦται μὲν γὰρ δι' αὐξήσεώς τε καὶ μειώσεως τὸ σῶμα, οἷον ἱμάτιά τινα τὰς καθεξῆς ἡλικίας μετενδυόμενον· ἕστηκε δὲ διὰ πάσης τροπῆς ἀμετάβλητον ἐφ' ἑαυτοῦ τὸ εἶδος, τῶν ἅπαξ ἐπιβληθέντων αὐτῷ παρὰ τῆς φύσεως σημείων οὐκ ἐξιστάμενον, ἀλλὰ πάσαις ταῖς κατὰ τὸ σῶμα τροπαῖς μετὰ τῶν ἰδίων ἐμφαινόμενον γνωρισμάτων. [27.4] Ὑπεξαιρείσθω δὲ τοῦ λόγου ἡ ἐκ πάθους ἀλλοίωσις, ἡ τῷ εἴδει ἐπισυμβαίνουσα· οἷον γάρ τι προσωπεῖον ἀλλότριον ἡ κατὰ τὴν νόσον ἀμορφία διαλαμβάνει τὸ εἶδος, [228] ἧς τῷ λόγῳ περιαιρεθείσης, καθάπερ ἐπὶ Νεεμὰν τοῦ Σύρου ἢ ἐπὶ τῶν κατὰ τὸ εὐαγγέλιον ἱστορηθέντων, πάλιν τὸ κεκρυμμένον ὑπὸ τοῦ πάθους εἶδος διὰ τῆς ὑγείας ἐν τοῖς ἰδίοις ἀνεφάνη γνωρίσμασι.

[27.5] Τῷ τοίνυν θεοειδεῖ τῆς ψυχῆς οὐ τὸ ῥέον ἐν τῇ ἀλλοιώσει καὶ μεθιστάμενον, ἀλλὰ τὸ μονιμόν τε καὶ ὡσαύτως [B] ἔχον ἐν τῷ καθ' ἡμᾶς συγκρίματι, τοῦτο προσφύεται· καὶ ἐπειδὴ τὰς κατὰ τὸ εἶδος διαφορὰς αἱ ποιαὶ τῆς κράσεως παραλλαγαὶ διαμορφοῦσιν, ἡ δὲ κρᾶσις οὐκ ἄλλη τις παρὰ τὴν τῶν στοιχείων μίξιν ἐστὶ—στοιχεῖα δέ φαμεν τὰ τῇ κατασκευῇ τοῦ παντὸς ὑποκείμενα, δι' ὧν καὶ τὸ ἀνθρώπινον συνέστηκε σῶμα—ἀναγκαίως τοῦ εἴδους οἷον ἐκμαγείῳ σφραγίδος τῇ ψυχῇ παραμείναντος, οὐδὲ τὰ ἐναπομαξάμενα τῇ σφραγίδι τὸν τύπον, ὑπ' αὐτῆς ἀγνοεῖται, ἀλλ' ἐν τῷ καιρῷ τῆς ἀναστοιχειώσεως ἐκεῖνα δέχεται πάλιν πρὸς ἑαυτὴν ἅπερ ἂν ἐναρμόσῃ τῷ τύπῳ τοῦ εἴδους· ἐναρμόσειε δὲ πάντως

20 μὲν] μὲν γὰρ D τῷ *om.* D E P S X 20–1 σωματικοῦ τινος W 21 ὁ *om.* L 21–2 ὁ πλούσιος οὐκ ἠγνοεῖτο M 23 οὐκοῦν] non igitur *Eri* οὐδὲν] οὐκ Æ B I O R T 24 ἀνάλυσιν] διάλυσιν D E γενέσθαι T γε *om.* D E P W X τῷ] τὸ W X 25 ἡμῶν] ἡμῖν O κατεξετάζοντι] ἐξετάζοντι D E οὔτε] οὐδὲ M δι' ὅλου] διόλου Æ I L : δι' ὅλων M Q 26 ἦ] si *Eri* ἂν ἄληπτον] reprehensibile *Eri* τὸ . . . ἔχον] τὸ . . . ἔχων Q : τῷ . . . ἔχον P^{ac} : τοῦτο . . . ἔχον P^{pc} : τῷ . . . ἔχειν *Ald Mign* 27 ἀκριβέστατον L τι *om.* T 28 μὲν *om.* I O τε *om.* M R 29 πάσης *om.* I 30 ἐφ'] ἀφ' Q ἑαυτὸ L S : ἑαυτῶν P^{ac} 31 ἐξισταμένων T 32 ὑφεξαιρείσθω P : ὑπεξηρήσθω Æ B L M O S T τῷ λόγῳ Æ B I M O 33 ἡ^{1} *om.* Q 35 ναιεμὰν O P : νεεμὰν S^{ac} (αι *sup. l.*) : νεμὰν W 36 ὑγιείας P S : ὑγίας Q 38 τὸ μόνιμον] τὸ ἀεὶ μένον R : μόνον T τοῦτο] *ita* B D L O P R S T W X *Forb* : τούτῳ *Ald Mign* 40 διαμορφοῦσιν] *ita* Æ B D E I L M O P Q R S W X *Forb* : μεταμορφοῦσιν *Ald Mign* ἡ δὲ] ἤτε Q κράσις I L P R S X 41 δὲ] μὲν B ὧν] ἦν T 42 σύνετσι R^{ac} : συνέστη R^{2} οἷον] οἷον ἐν Æ B P S T W X ἐκμαγεῖος R$^{ac?}$: ἐκμαγείου L 43 σφραγῖδος Æ I M S σφραγῖδι M S τὸν *om.* Q 44 ὑπ'] ἀπ' Q αὐτῆς] ea (uidelicet anima) *Eri* ἀγνοεῖτε O^{ac} (αι *supr. l.*) ἀναστοιχειώσεως] resurrectionis *Dion* 45 τῷ τύπῳ τοῦ εἴδους] formae ipsi *Dion* : formae characteri *Eri* ἐναρμόσῃ I : ἐναρμόση B W : ἐναρμόσει Æ M O Q R

even after the dissolution, is shown by the dialogue in Hades, with the bodies having been delivered to the tomb, but some bodily token remaining, by which both Lazarus was recognized and the rich man was not unknown.[105]

[27.3] There is, therefore, nothing beyond probability in believing that there will be a return from the common [pool] to the particular for the bodies that rise again, especially for one who examines our nature with careful attention. For neither does our being consist altogether in flux and change, for that which had no stability at all by nature would be absolutely incomprehensible; but, according to the more accurate account, something of what is in us is stable, [while] the rest goes through a process of alteration: for the body, on the one hand, is altered by way of growth and diminution, changing, like garments, the vesture of its successive statures, while the form, on the other hand, remains in itself unaltered through every changing, not varying from the marks once imposed upon it by nature, but appearing with all its own identifying marks in all the changes of the body. [27.4] We must exempt from this account, however, the alteration to the form resulting from disease; for the deformity resulting from sickness takes possession of the form, like some strange mask, but when this is removed by the word, as in the case of Naaman the Syrian or of those whose who are mentioned in the Gospel, the form that had been hidden by the disease is once again by means of health brought to light with its own identifying marks.[106]

[27.5] It is not that which is subject to flux and change in alteration, but that which is stable and always remaining as it is in our composite being that is closely associated with the deiform aspect of the soul. And since the various kinds of combination produce differences of form (combination is nothing other than the mixture of elements; by elements we mean the substrata for the construction of the universe, from which the human body is also composed), while the form necessarily remains in the soul as the impression made by a seal, those things which have received the impression of the stamp from the seal are not unknown by the soul, but at the time of the reconstitution, it receives back to itself those things which correspond to the stamp of the form; and certainly those things which were stamped by the form in the beginning would so correspond. Thus, it is

[105] Cf. Luke 16:24–31; Irenaeus, *Haer.* 2.34.1.

[106] Cf. 4 Rgns 5; Matt. 8:16, etc.

ἐκεῖνα ὅσα κατ' ἀρχὰς ἐνετυπώθη τῷ εἴδει· οὐκοῦν οὐδὲν ἔξω τοῦ εἰκότος ἐστὶ, πάλιν ἐκ τοῦ κοινοῦ πρὸς τὸ καθέκαστον ἐπαναλύειν τὸ ἴδιον.

[27.6] *Λέγεται δὲ καὶ τὴν ὑδράργυρον προχεθεῖσαν τοῦ περιέχοντος* [C] *καθ' ὑπτίου τινὸς καὶ κονιορτώδους χωρίου, εἰς λεπτὰ σφαιρωθεῖσαν κατὰ τὴν γῆν διασκίδνασθαι, πρὸς οὐδὲν τῶν ἐπιτυχόντων ἐμμιγνυμένην· εἰ δέ τις πάλιν τὸ πολλαχῇ κατεσπαρμένον εἰς ἓν συναγείρειεν, αὐτομάτως ἀναχεῖσθαι πρὸς τὸ ὁμόφυλον, οὐδενὶ μέσῳ πρὸς τὴν οἰκείαν μίξιν διειργομένην. Τοιοῦτόν τι χρῆναι νομίζω καὶ περὶ τὸ ἀνθρώπινον σύγκριμα διανοεῖσθαι, εἰ μόνον γένοιτο παρὰ τοῦ Θεοῦ τὸ ἐνδόσιμον, αὐτομάτως τὰ κατάλληλα μέρη τοῖς οἰκείοις ἐπανακίρνασθαι, μηδεμιᾶς ἐργωδίας τῷ ἀναστοιχειοῦντι τὴν φύσιν διὰ τούτων ἐγγινομένης.* [27.7] *Καὶ γὰρ ἐπὶ τῶν ἐν τῇ γῇ φυομένων, οὐδένα πόνον ὁρῶμεν τῆς φύσεως ἐπὶ τὸν πυρὸν ἢ τὴν κέγχρον ἢ ἄλλο τι τῶν σιτηρῶν ἢ χεδροπῶν σπερμάτων, ἐν τῷ μεταβάλλειν εἰς καλάμην καὶ ἀθέρας καὶ ἀστάχυας·* [D] *ἀπραγματεύτως γὰρ κατὰ τὸ αὐτόματον ἡ κατάλληλος τροφὴ ἐκ τοῦ κοινοῦ πρὸς τὴν ἑκάστου τῶν σπερμάτων ἰδιότητα μεταβαίνει. Εἰ οὖν κοινῆς πᾶσι τοῖς φυομένοις τῆς ἰκμάδος ὑποκειμένης, ἕκαστον τῶν δι' αὐτῆς τρεφομένων τὸ κατάλληλον ἔσπασεν εἰς τὴν τοῦ οἰκείου προσθήκην, τί καινὸν εἰ καὶ ἐν τῷ τῆς ἀναστάσεως λόγῳ, παρ' ἑκάστου τῶν ἀνισταμένων, καθὼς ἐπὶ τῶν σπερμάτων, συμβαίνει οὕτω γίνεσθαι τὴν τοῦ οἰκείου ὁλκήν;* [27.8] *Ὥστε ἐξ ἁπάντων δυνατὸν εἶναι μαθεῖν, μηδὲν ἔξω τῶν τῇ πείρᾳ γνωριζομένων τὸ κήρυγμα περιέχειν τῆς ἀναστάσεως.*

[27.9] *Καίτοιγε τὸ γνωριμώτατον τῶν ἡμετέρων ἐσιωπήσαμεν—αὐτὴν λέγω τὴν πρώτην τῆς συστάσεως ἡμῶν ἀφορμήν. Τίς γὰρ οὐκ οἶδε τὴν θαυματοποιΐαν τῆς*

46 *ἐνετυπώθη τῷ εἴδει*] speciei probantur inserta *Dion* : in forma characterizata sunt *Eri* *οὐκοῦν*] non ergo *Eri* *οὐδὲν*] *οὐδὲ* R : *om.* Q *τοῦ εἰκότος*] *τούτου* M 47 *τὸ*[1]] *τὸν* Æ B I M O Q R[2] T W *ἐπαναλύει* R 48 *προσχεθεῖσαν* Q R[ac] S[ac] : *προτεθεῖσαν* P 49 *λεπτὰς* M 50 *διασκίνδνασθαι* W *οὐδὲν*] *οὐδὲ ἕν* I *ἐνμιγνυμένην* P : *ἐπιμιγνυμένην* D E : *ἐγκαταμιγνυμένην* R 51 *συναγείρῃ* D : *συναγείρει* P 52 *τοιοῦτο* Æ O *τι om.* B D P X 53 *τοῦ om.* I L 54 *ἐπανακιρνᾶσθαι* M W : *παρακίρνασθαι* Q : *ἐπανακρίνεσθαι* B : *ἐπανακρίνασθαι* R[ac] (*sed corr. a pr. m.*) : reflorerent *Eri* 56 *ἐν om.* L R S *οὐδὲν ἄπονον* Q 57 *τὸν πυρὸν*] *τὴν πυρρὸν* M *χεδροπῶν ἢ σιτηρῶν* D E *χεδρόπων* D[ac] N : *χεδρωπῶν* M O P Q : *χιδροπῶν* D[2] L : *χιδρωπῶν* R T : *χεδροποιὼν* B : *χεδροποιῶν* ß W : *ἤγουν ὀσπρίων* I 58 *καὶ om.* R *ἀθέρας*] *ita* L O Q S W X *Ald Forb* : *ἀθέρα* Æ B D E N : *ἀθέρ* I (*α sup. l.*) : *ἐθέρα* P : *θεραν* T[ac] : *ἀνθέρα* R : *ἀνθέρικας* M T[pc] : *ἀθέρικας Mign* *καὶ*[2]] *τοὺς* E *ἀστάχυας*] *στάχυας* D E M P Q X 59 *ἡ om.* M 60 *κοινῇ* M *ἰκμάδος*] *ἰκμάδος ἐγγινομένος ἢ* N 61 *ἔσπασε τὸ κατάλληλον πρὸς* D E L P S X 62 *εἰ om.* Æ B I M N O Q *παρ'*] *ἐφ'* D E P S X 63 *οὕτω*] *ita* Æ I L O P Q R S X *Forb* : *οὕτως* W *Ald Mign*

not outside probability that one's own should once more return from the common [pool] to each.

[**27.6**] It is said also that quicksilver, when poured out from the vessel that contains it down a dusty slope, forms small globules and scatters over the ground, mingling with none of the things it encounters; but if one should collect at one place the substance dispersed in many directions, it spontaneously flows back to its kindred substance, if nothing intervening separates it from mixing with its own. Something of this kind, I think, ought to be understood also of the human composite, that, if the signal is but given by God, the appropriate parts would spontaneously be reunited with those belonging to them, without any obstruction arising from them to him who reconstitutes nature. [**27.7**] In the case of plants growing in the ground also, we do not see any toil on the part of nature towards the wheat or the millet or any other of the seeds of grain or pulse, in changing them into stalk or spike or ears; for the proper nourishment passes without trouble, spontaneously, from the common [pool] to each of the seeds. If, then, while the moisture supplied to all the plants is common, each of those plants which is nourished by it draws the appropriate supply for its own growth, what new thing is it if in the account of the resurrection also, as in the case of the seeds, it happens that for each of those who arise there is the attraction of what is its own? [**27.8**] As such, it is possible to learn from all sides that the preaching of the resurrection contains nothing beyond those things known to us by experience.

[**27.9**] And yet we have been silent on the most remarkable point concerning ourselves: I mean the very first beginning of our constitution. Who does not know

φύσεως, τί λαβοῦσα ἡ μητρώα νηδὺς, τί ἀπεργάζεται; [229] ὁρᾷς ὅπως ἁπλοῦν τρόπον τινὰ καὶ ὁμοιομερές ἐστι τὸ εἰς ἀφορμὴν τῆς συστάσεως τοῦ σώματος τοῖς σπλάγχνοις καταβαλλόμενον· τὴν δὲ ποικιλίαν τοῦ κατασκευαζομένου συγκρίματος, τίς λόγος ἐκδιηγήσεται; τίς δ᾽ ἄν, μὴ τῇ κοινῇ φύσει τὸ τοιοῦτον μαθών, δυνατὸν ἡγήσαιτο τὸ γινόμενον, ὅτι τὸ βραχύ τε καὶ ἀντ᾽ οὐδενὸς ἐκεῖνο τοῦ τοσούτου πράγματός ἐστιν ἀρχή; μέγα δέ φημι, οὐ μόνον εἰς τὴν κατὰ τὸ σῶμα βλέπων διάπλασιν, ἀλλ᾽ ὃ πρὸ τούτου θαυμάζειν ἄξιον, αὐτὴν λέγω τὴν ψυχὴν καὶ τὰ περὶ αὐτὴν θεωρούμενα.

Πρὸς τοὺς λέγοντας προϋφεστάναι τὰς ψυχὰς τῶν σωμάτων ἢ τὸ ἔμπαλιν πρὸ τῶν ψυχῶν διαπεπλάσθαι τὰ σώματα· ἐν ᾧ τις καὶ ἀνατροπὴ τῆς κατὰ τὰς μετεμψυχώσεις μυθοποιΐας.

[28.1] Τάχα γὰρ οὐκ ἔξω τῆς προκειμένης ἡμῖν πραγματείας ἐστὶ, τὸ διεξετάσαι τὸ ἀμφιβαλλόμενον ἐν ταῖς ἐκκλησίαις περὶ ψυχῆς τε καὶ σώματος. Τοῖς μὲν γὰρ τῶν πρὸ ἡμῶν δοκεῖ οἷς ὁ περὶ τῶν ἀρχῶν ἐπραγματεύθη λόγος, καθάπερ τινὰ δῆμον ἐν ἰδιαζούσῃ πολιτείᾳ τὰς ψυχὰς προϋφεστάναι λέγειν· προκεῖσθαι δὲ κἀκεῖ τά τε τῆς κακίας καὶ τῆς ἀρετῆς ὑποδείγματα· καὶ παραμένουσαν μὲν ἐν τῷ καλῷ τὴν ψυχὴν, τῆς πρὸς τὸ σῶμα συμπλοκῆς μένειν ἀπείρατον· εἰ δὲ καὶ ἀπορρυῇ τῆς τοῦ ἀγαθοῦ μετουσίας, πρὸς τὸν [C] τῇδε βίον κατολισθαίνειν, καὶ οὕτως ἐν σώματι γίνεσθαι. Ἕτεροι δὲ τῇ κατὰ τὸν Μωϋσέα τάξει τῆς κατασκευῆς τοῦ ἀνθρώπου προσέχοντες, δευτέραν εἶναι τὴν ψυχὴν τοῦ σώματος κατὰ τὸν χρόνον φασίν· ἐπειδὴ πρῶτον **λαβὼν** ὁ Θεὸς **χοῦν ἀπὸ τῆς γῆς, τὸν ἄνθρωπον ἔπλασεν**, εἶθ᾽ οὕτως ἐψύχωσε διὰ τοῦ ἐμφυσήματος· καὶ τούτῳ τῷ λόγῳ προτιμοτέραν ἀποδεικνύουσι τῆς ψυχῆς τὴν σάρκα, τῆς ἐπεισκρινομένης τὴν προδιαπεπλασμένην· λέγουσι γὰρ διὰ τὸ σῶμα τὴν

68 φύσεως] φύσεως ἡμῶν R τί λαβοῦσα ἡ μητρώα νηδὺς] quid in utero informe accipit *Eri* μητρῶα P ἀπειργάσατο N R ὁρᾷς] *ita* Æ B E I M N O P Q R T X *Forb* : ὀυχ ὁρᾷς W : ἢ ὀυχ ὁρᾷς *Ald Mign* ὅπως] *om.* T : πῶς P^pc R ἁπλοῦν ὅπως L 69 τρόπον] καὶ τρόπον P W X τινὰ τρόπον Q 71 τίς] τίς ἄρα Æ B E : τίς ἆρα I O 71–3 τίς δ᾽ ἂν—ἀρχή] quis nisi communi natura discens quod talens potens est quod factum est narrarit quia illud paruum ac prope nihil tantae rei fit principium *Eri* 71 τοιοῦτο Æ L N O W 72 ἡγήσατο B O T : ἡγήσεται R γενόμενον M βραχύ τε καὶ] βραχύτερον L τε] γε T : *om.* D E τοῦ *om.* T 73 ἀρχή] ἡ ἀρχή N 74 πρὸ τούτου] τούτου μᾶλλον I : τούτου O 75 θεωρούμενα] θεωρούμενα πάντα N (ἅ *sup.* π)

Cap. 29 Æ I N O Q R T *Dion*

28.4–14 (τάχα—ἐμφυσήματος): Justinian, *Ep. ad Mennam* (ACO 3, 199.22–31) 28.28–74 (οἱ τῷ προτέρῳ—σώμασι): Justinian, *Ep. ad Mennam* (ACO 3, 199.32–200.37) 28.4–17, 28.20–29.98 (τάχα—γίνεται, ἐπεὶ—βλαστημάτων ἐγένετο): John (of Damascus), *Sacra Parallela* II[1]39 / K cap. A 1, 39 (Thum, 68.8–74.21)

1–3 πρὸς—μυθοποιΐας] de diversis opinionibus originis animae *Λ* 1 τῶν σωμάτων τὰς ψυχὰς Æ B N R T W τὸ] ἐν τῷ W 1–2 διαπεπλάσθαι τὰ σώματα τῶν ψυχῶν M 2 διαπεπλάσθαι Æ I L M P R² S W X : διεπλάσθαι B : διεπλάσθη ß : διαπεπλᾶσθαι *Ald Mign* καὶ ἀνατροπὴ τις M 4 τάχα] ἀλλὰ Æ B I O διεξετάσαι] ἐξετάσαι D E P S W X *SP* 5 διαμφιβαλλόμενον *SP* ἐν *om.* T *Ius* τοῖς] τισὶ *Ius* τῶν] τοῖς T : *om.* D P X 5–6 δοκεῖ τῶν πρὸ ἡμῶν Æ B I N O Q R T W *Ius SP* 6 δοκεῖ *om.* M ἀρχῶν] ἀρχαίων D E N P S X : ψυχῶν M λόγος *om.* L δῆμον] pestilientiam *Dion* (*forte* λοῖμον) 7 πολιτείᾳ] πόλει D E P^ac? X *Ius* τε *om.* *Ius* 8 καὶ] καὶ τὰ Æ B N O Q R *SP* μὲν *om.* D P X ἐν *om.* S 9 ἀπείσρατον O καὶ *om.* Æ B I M N (*sed add. a pr. m*) O Q R T *Dion Ius Eri* ἀπορρύει B O P^ac R^ac 11 μωσέα *Ius* τῇ κατασκευῇ M R ἀνθρώπου] τελείου ἀνθρώπου M 12 ἐπειδὴ] ἐπειδὴ γὰρ R 13 χοῦν ὁ θεὸς L ἔπλασε τὸν ἄνθρωπον W *Ald Mign* ἔπλασεν] ἐποίησεν D εἶθ᾽] ἔπειτα *Ius* 14 ἐμφυσήματος] προσφυσήματος M *SP* : ἐμπροσφυσήματος Q 15 εἰσκρινομένης N διαπεπλασμένην D M P

the miraculous working of nature, what the maternal womb receives, what it produces? You see how what is implanted in the womb to be the beginning of the constitution of the body is, in a way, simple and homogenous; but what language can describe the variety of the composite body being formed? And who, not learning of such a thing in nature generally, would think that which does take place is possible, that that small thing, and nothing else, is the beginning of something so great? Great, I say, not only considering the bodily construction, but what is more worthy of marvel than this, I mean the soul itself and the things we contemplate regarding it.

To those who say 'souls pre-exist bodies', or the reverse, 'bodies were formed before souls'; in which is also a refutation of the myth-making concerning transmigrations of souls.[107]

[**28.1**] It is perhaps not beyond our present subject to discuss the matter debated in the churches regarding soul and body. Some of those before us, by whom the topic of principles has been treated, have thought it appropriate to say that souls pre-existed as a people in a polity of their own, and that there are set forth there the paradigms of vice and virtue, and that the soul residing there in goodness remains without experience of conjunction with the body, but if it flows away from its participation in the good, it falls down to this present mode of life and so comes to be in a body.[108] Others, taking note of the order, as related by Moses, of the formation of the human being, say that the soul is chronologically second to the body, since God first taking *dust from the earth, fashioned the human being,*

[107] *Bodl. 238* (as Chap. 29): 'On different views of the origin of the soul'.

[108] Cf. Plato, *Phaedr.* 245c–249d. Although many authors, from the time of Thales, had dealt with the question of 'principles' or 'first principles', and Longinus had written a text with this as the title (cf. Porphyry, *Vita Plot.* 14; Clement of Alexandria mentions that he intends to: *Strom.* 3.3.13.2, 21.2; cf. 5.14.140.3), Justinian, in 543, took these lines to be a reference to Origen (cf. *Ep. Mennam*; ACO 199). Yet in his letter to the Council of 553, while again attributing such teaching to Origen, in words that echo this passage and which are lifted verbatim from Theodoret of Cyrrhus, the originators of such teaching are identified otherwise: 'and again Pythagoras and Plato, after asserting there is a whole company of bodiless souls [*δῆμόν τινα ψυχῶν ἀσωμάτων*], say that those who fall into some sin or other are made to descend into bodies as a punishment. Plato in consequence called the body a fetter and a tomb.' Letter in Georgius Monachus, *Chronicon*, ed. de Boor, 2, 631–2 (Price, 2.283); cf. Theodoret, *affect.* 5.13 (Canivet, 1, 229–30); Plato, *Gorg.* 493a. And then, a few lines later: 'So Pythagoras, Plato, Plotinus and their followers, who agreed that souls are immortal, declared that they exist prior to bodies and that there is a great company of souls [*ἀθανάτους εἶναι τὰς ψυχὰς... προϋπάρχειν ταύτας ἔφησαν τῶν σωμάτων καὶ δῆμον εἶναι ψυχῶν* (Theodoret *add. ἀναρίθμων*), of which those that transgress descend into bodies.' *Chronicon*, de Boor 2, 632–3 (Price, 2.283); cf. Theodoret, *haer.* 5.9 (PG 83.480c). Origen, of course, repeatedly denied that he taught any such thing, deriding it as 'folly', 'myth', 'false teaching', 'introduced by the Greeks', borrowed from the Egyptians by Pythagoras and Plato: cf. *Cels.* 1.13 (= *Philoc.* 18.7); *Cels.* 1.20 (= *Philoc.* 18.5), *Cels.* 5.49; *Com. John* 6.64–73; see also *Cels.* 3.75, 5.29; 7.32; 8.30; *Com. Matt.* 10.20, 13.1–2; and the passages presented by Pamphilus, *Apol.* 173–88. Origen claimed that the proper view of 'the essence and principles' of the soul, 'the immortal entering a mortal body', is 'not according to the Platonic transmigration, but according to a more sublime contemplation' (*οὐ κατὰ τὴν Πλάτωνος μετενσωμάτωσιν ἀλλὰ κατ' ἄλλην τινὰ ὑψηλοτέραν θεωρία*, *Cels.* 4.17), so that 'incarnation' is different from 'reincarnation' (*ἐνσωμάτωσις—μετενσωμάτωσις*, *Com. John* 6.86). Gregory of Nyssa, no doubt, was aware of this, just as Basil and Gregory certainly were when excerpting passages from *Cels.* for their *Philocalia*. See further: *An. et res.* 8.3–6; 8.20–1; 9.13–14 (Spira, 80.8–81.9; 84.14–85.9; 94.16–95.3); *Vit. Moys.* 2.40 (Musurillo, 44.11–19); Gregory of Nazianzus, *Or.* 37.15.

ψυχὴν γενέσθαι, ὡς ἂν μὴ ἄπνουν τε καὶ ἀκίνητον εἴη τὸ πλάσμα· πᾶν δὲ τὸ διά τι γινόμενον, ἀτιμότερον πάντως ἐστὶ τοῦ δι' ὃ γίνεται, καθὼς τὸ εὐαγγέλιον λέγει ὅτι ***πλεῖόν ἐστι τῆς τροφῆς ἡ ψυχὴ καὶ τὸ σῶμα τοῦ ἐνδύματος****, διότι τούτων* [D] *ἕνεκεν ἐκεῖνα—οὐ γὰρ διὰ τὴν τροφὴν ἡ ψυχὴ οὐδὲ τοῦ ἐνδύματος χάριν κατεσκευάσθη τὰ σώματα, ἀλλά, τούτων ὄντων, ἐκεῖνα διὰ τὴν χρείαν προσεξηυρέθη.* [28.2] *Ἐπεὶ οὖν ἐν ἀμφοτέραις ταῖς ὑπολήψεσιν ὁ λόγος ὑπαίτιος, τῶν τε προβιοτεύειν τὰς ψυχὰς ἐν ἰδίᾳ τινὶ καταστάσει μυθολογούντων καὶ τῶν ὑστέρας τῶν σωμάτων κατασκευάζεσθαι νομιζόντων, ἀναγκαῖον ἂν εἴη μηδὲν τῶν ἐν τοῖς δόγμασι λεγομένων περιϊδεῖν ἀνεξέταστον. Ἀλλὰ τὸ μὲν δι' ἀκριβείας τοὺς ἑκατέρωθεν γυμνάζειν λόγους καὶ πάσας ἐκκαλύπτειν τὰς ἐγκειμένας ἀτοπίας ταῖς ὑπολήψεσι, μακροῦ ἂν δέοιτο καὶ λόγου καὶ χρόνου· δι' ὀλίγων δέ, καθώς ἐστι δυνατόν, ἑκάτερον τῶν εἰρημένων ἐπισκεψάμενοι,* [232] *πάλιν τῶν προκειμένων ἀντιληψόμεθα.*

[28.3] *Οἱ τῷ προτέρῳ παριστάμενοι λόγῳ καὶ πρεσβυτέραν τῆς ἐν σαρκὶ ζωῆς τὴν πολιτείαν τῶν ψυχῶν δογματίζοντες, οὔ μοι δοκοῦσι τῶν Ἑλληνικῶν καθαρεύειν δογμάτων τῶν περὶ τῆς μετενσωματώσεως αὐτοῖς μεμυθολογημένων· εἰ γάρ τις ἀκριβῶς ἐξετάσειε, πρὸς τοῦτο κατὰ πᾶσαν ἀνάγκην τὸν λόγον αὐτοῖς εὑρήσει κατασυρόμενον. Φασί τινα τῶν παρ' ἐκείνοις σοφῶν εἰρηκέναι, ὅτι ἀνὴρ γέγονεν ὁ αὐτός, καὶ γυναικὸς σῶμα μετημφιάσατο, καὶ μετ' ὀρνέων ἀνέπτη, καὶ θάμνος ἔφυ, καὶ τὸν ἔνυδρον ἔλαχε βίον—οὐ πόρρω τῆς ἀληθείας, κατά γε τὴν ἐμὴν κρίσιν, φερόμενος ὁ περὶ ἑαυτοῦ ταῦτα λέγων· ὄντως γὰρ βατράχων τινῶν ἢ κολοιῶν φλυαρίας ἢ ἀλογίας ἰχθύων ἢ δρυῶν ἀναισθησίας ἄξια τὰ τοιαῦτα δόγματα, τὸ μίαν ψυχὴν* [B] *λέγειν διὰ τοσούτων ἐλθεῖν.*

[28.4] *Τῆς δὲ τοιαύτης ἀτοπίας αὕτη ἐστὶν ἡ αἰτία, τὸ προϋφεστάναι τὰς ψυχὰς οἴεσθαι· δι' ἀκολούθου γὰρ ἡ ἀρχὴ τοῦ τοιούτου δόγματος ἐπὶ τὸ προσεχές τε καὶ*

16 *γεγενῆσθαι* N R *τε*] *τι* T : *om.* D E L P S *πλάσμα*] *σῶμα* I 17 *γενόμενον* L *δι' ὃ*] *διὸ* M R : *δι' ὅτι* T *γέγονε* D E L P S X 18 *πλείων* B D E M R : *πλεῖον* S[ac] (*ω sup. l.*) *ἡ ψυχὴ τῆς τροφῆς* M N *διότι*] *διότι οὐ* T *ἕνεκα* D I L N P X 19 *ἐκεῖνο* M *γὰρ om.* L 19–20 *τὸ σῶμα* D E 20 *ὄντων om.* D L *προσεξηυρέθη διὰ τὴν χρείαν* N *προσεξευρέθη* Æ B E I M O X : *προεξευρέθη* L N : *προσεξερεύθη* R : *προσεξηυρέθη* S[ac] (*ε sup. l.*) 21 *ἐν om.* I *ἐπ' ἀμφότερα* R 22 *τινὶ om.* Æ I *καταστάσει*] *τάξει* Æ B O Q : *διατάξει* I 22–3 *καὶ τῶν—νομιζόντων om. SP* 23 *κατεσκευάσθαι* M : *κατεσκευᾶσθαι* Q 23–4 *λεγομένων ἐν τοῖς δόγμασι Ald Mign* 23 *τοῖς om.* M 25 *ἐγκαλύπτειν* Q R[ac] W X *ἐκκειμένας* T : *ἐγγινομένας* R 26 *καὶ*[1] *om.* N *λόγου καὶ χρόνου*] *ita* D E I L M O P Q R S X *Forb* : *χρόνου καὶ λόγου* W *SP Ald Mign* *ἑκατέρων* Q 27 *προκειμένων*] *εἰρημένων* Q *Dion Eri* *ἀντιληψώμεθα* L 28 *τὴν om.* T 29 *δακοῦσι Ius* 30 *δογμάτων om. Ius* *τῶν om.* T *περὶ τῶν τῆς* N (*et in mg, a pr. m.*: *ἐν ἄλλοις περὶ τῆς μετεμψυχώσεως*) *μετενσωματώσεως*] *μετεμψυχώσεως Ius* *αὐτοῖς om. Ius* *μυθολογημένων SP* 32 *φασί*] *ita* D L P X *Forb* : *φασὶ γὰρ* Æ I N O S : *ὅν φασί* W *SP Ald Mign* : quod aiunt *Dion Eri* *ὅτι*] *ὅτι καὶ* Æ B I M N O Q R T W *Ius SP* 32–3 *ὁ αὐτὸς om. Ius* 33 *σῶμα μετημφιάσατο*] *ἠμφιάσατο σῶμα* N : *σῶμα ἠμφιάσατο* T *Ius* *θάμνοις* D E P[ac] : *ἐν θάμνοις* T *ἔφυ*] *ἐφοίτα* D E : *ἔφυτα* L 34 *κατά γε τὴν ἐμὴν κρίσιν*] recessit nostrum iudicum *Eri* *γε om.* D L P S X *Ius* 35 *ἑαυτοῦ*] *ita* Æ B D I L M N O P R S W X *Forb* : *αὑτοῦ Ald* : *αὐτοῦ Mign* 36 *φλυαρίας*] *καὶ φλυαρίας* S *δόγματα*] *ῥήματα SP* 39 *προσέχετε SP*

and then animated it by breathing into it,[109] and by this argument they show that the flesh is more noble than the soul, that which was previously formed than what is additionally introduced. For they say that the soul came to be for the body, so that the moulded figure might not be breathless and motionless; and that everything that comes to be for the sake of something else is surely less precious than that for which it comes to be, just as the Gospel says that *the soul is more than food and the body more than clothing*,[110] because the latter things exist for the sake of the former; for the soul was not formed for the sake of food nor our bodies for clothing, but when the former things exist, the latter were provided for their needs. [**28.2**] Since then the argument involved in both these positions—of those who mythologize about souls previously living in some special state, and of those who think that they were formed later than the bodies—is open to charge, it is perhaps necessary to let none of the statements in these doctrines pass by unexamined. But to wrestle with the arguments on each side with precision, and to reveal all the absurdities residing in the assumptions, would require a great deal of both argument and time; we shall, however, briefly survey, as far as it is possible, each of the views mentioned, and then resume again our subject.

[**28.3**] Those who stand by the former argument, and dogmatize that the polity of souls is prior to their life in the flesh, do not seem to me to be clear of the Greek mythological doctrines about their successive embodiments; for if one search carefully, he will find that their argument is, by every necessity, brought down to this. They say that one of their wise men said that he, the very same, became a man, was changed into a body of a woman, and flew with the birds, and grew as a bush, and obtained the life of an aquatic creature[111]—the one saying these things about himself did not, so far as I can judge, stray far from the truth; for doctrines such as this, saying one soul passed through so many changes, really are fitting for the nonsense of frogs or jackdaws, or the stupidity of fish or the insensibility of trees!

[**28.4**] The cause of such stupidity is this, supposing souls to pre-exist; for the first principle of such a doctrine, leading on the argument by consequence to the next and adjacent step, passes even to talking such fables. For if the soul, being dragged

[109] Gen. 2:7. [110] Matt. 6:25.

[111] Cf. Gregory of Nyssa, *An. et res.* 8.4–5, 31 (Spira, 80.12–81.6; 87.5–12); for Pythagoras, see Iamblichus, *Vit. Pythag.* 14; Porphyry, *Vit. Pythag.* 45; Diogenes Laertius, 8.4. See also Empedocles, Frag. B117 (DK, 358–9); Orpheus, Frag. 224b (Kern, 241=Proclus, *In Plat. Resp.*, ed. Kroll, 2.339.4–9); Plato, *Phaed.* 81e–82b; Calcidius, *Pl. Tim.* 2.197.

παρακείμενον τὸν λόγον προάγουσα, μέχρι τούτου τερατευομένη διέξεισιν· εἰ γὰρ διά τινος κακίας ἀποσπασθεῖσα τῆς ὑψηλοτέρας ἡ ψυχὴ πολιτείας, μετὰ τὸ (καθώς φασιν) ἅπαξ γεύσασθαι τοῦ σωματικοῦ βίου πάλιν ἄνθρωπος γίνεται· ἐμπαθέστερος δὲ πάντως ὁ ἐν σαρκὶ βίος ὁμολογεῖται παρὰ τὸν ἀΐδιον καὶ ἀσώματον· ἀνάγκη πᾶσα, τὴν ἐν τῷ τοιούτῳ γενομένην βίῳ, ἐν ᾧ πλείους αἱ πρὸς τὸ ἁμαρτάνειν εἰσὶν ἀφορμαί, ἐν πλείονί τε κακίᾳ γενέσθαι καὶ ἐμπαθέστερον ἢ πρότερον διατεθῆναι· ἀνθρωπίνης δὲ ψυχῆς πάθος, ἡ πρὸς τὸ ἄλογόν ἐστιν ὁμοίωσις· τούτῳ δὲ προσοικειωθεῖσαν [C] *αὐτήν, εἰς κτηνώδη φύσιν μεταρρυῆναι· ἅπαξ δὲ διὰ κακίας ὁδεύουσαν, μηδὲ ἐν ἀλόγῳ γενομένην τῆς ἐπὶ τὸ κακὸν προόδου λῆξαί ποτε· ἡ γὰρ τοῦ κακοῦ στάσις ἀρχὴ τῆς κατ᾽ ἀρετήν ἐστιν ὁρμῆς· ἀρετὴ δὲ ἐν ἀλόγοις οὐκ ἔστιν· οὐκοῦν ἀεὶ πρὸς τὸ χεῖρον ἐξ ἀνάγκης ἀλλοιωθήσεται, πάντοτε πρὸς τὸ ἀτιμότερον προϊοῦσα καὶ ἀεὶ τὸ χεῖρον τῆς ἐν ᾗ ἐστι φύσεως ἐξευρίσκουσα· ὥσπερ δὲ τοῦ λογικοῦ τὸ αἰσθητὸν ὑποβέβηκεν, οὕτω καὶ ἀπὸ τούτου ἐπὶ τὸ ἀναίσθητον ἡ μετάπτωσις γίνεται.*

[28.5] [D] *Ἀλλὰ μέχρι τούτου προϊὼν ὁ λόγος αὐτοῖς, εἰ καὶ ἔξω τῆς ἀληθείας φέρεται, ἀλλά γε διά τινος ἀκολουθίας τὸ ἄτοπον ἐξ ἀτόπου μεταλαμβάνει· τὸ δὲ ἐντεῦθεν ἤδη διὰ τῶν ἀσυναρτήτων αὐτοῖς τὸ δόγμα μυθοποιεῖται. Ἡ μὲν γὰρ ἀκολουθία παντελῆ διαφθορὰν τῆς ψυχῆς ὑποδείκνυσιν· ἡ γὰρ ἅπαξ τῆς ὑψηλῆς πολιτείας ἀπολισθήσασα, ἐν οὐδενὶ μέτρῳ κακίας στῆναι δυνήσεται, ἀλλά, διὰ τῆς πρὸς τὰ πάθη σχέσεως, ἀπὸ μὲν τοῦ λογικοῦ πρὸς τὸ ἄλογον μεταβήσεται· ἀπ᾽ ἐκείνου δὲ πρὸς τὴν τῶν φυτῶν ἀναισθησίαν μετατεθήσεται· τῷ δὲ ἀναισθήτῳ γειτνιᾷ* [233] *πως τὸ ἄψυχον· τούτῳ δὲ τὸ ἀνύπαρκτον ἕπεται· ὥστε καθόλου διὰ τῆς ἀκολουθίας πρὸς τὸ μὴ ὂν αὐτοῖς ἡ ψυχὴ μεταχωρήσει· οὐκοῦν ἀμήχανος αὐτῇ πάλιν ἐξ ἀνάγκης ἔσται ἡ πρὸς τὸ κρεῖττον ἐπάνοδος· ἀλλὰ μὴν ἐκ θάμνου ἐπὶ τὸν ἄνθρωπον τὴν ψυχὴν ἐπανάγουσιν. Οὐκοῦν προτιμοτέραν τὴν ἐν θάμνῳ ζωὴν τῆς ἀσωμάτου διαγωγῆς ἐκ τούτων ἀποδεικνύουσι.*

40 *τὸν om. SP* 41 *ἀποσπασθεῖσα*] *ὑποσπασθεῖσα* B 41–2 *ἡ ψυχὴ—ἄνθρωπος γίνεται*] anima (sicut asserunt) efficitur homo *Dion* : anima homo efficitur *Eri* *μετὰ—πάλιν om.* M N[ac] (*in* N[mg2]) Q R T W *Ius SP* 42 *φασιν*] *φησιν* D I M N[mg] P S X 43 *ἐν σαρκὶ*] *ἔνσαρκος* N *ὁμολογεῖται om.* N (*in* N[mg2] *ante βίος*) : *ὡμολόγηται* R T *Ius* *τὸν*] *τὸν ἤδη* B I *ἀΐδιον*] *ἀειδῆ* Q R[ac] T W : *ἴδιον* O *ἀνάγκη πᾶσα*] necessarium est omnem animam *Eri* 44 *γενομένην*] *ita* Æ B L M N O P Q S W X *Forb* : *γινομένην* R *Ald Mign* *βίῳ*] *βίῳ ψυχὴν* M 45 *τε*] *τινι τῷ Ius* *γίνεσθαι* R *ἢ*] *τοῦ* D L P S X : *ἢ τοῦ* W *ἢ πρότερον om.* Q *Ius* 46 *δὲ om.* L *ἡ om.* T 47 *μεταρρυῆναι*] *καταρρυῆναι* B (*a 2[a] m.*) *ὁδεύουσαν*] *ὁδεύουσαν καὶ* D L *μηδ᾽* L : *μὴ δὲ SP* 48 *γινομένην* O R : *γεγενημένην SP* *λῆξαι*] *λήξειν Ius* *γὰρ*] *δὲ* D 49 *οὐκοῦν*] non ergo *Eri* *ἀεὶ om. Ius* 51 *τὸ αἰσθητὸν τοῦ λογικοῦ* Q *αἰσθητικὸν* I 52 *οὕτως* M N R *SP* *ἐπὶ τὸ ἀναίσθητον om. Ius* *ἡ om.* D L M P S X *μετάπτωσις*] *μετάστασις* I : *μετάβασις* Q : casus *Dion Eri* 53 *ἀλλὰ*] *ἀλλὰ τὸ* R 54 *τὸ*[1] *om.* Æ B I N[ac] O Q R *SP* 54–5 *ἄτοπον—ἤδη* : *ἤδη ἄτοπον ἐξ ἀτόπου μεταλαμβάνει· οὐδὲ ἐντεῦθεν καὶ* Q 55 *συναρτήτων* Q *τὸ om.* N[ac] P[ac] Q 56 *παντελῶς* R *διαφθορὰν*] *φθορὰν* L : *διαφορὰν* I *SP* 58 *τὸ om.* R 59 *τῶν φυτῶν om.* M *μετατεθήσεται*] *μεταχωρήσει* M 60 *γειτνιᾷ om. Ius* *τὸ ἄψυχον·*] exanime *Dion* : inanimale *Eri* *τούτῳ δὲ*] *τοῦτο δὲ* P : *τῷ δὲ ἀψύχῳ* N : exanime autem *Dion* : post hoc autem (id est inanimale) *Eri* *καθόλου*] *διόλου Ius* 61 *οὐκοῦν*] non ergo *Eri* *ἀμήχανον* M 62 *ἐξ ἀνάγκης om. Ius* *ἡ πρὸς τὸ κρεῖττον ἔσται* D L P S X 63 *ἄνθρωπον*] *ἄνθρωπον πάλιν* B *οὐκοῦν*] non igitur *Eri* 64 *διαγωγῆς*] *ζωῆς* O *ἀποδεικνύσιν SP*

away from the more exalted polity by some wickedness, after once having tasted (as they say) corporeal mode of life, becomes a human being again, [and if] the mode of life in the flesh is acknowledged, as it certainly is, to be more subject to passion compared with the eternal and incorporeal, by every necessity, then, that which comes to be in such a mode of life, in which there are more occasions to sin, comes to be disposed in great wickedness and more subject to passion than before, and, as passion for the human soul is likeness to the irrational, being assimilated to this it descends to the animal nature; and that once it sets out through wickedness, it never, having become irrational, ceases its advance towards evil, for the cessation of evil is the beginning of the impulse towards virtue, and in irrational creatures virtue does not exist. Thus, by necessity, it will always be changed for the worse, continually proceeding to what is more dishonoured and ever finding what is worse in the nature in which it is. Just as the sense-perceptive is lower than the rational, so too there is a change from this to the insensate.

[28.5] Now, proceeding so far, even if it is carried outside the truth, their argument nevertheless derives one absurdity from another absurdity by a kind of logical sequence; but henceforth their doctrine mythologizes through incoherent points. Logical sequence points to the complete destruction of the soul; for that which has once fallen away from the exalted polity will not be able halt at any measure of evil, but, through its relation to the passions, it will pass from the rational to the irrational, and from there it will be transferred to the insensibility of plants, and the inanimate is adjacent, somehow, to the insensate, and following this, the non-existent. So that by this sequence they will absolutely have the soul pass into non-being.[112] Therefore, the return to the better state will again be, by necessity, impossible for it, and yet they have the soul return from the bush to the human being. They thus prove that the life in a bush is more precious than the incorporeal course of life.

[112] Cf. Gregory of Nyssa, *An. et res.* 8.25–6 (Spira, 86.2–10).

[28.6] Δέδεικται γάρ, ὅτι ἡ πρὸς τὸ χεῖρον γενομένη πρόοδος τῆς ψυχῆς, πρὸς τὸ κατώτερον κατὰ τὸ εἰκὸς ὑποβήσεται. Ὑποβέβηκε δὲ τὴν ἀναίσθητον φύσιν τὸ ἄψυχον, εἰς ὃ δι᾽ ἀκολουθίας ἡ ἀρχὴ τοῦ δόγματος αὐτῶν τὴν ψυχὴν ἄγει· ἀλλ᾽ ἐπειδὴ τοῦτο οὐ βούλονται· ἢ τῷ ἀναισθήτῳ τὴν ψυχὴν ἐγκατακλείουσιν, ἢ εἴπερ ἐντεῦθεν ἐπὶ τὸν ἀνθρώπινον αὐτὴν ἐπανάγοιεν βίον, προτιμότερον (καθὼς εἴρηται) [B] τὸν ξυλώδη βίον τῆς πρώτης ἀποδείξουσι καταστάσεως, εἴπερ ἐκεῖθεν μὲν ἡ πρὸς κακίαν κατάπτωσις γέγονεν, ἐντεῦθεν δὲ ἡ πρὸς ἀρετὴν ἐπάνοδος γίνεται. [28.7] Οὐκοῦν ἀκέφαλός τις καὶ ἀτελὴς ὁ τοιοῦτος διελέγχεται λόγος, ὁ τὰς ψυχὰς ἐφ᾽ ἑαυτῶν πρὸ τῆς ἐν σαρκὶ ζωῆς βιοτεύειν κατασκευάζων καὶ διὰ κακίας συνδεῖσθαι τοῖς σώμασι· τῶν δέ γε νεωτέραν τοῦ σώματος τὴν ψυχὴν εἶναι λεγόντων, προκατεσκευάσθη διὰ τῶν κατόπιν ἡ ἀτοπία. [28.8] Οὐκοῦν ἀπόβλητος ἐπίσης ὁ παρ᾽ ἀμφοτέρων λόγος· διὰ δὲ τοῦ μέσου τῶν ὑπολήψεων εὐθύνειν οἶμαι δεῖν ἐν ἀληθείᾳ τὸ ἡμέτερον δόγμα· ἔστι δὲ τοῦτο, τὸ μήτε κατὰ τὴν Ἑλληνικὴν ἀπάτην ἐν κακίᾳ τινὶ βαρηθείσας τὰς τῷ παντὶ συμπεριπολούσας ψυχάς, ἀδυναμίᾳ τοῦ συμπαραθέειν τῇ ὀξύτητι τῆς τοῦ πόλου [C] κινήσεως ἐπὶ τὴν γῆν καταπίπτειν οἴεσθαι. [D] Μηδ᾽ αὖ πάλιν οἱονεὶ πήλινον ἀνδριάντα προδιαπλάσαντας τῷ λόγῳ τὸν ἄνθρωπον, τούτου ἕνεκεν τὴν ψυχὴν γίνεσθαι λέγειν· ἦ γὰρ ἂν ἀτιμοτέρα τοῦ πηλίνου πλάσματος ἡ νοερὰ φύσις ἀποδειχθείη.

Κατασκευὴ τοῦ μίαν καὶ τὴν αὐτὴν ψυχῇ τε καὶ σώματι τὴν αἰτίαν τῆς ὑπάρξεως εἶναι.

[29.1] Ἀλλ᾽ ἑνὸς ὄντος τοῦ ἀνθρώπου, τοῦ διὰ ψυχῆς τε καὶ σώματος συνεστηκότος, μίαν αὐτοῦ καὶ κοινὴν τῆς συστάσεως τὴν ἀρχὴν ὑποτίθεσθαι, ὡς ἂν μὴ αὐτὸς ἑαυτοῦ προγενέστερός τε καὶ νεώτερος γένοιτο, τοῦ μὲν σωματικοῦ προτερεύοντος ἐν αὐτῷ, τοῦ δὲ ἑτέρου ἐφυστερίζοντος· ἀλλὰ τῇ μὲν προγνωστικῇ τοῦ Θεοῦ δυνάμει (κατὰ τὸν μικρῷ πρόσθεν ἀποδοθέντα λόγον) ἅπαν προϋφεστάναι τὸ ἀνθρώπινον

65 ὅτι ἡ πρὸς] ὡς ἡ εἰς N   ἡ *om. Ius*   γινομένη ß I M N O Q R : γιγνομένη T   ἡ πρόοδος *Ius*   67 ἀκολουθίαν B   ἀνάγει M   68 βούλεται Æ   ἐγκατακλείσουσιν Æ   69 αὐτὴν] *om.* I : αὐτὴν καὶ οὐράνιον T   ἐπαναγάγοιεν T   69–70 προτιμότερον—βίον *quaedam excidisse uidentur SP*   70 τῆς] τῆς αἰθερίας B   ἀποδείξωσι Q : δείξουσιν *SP*   71 ἐγένετο D L M P S X   72 οὐκοῦν] non igitur *Eri*   τις] τι M : τε N R   73 πρὸ] πρὸς τὸ P X   74 συνδεῖσθαι] ἐνδεῖσθαι *Ius*   γε νεωτέραν] γενναιοτέραν R$^{ac?}$ T^{ac} 74–5 λεγόντων εἶναι *SP*   75 προκατεσκεύασται I O Q   οὐκοῦν] non ergo *Eri*   76 ἐπίσης] dixeris *Eri*   παρ᾽] παρὰ W   ἀμφοτέροις T   77 *post* δόγμα *inc. cap. 30* R   μηδὲ Q   78 περιπολούσας B N^{ac} 79 συμπαραθεῖν Æ B I N O T : συμαράγειν M : συμπαρέχειν Q : concurrere *Dion* : concurrendi *Eri*   81 προδιαπλάσαντας] *ita* Æ B C F M N^{2} P Q R T W X *Forb* : προδιαπλάσαντα D E I L S : προσδιαπλάσαντας N^{ac} : προδιαπλάσας A : προδιαπλασθέντα *Ald Mign*   ἕνεκεν] *ita* Æ ß I L M N O P Q R S W X *Ald Forb* : ἕνεκα *Mign*   82 πλάσματος] σώματος Q R   ἡ] ἢ M   ἀποδειχθῇ T
Cap. inc. post οἴεσθαι (*Cap. 28, l. 80*) A B D E F L M N P S T W *Forb*

Cap. 30 Æ I N O Q R *Dion*

1 κατασκευὴ—εἶναι] quod deus pariter animam et corpus fecerit *Λ*   1 ψυχῇ τε] ψυχῆς οἴεσαι B   σώματι] subsistentiae *Eri*

3 τοῦ^{1} *om.* I *SP*   συνεστῶτος *SP*   4 αὐτῷ D L N^{pc} P S X   τὴν κοινὴν τῆς συστάσεως I   5 νεώτερος] μεταγενέστερος D^{2} προτερεύοντος] προτέρου ὄντος Æ   6 δ᾽ I   μὲν *om.* B   δυνάμει τοῦ θεοῦ N   7 κατὰ—ἅπαν *om. SP*   ἅπασαν B

[**28.6**] It has been shown that the passage towards the worse which takes place in the soul will likely be extended downwards. Lower than the insensate nature is the inanimate, towards which, by consequence, the principle of their doctrine leads the soul; but since they will not have this, they either exclude the soul from the insensate, or, if they are to bring it back from there to the human mode of life, they claim, as has been said, that the life of a tree is more honourable than the first state—if, that is, the fall towards wickedness took place from the one, and the return towards virtue takes place from the other. [**28.7**] Therefore, this argument of theirs, which maintains that the souls are living by themselves before their life in the flesh and that through wickedness they are bound to bodies, is shown to be without beginning and without conclusion; regarding those who say that the soul is later than the body, the absurdity was already demonstrated through what follows. [**28.8**] Thus, the argument of both is to be equally rejected. I think that we ought to direct our own doctrine in the way of truth through the middle of these assumptions. This is, that it should not be supposed, following the Greek error, that the souls, revolving with the movement of the universe but being weighed down by some wickedness, fall to earth by the inability to keep up with the swiftness of the movement of the celestial sphere. Neither are we to say, in our account, that the human being was fashioned beforehand like some clay statue, the soul coming into being for the sake of this; for in that case the intellectual nature would be shown to be less precious than the clay figure.

An elaboration of the fact that the cause of existence for soul and body is one and the same.[113]

[**29.1**] Rather, as the human being is one, consisting of soul and body, it is to be supposed that the principle of his constitution is one and common to both, so that he should not be both older and newer than himself, with the bodily element coming first in him and the other coming later, but instead to affirm the whole human plenitude to have pre-existed in the power of God's foreknowledge

[113] *Bodl. 238* (as Chap. 30): 'That God equally made the body and the soul of the human being'. Forbes had Chapter 29 begin with the last sentence of the previous paragraph. Several manuscripts, together with the Latin translations of Dionysius Exiguus and Eriugena, followed by Migne, place it here.

πλήρωμα λέγειν, συμμαρτυρούσης εἰς τοῦτο τῆς προφητείας τῆς λεγούσης, **εἰδέναι τὰ πάντα** τὸν Θεὸν **πρὶν γενέσεως αὐτῶν**· ἐν δὲ τῇ καθ' ἕκαστον δημιουργίᾳ μὴ προτιθέναι τοῦ ἑτέρου τὸ ἕτερον, μήτε πρὸ τοῦ σώματος τὴν ψυχὴν, μήτε τὸ ἔμπαλιν· ὡς ἂν μὴ στασιάζοι πρὸς ἑαυτὸν ὁ ἄνθρωπος τῇ κατὰ τὸν χρόνον διαφορᾷ [236] μεριζόμενος. [29.2] Διπλῆς γὰρ τῆς φύσεως ἡμῶν νοουμένης, κατὰ τὴν ἀποστολικὴν διδασκαλίαν, τοῦ τε φαινομένου ἀνθρώπου καὶ τοῦ κεκρυμμένου· εἰ τὸ μὲν προϋπάρχοι τὸ δὲ ἐπιγένοιτο, ἀτελής τις ἡ τοῦ δημιουργοῦντος ἀπελεγχθήσεται δύναμις, οὐ τῷ παντὶ κατὰ τὸ ἀθρόον ἐξαρκοῦσα, ἀλλὰ διαιρουμένη τὸ ἔργον καὶ ἀνὰ μέρος περὶ ἑκάτερον τῶν ἡμισευμάτων ἀσχολουμένη.

[29.3] Ἀλλ' ὥσπερ ἐν τῷ σίτῳ φαμὲν ἢ ἐν ἑτέρῳ τινὶ τῶν σπερμάτων, ἅπαν ἐμπεριειλῆφθαι τῇ δυνάμει τὸ κατὰ τὸν στάχυν εἶδος, τὸν χόρτον, τὴν καλάμην, τὰς διὰ μέσου ζώνας, τὸν καρπόν, τοὺς ἀνθέρικας, καὶ οὐδὲν τούτων ἐν τῷ τῆς φύσεως λόγῳ προϋπάρχειν ἢ προγίνεσθαί φαμεν τῇ φύσει τοῦ σπέρματος, ἀλλὰ τάξει μέν τινι φυσικῇ τὴν ἐγκειμένην τῷ σπέρματι δύναμιν φανεροῦσθαι, [B] οὐ μὴν ἑτέραν ἐπεισκρίνεσθαι φύσιν—κατὰ τὸν αὐτὸν λόγον καὶ τὴν ἀνθρωπίνην σπορὰν ἔχειν ὑπειλήφαμεν, ἐν τῇ πρώτῃ τῆς συστάσεως ἀφορμῇ συνεσπαρμένην τὴν τῆς φύσεως δύναμιν· ἐξαπλοῦσθαι δὲ καὶ φανεροῦσθαι διά τινος φυσικῆς ἀκολουθίας πρὸς τὸ τέλειον προϊοῦσαν, οὐ προσλαμβάνουσάν τι τῶν ἔξωθεν εἰς ἀφορμὴν τελειώσεως· ἀλλ' ἑαυτὴν εἰς τὸ τέλειον δι' ἀκολουθίας προάγουσαν· ὡς μήτε ψυχὴν πρὸ τοῦ σώματος μήτε χωρὶς ψυχῆς τὸ σῶμα ἀληθὲς εἶναι λέγειν, ἀλλὰ μίαν ἀμφοτέρων ἀρχὴν, κατὰ μὲν τὸν ὑψηλότερον λόγον, ἐν τῷ πρώτῳ τοῦ Θεοῦ βουλήματι καταβληθεῖσαν, κατὰ δὲ τὸν ἕτερον, ἐν ταῖς τῆς γενέσεως ἀφορμαῖς συνισταμένην.

[29.4] Ὡς γὰρ οὐκ ἔστι τὴν κατὰ τὰ μέλη διάρθρωσιν ἐνιδεῖν τῷ πρὸς τὴν σύλληψιν τοῦ σώματος ἐντιθεμένῳ πρὸ τῆς διαπλάσεως· [C] οὕτως οὐδὲ τὰς τῆς ψυχῆς ἰδιότητας ἐν τῷ αὐτῷ δυνατόν ἐστι κατανοῆσαι, πρὶν προελθεῖν εἰς ἐνέργειαν· καὶ

8 *λέγειν πλήρωμα* A D E L M^{pc} P S X *λέγειν*] *λέγει* D R *εἰς*] *πρὸς* N *εἰς τοῦτο om.* D E *τῆς om.* I Q *λεγούσης om.* I 9 *τὰ om.* Æ B I M N^{ac} O Q R T *SP* 10 *πρὸ om.* Q 10–11 *μήτε τὸ ἔμπαλιν*] neque iterum ante animam corpus *Eri* 11 *στασιάζῃ* ß I : *στασιάζει* B 12 *μεριζόμενος*] *γνωριζόμενος* M 13 *τε om.* R *κεκρυμμένου*] *κρυπτομένου* O 14 *προϋπάρχοι*] *ὑπάρχοι* M : *προυπάρχει* B *ἐπιγίνοιτο* D F L N P Q S W X : *ἐπιγίνεται* R 15 *ἀπελεγχθήσεται*] *ἀπελέγχοιτο* B : *ἀποδειχθήσεται* D E : *ἀπελεχθήσεται* *SP* *ἐξαρκοῦσα*] *ἐπαρκοῦσα* L 16 *περὶ*] *περὶ τὸ* B 18 *ἄσταχυν* N O 19 *ἀθέρικας* *SP* *ἐν om.* D P S X 20 *προγενέσθαι* D L P S X : *προσγίνεσθαι* Æ^{2} M N T 21 *φανεροῦσθαι δύναμιν* L 22 *ἐπεισκρίνεσθαι*] *ἐπισπείρεσθαι* T *σπορὰν*] seminationem (hoc est generationem uel creationem) *Eri* 23 *ἔχειν σπορὰν* A D E F L P S X *ἔχειν*] *ἔχει* L : *om.* T *ἔχειν ὑπειλήφαμεν*] *ita* Æ B I M N Q R *Forb* : *ὑπειλήφαμεν ἔχειν* W *Ald Mign* *ὑπειλήφαμεν*] *παρειλήφαμεν* D E^{ac} (E *ὑπ sup. l.*) *ἐν om.* *SP* *συνεσπαρμένην*] *συνεσπαρμένην μὲν κατὰ* Q *Eri* : *συνεσπαρμένην μὲν* T 25 *προϊοῦσα* *SP* 26 *ἀκολουθίαν* X *προσάγουσαν* A^{ac} O T^{pc} *ὡς*] *ὥστε* I *μήτε*] *μήτε τὴν* T 27 *χωρὶς*] *χωρὶς τῆς* B 29 *τὸν*] *τὸ* R *γεννήσεως* *SP* *ἀμορφίαις* T 31 *ὡς—ἐνιδεῖν*] ut enim non est unum per membra diuisionem artuum scire *Eri* *τὴν om.* D E X *τὰ om.* *Mign* *διάθρωσιν* *SP* *ἐνιδεῖν*] *ἰδεῖν* O 31–2 *τῶν…ἐντιθεμένων* T 32 *ἐντιθεμένῳ τοῦ σώματος* N *ἐντιθεμένη* X *πρὸ*] *πρὸ διὰ* W *οὕτως om.* *SP* *τῆς ψυχῆς*] *τυχῆς* N^{ac} 33 *ἐν τῷ αὐτῷ om.* N^{ac} *προελθεῖν*] *ἐλθεῖν* N^{ac}

(according to the account given a little earlier), to which the prophecy bears witness, saying that God *knows all things before their genesis*,[114] and not, in the crafting of each, to place one before the other, neither the soul before the body, nor the contrary, so that the human being may not be at strife against himself, being divided by a chronological time. **[29.2]** For as our nature is conceived of as twofold, according to the apostolic teaching—the visible human being and the hidden one[115]—if one pre-existed and the other came to be later, the power of the Craftsman will be convicted of being in some way imperfect, as not being completely sufficient for the whole task at once, but dividing the work and busying itself with each of the halves in turn.

[29.3] But just as we say that in the grain, or in any other seed, the whole form of the ear of corn is potentially included—the leaves, the stalk, the joints in the middle, the fruit, the beard—and do not say in our account of its nature that any of these things pre-existed or came into being before the nature of the seed, but rather that the power abiding in the seed is manifested in a certain natural order, not that another nature is introduced, in the same way we suppose the human seed, at the first occasion of its construction, to have been sown with the potentiality of its nature, and that it is unfolded and manifested by a certain natural sequence as it proceeds to its perfect state, not taking to itself anything external as a means for being perfected, but advancing itself by sequence to the perfect state. So that it is not true to say either that the soul exists before the body, or that the body exists without the soul, but that there is one beginning of both, which, on the one hand, according to the lofty account, was laid as a foundation in the first will of God, and, on the other hand, according to the other account, is established in the occasions of genesis.

[29.4] As one cannot observe the articulation of the limbs in that which is implanted for the conception of the body before its being formed, so neither is it possible to perceive in the same the properties of the soul before they advance to

[114] Sus. (*Θ*) 42.

[115] Cf. 1 Pet. 3:4; Rom. 7:22; 2 Cor. 4:16; Eph. 3:16. Cf. Origen, *Dial.* 16–24; *Com. Songs* Prologue (Baehrens, 62.31–68.3; ET Lawson, 25–30).

ὥσπερ οὐκ ἄν τις ἀμφιβάλοι πρὸς τὰς τῶν ἄρθρων τε καὶ σπλάγχνων διαφορὰς ἐκεῖνο τὸ ἐντεθὲν σχηματίζεσθαι, οὐκ ἄλλης τινὸς δυνάμεως ἐπεισερχομένης, ἀλλὰ τῆς ἐγκειμένης φυσικῶς πρὸς τὴν ἐνέργειαν ταύτην μεθισταμένης· οὕτω καὶ περὶ ψυχῆς ἀναλόγως ἔστι τὸ ἶσον ὑπονοῆσαι, ὅτι κἂν μὴ διά τινων ἐνεργειῶν ἐν τῷ φαινομένῳ γνωρίζηται, οὐδὲν ἧττόν ἐστιν ἐν ἐκείνῳ· καὶ γὰρ καὶ τὸ εἶδος τοῦ μέλλοντος συνίστασθαι ἀνθρώπου ἐν ἐκείνῳ ἐστὶ τῇ δυνάμει, λανθάνει δὲ διὰ τὸ μὴ εἶναι δυνατὸν πρὸ τῆς ἀναγκαίας ἀκολουθίας ἀναφανῆναι· οὕτω καὶ ἡ ψυχή, ἔστι μὲν ἐν ἐκείνῳ καὶ μὴ φαινομένη, φανήσεται [D] δὲ διὰ τῆς οἰκείας ἑαυτῆς καὶ κατὰ φύσιν ἐνεργείας, τῇ σωματικῇ αὐξήσει συμπροϊοῦσα. **[29.5]** Ἐπειδὴ γὰρ οὐκ ἀπὸ νεκροῦ σώματος ἡ πρὸς τὴν σύλληψιν δύναμις ἀποκρίνεται ἀλλ᾽ ἐξ ἐμψύχου καὶ ζῶντος· διὰ τοῦτό φαμεν εὔλογον εἶναι μὴ νεκρὸν καὶ ἄψυχον οἴεσθαι τὸ ἀπὸ ζῶντος εἰς ζωῆς ἀφορμὴν προϊέμενον· τὸ γὰρ ἐν σαρκὶ ἄψυχον, καὶ νεκρόν ἐστι πάντως· ἡ δὲ νεκρότης κατὰ στέρησιν ψυχῆς γίνεται· οὐκ ἂν δέ τις ἐπὶ τούτου πρεσβυτέραν τῆς ἕξεως εἴποι τὴν στέρησιν, εἴπερ τὸ ἄψυχον, ὅπερ νεκρότης ἐστὶ, τῆς ψυχῆς εἶναί τις κατασκευάζοι πρεσβύτερον. [237] Εἰ δέ τις καὶ ἐναργέστερον ζητοίη τεκμήριον τοῦ ζῆν ἐκεῖνο τὸ μέρος ὅπερ ἀρχὴ τοῦ κατασκευαζομένου γίνεται ζώου, δυνατόν ἐστι καὶ δι᾽ ἄλλων σημείων δι᾽ ὧν τὸ ἔμψυχον ἐκ τοῦ νεκροῦ διακρίνεται, καὶ περὶ τούτου κατανοῆσαι· τεκμήριον γὰρ τοῦ ζῆν ἐπὶ τῶν ἀνθρώπων ποιούμεθα, τὸ θερμὸν εἶναί τινα καὶ ἐνεργὸν καὶ κινούμενον· τὸ δὲ κατεψυγμένον τε καὶ ἀκίνητον ἐπὶ τῶν σωμάτων, οὐδὲν ἕτερον εἰ μὴ νεκρότης ἐστίν.

[29.6] Ἐπειδὴ τοίνυν ἔνθερμόν τε καὶ ἐνεργὸν θεωροῦμεν τοῦτο περὶ οὗ τὸν λόγον ποιούμεθα, τὸ μηδὲ ἄψυχον εἶναι διὰ τούτων συντεκμαιρόμεθα· ἀλλ᾽ ὥσπερ κατὰ τὸ σωματικὸν αὐτοῦ μέρος, οὐ σάρκα φαμὲν αὐτὸ καὶ ὀστέα καὶ τρίχας καὶ ὅσα περὶ τὸ ἀνθρώπινον καθορᾶται, ἀλλὰ τῇ δυνάμει μὲν εἶναι τούτων ἕκαστον, οὔπω δὲ κατὰ τὸ ὁρώμενον [B] φαίνεσθαι· οὕτω καὶ ἐπὶ τοῦ ψυχικοῦ μέρους, οὔπω μὲν τὸ λογικὸν καὶ ἐπιθυμητικὸν καὶ θυμοειδὲς καὶ ὅσα περὶ ψυχὴν καθορᾶται, καὶ ἐν ἐκείνῳ χώραν ἔχειν φαμὲν, ἀναλόγως δὲ τῆς τοῦ σώματος κατασκευῆς τε καὶ τελειώσεως, καὶ τὰς

34 ἀμφιβάλλοι Æ P[ac] O Q(?) : διαμφιβάλλοι M 35 ἐντεθὲν] ἐντεῦθεν Æ P T 36 φυσικῶς] φύσεως N ταύτην] *ita* Æ B E I M N O Q R[pc] S *Forb* : ταύτης A D F L P R[ac] T W X *Ald* : αὐτῆς *Mign* οὕτως M N R *SP* περὶ] περὶ τῆς Æ B O 37 ἴσον I M S X νοῆσαι T τινων] τῶν N 38 γνωρίζεται I R[ac] καὶ[2] *om.* Æ D E F L P S W X 39 ἐκείνῳ] ἐκείνῃ M 40 πρὸ] πρὸς *Mign* οὕτως Æ R ἡ *om.* T ἔστι] *ita* Æ ß I L M O P R S W X *Ald Forb* : ἐστι *Mign* 41 ἑαυτῆς] ἑαυτῇ I R : αὐτῇ M *SP* 43 ἐπεισκρίνεται *SP* ζῶντος] ζῶντος καὶ S 43–4 διὰ τοῦτό— ζῶντος *om.* X 44 εἶναι] ἂν R : εἶναι καὶ I L S οἴεσθαι] οἴεσθαι εἶναι N : εἶναι Q *Eri* εἰς] πρὸς I 44–5 ζωῆς ἀφορμὴν] ζῶσαν μορφὴν M 45 σαρκὶ] ζωῇ O ἡ δὲ νεκρότης] εἰ δὲ νεκρὸν T 46 ψυχῆς στέρησιν N ψυχῆς] τῆς ψυχῆς D E 48 κατασκευάζει ß *Ald Mign* ἐναργέστερον] ἐναργὲς M : ἐνεργέστερον D (ερ *2[a] man.*) N[ac] P R[ac] X ζητοίει O 49 ζώου *om.* D 50 ἐκ] ὃ ἐκ *SP* 51 γὰρ] δὲ X 52 ἐνεργὸν] ἐνεργοῦντα M 54 ἐπειδὴ] ἐπεὶ N 55 ποιούμεθα] ποιησόμεθα M μηδ᾽ I 56 αὐτὸ] αὐτῷ I R τρίχα L 56–7 τὸν ἄνθρωπον L 57 καθορᾶται] θεωρεῖται L M εἶναι *om.* O τούτῶν ἕκαστον εἶναι W *Ald Mign* 58 φαίνεται T οὕτως M P X *SP* 58–9 οὔπω—θυμοειδὲς] nondum quidem totum animosum scilicet *Eri* 58 καὶ[2]] καὶ τὸ R 59 ἐπιθυμητικὸν καὶ θυμοειδὲς] θυμοειδὲς καὶ θυμικὸν *I* ψυχὴν] τὴν ψυχὴν Æ B T ἐκείνῃ M 60 ἔχει *SP*

activity; and just as no one would doubt that what is implanted is shaped into the different varieties of limbs and internal organs—not by some other power being imported, but by that residing in it naturally, transforming the same to this activity—so also, analogously, it may equally be supposed in the case of the soul, that even if it is not made known by any apparent activity, it is nonetheless in it. For even the form of the human being to come is in it potentially, but concealed because it is not possible for it to be made visible before the necessary sequence of events, so also the soul is in it, even though not visible, and will become apparent by means of its own proper and natural activity, as it advances along with the bodily growth. **[29.5]** Since the potential for conception is secreted not from a dead body, but from one which is animate and living, for this reason we say it is reasonable that what is sent forth from a living being to be the occasion of life is not supposed to be dead and inanimate; for in the flesh that which is inanimate is surely dead, and the condition of death arises from the withdrawal of the soul.[116] Would not one in this case be saying that the withdrawal is older than possession, if, that is, he maintains that the inanimate state, which is the condition of death, is older than the soul? And, if anyone should seek for still clearer evidence of the life that becomes the beginning of the living creature being fashioned, it is possible to gain an idea regarding this through other signs as well, by which what is animate is distinguished from what is dead. For in the case of human beings we consider it evidence of life that one is warm and active and moving; but the chill and motionless state in the case of bodies, is nothing other than the condition of death.

[29.6] Since then we see that of which we are speaking to be warm and active, we thereby draw the further inference that it is not inanimate; but, just as, with respect to its corporeal part, we do not say that it is flesh and bones and hair and all that is observed in humankind, but that it is potentially each of these things, although it does not yet visibly appear to be so, so also, with respect to the animated part, the rational faculty and the desirous and the incensive and anything else pertaining to the soul are not yet visible, yet we assert that they have their place in it, and that analogously to the formation and perfection of the

[116] Cf. *An. et res.* 2.3 (Spira, 14.16–22; ET 178); *Cat. Or.* 11.1 (Mühlenberg, 39.15–18).

τῆς ψυχῆς ἐνεργείας τῷ ὑποκειμένῳ συναύξεσθαι. [29.7] Ὥσπερ γὰρ τελειωθεὶς ὁ ἄνθρωπος, ἐν τοῖς μείζοσιν ἔχει διαφαινομένην τῆς ψυχῆς τὴν ἐνέργειαν· οὕτως ἐν ἀρχῇ τῆς συστάσεως τὴν κατάλληλόν τε καὶ σύμμετρον τῇ παρούσῃ χρείᾳ συνέργειαν τῆς ψυχῆς ἐφ' ἑαυτοῦ διαδείκνυσιν, ἐν τῷ κατασκευάζειν αὐτὴν ἑαυτῇ διὰ τῆς ἐντεθείσης ὕλης τὸ προσφυὲς οἰκητήριον· οὐδὲ γὰρ εἶναι δυνατὸν λογιζόμεθα, ἀλλοτρίαις οἰκοδομαῖς τὴν ψυχὴν ἐναρμόζεσθαι, ὡς οὐκ ἔστι τὴν ἐν τῷ κηρῷ σφραγίδα πρὸς ἀλλοτρίαν ἁρμοσθῆναι γλυφήν. [29.8] [C] Καθάπερ γὰρ τὸ σῶμα ἐκ βραχυτάτου πρὸς τὸ τέλειον πρόεισιν, οὕτω καὶ ἡ τῆς ψυχῆς ἐνέργεια καταλλήλως ἐμφυομένη τῷ ὑποκειμένῳ, συνεπιδίδωσι καὶ συναύξεται· προηγεῖται μὲν γὰρ αὐτῆς ἐν τῇ πρώτῃ κατασκευῇ οἷον ῥίζης τινὸς ἐν τῇ γῇ κατακρυφθείσης ἡ αὐξητική τε καὶ θρεπτικὴ δύναμις μόνη· οὐ γὰρ χωρεῖ τὸ περισσότερον ἡ τοῦ δεχομένου βραχύτης· εἶτα, προελθόντος εἰς φῶς τοῦ φυτοῦ καὶ ἡλίῳ τὴν βλάστην δείξαντος, ἡ αἰσθητικὴ χάρις ἐπήνθησεν· ἁδρυνθέντος δὲ ἤδη καὶ εἰς σύμμετρον μῆκος ἀναδραμόντος, καθάπερ τις καρπὸς διαλάμπειν ἡ λογικὴ δύναμις ἄρχεται, οὐ πᾶσα ἀθρόως ἐκφαινομένη, ἀλλὰ τῇ τοῦ ὀργάνου τελειώσει δι' ἐπιμελείας συναύξουσα, τοσοῦτον ἀεὶ καρποφοροῦσα ὅσον χωρεῖ τοῦ ὑποκειμένου ἡ δύναμις.

[29.9] Εἰ δὲ ζητεῖς ἐν [D] τῇ τοῦ σώματος πλάσει τὰς ψυχικὰς ἐνεργείας, **πρόσεχε σεαυτῷ**, φησὶ Μωϋσῆς, καὶ ἀναγνώσῃ καθάπερ ἐν βίβλῳ τῶν τῆς ψυχῆς ἔργων τὴν ἱστορίαν· αὐτὴ γάρ σοι διηγεῖται ἡ φύσις, λόγου παντὸς ἐναργέστερον, τὰς ποικίλας ἐν τῷ σώματι τῆς ψυχῆς ἀσχολίας ἔν τε ταῖς καθόλου καὶ ἐν ταῖς ἐπὶ μέρους κατασκευαῖς. [29.10] Ἀλλὰ περιττὸν οἶμαι λόγῳ τὰ καθ' ἡμᾶς αὐτοὺς διεξιέναι, καθάπέρ τι τῶν ὑπερορίων διηγουμένους θαυμάτων· τίς γὰρ ἑαυτὸν βλέπων, [240] λόγῳ δεῖται τὴν οἰκείαν φύσιν διδάσκεσθαι; δυνατὸν γάρ ἐστι, τὸν τῆς ζωῆς τρόπον κατανοήσαντα καὶ ὡς πρὸς πᾶσαν ζωτικὴν ἐνέργειαν ἐπιτηδείως ἔχει τὸ σῶμα καταμαθόντα, γνῶναι περὶ τί κατησχολήθη τὸ φυτικὸν τῆς ψυχῆς παρὰ τὴν πρώτην τοῦ γινομένου διάπλασιν· ὥστε καὶ διὰ τούτου φανερὸν εἶναι τοῖς οὐκ ἀνεπισκέπτοις, τὸ μὴ νεκρόν τε καὶ ἄψυχον ἐν τῷ ἐργαστηρίῳ γενέσθαι τῆς φύσεως ὃ πρὸς τὴν τοῦ

61 *συναύξεσθαι*] *συναίρεσθαι* M 62 *ἔχει διαφαινομένην*] *διαφαινομένην ἔχει* B^{pc} ß *τὴν τῆς ψυχῆς* *SP* 63 *χρείᾳ om.* O 64 *συνεργίαν* Æ I L N P^{2} S *ἑαυτοῦ*] *ἑαυτὴν* T *αὐτὴν*] *ἑαυτὴν* D^{ac} F^{ac} P X 65 *οὐδὲ*] *οὐ* B 67 *σφαγῖδα* I M O S *γὰρ*] *δὲ* Æ B^{2} ß I M N O Q R T : *om.* B^{ac} *SP* 68 *οὕτως* Æ R *τῆς ψυχῆς ἡ* N 69 *ἐμφυομένη*] *ἐμφαινομένη* B 70 *αὐτῆς*] *αὐτῇ* M *ἐν om.* Æ B I M N O Q R^{ac} T W *SP* *κατακρυβείσης* L 72 *τοῦ φυτοῦ*] *τούτου* A (*sed non* Æ) D E F L N^{mg} P S X 73 *διαδείξαντος* Q *SP* *ἐπήνθησεν*] superadicitur *Eri* *ἁδρυνθέντος*] *ἀδρυνθέντος* Æ N R^{ac} : *ἀνδρυνθέντος* A D^{ac} O Q W X : *ἀνδρινθέντος* B : *ἁδρυθέντος* D^{2} E F S : *ἀνδρυθέντος* P^{ac} : *ἀδρυθέντος* P^{pc} *δὲ om.* B E 77 *ψυχικὰς*] *τῆς ψυχῆς* A (*non* Æ) D E F L P S X *πρόσχες* I O 78 *μωϋσῆς*] *ὁ μωϋσῆς* R *βιβλίῳ* ß I M Q R W *ἔργων*] *ἐνεργειῶν* Æ B E I M N O Q R T : operationes *Dion Eri* 79 *αὕτη* R *σοι*] *σε* L P S X *ἐνεργέστερον* B N R^{ac} W *ποικιλίας* P 80 *τῷ om.* D L P R^{2} S X *τε om.* M *ἐν*^{2} *om.* L M P Q S X *κατασκευαῖς*] *ita* A D E F L M N^{mg} P S W X *Forb* : *διασκευαῖς* Æ O R *SP Ald Mign* 82 *ὑπερορίων*] *ὑπερόγκων* N $R^{ac?}$ T *διηγούμενον* T *θαυμάτων*] *πραγμάτων* M *λόγῳ*] *λόγων* Q *Dion* : *om.* L *δεῖται*] *δεῖ περὶ* Q 83 *οἰκείαν*] *ἰδίαν* Æ B I M N O Q R T W *SP* *ζωῆς*] *κατασκευῆς* M *κατανοήσαντας* Q 84 *ζωτικὴν*] *βιωτικὴν* M *καταμανθάνοντα* D E : *καταμαθόντας* Q 85–6 *τὸ φυτικὸν—διάπλασιν*] animae primordialis seu potius germinalis illa potentia *Dion* 85 *τὸ φυτικὸν τῆς ψυχῆς*] germinalis animae uita *Eri* *φυτικὸν* Æ B I O R^{ac} : *φυσικὸν al. codd. SP Ald Forb Mign* 86 *γενομένου* ß N *οὐκ om.* Æ

body, so also the activities of the soul grow with the subject. [**29.7**] For just as a perfected human being has an especially marked activity of the soul in greater matters, so also at the beginning of his constitution he clearly shows in himself the cooperation of the soul appropriate and commensurate with the present need, in preparing for itself its proper dwelling place by means of the implanted matter; for we do not reckon that it is possible for the soul be adapted to a strange building, just as it is not possible for the stamp in the wax to be matched to an engraving of something else. [**29.8**] For just as the body proceeds from a very small original to the perfect state, so also the activity of the soul, growing in step with the subject, gains and increases with it. For in its first formation, first of all comes the power of growth and nourishment alone, as though some root buried in the ground, for the smallness of the one receiving does not admit of more; then, as the plant comes to light and shows it shoot to the sun, the gift of sense-perception blossoms; and when at last it is ripened and has grown up to its proper height, the rational faculty begins to shine, just like some fruit, not all appearing at once, but by diligence growing with the perfection of the instrument, always bearing as much fruit as the power of the subject grants.[117]

[**29.9**] If, however, you seek to trace the activity of the soul in the moulding of the body, *take heed to yourself*, as Moses says,[118] and you will read, as in a book, the account of the works of the soul; for nature itself expounds to you, more clearly than any discourse, the varied occupations of the soul in the body, in the acts of construction both general and particular. [**29.10**] But I deem it superfluous to declare at length in word things regarding ourselves, as though expounding some wonder beyond ourselves: for who, when looking at himself, needs words to be taught his own nature?[119] For it is possible for one who considers the mode of life, and learns how well suited the body is for every vital activity, to know with what the vegetative aspect of the soul was occupied from the first-fashioning of what came to be, so that thereby it is also clear to those who are not inattentive, that it was not a dead or inanimate thing, implanted by separation from the living body

[117] Cf. Alexander of Aphrodisias, *De an.* (esp. Bruns, 74.17–21; 81.13–22).
[118] Deut. 4:23.
[119] Cf. Basil, *Hom. de creat. hom.* 2.14 (Hörner, 66.6–7).

ζώου φυτείαν ἐκ τοῦ ζῶντος σώματος ἀποσπασθὲν ἐνετέθη. [29.11] *Καὶ γὰρ καὶ τῶν καρπῶν τὰς ἐντεριώνας καὶ τὰς τῶν ῥιζῶν ἀποσπάδας οὐ νεκρωθείσας τῆς ἐγκειμένης τῇ φύσει ζωτικῆς δυνάμεως τῇ γῇ καταβάλλομεν, ἀλλὰ συντηρούσας ἐν ἑαυταῖς κεκρυμμένην μὲν ζῶσαν δὲ πάντως, τοῦ πρωτοτύπου τὴν ἰδιότητα· τὴν δὲ τοιαύτην δύναμιν οὐκ ἐντίθησιν* [B] *ἡ περιέχουσα γῆ ἔξωθεν παρ' ἑαυτῆς ἐπεισκρίνουσα—ἦ γὰρ ἂν καὶ τὰ νεκρὰ τῶν ξύλων εἰς βλάστην προήγετο—ἀλλὰ τὴν ἐγκειμένην ἔκδηλον ἀπεργάζεται, διὰ τῆς οἰκείας ἰκμάδος τιθηνουμένη, εἰς ῥίζαν καὶ φλοιὸν καὶ ἐντεριώνην καὶ τὰς τῶν κλάδων ἐκφύσεις τὸ φυτὸν τελειοῦσα· ὅπερ οὐχ οἷόν τε ἦν γίνεσθαι, μή τινος φυσικῆς δυνάμεως συνεντεθείσης, ἥτις τὴν συγγενῆ καὶ κατάλληλον ἐκ τῶν παρακειμένων τροφὴν εἰς ἑαυτὴν ἕλκουσα, θάμνος ἢ δένδρον ἢ στάχυς ἤ τι τῶν φρυγανικῶν βλαστημάτων ἐγένετο.*

88 *σώματος*] *ὕδατος* I *ἐνετέθη*] *ἀνετέθη* I : *ἐτίθη* Q 89 *ἐντερώνας SP* 90 *δυνάμεως ζωτικῆς* N *συντηρούσης* M 91 *ἑαυταῖς*] *αὐταῖς* M Q *ζῶσαν*] *σώζουσαν* R *τῷ πρωτοτύπῳ* L P S W X : occulti *Eri* : *om. Dion* 93 *βλάστησιν* R *προηγάγετο* R T : *προήχετο* Æ[ac] *ἀλλὰ*] *ἀλλ' ἀεὶ* T 94 *ἐπικειμένην Ald Mign* *οἰκείας*] *ἰδίας* Æ B I N O T *SP* 95 *ἅπερ* O 96 *ἦν om.* E *γενέσθαι* Æ D E I O Q *συντεθείσης* M 97 *κατάλληλον*] *κατάλληλον γῆν* N *τῶν παρακειμένων*] accumbentibus humoribus *Eri* *τροφὴν*] *οἱονεὶ τροφὴν* N (*sed exp.*) *ἑαυτὴν*] *αὐτὴν* T : *σεαυτὴν* R[ac] 98 *ἢ στάχυς om.* D E L *ἤ τι*] *ἐπὶ* X *ἤ τι τῶν φρυγανικῶν om.* D E *φρυγανικῶν*] fotarum *Eri* *τῶν φρυγανικῶν βλαστημάτων*] ex huiusmodi rebus *Dion* *ἐγένετο*] *ἐπεγένετο* R T

for the growth of a living being, in the workshop of nature. [**29.11**] Moreover, we sow in the earth kernels of fruits and portions torn from roots, not deadened [by being deprived] of the vital power naturally residing in them, but preserving in themselves—hidden indeed, but certainly living—the property of their prototype; the surrounding earth does not implant such a power from without, introducing it from itself (for then even dead wood would proceed to growth), but it makes manifest that which resides within them, nourishing by its own moisture, perfecting the plant into root and bark and pith and the shoots of branches. This could not happen were not some natural power implanted within, which, drawing to itself its natural and appropriate nourishment from the surroundings, becomes a bush or a tree or an ear of grain or one of the sprouting shrubs.

Θεωρία τις ἰατρικωτέρα περὶ τῆς τοῦ σώματος ἡμῶν κατασκευῆς δι' ὀλίγων.

[30.1] *Ἀλλὰ τὴν μὲν ἀκριβῆ τοῦ σώματος ἡμῶν διασκευὴν διδάσκει μὲν ἕκαστος ἑαυτὸν ἐξ ὧν ὁρᾷ τε καὶ ζῇ καὶ αἰσθάνεται, τὴν ἰδίαν ἑαυτοῦ φύσιν διδάσκαλον ἔχων. Ἔξεστι δὲ καὶ τὴν ἐν βίβλοις φιλοπονηθεῖσαν τοῖς τὰ τοιαῦτα σοφοῖς περὶ τούτων ἱστορίαν ἀναλαβόντι, πάντα δι' ἀκριβείας μαθεῖν· ὧν οἱ μὲν ὅπως ἔχει θέσεως τὰ καθ' ἕκαστον τῶν ἐν ἡμῖν, διὰ τῆς ἀνατομῆς ἐδιδάχθησαν· οἱ δὲ καὶ πρὸς ὅ τι γέγονε πάντα τὰ τοῦ σώματος μόρια κατενόησάν τε καὶ διηγήσαντο· ὡς ἀρκοῦσαν ἐντεῦθεν τῆς ἀνθρωπίνης κατασκευῆς τὴν γνῶσιν τοῖς φιλοπόνοις γενέσθαι. Εἰ δέ τις ἐπιζητοίη πάντων αὐτῶν τὴν ἐκκλησίαν διδάσκαλον γίνεσθαι, ὡς εἰς μηδὲν τῆς ἔξωθεν φωνῆς ἐπιδέεσθαι (οὗτος γὰρ τῶν πνευματικῶν* [D] *προβάτων ὁ νόμος, καθώς φησιν ὁ Κύριος, τὸ ἀλλοτρίας φωνῆς μὴ ἀκούειν), διὰ βραχέων καὶ τὸν περὶ τούτων λόγον διαληψόμεθα.*

[30.2] *Τρία περὶ τὴν τοῦ σώματος ἐνοήσαμεν φύσιν, ὧν χάριν τὰ καθ' ἕκαστον τῶν ἐν ἡμῖν κατεσκεύασται. Τὰ μὲν γὰρ διὰ τὸ ζῆν, τὰ δὲ διὰ τὸ καλῶς ζῆν, ἕτερα δὲ πρὸς τὴν διαδοχὴν τῶν ἐπιγινομένων ἐπιτηδείως ἔχει. Ὅσα μὲν οὖν ἐν ἡμῖν τοιαῦτά ἐστιν ὧν ἄνευ συστῆναι τὴν ἀνθρωπίνην ζωὴν οὐκ ἐνδέχεται, ἐν τρισὶ μορίοις κατενοήσαμεν· ἐν ἐγκεφάλῳ καὶ καρδίᾳ καὶ ἥπατι. Ὅσα δὲ προσθήκη τις ἐστὶ τῶν ἀγαθῶν καὶ φιλοτιμία, τῆς φύσεως τὸ εὖ ζῆν δι' ἐκείνων τῷ ἀνθρώπῳ χαριζομένης,* [241] *τὰ περὶ τὴν αἴσθησίν ἐστιν ὄργανα· τὰ γὰρ τοιαῦτα τὴν μὲν ζωὴν ἡμῖν οὐ συνίστησιν, ἐπεὶ καὶ λειπόντων τινῶν πολλάκις, οὐδὲν ἧττον ἐν τῷ ζῆν ἐστιν ὁ ἄνθρωπος· ἀλλ' ἀμήχανον δίχα τούτων τῶν ἐνεργειῶν, τῶν κατὰ τὴν ζωὴν ἡδέων τὴν μετουσίαν ἔχειν. Ὁ δὲ τρίτος σκοπὸς πρὸς τὸ ἐφεξῆς τε καὶ τὴν διαδοχὴν βλέπει. Ἔστι δὲ καὶ ἄλλα τινὰ παρὰ ταῦτα, ἃ πρὸς διαμονὴν κοινὰ τοῖς πᾶσιν ὑπόκειται, τὰς καταλλήλους προσθήκας δι' ἑαυτῶν ἐπεισάγοντα, ὡς κοιλία καὶ πνεύμων, ὁ μὲν τῷ*

Cap. 31 Æ I N O Q R T *Dion*

30.90–6 (*ἐπειδὴ—πνεῦμα*): John (of Damascus), *Sacra Parallela* II[1]1218 / K cap K 1, 19 (Thum, 687.3–11) 30.250–1 (*ἀλλὰ— φύσεως*): John (of Damascus), *Sacra Parallela* II[1]40 / K cap. 1, 40 (Thum, 74.24–5) 30.253–78 (*τὸ γὰρ προκείμενον—τέλειον*): John (of Damascus), *Sacra Parallela* II[1]40 / K cap. 1, 40 (Thum, 74.25–75.27)

1 *θεωρία—ὀλίγων*] de triplici natura corporis *Λ*

1 *τις om.* D H P X *ἱστορικωτέρα* K O *δι' ὀλίγων om.* N 2 *διασκευὴν*] *κατασκευὴν* M 3 *ὁρᾷ τε*] *ὁρᾶται* M Q R[ac] *φύσιν ἑαυτοῦ* Æ B M N Q R S T W 4 *ἐν*] *ἐν τοῖς* B 5 *ἱστορίαν*] *ἰατρείαν* H *ἀναλαμβάνοντι* N R[ac] *δι'*] *μετὰ* A (*sed non* Æ) D E F H L P S W X *ὅπως*] *πῶς* M *ἔχῃ* K O Q R[ac?] T 5–6 *καθ' ἕκαστιν* K M S : *καθέκαστα* B : *καθέκαστον Ald Mign* 6 *καὶ om.* I K O 7 *τὰ om.* T 9 *αὐτῶν*] *αὐτῷ* Æ B C I K M O Q T *γενέσθαι* Æ B C H I K O W 9–10 *ὡς εἰς—ἐπιδέεσθαι*] *om. Eri* 9 *εἰς*] *ἂν* R[ac?] : *om.* B I M *τῆς om.* B 10 *ἐπιδέεσθαι*] *ἐπιδέσθαι* T : *ἐπιδύεσθαι Ald* : *ἐπιδεῖσθαι Mign* *οὗτος*] *οὕτως* Q R[ac] *ὁ νόμος om.* X 11 *φωνῆς μὴ ἀκούειν*] *ita* A B D E F H L P S X *Forb* : *μὴ ἀκούειν φωνῆς* Æ O W *Ald Mign* 13 *ἐνενοήσαμεν* Q *καθέκαστον* Æ H L M R : *καθέκαστα* B 14 *ζῆν*[1]] *ζῇν Mign* *διὰ*] *πρὸς* N *ζῇν καλῶς* M *ζῆν*[2]] *ζῇν Mign* *πρὸς*] *περὶ* N 15 *ἐπιγιγνομένων* N *ἔχειν* Æ L P[ac] S *οὖν—διαθάλπει* (*l.* 39) *def.* K O 16 *συστῆναι*] *στῆναι* T *τὴν ἀνθρωπίνην συστῆναι ζωὴν* A (*non* Æ) D E F H L P S X : *τὴν ἀνθρωπίνην ζωὴν συστῆναι* I 18 *ἐν om.* N *καὶ*[1] *om.* N *τῶν om.* D H L P S X 18–19 *καὶ φιλοτιμία τῶν ἀγαθῶν* I 18 *τῆς φύσεως om.* D *ζῆν*] *ζῆν καὶ* D H P X *τῷ ἀνθρώπῳ δι' ἐκείνων* B *τῷ ἀνθρώπῳ om.* N[ac] 19 *τὴν μὲν ζωὴν ἡμῖν*] *ita* Æ B D H I M N P Q R T W X *Forb* : *τὴν ζωὴν μὲν Ald Mign* *μὲν om.* L S 20 *λειπόντων*] *ita* Æ ß D H I M N Q R S (*ι add. sup. l.*) T W X *Forb* : *λιπόντων Ald Mign* *ὁ om.* T 21 *ἀλλ'*] *ὅμως* R : *ἀλλὰ καὶ* S *δίχα τούτων τῶν ἐνεργειῶν*] ex his quae operantur *Eri* 22 *σκοπὸς*] *τρόπος* R *πρὸς om.* D T 23 *διαμονὴν*] *διαμονὴν καὶ* D H L P R[2] S W X *τοῖς πᾶσιν κοινὰ* N 24 *μὲν*] *μὲν ἐν* L S W

A brief, more medical, contemplation regarding the formation of our body.[1]

[**30.1**] Now the exact structure of our body each one teaches himself from what he sees and lives and perceives, having his own proper nature as a teacher. It is also possible to learn everything with accuracy by taking up the research, contained in books, concerning these things laboured over by those wise in such matters. Some of these learnt by dissection the position of the individual organs in us; others also considered and expounded the reason for which all the parts of the body came to be; so that the knowledge of the human formation gathered thus suffices for the industrious. But if anyone further seeks that the Church should be his teacher on all these points, so that he may not be in need of anything from the voice of those outside (for this is the law of the spiritual sheep, as the Lord says, that they do not hear another voice[2]), we shall briefly take in hand the account of these matters also.

[**30.2**] There are three things we conceive of regarding the nature of the body, for the sake of which each of our particular parts were formed. Some are for the sake of living, others for living well, others are adapted towards the succession of descendants. All things, then, in us which are of such a kind that without them it is not possible to sustain human life, we consider as being in three parts: in the brain and the heart and the liver. On the other hand, all that are a kind of an addition of goods and bounties on the part of nature, bestowing on the human being the gift of living well through them, are the organs of sense-perception; for such things do not constitute our life, since even where some are often lacking the human being is none the less living; but without these activities it is impossible to have a share in the pleasures of life. The third looks to what comes after and the succession of life.[3] There are also certain other organs besides these, which, in common with the others, are subordinated to purpose of the continuance of life, importing by their own means the appropriate supplements, such as the stomach and the lungs, the latter fanning by breath the fire in the heart, the former

[1] *Bodl. 238* (as Chap. 31): 'Of the threefold nature of the body'. [2] Cf. John 10:5.

[3] Cf. Gregory of Nyssa, *An. et res.* 10.57 (Spira, 100.9–14); Galen, *De usu part.* 6.7 (Helmreich, 1, 318.8–15, ET 1, 292), 14.1 (Helmreich, 2, 283.142–285.6; ET 620–1).

πνεύματι τὸ ἐγκάρδιον πῦρ ἀναρριπίζων, ἡ δὲ τοῖς σπλάγχνοις τὴν τροφὴν εἰσοικίζουσα. [30.3] *Οὕτω τοίνυν τῆς ἐν ἡμῖν κατασκευῆς διῃρημένης, ἔστιν ἀκριβῶς κατανοῆσαι, ὅτι οὐ μονοειδῶς ἡμῖν δι' ἑνός τινος ἡ πρὸς τὸ ζῆν δύναμις διεξάγεται, ἀλλὰ πλείοσι μορίοις ἡ φύσις* [B] *τὰς πρὸς τὴν σύστασιν ἡμῶν ἀφορμὰς ἐπινείμασα, ἀναγκαίαν ποιεῖ πρὸς τὸ ὅλον τὴν παρ' ἑκάστου συνεισφοράν· ὥστε καὶ ὅσα πρὸς ἀσφάλειαν τῆς ζωῆς καὶ κάλλος ἡ φύσις ἐπετεχνάσατο, πλείω τε ἐστὶ ταῦτα καὶ πολλὴν πρὸς ἄλληλα τὴν διαφορὰν ἔχει.* [30.4] *Ἀλλ' οἶμαι διελέσθαι πρότερον ἐν ὀλίγῳ χρῆναι τῶν πρὸς τὴν σύστασιν τῆς ζωῆς συντελούντων ἡμῖν τὰς πρώτας ἀρχάς. Ἡ μὲν οὖν τοῦ παντὸς σώματος ὕλη, κοινὴ τοῖς καθ' ἕκαστον μέλεσιν ὑποκειμένη, σιγάσθω τανῦν· οὐδὲν γὰρ ἡμῖν πρὸς τὸν σκοπὸν συντελέσει ἡ καθόλου φυσιολογία πρὸς τὴν μερικὴν θεωρίαν.* [30.5] *Ὁμολογουμένου τοίνυν παρὰ πᾶσι τοῦ πάντων ἐν ἡμῖν εἶναι τῶν στοιχειωδῶς ἐν τῷ κόσμῳ θεωρουμένων τὴν μοῖραν, τοῦ τε θερμοῦ καὶ τοῦ ψύχοντος καὶ τῆς ἑτέρας συζυγίας τῆς κατὰ τὸ ὑγρόν* [C] *τε καὶ ξηρὸν νοουμένης, τὰ καθ' ἕκαστον ἡμῖν διαληπτέον.*

[30.6] *Οὐκοῦν ὁρῶμεν τρεῖς τὰς διοικητικὰς τῆς ζωῆς δυνάμεις· ὧν ἡ μὲν διαθάλπει τὸ πᾶν τῇ θερμότητι, ἡ δὲ ὑπονοτίζει τῇ ἰκμάδι τὸ θερμαινόμενον, ὡς ἂν τῇ ἰσοκρατίᾳ τῆς τῶν ἐναντίων ποιότητος ἐπὶ τοῦ μέσου συντηροῖτο τὸ ζῶον, μήτε τοῦ ὑγροῦ καταφρυγομένου τῷ πλεονασμῷ τῆς θερμότητος μήτε τοῦ θερμοῦ σβεννυμένου τῇ ἐπικρατείᾳ τοῦ καθυγραίνοντος· ἡ δὲ τρίτη δύναμις συνέχει δι' ἑαυτῆς κατά τινα συμβολήν τε καὶ ἁρμονίαν τὰ διακεκριμένα τῶν ἄρθρων, τοῖς παρ' ἑαυτῆς συνδέσμοις ἁρμόζουσα* [D] *καὶ πᾶσιν ἐπιπέμπουσα τὴν αὐτοκίνητόν τε καὶ προαιρετικὴν δύναμιν, ἧς ἐπιλειπούσης, πάρετον γίνεται καὶ νεκρῶδες τὸ μέρος, τοῦ προαιρετικοῦ πνεύματος ἀμοιρῆσαν.* [30.7] *Μᾶλλον δὲ, πρὸ τούτων ἄξιον κατανοῆσαι τὸ τεχνικὸν τῆς φύσεως ἡμῶν ἐν αὐτῇ τῇ δημιουργίᾳ τοῦ σώματος. Ἐπειδὴ γὰρ τὸ σκληρόν τε καὶ ἀντίτυπον τὰς αἰσθητικὰς ἐνεργείας οὐ καταδέχεται,*

26 *οὔτως* Æ N 24–5 *τῆς ἐν ἡμῖν κατασκευῆς*] *ita* A Æ B D E F H I M P Q R S W X *Forb* : *τῆς κατασκευῆς τῆς ἐν ἡμῖν* *Ald Mign* 27 *ὅτι*] *ὡς* R 28 *ἡ φύσις* *post* *ἡμῶν* (*l.* 28) *pon.* N *φύσις*] *φύσις καὶ* M *πρὸς*] *εἰς* M *τὴν* *om.* D 29 *ἐπινείμασα*] inspirans *Eri* *ποιεῖ* *om.* R *ποιεῖ—συνεισφοράν*] *τὴν παρ' ἑκάστου τὴν* [*τὴν* *exp.*] *πρὸς τὸ ὅλον συνεισφορὰν ἐποιήσατο* R 30 *κάλος* H R^{mg} *ἐπετεχνήσατο* M Q W 31 *ἔχοι* Q 32 *ἡμῶν συντελούντων* M 33 *σώματος* *om.* N^{ac} T *ὕλη* *om.* T *καθέκαστον* I R 34 *τανῦν*] *νῦν* A D E F H L P S X : *τὰ νῦν* Æ R *οὐδὲ* N^{ac} R *ἡμῖν πρὸς τὸν σκοπὸν*] *ita* A D E F H L M P Q R S X *Forb* : *πρὸς τὸν σκόπον ἡμῖν* W *Ald Mign* *ἡμῖν*] *ἡμῶν* N 36 *πάντως* R *τῶν στοιχειωδῶς*] *στοιχείων τῶν* R *θεωρουμένων ἐν τῷ κόσμῳ* H L P S X *θεωρουμένων* *om.* D 37 *τε* *om.* M N P Q R *καί*[2]] *καὶ τοῦ* Q 39 *οὐκοῦν*] non ergo *Eri* *τὰς* *om.* T *διοικήσεις* L *διαθάλπει*] *θάλπει* K N O : *διαλάμπει* B 41 *ἰσοκρατίᾳ*] *ita* B D E F H I K L M O P Q S X *Ald Forb* : *ἰσοκρασίᾳ* N R : *ἰσοκρατείᾳ* *Mign* *συντηροῖ* D : *συντηροίη* R : *συντηρεῖ* B : *συρροῖτο* M *τὸ* *om.* W 43 *τῇ ἐπικρατήσει* Æ B I K M O Q R T W : *τῷ πλεονασμῷ* N *καθυγραίνοντος*] *ὑγραίνοντος* R : *ὑγρότητος* N 46 *ἧς—μέρος*] dum administrationem artuum reliquens deficit neglectum corpus *Eri* *ἐπιλιπούσης* D M S *πάρετον*] *ita* Æ ß H N O Q R S X W *Forb* : *πάραιτον* P X : *περάτον* *Ald Mign* *γίνεται*] *τὸ σῶμα γίνεται* Q *μέρος*] *μέρος τὸ* N : *μέρος οὐ* Q 48 *ἐν*] *ἐπ'* H P S 49 *τε* *om.* Æ B I K M N O Q R T *ἐνεργείας*] *συνεργείας* O *οὐ καταδέχεται*] *οὐκ ἀναδέχεται* Æ B I K M N O Q R^{ac} T

introducing nourishment for the internal organs.[4] **[30.3]** When our formation is thus divided, then, one must understand accurately that the power for living is not conducted uniformly by any single organ in us, but that nature, by distributing the means for our existence among several parts, makes the contribution of each necessary for the whole, just as the things which nature contrives for the security and beauty of life are also numerous and differ greatly among themselves.[5] **[30.4]** But I think we ought first to discuss briefly the first principles of the things that contribute to the constitution of our life. The material of the whole body, the substratum common to each of the parts, may be left unremarked for now, for a discussion regarding natural substance in general will not contribute to our purpose regarding the consideration of the particular parts. **[30.5]** As, then, it is acknowledged by all that there is in us a share of everything contemplated as elements in the world—of heat and of cold, and of the other pair conceived, moisture and dryness—we must discuss them severally.[6]

[30.6] We see, then, that the powers which regulate life are three, of which one by its heat warms everything, and the other by its moisture keeps damp that which is warmed, so that the living being is held in an intermediate condition by the equal balance of the qualities of the opposing powers (with neither the moisture being dried up by the excess of heat nor the warmth being quenched by the prevalence of that which is moist), and the third power holds together, through itself, the separate members of the assemblage in a certain concord and harmony, connecting them by bonds, which it itself supplies, and sending into them all that self-moving and self-determining faculty, lacking which the part becomes riven and deadened, left destitute of the self-determining spirit. **[30.7]**[7] Or rather, before dealing with these, it is proper to consider the skilled workmanship of nature in the actual crafting of the body. For as that which is hard and resistant is not able to

[4] Cf. Plato, *Tim.* 70b–d; Galen, *De usu part.* 4.1 (Helmreich, 1, 195, ET 1, 204), 6.2 (Helmreich, 1, 300.20–301.17; ET 1, 279–80).

[5] Cf. Galen, *De usu part.* 9.8 (Helmreich, 2, 23.2–7; ET 1, 439).

[6] Cf. Gregory of Nyssa, *An. et res.* 1.9–10 (Spira, 7.11–19).

[7] For the following paragraphs, see Galen, *De usu part.* 5.9 (Helmreich, 1, 276.26–278.13; ET 1, 263–4), 8.5 (Helmreich, 1, 458.25–459.6; ET 1, 396–7), 8.6 (Helmreich, 1, 461.1–463.15; ET 398–400), 9.14 (Helmreich, 2, 42.6–43.2; ET 1, 453–4), 11.28 (Helmreich, 2, 172.18–173.8: ET 2, 542–3), 12.2 (Helmreich, 2, 183.17–26; ET 2, 551), 16.2 (Helmreich, 2, 380.24–381.13; ET 2, 684); *Hipp. et Plat.* 1.10.12–14 (De Lacy, 1, 98).

ὡς ἔστιν ἰδεῖν ἐπί τε τῶν ἐν ἡμῖν ὀστέων καὶ τῶν ἐν τῇ γῇ φυτῶν, ἐν οἷς ζωῆς μέν τι κατανοοῦμεν εἶδος ἐν τῷ αὔξειν καὶ τρέφεσθαι, οὐ μὴν παρεδέξατο ἡ ἀντιτυπία τοῦ ὑποκειμένου τὴν αἴσθησιν· τούτου χάριν ἔδει καθάπερ κηροειδῆ τινα κατασκευὴν ὑποτεθῆναι ταῖς κατ' αἴσθησιν ἐνεργείαις, δυναμένην τοῖς ἀντιληπτικοῖς τύποις ἐνσφραγισθῆναι, μήτε συγχεομένην δι' ὑπερβαλλούσης ὑγρότητος (οὐ γὰρ [244] *ἂν διαμένοι ἐν τῷ ὑγρῷ τὸ τυπούμενον) μήτε ἀντιτυποῦσαν ἐν τῇ ἀμετρίᾳ τῆς πήξεως (ἀσήμαντον γὰρ πρὸς τοὺς τύπους ἐστὶ τὸ ἀνύπεικτον) ἀλλὰ μέσως ἔχουσαν μαλακότητός τε καὶ στερρότητος, ὡς ἂν μὴ τοῦ καλλίστου τῶν κατὰ τὴν φύσιν ἐνεργημάτων, τῆς αἰσθητικῆς λέγω κινήσεως, ἀμοιροίη τὸ ζῶον.* **[30.8]** *Ἐπειδὴ τοίνυν τὸ μαλακόν τε καὶ εὔεικτον, μηδεμίαν τὴν ἐκ τῶν στερρῶν ἔχον συνεργίαν ἀκίνητον ἂν ἦν πάντως καὶ ἀδιάρθρωτον κατὰ τοὺς θαλασσίους πνεύμονας· διὰ τοῦτο καταμίγνυσιν ἡ φύσις τῷ σώματι τὴν τῶν ὀστέων στερρότητα, καὶ ταῦτα πρὸς ἄλληλα διὰ τῆς προσφυοῦς ἁρμονίας ἑνώσασα, τοῖς τε διὰ τῶν νεύρων συνδέσμοις τὰς συμβολὰς αὐτῶν ἐπισφίγξασα, οὕτως αὐτοῖς τὴν δεκτικὴν τῶν αἰσθήσεων περιέφυσε σάρκα, δυσπαθεστέρᾳ τε καὶ εὐτονωτέρᾳ τῇ ἐπιφανείᾳ* [B] *διειλημμένην.*

[30.9] *Ταύτῃ τοίνυν τῇ στερρᾷ τῶν ὀστέων φύσει, οἷον στύλοις τισὶν ἀχθοφόροις, ὅλον τοῦ σώματος ἐπιθεῖσα τὸ βάρος, οὐκ ἀδιαίρετον ἐνέφυσε τῷ παντὶ τὸ ὀστέον· ἦ γὰρ ἂν ἀκίνητός τε καὶ ἀνενέργητος ἔμεινεν, εἰ οὕτω κατασκευῆς εἶχεν ὁ ἄνθρωπος, καθάπέρ τι δένδρον ἐφ' ἑνὸς τόπου μένον, μήτε τῆς τῶν σκελῶν διαδοχῆς ἐπὶ τὸ πρόσω προαγούσης τὴν κίνησιν μήτε τῆς τῶν χειρῶν ὑπουργίας χρησιμευούσης τῷ βίῳ· νυνὶ δὲ μεταβατικὸν εἶναι καὶ πρακτικὸν τὸ ὄργανον διὰ τῆς ἐπινοίας ταύτης*

50 *οἷς*] *οἷς καὶ* M *μέν τι ζωῆς* N 51 *κατανοούμενον* N : *κατὰ τὸ νοούμενον* T *αὔξειν*] *αὔξειν τε* M *παρεδέξατο*] *ita* A Æ B C D E H I K M N O P Q R T W X *Forb* : *ἐδέξατο* M : *παρεδέξατο ἐναντίως* N^mg S *Ald Mign* *ἀντιτυπία*] *σκληρότης* F^sup.l. P^mg 52 *ἔδει*] *δεῖ* N *καθάπερ ἔδει* R^ac *τινα κηροειδῆ* M *τινα*] *τὴν* N 53 *τὰς … ἐνεργείας* Q *κατ'*] *κατὰ τὴν* P *ἀντιληπτικοῖς*] *ἀντιτυπικοῖς* B 54 *οὐ*] *οὐδὲ* A *ἂν om.* A 55 *διαμένοι*] *ita* Æ C I K L N O Q S T W *Forb* : *διαμείνοι* M R *Ald Mign* : *διαμείνῃ* D E H : *διαμείνει* P X : *διαμήνει* A : *διαμένει* B : *διαμένῃ* F² : *ἀναμένῃ* F¹ *ἐν*² *om.* N 55–6 *πήξεως*] *πήξεως ἀσήμαντον εἶναι* Æ B C E I K O 56 *ἀσήμαντον—ἀνύπεικτον*] quia quod nescit cedere imaginem nequit impressione excipere *Dion* *πρὸς τοὺς τύπους*] ad characteres *Eri* 57 *ἂν om.* B *τὴν om.* D H N P S T X 59 *τὴν*] *τῶν* L T^ac : *om.* B D E *στερρῶν*] *ἑτέρων* T *συνεργίαν*] *ita* Æ C D E F H I K L M N O P² R S *Forb* : *συνέργειαν* A P^ac Q X : *ἐνέργειαν* W *Ald Mign* 60 *ἂν om.* N^ac *ἦν*] *εἴη* R *θαλαττίους* L M 61 *ὀστέων*] *ὀστέων ἀντιτυπίαν τε καὶ* N 62 *πρὸς ἄλληλα om.* N *ἁρμονίας*] *συμφυοῦς* M *ἑνώσασα*] *ἡνώσατο* B 63 *οὕτω* H L P S X *αὐτοῖς*] *τοῖς αὐτοῖς* A D E F H L P S X 64 *δυσπαθεστέρᾳ τε καὶ εὐτονωτέρᾳ*] *ita* A C D E F I K O P R S² T W (*δυσπαθετέρᾳ*) X *Forb* : *δυσπαθεστέραν τε καὶ εὐτονωτέραν* ß H *Ald Mign* *τῇ ἐπιφανείᾳ*] *τῆς ἐπιφανείας* P^ac : *om.* T 67 *ἐνέφυσε*] *ἐπέφυσε* M : *ἀνέφυσε* L *ἦ*] *ἢ* H N P 68 *τε om.* Q *οὕτως* Æ N R^ac 69 *ἐφ'*] *ἀφ'* I² K *μένων* B L M 70 *προαγούσης*] *προαγούσης τῆς φύσεως* B^ac (*sed non* ß) 71 *νῦν* N *μεταβατικὸν*] *καταβατικὸν* B *πρακτικὸν*] *προακτικὸν* B C O

contain the activity of the senses (as one can see in the case of our own bones, and in that of plants in the earth, in which we can indeed perceive a certain form of life, in that they grow and receive nourishment, yet in reverse the resistant character of their substrate does not allow them sense-perception), for this reason it was necessary that some wax-like formation, as it were, should be supplied for the activities of the senses, capable of being impressed with the stamp of things able to be apprehended, neither becoming confused by the excess of moisture (for the impress would not remain in moist substance), nor resisting by disproportionate solidity (for that which is unyielding is unmarked by the impresses), but holding a middle state between softness and hardness, so that the living being might not be destitute of the most beautiful of all the activities of nature, I mean the movement of sense-perception. **[30.8]** Since, then, something soft and yielding, having no assistance from the hard parts, would certainly be unmoving and without articulation, like sea molluscs,[8] for this reason nature mixes into the body the hardness of the bones, and uniting these by close connection one to another, knitting their joints together by the bonds of the sinews, and thus makes the flesh, which is receptive to the senses, grow around them, furnished with a harder and tauter appearance.

[30.9] While placing, then, the whole weight of the body on the firm nature of the bones, as on columns bearing something, [nature] did not implant the bones undivided through the whole structure, for in that case the human being would have remained without movement or activity, if he had been so constructed, just like a tree remaining on one spot, with neither the alternating of legs to advance its movement further, nor the ministry of the hands serving the mode of life. But as it is she contrived that the organism should be made capable of walking and working by means of this device, by the self-determining spirit which extends through the

[8] Cf. Aristotle, *De part. an.* 4.5 (681a18–20).

ἐμηχανήσατο, τῷ προαιρετικῷ πνεύματι τῷ διὰ τῶν νεύρων διήκοντι τὴν πρὸς τὰς κινήσεις ὁρμήν τε καὶ δύναμιν ἐνθεῖσα τῷ σώματι· [C] *ἐντεῦθεν ἡ τῶν χειρῶν ὑπουργία, ἡ ποικίλη τε καὶ πολύστροφος καὶ πρὸς πᾶσαν ἐπίνοιαν ἐπιτηδεία· ἐντεῦθεν αἱ τοῦ αὐχένος περιστροφαὶ καὶ τῆς κεφαλῆς ἐπικλίσεις τε καὶ ἀνανεύσεις καὶ ἡ κατὰ τὴν γένην ἐνέργεια καὶ ἡ τῶν βλεφάρων διαστολὴ ἅμα νοήματι γινομένη καὶ τῶν λοιπῶν ἄρθρων αἱ κινήσεις, νεύροις μέν τισιν ἀνασπωμένοις ἢ χαλωμένοις, καθάπερ ἐκ μηχανῆς τινος ἐνεργοῦνται· ἡ δὲ διὰ τούτων διεξιοῦσα δύναμις αὐτοκέλευστον ἔχει τινὰ τὴν ὁρμήν, προαιρετικῷ πνεύματι κατά τινα φύσεως οἰκονομίαν ἐν τοῖς καθ' ἕκαστον ἐνεργουμένη· ῥίζα δὲ πάντων ἀπεδείχθη καὶ ἀρχὴ τῶν κατὰ τὰ νεῦρα κινήσεων, ὁ τὸν ἐγκέφαλον περιέχων νευρώδης ὑμήν.* **[30.10]** *Οὐκέτι οὖν ἡγούμεθα δεῖν πολυπραγμονεῖν, περί τι* [D] *τῶν ζωτικῶν μορίων τὸ τοιοῦτόν ἐστιν, ἐν τούτῳ δειχθείσης τῆς κινητικῆς ἐνεργείας· ὅτι δὲ μέγιστόν τι συντελεῖ πρὸς τὴν ζωὴν ὁ ἐγκέφαλος, ἐναργῶς τὸ ἐξ ἐναντίου συμβαῖνον δηλοῖ· εἰ γάρ τινα τρῶσιν ἢ ῥῆξιν ὁ περὶ αὐτὸν ὑμὴν πάθοι, εὐθὺς ἐπηκολούθησε τῷ πάθει ὁ θάνατος, οὐδὲ πρὸς τὸ ἀκαρὲς τῆς φύσεως ἀντισχούσης τῇ τρώσει, ὥσπερ, θεμελίου τινὸς ὑποσπασθέντος, ὅλον τὸ οἰκοδόμημα συγκατεσείσθη τῷ μέρει· οὗ τοίνυν παθόντος πρόδηλός ἐστιν ἡ τοῦ παντὸς ζώου διαφθορά, τοῦτο κυρίως ἂν τῆς ζωῆς τὴν αἰτίαν ἔχειν ὁμολογοῖτο.*

[30.11] *Ἐπειδὴ δὲ καὶ τῶν παυσαμένων τοῦ ζῆν, κατασβεσθείσης τῆς ἐγκειμένης τῇ φύσει θερμότητος, τὸ νεκρωθὲν καταψύχεται,* [245] *διὰ τοῦτο καὶ ἐν τῷ θερμῷ τὴν ζωτικὴν αἰτίαν κατενοήσαμεν· οὗ γὰρ ἐπιλελοιπότος ἡ νεκρότης ἐπηκολούθησεν, ἀνάγκη πᾶσα τῇ παρουσίᾳ τούτου συνεστάναι τὸ ζῷον ὁμολογεῖσθαι· τῆς δὲ τοιαύτης δυνάμεως οἱονεὶ πηγήν τινα καὶ ἀρχὴν τὴν καρδίαν κατενοήσαμεν, ἀφ' ἧς αὐλοειδεῖς πόροι πολυσχιδῶς ἄλλος ἐξ ἄλλου διαφυόμενοι, παντὶ τῷ σώματι τὸ θερμόν τε καὶ πυρῶδες διαχέουσι πνεῦμα.* **[30.12]** *Ἐπεὶ δὲ πάντως καὶ τροφὴν ἔδει τινὰ τῷ θερμῷ συμπαρεῖναι παρὰ τῆς φύσεως—οὐ γὰρ ἐνδέχεται τὸ πῦρ ἐφ' ἑαυτοῦ*

72 *τῷ προαιρετικῷ πνεύματι τῷ*] *τοῦ προσηνῶσαι πνεύματι γὰρ* B (*sed non* ß) 73 *ἡ om.* L *ἡ τῶν χειρῶν om.* N^{ac} 74 *πολύστροφος*] *περίστροφος* B C I K O *πᾶσαν*] *ἅπασαν* M 75 *περιστροφαὶ*] *ἐπιστροφαὶ* N R^{ac} *ἐπικλήσεις* P Q R^{ac} S^{ac} X *τε om.* N T *καὶ ἀνανεύσεις om.* T 76 *ἐνέργεια om.* N^{ac} *διαστολὴ*] *διατροφὴ* L *νοήματι*] *νεύματι Ald Mign* *γιγνομένη* N : *γενομένη* B 77 *νεύροις*] *ita* Æ B H I K L M N O Q R S T X *Forb* : *ἐν νεύροις* W *Ald Mign* *μὲν om.* N Q *ἀνασπωμένοις*] *ἀναπεμπομένοις* N 78 *ἐνεργοῦσιν* T^{pc} *διεξιοῦσα*] *ἐξιοῦσα* D E R : *ἐξουσιάζουσα* N : *ἐξ ἴσου* Q : digna *Eri* 79 *τινὰ ἔχει* R *τινὰ*] *ἀεὶ* Q *προαιρετικῷ πνεύματι*] prompto spiritu *Eri* *πνεύματι*] *πνεύματι τῷ διὰ τῶν νεύρων διήκοντι* I L 80 *καθ' ἕκαστον*] *ita* K O P S X *Forb* : *καθέκαστον* W *Ald Mign* *ἐνεργουμένην* Æ C E I K O R T : *ἐνεργουμένοις* B : *ἐνεργοῦσαν* N *ἀπεδείχθη*] *ἀνεδείχθη* Æ *καὶ ἀρχὴ ἀπεδείχθη* B 82 *οὐκέτ'* D H P R S X : *οὐκ ἔτ'* L M : *οὐκ ἔτι* K *τι*] *ita* Æ B D H I K L M N O R S T W X *Ald Forb* : *τε Mign* : *om.* P Q 83 *τὸ τοιοῦτον*] *τί τοιοῦτον* M : *τοῦτο* K O : *om.* I *ἐστιν om.* I R *τούτῳ*] *τούτοις* H P *ἐνεργίας* K *δὲ om.* K 84 *μέγιστόν iterum inc.* G *ἐξ ἐναντίας* R T : *ἐξεναντίας* N 86 *ἀκερὲς* W^{ac} 87 *τῇ τρώσει*] *τῷ πάθει τῆς τρώσεως* N *ὥσπερ*] *ὥσπερ δὲ* N Q 88 *παντὸς om.* N 89 *τὰς αἰτίας* D E F G H L P S X *ὁμολογεῖτο* B I G 90 *ἐπεὶ* B I M Q T : *ἐπὶ* K *δὲ om.* N^{ac} *SP* 91 *τὸ*] *τὸ σῶμα* Q *SP* : *τὸ ἐν ἐκείνῃ* T *καταψύγεται* B 92 *αἰτίαν*] *ἐνέργειαν* D E R^{2} 93 *συνεστᾶναι* G N P : *συστῆναι SP* *ὁμολογεῖται* X 94 *οἱονεὶ*] *εἱονεὶ* B (*non* ß) : *οἷον Ald Mign* *κατανοεῖσθαι* B *ἀφ'*] *ἐφ'* W 95 *αὐλοειδῶς* I : *αὐλοειδῶς τινὲς* N : *αὐλώδεις SP* *πολυσχεδῶς* H S *διαφυομέναι* W^{ac} : *διαφυομένος* R$^{ac?}$ *τῷ om. SP* 96 *θερμόν τε καὶ πυρῶδες*] *πυρῶδες καὶ θερμόν Ald Mign* *ἐπεὶ*] *ἐπειδὴ* Æ I K N O *πάντως om.* B 97 *τῷ θερμῷ om.* Q *παρὰ om.* R^{ac} *ἐνδέχηται* K *ἑαυτὸ* T

nerves implanting in the body the impulse and power for movement, and hence the service of the hands, so varied and so versatile and adapted for every thought; from this comes, as by some mechanism, the turnings of the neck and the bending and raising of the head and the action of the chin and the separation of the eyelids, occurring with a thought, and the movements of the other joints, by the tightening or relaxing of certain nerves. The power that extends through these has a sort of self-bidden impulse, working with the self-determining spirit by a sort of economy of nature in each particular part; but the root of all and the principle of the movements of the nerves is shown to be the nervous tissue that surrounds the brain. **[30.10]** We suppose, then, that it is no longer necessary to concern ourselves regarding which of the vital members is such a thing, when the energy of movement is shown to be in this. But that the brain contributes a great amount to life is shown clearly by the occurrence of the opposite: for if the tissue surrounding it suffers any wound or lesion, death immediately follows the injury, nature not being able to endure the wound even for a moment, just as, when a foundation is removed, the whole building collapses with the part; as, then, when this member suffers it is clearly the destruction of the whole living being, it may properly be acknowledged to contain the cause of life.

[30.11] And, since, in those who have ceased to live, when the heat implanted in our nature is quenched, what has died grows cold, for this reason we recognize the vital cause also in the heat, for we must by all necessity acknowledge that the living being subsists by the presence of that which when it has failed the condition of death follows. And we understand the heart to be, as it were, the spring and principle of such a force, as from it pipe-like passages, growing one from another split into many parts, diffuse the warm and fiery spirit to the whole body.[9] **[30.12]** And since certainly some nourishment must also be provided by nature for the element of heat—for it is not possible for the fire to continue by itself, without being nourished by what is appropriate[10]—therefore the channels of the

[9] Cf. Plato, *Tim.* 70ab; Galen, *De usu part.* 6.7 (Helmreich, 1, 318.15–319.14; ET 1, 292–3).
[10] Cf. Gregory of Nyssa, *Hex.* 53 (Drobner, 64.12).

μένειν, μὴ διὰ τοῦ καταλλήλου τρεφόμενον—διὰ τοῦτο οἱ τοῦ αἵματος ὀχετοί, καθάπερ ἐκ πηγῆς τινος τοῦ ἥπατος ἀφορμηθέντες, τῷ θερμῷ πνεύματι πανταχῆ κατὰ τὸ σῶμα συμπαροδεύουσιν, ὡς ἂν μή, μονωθὲν τοῦ ἑτέρου τὸ ἕτερον, διαφθείρῃ τὴν φύσιν, [B] πάθος γενόμενον. Παιδευέτω τοῦτο τοὺς ἀτακτοῦντας περὶ τὸ ἶσον, διδαχθέντας παρὰ τῆς φύσεως ὅτι ἡ πλεονεξία φθοροποιόν τι πάθος ἐστίν.

[30.13] Ἀλλ' ἐπειδὴ μόνον ἀπροσδεές ἐστι τὸ θεῖον, ἡ δὲ ἀνθρωπίνη πτωχεία τῶν ἔξωθεν πρὸς τὴν ἰδίαν σύστασιν ἐπιδέεται, διὰ τοῦτο ταῖς τρισὶ ταύταις δυνάμεσι δι' ὧν ἔφαμεν ἅπαν οἰκονομεῖσθαι τὸ σῶμα, ἐπίρρυτον ἔξωθεν ἐπεισάγει τὴν ὕλην, διαφόροις εἰσόδοις τὸ κατάλληλον αὐταῖς εἰσοικίζουσα. [30.14] Τῇ μὲν γὰρ πηγῇ τοῦ αἵματος, ἥτις τὸ ἧπάρ ἐστι, τὴν διὰ τῆς τροφῆς χορηγίαν ὑπέθηκε· τὸ γὰρ ἐπεισαγόμενον ἀεὶ διὰ ταύτης τὰς τοῦ αἵματος πηγὰς βρύειν ἐκ τοῦ ἥπατος παρασκευάζει, καθάπερ ἡ ἐπὶ τοῦ ὄρους χιὼν διὰ τῆς οἰκείας ἰκμάδος τὰς κατὰ τὴν ὑπώρειαν αὔξει πηγάς, διὰ τοῦ βάθους [C] τὸ οἰκεῖον ὑγρὸν ἐπὶ τὰς κάτω φλέβας συνθλίβουσα. [30.15] Τὸ δὲ ἐγκάρδιον πνεῦμα διὰ τοῦ γείτονος ἐπεισάγεται σπλάγχνου, ὃ καλεῖται μὲν πνεύμων, ἔστι δὲ τοῦ ἀέρος δοχεῖον, διὰ τῆς ἐγκειμένης ἀρτηρίας τῆς ἐπὶ τὸ στόμα διηκούσης τὸ ἔξωθεν πνεῦμα ταῖς ἀναπνοαῖς ἐφελκόμενον· ᾧ κατὰ τὸ μέσον ἡ καρδία ἐνειλημμένη, (κατὰ μίμησιν τῆς τοῦ ἀεικινήτου πυρὸς ἐνεργείας ἀδιαλείπτως καὶ αὐτὴ κινουμένη) οἷόν τι ποιοῦσιν ἐν τοῖς χαλκείοις αἱ φῦσαι, ἕλκει τε πρὸς ἑαυτὴν ἐκ τοῦ παρακειμένου πνεύματος πληροῦσα τῇ διαστολῇ τὰς κοιλότητας, καί, τὸ πυρῶδες ἑαυτῆς ἐκριπίζουσα, ταῖς ἐχομέναις ἀρτηρίαις ἐμπνεῖ· καὶ τοῦτο ποιοῦσα οὐ διαλείπει, τὸ μὲν ἔξωθεν διὰ τῆς διαστολῆς εἰς τὰς ἰδίας κοιλότητας ἕλκουσα, τὸ δὲ παρ' ἑαυτῆς διὰ τῆς συμπτώσεως [D] ταῖς ἀρτηρίαις εἰσκρίνουσα.

[30.16] Ὅ μοι δοκεῖ καὶ τῆς αὐτομάτου ταύτης ἀναπνοῆς αἴτιον ἡμῖν γίνεσθαι· πολλάκις γὰρ ὁ μὲν νοῦς ἄσχολός ἐστι πρὸς ἑτέρους ἢ καὶ παντάπασιν ἠρεμεῖ, λυθέντος ἐν τῷ ὕπνῳ τοῦ σώματος, ἡ δὲ ἀναπνοὴ τοῦ ἀέρος οὐ διαλείπει, μηδ'

98 μένειν *om.* B ὀχετοὶ] ὑδραγωγοὶ R 99 ἐκ *om.* Æ ß I K M N O T τινος πηγῆς Æ B I K O τινὸς H M N P R ἀφορμισθέντες R^{ac} 99–100 πανταχῆ κατὰ] κατὰ πᾶν N 101 γινόμενον I L R τοῦτο *om.* X ἴσον H I X 102 διδαχθέντες I S^{ac} 103 ἐστι] τι Æ I O Q 105 σῶμα] ζῶον L ἐπεισάγει ἔξωθεν Æ B I K O R 106 εἰσόδοις] ὁδοῖς A D E G H M P Q X αὐταῖς] αὐτοῖς I : αὐτῆς M 107 χορηγείαν W ἐπέθηκε D E 108 ἐκ] *ita codd. Forb* : διὰ W *Ald Mign* 109 παρασκευάζει] κατασκευάζει T ἡ *om.* Æ οἰκίας W 112 ἔστι] *ita* Æ ß H I K L M O P R S W X *Ald Forb* : ἐστὶ *Mign* δοχεῖον] τὸ δοχεῖον B ἀρτηρίας] 113 αὐτηρίας W τῆς *om.* A (*non* Æ) B D E G H P X 114 ἐνειλημμένη] συνειλημμένη N κατὰ] κατὰ τὴν M 109 τοῦ *om.* M^{ac} 114–15 ἀεικινήτου τοῦ D E G H L P Q R S X 115 αὕτη K 116 φῦσσαι L : φῦσαι Æ R W S ἕλκεται T τε *om.* N T ἐκ *om.* Q πνεύματος] *ita codd. Ald Forb* : πνεύμονος *Mign* 117 ἑαυτῆς] αὐτῆς G H ἐκρίπτουσα R 118 ἐχομέναις] ἐγκειμέναις D E R^2 : ἐπιχεομέναις R^{ac} 119 συμπτώσεως] concasum hoc est per contractionem *Eri* 122 μὲν γὰρ ὁ B ἄσχολος] ἄσχολος τε R πρὸς *om.* B ἑτέρους] ἑτέροις M N Q R : ἑτέραις G H P X : ἕτερα I : *om.* B 123 ἀναπνοὴ δὲ N ἀναπνοὴ] πνοὴ Q 123–4 μηδ' ὁτιοῦν] μηδοτιοῦν M : *om.* B

blood, issuing from the liver as from a spring, accompany the warm spirit everywhere in its way throughout the body, that the one may not by isolation from the other destroy the nature, becoming a disease.[11] Let this instruct the undisciplined regarding fairness, as they learn from nature that covetousness is a destructive disease.

[**30.13**] But since the divinity alone is free from needs, while human poverty requires external aid for its own subsistence, nature therefore, in addition to those three powers by which we said that the whole body is administered, brings in imported matter from without, introducing by different entrances that which is appropriate for them. [**30.14**] For to the spring of the blood, which is the liver, she furnishes its supply by food; for what is brought constantly in this way furnishes the springs of blood to issue from the liver, just as the snow on the mountain by its own moisture increases the springs in the lower ground, forcing its own moisture through the depths into the veins below. [**30.15**] The breath in the heart is supplied by means of the neighbouring organ, which is called the lungs and is a receptacle for air, drawing the breath from without through the windpipe placed in it, which extends to the mouth. The heart being placed in the midst of this organ (and itself also moving incessantly in imitation of the activity of the ever-moving fire), draws to itself, somewhat as the bellows do in the forges, a supply from the adjacent air, filling its recesses by dilatation and, while it fans its own fiery element, breathes upon the adjoining tubes; and it does not cease to do this, drawing the external air into its own recesses by dilatation and by compression infusing the air from itself into the tubes.[12]

[**30.16**] And this seems to me to be the cause of this spontaneous respiration of ours. For often the intellect is occupied with other matters, or is entirely at rest when the body is relaxed in sleep, but the respiration of air does not cease, even

[11] Cf. Galen, *De usu part.* 6.10 (Helmreich, 1, 324.17–20; ET 1, 296), 16.13–14 (Helmreich, 2.431.21–343.13; ET 2, 720–2).

[12] For this, and the following paragraph, see Galen, *De usu part.* 6.7 (Helmreich, 1, 316.14–19; ET 1, 291), 6.10 (Helmreich, 1, 324–333; ET 1, 296–304), 6.15 (Helmreich, 1, 350.15–351.5; ET 1, 316).

ὁτιοῦν συνεργούσης εἰς τοῦτο τῆς προαιρέσεως· οἶμαι γάρ, ἐπειδὴ περιείληπται τῷ πνεύμονι ἡ καρδία καὶ προσπέφυκεν αὐτῷ κατὰ τὸ ὀπίσθιον ἑαυτῆς μέρος, ταῖς ἰδίαις διαστολαῖς καὶ συμπτώσεσι συγκινοῦσα τὸ σπλάγχνον, τὴν τοῦ ἀέρος ὁλκήν τε καὶ ἐμπνοὴν ἐκμηχανᾶσθαι τῷ πνεύμονι· ἀραιὸς γάρ τις ὢν καὶ πολύπορος καὶ πάσας τὰς ἐν αὐτῷ κοιλότητας πρὸς τὸν πυθμένα τῆς ἀρτηρίας ἀνεστομωμένας [248] ἔχων, συστελλόμενος μὲν καὶ συμπίπτων, τὸ ἐναπολειφθὲν τοῖς κοίλοις πνεῦμα κατ' ἀνάγκην ἐκπιέζων προΐεται· ὑποχωρῶν δὲ καὶ ἀνοιγόμενος, ἐπισπᾶται τῇ διαστάσει πρὸς τὸ κενούμενον διὰ τῆς ὁλκῆς τὸν ἀέρα. [30.17] Καὶ αὕτη ἐστὶ τῆς ἀπροαιρέτου ταύτης ἀναπνοῆς αἰτία, ἡ τοῦ ἀτρεμεῖν τὸ πυρῶδες ἀδυναμία· ἐπειδὴ γὰρ ἴδιόν ἐστι τοῦ θερμοῦ ἡ κατὰ τὴν κίνησιν ἐνέργεια, τούτου δὲ τὰς ἀρχὰς ἐν τῇ καρδίᾳ κατενοήσαμεν, τὸ διηνεκὲς τῆς ἐν τῷ μέρει τούτῳ κινήσεως τὴν ἀδιάλειπτον τοῦ ἀέρος ὁλκήν τε καὶ ἐκπνοὴν διὰ τοῦ πνεύμονος ἀπεργάζεται· διὸ καὶ παρὰ φύσιν ἐπιταθέντος τοῦ πυρώδους, τὸ ἄσθμα τῶν διακαιομένων τῷ πυρετῷ συνεχέστερον γίνεται, ὥσπερ ἐπειγομένης τῆς καρδίας τὸν ἐγκείμενον ἐν αὐτῇ φλογμὸν τῷ νεαρωτέρῳ πνεύματι κατασβεννύειν.

[30.18] [B] Ἀλλ' ἐπειδὴ πενιχρά τίς ἐστιν ἡμῶν ἡ φύσις καὶ τῶν πρὸς τὴν ἰδίαν σύστασιν διὰ πάντων ἐπιδεής, οὐκ ἀέρος μόνον ἰδίου πτωχεύει καὶ πνεύματος τοῦ τὸ θερμὸν διεγείροντος, ὅπερ ἔξωθεν πρὸς τὴν τοῦ ζώου συντήρησιν διηνεκῶς ἐπεισάγεται· ἀλλὰ καὶ τὴν ὑπερείδουσαν τὸν τοῦ σώματος ὄγκον τροφὴν ἐπίκτητον ἔχει. Διὰ τοῦτο σιτίοις τε καὶ ποτοῖς ἀναπληροῖ τὸ ἐνδέον, ἑλκτικήν τινα τοῦ λείποντος δύναμιν καὶ ἀπωστικὴν τοῦ περιττεύοντος ἐνθεῖσα τῷ σώματι, οὐδὲ πρὸς τοῦτο τοῦ ἐγκαρδίου πυρὸς μικρὰν παρεχομένου τῇ φύσει συνέργειαν. [30.19] Ἐπειδὴ γὰρ τὸ κυριώτατον τῶν ζωτικῶν μορίων κατὰ τὸν ἀποδοθέντα λόγον ἡ καρδία ἐστὶν ἡ τῷ θερμῷ πνεύματι ζωπυροῦσα τὰ καθ' ἕκαστον μέρη, πανταχόθεν αὐτὴν ἐνεργὸν εἶναι [C] τῷ δραστικῷ τῆς δυνάμεως ὁ πλάστης ἡμῶν ἐποίησεν, ὡς ἂν μηδὲν αὐτῆς μέρος ἄπρακτόν τε καὶ ἀνόνητον πρὸς τὴν τοῦ παντὸς

124 *συνεργούσης*] *συναιρούσης* N *εἰς*] *πρὸς* Q R *προαιρέσεως*] *προτάσεως* W *περιείληπται*] *προείληπται* D^{ac} R^{2} : *προσείληπται* D^{2} 125 *ἑαυτῆς*] *αὐτῆς* B D K L O Q 126 *συγκρινοῦσα* D^{ac} : *συγκρίνουσα* D^{2} *τῶν σπλάγχνων* R 127 *ἐμπνοὴν*] *ἐκπνοὴν* Æ B C E I K M N O Q W *Dion Eri* *ἐκμηχανήσασθαι* M N *ἀρεὸς* X 128 *αὐτῷ*] *ἑαυτῷ* R *ἀναστομομένας* B : *ἀναστομωμένας* ß 129 *ἐναποληφθὲν* G H M P^{pc} S : *ἐναπολυθὲν* Q 130 *ἐκπιέζων*] *ἐκπιαίζων* W 131 *κινούμενον* Æ B C I K M N O Q *Dion Eri* 132 *ἀπροαιρέτου*] *αὐτοπροαιρέτου* W *αἰτία*] *ἡ αἰτία* R *τὸ πυρῶδες*] *τοῦ ἀέρος* D F G H L P S X 133 *ἐστι om.* Æ ß D(?) N O R T *τὴν om.* Æ *κίνησιν*] *κίνησιν ἐστιν* Æ B I K M N O R T *ἐνέργεια*] *ἐνέργεια καὶ* M 134 *μέρει τούτῳ*] *βάρει τούτου* N 135 *ὁλκήν*] *ὁρμὴν Ald Mign* *ἐκπνοὴν*] *ita* Æ C E I K L M N O Q S T W *Forb* : *ἀναπνοὴν* B R^{ac} : *ἐμπνοὴν* X *Ald Mign* *διὰ τοῦ πνεύμονος*] *μόνον* B : *μόνος* ß *πνεύμονος*] *ita codd. Ald Forb* : *πνεύματος Mign* 136 *ἐπιταθέντος*] *ἐπισταθέντος* H : *ἐπιτεθέντος* R^{ac} *ἄσθμα*] *ita* Æ G H O P R S W X *Forb* : *ἆσθμα Ald Mign* *πυρετῷ*] *πυρετῷ σωμάτων* Q 137 *γίγνεται* N *ἐν αὐτῇ*] *αὐτῇ* M : *ἑαυτῇ* Æ B N : *ἐν ἑαυτῇ* I : *ἑαυτῆς* K O 139 *ἡμῶν ἐστὶν* Æ B I K M R T *ἡμῶν*] *om. Eri* *ἰδίαν*] *φυσικὴν* R^{2} 140 *ἰδίου om.* D G H P X *τοῦ om.* K 142 *ἐνεισάγεται* G H P S^{ac} X 143 *τε om.* I 144 *ἐλλείποντος* K O 145 *συνεργίαν* ß D I K M N O P^{pc} : *συνέργιαν* Æ : *ἐνέργειαν* L S 147 *πνεύματι*] *om. Eri* *ζωπυροῦσα—μέρη*] *τὰ καθ' ἕκαστον ζωπυροῦσα μερῶν* I *καθ' ἕκαστον*] *ita* D G K S *Forb* : *καθέκασον Ald Mign* 148 *ἡμῶν om.* N 149 *ἐνεποίησεν* I *ἀνόητον* H K

though the will gives no cooperation to this end. I suppose that, since the heart is surrounded by the lungs and in the back part of its own structure is attached to them, moving that organ by its own dilatations and compressions, the inhaling and exhaling of the air is brought about by the lungs; for being slight and porous and having all their recesses opening at the base of the windpipe, when they contract and are compressed the air that remains in their cavities, being squeezed, goes out, and, when they expand and open, they draw the air, by their distention, into the void by suction. [**30.17**] This then is the cause of this involuntary respiration, the impossibility that the fiery element should keep still; for since the activity of movement is proper to heat, we understand the beginnings of heat to be in the heart, the continual movement of this organ producing the incessant inspiration and exhalation of the air through the lungs. Therefore, also, when the fiery element is unnaturally enlarged, the breathing of those burning up with fever becomes more rapid, as though the heart were endeavouring to quench the flame lying in it by fresher breath.

[**30.18**] But since our nature is poor and in need of supplies from all quarters for its own constitution, it not only lacks air of its own and breath which arouses heat, which it brings in from without for the preservation of the living being, but the nourishment supporting the bulk of the body is something acquired. Therefore, it supplies the deficiency by food and drink, implanting in the body a certain faculty for appropriating what it requires and rejecting what is superfluous, and for this purpose, the fire of the heart gives to nature no small assistance.[13] [**30.19**] For since, according to the account given, the heart which kindles by its warm breath the individual parts is the most important of the vital organs, our Fashioner caused it to be operative with its efficacious power at all points, so that no part of it might be left ineffectual or unprofitable for the administration of the

[13] Cf. Gregory of Nyssa, *Orat. Cat.* 37.4–5 (Mühlenberg, 94.5–95.1); Galen, *De usu part.* 4.7 (Helmreich, 1, 200.11–203.9; ET 208–9); *De nat. fac.* 3.4–8.

οἰκονομίαν καταλειφθείη· διὰ τοῦτο κατόπιν μὲν ὑποβᾶσα τὸν πνεύμονα, διὰ τῆς διηνεκοῦς κινήσεως, καθέλκουσά τε πρὸς ἑαυτὴν τὸ σπλάγχνον, ἀνευρύνει πρὸς τὴν ὁλκὴν τοῦ ἀέρος τοὺς πόρους, ἀποθλίβουσά τε πάλιν, ἐκπνεῖσθαι τὸ ἐναπειλημμένον παρασκευάζει· ἐν δὲ τοῖς ἔμπροσθεν ἑαυτῆς προσφυεῖσα τῷ χωρήματι τῆς ἄνω γαστρὸς, ἔνθερμον αὐτὴν καὶ πρὸς τὰς ἰδίας ἐνεργείας κινουμένην ποιεῖ· οὐκ εἰς πνεύματος ὁλκὴν ἀνεγείρουσα, ἀλλ' εἰς ὑποδοχὴν τῆς καταλλήλου τροφῆς· πλησίον μὲν γὰρ πεφύκασιν ἀλλήλων αἱ εἴσοδοι τοῦ πνεύματός τε καὶ τῆς τροφῆς, ἀντιπαρεξιοῦσαι κατὰ τὸ πρόμηκες ἡ ἑτέρα πρὸς τὴν ἑτέραν, καὶ τῷ ἴσῳ μέτρῳ [D] κατὰ τὸ ἄνω πέρας συναπαρτίζονται, ὥστε καὶ συνεστομῶσθαι πρὸς ἀλλήλας καὶ ἑνὶ στόματι τοὺς πόρους ἐναπολήγειν· ὅθεν τῷ μὲν τῆς τροφῆς τῷ δὲ τοῦ πνεύματος ἡ εἴσοδος γίνεται.

[30.20] Ἀλλ' ἐπὶ τὸ βάθος οὐκέτι διαπαντὸς τὸ προσφυὲς παραμένει τῆς συζυγίας τῶν πόρων· μέση γὰρ τῆς ἑκατέρων ἕδρας ἡ καρδία παρεμπεσοῦσα, τῷ μὲν πρὸς ἀναπνοὴν τῷ δὲ πρὸς τροφὴν τὰς δυνάμεις ἐντίθησι· πέφυκε γὰρ τὸ πυρῶδες ἐπιζητεῖν τὴν ὑπεκκαίουσαν ὕλην, ὃ δὴ καὶ περὶ τὸ δοχεῖον τῆς τροφῆς κατ' ἀνάγκην συμβαίνει· ὅσῳ γὰρ διάπυρον διὰ τῆς γείτονος γίνεται θερμασίας, τοσούτῳ μᾶλλον ἐφέλκεται τὰ τὸ θερμὸν ὑποτρέφοντα. Τὴν δὲ τοιαύτην ὁρμὴν ὄρεξιν ὀνομάζομεν. [30.21] [249] Εἰ δὲ περιδράξαιτο τῆς ἀρκούσης ὕλης τὸ περιεκτικὸν τῆς τροφῆς, οὐδὲ οὕτως ἠρεμεῖ τοῦ πυρὸς ἡ ἐνέργεια· ἀλλὰ καθάπερ ἐν χωνευτηρίῳ σύντηξίν τινα τῆς ὕλης ποιεῖ, καὶ διαλύσασα τὰ συνεστῶτα καὶ ἀναχέασα, καθάπερ ἐκ χοάνης τινὸς μεταχεῖ πρὸς τοὺς ἐφεξῆς πόρους· εἶτα τὸ παχυμερέστερον τοῦ εἰλικρινοῦς διακρίνασα, τὸ μὲν λεπτὸν δι' ὀχετῶν τινων ἐπὶ τὰς τοῦ ἥπατος ἄγει πύλας, τὴν δὲ ὑλώδη τῆς τροφῆς ὑποστάθμην εἰς τοὺς εὐρυχωροτέρους πόρους τῶν ἐντέρων ἀπώσατο, καὶ, τοῖς πολυτρόποις αὐτῶν

150 καταληφθείη B Q   151 πρὸς *om.* M   152 τοῦ πόρου M   ἀποθλίβουσα] *ita* A D E F(?) G H N P R^2 S X *Forb* : ἀναμοχλίζουσα Æ B C K O : ἀναμοχλεύουσα I : ἀναχλιάζουσα M : ἀναχλίζουσα T^{ac} : ἀνακαχλάζουσα $T^{2?}$: ἀποθλίβουσα ἀναχλίζουσα $R^{ac?}$: ὑποθλίβουσα L : ἀνοχλίζουσα W *Ald Mign*   τε] δε   153 χωρήματι] στόματι N (ἐν ἄλλοις χωρήματι N^{1mg})   154 πρὸς τὰς ἰδίας ἐνεργείας] τὰς πρὸς τᾶς ἐνεργείας τὰς ἰδίας B   155 ἀνεγείρουσα] διεγείρουσα I   καταλλήλους I   τρυφῆς L   156 μὲν *om.* O   ἀλλήλων πεφύκασιν D G H L P S W X   157 ἀντιπαρεξάγουσαι N : ἀντιπαρεξιοῦσα M   κατὰ] *ita* D G H L M N P R^{ac} S T W X *Dion Forb* : δὲ κατὰ O *Eri Ald Mign*   158 πέρας] *ita* Æ B C D E F G H I K L N^2 O P R^2 S X *Dion Forb* : *om.* W *Ald Mign*   συνανεστομῶσθαι B E R   159 ἑνὶ] in *Eri*   τὸ μὲν... τὸ δὲ Æ L M P^{ac} Q R T^{ac} 160 πνεύματος] σώματος K O   ἡ *om.* M Q   161 τὸ² *om.* M   παραμένῃ K O   τῇ συζυγίᾳ Æ B C E N O Q R T W   162 ἑκατέρωθεν M   παραπεσοῦσα B N   162–3 τὸ μὲν... τὸ δὲ Q R T^{ac} 163 ἀναπνοὴν] τὴν ἀναπνοὴν Æ B I K M N O Q R   τροφὴν] τὴν τροφὴν Æ B I K M N O Q R W   164 τὴν *om.* B   165 ὅσῳ] ὅσον I R   διάπυρον] ἄπειρον *Ald* : ἔμπυρον *Mign*   θερμασία N^{ac} : θεραπείας M   166 τοσοῦτο N^{ac} O Q : τοσοῦτον L R : τοσούτο P   168 περιεκτικὸν] ὀρεκτικὸν D^{pc} L   ἠρεμεῖ] *ita* G H L N O R X *Forb* : ἠρεμεῖ W *Ald Mign*   169 σύνπηξίν X   διεστῶτα X   170 ἀναχέασα] διαχέασα M : ἀναχύσασα B   χοάνης] χώμης Æ Q R   μεταχεῖ] participat *Eri*   τοὺς *om.* B   *post* πόρους *rel. des.* K   τὸ *om.* I   171 εἰλικρινοῦς I M N R^2 διακρίνουσα L   ἐπὶ] εἰς *om.* N   172 τοῦ *om.* B   ἄγει] ἀπάγει A D E F G H L P S W X   ὑλώδη] ἰλυώδη Æ B C E M N^{ac} O R : λυώδη T : ξυλώδη T^{mg} 173 πόρους τῶν ἐντέρων] *ita* A D E F G H L M P Q S W X *Forb* : τῶν ἐντέρων πόρους O *Ald Mign*   πόρους *om.* Æ   καὶ τοῖς] τοῖς δὲ M   πολυστρόφοις T^2

whole organism. Therefore, standing behind the lungs and drawing that organ to itself by its continuous movement, it dilates the passages for the inhalation of the air and compressing them again it effects the exhalation of the air taken in; while, in front, attached to the space above the stomach, it warms it and sets it in motion towards its own activity, rousing it, not to inhale air, but to receive its appropriate nourishment; for the entrances for both breath and food have been produced nearby one another, extending lengthwise one alongside the other, and end together in their upper parts by the same measure, so that they are furnished with contiguous openings and the passages culminate together in one mouth, from which the entrance of food is by one opening and that of breath through the other.[14]

[30.20] Internally, however, the closeness of the conjunction of the passages is not maintained throughout; for the heart, intervening between the base of the two, implants in the one the faculty for respiration and in the other the faculty for nourishment. Now the fiery element is naturally inclined to seek the material serving as fuel, and this also necessarily happens regarding the receptacle of nourishment; for the more it becomes heated by the neighbouring warmth, the more it draws to itself what nourishes the heat. And this sort of impulse we call appetite. **[30.21]**[15] But if the organ which contains the food should obtain sufficient material, not even in this way does the activity of the fire become still; it rather produces a sort of melting of the material, just as in a foundry, and, dissolving the solids and pouring them out, as it were from a funnel, it transfers them to the neighbouring passages; then, separating the coarser from the purer material, it leads the fine part through certain channels to the gates of the liver, and expels the sedimentary matter of the food to the wider passages of the bowels; and, by turning it over in their manifold windings, retains the food for a time in the intestines, lest, if it were easily jettisoned by a straight passage it might

[14] Cf. Plato, *Tim.* 78b.

[15] For this paragraph, see Plato, *Tim.* 72c–73a; Aristotle, *De part. an.* 3.14 (675b22–6); Galen, *De usu part.* 4.1–2 (Helmreich, 1, 195–7; ET 1, 204–5), 4.17–18 (Helmreich, 1, 237–45 ; ET 1, 235–41).

ἑλιγμοῖς ἀναστρέφουσα, χρόνῳ παρακατέχει τὴν τροφὴν τοῖς σπλάγχνοις, ὡς ἂν μή, δι' εὐθύτητα τοῦ πόρου ῥᾳδίως ἀποβαλλόμενον, εὐθὺς ἀνακινοίη τὸ ζῷον πρὸς ὄρεξιν, καὶ μηδέποτε παύοιτο τῆς τοιαύτης ἀσχολίας κατὰ τὴν τῶν ἀλόγων φύσιν ὁ ἄνθρωπος.

[30.22] [B] Ἐπεὶ δὲ καὶ τῷ ἥπατι μάλιστα τῆς τοῦ θερμοῦ συνεργίας ἦν χρεία πρὸς τὴν τῶν ὑγρῶν ἐξαιμάτωσιν, ἀφέστηκε δὲ τοῦτο τῆς καρδίας κατὰ τὴν θέσιν (οὐδὲ γὰρ ἦν, οἶμαι, δυνατὸν, ἀρχήν τινα καὶ ῥίζαν ζωτικῆς οὖσαν δυνάμεως, περὶ τὴν ἑτέραν ἀρχὴν στενοχωρεῖσθαι) ὡς ἂν μή τι τῆς οἰκονομίας ἐν τῇ ἀποστάσει τῆς θερμαντικῆς οὐσίας παραβλαβείη, πόρος νευρώδης (ἀρτηρία δὲ τὸ τοιοῦτον παρὰ τῶν τὰ τοιαῦτα σοφῶν ὀνομάζεται) ἀναδεξάμενος τῆς καρδίας τὸ ἔμπυρον πνεῦμα φέρει παρὰ τὸ ἧπαρ, αὐτοῦ που παρὰ τὴν εἴσοδον τῶν ὑγρῶν συνεστομωμένος, καὶ ἀναζέσας διὰ τῆς θερμότητος τὴν ὑγρασίαν, ἐναποτίθεταί τι τῷ ὑγρῷ τῆς τοῦ πυρὸς συγγενείας, τῇ πυροειδεῖ χρόᾳ τὸ τοῦ αἵματος εἶδος καταφοινίξας. [30.23] Εἶτ' ἐκεῖθεν ἀφορμηθέντες δίδυμοί τινες ὀχετοί, τὸ [C] οἰκεῖον ἑκάτερος σωληνοειδῶς περιέχοντες, πνεῦμά τε καὶ αἷμα (ὡς ἂν εὐπόρευτον εἴη τὸ ὑγρόν, τῇ τοῦ θερμοῦ κινήσει συμπαροδεῦον καὶ κουφιζόμενον) ἐφ' ἅπαν τὸ σῶμα πολυσχιδῶς κατασπείρονται, εἰς μυρίας ὀχετῶν ἀρχάς τε καὶ διαφύσεις κατὰ πᾶν μέρος κατασχιζόμενοι· μιχθεῖσαι δὲ πρὸς ἀλλήλας τῶν ζωτικῶν δυνάμεων αἱ δύο ἀρχαί, ἥτε τὸ θερμὸν πανταχῇ κατὰ τὸ σῶμα καὶ ἡ τὸ ὑγρὸν ἐπιπέμπουσα, καθάπερ τινὰ δασμὸν ἀναγκαῖον ἐκ τῶν οἰκείων τῇ ἀρχηγικωτέρᾳ τῆς ζωτικῆς οἰκονομίας δυνάμει δωροφοροῦσιν.

[30.24] Ἔστι δε αὕτη ἡ κατὰ τὰς μήνιγγας καὶ τὸν ἐγκέφαλον θεωρουμένη, ἀφ' ἧς πᾶσα μὲν ἄρθρου κίνησις, πᾶσα δὲ μυῶν συνολκή, πᾶν δὲ προαιρετικὸν πνεῦμα καὶ τοῖς καθ' ἕκαστον μορίοις ἐπιπεμπόμενον, ἐνεργόν τε καὶ [D] κινούμενον τὸν γήϊνον ἡμῶν ἀνδριάντα καθάπερ ἐκ μηχανῆς τινος ἀποδείκνυσι. Τοῦ τε γὰρ θερμοῦ τὸ καθαρώτατον καὶ τοῦ ὑγροῦ τὸ λεπτότατον, παρ' ἑκατέρας δυνάμεως διά τινος

174 ἑλιγμοῖς] *ita* W *Ald Forb Mign* : ἐλιγμοῖς Æ ß H P S X : εἰλιγμοῖς R : ἰλιγμοῖς Q   ἀναστρέψασα Q : ἀνατρέφουσα G : ἀποστρέφουσα Æ   175 εὐθύτητα] εὐθείας I N[ac?] O Q R : εὐθέος Æ M T   ἀποβαλλόμενον] *ita codd. Forb* : ἀποβαλλομένη Q : ἀποβαλόμενον *Ald Mign*   εὐθὺς] εὐθέως I O   178 ἐπειδὴ O   δὲ *om.* B   μάλιστα καὶ τῷ ἥπατι M   συνεργείας G L P[ac] W X   179 δὲ] γὰρ M : *om.* X   οὐδὲ] *ita codd. Forb* : οὐ *Ald Mign*   181 ἑτέραν *om.* I O   τι *om.* M T   182 τὸ τοιοῦτον] *ita* D E F G H I L M R S X *Forb* : τὸ τοιοῦτο Q W : τῷ τοιούτῳ A : τῶν τοιοῦτων P : τοῦτο Æ ß O *Ald Mign*   183 τὰ τοιαῦτα] *ita* Æ B C D E F G H I L N[2] P R[2] S X *Forb* : εἰς ταῦτα M : ταῦτα W *Ald Mign*   ἀναλεξάμενος B C O : ἀναξάμενος I   ἔμπυρον *om.* M   185 ἐναποτίθεταί] ἀποτίθεται N   τι *om.* B I M O Q   186 χροίᾳ B : χροιᾷ Æ ß M R   εἶτ'] *ita* ß G I L M Q S X *Forb* : εἰτ' B D H P : εἴτ' R : εἶτα Æ O *Ald Mign* : *om.* T   187 σωληνοειδῶς τὸ οἰκεῖον ἑκάτερος I   188 εὐπόρρυτον I   εἴη] εἶναι A D F G H L P S X   τῇ] *ita* Æ D G H I L M N O P Q R S W X *Forb* : τε *Ald Mign*   189 καὶ] τε καὶ I   πολυσχεδῶς H B[ac] (ι *sup. l.*)   190 κατασπείρωνται I   μυριάδας M   ὀχετῶν *om.* T   ἀρχὰς ὀχετῶν I   τε *om.* I   διαφύσεις] διαχύσεις A D E F G H N P R[2] X   191 κατασχιζόμενοι] *ita* A Æ B D E F G H L M N P R S T X *Forb* : κατασχιματιζόμενοι W : καταδιασχιζόμενοι Q : διασχιζόμενοι C O *Ald Mign*   αἱ *om.* T   192 ἡ *om.* B T W   193 δασμὸν] *ita* Æ B C D E F G H I L N[mg] O P Q R[2] S T W X *Ald Forb* : δεσμὸν M R[ac] : δεσμῶν A : διαμερισμὸν N : δανεισμὸν *Mign*   ἀρχικωτέρα Æ L N O : ἀρχηκωτέρᾳ Q   οἰκονομίας] ἐνεργείας D R[2]   194 δορυφοροῦσιν R[ac]   195 δε] *ita* B G H L N O P Q R S W X *Forb* : δ' *Ald Mign*   αὐτὴ Q   μήνιγγας] membranas *Eri*   196 μὲν] μὲν οὖν N   συνολκὴ] ὁλκὴ M   καὶ *om.* Æ ß I M N O Q R[ac] W *Dion Eri* : *eras.* B D   197 καθ' ἕκαστον] *ita* L O W X *Forb* : καθέκαστον *Ald Mign*   μορίοις] ὁρίοις T   198 ἀποδεικνύουσι M W   199 καθαρώτερον N

immediately stir up again the living being to an appetite, and the human being, in accordance with the nature of an irrational animal, might never cease from this kind of occupation.

[30.22][16] Since the liver has a special need of the cooperation of heat for the conversion of the fluids into blood, but this organ is by position distant from the heart (for it would not be possible, I think, being a certain principle or root of the vital power, for it to be hampered by proximity to another principle), in order that it may not be damaged because of the distance from the administration of the heat-giving substance, a muscular passage (and this is called, by those skilled in such matters, the artery), receiving the heated breath from the heart, conveys it to the liver, having its opening somewhere besides the entry-point for the fluids, and, as it warms the moist element by its heat, it introduces into the liquid something akin to fire, reddening the form of the blood with the fiery tint. [30.23] Then, giving rise to certain twin channels from there, each enclosing its own current like a pipe, dispersing air and blood (that the liquid may have free course when accompanied and lightened by the movement of heat) in many directions over the whole body, being separated at every part into countless branches and partitions of channels; while, when the two principles of the vital powers are mixed together (both that which disperses heat and that which supplies moisture to every bodily part) they make, as it were, a sort of compulsory contribution from their own nature to the supreme force of the vital economy.

[30.24] Now this force is that perceived in the cerebral membranes and the brain, from which it comes that every movement of a joint, every contraction of the muscles, and every deliberate influence exerted upon the members of each person, renders our earthen statue active and mobile as though by some mechanism. For the most pure form of heat and the most subtle form of liquid, being united by

[16] For this paragraph, see Galen, *De usu part.* 4.2–6 (Helmreich, 1, 196–201; ET 1, 204–8), 4.14 (Helmreich, 1, 228–31; ET 1, 229–32).

μίξεώς τε καὶ ἀνακράσεως ἑνωθέντα, τρέφει τε καὶ συνίστησι διὰ τῶν ἀτμῶν τὸν ἐγκέφαλον· ἀφ' οὗ πάλιν ἐπὶ τὸ καθαρώτατον ἐκλεπτυνομένη ἡ ἀπ' ἐκείνου ἀνάδοσις, ὑπαλείφει τὸν περιεκτικὸν τοῦ ἐγκεφάλου ὑμένα, ὃς ἄνωθεν ἐπὶ τὸ βάθος αὐλοειδῶς διήκων, διὰ τῶν καθεξῆς σπονδύλων ἑαυτόν τὲ καὶ τὸν ἐγκείμενον αὐτῷ μυελὸν διεξάγων, τῇ βάσει συναπολήγει τῆς ῥάχεως· πάσαις ὀστέων τε καὶ ἁρμονιῶν συμβολαῖς καὶ μυῶν ἀρχαῖς οἷόν τις ἡνίοχος αὐτὸς ἐνδιδοὺς τῆς καθ' ἕκαστον κινήσεώς τε καὶ στάσεως τὴν ὁρμὴν καὶ τὴν δύναμιν. **[30.25]** [252] Διὰ τοῦτό μοι δοκεῖ καὶ ἀσφαλεστέρας ἠξιῶσθαι φρουρᾶς, κατὰ μὲν τὴν κεφαλὴν διπλαῖς ὀστέων περιβολαῖς ἐν κύκλῳ διειλημμένος, ἐν δὲ τοῖς σπονδύλοις ταῖς τε τῶν ἀκανθῶν προβολαῖς καὶ ταῖς πολυτρόποις κατὰ τὸ σχῆμα διαπλοκαῖς, δι' ὧν ἐν ἀπαθείᾳ πάσῃ φυλάττεται, διὰ τῆς περιεχούσης αὐτὸν φρουρᾶς τὸ ἀσφαλὲς ἔχων.

[30.26] Ὁμοίως δ' ἄν τις καὶ περὶ τῆς καρδίας στοχάσαιτο, ὅτι, καθάπερ τὶς οἶκος ἀσφαλής, αὐτὴ διὰ τῶν στερροτάτων περιηρμόσθη, ταῖς τῶν ὀστέων ἐν κύκλῳ περιοχαῖς ὠχυρωμένη· κατόπιν μὲν γάρ ἐστιν ἡ ῥάχις, ταῖς ὠμοπλάταις ἑκατέρωθεν ἠσφαλισμένη· καθ' [B] ἑκάτερον δὲ πλάγιον ἡ τῶν πλευρῶν θέσις περιπτύσσουσα, τὸ μέσον δυσπαθὲς ἀπεργάζεται· ἐν δὲ τοῖς ἔμπροσθεν, τὸ στέρνον καὶ ἡ τῆς κλειδὸς συζυγία προβέβληται, ὡς ἂν πανταχόθεν αὐτῇ τὸ ἀσφαλὲς ἀπὸ τῶν ἔξωθεν διοχλούντων φυλάσσοιτο.

[30.27] Οἷον δὲ κατὰ τὴν γεωργίαν ἐστὶν ἰδεῖν, τῆς ἐκ νεφῶν ἐπομβρίας ἢ τῆς τῶν ὀχετῶν ἐπιρροῆς διάβροχον ποιούσης τὸ ὑποκείμενον· κῆπος δέ τις ὑποκείσθω τῷ λόγῳ, μυρίας μὲν δένδρων διαφορὰς παντοδαπὰς δὲ τῶν ἐκ γῆς φυομένων ἰδέας ἐν

200 τὸν ἀτμὸν B 201 τὸ] *ita* Æ ß D G H I L M N O P Q R S W X *Ald Forb* : *om. Mign* καθαρώτερον N R 202 ὑμένα] membrana *Eri* 203 σφονδύλων O τὲ] *ita* Æ B D G H I L M N O P Q R S W X *Forb* : δὲ *Ald Mign* αὐτῷ] ἑαυτῷ D : ἐν αὐτῷ B I O 204 βάσει] φύσει M 204–5 πάσαις—ἀρχαῖς] *om. Eri* 204 τε *om.* H N Q R[ac] W 205 μυῶν] medullarum *Dion* καθ' ἕκαστον] *ita* L O S *Forb* : καθέκαστον W X *Ald Mign* 206 ὁρμὴν] ὁρμὴν τε Æ B I O R τὴν *om.* Æ I O 207 φρουρᾶς] *ita codd. Forb* : φρουρᾶς καὶ *Ald Mign* 208 ἐν[1]] ἐπὶ Q 208–9 ἐν[1]—προβολαῖς *om.* I 208 σφονδύλοις O τε *om.* B L W 209 τὸ *om.* B 210 φυλάσσεται I N O Q R τὸ *om.* L 211 ὅτι] ὅτιπερ D G H L P X τὶς] *ita Ald Forb* : τίς H : τις D G P S W X *Mign* 212 αὐτὴ] *ita* B D G H P Q R X *Forb* : αὐτῇ L S : αὕτη O W *Ald Mign* στερροτέρων M N περιήρμοσται R 213 ὠχυρωμένος Æ Q R[ac] μὲν *om.* D 213–14 ταῖς—ἠσφαλισμένη] aequalibus latitudinibus hinc inde munita *Eri* 213 τοῖς G H L M P R[2] S X 214 ἑκατέρωθεν] ἀμφοτέρωθεν Æ B C I M N O Q ἑκατέρωθεν ἠσφαλισμένη] ἀσφάλεια ἀμφοτέρων ἑκάτερον] ἕτερον T 215 τὸ][2] τὸ τε Æ ß I N O T 216 αὐτὴ B : αὐτῆς N ἀπὸ] ὑπὸ N 217 φυλάττοιτο D G H P S 218 δὲ] δὴ M N Q ἔστιν Æ I M O *Mign* 219 ἐπιρροῆς] ἐπομβρίας B 220 μὲν *om.* N δὲ] τε N τῶν] τὰς O ἰδέας] τὰς ἰδέας D

their respective forces through a certain mixture and combination, nourish and sustain the brain by their vapours, by which, in turn, being rarefied to the most pure condition, the exhalation that proceeds from that organ anoints the tissue containing the brain, which, reaching from above downwards like a pipe, extending (itself and the marrow which is contained in it) through the successive vertebrae, terminates together at the base of the spine, giving, like a charioteer, to all the meeting points of bones and joints and the branches of muscles the impulse and power of movement and rest for each particular part. [**30.25**] For this reason also, it seems to me, that it has been granted a more secure defence, being set apart, in the head, by a double shelter of bones around it, in the vertebrae of the neck formed by the projections of the spine, and by the diverse inter-lacings of the form of those vertebrae, by which it is kept safe in freedom from all injury, enjoying safety by the defence surrounding it.[17]

[**30.26**] Likewise one might suppose of the heart, that, like some safe house, it is itself fitted with the most solid defences, fortified by the enclosing walls of the bones around it; for in the rear there is the spine, fortified on either side by the shoulder-blades, and on each side the enfolding position of the ribs makes that which is in-between difficult to injure; while in front the breast-bone and the juncture of the collar-bone stand on defence, so that its safety may be guarded at all points from external troubles.

[**30.27**] One may see something of this in husbandry, when the heavy rain from the clouds or the overflow from the rivers causes the land beneath it to be sodden. Let us suppose for our argument a garden, nourishing in it countless varieties of

[17] Plato, *Tim.* 75c; Galen, *De usu part.* 8.9 (Helmreich, 1, 479.3–480.11; ET 410–11).

ἑαυτῷ τρέφων, ὧν καὶ τὸ σχῆμα καὶ ἡ ποιότης καὶ ἡ τῆς χρόας ἰδιότης ἐν πολλῇ διαφορᾷ τοῖς καθ' ἕκαστον ἐνθεωρεῖται· τοσούτων τοίνυν κατὰ τὸν ἕνα χῶρον τῷ ὑγρῷ τρεφομένων, ἡ μὲν ὑπονοτίζουσα τὰ καθ' ἕκαστον δύναμις μία [C] *τις ἐστὶ κατὰ τὴν φύσιν· ἡ δὲ τῶν τρεφομένων ἰδιότης εἰς διαφόρους τὸ ὑγρὸν μεταβάλλει ποιότητας· τὸ γὰρ αὐτὸ πικραίνεται μὲν ἐν τῇ ἀψίνθῳ, εἰς φθοροποιὸν δὲ χυμὸν ἐν τῷ κωνείῳ μεθίσταται· καὶ ἄλλο ἐν ἄλλῳ γίνεται, ἐν κρόκῳ, ἐν βαλσάμῳ, ἐν μήκωνι· τῷ μὲν γὰρ ἐκθερμαίνεται, τῷ δὲ καταψύχεται, τῷ δὲ μέσην ἔχει ποιότητα· καὶ ἐν δάφνῃ καὶ ἐν σχίνῳ καὶ τοῖς τοιούτοις εὔπνουν ἐστὶν, καὶ ἐν συκῇ δὲ καὶ ὄχνῃ κατεγλυκάνθη, καὶ διὰ τῆς ἀμπέλου βότρυς καὶ οἶνος ἐγένετο, καὶ ὁ τοῦ μήλου χυλὸς καὶ τὸ τοῦ ῥόδου ἐρύθημα καὶ τὸ λαμπρὸν τοῦ κρίνου καὶ τὸ κυανίζον τοῦ ἴου καὶ τὸ πορφύρεον τῆς ὑακινθίνης βαφῆς καὶ πάνθ' ὅσα κατὰ τὴν γῆν ἔστιν ἰδεῖν, ἐκ μιᾶς καὶ τῆς αὐτῆς ἰκμάδος ἀναβλαστάνοντα, εἰς τοσαύτας διαφορὰς κατά τε τὸ σχῆμα* [D] *καὶ τὸ εἶδος καὶ τὰς ποιότητας διακρίνεται·—τοιοῦτόν τι καὶ κατὰ τὴν ἔμψυχον ἡμῶν ἄρουραν θαυματοποιεῖται παρὰ τῆς φύσεως, μᾶλλον δὲ παρὰ τοῦ Δεσπότου τῆς φύσεως. Ὀστέα καὶ χόνδροι, φλέβες, ἀρτηρίαι, νεῦρα, σύνδεσμοι, σάρκες, δέρμα, πιμελαί, τρίχες, ἀδένες, ὄνυχες, ὀφθαλμοί, μυκτῆρες, ὦτα—πάντα τὰ τοιαῦτα καὶ μυρία πρὸς τούτοις ἄλλα διαφόροις ἰδιώμασιν ἀπ' ἀλλήλων κεχωρισμένα μιᾷ τῇ τῆς τροφῆς ἰδέᾳ καταλλήλως τῇ ἑαυτῶν τρέφεται φύσει, ὡς ἑκάστῳ τῶν ὑποκειμένων τὴν τροφὴν προσεγγίσασαν, ᾧπερ ἂν ἐμπελάσῃ, κατ' ἐκεῖνο καὶ ἀλλοιοῦσθαι, οἰκείαν καὶ συμφυῆ τῇ τοῦ μέρους ἰδιότητι γινομένην. Εἰ γὰρ κατὰ τὸν ὀφθαλμὸν γένοιτο, τῷ ὁρατικῷ μορίῳ* [253] *συγκατεκράθη, καὶ τῶν περὶ τὸν ὀφθαλμὸν χιτώνων ταῖς διαφοραῖς οἰκείως εἰς ἕκαστον κατεμερίσθη· εἰ δὲ τοῖς κατὰ τὴν ἀκοὴν μέρεσιν ἐπιρρυῇ, τῇ ἀκουστικῇ καταμίγνυται φύσει· καὶ ἐν χείλει γενόμενον χεῖλος ἐγένετο, καὶ ἐν ὀστέῳ πήγνυται, καὶ ἐν μυελῷ ἁπαλύνεται,*

221 *χροιᾶς* R *ἰδιότης*] *ἰδέα* M 222 *καθ' ἕκαστον*] *ita* G O X *Forb* : *καθέκαστον Ald Mign* *θεωρεῖται* D F G H P S X 223 *ἡ—ἕκαστον*] ueluti singula subirrigans *Eri* *καθέκαστον* Æ M R *Ald* 223–4 *ἐστὶ κατὰ τὴν φύσιν*] *ita* A D E F G H L M N P S X *Forb* : *κατὰ τὴν φύσιν ἐστὶν* O W *Ald Mign* 224 *τὴν om.* D E *εἰς*] *εἰς πολλὰς καὶ* N 225 *δὲ om.* L 226 *ἐν κρόκῳ, ἐν βαλσάμῳ*] in balsamo in croco *Dion* 226–7 *τῷ . . . τῷ . . . τῷ*] *τὸ . . . τὸ . . . τὸ* M N Q R T 227 *ἐκθερμαίνεται*] *θερμαίνεται* D E G H P X *καταψύχεται*] *ψύχεται* D E L *ἔχει*] *ἴσχει* Æ B C I N O R^{ac} : infundit *Eri* 228 *σχίνῳ*] *ita* A Æ B C D^{2} E F G H N O P Q R S T X *Dion Ald Forb* : *σχοίνῳ Mign* : schino *Eri* *εὔπνουν*] *ἔμπνουν* B D^{ac} E H R^{ac} W *καὶ*³] *ita* A $Æ^{2?}$ C D E F G H L N^{2} P R S X *Forb* : *om.* O W *Ald Mign* *δὲ*] *τε* N R *καὶ*⁴] et (*ΟΓΧΝΗ* est species spiri quam uolemam latini uocant: hinc Virgilius grauibus uolemis) *Eri* [cf. Verg. *Georg.* 2.88] *ὄχνῃ*] *ὄγχνῃ* Æ B N R^{2} : *ὄχνῃ et γ sup. l.* ß P S 229 *διὰ*] *ὁ* Æ B C E I O T : *ὁ διὰ* R^{2} *καὶ*² *om.* Æ B C E I O T 230 *χυλὸς*] *χυμὸς* N Q R^{ac} *ἐρύθημα*] *ita codd. Forb* : *ἐρύθρημα Ald Mign* *τοῦ κρίνου λαμπρὸν* W *Ald Mign* *τοῦ*² *om.* T 231 *πορφύρεον*] *ita* A Æ B C D E F^{ac} (*προφυρίζον sup. l.*) I M N O R S T *Forb* : *προφύραιον* G H : *προφυραῖον* W X *Ald Mign* *ὑακινθίνης*] *ita* A Æ C D E F G I L M N O Q S T W *Forb* : *οἰακινθίνης* P X : *ὑακινθίνου* H : *ὑακίνθης* B *Ald* : *ὑακιν* R (*θν sup. l.*) : *ὑακίνθου Mign* *πάνθ'*] *πάντα* Æ B I L M N O Q W 232 *εἰς*] *καὶ* X *τε*] *δὲ* T : *om.* Q 235 *τῆς om. Mign* *καὶ*] *τε καὶ* N : scilicet *Dion* : *om. Eri* *χόνδρος* T *φλέβαις* O : *om. Eri* *φλέβες ἀρτηρίαι*] *καὶ φλέβες καὶ ἀρτηρίαι* H 236 *δέρματα* M *πιμελαὶ—ὄνυχες om.* L *πιμέλη* I : aruina musculi *Dion* : adipes *Eri* *ἀδένες τρίχες* I *ἀδένες*] *ἀδεναὶ* I : *ὀδόντες* R^{mg} : *om. Dion* : adenes *Eri* *μυκτῆρες*] *om. Eri* 237 *ἄλλα*] *ἄλλα καὶ* L *ἰδιώμασιν*] *ita* Æ B C D E F G H I O P R S T X *Forb* : *ἰδιότησιν* A *Ald Mign* 238 *τῇ om.* L O Q *καταλλήλῶς τῇ τῆς τροφῆς ἰδέᾳ* N 239 *ᾧπερ*] *ὅπερ* D G H L P X *ἂν*] *γὰρ* B *ἐμπελάσῃ*] *ἐνπελάσῃ* Q : *ἐμπελάσει* B : *ἐν πελάσει* L : *πελάσῃ* N 240 *συμφυᾶ* I *ἰδιότητι*] *οἰκειότητι* N M^{ac} (*ἰδ sup. l.*) 241 *κατὰ τὸν ὀφθαλμὸν*] *ἐν τῷ ὀφθαλμῷ* I *τῶν ὀφθαλμῶν* W X *ὁρατικῷ*] spectivae *Eri* *συγκατεκρίθη* B F^{pc} S : *συνανεκράθη* M : *συνκράθη* C : *συνεκράθη* O 242 *τῶν ὀφθαλμῶν* D R^{ac} : *τοὺς ὀφθαλμοὺς* M : *ὁ ὀφθαλμὸν* O (*ω supr. l.*) *εἰς om.* D 243 *κατὰ τὴν*] *κατ'* D G H P S X *ἐπιρρυῇ*] *ἐπιρρύει* B C : *ἐπιρρυεῖ* G O P^{ac} R^{ac} X : *ἐπιρροὴ* T *καταμίγνυται*] *ἐπμίγνυται* N

trees and all the forms of plants that grow from the earth, of which one can see in each the figure and the quality and the particularity of colour in great variety—so many things, then, in one place are nourished by the moisture, the power which moistens each being one in nature, but the particularity of the plants being nourished changes the moisture into different qualities: for the same moisture becomes bitter in wormwood, and is changed into a deadly juice in hemlock, and becomes different in other plants, in saffron, in balsam, in the poppy; in one it becomes hot, in another cold, in another it obtains the middle quality; and in laurel and mastic and in such things it is scented, and in the fig and the pear it is sweetened; and by passing through the vine it becomes a cluster of grapes and wine; and the juice of the apple, the redness of the rose, the radiance of the lily, the blue of the violet, the purple of the hyacinthine dye, and all that one sees upon the earth, while arising from one and the same moisture, yet are separated into so many varieties in respect of figure and form and quality. The same sort of wonder is wrought in our animated soil by nature, or rather by the Lord of nature: bones and cartilages, veins, arteries, nerves, ligatures, flesh, skin, fat, hair, glands, nails, eyes, nostrils, ears—all such things as these and countless others in addition, while separated from one another by different properties, are nourished by the one form of nourishment in ways appropriate to their own nature, so that the nourishment, approaching each of the subjects, is changed according to that to which it approaches, becoming suitable for and akin to the particularity of the part.[18] For if it is near the eye, it blends with the visual part and is suitably distributed to each by the differences of the membranes around the eye; or, if it flows to the auditory parts, it is mingled with the acoustic nature; or if it is in the lip, it becomes lip; and it grows solid in bone, and grows soft in marrow, and is made tense with the sinew,

[18] Cf. Gregory of Nyssa, *Hex.* 49 (Drobner, 62. 7–14).

καὶ τονοῦται μετὰ τοῦ νεύρου, καὶ τῇ ἐπιφανείᾳ συμπεριτείνεται, καὶ εἰς ὄνυχας διαβαίνει, καὶ εἰς τριχῶν γένεσιν λεπτοποιεῖται τοῖς καταλλήλοις ἀτμοῖς· εἰ μὲν διὰ σκολιῶν προάγοιτο πόρων, οὐλοτέρας τε καὶ κατηγκυλωμένας τὰς τρίχας ἐκφύουσα, εἰ δὲ δι' εὐθείας ἡ τῶν τριχοποιῶν ἀτμῶν γένοιτο πρόοδος, τετανάς τε καὶ εὐθείας προάγουσα.

[**30.28**] *Ἀλλὰ πολὺ τῶν προκειμένων ὁ λόγος ἡμῖν ἀποπεπλάνηται, τοῖς ἔργοις ἐμβαθύνων τῆς φύσεως, καὶ ὑπογράφειν ἐπιχειρῶν ὅπως ἡμῖν καὶ ἐξ ὁποίων συνέστηκε τὰ* [B] *καθ' ἕκαστον, τά τε πρὸς τὸ ζῆν καὶ τὰ πρὸς τὸ εὖ ζῆν καὶ εἴ τι μετὰ τούτων ἕτερον κατὰ τὴν πρώτην διαίρεσιν ἐνοήσαμεν.* [**30.29**] *Τὸ γὰρ προκείμενον ἦν δεῖξαι τὴν σπερματικὴν τῆς συστάσεως ἡμῶν αἰτίαν μήτε ἀσώματον εἶναι ψυχὴν μήτε ἄψυχον σῶμα, ἀλλ' ἐξ ἐμψύχων τε καὶ ζώντων σωμάτων ζῶν καὶ ἔμψυχον παρὰ τὴν πρώτην ἀπογεννᾶσθαι ζῶον· ἐκδεξαμένην δὲ τὴν ἀνθρωπίνην φύσιν, καθάπερ τινὰ τροφὸν ταῖς οἰκείαις δυνάμεσιν αὐτὴν τιθηνήσασθαι· τὴν δὲ τρέφεσθαι κατ' ἀμφότερα καὶ καταλλήλως ἐν ἑκατέρῳ μέρει τὴν αὔξησιν ἐπίδηλον ἔχειν· εὐθὺς μὲν γὰρ διὰ τῆς τεχνικῆς ταύτης καὶ ἐπιστημονικῆς διαπλάσεως τὴν συμπεπλεγμένην αὐτῇ τῆς ψυχῆς ἐνδείκνυται δύναμιν, ἀμυδρότερον μὲν κατὰ τὴν πρώτην ἐκφαινομένην, καθεξῆς δὲ τῇ τοῦ ὀργάνου τελειώσει* [C] *συναναλάμπουσαν.*

[**30.30**] *Οἷον δὲ ἐπὶ τῶν λιθογλύφων ἔστιν ἰδεῖν· πρόκειται μὲν γὰρ τῷ τεχνίτῃ ζώου τινὸς εἶδος ἐν λίθῳ δεῖξαι· τοῦτο δὲ προθέμενος, πρῶτον μὲν τὸν λίθον τῆς συμφυοῦς ὕλης ἀπέρρηξεν, εἶτα περικόψας αὐτοῦ τὰ περιττὰ, προήγαγέ πως διὰ τοῦ πρώτου σχήματος τῇ μιμήσει τῇ κατὰ πρόθεσιν· ὥστε καὶ τὸν ἄπειρον διὰ τῶν φαινομένων τοῦ σκοποῦ τῆς τέχνης καταστοχάσασθαι· πάλιν ἐπεργασάμενος, προσήγγισε πλέον τῇ ὁμοιότητι τοῦ σπουδαζομένου· εἶτα τὸ τέλειον καὶ ἀκριβὲς εἶδος ἐγχειρουργήσας τῇ ὕλῃ, εἰς πέρας τὴν τέχνην προήγαγε· καὶ ἔστι λέων ἢ ἄνθρωπος ἢ ὅ τι ἂν τύχῃ παρὰ τοῦ τεχνίτου γενόμενον, ὁ πρὸ βραχέος ἄσημος λίθος· οὐ τῆς ὕλης πρὸς τὸ εἶδος ὑπαμειφθείσης ἀλλὰ τοῦ εἴδους ἐπιτεχνηθέντος τῇ*

245 *συμπαρατείνεται* D G H I N O P S T X *ὄνυχα* Æ B C I M O Q R T 246 *τοὺς καταλλήλους ἀτμοὺς* I N$^{ac?}$ Q 247 *προάγοιντο* L T W : *προάγοι το* N (*ν forte eras.*) : *προάγοι τῶν* Æ B C M O Q *κατηγκυκλωμένας* O 248 *γίνοιτο* N R *πρόοδος γένοιτο* A D E F G H P S X *τετανὰς*] *ita codd. Forb* : *τεταμένας* R^{ac} W *Ald Mign* 250 *ἡμῖν ὁ λόγος* Æ I N O R *ἀπεπλάνηται* D^{ac} Q 251 *ἐμβατεύων* L W 251–3 *καὶ ὑπογράφειν—ἕτερον*] et quodammodo quae in nobis constituta sunt et quae extrinsecus efficiunt quae per singula quae ad uiuendum sunt conantes subscribere, etiam cum his alia quaedam *Eri* 251 *ὅπως*] *ὅπως τε* O *καὶ ἐξ ὁποίων ἡμῖν* I O *καὶ*^{2} *om.* W 252 *καθ' ἕκαστον*] *ita* L O P *Forb* : *καθέκαστον* W X *Ald Mign* *καὶ*^{1}] *τε καὶ* I *τὰ om.* D E N R T *πρὸς om.* N R T *ζῆν εὖ* L *εἴ τι*] *ἔτι* L M 252–3 *τι . . . ἕτερον*] *τινα . . . ἕτερα* Q 253 *τούτων*] *τοῦτο* D G H L P S W X *διαίρεσιν*] *αἵρεσιν* Q *ἐνοήσαμεν*] *ἐννοήσαμεν* W : *ἐνομίσαμεν* T : *ἐποιήσαμεν* D E G H P X : *ἐποιήσαμεν* F^{ac} (*ἐνοήσαμεν sup. l.*) 255 *ἀψύχων* T^{ac} : *ἐμψύχων* T^{2} *ἐξ om.* D N^{ac} P(?) X *τε om. SP* 256 *σωμάτων*] *om. Eri* *ζῶν*] *ζῶον* Q : *ζῶσαν* R : *ζῶν τε* H : animantum *Eri* *ζῶον*] *ζωὴν* Æ Q R : *om.* B I M N^{ac} O T *SP* : constitutionem *Eri* *δὲ*] *τε* D G H L N^{2} P S W X 257 *δυνάμεσιν*] *τροφαῖς* Q *Eri* *αὐτὴν δυνάμεσιν* Æ B I N O R *αὐτὴν*] eam (dico causam) *Eri* 258 *τρέφεσθαι*] *τρέφεσθαι τε* Æ B C E I L M N O R *κατ' ἀμφότερα*] utramque uero partem (materiam uidelicet et utiam) *Eri* *καὶ om. SP* *ἐν om.* D *ἑκατέρῳ*] *ἑκάστῳ* Æ B C E I O R T 260–1 *δύναμιν ἐνδείκνυται* N 261 *ἀμυδρωτέραν* L *μὲν om.* O *κατὰ*] *παρὰ* Æ B C I M N O Q R T *SP* *ἐκφαινομένην*] *ἐμφαινομένην* N : *ἐκφαινομένην καὶ SP* 263 *δὲ*] *δὴ* Æ B Q : *δέ τι* R 264 *ἐν*] *ἐν τῷ* N 265 *προσήγαγε* ß H M N O R^{ac} S T *SP* 266 *τῇ*] *τὸ* I : *τοῦ* B C N O R^{ac} *SP* *πρόθεσιν*] *τὴν πρόθεσιν* B *ἄπειρον*] *ἀνεπιστήμονα ἄπειρον* B : *ἀνεπιστήμονα καὶ ἄπειρον* R 266–7 *τοῦ φαινομένου* N^{ac} *Dion* 267 *σκοποῦ*] *σκοτίου* Q : *κρυπτοῦ* M *ἐπεργασάμενος*] *ἀπεργασάμενος* L P^{ac} : *ἐπεξεργασάμενος* M : *προσεξεργασάμενος* I : *προσεργασάμενος* Æ B C O 268 *ἀκριβῶς* T 269–70 *ἢ ἄνθρωπος om. Mign* 270 *τύχοι* M 271 *ἐπιτεχνιθέντος* G I : *ἐπὶ τεχνιτευθέντος* N

and is extended with the surface, and passes into the nails; and is rendered fine for the growth of hair, by the corresponding exhalations—if it proceeds through winding passages, it produces hair that is more curly and wavy, but if the course of the exhalations that produce hair is straight, it induces flat and straight hair.[19]

[**30.28**] But our argument, however, has wandered far from the matters at hand, going deep into the works of nature, and endeavouring to describe how and from what our particular organs are constituted, those intended for life and those for good life, and any other category after these that we considered in the first division. [**30.29**] The purpose was to show that the seminal cause of our constitution is neither a soul without body, nor a body without soul, but that, from animated and living bodies a being, living and animated from the first, is generated, human nature receiving it to be cherished, like a nursling, with her own powers; it is nourished in both respects and makes its growth manifest appropriately in each part, for it immediately displays, by this artistic and scientific process of formation, the power of the soul interwoven with it, appearing at first somewhat obscurely, but afterwards increasing in radiance concurrently with the perfecting of the organism.[20]

[**30.30**] One may see this with stone-carvers: the artist's purpose is to produce in stone the figure of some animal; proposing this, he first severs the stone from its kindred matter, then, by chipping away the superfluous parts, he advances somehow through the first outline to the imitation that is his purpose, so that even someone inexperienced may, by what appears, conjecture the aim of the art; and again, working at it, he brings it closer to the likeness of the object in view; then, lastly, producing in the material the perfect and exact form, he brings his art to its conclusion and that which shortly before was shapeless stone is a lion, or a human, or whatever it may be that was made by the artist, not by the material being changed into the figure, but by the figure being wrought upon the matter. To suppose something similar in the case of the soul would not be far from probability; for we say that the all-contriving nature, taking from the kindred matter within herself the part that comes from the human being, crafts the statue.[21] And

[19] Cf. Plato, *Tim.* 76bc; Aristotle, *De part. an.* 2.14–15 (658ab); Galen, *De usu part.* 11.14 (Helmreich, 2, 155.6–15; ET 2, 531).

[20] Cf. Philo, *Opif.* 67; Origen, *Princ.* 1.1.6.

[21] Cf. Gregory of Nyssa, *Inscr.* 1.11.131–7 (McDonough, 115–17; ET 163–5); Plato, *Phaedr.* 252d7; Plotinus, *Enn.* 1.6.9; Gregory of Nazianzus, *Or.* 27.7.

ὕλη. [D] Τοιοῦτόν τι καὶ ἐπὶ τῆς ψυχῆς ὁ λογισάμενος, τοῦ εἰκότος οὐχ ἁμαρτήσεται· τὴν γὰρ πάντα τεχνιτεύουσαν φύσιν ἐκ τῆς ὁμογενοῦς ὕλης λαβοῦσαν, ἐν ἑαυτῇ τὸ ἐκ τοῦ ἀνθρώπου μέρος δημιουργεῖν ἀνδριάντα φαμέν. Ὥσπερ δὲ τῇ κατ' ὀλίγον ἐργασίᾳ τοῦ λίθου τὸ εἶδος ἐπηκολούθησεν, ἀμυδρότερον μὲν παρὰ τὴν πρώτην, τελειότερον δὲ μετὰ τὴν τοῦ ἔργου συμπλήρωσιν· οὕτω καὶ ἐν τῇ τοῦ ὀργάνου γλυφῇ τὸ τῆς ψυχῆς εἶδος κατὰ τὴν ἀναλογίαν τοῦ ὑποκειμένου προφαίνεται, ἀτελὲς ἐν τῷ ἀτελεῖ καὶ ἐν τῷ τελείῳ τέλειον· ἀλλ' ἐξ ἀρχῆς ἂν τέλειον ἦν εἰ μὴ διὰ τῆς κακίας ἡ φύσις ἐκολοβώθη· διὰ τοῦτο ἡ πρὸς τὴν [256] ἐμπαθῆ καὶ ζωώδη γένεσιν κοινωνία οὐκ εὐθὺς ἐκλάμπειν ἐν τῷ πλάσματι τὴν θείαν εἰκόνα ἐποίησεν ἀλλ' ὁδῷ τινι καὶ ἀκολουθίᾳ διὰ τῶν ὑλικῶν τε καὶ ζωωδεστέρων τῆς ψυχῆς ἰδιωμάτων ἐπὶ τὸ τέλειον ἄγει τὸν ἄνθρωπον.

[30.31] Τὸ δὲ τοιοῦτον δόγμα καὶ ὁ μέγας ἀπόστολος ἐν τῇ πρὸς Κορινθίους διδάσκει, λέγων· **Ὅτε ἤμην νήπιος, ὡς νήπιος ἐλάλουν, ὡς νήπιος ἐφρόνουν, ὡς νήπιος ἐλογιζόμην· ὅτε δὲ γέγονα ἀνὴρ, κατήργηκα τὰ τοῦ νηπίου·** οὐκ ἄλλης ἐν τῷ ἀνδρὶ τῆς ψυχῆς ἐπεισελθούσης παρὰ τὴν ἐν τῷ μειρακίῳ νοουμένην, ἡ νηπιωδεστέρα καταργεῖται διάνοια καὶ ἡ ἀνδρώδης ἐγγίνεται· ἀλλὰ τῆς αὐτῆς, ἐν ἐκείνῳ μὲν τὸ ἀτελὲς, ἐν τούτῳ δὲ διαδεικνυούσης τὸ τέλειον. [30.32] Ὥσπερ γὰρ τὰ φυόμενά τε καὶ αὐξάνοντα ζῆν λέγομεν, πάντα δε τὰ ἐν μετουσίᾳ ζωῆς καὶ φυσικῆς [B] ὄντα κινήσεως οὐκ ἄν τις ἄψυχα φήσειεν, οὐ μὴν οὐδὲ τελείας ψυχῆς μετέχειν τὴν τοιαύτην ζωήν ἐστιν εἰπεῖν· γενομένη γὰρ ἐν τοῖς φυτοῖς ψυχική τις ἐνέργεια, μέχρι τῶν κατ' αἴσθησιν κινημάτων οὐκ ἔφθασε· πάλιν δὲ κατὰ προσθήκην δύναμίς τις ψυχικὴ τοῖς ἀλόγοις ἐγγινομένη, οὐδὲ αὐτὴ τοῦ τέλους ἐφίκετο, λόγου τε καὶ διανοίας χάριν ἐν ἑαυτῇ μὴ χωρήσασα. [30.33] Διὰ τοῦτό φαμεν τὴν μὲν ἀληθῆ καὶ τελείαν ψυχὴν τὴν ἀνθρωπίνην εἶναι, διὰ πάσης ἐνεργείας γνωριζομένην· εἰ δέ τι ἄλλο μετέχει ζωῆς, ἐν καταχρήσει τινὶ συνηθείας ἔμψυχον λέγομεν, ὅτι μὴ τελεία ἐν τούτοις ἐστὶν ἡ ψυχὴ, ἀλλά τινα μέρη ψυχικῆς ἐνεργείας, ἃ καὶ ἐν τῷ ἀνθρώπῳ κατὰ τὴν μυστικὴν τοῦ Μωϋσέως ἀνθρωπογονίαν ἐπιγεγενῆσθαι, διὰ τὴν πρὸς τὸ ἐμπαθὲς οἰκειότητα μεμαθήκαμεν· [C] διὰ τοῦτο συμβουλεύων ὁ Παῦλος τοῖς ἀκούειν αὐτοῦ δυναμένοις, τῆς τελειότητος ἔχεσθαι, καὶ τὸν τρόπον ὅπως ἂν τοῦ

272 τοιοῦτο Æ N O   τι] τις B C M N O P[2] : τί τις I : τε A   ὁ *om.* X *SP*   εἰκότος] εἶναι τὸ T   273 ἁμαρτήσει B M   φύσιν] φύσιν καὶ X   274 λαβοῦσαν] ἀναλαβοῦσαν R   ἑαυτῇ] αὐτῇ L R[ac]   ἐκ *om.* N   δημιουργεῖν] δημιουργεῖν τὸν N : δημιουργεῖ *SP*   276 παρὰ *om.* Æ   276–300 τελειότερον—τρόπον *def. Eri*   276 τελεώτερον H   τοῦ *om.* B L   οὕτως L   277 τοῦ[1]] τοῦ ἀνθρωπίνου L   ψυχῆς] γλυφῆς M   278 τῷ[1] *om.* M   ἀτελεῖ] ἀτελεῖ ὂν N   τῷ[2] *om.* G M P Q R S W X : *des.* Q   280 γέννησιν D E F G H P S W X : γεννήσει A   ἐκλάμπειν] ἀναλάμπειν R   τὴν θείαν εἰκόνα ἐν τῷ πλάσματι *Ald Mign* (*repugn. codd.*)   281 τε *om. Ald Mign*   283 τοιοῦτο Æ L N O   283–4 τῇ . . . λέγων] τῷ . . . λόγῳ Æ B I M O R   284–5 ὡς νήπιος—ἐλογιζόμην] *ita* A B C D E F G H L M P R S T W X *Forb* : ἐλάλουν ὡς νήπιος ἐφρόνουν ὡς νήπιος ἐλογιζόμενην ὡς νήπιος Æ I N O : ἐλάλουν ὡς νήπιος ἐλογιζόμενην ὡς νήπιος *Ald Mign*   285 κατήργηκα] κατήργησα *Ald Mign*   τὰ τοῦ νηπίου καρήργηκα G H P R S X   ἄλλης] ἄλλης δὲ L   286 τῆς *om.* Æ B O R   287 κατήργηται M   ἀνδρώδης] ἀνδρειότης D E : ἀνδρειώδης F G H S X   γίνεται D E   ἐν *om.* L   288 διαδεικνύσης Æ I N O : δεικνυούσης R T : δεικνούσης L   289 τε *om.* Æ   αὔξοντα A D E F G H M N P S X   δε] *ita* Æ G H I L M N O P R S X *Ald Forb* : τε *Mign*   τὰ *om.* T   ζωῆς] ζωτικῆς N   293 ψυχικὴ *om.* T   ἐγγιγνομένη L : ἐγγενομένη M   αὐτὴ] αὕτη B I N   ἐφίκεται A D[ac] F G H P S : ἐφικνεῖται D[2] E L T : ἀφήκεται X   *post* καὶ *des.* I   294 ἀληθῆ καὶ τελείαν] τελείαν τε καὶ ἀληθῆ N   295 τὴν *om. Mign*   γνωριζομένην] χωριζομένην M   296 τινὶ *om.* D   ὅτι μὴ] *ita codd. Ald Forb* : μὴ ὅτι *Mign*   297 ἐστὶν] ἦν R   ἡ *om.* M P W X   298 κατὰ] μετὰ L   299 Παῦλος] μέγας Παῦλος B   αὐτοῦ δυναμένοις] *ita codd. Forb* : αὐτοῦ βουλομένοις *Ald* : βουλομένοις *Mign*   300 *post* τρόπον *habet* T ὁ θεὸς εἰπὼν, ὅτι ποιήσωμεν ἄνθρωπον ὡς οὐκ εἶχε φύσεως τὸ κακὸν ἐκ τοῦ προφανοῦς ἐπιδείξας· οὐ γὰρ ἂν ἠπατήθη ὁ ἄνθρωπος τῷ προδήλῳ κακῷ κινήσει δοὺς· οὐκ ἀμφιβάλλει πάντως ὅπως ἂν τοῦ σπουδαζομένου τύχοιεν ὑποτίθεσθαι λέγων· ἀπεκδύσασθε τὸν παλαιὸν *et rel. des.*

just as the form follows upon the gradual working of the stone, at first somewhat indistinct, but more perfect after the completion of the work, so also in the carving of the organism the form of the soul, by the analogy, is displayed in the substratum, incompletely in that which is incomplete, and perfectly in that which is perfect; but it would have been perfect from the beginning had nature not been maimed by evil. For this reason our sharing in that impassioned and animal-like genesis brings it about that the divine image does not shine forth immediately in the moulded figure, but, by a certain method and sequence, through those material and more animal-like properties of the soul, brings to perfection the human being.

[30.31] Some such doctrine as this the great Apostle also teaches in his Epistle to the Corinthians, saying, *When I was a child, I spoke as a child, I understood as a child, I thought as a child; but when I became an adult I put away childish things*;[22] not that the soul which arises in the adult is conceived otherwise than that which we know to be in the boy, [as if] the childish mind is abolished when the adult mind intervenes, but that the same soul displays its imperfect condition in that one and the perfect state in this. **[30.32]** For just as we say that those things which sprout and grow are alive, and no one would say that all things that participate in life and natural movement are inanimate, yet one does not say that such life partakes of a perfect soul, for although a certain animate activity exists in plants, it does not attain to the movements of sense-perception, and, again, though a certain further animate power arises in the irrational animals, neither does this reach perfection, for it does not contain in itself the grace of reason and mind. **[30.33]** Therefore, we say that the true and perfect soul is the human, known by every activity. If anything else shares in life we speak of it as animate by a sort of customary misuse of language, because in these cases the soul is not perfect, but only certain parts of the animated activity, which, we have learnt, have also arisen in the human being, according to Moses' mystical anthropogony, through kinship with the impassioned. Therefore, Paul, advising those able to hear him to lay hold of perfection, proposes the way by which they may attain to that which is earnestly

[22] 1 Cor. 13:11.

σπουδαζομένου τύχοιεν ὑποτίθεται, λέγων **ἀπεκδύσασθαι** δεῖν **τὸν παλαιὸν ἄνθρωπον** καὶ **ἐνδύσασθαι τὸν ἀνακαινούμενον κατ' εἰκόνα τοῦ κτίσαντος.**

[30.34] Ἀλλ' ἐπανέλθωμεν πάντες ἐπὶ τὴν θεοειδῆ χάριν ἐκείνην ἐν ᾗ ἔκτισε τὸ κατ' ἀρχὰς τὸν ἄνθρωπον ὁ Θεὸς, εἰπών· ὅτι **ποιήσωμεν ἄνθρωπον κατ' εἰκόνα καὶ ὁμοίωσιν ἡμετέραν**· ᾧ ἡ δόξα καὶ τὸ κράτος εἰς τοὺς αἰῶνας τῶν αἰώνων. Ἀμήν.

301 *ὑποτίθεται*] *ὑποδεικνύει* N *post ἀπεκδύσασθαι des.* W 302 *ἐνδύσασθαι*] *ita* A Æ B C D E F G H L M O P S X *Forb* : *ἐνδύσασθαι τὸν νέον* R *Ald Mign* 303 *ἐπανέλθωμεν*] *ἐπανέλθοιμεν* Æ B C D E[pc] (*οι sup. l.*) F L N : *ἐπανέλθωμεν πάλιν* B N R 303–4 *τὸ κατ' ἀρχὰς τὸν*] *τὸν κατ'ἀρχὰς* D E 305 *ὁμοίωσιν*] *καθ' ὁμοίωσιν* Æ B N O *καὶ τὸ κράτος om.* Æ B N O *Dion* *κράτος*] *κράτος νῦν καὶ ἀεὶ καὶ* R : potentia Patri et Filio et Sancto Spiritui *Eri*

desired, saying it is necessary *to put off the old human being* and *put on the one being renewed in accordance with the image of the Creator.*[23]

[**30.34**] Now may we all ascend to that divine grace in which God at the first created the human being, saying, *Let us make the human being in accordance with our image and likeness*; to whom be glory and might unto ages of ages. Amen.

[23] Col. 3:9–10.

Appendix

In their work on the manuscript tradition of Basil's *Hexaemeron*, Emmanuel Amand de Mendieta and Stig Y. Rudberg identified three different collections in which that work appears.[1] The first is the 'small' collection, including Basil's *Hexaemeron* and the two homilies *On the Words: Let us Make the Human Being* (also called *Homilies on the Creation of the Human Being*; CPG 3217) to which the apocryphal homily *On Paradise* (CPG 3217) is sometimes added. The second is the 'normal' collection, in which Basil's *Hexaemeron* is supplemented by Gregory's *On the Human Image of God* and sometimes his *Hexaemeron*. The third is a larger collection, bringing together all the texts that are in the small and normal collection: Gregory's *On the Human Image of God*, the *Hexaemeron*, the two homilies *On the Words: Let us Make the Human Being*, and occasionally the *Hexaemeron* and *On Paradise*. Of the manuscripts that they list, 68 contain Gregory's treatise (18 in the large collection; 50 in the normal collection), 14 of which had been used by Forbes. This appendix provides a full list of these 68 manuscripts, together with the details they supplied and further details gained from the collation undertaken for this volume. The online database 'Pinakes|*Πίνακες* Textes et manuscrits grecs' lists 166 manuscripts of Gregory's treatise.[2]

9th to 10th Centuries

Vatican, Biblioteca Apostolica Vaticana, *grec 413*, 374^v–413^r (M–R, 117–19: E 2, normal) Missing Ep. to Peter. 374^v–375^r list of 31 headings. 375^v–413^r complete treatise, entitled *περὶ εἰκόνος ἀνθρώπου*.

Vatican, Biblioteca Apostolica Vaticana, *grec 2053*, 247^r–283^v (M–R, 124–5: G 1, normal) No initial title. 248^r (M–R and Pinakes have 247^r) *Τῷ ἀδελφῷ δούλῳ Θεοῦ Πέτρῳ ἐπισκόπῳ Γρηγόριος ἐπίσκπος Νύσης*. 248^{rv} Ep. to Peter. 248^v *Τοῦ ὁσίου πατρὸς ἡμῶν Γρηγορίου Νύσης. σύνταξις κεφαλαίων λ*, but no list of headings. 248^v–283^v treatise in 30 chapters, with headings and numbers ornately marked out. Text breaks off a few lines before the end of the treatise, at last line of 283^v, with *ὑποτίθεται, λέγων ἀπεκδύσασθαι* (PG 44, 256 C 4).

Vatican, Biblioteca Apostolica Vaticana, *grec 2066*, 299^r–316^v (M–R, 115–17 E 1, normal) No initial title. 299^r *Τῷ ἀδελφῷ δούλῳ Θεοῦ Πέτρῳ ἐπισκόπῳ Γρηγόριος ἐπίσκπος Νύσης*. 299^r–300^r Ep. to Peter. 300^r–301^r list of 30 headings with numbers in margin. 301^r heading

[1] Emmanuel Amand de Mendieta and Stig Y. Rudberg, *Basile de Césarée: La tradition manuscrite directe des neuf homélies sur l'Hexaéméron*, TU 123 (Berlin: Akademie, 1980).

[2] https://pinakes.irht.cnrs.fr (accessed 23 October, 2021); the information it supplies, however, should be treated with caution: it lists the 8th to 9th century Athens, *EBE 223* as containing exclusively works by Basil but also as including Gregory's treatise; and it dates Moscow, Musée historique, *grec 81 Vladimir* to the 10th century, which as M–R observe is correct for folios 2–120, but folios 121–235, in which we have Gregory's work, date to the 12th century.

Τοῦ ἁγίου Γρηγορίου ἐπίσκοπου Νύσης, then title of first chapter. 301^{r}–316^{v} incomplete text, containing first eleven chapters and part of chapter 12; text of treatise breaks off at last line of 316^{v}, with *κάτοπτρον γινομένην κρατεῖ* (PG 44, 161 D 1). Chapters' divisions are clearly indicated by line of ornamentation and the chapter numbers are written in the margin.

Venice, Biblioteca Nazionale di San Marco, *grec. 58*, 65^{v}–116^{r} (M–R, 119–21: E 3, normal) 65^{v} title in red uncials: *Τοῦ μακαρίου καὶ ἐν ἁγίοις Γρηγορίου ἐπισκόπου Νύσσης· εἰς τὴν ἀναπλήρωσιν τῶν προκειμένων τῆς ἑξαημέρου.* 65^{v}–66^{v}: *πρόλογος τῷ ἀδελφῷ δούλῳ Θεοῦ Πέτρῳ ἐπισκόπῳ Γρηγόριος ἐπίσκοπος Νύσης.* 66^{v}–67^{v} list of 31 headings, under the title: *κεφάλαια ἐμπιλόσοφα περὶ τῆς τοῦ ἀνθρώπου κτίσεως· καὶ περὶ τῆς τοῦ κόσμου δὲ μερικῶς· ἅπερ ἦν λείποντα τῇ ἑξαημέρῳ· ἥν προείρηκεν ὁ μακάριος καὶ ἐν ἁγίοις Βασίλειος.* 67^{v}–116^{r} text in 31 chapters, with scholia.

10th Century

Florence, Biblioteca Laurenziana, *grec. 4.27*, 186^{v}–240^{v} (M–R 27–9: A 3, normal)
Dated to the first part of the 10th century. No initial title. 186^{v} *Τῷ ἀδελφῷ δούλῳ Θεοῦ Πέτρῳ ἐπισκόπῳ Γρηγόριος ἐπίσκπος Νύσης.* 186^{v}–187^{v} Ep. to Peter. 187^{v}–188^{v} list of 30 headings with numbers. 188^{v}–240^{v} treatise in 30 chapters with numbers in the margins, and scholia.

Genova, Biblioteca Franzoniana, *grec 17*, 209^{v}–305^{v} (M–R, 126–9: G 2, large)
Second part of 10th century. No general title of treatise. 209^{v}–211^{r} Ep. to Peter. 211^{r}–212^{v} list of 30 headings. 213^{r}–305^{v} treatise in 30 chapters, beginning with heading of chapter 1.

Lesbos, Gymnase de Mytilène, *grec 1*, 54^{v}–85^{v} (M–R, 42–3: A 6, normal, M–R)
Perhaps late 10th or early 11th century. 54^{v}–85^{v} incomplete text.

Milan, Biblioteca Ambrosiana, *grec 189*, 50^{v}–126^{v} (M–R, 39–40: A 4, normal)
Probably last part of 10th century. 50^{v}–52^{r} Ep. to Peter. 52^{r}–53^{v} list of 30 headings; 54^{r}–126^{v} treatise in 30 chapters.

Milan, Biblioteca Ambrosiana, *grec 359*, 75^{r}–103^{v} (M–R, 64–5: B 3, normal)
Probably beginning of 10th century. 75^{r}–103^{v} order of folios disrupted; Ep. to Peter; list of headings and fragments.

Moscow, Bibliothèque de l'Université, *grec 1*, 83^{v}–153^{v} (M–R, 136–8: E 5, normal)
First part of 10th century. 83^{v}–85^{r} Ep. to Peter. 85^{r}–86^{r} list of 31 headings; 86^{r}–153^{v} treatise in 31 chapters.

Oxford, Bodleian, *Barocci grec. 144*, 98^{r}–174^{v} (M–R, 56–7: A*15, normal)
Dated to the second part of the 10th century. No initial title. 98^{v} *Τῷ ἀδελφῷ δούλῳ Θεοῦ Πέτρῳ ἐπισκόπῳ Γρηγόριος ἐπίσκπος Νύσης.* 98^{v}–100^{r} Ep. to Peter. 100^{r}–101^{r} list of 30 headings. 101^{v}–174^{v} treatise in 30 chapters, with numbers in the margins. 174^{v} *explicit* in black uncials: *τοῦ ἐν ἁγίου Γρηγορίου ἐπισκόπου νύσης θεωρία εἰς τὴν κατασκευὴν τοῦ ἀνθρώπου.*

Paris, Bibliothèque nationale de France, *grec. 476*, 64^{v}–116^{v} (M–R, 22–5: A 1, normal)
Dated to the first part of the 10th century. No initial title. 64^{v} *Τῷ ἀδελφῷ δούλῳ Θεοῦ Πέτρῳ ἐπισκόπῳ Γρηγόριος ἐπίσκπος Νύσης.* 64^{v}–65^{v} Ep. to Peter. 65^{v}–66^{v} list of 30 headings. 66^{v}–116^{v} treatise in 30 chapters, with numbers in the margins, and scholia.

116^{v} *explicit*: *Τοῦ ἁγίου Γρηγορίου ἐπισκόπου Νύσης θεώρια εἰς τὴν κατασκευὴν τοῦ ἀνθρώπου*, written around an image of the cross.

Vatican, Biblioteca Apostolica Vaticana, *grec. 408*, 89^{v}–161^{v} (M–R, 36–7: C 1, normal)
Dated to the second part of the 10th century. No initial title. 89^{v} *Τῷ ἀδελφῷ δούλῳ Θεοῦ Πέτρῳ ἐπισκόπῳ Γρηγόριος ἐπίσκπος Νύσσης*. 89^{v}–91^{r} Ep. to Peter. 91^{r}–92^{v} list of 31 headings. 92^{v}–161^{v} treatise in 31 chapters, with numbers written in the margins and scholia.

10th to 11th Centuries

Florence, Biblioteca Laurenziana, *grec 4.18*, 137^{r}–219^{r} (M–R, 201–4: G 5, large)
137^{r}–138^{v} Ep. to Peter. No list of headings. 138^{v}–219^{r} treatise in 30 chapters; folios 138–45 are inserted between folios 153 and 154.

Oxford, Bodleian, *Barocci grec 228*, 65^{r}–118^{v} (M–R, 138–41: E 6, normal)
65^{r} two dodecasyllables in the hand of the copyist:

> *ὡς αὐτάδελφος καὶ ὁμότροπος πέλων,*
> *πληροῖ τὸ λεῖπον τοῦ σοφοῦ Βασιλείου.*

65^{r} title: *περὶ εἰκόνος ἀνθρώπου τοῦ μακαρίου Γρηγορίου ἀδελφοῦ τοῦ ἁγίου Βασιλείου*. 65^{r}: *Τῷ τιμιωτάτῳ ἀδελφῷ δούλῳ Θεοῦ Πέτρῳ ἐπισκόπῳ Γρηγόριος ἐν κυρίῳ χαίρειν*. 65^{r}–66^{r} Ep. to Peter. 66^{r}–67^{r} list of 31 headings. 67^{r}–118^{v} treatise in 31 chapters, with numbers in margin, and scholia. 118^{v}, *explicit* in black uncials: *Γρηγορίου ἐπισκόπου Νύσσης ἀδελφοῦ τοῦ ἁγίου Βασιλείου θεωρία εἰς τὴν τοῦ ἀνθρώπου κατασκευήν*.

Paris, Bibliothèque nationale de France, *Coislin grec. 235*, 121^{r}–208^{v} (M–R, 249–52: I 1, normal)
No initial title. 121^{r} *Τῷ ἀδελφῷ δούλῳ Θεοῦ Πέτρῳ ἐπισκόπῳ Γρηγόριος ἐπίσκπος νύσης εἰς τὸν ἄνθρωπον*. 121^{r}–123^{r} Ep. to Peter. 123^{r}–124^{v} list of 31 headings. 124^{v}–208^{v} treatise in 31 chapters, with numbers in the margins. Text breaks off a few lines before the conclusion of chapter 31, with *ἐν τῷ ἀτελεῖ καὶ ἐν* (PG 44, 255 D 10).

Patmos, Monastery St John, *grec 47*, 67^{v}–121^{v} (M–R, 79–80: C 2, normal)
67^{v}–68^{v} Ep. to Peter. 69^{rv} list of 30 headings. 70^{r}–121^{v} treatise in 30 chapters, entitled *εἰς τὴν τοῦ ἀνθρώπου κατασκευήν*.

Vienna, Österreichische Nationalbibliothek, *theol. gr. 160*, 60^{r}–113^{v} (M–R, 80–1: C 3, normal)
Beginning damaged; Ep. to Peter missing. 60^{r} *Τοῦ ἐν ἁγίοις πατρὸς ἡμῶν Γρηγορίου ἐπισκόπου Νύσσης κεφάλαια τριάκοντα εἰς τὴν τοῦ ἀνθρώπου κατασκευήν* followed by list of 30 headings. 61^{r}–113^{v}, text of treatise missing first seven chapters and first part of chapter 8.

11th Century

Athens, *Ἐθνικὴ Βιβλιοθήκη*, *grec 415*, 94^{v}–96^{v} (M–R, 142–3: E 8, large)
Restored in 16th. Only contains the Ep. to Peter.

Athos, Iviron, *grec 335*, 136^{v}–152^{v}, 161^{r}–258^{r} (M–R, 81–2: C 4, normal)
136^{v}–139^{r} Ep. to Peter. 139^{r}–141^{v} list of 31 headings. 141^{v}–152^{v}, 161^{r}–258^{r} treatise in 31 chapters with each title written in full in uncials.

Athos, Lavra, *grec B.77*, 66^{r}–120^{v} (M–R, 82–3: C 5, normal)
Perhaps end of 11th century. 66^{r} title: *Γρηγορίου ἐπισκόπου περὶ εἰκόνος· εἰς τὰ ἐλλειφθέντα τῶν παρὰ τοῦ ἀδελφοῦ αὐτοῦ Βασιλείου ἐπισκόπου γεγραμμένων εἰς τὴν ἑξαήμερον.* 66^{r}–67^{v} Ep. to Peter. 67^{r}–68^{r} list of 31 headings. 68^{r}–120^{v} incomplete text in 31 chapters, lacking end of chapter 31.

Athos, Lavra, *grec. B.105*, 78^{r}–172^{v} (M–R, 83–5: C 6, normal)
Perhaps copied in 1092. 78^{r} title in uncials red ink: *Τοῦ ἐν ἁγίοις ἡμῶν Γρηγορίου ἐπισκόπου Νύσσης· λόγος κεφαλαιώδης εἰς τὴν κατασκευὴν τοῦ ἀνθρώπου.* 78^{r}–79^{r} Ep. to Peter. 79^{r}–80^{v} list of 30 headings. 89^{r}–140^{r} treatise in 30 chapters.

Athos, Vatopedi, *grec. 54*, 83^{r}–146^{r} (M–R, 85–6: C 7, normal)
83^{r}–84^{r} Ep. to Peter. 84^{r}–146^{r} treatise in 30 chapters, with titles written in margins.

Milan, Biblioteca Ambrosiana, *grec 833*, 51^{r}–122^{v} (M–R, 45–6: A 8, normal)
51^{r}–52^{v} Ep. to Peter; no list of headings; 52^{v}–122^{v} treatise in 30 chapters; text (and the manuscript) breaks off a few lines before end: *ψυχὴν τὴν ἀνθρωπίνην εἶναι* (PG 44, 256 B 8–9).

Modène, Biblioteca Estense, *grec 72*, 109^{r}–208^{r} (M–R, 96–7: D 1, normal)
Incomplete text preceded by Ep. to Peter.

Paris, Bibliothèque nationale de France, *Coislin grec 228*, 62^{r}–74^{v}, only 12 chaps. (M–R, 90–1: C*10, normal)
62^{rv} Ep. to Peter. 63^{r}–74^{v} incomplete treatise, entitled: *Γρυγορίου ἐπισκόπου Νύσσης ἀδελφοῦ τοῦ μεγάλου Βασιλείου εἰς τὴν τοῦ ἀνθρώπου κατασκευήν.* Chapters are numbered in the margin, and their titles marked in the text in red ink; treatise breaks off at end of 74^{v}, towards the close of chapter 12, with words *καθορᾶσθαι τοῦ πλάσματος* (PG 44, 164A2–3).

Vatican, Biblioteca Apostolica Vaticana, *grec 405*, 111^{r}–229^{v} (M–R, 91–2: C*11, normal)
111^{r}–112^{v} Ep. to Peter. 113^{r}–114^{r} same letter copied by a later hand (11th–13th cent.). 114^{r}–115^{v} list of 30 headings. 116^{r}–203^{v} complete treatise in 30 chapters.

Vatican, Biblioteca Apostolica Vaticana, *grec 407*, 117^{v}–199^{r} (M–R, 51–2: A 12, normal)
117^{v}–119^{r} Ep. to Peter. 119^{r}–120^{v} list of 30 headings. 121^{r}–199^{r} complete treatise in 30 chapters.

12th Century

Athos, Koutloumousiou, *grec 4*, 101^{r}–171^{v} (M–R, 204–5: G 6, normal)
101^{r}–102^{v} Ep. to Peter. 102^{v}–103^{v} list of 30 headings. 103^{v}–171^{v} treatise in 30 chapters; last folio torn, thus missing end of chapter 30.

Brussels, Bibliothèque Royale, *11.354*, 73^{r}–124^{v} (M–R, 255–7: I 3, normal)
73^{r} general title in red ink: *Τοῦ ἐν ἁγίοις πατρὸς ἡμῶν Γρηγορίου ἀρχιεπισκόπου Νύσης ἡ γένεσις.* 73^{r}–74^{r} list of 30 headings. 74^{r}–75^{r} Ep. to Peter. 75^{r}–124^{v} treatise in 30 chapters; treatise (and manuscript) breaks off at end of chapter 29 with *κεκρυμμένην μέν, ζῶσαν* (PG 44, 240 A 14).

Escurial, Biblioteca de El Escorial, *Ψ II.18 (grec 453)*, 70^{v}–118^{v} (M–R, 69–70: B 6, normal)
70^{v}–71^{v} Ep. to Peter. 71^{v}–72^{v} list of 30 headings. 72^{v}–118^{v} complete treatise in 30 chapters.

Lesbos, Monastery of St John, *grec 6*, 117–90 (M–R, 148–9: E 12, large)
Title:... *πρὸς Πέτρον τὸν ἴδιον ἀδελφόν· καὶ εἰς τὰ λοιπὰ τῆς ἑξαημέρου τοῦ ἀδελφοῦ αὐτοῦ Βασιλείου τουτέστιν εἰς τὴν κατασκευὴν τοῦ ἀνθρώπου.*

Moscow, Musée historique, *grec 81 Vladimir*, 189ʳ–234ᵛ (M–R, 150: E 13, normal)
189ʳ–191ʳ Ep. to Peter. 191ʳ title, *Γρηγορίου ἐπισκόπου Νύσσης θεωρία εἰς τὴν τοῦ ἀνθρώπου κατασκευήν* followed by list of 31 headings. 191ʳ–243ʳ treatise in 31 chapters; last chapter damaged.

Naples, Biblioteca Nazionale, *grec 18*, 91ᵛ–168ʳ (M–R, 176–7: F 2, normal)
Copied before 13 Sept. 1175. 91ᵛ title in red ink: *Γρηγορίου ἐπισκόπου τοῦ ἀδελφοῦ Βασιλείου θεωρία εἰς τὴν τοῦ ἀνθρώπου κατασκευήν.* 91ᵛ–93ʳ Ep. to Peter. 93ʳ–94ᵛ list of 30 headings; 94ᵛ–168ʳ treatise in 30 chapters.

Paris, Bibliothèque nationale de France, *grec 479*, 76ʳ–140ᵛ (M–R, 97–9: D 2, normal)
Probably copied in first part of century, restored and supplemented in 15th century. 76ʳ–77ʳ title in red ink: *Τοῦ ἁγίου Γρυγορίου ἐπισκόπου Νύσσης, ἀδελφοῦ τοῦ μεγάλου ̣βασιλείου, εἰς τὸν ἄνθρωπον θεωρία*, followed by Ep. to Peter; 77ᵛ–78ᵛ list of 31 headings. 79ʳ–140ᵛ treatise in 31 chapters.

Vatican, Biblioteca Apostolica Vaticana, *Pii II grec 25*, 77ʳ–80ᵛ fragment (M–R, 205–8: G 6, large)
Chapter 1 is damaged at the beginning; chapters 2–5 complete; chapter 6 incomplete: 77ʳ begins *καὶ τῇ ποικίλῃ τῶν δένδρων ὥρᾳ* (PG 44, 132 B 1); 80ᵛ ends *ποιήσωμεν γὰρ ἄνθρωπον κα* (PG 44, 140 B 6).

13th Century

Athens, *Ἐθνικὴ Βιβλιοθήκη*, *grec 433*, 220ʳ–259ᵛ (M–R, 224–6: H 1, normal)
Manuscript restored in 15th century. 220ʳᵛ Ep. to Peter. 220ᵛ–221ᵛ list of 30 headings, *κεφάλαια τριάκοντα εἰς τὴν τοῦ ἀνθρώπου κατασκευήν.* 221ᵛ–258ᵛ treatise in 30 chapters; treatise, and manuscript, breaks off in the middle of chapter 30, at bottom of 259ᵛ with *ἐκ μηχανῆς τινὸς ἀποδείκνυσι* (PG 44, 249 D1–2).

Athos, Dionysiou, *grec 55 (93)*, 74ʳ–142ᵛ (M–R, 152–3: E 15, normal)
74ʳ–75ʳ Ep. to Peter. 75ʳ–76ʳ list of 31 headings, title and *incipit* for each chapter. 76ʳ–142ᵛ treatise in 31 chapters, entitled: *Τοῦ μακαρίου καὶ ἐν ἁγίοις πατρὸς ἡμῶν Γρηγορίου ἐπισκόπου Νύσσης περὶ τῆς τοῦ ἀνθρώπου κατασκευῆς.*

Escurial, Biblioteca de El Escorial, *Ψ II.12 (grec 447)*, 74ʳ–126ᵛ (M–R, 70: B 7, normal)
74ʳᵛ Ep. to Peter. 74ᵛ–75ᵛ list of 30 headings. 76ʳ–126ᵛ, complete treatise, titled *εἰς τὰ λοιπὰ τῆς ἑξαημέρου*, in 30 chapters.

Escurial, Biblioteca de El Escorial, *Ψ III.5 (grec 460)*, 124ᵛ–215ᵛ (M–R, 177–8: F 3, normal)
124ᵛ–126ᵛ Ep. to Peter. 126ᵛ–215ᵛ treatise in 30 chapters; incomplete, breaking off with *ἐρύθημα καὶ τὸ λαμπρὸν τοῦ κρίνου* (PG 44, 252 C 12).

Oxford Christ Church Library, *grec. 45*, 115ʳ–194ʳ, 13th (M–R, 57–8: A*16, normal)
115ʳ–116ᵛ Ep. to Peter. 116ᵛ–118ʳ list of 30 headings; 118ʳ–194ʳ text in 30 chapters, with scholia. 194ʳ *explicit*: *τοῦ ἐν ἁγίου Γρηγορίου ἐπισκόπου Νύσης θεωρία εἰς τὴν κατασκευὴν τοῦ ἀνθρώπου* and this dodecasyllable verse:

+ *ὁ σταυρὸς ἀρχὴ καὶ τέλος καλῶν πέλει.*

Rome, Biblioteca Angelica, *grec 69 (B 3.3)*, 72ʳ–115ᵛ (M–R, 157–8: E 19, large)
72ʳ–73ʳ Ep. to Peter. 73ʳ–115ᵛ list of headings followed by treatise.

Vienna, Österreichische Nationalbibliothek, *theol. gr. 134*, 95ʳ–150ᵛ (M–R, 101–2: D 4, large)
Dated by ÖNB to 1200 Constantinople; by Pinakes to *c*.1300. No initial title. 95ʳ *τῷ ἀδελφῷ δούλῳ Θεοῦ Πέτρῳ ἐπισκόπῳ Γρηγόριος ἐπίσκπος νίσης*. 95ʳ–96ᵛ Ep. to Peter. 96ᵛ–98ʳ list of 30 headings. 98ʳ–150ᵛ text; headings and numbers, in margins, in red ink.

14th Century

London, British Library, *Harleianus 5576*, 52ʳ–72ʳ (M–R, 58–9: A*17, normal)
52ʳ list of 12 first chapters. 53ʳ title *Τοῦ ἐν ἁγίοις πατρὸς ἡμῶν Γρηγορίου ἀρχιεπισκόπου Νύσσης εἰς τὰ ἐπίλοιπα τῆς ἑξαημέρου*. 53ʳ–53ᵛ Ep. to Peter. 53ᵛ–72ʳ treatise in 30 chapters, breaking off at end of 72ʳ with: *τὸ φυτὸν τελειοῦσας ὅπερ οὐχ οἷόν τε ἦν* (PG 44, 240 B 6–7).

Milan, Biblioteca Ambrosiana, *grec 96 (B 63 sup.)*, 87ʳ–136ᵛ (M–R, 179–80: P F 4, normal)
87ʳ–88ᵛ Ep. to Peter. 88ᵛ incomplete list of first six headings. 89ʳ blank. 89ᵛ–136ᵛ, incomplete treatise, lacking most of chapter 30, breaking off at end of 136ᵛ with words *ἔστι δὲ καὶ ἄλλα τινὰ* (PG 44, 241 A 7).

Moscow, Musée historique, *grec 126 Vladimir*, 70ʳ–111ᵛ (M–R, 144–6: E 9, normal)
70ʳᵛ Ep. to Peter; 71ʳ–111ᵛ list of 30 headings; treatise in 30 chapters, entitled: *Τοῦ ἐν ἁγίοις πατρὸς ἡμῶν Γρηγορίου τοῦ Νύσσης ὑπόθεσις εἰς τὴν τοῦ ἀνθρώπου κατασκευήν, ἐν λόγοις ἤγουν ἐν κεφαλαίοις λ'*

Moscow, Musée historique, *grec 132 Vladimir*, 96ʳ–148ᵛ (M–R, 160–1: E 21, normal)
Dated 1339. 96ʳ–148ᵛ *Κεφάλαια τριάκοντα εἰς τὴν τοῦ ἀνθρώπου διάπλασιν*; list of 30 headings; treatise in 30 chapters.

Munich, Bayerische Staatsbibliothek, *Cod. graec. 192*, 111ᵛ–166ᵛ (M–R, 232–4: H 4, normal)
Dated *c*.1370. 111ᵛ title: *Τοῦ ἁγίου Γρηγορίου ἐπισκόπου Νύσης, εἰς τὴν ἑξαήμερον· τοῦ μακαρίου Γρηγορίου ἐπισκόπου Νύσης ἀδελφοῦ τοῦ ἁγίου βασιλείου περὶ εἰκόνος ἀνθρώπου τῷ τιμιωτάτῳ ἀδελφῷ δούλῳ τοῦ Θεοῦ Πέτρῳ γρηγόριος ἐν Κυρίῳ χαίρειν*. 111ᵛ–112ᵛ Ep. to Peter. 112ᵛ–113ᵛ list of 31 headings. 114ʳ–166ᵛ treatise in 31 chapters, with headings and numbers (placed before the heading) in red ink.

Munich, Bayerische Staatsbibliothek, *Cod. graec. 240*, 65ʳ–109ᵛ (M–R, 155: E 17, normal)
Dated by BSB and Pinakes to the 15th century; by M–R to the 14th century. 65ʳ title: *Τοῦ ἐν ἁγίοις πατρὸς ἡμῶν Γρηγορίου ἐπισκόπου Νύσης κεφάλαια τριάκοντα εἰς τὴν τοῦ ἀνθρώπου κατασκευήν*. 65ʳ–66ʳ Ep. to Peter. 66ʳ–109ᵛ text divided into 30 chapters; headings marked by large capital in the margin together with number, in red ink.

Munich, Bayerische Staatsbibliothek, *Cod. graec. 570*, 108ʳ–170ᵛ (M–R, 161–3: E 22, large)
108ʳ *τοῦ ἐν ἁγίοις πατρὸς Γρηγορίου ἐπισκόπου Νύσσης πρὸς Πέτρον ἴδιον ἀδελφὸν εἰς τὰ λοιπὰ τῆς ἑξαημέρου τοῦ ἀδελφοῦ αὐτῷ Βασιλείου· τουτέστιν εἰς τὴν κατακσκευὴν τοῦ ἀνθρώπου*. Ep. to Peter. List of 30 headings; treatise in 30 chapters.

Oxford, Bodleian, *Aucarium E.1.6 (Misc. graecus 20)*, 319ʳ–363ʳ (M–R, 212–5: G 10, large)
319ʳᵛ Ep. to Peter, damaged at beginning (beginning at PG 44, 125 B 6). 319ᵛ–320ᵛ list of 31 headings. 320ᵛ–363ʳ text in 31 chapters.

Paris, Bibliothèque nationale de France, *grec 503*, 165r–203r (M–R, 226–30: H 2, large)
165rv Ep. to Peter; *Τοῦ αὐτοῦ Γρηγορίου τῆς Νύσσης πρόγραμμα εἰς τὴν περὶ διαπλάσεως τοῦ ἀνθρώπου φιλοσοφίαν ἢ φυσιολογίαν.* 165v–203r treatise in 31 chapters; titles of chapters written in margins in red ink.

Paris, Bibliothèque nationale de France, *grec 956*, 90v–143v (M–R, 230–2: H 3, large)
90v title in red ink: *Τοῦ ἐν ἁγίοις πατρὸς ἡμῶν Γρηγορίου ἐπισκόπου Νύσσης πρὸς Πέτρον τὸν ἴδιον ἀδελφοῦ εἰς τὰ λοιπὰ τῆς ἑξαημέρου τοῦ ἀδελφοῦ αὐτοῦ Βασιλείου, τουτέστιν εἰς τὴν κατασκευὴν τοῦ ἀνθρώπου.* 90v–91v Ep. to Peter. 92r–93r list of 30 headings. 93r–143v treatise in 30 chapters.

Paris, Bibliothèque nationale de France, *grec 940*, 140r–177v (M–R, 257–9: I 4, normal)
140r–141r Ep. to Peter: *Τοῦ αὐτοῦ Γρηγορίου πρόγραμμα εἰς τὴν περὶ διαπλάσεως τοῦ ἀνθρώπου φυσιολογίαν.* 141rv list of 31 headings. 142r–177v treatise in 31 chapters, with the title: *Τοῦ αὐτοῦ φυσιολογία περὶ τῆς τοῦ ἀνθρώπου κατασκευῆς, ἤτοι εἰς τὰ ὑπόλοιπα τῆς ἑξαημέρου.* Titles not repeated in text nor margin; the chapter number is indicated in margin with red ink.

Paris, Bibliothèque nationale de France, *grec 777 A*, 246v–327v (M–R, 259–63: I 5, large)
14th to 15th century. 246v–248r Ep. to Peter. Title: *Τοῦ αὐτοῦ πρόγραμμα εἰς τὴν περὶ διαπλάσεως τοῦ ἀνθρώπου φυσιολογίαν.* 248r–249v list of 31 headings. 249v–327v *Τοῦ αὐτοῦ φυσιολογία τῆς τοῦ ἀνθρώπου κατασκευῆς, ἤτοι εἰς τὰ ὑπόλοιπα τῆς ἑξαημέρου.* Treatise in 31 chapters.

Paris, Bibliothèque nationale de France, *grec 1277*, 54v–82v (M–R, 102–4: D 5, large)
54v–55r list of 30 headings. 55r–56r Ep. to Peter: *Τοῦ ἐν ἁγίοις πατρὸς ἡμῶν Γρηγορίου ἐπισκόπου Νύσσης θεωρία εἰς τὴν τοῦ ἀνθρώπου κατασκευὴν· πρὸς τὸν ἐπίσκοπον ἀδελφὸν αὐτοῦ Πέτρον.* 56r–82v treatise in 30 chapters, with chapter numbers in the margins.

Vatican, Biblioteca Apostolica Vaticana, *grec 1857*, 111r–139r (M–R, 72–3: B 8, large)
No title. Ep. to Peter. Treatise breaks off in chapter 21 (PG 44, 201 B 1); some marginal scholia; folios 139v–142v blank.

15th Century

Bucarest, Bibliothèque de l'Academie de Romanie, *grec 559 (165)*, 104v–165r (M–R, 165–6: E 25, large)
Ep. to Peter. List of 30 headings; treatise in 30 chapters.

Florence, Biblioteca Laurenziana, *grec 10.12*, 117v–176r (M–R, 93–4: C*12, normal)
117v–119r Ep. to Peter. 119v–121r list of 31 chapters. 121r–176r treatise in 31 chapters: *Γρηγορίου ἐπισκόπου Νύσσης ἀδελφοῦ τοῦ μέγαλου Βασιλείου· εἰς τὴν τοῦ ἀνθρώπου κατασκευήν.*

Madrid, Biblioteca Nacional, *4806 (grec O. 87)*, 155r–245r (M–R, 215–17: G 11, large)
115r–242r treatise in 30 chapters; text incomplete with lacunae. 242v–245r Ep. to Peter.

Milan, Biblioteca Ambrosiana, *grec 668 (Q. 14 sup.)*, 96r(90r)–162v(156v) (M–R, 74: B 9, normal)
96r *Τὸ ἐπίλοιπον τῶν ὁμιλιῶν τῆς ἑξαμέρου Γρηγορίου Νύσης: εἰς τὴν κατασκευὴν τοῦ ἀνθρώπου κεφάλαια τριάκοντα καὶ δύο ὧν τὸ πρῶτὸν περὶ τῆς κατασκευῆς τοῦ ἀνθρώπου.* 96r–97v list of 32 headings. 97v–99r Ep. to Peter. 99r–162v treatise in 32 chapters.

Paris, Bibliothèque nationale de France, *grec 968*, 135^{r}–204^{v} (M–R, 106–8: D 7, large)
135^{r} *Τοῦ ἐν ἁγίοις πατρὸς ἡμῶν Γρηγορίου ἀρχιεπισκόπου Νύσσης θεωρία εἰς τὴν του ἀνθρώπου κατασκευήν.* 135^{r}–136^{v} Ep. to Peter. 136^{v}–138^{v} list of headings. 138^{v}–204^{v} treatise; titles of chapters written in full in red ink in the text.

Sinai, St Catherine, *grec 328*, 60^{r}–100^{v} (M–R, 241–2: H9, normal)
60^{r}–61^{r} Ep. to Peter. 61^{rv} list of 30 headings.

Vatican, Biblioteca Apostolica Vaticana, *grec 1568*, 108^{r}–193^{v} (M–R, 169–70: E 28, large)
108^{r}–109^{v} Ep. to Peter. 109^{v}–111^{r} list of 30 headings. 111^{r}–193^{v} treatise in 30 chapters, *εἰς τὰ ἐπίλοιπα τοῦ ἑξαημέρου.* 113^{v}, two dodecasyllables in the hand of the copyist.

> *Καὶ Γρηγορίου τοῦ σοφοῦ πέρας φθάνει*
> *ἔκφρασις ἀνθρώπου νῦν ἠγλαϊσμένη.*

Vienna, Österreichische Nationalbibliothek, *theol. gr. 113*, 79^{r}–138^{r} (M–R, 180–1: F 5, normal)
Dated 27/8/1412. 79^{r} title: *περὶ εἰκόνος ἀνθρώπου· τοῦ μακαρίου Γρηγορίου ἀδελφοῦ τοῦ ἁγίου Βασιλείου τῷ τιμιωτάτῳ ἀδελφῷ δούλῳ Θεοῦ πέτρῳ ἐπισκόπῳ Γρηγόριος ἐν Κυρίῳ χαίρειν.* 79^{r}–80^{r} Ep. to Peter. 80^{r}–81^{r} list of 31 headings; 81^{v}–138^{r}, treatise in 31 chapters.

Vienna, Österreichische Nationalbibliothek, *theol. gr. 168*, 73^{v}–120^{r} (M–R, 237–8: H 7, normal)
Dated M–R to 15th century; Pinakes to the 14th century. Lacking Ep. to Peter and list of headings; begins immediately, 73^{v}, with title: *εἰς τὴν τοῦ ἀνθρώπου κατασκευήν.*

16th Century

Vatican, Biblioteca Apostolica Vaticana, *Palatinus graecus 327*, 64^{r}–123^{r} (M–R, 60–1: A*18, normal)
List of headings, followed by Ep. to Peter and treatise.

Bibliography

Gregory of Nyssa, *On the Human Image of God*

Editions

Editio Princeps: *Gregorii Nazanzeni Theologi orationes novem elegantissimae, Gregorii Nysseni liber de homine, quae omnia nunc primum, emendatissima, in lucem prodeunt* (Aldus, 1536); and in the final colophon: *Venetiis, in aedibus haeredum Aldi, et Andreae Asulani soceri. MDXXXVI.*

Löwenklau (Levvencklaius), Johannes, ed., *Γρηγορίου τοῦ Νύσσης ἐπισκόπου θαυμαστὴ βίβλος, περὶ κατασκευῆς ἀνθρώπου. Opus admirandum Gregorii Nysseni antistitis de hominis opificio*, interprete Iohanne Levvenklaio, annotationibus estiam necessariis additis. Liber medicinae, philosophiae sacrarumque litterarum studiosis perutilis (Basel: Ioannis Oporini, 1567).

Forbes, George Hay, ed., *Τοῦ ἐν ἁγίοις πατρὸς ἡμῶν Γρηγορίου ἐπισκόπου Νύσσης* (*ἀδελφοῦ τοῦ μεγάλου Βασιλείου*) *τὰ εὑρισκόμενα πάντα. Sancti patris nostri Gregorii Nysseni Basilii Magni fratris quae supersunt omnia. In unum corpus collegit, ad fidem codd. mss. recensuit, Latinis versionibus quam accuratissimis instruxit et genuina a supposititiis discrevit*, Tomus primus, Fasc. 1 and 2 (Burntisland: Pitsligo Press, 1855, 1861).

Migne, J.-P., ed., PG 44.125–256 (Paris, 1858).

Versions

Latin: Dionysius Exiguus. See Forbes.

Latin: John Scottus Eriugena. Ed. Cappuyns, M., ‘Le “De imagine” de Grégoire de Nysse traduit par Jean Scot Érigène’, in *Recherches de théologie ancienne et médiévale* 32 (Louvain, 1965), pp. 205–62; ed. Giovanni Mandolino, in Iohannis Scotti Eriugenae, *Carmina; De Imagine*, ed. Michael W. Herren, Andrew Dunning, Giovanni Mandolino, and Chiara O. Tommasi, CCCM 167 (Turnhout: Brepols, 2020), 67–165.

Syriac: ‘La versione siriaca del “De opificio hominis” di Gregorio di Nissa’: T. Clementoni, on Chapters 13–14, *SROC* 5 (1982), 81–101, 157–71; M. R. De Deo, further on Chapter 14, *SROC* 3 (1983) 39–56, 181–95; F. Grassi, on Chapters 9–11, *SROC* 7 (1984), 25–50, 191–206; and A. Bonanni, on Chapter 22, *SROC* 10 (1987), 149–70.

Slavonic: ed. Sels, Lara, *Gregory of Nyssa,* De hominis opificio О Образѣ Чловѣка*: The Fourteenth-Century Slavonic Translation: A Critical Edition with Greek Parallel and Commentary*, Bausteine zur Slavischen Philologie und Kulturgeschichte NF 21 (Köln: Böhlau, 2009).

Translations

Wilson, Henry Austin, in William Moore and Henry Austin Wilson, *Select Writings and Letters of Gregory, Bishop of Nyssa*, NPNF, second series, vol. 5 (1893; reprinted Grand Rapids, MI: Eerdmans, 1994), 387–427.

LaPlace, Jean, and Jean Daniélou, *Grégoire de Nysse: La création de l’homme*, SC 6 (Paris: Cerf, 2002 [1943]).

Guillaumin, J. Y., and A. G. Hamman, *Grégoire de Nysse: La création de l'homme* (Paris: Desclée de Brouwer, 1982).

Salmona, B., *Gregorio di Nissa. L'uomo*, Collana di testi patristici 32 (Rome: Città Nuova, 1982, reprinted 2000).

Лурье, В., *Об устроении человека* (St Petersburg, 2000).

Editions and Translations of Other Works of Gregory

Catechetical Oration (*Cat. Or.*). Ed. Ekkehard Mühlenberg, GNO 3.4 (Leiden: Brill, 1996); ET, with parallel Greek text, Ignatius Green, PPS 60 (Yonkers: St Vladimir's Seminary Press, 2019).

Homilies on Ecclesiastes (*Eccl.*). Ed. P. Alexander GNO 5 (Leiden: Brill, 1986), 277–442; ET Stuart G. Hall, in idem, ed. *Gregory of Nyssa, Homilies on Ecclesiastes* (Berlin: De Gruyter, 1993), 31–144.

Hexameron (*Hex.*). Ed. Hubertus R. Drobner, GNO 4.1 (Leiden: Brill, 2009); ET Robin Orton, FC Shorter Works 1 (Washington, DC: Catholic University of America Press, 2021).

On the Inscriptions of the Psalms (*Inscr.*). Ed. James McDonough, GNO 5 (Leiden: Brill, 1986), 24–175; ET Ronald E. Heine, OECS (Oxford: Clarendon Press, 1995).

Letters (*Ep.*). Ed. G. Pasquali, GNO 8.2, 2nd edn. (Leiden: Brill, 1998); ET Anna M. Silvas, Suppl. *VC* 83 (Leiden: Brill, 2007).

On the Life of Moses (*Vit. Moys.*). Ed. Herbert Musurillo, GNO 7.1 (Leiden: Brill, 1991); ET Abraham J. Malherbe and Everett Ferguson, CWS (New York: Paulist Press, 1978).

Homilies on the Song of Songs (*Cant.*). Ed. Hermann Langerbeck, GNO 6 (Leiden: Brill, 1986); ET, with parallel Greek Text, Richard A. Norris, WGRW 13 (Atlanta: SBL Press, 2012).

On the Soul and Resurrection (*An. et res.*). Ed. Andreas Spira, GNO 3.3 (Leiden: Brill, 2014); ET in Anna M. Silvas, *Macrina the Younger: Philosopher of God*, Medieval Women: Texts and Contexts, 22 (Turnhout: Brepols, 2008), 117–246.

On Those Who Have Fallen Asleep (*Mort*). Ed. Gunter Heil, in GNO 9.1 (Leiden: Brill, 1967), 28–68; ET by Rowan A. Greer in *One Path for All: Gregory of Nyssa on the Christian Life and Human Destiny* (Eugene, OR: Cascade, 2014), 94–117.

On Virginity (*Virg.*). Ed. John P. Cavarnos, GNO 8.1 (Leiden: Brill, 1986), 215–343; ed. with French trans. Michel Aubineau, SC 119 (Paris: Cerf, 1966); ET Virginia Woods Callahan, FC 58 (Washington, DC: Catholic University of America Press, 1999), 6–75.

On the Three Day Period (*Trid. spat.*). Ed. E. Gebhardt, GNO 9 (Leiden: Brill, 1967), 273–306; ET Stuart Hall, in Andreas Spira and Christoph Klock, *The Easter Sermons of Gregory of Nyssa: Translation and Commentary: Proceedings of the Fourth International Colloquium on Gregory of Nyssa, Cambridge, England: 11–15 September, 1978*, Patristic Monograph Series, 9 (Cambridge, MA: Philadelphia Patristic Foundation, 1981), 31–50.

Editions and Translations of Ancient Texts

Alcinous, *Epitome* (*Epi*). *Alcinoos: Enseignement des doctrines de Platon*, ed. J. Whittaker (Paris: Belles Lettres, 1990); ET J. Dillon, *The Handbook of Platonism* (Oxford: Clarendon Press, 1993).

Alexander of Aphrodisias, *On Mixture* (*Mixt.*). Ed. I. Bruns, *Alexandri Aphrodisiensis praeter commentaria scripta minora*, CAG, Suppl. 2.2 (Berlin: Reimer, 1892); ed. and ET Robert B. Todd (Leiden: Brill, 1976).

Alexander of Aphrodisias, *On the Soul* (*De an.*). Ed. Ivor Bruns, CAG, Suppl. 2.1 (Berlin: Reimer, 1887); Partial ET Victor Caston, ACA (London: Bloomsbury, 2012); full ET Athanasios P. Fotinis (PhD thesis: Milwaukee: Marquette University, 1978).

Alexander of Aphrodisias, *Supplement* (*Mantissa*). Ed. Robert W. Sharples, Peripatoi: Philologisch-historische Studien zum Aristotelismus, 21 (Berlin: De Gruyter, 2008); ET Robert W. Sharples, *Alexander of Aphrodisias: Supplement to* On the Soul, ACA (London: Bloomsbury, 2014).

Alexander of Aphrodisias, *Meteorology* (*Meteor.*). Ed. M. Hayduck, CAG, Suppl. 3.2 (Berlin: Reimer, 1899); ET Eric Lewis, ACA (London: Bloomsbury, 2014).

Anastasius of Sinai, *Hexaemeron* (*Hex.*). Ed. and ET Clement A. Kuehn and John D. Baggarly, OCA 278 (Rome: Pontificio Istituto Orientale, 2007).

Anaxagoras, Fragments. Ed. and ET André Laks and Glenn W. Most, *Early Greek Philosophy*, vol. 6, LCL 529 (Cambridge, MA: Harvard University Press, 2016); ed. and ET David Sider, *The Fragments of Anaxagoras*, 2nd edn. (Sankt Augustin: Academia Verlag, 2005); ed. and ET Patricia Curd, *Anaxagoras of Clazomenae: Fragments and Testimonia* (Toronto: University of Toronto Press, 2007).

Apocryphon of John (*Ap. John*). NHC II.1; ET in James M. Robinson, ed., *The Nag Hammadi Library in English* (Leiden: Brill, 1988), 104–23.

Aristotle, *Generation and Corruption* (*Gen. corr.*). Ed. and ET E. S. Forster, LCL 400, Aristotle 3 (Cambridge, MA: Harvard University Press, 1955).

Aristotle, *History of Animals* (*Hist. an.*). Books 1–6, ed. and ET A. L. Peck, LCL 437–8, Aristotle 9–10 (Cambridge, MA: Harvard University Press, 1970); Books 7–10, ed. and ET D. M. Balme, LCL 439, Aristotle 11 (Cambridge, MA: Harvard University Press, 1991).

Aristotle, *Metaphysics* (*Metaph.*). Ed. and ET Hugh Tredennick, LCL 271, 287, Aristotle 17–18 (Cambridge, MA: Harvard University Press, 1933, 1935).

Aristotle, *Meteorology* (*Meteor.*). Ed. and ET H. D. Lee, LCL 397 (Cambridge, MA: Harvard University Press, 1998).

Aristotle, *Parts of animals* (*Part. an.*). Ed. and ET A. L. Peck, LCL 323, Aristotle 12 (Cambridge, MA: Harvard University Press, 1937).

Aristotle, *Physics* (*Phys.*). Ed. and ET Philip H. Wicksteed and Francis M. Cornford, LCL 228, 255, Aristotle 4, 5 (Cambridge, MA: Harvard University Press, 1929, 1934).

Aristotle, *Problems* (*Probl.*). *Prob.* 1–19, ed. and ET Robert Mayhew, LCL 316, Aristotle 15 (Cambridge, MA: Harvard University Press, 2011); *Prob.* 20–38, ed. and ET David C. Mirhady, LCL 317, Aristotle 16 (Cambridge, MA: Harvard University Press, 2011).

Aristotle, *On the Soul* (*De an.*). Ed. and ET W. S. Hett, LCL 288, Aristotle 8 (Cambridge, MA: Harvard University Press, 1938).

Athenagoras, *On the Resurrection* (*De res.*). Ed. and ET William R. Schoedel, OECT (Oxford: Oxford University Press, 1972).

Basil of Caesarea, *Homilies on the Hexameron* (*Hex.*). Ed. Amand de Mendieta and Stig Y. Rudberg, *Basilius von Caesarea: Homilien zum Hexaemeron*, GCS NF 2 (Berlin: Akademie Verlag, 1997); ed. and French trans. Alexis Smits and Michel van Esbroeck, *Basile de Césarée: Sur l'origine de l'homme*, SC 160 (Paris: Cerf, 1970).

Basil of Caesarea, 'First Homily on the Origin of Humanity' (*Hom. de creat. hom.* 1). Ed. Hadwig Hörner, GNO Supplementum (Leiden: Brill, 1971), 2–40; ET Nonna Verna Harrison, *St Basil the Great: On the Human Condition*, PPS (Crestwood, NY: SVS Press, 2005), 31–48.

Basil of Caesarea, 'Second Homily on the Origin of Humanity' (*Hom. de creat. hom.* 2). Ed. Hadwig Hörner, GNO Supplementum (Leiden: Brill, 1971), 41–72; ET Nonna Verna

Harrison, *St Basil the Great: On the Human Condition*, PPS (Crestwood, NY: SVS Press, 2005), 49–64.

Calcidius, *On Plato's* Timaeus (*Pl. Tim.*). Ed. J. H. Waszink, Corpus Platonicum Medii Aevi, 4 (London/Leiden: Warburg Institute/Brill, 1975); ed. and ET John Magee, DOML 41 (Cambridge, MA: Harvard University Press, 2016).

Cicero, *On Ends* (*Fin.*). Ed. and ET H. Rackham, LCL 40, Cicero 17 (Cambridge, MA: Harvard University Press, 1914).

Clement of Alexandria, *Paedagogue* (*Paed.*). Ed. O. Stählin, 3rd ed. rev. U. Treu, GCS 12 (Berlin: Akademie Verlag, 1972). ET in ANF 2.

Clement of Alexandria, *Protreptikos* (*Protr.*). Ed. O. Stählin, 3rd ed. rev. U. Treu, GCS 12 (Berlin: Akademie Verlag, 1972). ET in ANF 2.

Clement of Alexandria, *Stromata* (*Strom.*). *Stromata I–VI*, ed. O. Stählin, 3rd edn., rev. L. Früchtel, GCS 52 (Berlin: Akademie Verlag, 1972); trans. in ANF 2; *Stromata VII, VIII*, ed. O. Stählin, 2nd edn. rev. L. Früchtel and U. Treu, GCS 17 (Berlin: Akademie Verlag, 1970); ET in ANF 2.

Diogenes Laertius, *Lives of the Eminent Philosophers* (DL). Ed. and ET R. D. Hicks, LCL 184–5 (Cambridge, MA: Harvard University Press, 1989); ET Pamela Mensch, ed. James Millar (Oxford: Oxford University Press, 2018).

Doctrina Patrum De Incarnatione Verbi. Ed. Franz Diekamp, rev. B. Phanourgakis and E. Chrysos (Münster: Aschendorff, 1981).

Empedocles, Fragments. See 'Presocratics'.

Eusebius of Caesarea, *Ecclesiastical* History (*Hist. eccl.*). Ed. and ET K. Lake, LCL, 2 vols (Cambridge, MA: Harvard University Press, 1989); ET H. J. Lawlor and J. E. L. Oulton, *Eusebius Bishop of Caesarea: The Ecclesiastical History and the Martyrs of Palestine*, 2 vols (London: SPCK, 1927).

Eusebius of Caesarea, *Preparation for the Gospel* (*Praep. Ev.*). Ed. Karl Mras, GCS 43.1–2, Eusebius Werke 8, 1–2 (Berlin: Akademie, 1954, 1956).

Eriugena, John Scottus, *Periphyseon*. Ed. É. Jeauneau, CCCM 161–5 (Turnhout: Brepols, 1996–2003); and I. P. Sheldon-Williams, Scriptores Latini Hiberniae, 7, 9, 11, 13 (Dublin: Dublin Institute for Advanced Study, 1999 [1968], 2017 [1972], 2005 [1981], 2009 [1995]).

Galen, *On the Doctrines of Hippocrates and Plato* (*Hipp. et Plat.*). Ed. and ET Phillip De Lacy, CMG V, 4, 1, 2, in 2 parts (Berlin: Akademie Verlag, 2005).

Galen, *Medical Definitions* (*Def.*). Ed. Karl Gottlob Kühn (Leipzig: Car Cnoblochi, 1830), vol. 19, 346–462.

Galen, *On the Natural Faculties* (*De nat. fac.*). Ed. and ET Arthur John Brock, LCL 71 (Cambridge, MA: Harvard University Press, 1916).

Galen, *On the Shaping of the Embryo* (*De foet. form.*). Ed. and German trans. D. Nickel, CMG V, 3.3 (Berlin: Akademie Verlag, 2001).

Galen, *On the Usefulness of the Parts of the Body* (*De usu part.*). Ed. Georg Helmreich, 2 vols (Leipzig: Teubner, 1907, 1909); ET Margaret Tallmadge May, 2 vols (Ithaca, NY: Cornell University Press, 1968).

Gregory of Nazianzus, *Epistles to Cledonius* (*Ep.* 101, 102). Ed. and French translation, P. Galla with M. Jourjon, *Grégoire de Nazianze: Lettres Théologiques*, SC 208 (Paris: Cerf, 1974). ET in L. Wickham and F. Williams, *St Gregory of Nazianzus: On God and Christ: The Five Theological Orations and Two Letters to Cledonius*, PPS 23 (Crestwood, NY: St Vladimir's Seminary Press, 2002).

Gregory of Nazianzus, *Oration* 2. Ed. and French trans. Jean Bernardi, SC 247 (Paris: Cerf, 1978); ET Charles Gordon Browne and James Edward Swallow, NPNF 2.7, 204–27.

Gregory of Nazianzus, *Oration* 28. Ed. and French trans. Paul Gallay, SC 250 (Paris: Cerf, 1978); ET Lionel Wickham, *St Gregory of Nazianzus: On God and Christ*, PPS 23 (Crestwood, NY: St Vladimir's Seminary Press, 2002).

Gregory of Nazianzus, *Oration* 37. Ed. and French trans. Claudio SC 318 Moreschini, SC 358 (Paris: Cerf, 1990); ET Charles Gordon Browne and James Edward Swallow, NPNF 2.7, 338–44.

Gregory of Nazianzus, *Oration* 38. Ed. and French trans. Claudio Moreschini, SC 358 (Paris: Cerf, 1990); ET Nonna Verna Harrison, *St Gregory of Nazianzus: Festal Orations*, PPS 36 (Crestwood, NY: St Vladimir's Seminary Press, 2008).

Heraclitus, Fragments. See 'Presocratics'.

Iamblichus, *Life of Pythagoras* (*Vit. Pythag.*). Ed. and trans. John Dillon and Jackson Hershbell, *Iamblichus: On the Pythagorean Way of Life: Text, Translation, Notes*, SBL Texts and Translations 29, Graeco-Roman Religion Series 11 (Atlanta: Scholars Press, 1991).

Irenaeus of Lyons, *Against the Heresies* (*Haer.*). *Haer.* 1–3 ed. and French trans. A. Rousseau and L. Doutreleau, SC 263–4, 293–4, 210–11 (Paris: Cerf, 1979, 1982, 1974); *Haer.* 4 ed. and French trans. A. Rousseau, B. Hemmerdinger, L. Doutreleau, and C. Mercier, SC 100 (Paris: Cerf, 1965); *Haer.* 5 ed. and French trans. A. Rousseau, L. Doutreleau, and C. Mercier SC 152–3 (Paris: Cerf, 1969); ET ANF 1; *Haer. 1*, D. J. Unger, rev. J. J. Dillon, ACW 55 (New York: Paulist Press, 1992); *Haer.* 2, ACW 65 (New York: Paulist Press, 2012); *Haer.* 3, D. J. Unger, rev. Irenaeus M. C. Steenberg, ACW 64 (New York: Newman Press, 2012).

Irenaeus of Lyons, *Demonstration of the Apostolic Preaching* (*Dem.*). ET John Behr, PPS 17 (Crestwood, NY: Saint Vladimir's Seminary Press, 1997).

John of Damascus, *On the Holy Images* (*Imag.*). Ed. Bonifatius Kotter, *Die Schriften des Johannes von Damaskos*, 2, PTS 12 (Berlin-New York: Walter de Gruyter, 1973); ET Andrew Louth, PPS 24 (Crestwood, NY: St Vladimir's Seminary Press, 2003).

John of Damascus (?), *Sacra Parallela* (*SP*). Ed. Tobias Thum, *Die Schriften des Johannes von Damaskos*, VIII/4–5, PTS 74–5 (Berlin: De Gruyter, 2018).

Josephus, *Against Apion* (*C. Ap.*). Ed. and ET H. St. J. Thackeray, LCL 186, Josephus 1 (Cambridge, MA: Harvard University Press, 1926).

Justinian, *Ep. ad Mennam* (*Mennam*). Ed. Eduard Schwartz, *ACO* 3 (1940), *Collectio Sabbaitica contra Acephalos et Origeniastas destinata*, 189–214.

Justinian, 'Letter to the Holy Council about Origen and Those Like-Minded' (*Ep. ad 553*). Text in Georgius Monachos, *Chronicon*, ed. Carolus de Boor (Leipzig: Teubner, 1904), 2.631–2; ET in Richard Price, *The Acts of the Council of Constantinople 553*, TTH 51 (Liverpool: Liverpool University Press, 2009), 2.282–4.

Maximos the Confessor, *Responses to Thalassios* (*Ad. Thal.*). Ed. Carl Laga and Carlos Steel, CCSG 7, 22 (Turnhout: Brepols. 1980, 90); ET in Maximos Constas, *On Difficulties in Sacred Scripture: The Responses to Thalassios*, FC 136 (Washington, DC: Catholic University of America Press, 2018).

Maximos the Confessor, *Ambigua* (*Ambig.*). Ed. and ET Nicholas Constas, *On Difficulties in the Church Fathers: The Ambigua*, DOML 2 vols (Cambridge, MA: Harvard University Press, 2014); French trans. Emmanuel Ponsoye, with an introduction by Jean-Claude Larchet and commentary by Dumitru Staniloae, *Saint Maxime le Confesseur: Ambigua*, Collection l'Arbre de Jessé (Paris–Suresnes: Éditions de l'Ancre,

1994); further ET of *Ambig.* 41 in Andrew Louth, *Maximus the Confessor*, Early Christian Fathers (London: Routledge, 1996), 156–62.

Maximos the Confessor, *Commentary on the Our Father* (*Or. dom.*). Ed. Peter van Deun, CCSG 23 (Turnhout: Brepols, 1991); ET George Berthold, CWS (London: SPCK, 1985).

Methodius of Olympus, *Aglaophon: On the Resurrection* (*Res.*). Ed. G. N. Bonwetsch, *Methodius: Werke*, GCS 27 (Leipzig, 1917), 217–424.

Nemesius of Emesa, *On the Nature of Man* (*De nat. hom.*). Ed. M. Morani (Leipzig: Teubner, 1987); ET R. W. Sharples and P. J. van der Eijk, TTH 49 (Liverpool: Liverpool University Press, 2008).

Origen, *Hexapla*. Ed. Frederick Field, *Origenis Hexaplorum*, 2 vols (Oxford: Clarendon Press, 1875).

Origen, *Commentary on Genesis*, Fragments (*Com. Gen.*). Ed. and German trans. Karin Metzler, *Origenes: Die Kommentiering des Buches Genesis*, Origenes Werke Mit Deutscher Übersetzung 1/1 (Berlin: De Gruyter, 2010).

Origen, *Homilies on Genesis* (*Hom. Gen.*). Ed. W. A. Baehrens, GCS 29, Origenes Werke 6 (Leipzig: Hinrichs, 1920); ed. and French trans., L. Doutreleau, SC 7 (Paris; Cerf, 1976); ET Ronald E. Heine, FC 71 (Washington, DC: Catholic University of America Press, 1981).

Origen, *Homilies on Exodus* (*Hom. Exod.*). Ed. W. A. Baehrens, GCS 29, Origenes Werke 6 (Leipzig: Hinrichs, 1920); ed. and French trans. M. Borret SC 321 (Paris: Cerf, 1985); ET Ronald E. Heine, FC 71 (Washington, DC: Catholic University of America Press, 1981).

Origen, *Homilies on the Psalms* (*Hom. Ps.*). Ed. Lorenzo Perrone, GCS ns 19, Origenes Werke 13 (Berlin: De Gruyter, 2015); ET Joseph W. Trigg, FC 141 (Washington, DC: Catholic University of America Press, 2020).

Origen, *Commentary and Homilies on Song of Songs* (*Com. & Hom. Songs*). Ed. W. A. Baehrens, GCS 33, Origenes Werke 8 (Leipzig: Hinrichs, 1925); ed. and French trans. L. Brésard et al., SC 375–6 (Paris: Cerf, 1991–2); ET R. P. Lawson, ACW 26 (New York/Mahwah, NJ: Newman Press, 1956).

Origen, *Commentary on Isaiah* (*Com. Isa.*). Ed. W. A. Baehrens, GCS 33, Origenes Werke 8 (Leipzig: Hinrichs, 1925); ET Thomas P. Scheck, ACW 68 (New York/Mahwah, NJ: Newman Press, 2015).

Origen, *Homilies on Jeremiah* (*Hom. Jer.*). Ed. Erich Klostermann, rev. P. Nautin, GCS 6, Origenes Werke 3, 2nd edn. (Berlin: Akademie Verlag, 1983); ed. and French trans. P. Nautin et al., SC 232, 238 (Paris: Cerf, 1976, 1977); ET John Clark Smith, FC 97 (Washington, DC: Catholic University of America Press, 1998).

Origen, *Homilies on Ezekiel* (*Hom. Ezek.*). Ed. W. A. Baehrens, GCS 33, Origenes Werke 8 (Leipzig: Hinrichs, 1925); ed. and French trans. M. Borret, SC 352 (Paris: Cerf, 1989); ET Thomas P. Scheck, ACW 62 (New York/Mahwah, NJ: Newman Press, 2010).

Origen, *Commentary on Matthew* (*Com. Matt.*). Ed. Erich Klostermann with Ernst Benz, GCS 40, Origenes Werke 10, *Die Griechisch erhaltenen Tomoi* (Leipzig: Hinrichs Verlag, 1935); ed. Erich Klostermann with Ernst Benz, revised Ursula Treu, GCS 44, Origenes Werke 11.2, *Die Lateinische Übersetzung der Commentariorum Series* (Berlin: Akademie Verlag, 1976 [1933]); ed. Erich Klostermann with Ernst Benz GCS 41, Origenes Werke 12.1, *Fragmente und Indices* (Leipzig: Hinrichs Verlag, 1941); ed. Erich Klostermann and Ludwig Früchtel, GCS 41, Origenes Werke 12.2, *Fragmente und Indices* (Leipzig: Hinrichs Verlag, 1955); ET Ronald E. Heine, OECT (Oxford: Oxford University Press, 2018).

Origen, *Commentary on John* (*Com. John*). Ed. Erwin Preuschen, GCS 10, Origenes Werke 4 (Leipzig: Hinrichs, 1903); ed. and French trans. C. Blanc, SC 120, 157, 222, 290, 385

(Paris: Cerf, 1966, 1970, 1975, 1982, 1992); ET R. E. Heine, FC 80, 89 (Washington, DC: Catholic University of America Press, 1989, 1993).

Origen, *Fragments on John*. Ed. Erwin Preuschen, GCS 10, Origenes Werke 4 (Leipzig: Hinrichs, 1903).

Origen, *On First Principles* (*Princ.*). Ed. and trans. John Behr, OECT (Oxford: Oxford University Press, 2017).

Origen, *Against Celsus* (*Cels.*). Ed. Paul Koetschau, GCS 2 and 3, Origenes Werke 1 and 2 (Leipzig: Hinrichs, 1899); ed. and French trans. M. Borret, SC 132, 136, 147, 150, 227 (Paris: Cerf, 1967, 1968, 1969, 1976); ET H. Chadwick (Cambridge: Cambridge University Press, 1953).

Origen, *On Prayer* (*Ora.*). Ed. Paul Koetschau, GCS 3, Origenes Werke 2 (Leipzig: Hinrichs, 1899); ET Alistair Stewart-Sykes, *Tertullian, Cyprian, Origen: On the Lord's Prayer*, PPS (Crestwood, NY: St Vladimir's Seminary Press, 2004).

Origen, *Exhortation to Martyrdom* (*Martyr.*). Ed. Paul Koetschau, GCS 2, Origenes Werke 1 (Leipzig: Hinrichs, 1899); ET Rowan A. Greer, *Origen: An Exhortation to Martyrdom, Prayer and Selected Works*, CWS (New York: Paulist Press, 1979).

Origen, *Dialogue with Heraclides* (*Dial.*). Ed. Jean Scherer, *Entretien D'Origène avec Héraclide et les évêques ses colleges sur le Père, le Fils, et l'âme*, Publications de la Société Fouad I de Papyrologie, Textes et Documents 9 (Cairo: Institute Français d'Archéologie Orientale, 1949); ed. and French trans. Jean Scherer, SC 67 (Paris: Cerf, 1960); ET Robert J. Daly, ACW 54 (New York/Mahwah, NJ: Paulist Press, 1992).

Origen, *On Pascha* (*Pasch.*). Ed. and French trans. O. Guéraud and P. Nautin, *Origène: Sur la Pâque: Traité inédit publié d'apres un papyrus de Toura*, Christianisme Antique 2 (Paris: Beauchesne, 1979); ed. and German trans. Bernd Witte, *Die Schrift des Origenes 'Über das Passa': Textausgabe und Kommentar* (Altenberge: Oros Verlag, 1993); ET Robert J. Daly, ACW 54 (New York/Mahwah, NJ: Paulist Press, 1992).

Origen, *Philocalia* (*Philoc.*). Ed. Marguerite Harl, *Origène: Philocalie 1–20: Sur les Écritures*; together with Nicholas de Lange, ed. and trans. *La Lettre à Africanus sur l'histoire de Suzanne*, SC 302 (Paris: Cerf, 1983); Éric Junod, *Origène: Philocalie 21–27: Sur le libre arbitre*, SC 226 (Paris: Cerf, 1976); ET George Lewis, *The Philocalia of Origen* (Edinburgh: T. & T. Clark, 1911).

Orpheus, Fragments. Ed. Otto Kern, *Orphicorum Fragmenta* (Berlin: Weidmann, 1922).

Pamphilus of Caesarea, *Apology for Origen* (*Apol.*). Ed. and trans. R. Amacker and E. Junod, SC 464, 465 (Paris: Cerf, 2002); ET Thomas P. Scheck, FC 120 (Washington, DC: Catholic University of America Press, 2010).

Philo, *On the Creation of the World* (*Opif.*). Ed. F. H. Colson and G. H. Whitaker, LCL 226, Philo 1 (Cambridge, MA: Harvard University Press, 1929); ET David T. Runia, *Philo, On the Creation of the Cosmos according to Moses: Introduction, Translation, and Commentary*, Philo of Alexandria Commentary Series 1 (Atlanta: Society of Biblical Literature, 2001).

Philo, *On the Special Laws* (*Spec.*). Ed. and ET F. H. Colson, LCL 320, 341, Philo 7–8 (Cambridge, MA: Harvard University Press, 1937, 1939).

Philo, *Who is the Heir?* (*Her.*). Ed. and ET F. H. Colson and G. H. Whitaker, LCL 261, Philo 5 (Cambridge, MA: Harvard University Press, 1935).

Philoponos, John, *De Opificio Mundi* (*Opif. mund.*). Ed. and German translation by C. Scholten, FChr 23, 3 vols (Freiburg i. Br. 1997).

Pindar. Ed. Bruno Snell and Herwig Maehler, *Pindari Carmina cum fragmentis*, 2 vols (Leipzig: Teubner, 1959, 1964).

Plato, *Cratylus* (*Crat.*). Ed. and ET H. N. Fowler, LCL 167, Plato 6 (Cambridge, MA: Harvard University Press, 1924).

Plato, *Critias* (*Crit.*). Ed. J. Burnet, OCT, Platonis Opera 4 (Oxford: Clarendon Press, 1902); ET R. G. Bur, LCL 234, Plato 9 (Cambridge, MA: Harvard University Press, 1981).

Plato, *Gorgias* (*Gorg.*). Ed. and ET W. R. M. Lamb, LCL 166, Plato 3 (Cambridge, MA: Harvard University Press, 1983).

Plato, *Phaedo* (*Phaed.*). Ed. and ET Harold North Fowler, LCL 36, Plato 1 (Cambridge, MA: Harvard University Press, 1914).

Plato, *Phaedrus* (*Phaedr*). Ed. J. Burnet, OCT, Platonis Opera 2 (Oxford: Clarendon Press, 1902); Ed. and ET Harold North Fowler, LCL 36, Plato 1 (Cambridge, MA: Harvard University Press, 1914).

Plato, *Republic* (*Resp.*). Ed. J. Burnet, OCT, Platonis Opera 4 (Oxford: Clarendon Press, 1902); ET Robin Waterfield, Oxford World's Classics (Oxford: Oxford University Press, 1993).

Plato, *Timaeus* (*Tim.*). Ed. J. Burnet, OCT, Platonis Opera 4 (Oxford: Clarendon Press, 1902); ET Donald J. Zeyl (Indianapolis, IN: Hackett, 2000), occasionally modified.

Pliny, *Natural History* (*Nat. hist.*). Ed. and ET H. Rackham, LCL (Cambridge, MA: Harvard University Press, 1967).

Plotinus, *Enneads* (*Enn.*). Ed. Paul Henry and Hans-Rudolf Schwyzer, Plotini Opera, 3 vols, OCT (Oxford: Clarendon Press, 1964, 1977, 1983); ET Lloyd P. Gerson, ed. (Cambridge: Cambridge University Press, 2018).

Porphyry, *Life of Plotinus* (*Vita Plot.*). In Henry and Schwyzer, ed., Plotini Opera 1; ET Gerson, ed., *Plotinus*, 17–37.

Porphyry, *Isagoge* (*Isag.*). Ed. A. Busse, *Porphyrii isagoge et in Aristotelis categorias commentarium*, CAG 4.1 (Berlin: Reimer, 1887); ET in Jonathan Barnes, *Porphyry: Introduction*, Clarendon Later Ancient Philosophers (Oxford: Clarendon Press, 2003), 1–19.

Posidonius, Fragments. Ed. L. Edelstein and Ian Gray Kidd, Cambridge Classical Texts and Commentary, 13, 2nd ed. (Cambridge: Cambridge University Press, 2004); ET Ian Gray, Cambridge Classical Texts and Commentary, 36 (Cambridge: Cambridge University Press, 2004).

Procopius of Gaza, *Commentary on Genesis* (*Com. Gen.*). Ed. Karin Metzler, GCS NF 22, Prokop von Gaza 1 (Berlin: De Gruyter, 2015).

Presocratics, Fragments. Ed. Herman Diels, *Die Fragmente der Vorsokratiker*, ed. Walther Kranz, 6th edn., 3 vols (Berlin: Weidmann, 1951–2); ed. and ET Daniel W. Graham, *The Texts of Early Greek Philosophy: The Complete Fragments and Selected Testimonies of the Major Presocratics*, 2 vols (Cambridge: Cambridge University Press, 2010).

Simplicius, *In Aristotelis Physicorum, Libros Quattor Priores, Commentaria* (*In Phys.*). Ed. Herman Diels, CAG 9 (Berlin: Reimeri, 1882). ET Pamela Huby and C. C. W. Taylor, *On Aristotle Physics 1.3–4*, ACA (London: Bloomsbury, 2011); J. O. Urmson, *Simplicius: On Aristotle Physics 3*, ACA (London: Bloomsbury, 2013).

Socrates, *Historia ecclesiastica* (*Hist. eccl.*). Ed. G. C. Hansen, with M. Širingan, GCS NF 1 (Berlin: Akademie Verlag, 1995); ET in NPNF 2.

Stoicorum Veterum Fragmenta. Ed. J. von Arnim (Leipzig: Teubner, 1903–24).

The Testimony of Truth (*Testim. Truth*). NHC IX.3; ET in James M. Robinson, ed., *The Nag Hammadi Library in English* (Leiden: Brill, 1988), 448–59.

Theodoret of Cyrus, *Cure of the Greek Maladies* (*affect*). Ed. and French trans. Pierre Canivet, SC 57, 2 vols (Paris: Cerf, 1958).

Theodoret of Cyrus, *Compendium of Heretical Accounts* (*haer.*). PG 83.335–556.

Victorinus, *On the Making of the World* (*De fab. mun.*). Ed. and French trans. M. Dulaey, SC 423 (Paris: Cerf, 1997).

Xenophon, *Memorabilia* (*Mem.*). Ed. and ET E. C. Marchant, LCL 168, Xenophon 4 (Cambridge, MA: Harvard University Press, 1979).

Secondary Material

Aaron, David H., 'Shedding Light on God's Body in Rabbinic Midrashim: Reflections on the Theory of a Luminous Adam', *HTR* 90.3 (1997), 299–314.

Abecina, Alexander L., *Time and Sacramentality in Gregory of Nyssa's* Contra Eunomium, Early Christian Studies 16 (Strathfield, Australia: St Paul's Publications, 2013).

Abecina, Alexander L., 'Gregory of Nyssa's Change of Mind about the Heart', *JTS*, NS 68.1 (2017), 121–40.

Alexandre, Monique, 'La théorie de l'exégèse dans le *De hominis opificio* et l'*In hexameron*', in Harl, ed., *Écriture et culture*, 87–110.

Alexandre, Monique, 'Protologie et eschatologie chez Grégoire de Nysse', in Bianchi and Crouzel, eds., *Arché et Telos*, 122–60.

Allers, Rudolf, 'Microcosmus: From Anaximandros to Paracelsus', *Traditio* 2 (1944), 319–407.

Altenburger, Margarete, and Friedhelm Mann, *Bibliographie zu Gregor von Nyssa: Editionen—Übersetzungen—Literatur* (Leiden: Brill, 1988).

Anderson, Gary A., *The Genesis of Perfection: Adam and Eve in Jewish and Christian Imagination* (Louisville, KY: Westminster John Knox Press, 2001).

Andrist, Patrick, 'Towards a Definition of Paratexts and Paratextuality: The Case of Ancient Greek Manuscripts', in Liv Ingeborg Lied and Marilena Maniaci, eds., *Bible as Notepad: Tracing Annotations and Annotation Practices in Late Antique and Medieval Biblical Manuscripts*, Manuscripta Biblica 3 (Berlin: de Gruyter, 2018), 130–50.

Assemanus, S. E. and J. S. Assemanus, *Bibliothecae Apostolicae Vaticanae: Codicum manuscriptorum catalogus, in tres partes distributus* (Rome, 1759; reprinted Paris: Libraire Orientale et Américaine, 1926), Partis primae, tomus tertius.

Astruc, Charles, 'Deux fragments anciens (en minuscule de type "Anastase") du *De hominis opificio* de Grégoire de Nysse', *Scriptorium: revue internationale des études relatives aux manuscrits*, 39.1 (1985), 265–9.

Balás, David L., *Μετουσία Θεοῦ: Man's Participation in God's Perfections according to Saint Gregory of Nyssa*, SA 55 (Rome: Herder, 1966).

Balás, David L., 'Plenitudo Humanitatis: The Unity of Human Nature in the Theology of Gregory of Nyssa', in Donald F. Winslow, ed., *Disciplina nostra: Essays in Memory of Robert F. Evans* (Philadelphia, PA: Philadelphia Patristic Foundation 1979), 115–31, 205–8.

Balthasar, Hans Urs von, *Presence and Thought: An Essay on the Religious Philosophy of Gregory of Nyssa*, trans. Mark Sebanc (San Francisco, CA: Ignatius, 1995 [1952/1988]).

Behr, John, 'The Rational Animal: A Rereading of Gregory of Nyssa's *De hominis opificio*', *JECS* 7.2 (1999), 219–47.

Behr, John, *Irenaeus of Lyons: Identifying Christianity*, CTC (Oxford: Oxford University Press, 2013).

Behr, John, *John the Theologian and His Paschal Gospel: A Prologue to Theology* (Oxford: Oxford University Press, 2019).

Behr, John, '"Since the Saviour Pre-exists": A Reconsideration of Irenaeus 3.22.3', *StP* 109, vol. 6 (Leuven: Peeters, 2021), 43–54.

Bianchi, Ugo, 'Presuppostí platonici e dualistici nell' antropogonia di Gregorio di Nissa', in idem, ed., *La 'doppia creazione' dell'uomo negli Alessandrini nei Cappadoci e nella gnosi* (Rome: Edizione dell'Ateneo & Bizzarri, 1978), 83–115.

Bianchi, Ugo, with Henri Crouzel, *Arché e Telos: L'antropologia di Origene e di Gregorio di Nissa, Analisi storico-religiosa, Atti del Colloquio Milano, 17–19 Maggio, 1979*, SPM 12 (Milan: Università Cattolica del Sacro Cuore, 1981).

Biriukov, Dmitry, '"The Ascent of Nature from the Lower to the Perfect": A Synthesis of Biblical and Logical-Philosophical Descriptions of the Order of Natural Beings in *De opificio hominis* 8 by Gregory of Nyssa', *Scrinium* 11 (2015), 197–217.

Blowers, Paul, *The Drama of the Divine Economy: Creator and Creation in Early Christian Theology and Piety* (Oxford: Oxford University Press, 2012).

Boer, S. de, *De anthropologie van Gregorius van Nyssa* (Assen, Netherlands: Van Gorcum, 1968).

Boersma, Hans, *Embodiment and Virtue in Gregory of Nyssa: An Anagogical Approach*, OECS (Oxford: Oxford University Press, 2013).

Brown Dewhurst, E., 'On the Soul and the Cyberpunk Future: St Macrina, St Gregory of Nyssa and Contemporary Mind/Body Dualism', *SCE* 33.4 (2020), 443–62.

Bulgakov, Sergius, *The Sophiology of Death*, trans. Roberto J. De La Noval (Eugene, OR: Cascade, 2021).

Cadenhead, Raphael A., *The Body and Desire: Gregory of Nyssa's Ascetical Theology*, CLA 4 (Berkeley, CA: University of California Press, 2018).

Casey, R. P., 'Armenia Inedita', *Le Muséon, Revue d'études orientales* 68 (1955), 55–9.

Cassin, Matthieu, *L'écriture de la polémique à la fin du IVe siècle: Grégoire de Nysse,* Contra Eunome III (PhD thesis: Paris: Sorbonne, 2009).

Cassin, Matthieu, 'Text and Context: The Importance of Scholarly Reading: Gregory of Nyssa, "Contra Eunomium"', in Scott Douglass and Morwenna Ludlow, *Reading the Church Fathers* (London: T&T Clark, 2011), 109–31, 161–5.

Cassin, Matthieu, 'Contra Eunome III: une introduction', in Johan Leemans and Matthieu Cassin, eds., *Gregory of Nyssa: Contra Eunomium III. An English Translation with Commentary and Supporting Studies*, Suppl. *VC* 124 (Leiden: Brill, 2014), 3–33.

Cavarnos, J. P., 'The Relation of Body and Soul in the Thought of Gregory of Nyssa', in H. Dörrie, M. Altenburger, and U. Schramm, eds., *Gregor von Nyssa und die Philosophie* (Leiden: Brill, 1976), 61–78.

Cherniss, Harold Fredrik, 'The Platonism of Gregory of Nyssa', UCPCP 11.1 (Berkeley, CA: University of California Press, 1930).

Clark, Elizabeth A., *The Origenist Controversy: The Cultural Construction of an Early Christian Debate* (Princeton, NJ: Princeton University Press, 1992).

Coakley, Sarah, 'The Eschatological Body: Gender, Transformation, and God', *MTh* 16 (2000), 61–73.

Coogan, Jeremiah, 'Transforming Textuality: Porphyry, Eusebius, and Late Ancient Tables of Contents', *Studies in Late Antiquity*, 5.1 (2021), 6–27.

Coogan, Jeremiah, *Eusebius the Evangelist* OECS (Oxford: Oxford University Press, 2022).

Cornford, Francis MacDonald, *Plato's Cosmology: The* Timaeus *of Plato* (Indianapolis, IN: Hackett, 1997 [1937]).

Corsini, Eugenio, 'L'harmonie du monde et l'homme microcosme dans le *De hominis opificio*', in Jacques Fontaine and Charles Kannengiesser, eds., *Epektasis: mélanges patristiques offerts au Cardinal Jean Daniélou* (Paris: Beauchesne, 1972), 455–62.

Corsini, Eugenio, 'Plérôme humaine et plérôme cosmique chez Grégoire de Nysse', in Harl, ed., *Écriture et culture philosophique*, 111–26.

Costache, Doru, 'Living Above Gender: Insights from Saint Maximus the Confessor', *JECS* 21.2 (2013), 261–90.

Crawford, Matthew R., *The Eusebian Canon Tables: Ordering Textual Knowledge in Late Antiquity*, OECS (Oxford: Oxford University Press, 2019).

Cross, Richard, 'Gregory of Nyssa on Universals', *VC* 56 (2002), 372–410.

Daley, Brian E., 'Origen's *De Principiis*: A Guide to the Principles of Scriptural Interpretation', in John Petruccione, ed., *Nova et Vetera: Patristic Studies in Honor of Patrick Halton* (Washington, DC: Catholic University of America Press, 1998), 3–21.

Daley, Brian E., '"The Human Form Divine": Christ's Risen Body and Ours according to Gregory of Nyssa', *SP* 41 (2006), 301–18.

Dames, Nicholas, 'Chapter Heads', in Duncan and Smith, eds., *Book Parts*, 153–64.

Daniélou, Jean, 'L'Apocatastase chez saint Grégoire de Nysse', *RSR* 35 (1948), 382–411.

Daniélou, Jean, 'Akolouthia chez Grégoire de Nysse', *RSR* 27 (1953), 219–49.

Daniélou, Jean, *Platonisme et théologie mystique* (Paris: Aubier, nouvelle édition, 1954 [1944]).

Daniélou, Jean, 'La Notion des confins (*methorios*) chez Grégoire de Nysse', *RSR* 49 (1961), 161–87.

Daniélou, Jean, 'Les tuniques de peau chez Grégoire de Nysse', in Gerhard Müller and Winfried Zeller, eds., *Glaube, Geist, Geschichte: Festschrift für Ernst Benz zum 60. Geburtstage am 17.November 1967* (Leiden: Brill, 1967), 355–67.

Daniélou, Jean, 'Philon et Grégoire de Nysse', in *Philon d'Alexandrie. Lyon 11–15 septembre 1966: colloques nationaux du Centre National de la Recherche Scientifique* (Paris: Center National de la Recherche Scientifique, 1967), 333–45.

Daniélou, Jean, *L'être et le temps chez Grégoire de Nysse* (Leiden: Brill, 1970).

Do Vale, Fillipe, 'Cappadocian or Augustinian? Adjudicating Debates on Gender in the Resurrection', *International Journal of Systematic Theology* 21.2 (2019), 182–98.

Dodds, E. R., *Proclus: The Elements of Theology*, 2nd edn. (Oxford: Clarendon Press, 1963).

Dolidze, Tina, and Ekvtime (Tamaz) Kochlamazashvili, 'Old Georgian Translations of Gregory of Nyssa's Works', in Volker Henning Drecoll and Margitta Berghaus, eds., *Gregory of Nyssa: The Minor Treatises on Trinitarian Theology and Apollinarism*, Suppl. *VC* 106 (Leiden: Brill, 2011), 577–92.

Doody, Aude, *Pliny's Encyclopedia: The Reception of the Natural History* (Cambridge: Cambridge University Press, 2010).

Drioton, Étienne, 'La Discussion d'un moine anthropomorphite Audien avec le patriarche Théophile d'Alexandrie en l'année 399', *Revue de l'Orient Chrétien*, 2nd series 10 (=20) (1915–17), 92–100, 113–28; partial ET in Georges Florovsky, 'The Anthropomorphites in the Egyptian Desert', in idem, *Aspects of Church History*, Collected Works 4 (Vaduz, Liechtenstein: Büchervertiebsanstalt, 1987), 89–96.

Drobner, Hubertus R., 'Gregory of Nyssa as Philosopher: *De anima et resurrectione* and *De hominis opificio*', *Dionysius* 18 (2000), 69–102.

Duncan, Dennis, and Adam Smith, *Book Parts* (Oxford: Oxford University Press, 2019).

Edwards, Mark, *Origen against Plato* (Aldershot: Ashgate, 2002).

Edwards, Mark, 'Origen in Paradise: A Response to Peter Martens', *ZAC* 23.2 (2019), 163–85.

Eijk, Ton H. C. van, 'Marriage and Virginity, Death and Immortality', in J. Fontaine et C. Kannengiesser, eds., *Epektasis: mélanges patristiques offerts au Cardinal Jean Daniélou* (Paris: Beauchesne, 1972), 209–35.

Esbroeck, M. van, and U. Zanetti, 'Le manuscrit Érevan 993. Inventaire des pièces', *Revue des études Arméniennes* 12 (1977), 123–67.

Floeri, F., 'Le sens de la "division des sexes" chez Grégoire de Nysse', *RevScRel* 27 (1953), 105–11.

Fredouille, J.-C., Marie-Odile Goulet-Cazé, Philippe Hoffmann, and Pierre Petitmengin, *Titres et articulation du texte dans les ouvrages antiques: Actes du Colloque International de Chantilly, 13–15 décembre 1994*, CÉA, SA 152 (Paris: Institut d'Études Augustiniennes, 1997).

Gadamer, Hans-Georg, 'Idea and Reality in Plato's *Timaeus*', in idem, *Dialogue and Dialectic: Eight Hermeneutical Studies on Plato*, trans. P. Christopher Smith (New Haven: Yale University Press, 1980), 156–93.

Genette, Gérard, *Paratexts: Thresholds of Interpretation*, trans. Jane E. Lewin, Literature, Culture, Theory 20 (Cambridge: Cambridge University Press, 1997 [French edn. 1987]).

Gottstein, Alon Goshen, 'The Body as Image of God in Rabbinic Literature', *HTR* 87.2 (1994), 171–95.

Gregorios, P., *Cosmic Man: The Divine Presence: The Theology of St Gregory of Nyssa (ca 330–395 A.D.)* (New Delhi, 1980; repr. New York: Paragon, 1988).

Harl, Marguerite, ed., *Écriture et culture philosophique dans la pensée de Grégoire de Nysse: Actes du Colloque de Chevetogne (22–26 septembre 1969)* (Leiden: Brill, 1971).

Harl, Marguerite, 'La préexistence des âmes dans l'oeuvre d'Origène', in Lothar Lies, ed., *Origeniana Quarta* (Innsbruck-Vienna: Tyrolia, 1987), 238–58.

Harrison, Verna E., 'Male and Female in Cappadocian Theology', *JTS*, NS 41.2 (1990), 441–71.

Harrison, Verna E., 'Gender, Generation, and Virginity in Cappadocian Theology', *JTS*, NS 47 (1997), 38–68.

Hauke, M., *Heilsverlust in Adam. Stationen griechischer Erbsündenlehre: Irenäus—Origenes—Kappadozier* (Paderborn: Bonifatius, 1993).

Heine, Ronald E., 'The Testimonia and Fragments Related to Origen's *Commentary on Genesis*', *ZAC* 9 (2005), 122–42.

Heine, Ronald E., *Origen: Scholarship in Service of the Church*, CTC (Oxford: Oxford University Press, 2010).

Heine, Ronald E., *Origen: An Introduction to His Life and Thought* (Eugene, OR: Wipf and Stock, 2019).

Holsinger-Friesen, Thomas, *Irenaeus and Genesis: A Study of Competition in Early Christian Hermeneutics*, *JTI* Suppl. 1 (Winona Lake, IN: Eisenbrauns, 2009).

Hörner, Hadwig, 'Über Genese und Derzeitigen Stand der Grossen Edition der Werke Gregors von Nyssa', in Harl, ed., *Écriture et culture philosophique*, 18–50.

Howley, Joseph A., 'Tables of Contents', in Duncan and Smith, *Book Parts*, 67–79.

Hübner, Reinhard M., *Die Einheit des Leibes Christi bei Gregor von Nyssa: Untersuchungen zum Ursprung der 'Physischen' Erlösungslehre*, Philosophia Patrum: Interpretations of Patristic Texts, 2 (Leiden: Brill, 1974).

Jacobsen, Anders Lund, 'Genesis 1–3 as Source for the Anthropology of Origen', *VC* 62 (2008), 213–32.

Jaeger, Werner, 'Greek Uncial Fragments in the Library of Congress in Washington', *Traditio*, 5 (1947), 79–102.

Jaeger, Werner, *Two Rediscovered Works of Ancient Christian Literature: Gregory of Nyssa and Macarius* (Leiden: Brill, 1954).

Jansen, Laura, *The Roman Paratext: Frame, Texts, Readers* (Cambridge: Cambridge University Press, 2014).

Johansen, T. K., *Plato's Natural Philosophy: A Study of the* Timaeus-Critias (Cambridge: Cambridge University Press, 2004).

Karatzoglou, Orestis, *The Embodied Self in Plato:* Phaedo–Republic–Timaeus, Trends in Classics (Berlin: De Gruyter, 2021).

Karras, Valerie A., 'Sex/Gender in Gregory of Nyssa's Eschatology: Irrelevant or Non-Existent?', *StP* 41 (2006), 363–8.

Kern, Cyprien, *Les traductions russes des textes patristiques: Guide bibliographique* (Chevetogne: Éditions de Chevetogne, 1957).

Kochlamazanashvili, Ekvtime, and Tina Dolidze, *Description of Georgian Manuscripts Including St. Gregory of Nyssa's Works* (Tbilisi, 2009; in Georgian).

Köckert, Charlotte, *Christliche Kosmologie und kaiserzeitliche Philosophie*, STAC 56 (Tübingen: Mohr Siebeck, 2009).

Ladner, G., 'The Philosophical Anthropology of Saint Gregory of Nyssa', *DOP* 12 (1958), 59–94.

Lambeck, Peter, *Commentariorum de augustissima bibliotheca caesarea Vindobonensis, Liber Tertius, editio altera* (Vienna: J. Thomae, 1776), and *Liber Quartus, editio altera* (Vienna: J. Thomae, 1778).

LeCron Foster, Mary, 'Symbolism: the Foundation of Culture', in Tim Ingold, ed., *Companion Encyclopedia of Anthropology: Humanity, Culture, Social Life* (London: Routledge, 1993), 366–95.

Levine, Philip, 'Two Early Versions of St. Gregory of Nyssa's *Περὶ κατασκευῆς ἀνθρώπου*', *Harvard Studies in Classical Philology* 63 (1958), 473–92.

Leys, Roer, *L'image de Dieu chez Grégoire de Nysse. Esquisse d'une doctrine* (Brussels: L'Édition universelle; Paris: Desclée de Brouwer, 1951).

Liddell, H. G., and R. Scott, *A Greek-English Lexicon*, rev. H. S. Jones with R. McKenzie. 9th edn. with revised supplement (Oxford: Clarendon Press, 1996).

Ludlow, Morwenna, *Universal Salvation: Eschatology in the Thought of Gregory of Nyssa and Karl Rahner* (Oxford: Oxford University Press, 2000).

Ludlow, Morwenna, *Gregory of Nyssa: Ancient and (Post)modern* (Oxford: Oxford University Press, 2007).

Ludlow, Morwenna, 'Science and Theology in Gregory of Nyssa's *De Anima et resurrectione*: Astronomy and Automata', *JTS*, NS 60 (2009), 467–89.

Ludlow, Morwenna, 'Christian Formation and the Body-Soul Relationship in Gregory of Nyssa', in Marmodoro and McLynn, eds., *Exploring Gregory of Nyssa*, 160–78.

Marmodoro, Anna, *Everything in Everything: Anaxagoras's Metaphysics* (Oxford: Oxford University Press, 2017).

Marmodoro, Anna, 'Gregory of Nyssa on the Creation of the World', in Anna Marmodoro and Irini-Fotini Viltanioti, *Divine Powers in Late Antiquity* (Oxford: Oxford University Press, 2017), 218–34.

Marmodoro, Anna, and Neil B. McLynn, eds., *Exploring Gregory of Nyssa: Philosophical, Theological, and Historical Studies* (Oxford: Oxford University Press, 2018).

Martens, Peter W., 'Origen's Doctrine of Pre-Existence and the Opening Chapters of Genesis', *ZAC* 16 (2012), 516–49.

Martens, Peter W., 'Response to Edwards', *ZAC* 23.2 (2019), 186–200.

Marunová, Magdalena, 'Gregory of Nyssa's Anthropological Doctrine of Human Beings Created as the Image of God', *Communio Viatorum*, 63.2 (2020), 250–65.

Maspero, G., *Trinity and Man: Gregory of Nyssa's* Ad Ablabium (Leiden: Brill, 2007).

Mateo-Seco, Lucas Francisco, and Giulio Maspero, eds., *The Brill Dictionary of Gregory of Nyssa*, trans. Seth Cherney (Leiden: Brill, 2009).

McClear, Ernest V., 'The Fall of Man and Original Sin in the Theology of Gregory of Nyssa', *TS* 9 (1948), 175–212.

Mendieta, Emmanuel Amand de, and Stig Y. Rudberg, *Basile de Césarée: La tradition manuscrite directe des neuf homélies sur l'Hexaéméron*, TU 123 (Berlin: Akademie, 1980).

Meredith, Anthony, 'The Concept of Mind in Gregory of Nyssa and the Neoplatonists', *StP* 22 (1989), 35–51.

Merki, Hubert, *ΟΜΟΙΩΣΙΣ ΘΕΩ: Von der platonischen Angleichung an Gott zur Gottähnlichkeit bei Gregor von Nyssa*, Paradosis: Beiträgeg zur Geschichte der altchristlichen Literature und Theologie, 7 (Fribourg: Paulus, 1952).

Meyer, Eric Daryl, 'Gregory of Nyssa on Language, Naming God's Creatures, and the Desire of the Discursive Animal', in Nathan MacDonald, Mark Elliot, and Grant Macaskill, eds., *Genesis and Christian Theology* (Grand Rapids, MI: Eerdmans, 2012), 103–16.

Meyer, Eric Daryl, 'On Making Fleshly Difference: Humanity and Animality in Gregory of Nyssa', *Relegere: Studies in Religion and Reception* 7.1–2 (2017), 39–58.

Mohr, Richard D., and Barbara M. Sattler, *One Book, The Whole Universe: Plato's* Timaeus *Today* (Las Vegas-Zurich-Athens: Parmenides Publishing, 2010).

Moutsoulas, Elias D., *The Incarnation of the Word and the Theosis of Man according to the Teaching of Gregory of Nyssa* (Athens: Eptalofos, 2000).

Naldini, M., 'Per una esegesi de *De hominis opificio* di Gregorio Nisseno (Cap. V e XVI)', *Studi Italiani di Filologia Classica* 45 (1973), 88–123.

Nasrallah, Joseph, 'Dossier arabe des oeuvres de saint Basile dans la littérature melchite', *Proche-Orient Chrétien* 29 (1979), 17–43.

Nessel, Daniel de, *Catalogus sive Recensio specialis omnium codicum manuscriptorum graecorum, nec non linguarum orientalium, Augustissimae Bibliothecae Caesareae Vindobonensis* (Vienna: L. Voigt & J. B. Endteri, 1690).

Norris, Richard A., 'Two Trees in the Midst of the Garden (Genesis 2:9b): Gregory of Nyssa and the Puzzle of Human Evil', in Paul Blowers, ed., *In Dominico eloquio: In Lordly Eloquence: Essays on Patristic Exegesis in Honor of Robert Louis Wilken* (Grand Rapids, MI: Eerdmans, 2002), 218–41.

Oesterle, Hans J., 'Probleme der Anthropologie bei Gregor von Nyssa. Zur Interpretation seiner Schrift *De hominis opificio*', *Hermes* (Wiesbaden) 113 (1985), 101–14.

O'Meara, Dominic J., *Cosmology and Politics in Plato's Later Works* (Cambridge: Cambridge University Press, 2017).

Otis, B., 'Cappadocian Thought as a Coherent System', *DOP* 12 (1958), 97–124.

Otis, B., 'Gregory of Nyssa and the Cappadocian Concept of Time', *StP* 14.3 (1976), 327–57.

Parmentier, M., 'Syriac Translations of Gregory of Nyssa', *OLP* 20 (1989), 143–93.

Patterson, Paul A., *Visions of Christ: The Anthropomorphite Controversy of 399 CE*, STAC 68 (Berlin: Mohr Siebeck, 2012).

Perry, W., *George Hay Forbes: A Romance in Scholarship* (London: SPCK, 1927).

Pierce, Alexander H., 'Apokatastasis, Genesis 1:26–27, and the Theology of History in Origen's *De Principiis*', *JECS* 29.2 (2021), 169–91.

Pisi, P., *Genesis e phthorà: Le motivazioni protologiche della verginità in Gregorio di Nissa e nella tradizione dell'enkrateia* (Rome: Ateneo, 1981).

Pitra, Jean-Baptiste-François (Cardinal), *Analecta Sacra Spicilegio Solesmensi Parata* tome 3, *Patres Antenicaeni* (Venice: Mechitaristarum Sancti Lazari, 1883).

Rabinowitz, Celia E., 'Personal and Cosmic Salvation in Origen', *VC* 38 (1984), 319–29.

Ramelli, Ilaria L. E., '"Preexistence of Souls"?: The ἀρχή and τέλος of Rational Creatures in Origen and Some Origenians', in *StP*, 56.4, *Rediscovering Origen*, ed. Markus Vinzent (Leuven: Peeters, 2013), 167–226.

Ramelli, Ilaria L. E., '*Οἰκείωσις* in Gregory's Theology: Reconstructing His Creative Reception of Stoicism', in Johan Leemans and Matthieu Cassin, *Gregory of Nyssa* Contra Eunomium III: *An English Translation with Commentary and Supporting Studies: Proceedings of the 12th International Colloquium on Gregory of Nyssa (Leuven, 14–17 September 2010)*, Suppl. *VC* 124 (Leiden: Brill, 2014), 643–59.

Ramelli, Ilaria L. E., 'The Stoic Doctrine of *Oikeiosis* and its Transformation in Christian Platonism', *Apeiron*, 47 (2014), 116–40.

Rasmussen, Adam, *Genesis and Cosmos: Basil and Origen on Genesis 1 and Cosmology*, The Bible in Ancient Christianity, 14 (Leiden: Brill, 2019).

Reydams-Schils, Gretchen, *Calcidius on Plato's* Timaeus*: Greek Philosophy, Latin Reception, and Christian Contexts* (Cambridge: Cambridge University Press, 2020).

Riggsby, Andrew M., 'Guides to the Wor(l)d', in Jason König and Tim Whitmarsh, eds., *Ordering Knowledge in the Roman Empire* (Cambridge: Cambridge University Press, 2007).

Röder, J. A., *Gregor von Nyssa, Contra Eunomium I, 1–146, eingeleitet, übersetzt und kommentiert*, Patrologia 2 (Frankfurt am Main: Peter Lang, 1993).

Ross, Taylor, 'Cultivation as Immanent Critique: Horticultural Metaphors in Gregory of Nyssa's Reception of Origen and Basil', *Open Theology* 7 (2021), 388–400.

Ross, Taylor, '"Reformulating" Gregory of Nyssa's Reception of Origen', in Markus Vinzent, ed. *StP 115.12, The Cappadocians* (Leuven: Peeters, 2021), 88–98.

Ross, Taylor, 'The Inextricability of Hermeneutics and Metaphysics in Late Neoplatonism and Patristic Theology', in Athanasios Despotis and James Buchanan Wallace, *Greek and Byzantine Philosophical Exegesis*, Eastern Church Identities 5 (Leiden: Brill, 2022), 188–216.

Runia, David T., *Philo of Alexandria and the Timaeus of Plato*, Philosophia Antiqua 44 (Leiden: Brill, 1986).

Runia, David T., *Philo in Early Christian Literature: A Survey*, Compendia rerum judaicarum ad Novum Testamentum, Section III, Jewish Traditions in Early Christian Literature 3 (Assen, Netherlands: Van Gorcum; Minneapolis: Fortress Press, 1993).

Schoemann, J. B., 'Gregor von Nyssa's Anthropologie als Bildstheologie', *Scholastik* 18 (1943), 31–53, 175–200.

Schwartz, Eduard, 'Überschriften und Kephalaia', GCS 9.3 (1909), CXLVII–CLII.

Schröder, Bianca-Jeanette, *Titel und Text: Zur Entwicklung lateinischer Gedichtüberschriften. Mit Untersuchungen zu lateinischen Buchtiteln, Inhaltsverzeichnissen und anderen Gliederungsmitteln* (Berlin: De Gruyter, 1999).

Sedley, David, *Creationism and Its Critics in Antiquity* (Berkeley, CA: University of California Press, 2007).

Skinner, Quentin, 'Meaning and Understanding in the History of Ideas', *History and Theory* 8 (1969), 3–53; reprinted in idem, *Visions of Politics*, vol. 1, *Regarding Method* (Cambridge: Cambridge University Press, 2002), 57–89.

Smith, J. Warren, *Passion and Paradise: Human and Divine Emotion in the Thought of Gregory of Nyssa* (New York: Crossroad, 2004).

Smith, J. Warren, 'The Body of Paradise and the Body of the Resurrection: Gender and the Angelic Life in Gregory of Nyssa's *De hominis opificio*', *HTR* 92.2 (2006), 207–28.

Sorabji, Richard, *Time, Creation and the Continuum: Theories in Antiquity and the Early Middle Ages* (London: Duckworth, 1983).

Staats, Reinhart, *Gregor von Nyssa und die Messalianer: Die Frage der Priorität zweier altkirchlicher Schriften*, PTS 8 (Berlin: De Gruyter, 1968).

Sutcliffe, E. F., 'St. Gregory of Nyssa and Paradise', *EcRev*, NS 4 (1931), 342–4.

Tobin, T. H., *The Creation of Man: Philo and the History of Interpretation*, CBQ MS 14 (Washington, DC: Catholic Biblical Association of America, 1983).

Tzamalikos, Panayiotis, *The Concept of Time in Origen* (Bern: Peter Lang, 1991).

Tzamalikos, Panayiotis, *Origen: Cosmology and Ontology of Time*, Suppl. *VC* 77 (Leiden: Brill, 2005).

Tzamalikos, Panayiotis, *Origen: Philosophy of History and Eschatology*, Suppl. *VC* 85 (Leiden: Brill, 2007).

Tzamalikos, Panayiotis, *Anaxagoras, Origen, and Neoplatonism: The Legacy of Anaxagoras to Classical and Late Antiquity*, Arbeiten zur Kirchengeschichte 128, 2 vols (Berlin: De Gruyter, 2016).

Wessel, Susan, 'The Reception of Greek Science in Gregory of Nyssa's *De hominis opificio*', *VC* 63 (2009), 24–46.

Williams, R. D., 'Macrina's Deathbed Revisited: Gregory of Nyssa on Mind and Passion', in Lionel R. Wickham and Caroline P. Bammel, with Erica C. D. Hunter, eds., *Christian Faith and Greek Philosophy in Late Antiquity. Essays in Tribute to George Christopher Stead*, Suppl. *VC* 19 (Leiden: Brill, 1993), 227–46.

Wood, Jordan, *The Whole Mystery of Christ: Creation as Incarnation in Maximus Confessor* (Notre Dame, IN: Notre Dame Press, 2022).

Young, Frances M., 'Adam and Anthropos: A Study of the Interaction of Science and the Bible in Two Anthropological Treatises of the Fourth Century', *VC* 37 (1983), 110–40.

Young, Robin D., 'Gregory of Nyssa's Use of Theology and Science in Constructing Theological Anthropology', *Pro Ecclesia* 2.3 (1993), 345–63.

Zachhuber, Johannes, *Human Nature in Gregory of Nyssa: Philosophical Background and Theological Significance* (Leiden: Brill, 2014 [2000]).

Zachhuber, Johannes, 'Once Again: Gregory of Nyssa on Universals', *JTS* NS 56.1 (2005), 75–98.

Zachhuber, Johannes, 'The Soul as *Dynamis* in Gregory of Nyssa's *On the Soul and Resurrection*', in Marmodoro and McLynn, eds., *Exploring Gregory of Nyssa*, 142–59.

Index of Ancient Sources

Where texts are not divided into books and chapters, in either editions or translations, reference is given to the page number of the edition cited in the Bibliography.

I: Scripture

II: Gregory of Nyssa

III: Other Ancient Sources

Index of Modern Authors